AIA GUIDE TO CHICAGO

Introduction by Perry R. Duis

Preface by John F. Hartray, Jr., FAIA

Alice Sinkevitch, Editor

Laurie McGovern Petersen, Associate Editor

AIA
GUIDE TO
CHICAGO

American Institute
of Architects Chicago

Chicago Architecture Foundation

Landmarks Preservation
Council of Illinois

with special assistance from the
Commission on Chicago Landmarks

HARCOURT BRACE & COMPANY
New York   San Diego   London

HARCOURT
BRACE

Copyright © 1993
by Guide to Chicago Architecture Joint Venture

Library of Congress Catalog Card Number: 93-078329
ISBN 0-15-138018-X

Designed by Linda Lockowitz

Printed in the United States of America

First edition

A B C D E

Photo credits for section openers: Central City, pages
26–27, Courtesy of the Commission on Chicago
Landmarks; North Side, pages 152–153, © 1993 The Art
Institute of Chicago. All rights reserved.; Northwest Side,
pages 244–245, Photo by Dennis Pratt; West Side, pages
268–269, Courtesy of Chicago Park District Special
Collections; Oak Park, pages 308–309, Photo by Thomas A.
Heinz; Southwest Side, pages 334–335, Photo © by
Lawrence Okrent; South Side, pages 352–353, Hedrich-
Blessing photograph, courtesy Chicago Historical Society.

CONTENTS

GUIDE TO
THE GUIDE

The *AIA Guide to Chicago* is the largest portable source of information on the city's built environment. The book will serve as both an introduction to Chicago's architecture for neophytes and as a sourcebook for those seeking to expand their knowledge beyond the well-documented buildings. The city's "greatest hits" are included and many are discussed in essay form; numerous neighborhood buildings are documented in print for the first time. Much information available in other books—biographical, theoretical, statistical, and critical—is deliberately minimized, while details concerning functional requirements, client tastes, and materials are often included. The purpose of the *Guide* is to encourage the reader to discover, look at, and appreciate man-made Chicago.

Genesis of the book: The *Guide* was created for, and is intended as, a legacy of the 1993 American Institute of Architects/International Union of Architects World Congress, the first national convention of the AIA held in Chicago since 1969. The three sponsoring organizations—the AIA Chicago, the Chicago Architecture Foundation, and the Landmarks Preservation Council of Illinois—provided the core of the Editorial Committee, which was expanded to include experts from the Chicago Park District, the Commission on Chicago Landmarks, and other groups. The Editorial Committee chose the featured tour areas and selected the bylined essayists. Each tour area had a "chapter captain" in charge of research and recommending entries. One important source of new information was the citywide Historic Resources Survey of pre-1940 buildings, conducted from 1984 to 1992 by the Commission on Chicago Landmarks. Many other new facts were uncovered by the authors and by the dedicated group of volunteer researchers.

Many photographs came from architectural firms and their clients, libraries, and other archives. Others were taken by architectural photographers, who, working as volunteers, traveled throughout the city to document neighborhood buildings.

Criteria for inclusion: Even at its present length, the *Guide* is illustrative rather than encyclopedic, presenting a representative selection of buildings in addition to the essential landmarks. The neighborhoods chosen display a range of types, styles, and eras.

The criteria for selecting buildings, landscape and park features, bridges, public art, and cemetery monuments included not only the quality of their design but also the degree to which they either exemplified a style, trend, or functional type or stood out as unusual. Other important factors included visibility, historical significance, and the "what the heck is that" curiosity factor. Practical considerations included the geographical "fit" with the tour itineraries, which were laid out to connect major points of interest. Good examples of common types—the CTA station, the modernized storefront, the grain elevator—on a route connecting featured structures were chosen over those in more remote locations.

The availability of information also played a part. If dedicated research failed to produce specific data for a post-1870s building, it was likely to be omitted in favor of another, better-documented example.

Building types were weighted, with criteria varying from one area to another. Houses get more attention than churches in Oak Park, for example, because of the important evolution of residential styles to be seen there.

The authors' likes and dislikes were significant factors, and no pretense is made of objectivity. Due to limited space, many of the city's prominent but dull buildings are omitted or only briefly noted in order to include a greater range and number of structures. Few buildings of historic rather than architectural interest are included.

Organization: The *Guide* is organized by neighborhood chapters, beginning with the central city and radiating outward. Each chapter has its own map that displays wherever possible each building's name next to its entry number. A small inset map locates the area within Chicago. All maps have north at the top.

Because of the large areas covered in each chapter, all but the Loop have their entries ordered to facilitate driving tours. Quirks in the numerical ordering are usually the result of accommodating one-way and dead-end streets, railway embankments, and other automotive impediments. Separate maps are provided for groups of entries, such as campuses and cemeteries, that lack street addresses.

Chapter introductions outline each area's historical development and describe its neighborhoods and prominent demarcations. All neighborhoods are within the city of Chicago except for suburban Oak Park, whose concentration of Frank Lloyd Wright designs compelled its inclusion.

Information on the entries: The heading for each nonresidential entry begins with the building's current name or address, followed by a parenthetical listing of the original name and, occasionally, well-known subsequent appellations. The use of current rather than historical names is intended to make it easier to locate buildings. In the case of a house, the name of the original owner is used.

Dashes between house numbers indicate a row of contiguous structures (such as row houses); an ampersand or the word "through" is used for a group of freestanding buildings unless they are commonly known as something else—as, for example, 860–880 N. Lake Shore Dr. Dates generally indicate the year of completion (except for prolonged construction) and are followed by the contemporaneous name of the responsible architecture firm. An ampersand joins the names of a single firm; "and" links the names of two or more separate firms.

The design architect's firm is listed first, except in the case of buildings commissioned by the City of Chicago. Subsequent work that is visually apparent is included with its year of completion and architect. Most major buildings more than ten years old have had many alterations; only major renovations and additions are cited. "Restored" means the building was returned to its original appearance, but "renovated" or "converted" entries may look substantially different as a result of the work.

Interiors are generally described only if they are open to the public or are especially noteworthy. Churches are usually open only during services and welcome visitors at those times.

A final word: The opinions expressed in the *Guide* are those of its many authors and in no way represent views or opinions of any sponsoring organization. Information is current as of 1992; in a city as dynamic as Chicago many changes will already have occurred before publication. Most buildings are privately owned and not open to the public; investigation of anything not visible from the street or from a public space constitutes trespassing. Neighborhoods that are off the usual traveler's itinerary do not always treat every tourist well. Italicized commentary flags a few—but by no means all—of these areas. Readers are urged to travel by car and in groups when exploring unfamiliar territory; visitors are encouraged to consult with a Chicago resident before planning a tour.

Ideally, this book will serve as a net in which much new information will be captured. Become a contributor to the second edition of the *AIA Guide to Chicago* by submitting corrections, additions, or information on alterations and demolitions to AIA Chicago, 222 Merchandise Mart Plaza, Suite 1049, Chicago, Illinois 60654.
—Alice Sinkevitch and Laurie McGovern Petersen

ACKNOWLEDGMENTS

DONORS

The commitment of Chicago's business community, grants from many foundations, and the generosity of individuals passionately committed to the built environment made this book possible.

Benefactors
The Chicago Community Trust; Graham Foundation for Advanced Studies in the Fine Arts; National Endowment for the Arts; AIA Chicago; John D. and Catherine T. MacArthur Foundation

Patrons
American Architectural Foundation; Chicago Architecture Foundation; The Joyce Foundation; Landmarks Preservation Council of Illinois

Sponsors
William B. Hinchliff; John A. Holabird, Jr., FAIA; Illinois Arts Council; Henry H. Kuehn; Lohan Associates; Petersen Aluminum Corporation

Contributors
Baird Foundation; Chicago Dock & Canal Trust; D & K Foundation; Ernst & Young; Greater North Michigan Avenue Association; Holabird & Root; Richard J. Hoskins; Knight Architects Planners, Inc.; Lucia Woods Lindley; Pamela Lohan; McClier, Inc.; Hope McCormick; Murphy/Jahn; O'Donnell Wicklund Pigozzi & Peterson Architects; The Pepper Companies; Perkins & Will; Seymour H. Persky; Schal Associates, Inc.; The Law Firm of Schiff Hardin & Waite; John I. Schlossman, FAIA; Jacqueline & Gene Summers, FAIA; U.S. Equities Realty, Inc.; Harry Weese Associates; Weese Langley Weese Architects; Doreen & Steven Weiss, AIA

Friends
Anonymous; Susan M. Baldwin; Beer Gorski & Graff, Ltd.; Anthony Belluschi, AIA; The John Buck Company; Chicago Architecture Foundation Docents; Continental Bank Foundation; Employees of Loebl, Schlossman & Hackl; John Engman; Gerhardt Meyne Company; Gilbane Building Company; Ernest A. Grunsfeld III, FAIA; John F. Hartray, Jr., FAIA; Hinshaw & Culbertson; Edward C. Hirschland; Harold S. Jensen; Joseph D. La Rue; The Linpro Company; Jane Lucas; Robert G. Lyon Associates, Inc.; Lynn & Eva Maddox, AIA; Matthei & Colin; Mekus Johnson Inc.; The Monadnock Building; Power Contracting & Engineering; Linda Searl, AIA; Sears Tower; Bruce A. Simons; Stein & Company; Stein, Ray & Conway; Michael Tobin; Turner Construction Company; Carol Wyant

CREDITS

AIA Chicago is a chapter of the American Institute of Architects, the nation's largest professional association for architects. Since its founding in 1869, the Chapter has worked to advance the architect's professional development and to enrich the cultural, economic, and environmental vitality of the local community.

The Chicago Architecture Foundation, founded in 1966, is a non-profit organization dedicated to advancing public interest and education in architecture and design. The Foundation pursues this educational mission through a comprehensive program of tours, exhibitions, lectures, special events, and the operation of the Clarke and Glessner House museums, all designed to further the general public's awareness and appreciation of the architecture of metropolitan

Chicago.

Landmarks Preservation Council of Illinois is a private, nonprofit membership organization dedicated to promoting the vitality of Illinois's historic architecture. LPCI is committed to community revitalization by preserving the economic and social strength of neighborhoods throughout Illinois.

AIA Chicago, the Chicago Architecture Foundation, and the Landmarks Preservation Commission of Illinois formed a joint venture to produce this guidebook. Representatives of each organization served on each major committee. The Management Committee provided basic direction and structure; the Editorial Committee chose the primary essayists and set editorial direction; and the Fund-raising Committee made the project happen.

Management Committee

Steven F. Weiss, AIA, Chair; Susan Baldwin; John Engman; Richard Hoskins; Henry H. Kuehn; Jane Lucas; Thomas R. Samuels, AIA; Linda Searl, AIA; Emese Wood; Carol Wyant

Editorial Committee

Wim de Wit; John F. Hartray, Jr., FAIA; Robert F. Irving; Joseph D. La Rue; Vincent Michael; Joan Pomaranc; Deborah Slaton; Julia Sniderman; Cynthia Weese, FAIA

Fund-raising Committee

Pamela Lohan, Chair; Susan Baldwin; Kathryn Godfrey Benish; Joan Goldstein; John A. Holabird, Jr., FAIA; Henry H. Kuehn; John I. Schlossman, FAIA; Steven F. Weiss, AIA

Project Team

Alice Sinkevitch, Editor; Laurie McGovern Petersen, Associate Editor; Joan Pomaranc, Assistant Editor; Mary Alice Molloy, Special Projects Editor; Emese Wood, Photo Coordinator; Dennis McClendon, Map Designer

Our book also benefited from the efforts of many other individuals. The editorial guidance of John Radziewicz and Dan Janeck of Harcourt Brace and the excellent copy editing of Joel Honig gave our efforts form and refinement. Michael Smith compiled the index. Important to the production of the book were the efforts of production manager David Hough, book designer Linda Lockowitz, layout artist Barry Age, and proofreader Phyllis DeBlanche.

This book had many authors. The following individuals contributed research or wrote essays and entries: Rolf Achilles; Deborah Allen; Margaret Babcock; Marguerite Bailey; Margaret Balanoff; Susan Baldwin; Barry Bebart, AIA; Kathryn Godfrey Benish; Susan Benjamin; Ellen S. Berkelhamer; Alice Blum; Robert W. Blythe; Elizabeth Borden; Michael Bordenaro; Robert Bruegmann; Adam Burck; Joan Campbell; Cathy Capriglione; Constance K. Casey; Sally A. Kitt Chappell; Jane H. Clarke; Earl Clendenon; Patricia Lee Cody; Carole Cosimano; Kathleen Cummings; Barbara Cunningham; Eric Emmett Davis, AIA; Mary Dawson; Wim de Wit; Yvonne DeMuyt; Karen Dimond; Thomas Drebenstedt; David DuPre; Perry R. Duis; Joan Eggers; Janice M. Elliott; Roy Forrey; Ferne Winifred Gerulat; Ann Erickson Gifford; Blair Gifford; Paul Glassman; Patricia Goldfein; Norma Green; Mary Griffin; Florence Gurke; Louise B. Haack; T. Gunny Harboe; Elaine Harrington; Kevin Harrington; Neil Harris; John F. Hartray, Jr., FAIA; Frances B. Hedlund; John Hern; Mary Beth Herr; William B. Hinchliff; Mark Hinchman; Richard Hoskins; Robert F. Irving; Leo Jung; Nancy Kayman; Donald G. Kalec; Blair Kamin; Paul Kendall; Donald Kepler; Paul Kruty; Henry H. Kuehn; Joseph D. La Rue; Heather M. Lange; Bill Latoza, AIA; Beth LeGros; Margaret Lehto, AIA; Aldarcy C. Lewis; Jane Lucas; William Q. Lucas; Patricia Marks Lurie; John M. MacDonald; Laurel McCain; Harriet McShane; Suzanne Carter Meldman; Thomas Michael II; Vincent

Michael; Frank P. Michalski, AIA; Mary Alice Molloy; Aurelia Moody; Harold Moody; Charlotte Myhrum; Kathleen Nagle; Kathryn Neary; Anders Nereim; Pat O'Brien; Dan O'Dair; Penny Obenshain; Lawrence Okrent; Maria Olson; Mary Lou Oswalt; Laurie McGovern Petersen; Charles Pipal; Joan Pomaranc; Helen Poot; Stephen W. Radke, AIA; Michael Ramirez; Judith Randall; John Ravitch; Diane Richard; Katherine Ross; Anne Royston; Bart H. Ryckbosch; Pauline Saliga; Thomas R. Samuels, AIA; Timothy Samuelson; John I. Schlossman, FAIA; Franz Schulze; Vincent Scully; Linda Searl, AIA; R. Stephen Sennott; Robert A. Sideman; Joseph Siry; Deborah Slaton; Alice Sinkevitch; Julia Sniderman; C. Richard Spurgin; Joan Stinton; Patricia Talbot; Terry Tatum; Meredith Taussig; Laurence Terp; William W. Tippens; John Tomassi, AIA; Theodore Turak; David Van Zanten; John Vinci, FAIA; Gloria Wallace; Dina Wayne; Ben Weese, FAIA; Catharine Weese; Cynthia Weese, FAIA; Michael Weiland; Lauren S. Weingarden; Timothy Wittman; Carol Wyant; Ethel Zitnik; and Atie Zuurdeeg.

The "chapter captains" who led the research teams for each chapter were Adam Burck (Beverly/Morgan Park); Wim de Wit and Robert F. Irving (Lakeview/Uptown/Ravenswood); William B. Hinchliff (N. Michigan Ave./Streeterville and Edgewater/Rogers Park); Joseph D. La Rue (Near South Side and Oakland/Kenwood); Patricia Marks Lurie (Gold Coast/Old Town and Lincoln Park); Vincent Michael (Near West Side and Lower West Side); Mary Alice Molloy (Loop, River North, South Loop, and Pullman/Roseland); Kathleen Nagle (Bridgeport/Canaryville/McKinley Park/Back of the Yards); Anne Royston (Chicago–O'Hare International Airport); R. Stephen Sennott (Hyde Park/South Shore); Alice Sinkevitch (Garfield Park/Austin and Oak Park); Julia Sniderman (Northwest Side); and John Tomassi, AIA (Chicago–Midway Airport).

Among the photographers listed in the photo credits at the end of this volume, the following contributed work done especially for this book: Ben Altman; Mark Ballogg; Barry Bebart, AIA; Judith Bromley; Suzette Bross; Wayne Cable; David Clifton; Don DuBroff; David Vincent Forte, AIA; Josh Goldman; Ron Gordon; Howard N. Kaplan; William Kildow; George Lambros; Fred Leavitt; Margaret Lehto, AIA; Harold A. Nelson; James Norris; Lawrence Okrent; Jamie Padgett; Dennis Pratt; Sean Reidy; Felicity Rich; Katherine Roth; Barry Rustin; Dennis M. Ryan, AIA; Leslie Schwartz; James Steinkamp; Neal A. Vogel; and Helena Chapellin Wilson.

The category of special supporters and advisers is large and includes attorneys Ross Altman and Mark Feldman of Rudnick & Wolfe; the Law Firm of Jenner & Block; and the Law Firm of Sidley & Austin; each helped to structure the sponsoring joint venture and our contracts. Also critically important were the librarians and photo specialists at the Art Institute of Chicago and the Chicago Historical Society, including Patrick Ashley, Emily Clark, Denise English, Lorraine Estreich, Eileen Flanagan, Charles McMorris, Janice McNeill, Susan Perry, Larry Viskochil, and Mary Woolever. Past AIA Chicago Presidents Frank Heitzman, AIA, Sherwin Braun, AIA, and Leonard Peterson, FAIA, were instrumental in supporting the project in its infancy. Key advice and assistance were also given by Timothy Barton; Daniel Bluestone; Eric Brightfield; Janice Curtis; Jan Dubin; Ann Dumas; Charles Fiori; Mary Jo Graf; T. Gunny Harboe, AIA; Jack Hedrich; Sally Hess; Michael Houlihan; Bob Johnson; Mary Sue Kranstover; Bonita Mall; William McLenahan; Lawrence Okrent; Kevin Putz; Pat Rosenzweig; Rick Solomon, AIA; Ben Weese, FAIA; and John Zukowsky.

The invaluable Project Coordinators who worked in the AIA Chicago office and made the project happen administratively were Aldarcy C. Lewis, Audrey Cusack, Eva Silverman, and Joyce de Vries.

A special thank you goes to the late Paul Gapp, the architecture critic for the *Chicago Tribune*, who gave us enthusiastic interest and support when we needed it the most.
—Steven F. Weiss, AIA, and Alice Sinkevitch

PREFACE

Chicago's eminent position in the history of architecture has been so firmly established that it borders on cliché. The modernist myth describes our past in terms of a succession of great episodes: the heroic Chicago School of the 1880s and 1890s, the Beaux Arts fall from grace, a sophisticated Art Deco interlude in the 1920s and 1930s, and the triumphal flowering of modernism after World War II. Louis H. Sullivan, John Wellborn Root, and Ludwig Mies van der Rohe are the central heroes. The steel frame, the high-speed elevator, and the curtain wall provided their technological expressions. But in the best biblical sense, each golden age has ended in disaster. Burnham tempts us to leave Sullivan's paradise, Root is toppled by Herbert Hoover's economic depression, and a postmodern plague descends upon us after Mies dies.

This legend is illustrated by photos of buildings that we have learned to admire, but the story is too simplistic to be of much use when we actually look at the city. Frank Lloyd Wright is too complex both as a person and as an artist to fit into any historic theory; and when we examine the work of Burnham, Sullivan, Root, and Mies, we find many plausible but contradictory interpretations. Bertrand Goldberg exemplifies the architect who has consistently followed a vision that does not fit neatly into a simple view of history, while the buildings of gifted experimenters like Harry Weese seem to fit into history in several places.

Some of our most productive architects never became aware of an overriding historic mission; they simply sought to design useful buildings. Firms like Hausner & Macsai, Gordon & Levin, and Solomon, Cordwell & Buenz invented a form of urban housing so well adapted to the economy and technology of our time that it has become almost invisible.

There is also a large body of work that those of us who were educated as architects were trained not to see: Rapp & Rapp, in their great movie palaces, adapted the formal vocabulary of the opera house to an unprecedented optical and acoustic technology, culminating in a seating geometry that enabled every spectator to have an undistorted view of a vast rectangle of space. But the quality and originality of their work, like that of the movies themselves, was not immediately apparent.

Some dedicated architects endured isolation and ridicule to do what they felt was right. Belli & Belli responded to the programs of scores of Catholic congregations, which wanted recognizable polychrome saints at a time when the professional elite was searching for salvation in the structural grid. Their work now seems to have been prematurely postmodern, but their practice displayed a tough-minded consistency and commitment that sets them worlds apart from more recent trend followers.

This guide should clarify our vision of Chicago. For the past two years Alice Sinkevitch has sent into our neighborhoods a dedicated troop of scouts who have trained themselves to see the city with open minds and keen eyes. There were a few practicing architects among them, but the majority were amateurs in the most loving sense of the word. Many are docents for the Chicago Architecture Foundation and have had a critical part in creating a political and educational environment in which preservation is possible. Others are dedicated preservationists who have worked within the city government and cultural institutions.

Their greatest accomplishment, however, was not only to have catalogued the city's famous buildings but also to have captured the rich diversity of the built environment. There is a gritty integrity to Chicago's neighborhoods. Their buildings remind us that, until quite

recently, architecture was a craft handed down through the generations. Our city was built largely by people who could not legally be
called architects today. This book amply demonstrates that the loss
of this craft tradition has not improved the quality of our lives.

This guide is a monument to the breadth of our scouts' interests
and to the clarity of their observations. It will help us to see Chicago as
a whole and to recognize in it a much richer architectural culture than
many of us might have expected.

Now that we have the book, let's go out and look at the city. It's all
here—the vain efforts to scratch out a place in architectural history, the
confident works of genius, and the spontaneous outpourings of decorative invention that sometimes result from the simple task of laying brick.
—John F. Hartray, Jr., FAIA

AIA GUIDE TO CHICAGO

THE SHAPING OF CHICAGO

Perry R. Duis

C hicago holds a special place in the history of American cities.

It frequently assumes the role of the great American exaggeration, the place where common characteristics are stretched to their limits. Other cities grew during the nineteenth century, but Chicago mushroomed. Every town had its boosters, but the Windy City's were obstreperously boastful. Crime and political corruption were everywhere, but in Chicago they seemed to be elevated to an art. More positively, Chicago became a synonym for "the new" and "the first," leading the way in architecture, literature, and social reform—in part because, as a brash upstart, it possessed few encumbering traditions.

As the archetypal American industrial city, Chicago's rise and metamorphoses not only illustrate the urbanization process at its most basic. They also demonstrate how the compelling forces of concentration, which allow efficiencies of space and time to outweigh all other considerations, both attract people and activities into cities and drive them outward toward the fringes.

The creative efforts of talented individuals are the substance of this book. But location, challenges, opportunities, and calamities also shaped Chicago and stimulated the city's problem-solvers to reach inventive solutions. Many conditions, events, and movements have shaped the city; the following are some that have had a special impact on the built environment.

The Power of Place

Chicago's location was both a curse and a blessing. The land at the banks of the Chicago River was swampy, and the stream itself flowed too slowly to turn a waterwheel or clear the mouth of silt. But it sat at the southwestern end of the massive Great Lakes navigation system. Via these waterways, prerailroad commerce penetrated the midsection of the continent and, interrupted only by a dry-weather portage, was linked to the Mississippi and Missouri rivers via the

Illinois & Michigan Canal in Bridgeport

Illinois and Des Plaines rivers and the south branch of the Chicago River. Its advantages made Chicago's site a spot to control. When the first outsiders, Jacques Marquette and Louis Jolliet, explored the region in 1673, the warlike Potawatomi had already displaced peaceful Indian tribes. Around 1779 Jean Baptiste Point Du Sable built a cabin roughly where the Equitable Building stands today and became Chicago's first permanent resident. A French-speaking black man, Du Sable was one of many Great Lakes traders who exchanged iron and cloth goods for furs.

In 1803, the year of the Louisiana Purchase, the United States established Fort Dearborn, the nation's westernmost military post, near what is now the south end of the Michigan Avenue Bridge. In 1812, in an incident known as the Fort Dearborn Massacre, the Potawatomi attempted to regain the valuable site. They burned the stockade, while three miles to the south, a raiding party killed most of the garrison and their families as they fled along the lake shore.

The fort was rebuilt in 1816, the same year that surveying began for the Illinois & Michigan Canal, which would provide a year-round link between the Chicago River and the Illinois-Mississippi river system some seventy-five miles away. A national financial panic in 1819 and fears of Indian unrest halted progress until the 1830s. On August 5, 1833, thirteen electors gathered to incorporate the Town of Chicago, and newcomers—many of whom were land speculators—began arriving in droves. By 1836, when work on the canal began in earnest, optimism about Chicago's future had boosted land prices to astronomical levels and attracted over 3,000 more residents. In March 1837 Chicagoans demanded and received a city charter from the state legislature.

The Golden Funnel and the Growth of Transportation

In the mid-1840s Chicago's merchants began to exploit the city's site by creating what might be called the golden funnel. The settlement of farmland throughout the West produced agricultural surpluses that could be shipped to eastern markets most efficiently via Chicago's water linkage. Wheat shipped through Chicago rose from a meager few bushels in 1840 to nearly two million bushels seven years later.

In 1848 several events improved the funnel's flow. The Illinois & Michigan Canal was finally opened; plank roads to the hinterlands made it easier for farmers to roll their grain wagons into town; and the telegraph linked national and international markets to the Chicago Board of Trade, newly formed to provide a standardized, self-policing market that farmers could trust. Most significant, on October 25,

Union Stock Yards Entrance Gate

1848, a tiny locomotive named the Pioneer made its inaugural run between Chicago and present-day Oak Park.

The promises of the 1840s became prosperous realities in the 1850s. Rail lines extending west to the Mississippi and east to Philadelphia and New York transformed Chicago into a national transportation hub. Grain elevators now towered over the city, while huge stacks of timber along the river banks proved that Chicago was the nation's leading lumber center.

The Civil War ushered in a new era for Chicago. The city's size and remoteness from military action made it an ideal site for producing war goods. The golden funnel now supplied the Union Army with horses and hay and fed its troops with carloads of bread, condensed milk, dried fruit, and cans of cooked meats from Chicago slaughterhouses. So great was the movement of livestock into the city that the need for efficiency forced packers and shippers to consolidate. On Christmas Day, 1865, they opened the Union Stock Yards four miles southwest of the city. The yards soon enabled Chicago to displace Cincinnati as the nation's pork-packing capital.

Dire Necessities and Creative Technologies

The new city offered few amenities. Depending on the season, the streets were graded dust or mud that regularly disappeared under ponds left by springtime rain. Visitors were uniformly unimpressed by the buildings. Shortages of structural wood and skilled labor led to lightweight "balloon frame" construction, invented in 1833, which gave the mushrooming population housing easily built by unskilled laborers.

Only gradually did more substantial masonry structures join the tiny buildings of logs or crudely cut boards. In 1837 William B. Ogden, the city's first mayor, enticed John M. Van Osdel, a carpenter and architect, from New York to Chicago to begin providing something more than an architecture of expediency.

"Balloon Frame" Construction

City officials also turned to engineering experts to solve problems generated by exploding growth. To combat epidemics by improving drainage flow, the city's chief engineer, Ellis S. Chesbrough, designed a sewer system to be constructed on top of the existing streets, an expensive project that began in 1855 and continued for decades. The pavement grade was then raised a dozen feet, and building owners turned to youthful talents such as George Westinghouse and George M. Pullman to jack up old structures and insert new foundations. In older neighborhoods, such as Pilsen, these raised street grades are still visible.

Public health reformers began a long crusade against unsanitary burial practices in 1858. Their efforts eventually closed the city cemetery, now the southern part of Lincoln Park, and increased the attractiveness of landscaped plots in rural areas. Cemeteries such as Graceland, Rosehill, and Oak Woods became accessible to city dwellers because of advances in public transportation. These improvements included steam railroad commuter service, a horse-drawn street railway system, and a pivoting span bridge over the river at Rush Street (1856), touted as the first iron bridge west of the Alleghenies. Architects such as W. W. Boyington, Edward Burling, and Otis L. Wheelock joined Van Osdel as designers of specialized structures for stores, public buildings and homes.

With heavy maritime traffic keeping bridges open almost perpetually, tunnels were excavated under the river at Washington (1869) and La Salle (1871) streets. When pollution from the sewage-laden river threatened the water supply, engineers designed a new water plant, the Chicago Water Tower & Pumping Station (1869), with an intake crib two miles from shore.

The Great Conflagration

To this day no one really knows how the fire of October 8–9, 1871, started. Whether it was lightning, raucous tenants, a drunken neighbor, or even a cantankerous cow kicking over a lantern, the blaze definitely began in the barn behind Patrick and Katherine O'Leary's DeKoven St. home. Incompetent dispatchers and lookouts allowed it to flare out of control, and an intense firestorm proceeded to consume block after block of a city that had had no rain since July. The conflagration raged for thirty-six hours, sweeping away a third of the city before burning itself out four miles away on the northern edge of town. Over 300 people perished, 17,450 structures were

Aftermath of the Fire of 1871

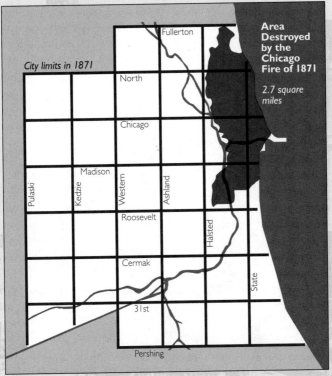

Map of the Fire's Destruction

reduced to ashes, the downtown was devastated, and on the North Side only a few scattered houses and the Water Tower were spared. At least 90,000 people were left homeless, and the livelihoods of thousands more had disappeared with their workplaces.

Residential Chicago would never be the same. The Common Council soon banned any new nonmasonry construction within the city limits (roughly Fullerton Ave. on the north, Pulaski Rd. on the west, and Pershing Rd. on the south). Thousands of North Siders who could not afford to rebuild in brick were forced to sell their lots and move just over the border, where developers were only too happy to put them in inexpensive new wooden houses. The contrast between the masonry city and the wooden suburbs on the old city borders can still be seen in spots along Fullerton Ave. west of Halsted St. The undamaged South and West sides were also dramatically transformed. Owners subdivided houses near the "burnt district" and rented space at premium rates. Overcrowding quickly deteriorated thousands of these structures and hastened inner-city decay.

In contrast to the neighborhoods, the problem downtown was the seemingly impossible one of reestablishing as quickly as possible the heart of Chicago's economic and cultural life. Rebuilding began even before the rubble cooled, and Chicagoans turned to their architects and engineers. John M. Van Osdel, Edward Burling, W. W. Boyington, Otis L. Wheelock, Gurdon P. Randall, Augustus Bauer, Asher Carter, and Peter B. Wight had as many commissions as they could handle, and for two years, as crews worked around the clock and throughout the winters, they kept track of their designs in terms of miles of building fronts constructed. The new structures appeared to be much the same as pre-Fire ones, but most were slightly taller and had more elevators. Innovations were limited to improved fire-proofing techniques.

The Fire hastened the evolution of city-use patterns. Downtown residential use, which had been declining, was not reestablished, and most of the manufacturers whose North Side factories were destroyed soon relocated in outlying industrial districts along rail lines or the river's branches. The McCormick Reaper Company, for example, replaced its plant on the north bank of the river's mouth with what would eventually be one of the nation's largest manufacturing facilities (now demolished) at Western and Blue Island avenues. The new factories were generally much larger than their predecessors and housed heavier, more complex equipment. This reduced the mobility of the enterprises, and land-use patterns were thereby fixed for decades to come.

The Logic of Centralization

By 1870 the city's population surged to 298,977, but wartime shortages of building materials and carpenters had hampered housebuilding, and many areas were overcrowded. This congestion, aggravated by the noise and smoke of postbellum factories, instilled thoughts of escape. The middle and upper classes could choose to move to quiet, orderly sections of the city serviced by expanded horsecar lines and commuter railways. Those seeking permanent residential refuge found homes in subdivisions and suburban towns that sprang up along railroad routes.

The population of Chicago exploded to 500,000 in 1880 and to more than a million in 1890. The city had become big, and in this largeness was an overwhelming logic of concentration, of which post-Fire factories were only one example. The savings of time and economies of scale that resulted from putting many departments under one roof—so that belts and pulleys from one huge stationary steam engine could drive the greatest number of machines—more than paid for the cost of building the structure. Downtowns were seen as also benefiting from economies of size and geographic convenience. In Chicago most of the public transit lines, which included the world's largest cable car system, were built to carry passengers into the central business district. This area acquired the nickname the Loop in the early 1880s because it was encircled by transit tracks. Electric trolleys went into service in 1890, and two years later an elevated "iron highway" was inaugurated—the first of five radial rapid transit lines that would be united in 1897 by the Union Loop built above the downtown's perimeter. Steam suburban lines brought an estimated 100,000 additional daily passengers into their six depots, which also ringed the downtown.

Nineteenth-century urban residents also exercised the logic of concentration in their division of city spaces. For them, domestic

"The Rookery" Lobby by Burnham & Root

dwellings were clearly private spaces, and the wealthy were better able than others to use private areas for sheltering their affairs. They built their homes in exclusive districts, like Prairie Ave. on the South Side or Astor St. on the Near North, and their luxurious world of private clubs, schools, opera boxes, and carriages permitted selective contact with the rest of Chicago. Conversely, the streets, sidewalks, parks, river, and government facilities made up the public places. These were commonly owned, primarily utilitarian, and usually undistinguished in design—with one great exception, Chicago's well-landscaped parks and boulevards. In 1869 Illinois Health Board member Dr. John H. Rauch, along with real estate developers and civic boosters, persuaded voters and the Illinois General Assembly to create three tax districts to fund an ambitious ring of parks several miles beyond the built-up neighborhoods.

A third category of city space might be called semipublic places, privately owned areas to which the public had access. Some were noncommercial, such as churches, which by the 1890s were often grand buildings with Sunday school or meeting facilities at least partly available to all. Most semipublic spaces, however, were profit-making, and the degree to which they had become objects of civic pride reflected the progress of urbanization and centralization. The office building was an example. Although it featured private offices, it offered services ranging from barbershops to restaurants, and its elevator lobby had evolved into a showplace meant to make a good impression and attract tenants. In the (now demolished) Chicago Stock Exchange Building, for instance, the elevator cages were enclosed in delicate metalwork; the Marquette Building presents a Chicago history lesson in mosaic tiles; and the Rookery has an airy, naturally illuminated core.

The concentration of activities downtown encouraged the creation of districts within the Loop. The railway stations girding the central business district, for example, encouraged a similarly shaped placement of hotels for the convenience of passengers. The Chicago Board of Trade at the foot of La Salle St. drew not only brokers but also law firms, banks, and insurance companies to adjacent blocks. To the east, Marshall Field had moved his retail business from Lake St. to State St. just prior to the Fire. His competitors followed, so that within months a residential area had been transformed into the city's main mercantile district. Randolph St. emerged as Chicago's theater row, as well as the home of a thriving music publishing industry. Warehousing, printing, and clothing concerns located on the edges of downtown to be near suppliers and customers.

Department stores were examples of semipublic spaces designed for public use. Before the Fire, merchants had offered undifferentiated varieties of wholesale and retail goods. Eventually, merchandise and services were centralized under one roof, and the stores functioned as "factories of consumption" that saved consumers time and steps. The store that Marshall Field built after the Fire was one of America's most lavishly furnished. By the end of the century, Field had begun what would become a complex that would cover more than a square block on State St.; Schlesinger & Mayer had commissioned the Louis H. Sullivan building at State and Madison streets (later known as the Carson, Pirie, Scott store); and Siegel, Cooper & Co. had fifteen acres of floor space in the Second Leiter Building. Elsewhere on "That Great Street," new buildings for Maurice Rothschild, Mandel Brothers, and the Boston Store would soon create a retail district of enormous drawing power. Huge plate glass windows allowed each store to display its wares to lure passersby, while lighting counters deep within the buildings.

Hotels had matured from rude inns into spectacularly appointed rivals to the palaces of European nobility. They offered such specialized amenities as billiard parlors, sun rooms, and ballrooms, as well as several classes of guest rooms and dining facilities. The six major railway stations near which the hotels were concentrated had in turn evolved from homely barns into spectacular urban gateways featuring so many services that they were called "cities within cities." The Auditorium, the most remarkable structure of all, combined three types of grand semipublic places. It had an office block on its Wabash Ave. side, a luxurious, 400-room hotel fronting on Michigan Ave., and an acoustically perfect theater, the world's largest when it opened in 1889.

In the 1890s the battle between centralization and dispersal continued, with new factors favoring decentralization. One of these was the replacement of the steam engine as the power source for an entire factory by small electrical motors for each machine. This spawned "electrical manufacturing suburbs," such as Harvey, Maywood, and Chicago Heights, which had room for both new factories and cheap workers' housing. Another element was the continuing migration to the urban fringe by those who could afford spacious homes.

Labor Unrest in the Industrial City

Raw materials flowed through the golden funnel to post-Fire industries, where many tasks carried on in the new plants created a dependence on repetitive jobs requiring few skills. Long hours and low wages fomented worker dissatisfaction, which led to an era of labor unrest and violence. The nation's attention focused on Chicago in 1886, when demands for an eight-hour workday produced a series of strikes at the McCormick works. On the night of May 4 police charged into a labor rally at Haymarket Sq., near the corner of Randolph and Desplaines streets. A bomb exploded, and the police opened fire. This Haymarket Riot led to a conspiracy trial, executions, and international protests.

The self-sufficient model factory and town thirteen miles south of Chicago, begun in 1880 by George M. Pullman, was the epitome of the new industrial order. Architect Solon S. Beman designed an efficient factory, workers' housing, and amenities such as a shopping arcade, stables, a market, a park, a hotel, and a church. It was hardly utopia, however. Pullman sought a sober, dependable work force that did not have to live in the city's slums, but workers chafed under planning that kept them isolated from executives and placed controls on how they lived and where they shopped. During a serious depression that began in 1893 the company slashed wages and laid off workers, but Pullman refused to lower his rents. The Pullman strike of 1894 and nationwide boycott resulted in the firebombing of Pullman's cars and occupation of his town by federal militia. Although the

First Infantry Armory by Burnham & Root (demolished)

company won the struggle, the courts eventually forced it to sell the houses and to hire nonresidents. The Haymarket and Pullman incidents produced front-page headlines worldwide, not only because they were startling events but also because Chicago's economic importance and position as the nation's fastest-growing city prompted widespread concern that battles between workers and police might eventually be repeated everywhere.

The Development of the Skyscraper

Downtown centralization required special buildings to draw together thousands of people simultaneously, and a rapid succession of technological developments made this possible. Advances in foundation engineering and in metal-frame construction, reliable lighting systems (first gas, then electric), improvements in steam heating and fireproofing, and faster, safer elevators made vertical expansion possible. Soaring land values demanded the intensive use of downtown lots, just as telephone and telegraph communications were enabling business leaders to move away from their manufacturing facilities and near their lawyers, bankers, and other downtown services.

It took more than demand, however, to create tall buildings. Chicago was blessed with a talented cadre of architects and engineers. John M. Van Osdel and Peter B. Wight were seasoned veterans among a group of varied talents. William Le Baron Jenney and William Sooy Smith concentrated on foundations and structure. Dankmar Adler, an expert in acoustics, teamed with Louis H. Sullivan, the master of detail. Daniel H. Burnham, who understood the business of architecture, formed a partnership with John Wellborn Root, who

Construction of the Marquette Building

excelled in its artistry. William Holabird and Martin Roche were among the steadiest producers, with a stream of successful designs.

The architects and engineers had to find ways to secure tall buildings in Chicago's spongy soil. Initially, following suggestions from structural engineer Frederick Baumann, they designed raft foundations that spread a building's weight over as much of the subsurface soil as possible, and they set entrance levels high enough to compensate for expected settling. Particularly heavy or tall buildings required more substantial support. Adler & Sullivan, for instance, placed the structural walls of the Auditorium on continuous reinforced concrete foundations and carried the massive weight of the seventeen-story tower on a floating raft of crisscross layers of timbers, steel rails, and I-beams. In their seventeen-story Schiller Building raft foundations were supported on wooden pilings driven to refusal; the same architects subsequently made an important breakthrough in settlement problems when they supported the west party wall of the Chicago Stock Exchange with tubular concrete caissons (the first used in Chicago) that reached fifty-five feet down to hard pan, an oxidized clay.

Framing problems also had to be resolved. The six-foot-thick walls and tiny windows of the lower floors of Burnham & Root's Monadnock Building demonstrated that extending load-bearing construction to sixteen stories limited interior space and light so severely that taller masonry projects were pointless. But a feasible way to go higher had already been worked out gradually, so that in Jenney's Home Insurance Building (1885), metal framing had eliminated the need for exterior load-bearing walls. As the construction of tall buildings evolved into all-steel structures, "curtain walls" came to function only as skins and could be made of almost any material, including glass or terra-cotta. Interiors were flooded with light through Chicago windows, which were bay-filling frames holding movable sashes on either side of large fixed panes. Most important, there were now almost no theoretical limits to a building's height.

Chicago's skyline altered at a dizzying pace after 1880, and what was daringly tall in one decade became the norm of the next and small twenty years later. The distinction of being the city's tallest building passed quickly from the ten-story Montauk Building (1882), the first labeled a skyscraper, to the thirteen-story Royal Insurance Building (1885). The Rookery, Austin, and Adams Express Co. buildings (all eleven stories) were exceptionally large when built in 1886—but of only average size once the Auditorium was under way. The Monadnock, with its load-bearing walls, and the Manhattan, with its metal frame, both reached a world's-record sixteen stories in 1890. Two years later they would be dwarfed by the twenty-one-story Masonic Temple.

Rampant Growth and Annexation

Few cities had less geographical constraint on dispersal than Chicago. The abundance of land kept down the cost of a lot or factory site, while the transportation networks that brought passengers downtown to work or shop also made it convenient for them to live great distances away. Developers aggressively marketed life on the urban fringe. They cut building costs by mass-producing limited varieties of designs, advertised their developments heavily in every language, and even gave away samples—weekend excursion rides to their subdivisions. Housing for every budget was available beyond Chicago's borders, while the congestion, crime, disease, and political corruption within them made daily headlines and provided the motivation to leave.

By the 1880s Chicago risked being rivaled by its adjacent areas, which were growing far faster than the city. Since its founding, the city had grown steadily by annexation. Now, the municipal government proposed a massive annexation that would take in such com-

The Growth of Chicago
area within city limits

1837	10 square miles
1870	35 square miles
1890	170 square miles
1900	190 square miles
1930	207 square miles
1960	225 square miles

Map of Major Annexations

munities as Hyde Park, Kenwood, and Pullman to the south and Lake View and Jefferson to the north. Many of those affected realized annexation would offer the benefits of Chicago's more advanced municipal infrastructure and better services, including schools. Others, feeling safer and morally superior to their city counterparts, earnestly wanted the status quo. Nonetheless, on June 29, 1889, by a thin majority, suburbanites spread over 125 square miles—much of it farmland—voted to join with Chicago. The city's territory almost quadrupled in one day, and its population was recorded at one million in the following year's census. Among American cities only New York was larger.

"A World of Unmixed Bliss"

The success of the annexation vote aided Chicago's efforts to become host to an international exposition being proposed to celebrate the 400th anniversary of the discovery of America. Not only did it help the negotiations for the host city to be as large as possible, but the best sites for the fairgrounds were now inside the city limits. The self-promotion of the Chicago delegation seeking congressional approval was so aggressive that it earned for the city its "Windy City" nickname. A struggle at home over location ended with the commissioners' choice of Jackson Park on the South Side. An illustrious group of architects from the East Coast and Chicago, led by Daniel H. Burnham, designed an immense architectural wonderland. Workers constructed a neo-Classic "White City" from steel frames finished in lath and staff, a mixture of plaster, cement, and jute.

To help the city look its best for the fair, several cultural institutions opened new buildings, including the Chicago Historical Society, the Chicago Academy of Sciences, and the Newberry Library. The

Palace of Fine Arts by Charles B. Atwood, World's Columbian Exposition

Art Institute rented its new home to the exposition congresses, a series of international scholarly meetings. The realization that visitors would also note what Chicago lacked motivated the founding of the Chicago Symphony Orchestra and a second University of Chicago (the first one had gone bankrupt in 1886). The World's Columbian Exposition opened amid a severe national depression, but when visitors passed through its gates in numbers that reached 750,000 a day, they found a plaster paradise in which the world's technical knowledge, mechanical skills, and manufacturing prowess had been collected, classified, subdivided, and displayed as never before. More than a million objects filled more than a hundred buildings. No exposition before or since ever aspired to such comprehensiveness.

The exposition left Chicago with two significant legacies. First, the fair drew hundreds of talented young people to the city, and despite a persistently depressed economy that hampered the arts in general, they created an innovative cultural milieu. Experimental theaters staged avant-garde productions. Small-scale publishers and little magazines, such as the *Chap-Book*, commissioned Art Nouveau illustrations and featured works by new authors, including Theodore Dreiser and George Ade. This creative community gathered in buildings especially designed for the arts, such as the low-rent artists' studios that Judge Lambert Tree erected in 1894 in the backyard of his N. Wabash Ave. house. The former Studebaker carriage works was remodeled by new owners in 1898 into the Fine Arts Building, housing a unique collection of studios, theaters, and music schools.

Second, Chicago's first elevated line was built to carry visitors between the downtown and the fairgrounds, and hundreds of small hotels and apartments were built along it and other South Side transit routes. Often hastily and poorly constructed by underfinanced opportunists whom the depression bankrupted, these buildings quickly fell into disrepair. From 1900 to 1930 African-Americans arriving from the South could find few housing opportunities outside this broad band of exposition housing, and the so-called Black Belt emerged.

"Make Big Plans, Aim High in Hope"

By the 1890s Chicago seemed to be choking on its own success. Each new downtown skyscraper added to traffic woes. The clatter of hoofs and metal wheels, peddlers' shouts, and streetcar bells had reached an unbelievable din. Some health officials worried that the darkness of the skyscraper canyons would turn the ubiquitous layers of horse manure and refuse into germ incubators. Finding one's way

Jules Guerin rendering from Plan of Chicago

around was complicated by a house-numbering system that used the meandering river as its baseline and allowed countless duplicate addresses.

Proposals to relieve the city's woes took several forms. To reduce street congestion the elevated system was extended, and a network of tunnels enabled miniature electric locomotives to haul freight, coal, and ashes to and from downtown buildings. (In 1992 a leak from the Chicago River flooded the long-abandoned system, creating an estimated $1 billion in damage.) By the beginning of the new century the extensive use of automobiles was being proposed as a solution to several ills. Their maneuverability would help relieve traffic jams involving fixed-route vehicles, they would eliminate the health hazards connected with manure and animal carcasses, and they would reduce the dense smoke from commuter trains because fewer trains would be needed. There were also several governmental efforts to untangle Chicago's street chaos. The City Council voted in 1893 to limit building heights to 130 feet. (Lobbying interests successfully raised the ceiling in following years.) The aldermen also renamed hundreds of streets and in 1909 instituted a rational house-numbering system with State and Madison streets as baselines.

The most significant proposal combined careful restructuring of the street system with strict planning for future development. Calling upon his experience with the Columbian Exposition, Daniel H. Burnham and his assistant, Edward H. Bennett, backed by the Merchants' and Commercial clubs, began work in 1906 on a master plan for the city. When published three years later, the *Plan of Chicago* presented a grand blueprint of transportation for the entire region and a demonstration of how public spaces could be made as magnificent as semipublic ones. The plan reserved the lakefront for recreation and proposed a string of offshore islands. Monroe Harbor and Grant Park would became a formal "front door," while the seat of government would be relocated to an immense plaza at the junction of Congress and Halsted streets. Burnham and Bennett took great pains to demonstrate how railroad facilities could be efficiently concentrated in outlying districts, how commercial and recreational use of the river's downtown banks could be compatible, and how attractive a city of uniform height might be. The most important feature, however, was the treatment of streets as the veins and arteries of a living organism. Impediment-free circulation required widening many streets, including Michigan Ave., designated as the new gateway to the North Side. Diagonal streets would improve crosstown travel. The plan was lavishly illustrated by artist Jules Guerin, who purposely depicted the streets as low-density mixtures of automobiles, horse-drawn vehicles, and pedestrians to demonstrate the benefits of proper urban planning.

To promote Burnham's grand scheme, the Commercial Club established the Chicago Plan Commission of civic and business leaders, chaired by brewer Charles H. Wacker and with Burnham as its chief architect. The commission not only lobbied for individual projects that would conform to the plan but also campaigned intensively to sell it to the citizenry. Pamphlets on the plan blanketed the city, nickelodeon audiences found promotional movies on it sandwiched between standard features, and eighth-grade children were required to pass examinations based on *Wacker's Manual of the Plan of Chicago*, a textbook version published in 1912.

Many people objected to the plan. The Army Corps of Engineers, which was responsible for harbor development along the Lake Michigan shore, thought Chicago would be foolish to relinquish miles of potential docking facilities for recreation. The city negotiated a compromise under which Municipal (later Navy) Pier was built to combine both uses. Property owners objected to street-widening plans that destroyed their front yards or buildings. Railroads resisted consolidation. And A. Montgomery Ward, the mail-order baron, opposed the idea of clustering public buildings in the downtown lakefront park. Ward's lawyers invoked an obscure clause in the original federal land grant that gave Michigan Ave. property owners, of which he was one, veto power over any construction there. Ward did not challenge building the Art Institute, but he pursued lawsuits to the Illinois Supreme Court to prevent the construction in the park of the John Crerar Library and the Field Columbian Museum.

The Burnham Plan shaped public-works construction for decades. Its success depended on a bold government to borrow and spend on a grand scale, and William Hale ("Big Bill") Thompson, who was elected mayor in 1915, was willing to do just that. During the next eight years Thompson began a physical transformation of the city. He enhanced the southern bank of the river with a bilevel street named in honor of Wacker; and he built new bridges, including the double-decker at Michigan Ave., thereby making that street a major thoroughfare on both sides of the river. Thompson also extended Ogden Ave. and elevated Roosevelt Rd. to speed traffic across the city, and he even straightened out an obtrusive bend in the Chicago River between 12th and 16th streets.

The plan also inspired passage in 1923 of Chicago's first comprehensive zoning law, in an attempt to regulate both vertical and horizontal sprawl. The law replaced the rigid height limit with an elaborate formula that allowed towers above the twenty-second story—provided they did not occupy more than one-fourth of the area of the lot and that tower space was not more than one-sixth of the entire building. While this did not help traffic problems, it slightly reduced canyon effects. The zoning law proved quite compatible with skyscraper developments of the 1920s, a decade that witnessed an enormous building boom and the first significant appearance of tall buildings outside the Loop. The Burnham Plan urged making the Chicago River a focal point, and by 1929 the Merchandise Mart—with more than four million square feet of floor space the world's largest building—was gracing the northern bank of the main branch, while the Chicago Daily News Building peered across the river at the forty-five-story Civic Opera Building, built by utilities magnate Samuel Insull. The opening of the Michigan Avenue Bridge in 1920 extended development north of the river, much as Burnham had envisioned. The dazzling white Wrigley Building was soon joined by hotels, a Northwestern University campus, and other office buildings, most notably the Tribune Tower, whose design was chosen in an international competition. A string of new apartment buildings stretched northward along Lake Shore Dr. In the Loop itself buildings of twenty and twenty-five stories became the norm, while the Chicago Board of Trade, at 605 feet, loomed over its neighbors.

Elsewhere the zoning law not only protected property values in built-up areas from incompatible or detrimental intrusions but also provided a general guideline for developing the remaining open lands. Throughout the 1920s developers lured workers into almost endless rows of sturdy, spacious, one-story brick bungalows. Shopping in the "bungalow belt" was usually nearby, because the zoning law fostered the development of outlying business districts centered on major transit intersections where heavy pedestrian traffic was generated. These shopping districts were also likely to include the "popcorn palace" movie theaters in which architects such as Rapp & Rapp had mastered sight lines and acoustics and created spectacular interiors based on escapist themes.

Poverty, Racism, and the Growth of Slums

In stark contrast to the Loop's nineteenth-century splendors were the slums adjacent to them. Owners had deferred maintenance on properties that they expected to raze as the downtown expanded outward. Tall-building construction had instead restricted development to the core of downtown, and decrepit transient housing soon ringed the Loop on all sides. On the South Side was the Levee, one of the nation's largest vice districts, controlled by colorful turn-of-the-century scoundrels, First Ward aldermen "Bathhouse John" Coughlin and Michael ("Hinky Dink") Kenna.

The residential slums began about a mile west and south of the Loop. The poor, many of them immigrants, lived in old wooden houses standing cheek by jowl with factories and bars or in once elegant apartments and mansions converted into rooming houses and then tenements. Some lots were filled front to back with ramshackle frame houses; others became refuse pits in front of houses that had not been elevated when the street grade was raised. Many of the tiny units had no bathroom or kitchen. While other neighborhoods were adopting electricity and steam heat, the slums had yet to see gas lighting or coal stoves in every room.

Among the few constant features of slum life were the buildings themselves, the high death rates, and political bosses who prevented reforms. By doling out city jobs, they got enough votes to remain on the City Council for decades. Efforts were largely ineffectual to end the hegemony of the gray wolves, as the press called such grafters as Coughlin, Kenna, "Foxy Ed" Cullerton and "Johnny De Pow" Powers. Political reformers could count on support only from the middle-class

CHA—Stateway Gardens under Construction

residents of the neighborhoods adjacent to the slums, and the political parties could not supply sufficiently strong challengers.

The multiplicity of slum problems called for a multifunctional solution. Such a "department store" approach to social reform was pioneered by Jane Addams, who arrived on the West Side in 1889 with Ellen Gates Starr to establish Hull House. The traditional approach to charity had been to dole out food and money from a downtown office or to intrude on humble homes with prying questions about worthiness. Addams felt that the proper way to help the poor was to live among them and create a semipublic place, the settlement house, where those in need could find a variety of services. Hull House offered the arts, job training, health services, child care, physical education, domestic science, a library, and a savings bank. Hull House expanded to thirteen buildings covering a square block and inspired the creation of fifty similar facilities across the city, most notably the University of Chicago and Northwestern University settlements and Chicago Commons. Ironically, by teaching job skills and thrift, settlement houses—instead of instilling neighborhood loyalty and cohesiveness—contributed to the transience of the slum by showing its occupants how to move on to better lives elsewhere.

Burnham's vision of the City Beautiful made only vague comments about how deconcentration could solve slum problems, and it failed to recognize that racial discrimination and poverty are perversely centralizing forces. So while preservation or dispersal were options elsewhere in Chicago, the Madison St. skid row still sheltered the homeless, and the dense ring of slums surrounding the downtown continued to house those too poor to afford anything else. The 50,000 African-Americans who migrated to Chicago during World War I were trapped by racial discrimination within overcrowded areas, regardless of their economic circumstances. Their competition with returning veterans for jobs and housing led to a bloody race riot in July 1919. Threats of violence, combined with racial covenants in sale and rental agreements, kept the Black Belt a firmly walled enclave.

After World War II, although vast neighborhood-clearance lands lay vacant, the Chicago Housing Authority began a policy of erecting high-rise buildings on compact sites, claiming as its motives the high costs of land and federal pressure to save money on construction. It was clear to critics, however, that the policy ensured that the maximum number of African-Americans arriving from the South would be absorbed within the existing Black Belt, thereby decreasing the possibility that middle-class black families near its edges might move into adjacent white neighborhoods. By the early 1960s Chicago officials had accepted the widespread belief that it was easier and cheaper to demolish whole neighborhoods of substandard old flats and bungalows than to renovate structures on an individual basis. The result was massive land clearance in a swath that encircled the downtown and expanded several miles into the South Side.

The Depression and Public Works

For most Chicagoans, prosperity disappeared as the 1920s ended. Declines in construction and other economic indicators had begun around 1927, and by the time Wall Street crashed in October 1929, welfare cases were beyond the capabilities of private agencies. Ironically, the central location that underlay much of Chicago's past prosperity made the city a prime destination for the homeless traveling in boxcars. Unfinished lower Wacker Dr. provided temporary shelter for both transients and residents who found themselves evicted or foreclosed. The "Winded City" seemed to be moving backward. Health and education services were cut to nineteenth-century levels, streets were strewn with garbage, and at least thirty downtown build-

Chrysler Building by Holabird & Root, 1933 World's Fair

ings were demolished to save paying taxes. Among them were Henry
Hobson Richardson's Marshall Field Wholesale Building and Burnham
& Root's Masonic Temple.

Chicago turned to dramatic solutions. Where Republican Mayor
Thompson had built with bonds, voters in 1931 backed a new Democratic machine under Anton Cermak and his successor, Edward J.
Kelly, who funneled federal New Deal money into massive public
works projects. Not only was the Outer Drive Bridge opened in
1937 and Municipal (now Midway) Airport upgraded into a major
facility, but new viaducts, sidewalks, school athletic fields, and other
projects put paychecks in thousands of hands. Mayor Kelly enthusiasti-
cally backed the wholesale replacement of the slum belt with public
housing projects. The first three were built in 1935: the Jane Addams
Homes, the Julia C. Lathrop Homes, and Trumbull Park Homes. Chicago also began work on a long-delayed subway system, the first section of which opened under State St. in 1943.

In the boldest of all moves, at the nadir of the Depression in 1933
Chicago celebrated its centennial with the Century of Progress Exposition, sprawled along the lakefront and focused on what is now the
current site of Meigs Field. The fair offered an optimistic statement
that science, industry, and business would bring a return of prosperity.
Its futuristic buildings were made of such unconventional materials as
rolled steel, Masonite, and plywood; bright colors, accents of neon
and fluorescent lights, and a whimsical Midway gave the fair an escapist atmosphere.

The Depression ended with the military buildup of World War II,
and Chicago's central location again shaped its role. Its diverse industrial base made the metropolis second only to Detroit as a produc-
er of war materiel, but to fulfill 1,400 federal contracts, companies
sought larger quarters outside the city. The gigantic Dodge-Chicago
plant at 76th St. and Cicero Ave., in what is now Ford City Shopping Center, the Buick aircraft engine plants in Melrose Park, and the
Amertorp torpedo plant in Forest Park led the industrial suburbanization, which also drew the latest influx of workers to suburban "defense housing."

The Loop Reborn versus
the Logic of Decentralization

Urban patterns entrenched by the Great Depression and wartime
controls crumbled with the arrival of postwar prosperity and mobility
and although few noticed at first, among the traditions in decline was
centralization itself.

Many businesses remained eager to locate downtown. Beginning with the ground breaking in 1952 for the Prudential Building, the first Loop skyscraper since the Field Building of the 1930s, tower after tower appeared in rapid succession. "The tall boys are sprouting in bunches," proclaimed one journalist in 1967. The Loop seemed reborn: the Inland Steel, the Chicago Civic Center (now Richard J. Daley Center), the Brunswick, and the First National Bank buildings were just a few of the additions. Most buildings of the 1960s and 1970s were at least indirectly influenced by the careful, ordered style of Ludwig Mies van der Rohe, whose strong, black-framed glass towers became the ultimate statement of the curtain wall. Innovations gradually came into the style, as in the graceful curves of Lake Point Tower and the bold bracing of the John Hancock Center. The greatest structural achievement of the era was the Sears Tower, at 1,454 feet the world's tallest building. Although pundits questioned its site west of the Loop, Sears chairman Arthur M. Wood defended it, using the logic of the centralization argument. The major factor in choosing the location was "our employees—how they would get to and from work," he explained. "The site we chose offers all the advantages we were looking for . . . close to the post office, financial district, government offices, and the major attractions."

For many others, the trend toward dispersal greatly accelerated in the postwar years. The first evidence was the suburban exodus of industry made possible by a superhighway system that had begun in 1954 with the Congress (later Eisenhower) Expressway. By 1960 work was either finished or under way on the Northwest (later Kennedy), Southwest (later Stevenson), Edens, and Kingery; the Dan Ryan would soon follow. Industrial developers, who had long complained that zoning in Chicago stunted expansion by preserving too much land for residential purposes, grabbed at the irresistible lure of lower taxes and cheaper land in suburbia. They were quick to take advantage of the independence from rail depots that was made possible by the increasing use of truck transportation. The opening of O'Hare International Airport in 1962, on a former Douglas Aircraft Co. plant site, provided a new form of transportation hub particularly suited for manufacturers of high-value, low-bulk goods such as electronics. Chicago reached its peak population of 3.6 million in 1950, as developers were filling in the open tracts on the Northwest and Southwest sides. But land in the suburbs was cheaper, and by the early 1960s virtually all new single-family construction was taking place beyond the city limits. In some suburbs, failed developments from the 1920s were completed near commuter lines; in others, the dominance of the automobile was recognized and developments were oriented toward highways.

Within the city, neighborhoods became less cohesive and no longer the focus of residents' lives. Many Chicagoans had traditionally

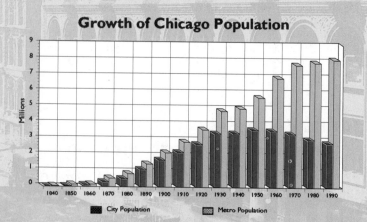

Growth of Chicago Population

Millions

| 1840 | 1850 | 1860 | 1870 | 1880 | 1890 | 1900 | 1910 | 1920 | 1930 | 1940 | 1950 | 1960 | 1970 | 1980 | 1990 |

■ City Population   ▨ Metro Population

met most of their needs with local churches, stores, saloons, news-papers, movie theaters, and schools. Outings to a major park or shopping expeditions to the Loop were special events. That world evaporated after World War II, especially in the wake of 1949 federal legislation that made it easier to obtain a GI Bill or FHA mortgage on a house in the suburbs than on one in the city. Two new phenom-ena, malls anchored by large chain stores and franchise food outlets, drew clientele from wide areas, forcing many neighborhood busi-nesses to close; while television sealed the fate of the local movie house and local newspaper. Small manufacturing plants also closed, and more breadwinners had to travel longer distances to work, of-ten by auto. As neighborhood populations aged, their schools and churches struggled to survive.

The disintegration of neighborhoods affected the fate of Chicago's Democratic machine, which had begun the postwar years in a swirl of scandals that ended the fourteen-year mayoralty of Edward J. Kelly. His successor, Martin H. Kennelly, a moving-and-storage company ex-ecutive, presented enough of a good-government image to hold the organization together while planners were laying out the expressway and urban renewal programs, but in 1955 the aloof incumbent found himself ousted by the city clerk, Richard J. Daley. Promising greater emphasis on neighborhood and family concerns, the new mayor kept the machine alive for the next twenty-one years, in part because he functioned as a symbolic bulwark against change. His early years in office benefited from the infusions of federal money that built O'Hare, the expressways, and a new water-filtration plant, and he adjusted the machine to reflect Chicago's changing ethnic and racial makeup—while critics charged that his moves were too slow and too limited. He even survived the charge of a "police riot" at the 1968 Democratic National Convention.

But Daley's ability to deliver the vote began to wane in the early 1970s, and the city's Democratic political organization was slowly un-raveling when he died in office in 1976. Voters now paid more atten-tion to the media than to their precinct captains, and middle-class African-Americans felt alienated. A half-century of political stability was replaced by a succession of five chief executives in just over twelve years. In 1979 a political maverick, Jane M. Byrne, upset Daley's machine successor, Michael A. Bilandic, but she, in turn, lost four years later to Chicago's first black mayor, Harold Washington, who proclaimed that the machine was dead. Washington's sudden death in November 1987 was followed by the interim mayorality of Eugene Sawyer, who was defeated in a special election by Daley's son, Richard M. Daley. In 1989 Daley won a full term—but not as the head of the centralized, cohesive machine that had put his father in office.

The Birth of the Preservation Movement

The creation of the magnificent postwar skyline forced Chicagoans to deal with the constraints invariably imposed by each generation of ur-banites on its successors. Should they destroy the institutional artifacts of earlier ages, modify them to conform to present needs, or pre-serve them as is? The earliest response was destruction. Federally funded urban renewal and land-clearance programs leveled entire neighborhoods, including churches, small businesses, and social insti-tutions. Demolition occasionally had a specific intention, such as the clearance of the Hull House area to build the Chicago campus of the University of Illinois (opened in 1965), but more often the land was left vacant for decades.

In the Loop the wrecker's ball was in the hands of private specu-lators who claimed many first-generation skyscrapers before Chica-

Chicago Stock Exchange by Adler & Sullivan (demolished)

goans began to realize that the demolished structures included some
of the best examples of Chicago School architecture. In 1957 the
City Council created a landmarks commission, but all it could do was
issue plaques. Its inadequacy was underscored by the demolition of
Adler & Sullivan's Schiller Building in 1960 and by its replacement
with a parking structure whose facade parodies the lost classic. Nonetheless it took eight years before Chicago had a preservation law and
a commission (now the Commission on Chicago Landmarks) empowered to administer it. The subsequent loss of Adler & Sullivan's Chicago Stock Exchange in 1972 and the McCarthy Building in 1990
demonstrated that the commission could do little more than delay
demolition unless the City Council designated a building and enforced
its decision. Meanwhile, the Landmarks Preservation Council of Illinois,
the Chicago Architecture Foundation, the Chicago Chapter of the
American Institute of Architects, neighborhood groups, and countless
newspaper articles worked to foster a sense of pride in the city's physical heritage.

The Emergence
of a Service Economy

A most significant postwar change was the gradual shift in employment from a preeminence of manufacturing to service-sector jobs.
Although Chicago was still a leading industrial center, blue-collar jobs
dropped by 77 percent between 1947 and 1982. By the early 1980s
more employment dollars were earned in nonmanufacturing employment than in industry. Chicago's role as the nation's transportation

hub, strengthened by O'Hare's steady growth, attracted corporate headquarters and research facilities, rekindling intense competition between the city center and periphery for buildings. The continued lure of lower taxes and quick access by expressway, combined with the available acreage on which to build horizontally oriented office parks, generated a new wave of exurban construction. One hub for this was the O'Hare area; another was the East–West Tollway between Oak Brook and Naperville. Even Sears, which had found the downtown so advantageous in 1974, moved in 1992 to a "campus" of low buildings in the northwestern suburbs.

The service-sector world, held together by silicon chips and fiber optics, is also potentially much more mobile than the industrial one. It is no easy task to move heavy equipment; outmoded factories, such as steel mills, are simply closed. But service businesses can be transferred quickly and constantly seek newer, more flexible spaces that can accommodate rapidly evolving office technology. This mobility has increased the competition for tenants in the downtown towers.

The most exciting result of Chicago's transition to a service economy has been the latest generation of downtown construction. Since

W. Wacker Drive in 1964

W. Wacker Drive in 1992

the completion of the Sears Tower, well over 100 buildings have appeared in the central area. They represent a construction boom even greater than that of the Richard J. Daley years. On many of these buildings the Miesian frame box has yielded to shimmering glass and mirrors cast in curves and points. Michigan Avenue's Magnificent Mile is the hub of a second downtown, an idea that had been promoted since the late 1940s by real estate mogul Arthur Rubloff.

Summary

Chicagoans have discovered the depth and variety of their architectural heritage. Not only has popular interest in downtown gems expanded, but the Tax Reform Act of 1981 sparked the interest of commercial developers who invested heavily in renovating historic buildings. Although these incentives were subsequently reduced, older neighborhoods have been rediscovered and rebuilt, and many old factories adjacent to downtown have been reborn as lofts and galleries.

There are negatives, of course, most notably in the loss of semipublic spaces in the Loop. Except for the waiting room at Union Station, the great railway depots are only memories; no Loop movie theater functions, and few restaurants remain open for the after-lunch trade. The vertical malls that draw crowds to the Magnificent Mile exemplify a new breed of semipublic space that seems to shield customers from the city rather than immerse them in it, as the Loop stores did. One of the most dramatic interior spaces of the type previously associated with department stores is a public one: the atrium of the State of Illinois Center, which reinterprets the rotunda of a capitol building.

But cities change constantly, and in Chicago that is always cause for optimism. For if history proves anything about Chicago, the city will continue to find new ways to be a leader, both as a special place and as the quintessential American metropolis. Chicago is both a museum and a laboratory in which to observe how an agglomeration of peoples deploys the finite space within the city's borders and how architects respond to the challenge of designing for them. Chicago's story relates the triumphs and failures, the problems and prospects, of all American cities.

Key to Maps

*detailed feature maps are not shown on this key map

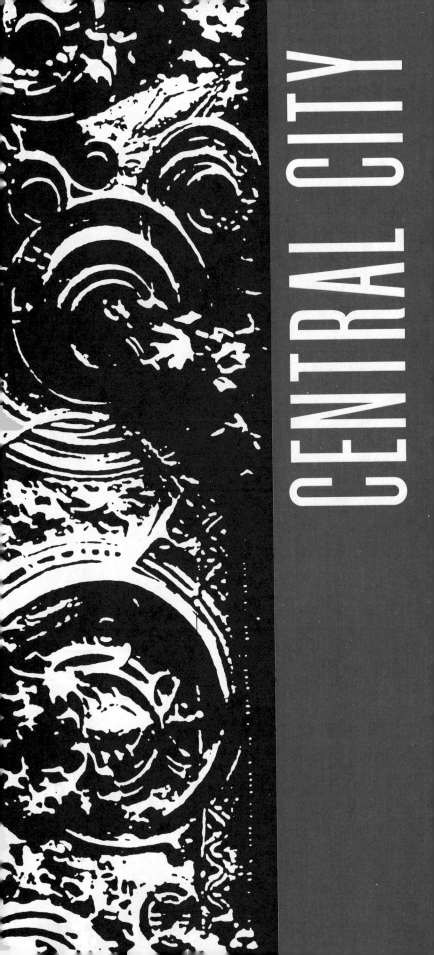

CENTRAL CITY

THE LOOP

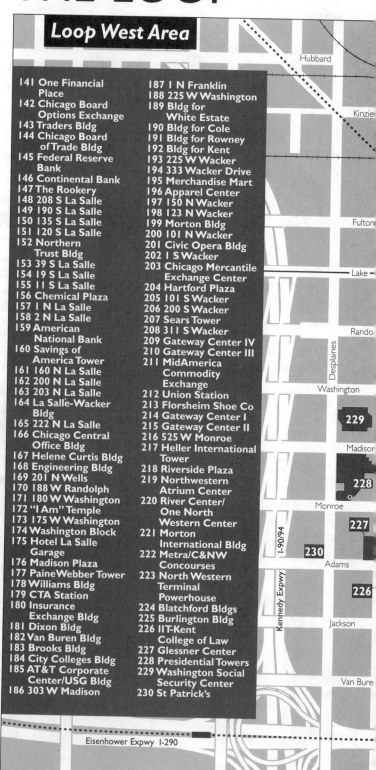

Loop West Area

141 One Financial Place
142 Chicago Board Options Exchange
143 Traders Bldg
144 Chicago Board of Trade Bldg
145 Federal Reserve Bank
146 Continental Bank
147 The Rookery
148 208 S La Salle
149 190 S La Salle
150 135 S La Salle
151 120 S La Salle
152 Northern Trust Bldg
153 39 S La Salle
154 19 S La Salle
155 11 S La Salle
156 Chemical Plaza
157 1 N La Salle
158 2 N La Salle
159 American National Bank
160 Savings of America Tower
161 160 N La Salle
162 200 N La Salle
163 203 N La Salle
164 La Salle-Wacker Bldg
165 222 N La Salle
166 Chicago Central Office Bldg
167 Helene Curtis Bldg
168 Engineering Bldg
169 201 N Wells
170 188 W Randolph
171 180 W Washington
172 "I Am" Temple
173 175 W Washington
174 Washington Block
175 Hotel La Salle Garage
176 Madison Plaza
177 Paine Webber Tower
178 Williams Bldg
179 CTA Station
180 Insurance Exchange Bldg
181 Dixon Bldg
182 Van Buren Bldg
183 Brooks Bldg
184 City Colleges Bldg
185 AT&T Corporate Center/USG Bldg
186 303 W Madison

187 1 N Franklin
188 225 W Washington
189 Bldg for White Estate
190 Bldg for Cole
191 Bldg for Rowney
192 Bldg for Kent
193 225 W Wacker
194 333 Wacker Drive
195 Merchandise Mart
196 Apparel Center
197 150 N Wacker
198 123 N Wacker
199 Morton Bldg
200 101 N Wacker
201 Civic Opera Bldg
202 1 S Wacker
203 Chicago Mercantile Exchange Center
204 Hartford Plaza
205 101 S Wacker
206 200 S Wacker
207 Sears Tower
208 311 S Wacker
209 Gateway Center IV
210 Gateway Center III
211 MidAmerica Commodity Exchange
212 Union Station
213 Florsheim Shoe Co
214 Gateway Center I
215 Gateway Center II
216 525 W Monroe
217 Heller International Tower
218 Riverside Plaza
219 Northwestern Atrium Center
220 River Center/ One North Western Center
221 Morton International Bldg
222 Metra/C&NW Concourses
223 North Western Terminal Powerhouse
224 Blatchford Bldgs
225 Burlington Bldg
226 IIT-Kent College of Law
227 Glessner Center
228 Presidential Towers
229 Washington Social Security Center
230 St Patrick's

Hubbard
Kinzie
Fulton
Lake
Rando
Desplaines
Washington
229
Madisor
228
Monroe
227
I-90/94
230
Adams
Kennedy Expwy
226
Jackson
Van Bure
Eisenhower Expwy I-290
Harrison

Illinois

Hubbard

Orleans

Kinzie

196

195

167

166

CHICAGO RIVER

223

24

Wacker

193 168

165 164

Clark

169 162 163

Lake

220

189-192

131

197

170 161

Randolph

198

LaSalle

221

199

171-172

160

133

220

200

222

Washington

174

219

218

201

188 175

173

159 134

187 176

158 157

Canal

Wacker

Madison

177 156

155 154

136

Clinton

202

Franklin

28

217

214

203

186

152

153

Monroe

28

Wells

Monroe

216

204

205

178

151

137

215

185

213

149 150

Adams

206

207

179

148

147 138

212

210

Quincy

184

145

146

211

Jackson

183

209

208

180

144

182

225

Van Buren

Wells

Financial

142 143

181

141

LaSalle

Clark

Congress

Harrison

The Loop   29

Loop East Area

1 333 N Michigan
2 360 N Michigan
3 320 N Michigan
4 Old Republic Bldg
5 Carbide &
  Carbon Bldg
6 One Illinois Center

7 Two Illinois Center
8 Boulevard Towers
9 Three Illinois Center
10 Fire Station
11 Hyatt Regency
12 Columbus Plaza
13 Swissotel

14 Fairmont Hotel
15 Sporting Club
16 Amoco Bldg
17 One Prudential Plaza
18 Two Prudential Plaza
19 150 N Michigan
20 Cultural Center
21 Illinois State
   Medical Society

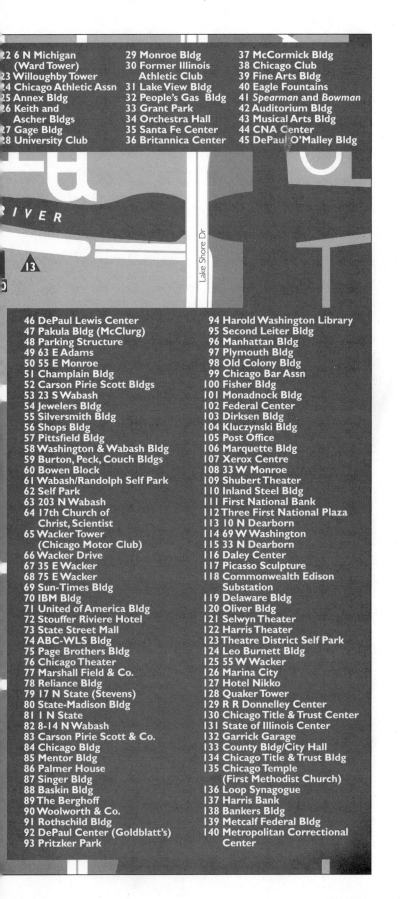

22 6 N Michigan
(Ward Tower)
23 Willoughby Tower
24 Chicago Athletic Assn
25 Annex Bldg
26 Keith and
Ascher Bldgs
27 Gage Bldg
28 University Club

29 Monroe Bldg
30 Former Illinois
Athletic Club
31 Lake View Bldg
32 People's Gas Bldg
33 Grant Park
34 Orchestra Hall
35 Santa Fe Center
36 Britannica Center

37 McCormick Bldg
38 Chicago Club
39 Fine Arts Bldg
40 Eagle Fountains
41 *Spearman* and *Bowman*
42 Auditorium Bldg
43 Musical Arts Bldg
44 CNA Center
45 DePaul O'Malley Bldg

46 DePaul Lewis Center
47 Pakula Bldg (McClurg)
48 Parking Structure
49 63 E Adams
50 55 E Monroe
51 Champlain Bldg
52 Carson Pirie Scott Bldgs
53 23 S Wabash
54 Jewelers Bldg
55 Silversmith Bldg
56 Shops Bldg
57 Pittsfield Bldg
58 Washington & Wabash Bldg
59 Burton, Peck, Couch Bldgs
60 Bowen Block
61 Wabash/Randolph Self Park
62 Self Park
63 203 N Wabash
64 17th Church of
Christ, Scientist
65 Wacker Tower
(Chicago Motor Club)
66 Wacker Drive
67 35 E Wacker
68 75 E Wacker
69 Sun-Times Bldg
70 IBM Bldg
71 United of America Bldg
72 Stouffer Riviere Hotel
73 State Street Mall
74 ABC-WLS Bldg
75 Page Brothers Bldg
76 Chicago Theater
77 Marshall Field & Co.
78 Reliance Bldg
79 17 N State (Stevens)
80 State-Madison Bldg
81 1 N State
82 8-14 N Wabash
83 Carson Pirie Scott & Co.
84 Chicago Bldg
85 Mentor Bldg
86 Palmer House
87 Singer Bldg
88 Baskin Bldg
89 The Berghoff
90 Woolworth & Co.
91 Rothschild Bldg
92 DePaul Center (Goldblatt's)
93 Pritzker Park

94 Harold Washington Library
95 Second Leiter Bldg
96 Manhattan Bldg
97 Plymouth Bldg
98 Old Colony Bldg
99 Chicago Bar Assn
100 Fisher Bldg
101 Monadnock Bldg
102 Federal Center
103 Dirksen Bldg
104 Kluczynski Bldg
105 Post Office
106 Marquette Bldg
107 Xerox Centre
108 33 W Monroe
109 Shubert Theater
110 Inland Steel Bldg
111 First National Bank
112 Three First National Plaza
113 10 N Dearborn
114 69 W Washington
115 33 N Dearborn
116 Daley Center
117 Picasso Sculpture
118 Commonwealth Edison
Substation
119 Delaware Bldg
120 Oliver Bldg
121 Selwyn Theater
122 Harris Theater
123 Theatre District Self Park
124 Leo Burnett Bldg
125 55 W Wacker
126 Marina City
127 Hotel Nikko
128 Quaker Tower
129 R R Donnelley Center
130 Chicago Title & Trust Center
131 State of Illinois Center
132 Garrick Garage
133 County Bldg/City Hall
134 Chicago Title & Trust Bldg
135 Chicago Temple
(First Methodist Church)
136 Loop Synagogue
137 Harris Bank
138 Bankers Bldg
139 Metcalf Federal Bldg
140 Metropolitan Correctional
Center

The Loop is quintessential Chicago! Here the "city of big shoulders" flaunts its continuing vitality with an unequalled display of dazzling towers and crowded streets. Jammed with a medley of cars, trucks, buses, and darting pedestrians, the Loop is an urban canvas framed by its famous "El." It is home to banks, national and international corporate headquarters, stock and commodities trading centers, and a myriad of shops, restaurants, and other support services.

The small tongue of land on which the Loop is situated, bounded by Lake Michigan on the east and the Chicago River on the north and west, determined not only the shape but also the nature of Chicago's downtown, for it demanded the utmost in concentration. Land for efficient corporate enterprise was at such a premium here that almost all other competing uses—factories, residences, civic institutions, and cultural facilities—were soon priced out of the area. The dynamics of American business required that the successful businessman be on the scene, close to where "the action" was. Thus, the second half of the nineteenth century in the Loop witnessed an increasing concentration of fewer and fewer business and support functions crowded into congested streets. Even before the Great Fire of 1871, Chicago's downtown had become a business hub. Horse-drawn omnibuses, introduced on State St. in 1859, laid the groundwork for a network of transit lines to serve a commuter population.

The Fire of 1871 reinforced these tendencies. The gridded streets of pre-Fire downtown were re-created as the most efficient pattern for the rapid development of business and commerce. Chicago's "new" downtown would provide little space for parks, churches, or recreational facilities, and none at all for residences. The 1880s saw the introduction of cable car lines, which, circling part of the downtown area, gave that area the name "Loop." The term was firmly fixed when the Union Loop Elevated Railway was completed in 1897.

Technology stood ready in that same decade to generate a forest of office towers. The safety elevator, the telegraph and telephone, the flush toilet, the modern coal furnace—all already existed. Construction methods using iron and then steel developed rapidly, as well as revolutionary foundation techniques to anchor the new skyscraper city firmly to the ground.

So rapid, indeed, were these developments that some historians have posited a whole new architecture—the Chicago School—that they claim emerged in the Loop from the early 1880s to 1910. They suggest that this architecture, direct, pragmatic, and ahistorical, rests upon the pioneering efforts of designers like Burnham & Root, Holabird & Roche, William Le Baron Jenney, and, perhaps most notably, Louis H. Sullivan. The dictum attributed to Sullivan, "Form follows function," encapsulates the school's aesthetic and characterizes its importance as a forerunner of modernism.

More recently, some critics have challenged the concept of a "Chicago School," noting that many of its designs are neither functionalist nor ahistorical. Though Sullivan had suggested the elimination of architectural ornament to the young Viennese architect Adolf Loos when the latter visited Chicago in 1893, he himself certainly did not follow his own advice.

Perhaps the wisest way to resolve this controversy is by reverting to a term frequently used at the turn of the century: Chicago construction. The great Chicago architects devised less a new architecture than a new means of creating it—efficient, cost-effective, and speedy. The Reliance Building, for example, whose glassy facade is often hailed as the prototype of the glass curtain-wall skyscraper, was praised in the 1890s for the rapidity with which its steel frame was erected, and for the practicality of its washable terra-cotta sheathing. The speed with which Chicago's architects adopted a new and changing technology can be demonstrated in the shift from almost full bearing-wall construction in the 1891 or northern portion of the Monadnock Building to the almost full skeletal construction of its 1893 or southern section.

Chicago designers maintained a sense of decorum or "keeping" in their works. Martin Roche could design a simple, straightforward loft building, the Great Lakes Building, in 1910, the verticals and horizontals of its skeletal frame neatly and modestly encased in brick and clearly expressed on its facades. That year he also designed the lavishly ornamented Monroe Building, whose gabled roof and facades sheathed in terra-cotta reflected the building's more prestigious location and "higher calling" as an office building.

Today's movement toward decentralization, ever more efficient transportation and communication, and the suburbanization of the white-collar class are again changing the future of the Loop. After decades of confinement within the "old" Loop, business has burst these bonds, and new "downtowns" are springing up to the north and west of the old central city. Some planners suggest that these movements spell the inevitable demise of the Loop as Chicago's hub. Others envision a new and more variegated life for the area, pointing out that, for the first time in well over a century, residential construction is once more under way in the Loop. Major State St. retail stores have spent millions to remodel and update their facilities, and new retail outlets have begun to appear. Cultural and educational institutions have expanded and remodeled, revivifying sections of the Loop. Despite the inevitable changes that will continue to confront Chicago's Loop, there is little doubt that it will remain an impressive urbanistic symbol. Those who have doubts about the Loop's vitality are invited to stand at the foot of La Salle St. on the morning of an active market day. They'll need no further convincing!

—Robert F. Irving

■ 333 N. Michigan Ave.
1928, Holabird & Root

Its pronounced verticality, spare lines, and dramatic setbacks were inspired by Eliel Saarinen's second-prize entry in the 1922 Chicago Tribune Tower Competition. The polished marble base and stylized bands of ornament are the only embellishments on this elegant limestone tower. Low reliefs by Fred M. Torrey depict pioneers, traders, hunters, and Native Americans at Fort Dearborn, which occupied part of this site.

■ 360 N. Michigan Ave.
(London Guarantee & Accident Building)
1923, Alfred S. Alschuler

The river's bend dictated the building's unusual shape, which provides a graceful forecourt. The neo-Classical ornament includes a triumphal-arch entry with colossal Corinthian columns, a second rank of columns in a three-story top, and a crowning belvedere.

■ 320 N. Michigan Ave.
1983, Booth/Hansen & Assocs.

This stylish infill building was designed for residences but was leased as offices, which accounts for some unpleasant accretions. Concrete was shaped into moldings, curves, and capitals on the main facade and expresses the building's structural grid on the sides.

■ Old Republic Building
(Bell Building)
307 N. Michigan Ave.
1925, Vitzthum & Burns

Classicism is stressed throughout, from the beige granite base with its triumphal-arch entrance through the cream terra-cotta shaft and colonnaded top.

■ Carbide & Carbon Building
230 N. Michigan Ave.
1929, Burnham Bros.

The polished granite base has a black marble and bronze entrance, ornamented with delicate grillework. The dark green and

Carbide & Carbon Building

gold terra-cotta shaft rises without horizontal cornices or projections to a fifty-foot tower trimmed with gold leaf.

Illinois Center
Bounded by the Chicago River, N. Lake Shore Dr., N. Michigan Ave. (excluding 151, 333 & 307 N. Michigan Ave.), and E. Lake St.
Master plan begun 1967, Ludwig Mies van der Rohe

6 One Illinois Center
111 E. Wacker Dr.
1970, Office of Mies van der Rohe

7 Two Illinois Center
233 N. Michigan Ave.
1973, Office of Mies van der Rohe

8 Boulevard Towers
205–225 N. Michigan Ave.
1981, 1985, Fujikawa, Johnson & Assocs.

9 Three Illinois Center
303 E. Wacker Dr.
1980, Fujikawa, Conterato, Lohan & Assocs.

10 Fire Station CF-21
259 N. Columbus Dr.
1982, Fujikawa, Johnson & Assocs.

11 Hyatt Regency Chicago
151 E. Wacker Dr.
West Tower 1974, East Tower and Atrium Lobby 1980, A. Epstein & Sons

12 Columbus Plaza
233 E. Wacker Dr.
1980, Fujikawa, Conterato, Lohan & Assocs.

This mixed-use development, one of the nation's largest, is a densely packed mixed bag of colors, materials, and styles, built to a colossal scale around dark, cramped plazas. Development of the eighty-three-acre site, which uses air rights over former Illinois Central Gulf Railroad tracks, has followed the original plan for a self-contained city of offices, shops, apartments, and hotels. Master planning in this case seems to have been a euphemism for a means of squeezing the highest density onto the land. There is no hierarchy of buildings or spaces, just a thicket of structures competing for land, light, and—in the postmodern era—visual dominance. A trilevel street system segregates service vehicles, arterial traffic, and local traffic; dreary and confusing pedestrian concourses link most of the buildings.

A commercial success, the project has continued to expand and is slated for completion in the late 1990s. The urbanistic amenities are nil; the project lacks even a meaningful relationship to the river. Architectural discord has been the rule from the early days of construction, when the Miesian steel-and-glass towers of One and Two Illinois Center were made to share their site with the clunky, brick-faced Hyatt Regency hotel. One of Mies's successor firms, Fujikawa, Johnson & Assocs., has stayed remarkably faithful to the original design aesthetic—for better or worse—in its office buildings, while compounding the visual incoherence of Wacker Dr. with the concrete Columbus Plaza apartment building. They did, however, provide a small grace note of Miesian modernism in the fire station at the base of Three Illinois Center.

**13 Swissôtel Chicago
(Swiss Grand Hotel)**
323 E. Wacker Dr.
1989, Harry Weese & Assocs.

Wrapped in alternating bands of opaque and reflective glass, the tower reiterates the triangular massing of Weese's Metropolitan Correctional Center.

14 Fairmont Hotel
200 N. Columbus Dr.

1987, Hellmuth, Obata & Kassabaum; Fujikawa, Johnson & Assocs., assoc. archs.

The towered top and pink granite walls offer a deliberate contrast to the surrounding austerity.

15 Sporting Club
211 N. Stetson Ave.
1990, Kisho Kurokawa; Fujikawa, Johnson & Assocs., assoc. archs.

This small building, the nation's first by Japanese architect Kurokawa, is the gem of the Illinois Center complex. The white-painted steel frame and window mullions are scaled to elements of traditional Japanese wooden buildings. The quartet of steel-frame rooftop towers, which pay homage to the towers of Louis H. Sullivan's People's Savings Bank (1911) in Cedar Rapids, Iowa, sport seventeen-foot wind sculptures by Osamu Shingu entitled *Children of the Sun*. They also mark a dramatic interior space that extends an additional three stories below Stetson Ave.: a six-story skylit atrium with a curving staircase and a 100-foot rock-climbing wall.

16 Amoco Building
(Standard Oil Building)
200 E. Randolph St.
1973, Edward Durell Stone; Perkins & Will, assoc. archs.

Chicago's second-tallest building was originally the world's tallest marble-clad structure but is now most famous—or notorious—as a colossal failure of building technology. In order to sheath the eighty-two-story skyscraper, the architect and the client depleted the Carrara marble quarry that had served Michelangelo. Perhaps in retribution for their hubris, the slabs began to buckle at the southeast corner. Cut as thin as permitted by then-new methods, the material was unable to withstand extremes of temperature. Total recladding was the only solution; from 1990 to 1992, the marble was replaced by thicker slabs of speckled North Carolina granite.

With a new skin that is matte rather than glossy, the building's banality is even more pro-

nounced. Structurally, it is a long hollow tube. The V-shaped perimeter columns house pipes and utility lines and allow column-free interiors. The plaza facing Grant Park features Harry Bertoia's *Untitled Sounding Sculpture* (1975). Northerly Plaza (1986, Perkins & Will) is an attractive gateway.

17 One Prudential Plaza
(Prudential Building)
130 E. Randolph St.
1955, Naess & Murphy

Although lacking their soaring verticality, this limestone and aluminum-clad skyscraper looks back to the towers of the 1920s rather than emulating the steel and glass curtain walls coming into favor after World War II. Construction ended a twenty-year hiatus in major downtown building and created what was then Chicago's tallest building, complete with observation deck. The first project to use the air rights of the Illinois Central Railroad yards, it established a pattern for developers. The enormous sculpted relief of Prudential's trademark Rock of Gibraltar is by Frank Lloyd Wright collaborator Alfonso Iannelli.

18 Two Prudential Plaza
180 N. Stetson Ave.
1990, Loebl, Schlossman & Hackl

With its soaring spire and chevroned top, Two Pru seems determined to compensate for its earlier neighbor's modesty. Although the architects cite the Chrysler Building as design inspiration, a closer parallel can be found in the work of Helmut Jahn, especially his One Liberty Place in Philadelphia (1987) and his unbuilt 1982 design for the Bank of the Southwest Tower in Houston. The best feature is the landscaped plaza to the northwest, which leads to an atrium lobby serving both Prudential buildings.

19 150 N. Michigan Ave.
1984, A. Epstein & Sons

Ten more floors would be needed for the height to balance the overwhelming slice cut through the top. The light color and aggressive orientation commands attention, but the proportions and detailing are a disappointment. Yaacov Agam's colorful sculpture *Communication X9* promises less and delivers more.

20 Chicago Cultural Center (Chicago Public Library)
78 E. Washington St.
1897, Shepley, Rutan & Coolidge
Renovated 1977 and 1993, Holabird & Root

This latter-day Renaissance palace belongs to an illustrious family of civic and social institutions that grace Michigan Ave. and Grant Park. The spur to the founding of a free public library for the city came, ironically, from the Fire of 1871. Responding to the devastation, British sympathizers sent over 8,000 books, many of them autographed by such noted donors as Disraeli, Carlyle, Tennyson, and even Queen Victoria. To circulate the "English book donation," the Chicago Public Library was established in 1872 and temporarily housed in an old water tank, while the board sought a permanent site in Dearborn Park, a remnant of the Fort Dearborn military outpost. Contending for the same parcel was a Civil War veterans' organization. A compromise reached in 1891 permitted the erection of a public library that contained a memorial hall dedicated to the Grand Army of the Republic.

The commission was awarded to the Boston-based successors to the practice of Henry Hobson Richardson, the firm of Shepley, Rutan & Coolidge, which was then completing the Art Institute. Responsibility for designing and testing the foundation went to engineer William Sooy Smith; to this day there has been no appreciable settlement. The library board stipulated that the new building should "convey to the beholder the idea that it is an enduring monument worthy of a great and public-spirited city." To fulfill this dictum the final design was an amalgam of Italian Renaissance, Greek, and neo-Grec elements executed in Bedford limestone and granite.

The interior decoration is of majestic splendor, realized in rare marble, fine hardwood, stained glass, and polished bronze. Most sumptuous of all is the jewellike luster of the cosmati work: mosaics of Favrile glass, colored stone, mother-of-pearl,

Chicago Cultural Center exterior

Chicago Cultural Center interior

and gold leaf inlaid in white marble. The mosaics and marble were practical as well, durable against the onslaught of Chicago's sooty air. Among the more interesting motifs are Renaissance printers' marks and quotations in ten languages. Robert C. Spencer, Jr., later famed as a Prairie School architect, designed the mosaics, which were executed by Tiffany-trained J. L. Holzer.

In 1977 the building was renovated and modernized into a popular library and cultural center. It remains emblematic of Chicago in the 1890s when, eager to no longer be identified solely for meat packing and merchandising, the city sought to secure its status as a sophisticated and culturally conscious metropolis.
—Meredith Taussig

21 Illinois State Medical Society (Ward Building)
20 N. Michigan Ave.
*1885, Beers, Clay & Dutton;
Addition 1892
Renovated 1985, Nagle, Hartray
& Assocs.*

A red brick, timber-frame warehouse for Montgomery Ward's catalog operations was converted into a modern office building sympathetic to its past.

22 6 N. Michigan Ave. (Montgomery Ward & Co. "Tower Building")
*1899, Richard E. Schmidt
Four-story addition 1923, Holabird
& Roche
Remodeled 1955, Loebl,
Schlossman & Bennett*

The design is attributed to Schmidt's employee Hugh M. G. Garden, who later became his partner. The firm's first major commission was much grander when new, when it sported a ten-story tower topped by a three-story pyramidal roof, tempietto, and an eighteen-foot gilded female weather vane called *Progress Lighting the Way for Commerce.* Although the addition of four floors and the demolition of the tower (1947) have drastically altered the massing, interesting details such as plants, birds, and fish are still dimly visible through the dirt on the terra-cotta spandrels. Images of the long-lost *Progress* are on the bronze elevator doors.

23 Willoughby Tower
8 S. Michigan Ave.
1929, Samuel N. Crowen & Assocs.

The graceful profile is complemented by the foyers and lobbies, with their spectacular green marble walls, rich bronze ornament, and strapwork ceilings.

24 Chicago Athletic Association Building
12 S. Michigan Ave.
1893, Henry Ives Cobb
25 Annex Building
71 E. Madison St.
1907, Richard E. Schmidt, Garden & Martin
Seven-story addition 1926, Richard E. Schmidt, Garden & Martin

Built to impress the crowds that flocked to the World's Columbian Exposition of 1893, the building is a lavish display of Venetian Gothic inside and out. The far simpler annex suggests Chicago's own Prairie School.

ern facades clearly express their framing systems. At the request of the Gage Brothers, the third facade was designed by Sullivan because they felt it would benefit their business. It is finished in buff terra-cotta and displays his philosophy that a skyscraper's design should express its height. He did this by presenting the facade as a hung curtain. Because the base, originally framed in foliate cast iron, hid the first-floor columns, the piers would have appeared to exert insupportable weight on the first-floor spandrel without the pair of "clasps" on the cornice.

Gage Building

Gage Group
26 Edson Keith and Theodore Ascher Buildings
24 & 30 S. Michigan Ave.
1899, Holabird & Roche
Ascher Building addition 1971, Altman-Saichek Assocs.
27 Gage Building
18 S. Michigan Ave.
1899, Holabird & Roche; facade, Louis H. Sullivan
Addition 1902, Holabird & Roche
Renovated 1986, Bovine Group, for Aubrey Greenberg Assocs.

These steel-frame loft buildings were built on Michigan Ave. because of the unobstructed daylight needed for the millinery businesses that they housed. Clad in the red brick common to Chicago lofts, the two south-

28 University Club of Chicago
76 E. Monroe St.
1908, Holabird & Roche
29 Monroe Building
104 S. Michigan Ave.
1912, Holabird & Roche

The University Club's details recall the University of Chicago's Gothic inspirations. Inside are two multistory rooms, one of which features medieval hunt murals by Frederic Clay Bartlett. The height of the gabled Monroe Building was chosen to complement its neighbor. Step inside to see the vaulted lobby with its glazed Rookwood tile.

Monroe Building

30 Former Illinois Athletic Club
112 S. Michigan Ave.
1908, Barnett, Haynes & Barnett
Addition 1985, Swann & Weiskopf

The six-story limestone and glass addition was intended to complement the original but doesn't. Leon Harmant's frieze depicts Zeus presiding over athletic contests.

31 Lake View Building
(Municipal Court Building)
116 S. Michigan Ave.
1906, 1912, Jenney, Mundie & Jensen

This white terra-cotta pencil of a building was commissioned by Jacob L. Kesner to lease as courtrooms while City Hall was being demolished and rebuilt. When the City moved out, Kesner added four stories and a vaulted ceiling in the lobby to attract other tenants.

32 People's Gas Co. Building
122 S. Michigan Ave.
1910, D. H. Burnham & Co.
Restored 1987, Eckenhoff Saunders Architects

To keep the weight of the upper stories off the ornamental granite columns, steel cantilevers at the third floor transfer the load to an interior steel frame.

33 Grant Park and Burnham Park
Between Michigan Ave. and Lake Michigan, from Randolph St. to Roosevelt Rd.
1903–1907, Olmsted Bros.; 1915–1930, Bennett, Parsons, Frost, & Thomas and predecessors

Chicago's formal front garden was created from sandbars, landfill, and Chicago Fire debris and was shaped by the guiding visions of the 1893 World's Columbian Exposition and the 1909 Plan of Chicago. Its origins as a public open space date from 1835, when the federal government gave its reservation on the south side of the river, east of State St., to the commissioners of the Illinois & Michigan Canal. In 1836 they platted it and sold lots to help fund the canal's construction. To provide for a town common on the lakeshore, they wrote on their map, on the space defined by Michigan Ave. and the lake, Randolph St., and what is now 11th St., "Public Ground—A Common to Remain Forever Open, Clear and Free of any Buildings, or Other Obstruction whatever." The public ground was named Lake Park in 1847, but wave action caused continual erosion of the undeveloped site. In 1852 the Illinois Central Railroad offered to build a stone breakwater in the lake, in exchange for an easement permitting the construction of an offshore trestle as far north as the mouth of the Chicago River. Sand, which accumulated in the lagoon created by the breakwater, was augmented by the unofficial dumping of garbage and rubble from the Fire of 1871.

In 1861 the state legislature had passed a law confirming the establishment of Lake Park and requiring the consent of all adjacent property owners for any encroachments on the public ground. Nearly thirty years later, however, the park contained little more than squatters' shacks,

Grant Park before the creation of Congress Dr.

two federal armories, and staging areas for refuse awaiting removal by train. In 1890 Aaron Montgomery Ward, creator of the mail-order business with headquarters at Michigan Ave. near Madison St., brought a lawsuit to force the City to clean up and improve the site. The response was to draw up a plan creating a civic center in the park and to clean the site of all buildings except the armories.

At this time, planning for the World's Columbian Exposition was under way; so, too, were plans for a new Art Institute, the museum having outgrown its home on the west side of Michigan Ave. at Van Buren St. A park site was proposed for the museum and approved by adjacent property owners. After the fair, several plans were made for developing Lake Park. All called for placing more buildings in the park, but Ward drew the line. He won three more lawsuits concerning construction in the park. Frequently vilified as an impediment to progress by newspaper editorials and fellow businessmen, he never wavered in his fight to protect the park "for the poor people of Chicago, not for the millionaires."

Responsibility for Lake Park was transferred to the South Park Commission in 1896 and 1903. The commission renamed it Grant Park in 1901 and two years later entrusted its design to the Olmsted Brothers, successors to the firm of Frederick Law Olmsted. Their plan, published in 1907, created a formal park based on the landscape principles embodied in the gardens of Versailles. The park was designed as a series of symmetrical spaces, or "rooms," defined by paths and plantings, with small enclosed spaces for passive recreation and large open areas for active pursuits. Promenades extended along Michigan Ave., under an allée of trees, and along the lake shore. Sculptures and fountains created focal points for vistas, with a great fountain planned to serve as the central point of reference.

In 1915 Edward H. Bennett, who had helped Daniel H. Burnham create the 1909 Plan of Chicago, was retained by the South Park Commission to take charge of Grant Park. He was already serving as consulting architect to the Chicago Plan Commission and thus had two positions in which he could promote the plan's Beaux Arts principles.

As part of a 1919 agreement between the South Park Commission, the City, and the Illinois Central to cooperate on planning, the railroad electrified its trains, depressed its tracks below street level, and offered a landfill site at the park's south end for the Field Museum.

In 1924 the commission adopted a comprehensive plan for the park, and the following year philanthropist Kate Buckingham provided funds for a centerpiece in the form of Buckingham Fountain. Bennett oversaw the plan's implementation until his association with the park ended in 1930, when the onset of the Depression put an end to major improvements.

In 1955 Congress Pkwy. was widened and extended through the park, destroying a grand plaza and stairway. Between the 1950s and 1970s three underground garages replaced surface lots in the park; concrete benches along Michigan Ave. disguise their ventilation stacks. The Daley Bicentennial Plaza (1976) added an ice rink and a bermed field house under Randolph St. The 1986 realignment of Lake Shore Dr. where it crosses the Chicago River created additional land at the park's northeast corner. In the 1980s Grant Park became the setting for a summerlong series of festivals that attract huge crowds and enhance the liveliness of downtown Chicago but not without a detrimental effect on the landscape.

In the early 1990s, after some thirty years of planning, the City announced its intention to relocate the lanes of Lake Shore Dr. that divide the Field Museum from the Shedd Aquarium and Adler Planetarium to the west of the museum, fulfilling the goal of a cultural campus. At the same time, the Chicago Park District

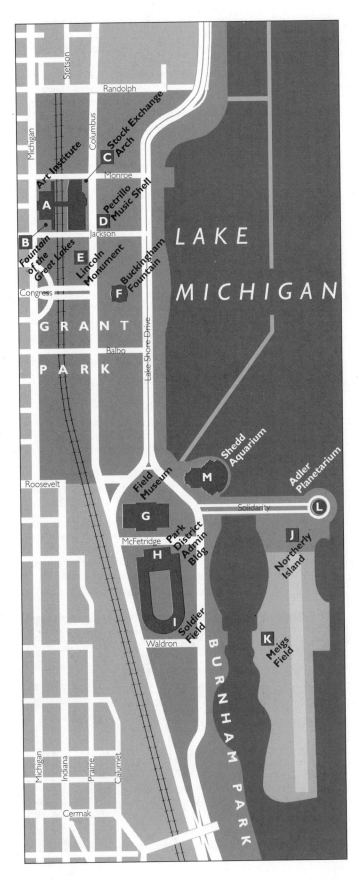

Michigan

Stetson

Randolph

Columbus

Stock Exchange Arch

Art Institute

C

Monroe

Michigan

A

Petrillo Music Shell

D

Jackson

B

Fountain of the Great Lakes

E

Lincoln Monument

F

Buckingham Fountain

Congress

LAKE

MICHIGAN

G R A N T

Balbo

P A R K

Lake Shore Drive

Roosevelt

Shedd Aquarium

Field Museum

M

Adler Planetarium

Solidarity

L

G

Park District Admin Bldg

J

McFetridge

Northerly Island

H

Soldier Field

I

K

Meigs Field

Waldron

B U R N H A M

Michigan

Indiana

Prairie

Calumet

P A R K

Cermak

began to create a long-range plan for preservation and improvement that seeks to ensure the well-being of Chicago's front garden.

—Joan Pomaranc

A Art Institute of Chicago
Michigan Ave. at Adams St.
1893–1916, Shepley, Rutan & Coolidge
Additions include:
Ryerson and Burnham Libraries 1901, Shepley, Rutan & Coolidge
McKinlock Court 1924, Coolidge & Hodgdon
Goodman Theater 1926, Howard Van Doren Shaw
Ferguson Building 1958, Holabird & Root & Burgee
Morton Wing 1962, Shaw, Metz & Assocs.
Columbus Drive Addition and School of the Art Institute 1977, Skidmore, Owings & Merrill
Daniel F. & Ada L. Rice Building 1988, Hammond, Beeby & Babka

Along with the art treasures guarded by Edward Kemeys's famous bronze lions flanking the entrance (1894) are several special architectural spaces; a map available in the main lobby will guide your exploration. The restored lobby (1987, Office of John Vinci) is the museum's oldest and grandest space; atop the staircase (1910) is an exhibit of fragments of Chicago's architectural past. The Trading Room, salvaged from Adler & Sullivan's demolished Chicago Stock Exchange Building, was restored

and installed in the Columbus Dr. addition in 1977 by the Office of John Vinci. Its virtuoso stenciling is one of the most lyrical examples of Sullivan's decorative talent. McKinlock Court is an unexpected oasis, open for dining in the summer months. The serene, neo-Classical Rice Building galleries are newer favorites.

B Fountain of the Great Lakes
S. Michigan Ave. south of main entrance
1914, Lorado Taft; basin Shepley, Rutan & Coolidge

This sculpture represents the five Great Lakes as they flow into each other. Superior pours water to the central figure of Huron, with Michigan to her right, Erie to the left, and Ontario kneeling below.

C Chicago Stock Exchange Arch
Monroe St. and Columbus Dr.
1893, Adler & Sullivan

This building fragment is the Wailing Wall of Chicago's preservation movement.

D Petrillo Music Shell
Columbus Dr. and Jackson Blvd.
1978, Chicago Park District

Technically a demountable structure that could be disassembled every fall (although the cost would be prohibitive), the music shell thus escaped the ban on structures in the park.

Art Institute of Chicago—Chicago Stock Exchange Trading Room

E Abraham Lincoln ("The Seated Lincoln") Court of the Presidents
Between Columbus Dr. and Illinois Central tracks at Van Buren St.
1908, Augustus Saint-Gaudens; exedra McKim, Mead & White

Installed in 1926, Saint-Gaudens's second Lincoln statue in Chicago was intended as the centerpiece of a collection of presidential statues, but it stands—or sits—alone.

F Clarence Buckingham Fountain
East end of Congress Dr. at Columbus Dr.
1927, Marcel François Loyau & Jacques Lambert; Bennett, Parsons & Frost, archs.

The fountain is the focal point of the park, terminating the Congress Pkwy. axis as envisioned in the 1909 Plan of Chicago. Built of pink Georgia marble, it is based on the Bassin de Latone at Versailles, doubled in size. Four pairs of fanciful bronze sea creatures symbolize the states bordering Lake Michigan, which the fountain is intended to represent.

G Field Museum of Natural History
Roosevelt Rd. and S. Lake Shore Dr.
1909–1912, D. H. Burnham & Co.; 1912–1917, Graham, Burnham & Co.; 1917–1920,

Graham, Anderson, Probst & White
Renovated 1977, Harry Weese & Assocs.

Exhibits from the 1893 World's Columbian Exposition were the nucleus of the collections, housed for the first twenty-seven years in what was later reconstructed as the Museum of Science and Industry. The design was inspired by the Greek temple; the caryatids are especially reminiscent of the Erechtheion. The great central hall, ringed by Ionic columns, is one of Chicago's grandest neo-Classical spaces, monumental yet serene.

H Chicago Park District— Administration Building
425 E. McFetridge Dr.
1939, Holabird & Root

The consolidation in 1934 of separate park commissions into the Chicago Park District was the impetus for this remarkably dull structure.

I Soldier Field
425 E. McFetridge Dr.
1922–1926, Holabird & Roche

This enormous colonnaded stadium has been used for sports events, religious gatherings, and concerts. It was named to honor soldiers of the first World War; at the same time, Municipal Pier was renamed Navy Pier to honor sailors. The U-shaped structure was designed to harmonize

Buckingham Fountain

with the Field Museum, but the axial connection was lost when the Park District Administration Building was erected just to the north.

J Burnham Park & Northerly Island
From Solidarity Dr. south to 57th St., east of Illinois Central tracks
1917–1930

Northerly Island (1928–1930) was the only actualization of the chain of man-made islands proposed in the 1909 Plan of Chicago. It was intended to be a park, but its first role, and that of the parallel section of Burnham Park, was as the site for the 1933–1934 World's Fair, "A Century of Progress." After the fair, one of the temporary connections between the mainland and the island (Solidarity Dr.) was made permanent.

K Merrill C. Meigs Field
South portion of Northerly Island
Air Traffic Control Tower *1952, Consoer & Townsend*
Terminal Building *1961, Consoer & Morgan*

Despite criticism that an airfield was inappropriate for the lakefront, this part of the 1933–1934 World's Fair site was turned over to the Park District in 1937 and leased to the City. The unsuitability is aeronautical as well as aesthetic; Chicago's winds blow almost perpetually from the west, making for sometimes fierce crosswinds on the north–south runway.

L Adler Planetarium & Astronomical Museum
1300 S. Lake Shore Dr.
1930, Ernest A. Grunsfeld, Jr.
Entrance addition 1981, Lohan Assocs.

While the architects of nearby museums looked to the past, Grunsfeld found an ahistorical form to house the nation's first public planetarium. The twelve-sided structure of beautifully variegated rainbow granite, each corner adorned with a zodiacal sign, accommodates a domed room for viewing images created by the planetarium's projector. Alfonso Iannelli's bronze plaques depict the constellations as described in the second century by the Greek astronomer Ptolemy.

M John G. Shedd Aquarium
1200 S. Lake Shore Dr.
1929, Graham, Anderson, Probst & White
Oceanarium addition 1991, Lohan Assocs.

Designed to harmonize with the Field Museum, the original building is covered inside and out with aquatic motifs. The Oceanarium's lakeside curtain wall offers the illusion of an unbroken line of water from the interior pools to Lake Michigan. The marble on the facade was created by removing slabs from the original east wall and splitting them; the color will eventually dull to match the rest of the building.

Adler Planetarium

34 Theodore Thomas Orchestra Hall

220 S. Michigan Ave.
1905, D. H. Burnham & Co.
Top-floor addition for Cliff Dwellers Club 1908, Howard Van Doren Shaw
Remodeled 1967, Harry Weese & Assocs.
Rehabilitated 1981, Skidmore, Owings & Merrill

A member of the orchestra's board, Burnham encouraged efforts to acquire a hall of its own and, as owner of this land, was the logical choice for architect. Behind the Georgian facade is an auditorium, a ballroom at the second level, offices, and the Cliff Dwellers Club.

Santa Fe Center

35 Santa Fe Center

(Railway Exchange Building)
80 E. Jackson Blvd./224 S. Michigan Ave.
1904, D. H. Burnham & Co.
Renovated 1985, Metz, Train & Youngren and Frye Gillan & Molinaro

A building around a light well, a form common to Daniel H. Burnham's work from the mid-1880s onward, received an undulating white-glazed terra-cotta skin, oriel bays, and a top floor of distinctive porthole windows. As in the Rookery, there is a two-story covered court at the base of the light well dominated by a grand staircase. In the renovation a new skylight was placed at the top, and the light well's inner walls were opened up. The building housed Daniel H. Burnham's offices, where the 1909 Plan of Chicago was worked out and a decade of buildings were planned.

36 Britannica Center

(Straus Building)
310 S. Michigan Ave.
1924, Graham, Anderson, Probst & White

This was the first building to take advantage of Chicago's 1923 zoning ordinance, which permitted the erection of occupied towers above 260 feet if setback provisions were satisfied. In most other ways the main block is a variant of the firm's La Salle St. banking buildings, which featured second-story banking floors behind Classical facades. Behind the tall windows was the elegant banking floor of the investment firm of S. W. Straus & Co. The glass beehive atop the pyramidal roof symbolized industry and thrift and originally housed a directional beacon signifying the company's global reach.

37 McCormick Building

332 S. Michigan Ave.
1910, 1912 (northern expansion), Holabird & Roche

Although dismissed by *Architectural Record* as "not calculated to attract remark," the McCormick Building is one of the firm's more prominent and solidly designed office buildings. Its windows are punched out uniformly across a neutral facade, in a negation of the steel frame. The Michigan Ave. site, where legislation ensured that no building would ever block the light, allowed exceptionally deep offices.

38 Chicago Club

81 E. Van Buren St.
1929, Granger & Bollenbacher

This building was designed in the spirit of an earlier structure by Burnham & Root that housed the Art Institute in the late 1880s. It collapsed in 1929 while being remodeled for this private club's use.

39 Fine Arts Building
(Studebaker Building)
410 S. Michigan Ave.
1885, Solon S. Beman
Three-story addition and conversion to Fine Arts Building 1898, Solon S. Beman
Renovated for Studebaker Theater 1917, Andrew N. Rebori

The Romanesque rough stone base and ranks of floors under arches established a prototypical rhythm for this stretch of S. Michigan Ave. The arches and the huge red granite columns that carry them were a means of opening the load-bearing east wall for the Studebaker carriage showrooms, which occupied the first five floors. A shift in function within was recorded in the upper stories; groupings of smaller windows mark where wagons and carriages were assembled.

When the building no longer suited Studebaker's needs, Beman altered it for music publisher and real estate developer Charles C. Curtiss into a proto-arts center with two theaters, offices, shops, and studios for musicians, artists, and writers. This included the replacement of the top story with three new ones, including skylit studios. The building was a locus of activity for women's suffrage efforts and, later, of the Chicago literary movement of the 1920s. Inside it has a rabbit warren of woody hallways, a light well with internal balconies appropriately called Venetian Court, and tenth-floor muraled walls as reminders of former tenants.

40 Eagle Fountains
Michigan Ave. at Congress Dr.
1931, Frederick C. Hibbard

These graceful eagles grasping fish in their talons made more sense years ago, when the pools were filled with water.

The Bowman

41 *The Spearman and the Bowman*
Michigan Ave. at Congress Dr.
1928, Ivan Mestrovic

The sculptor proposed a cowboy and an Indian, but two Native Americans were felt to be more suitable for so prominent a site, which originally featured a grand stair and plaza leading to Buckingham Fountain. Their weapons must be supplied by the viewer's imagination.

42 Auditorium Building
430 S. Michigan Ave.
1887–1889, Adler & Sullivan
Auditorium Theater restored 1967, Harry Weese & Assocs.

The Auditorium Building commission was the single most important factor in establishing the internationally recognized role of Dankmar Adler and Louis H. Sullivan in the evolution of modern architectural thought. Adler's previous successes as a theater designer secured the coveted job, while the publicity generated by the project promulgated Sullivan's innovative architectural ideals.

Created to provide a permanent home for Chicago's

Auditorium Building exterior

operatic, symphonic, and other cultural events, the building was planned with large multiuse commercial components, a 400-room hotel, and rental offices in order to offset possible losses from the operation of the 4,300-seat theater. It was a civic achievement of enormous stature, made even more impressive by the modernist style of its design.

The composition of the street facades, suggesting the Romanesque character of H. H. Richardson's demolished Marshall Field Wholesale Store (1887), is a highly original expression of the building's bearing-wall construction: a rugged base of supporting rusticated granite contrasts with the smooth, machined Bedford limestone skin above. Except for the entrance, the theater was almost completely enclosed from the street by the hotel, which was located along the Michigan Ave. and Congress Pkwy. frontages, and by the office section along Wabash Ave. Rising above the ten-story block on Congress Pkwy. is an eight-story tower that originally housed additional offices, tanks for the hydraulic stage equipment, and a rooftop observatory, initially the highest point in the city. Adler & Sullivan's own offices were behind the stone colonnade at what is now the sixteenth floor.

In contrast to the heavy

Auditorium Building interior

treatment of the masonry exterior, the interiors are reflections of the light, modular, post-and-beam metal frame, and of the fireproof tile partitions, articulated by the creative manipulation of interior finishes in plaster, wood, cast iron, art glass, mosaic, and other materials. The primary space is the theater itself, enclosed within a fireproof brick shell. Its excellent acoustics and sight lines are testament to Adler's theater expertise and were given creative form through Sullivan's integral collaboration.

Other significant interior spaces can be seen by touring the facilities of Roosevelt University, which has owned the building since 1946. The former hotel lobby is entered on Michigan Ave., and its central grand staircase leads to the second-floor parlor. The finely restored Ladies' Parlor, now the Sullivan Room and usually closed, is partially visible through a door at the south end of the loggia. The barrel-vaulted tenth-floor hotel dining room is now the university's library. The restored southern alcove reflects its original appearance, while the main room's restoration awaits funding. One of Adler & Sullivan's finest interior spaces is the hotel's banquet hall/ballroom, built of lightweight plaster and birch paneling. Now the Rudolph Ganz Memorial Recital Hall (Room 745), it was an afterthought planned when the building was largely complete. The remarkable room spans forty feet over the theater's roof on twin bridge trusses bearing on the theater's perimeter masonry walls.
—John Vinci

43 Musical Arts Building
(Fine Arts Building Annex)
421 S. Wabash Ave.
1924, Rebori, Wentworth, Dewey & McCormick

This charming sliver was built to house the Fine Arts Building's heating plant and five floors of studio space, connected by a bridge to the main building. The polychrome facade of verde antique marble is accented with pale yellow and green, matte-glazed terra-cotta and iron balconettes.

44 CNA Center
(Continental Center)
55 E. Jackson Blvd.
North tower 1962, C. F. Murphy Assocs.
South tower 1972, Graham, Anderson, Probst & White

The bays of the northern building, originally connected to 310 S. Michigan Ave., have forty-two-foot spans; they were the largest constructed to that time but were soon surpassed by the Richard J. Daley Center's gargantuan bays. The unclad skin of carbon steel, originally painted black, received a red coating to match the south tower.

45 DePaul University— O'Malley Building
(Finchley Building)
23 E. Jackson Blvd.
1928, Alfred S. Alschuler

The Gothic style of the stone base changes incongruously to a Tudor half-timbered treatment at the top.

46 DePaul University—Lewis Center (Kimball Building)
25 E. Jackson Blvd.
1917, Graham, Anderson, Probst & White

Step inside to see the well-preserved L-shaped lobby of buff ceramic tile.

47 Pakula Building
(formerly McClurg Building, originally Ayer Building)
218 S. Wabash Ave.
1899, Holabird & Roche

This steel-frame loft building is a small but resonant example of the qualities for which the Chicago School—especially the work of Holabird & Roche—is famous. The grid of the wall clearly expresses the underlying structure, with large Chicago windows set between the thinnest possible piers and spandrels. As with Mies's I-beams of a half-century later, the deep fluted piers and mullions give dimensionality and rhythm to the skeletal facade. Unfortunately, the cornice that once capped the composition is missing.

48 Parking Structure
209 S. Wabash Ave.
1929, Loebl, Schlossman & Demuth

A garage with first-floor shops fits behind a four-story Art Deco facade.

63 E. Adams St. (Chapin & Gore Building)

49 63 E. Adams St.
(Chapin & Gore Building)
1904, Richard E. Schmidt and Hugh M. G. Garden

The facade's unusual composition reflects the special retail, storage, and office needs of the client's liquor business. Between the retail base and the office stories are two storage floors, which needed a sturdier structure and less window space. The second- and third-floor windows are joined by ornamental spandrels that show Garden's adaptation of Louis H. Sullivan's geometric forms. The windows' width matches that of the central panes in the Chicago windows of the office floors, while a decorative terra-cotta frame expands

the composition to the larger overall width. The incongruously stark upper floors originally had foliate capitals crowning the piers and a projecting cornice.

50 55 E. Monroe St.
(Mid-Continental Plaza)
1972, Alfred Shaw & Assocs.

This International Style behemoth has closely spaced piers, clad in stainless steel and ascending uninterrupted to the flat roof. A 1991 renovation by Swanke Hayden Connell gave the building a presence on the night skyline with three bands of light that surround the mechanical penthouse.

51 Champlain Building
(Powers Building)
37 S. Wabash Ave.
1903, Holabird & Roche

This archetypal Holabird & Roche office building follows the firm's successful formula exploited between 1895 and 1910. Features include continuous piers, recessed spandrels, wide Chicago windows, and a tripartite organization of base, shaft, and cornice. The simple treatment maximized light and air while expressing the structural steel frame.

52 Carson Pirie Scott Buildings
(Haskell and Barker Buildings)
18–24 S. Wabash Ave.
1875, Wheelock & Thomas Haskell Building remodeled 1896, Louis H. Sullivan
(J. P. Atwater Building)
26–28 S. Wabash Ave.
1877, John M. Van Osdel

In the 1890s the Schlesinger & Mayer store began acquiring space on Wabash Ave. near the planned Madison St. elevated station. Sullivan was commissioned to open the first two stories of the Haskell Building's load-bearing facade, by spanning it with ironwork finished in his own decorative style and painted white. It is the only surviving exterior example of Sullivan's alterations to the company's buildings before receiving the commission for their State St. store.

53 23 S. Wabash Ave.
(Rae Building)
1872, Frederick Baumann
Remodeled 1928, Graven &
Mayger

This sober Italianate facade,
which follows the design of earlier cast-iron fronts, is the perfect
foil for Sullivan's exuberant Jewelers Building.

Jewelers Building

54 Jewelers Building
19 S. Wabash Ave.
1882, Adler & Sullivan

Disregard the ground-floor alterations and look up, or view this
oldest surviving Adler & Sullivan
design from the El platform. The
color and materials are Ruskinian
Gothic; the details exhibit the
emergence of Sullivan's distinctive ornament. The chunky,
rather stiff plant forms are akin
to the work of Philadelphia architect Frank Furness, or the designs of Owen Jones as found in
such publications as *The Grammar of Ornament* (1854).

55 Silversmith Building
10 S. Wabash Ave.
1897, D. H. Burnham & Co.

On a richly colored facade composed of expressed structural
elements, brick mullions placed
on the spandrels and the column
faces emphasize verticality.

56 Shops Building
21 N. Wabash Ave.
1875, architect unknown
Remodeled 1912, Alfred S.
Alschuler

An old loft building became a retail center with the addition of a
metal-frame facade covered with
polychrome terra-cotta.

57 Pittsfield Building
55 E. Washington St.
1927, Graham, Anderson, Probst
& White

This tower was briefly Chicago's
tallest building. Its emphasis on
verticality and use of setbacks recall the era's Art Deco high rises,
but it uses the Gothic vocabulary
of earlier skyscrapers. The building accommodated the special
electrical and plumbing needs of
medical and dental offices and
the security requirements of jewelers. Beyond the Washington St.
lobby is a well-preserved five-story shopping arcade surrounded by balconies and shop
windows.

58 Washington & Wabash
Building (Marshall Field & Co.
Annex)
25 E. Washington St.
1914, Graham, Burnham & Co.

Field's established a popular
practice of offering a separate
men's store. The six retail levels
of this mixed-use building are
surmounted by fourteen office
floors.

59 Burton Estate, Peck, and
Couch Estate Buildings
129, 137 & 139 N. Wabash
Ave.
1872, 1877 (Burton Estate), John
M. Van Osdel

This fragment of a post-Fire
commercial streetscape shows
the variations possible in Italianate facades.

60 Bowen Block
70 E. Randolph St.
1872, William W. Boyington

This building, the central third of
the original block, is a rare reminder of the immediate post-Fire years, when the construction
of commercial buildings was
measured in miles of frontage.
Ornamentation was limited to
sheet-metal Italianate window
caps.

61 Wabash/Randolph Center Self Park
20 E. Randolph St.
1990, Lucien Lagrange & Assocs.;
Desman Assocs., assoc. archs.

The facades pay homage to the Chicago School with their tripartite organization and vertical green pipes set against the concrete to suggest Chicago windows.

62 Self Park
60 E. Lake St.
1986, Stanley Tigerman & Assocs.

A classic touring car inspired the facade. The turquoise of the baked enamel panels was selected from the 1957 Chevrolet color schedule.

63 203 N. Wabash Ave.
(Old Dearborn Bank Building)
1928, Rapp & Rapp

Movie palace confectioners Rapp & Rapp also designed sober business buildings. This tower's only indulgence is in the ornament of the spandrels.

64 Seventeenth Church of Christ, Scientist
55 E. Wacker Dr.
1968, Harry Weese & Assocs.

A 200-foot travertine curve marks the auditorium and creates a commanding presence for this low building set among skyscrapers. Structural elements, including the lower columns and roof ribs, are clearly visible. A school is located under the auditorium level; offices are slipped in behind.

65 Wacker Tower
(Chicago Motor Club)
68 E. Wacker Pl.
1928, Holabird & Root

This modestly scaled tower equals the firm's more celebrated Art Deco skyscrapers in refinement and soaring verticality. The theme of travel was beautifully elaborated in a large lobby mural by John W. Norton.

66 Wacker Drive
East–West segment
1926, Edward H. Bennett

Along the south bank of the main branch of the Chicago River is a double-level street and embankment built of reinforced-concrete construction with Bedford limestone details. Called Wacker Dr., it honors the first president of the Chicago Plan Commission. The initial conception was part of Daniel H. Burnham's 1909 Plan of Chicago; the design was elaborated with businessmen's needs in mind. The world's first two-level street replaced the congested, dilapidated South Water Street Market in little more than two years. Demolition and construction had to safeguard existing buildings and tunnels, contain the river, and mesh with streets, bridges, and ramps.

The upper level is a flat slab system, supported by octagonal columns that carry a roadway 110 to 115 feet wide plus sidewalks and a riverfront promenade. Images of the banks of the Seine are deliberately encouraged by such garniture as balustrades similar to those on the Pont de la Concorde, grand staircases from street to dock level, and obelisk lampposts modeled on a Parisian example. The lower level provides truck access to the area and carries four lanes of through traffic. There is also an uncovered dock at the river's edge, as well as a right-of-way and ventilation system for a rail line that never materialized.

Wacker Dr. was extended southward to W. Congress Pkwy. along the former Market St. from 1949–1958 but this time without water contact. East of Michigan Ave. it was extended to Lake Michigan as Illinois Center developed.

67 35 E. Wacker Dr.
(formerly Pure Oil Building, originally Jewelers Building)
1926, Thielbar & Fugard; Giaver & Dinkelberg, assoc. archs.

The initials "JB" in the terra-cotta commemorate the original plan to attract tenants in the jewelry trade. When new, the building was noted for its internal garage. Tenants could drive in from

35 E. Wacker Dr.

lower Wacker Dr. and have their cars taken by elevator to assigned stalls on the lower twenty-two floors. In 1940 the system was abandoned due to mechanical failures and larger cars, and the garage space was converted to office use. The setbacks at Floors 24 and 26 created terraces punctuated by corner tempietti that artfully hid water towers. "The Belvedere" on top, whose dome hides mechanical equipment, provided an expansive view above a restaurant and lounge. More recently, it has served as a dramatic presentation room for Murphy/Jahn, which occupies space below.

75 E. Wacker Dr.

68 75 E. Wacker Dr.
(formerly Lincoln Tower, originally Mather Tower)
1928, Herbert Hugh Riddle
Renovated 1983, Harry Weese & Assocs.

The city's slenderest skyscraper, a twenty-four-story rectangle topped by a telescoping eighteen-story octagon, is like a terra-cotta Gothic rocket poised for takeoff.

69 Sun-Times Building
401 N. Wabash Ave.
1957, Naess & Murphy
Rush St. river plaza 1958, Atkinson & Fitzgerald, landscape archs.

An undistinguished building has elevations enlivened by views of the pressroom in action and by one of the city's earliest riverfront plazas.

70 IBM Building
330 N. Wabash Ave.
1971, Office of Mies van der Rohe; C. F. Murphy Assocs., assoc. arch.

Mies's last American building, and his largest, follows his familiar model but is executed in dark aluminum and bronze-tinted glass, not basic black. It is sited so as to avoid obstructing Marina City and to capture the lake views made possible by a jog in the river.

71 United of America Building (United Insurance Building)
1 E. Wacker Dr.
1962, Shaw, Metz & Assocs.
Renovated 1989, Lucien Lagrange & Assocs.

The *luxe* marble finish does little to disguise the absence of the pristine detailing and proportions of stronger modernist designs. The 1989 renovation interrupted the rhythm of the facades—which had never been better than dull—with new, elegantly detailed entries.

72 Stouffer Riviere Hotel
1 W. Wacker Dr.
1991, William B. Tabler Architects; Mann, Gin, Ebel & Frazier Ltd., assoc. archs.

Pedestrian access to this auto-mobile-oriented hotel is death-defying. Set back from the streetline, it claims to be upholding Chicago traditions in the large proportions of the windows in its base and in the bay windows in the setback tower.

73 State Street Mall
1979, City of Chicago, Dept. of Public Works, Bureau of Architecture

In an effort to attract shoppers who had deserted the Loop in favor of N. Michigan Ave. or suburban malls, State St. from Lake St. to Congress Pkwy. was converted in 1979 into a two-lane thoroughfare restricted to buses. The new pedestrian mall featured widened sidewalks, new subway entrances and bus shelters, and art installations; sidewalk vendors were encouraged. The elimination of automobile traffic had the contrary effect: activity here was reduced and encouraged on adjacent streets. While that once Great Street declined, shabbier Wabash Ave. began to flourish. Plans announced in 1992 call for re-creating a four-lane vehicular thoroughfare linking newly emerging academic, retail, and entertainment "districts."

74 ABC–WLS Building
(State–Lake Theater)
190 N. State St.
1917, Rapp & Rapp

Renovated 1984, Skidmore, Owings & Merrill

This former movie palace and office building now serves the television industry.

75 Page Brothers Building
177–191 N. State St.
1872, John M. Van Osdel
State St. facade 1902, Hill & Woltersdorf
Renovated 1986, Daniel P. Coffey & Assocs.

Built immediately after the Fire, and in the same style and materials as the destroyed buildings, this building has one of the Loop's two remaining cast-iron facades. Such facades became unpopular after the Fire because they had melted in the heat, bringing down masonry walls with them. The Page Building originally fronted on Lake St.; its brick side wall was given a fancy facade after State St. had become the city's premier mercantile address. In 1986 the building was rehabilitated to provide speculative office space that would support the Chicago Theater, which wraps around it in an L-shaped plan. The linkage could be accomplished only after upgrading the Page Building's wood-frame structure, which did not conform to building codes. In order to preserve the delicate Lake St. cast-iron facades, the original structure was used as formwork for the new concrete system and was then replaced in stages.

Page Brothers Building

76 Chicago Theater

175 N. State St.
1921, Rapp & Rapp
Restored 1986, Daniel P. Coffey &
Assocs.

Though the architects went on to design larger movie palaces, the Chicago, along with the Tivoli Theater (1921, demolished) at Cottage Grove Ave. and 63rd St., set the standards for the type. Their success was so great that Rapp & Rapp became architects "in residence" for their client, Balaban & Katz, and later for the entire Paramount/Publix theater chain.

The theater has been restored to its condition in 1933, when it was refurbished in preparation for the World's Fair. The triumphal-arch facade of off-white terra-cotta opens into a series of lavish, Versailles-inspired spaces. The 3,800-seat auditorium's excellent sight lines derive from the unusually shaped site.

77 Marshall Field & Co.

111 N. State St.
On N. Wabash Ave.: south section
1892, D. H. Burnham; middle
section 1906, D. H. Burnham &
Co.; north section 1914, Graham,
Burnham & Co.; on N. State St.:
north section 1902 and south
section 1907, D. H. Burnham
& Co.
Renovation 1992, HTI/Space
Design International

The grande dame of State St. has an appropriately massive, stolid design that contrasts with the more skeletal facades of its competitors. The southeastern structure is the earliest, designed with load-bearing walls and heavy arched windows by Charles B. Atwood in complete contrast to his contemporaneous Reliance Building. The high ceilings are supported by forests of decorated columns; the two arcades are topped by a skylight and by shimmering Tiffany mosaics.

78 Reliance Building

32 N. State St.
Foundations and base 1891,
Burnham & Root
Additional stories 1895, D. H.
Burnham & Co.

Its chief virtue is as clear support for the Chicago School's claim to be a precursor of modern architecture: it is very glassy. Designer Charles Atwood used glass at every opportunity. He folded the bay windows out from the frame to completely hide the columns, and he balanced huge picture windows with narrow ones of double-hung sashes in the fullest early example of the Chicago window. His achievement is all the more remarkable because his work had to use the foundations and base executed four years earlier according to John Wellborn Root's plans. Root, Daniel H. Burnham's original design partner, died in 1891, and his plans for the elevations are lost.

Reliance Building

On the terra-cotta facades Atwood stressed the overriding continuity of the horizontal spandrels. This was a clear break with the prevailing tradition of letting vertical load-bearing piers carry down to the ground. At the corner, where the structural column could not be suppressed behind the glass, two bundled sets of colonnettes slide up the covering pier to dematerialize it, a technique used by Gothic stone masons for exactly the same purpose. This corner treatment makes an interesting comparison with those on tall buildings designed by Mies van der Rohe.

The Reliance Building is almost as weightless as it looks. The vertical loads are borne down to preexisting foundations by lightweight, open, trusswork columns. Constructing the frame out of factory-assembled two-story columns with staggered joints reduced the number of field connections and allowed the steel for the top ten stories to be erected in fifteen days. Structural engineer Edward C. Shankland relied for wind bracing on these tall, stiff columns rigidly coupled to extradeep girders. This method of construction was a significant departure from the heavier portal bracing derived from railroad viaducts and used frequently for such tall buildings as Holabird & Roche's Old Colony Building (1894) and Cass Gilbert's Woolworth Building (1913) in New York. The Reliance's construction methods have much in common with more recent construction and wind-bracing techniques, such as those used in the Amoco Building (1974).

Predominantly glassy facades could be found before 1895 on, for example, the Crystal Palace in London (Joseph Paxton, 1851) and on Oriel Chambers in Liverpool (Peter Ellis, Jr., 1864), but the promise of these early aesthetic speculations had to wait a generation for delivery. The perfection of the high-speed elevator made the Reliance Building's height possible; the explosive demand for modern office space in Chicago after the Fire of 1871 made it essential. Today the building exudes the logic of engineering under clear commercial pressure.
—Anders Nereim

79 17 N. State St./16 N. Wabash Ave. (Charles A. Stevens Store Building)
1912, D. H. Burnham & Co.

Recognizing the need to accommodate small retailers on a street that had become filled with grand emporiums, the Stevens brothers topped the seven floors of their own department store with eleven levels of shops for others.

80 State-Madison Building (Boston Store)
22 W. Madison St./1 N. Dearborn St.
1905, 1917, Holabird & Roche

The Chicago School formula is weakened by a heavy-handed colonnaded top.

81 1 N. State St. (formerly Wieboldt's Department Store, originally Mandel Bros. Store)
1912, Holabird & Roche
82 8–14 N. Wabash Ave (Mandel Brothers Annex)
1900, Holabird & Roche
Top two floors added 1905, Holabird & Roche

The restored State St. building has been subdivided to accommodate smaller retailers. The more distinguished Wabash Ave. structure has unusually wide bays, very narrow spandrels, and slim projecting courses, all of which stress horizontality. The most precocious feature is the continuous glazing of the second floor, which is like an International Style ribbon window.

83 Carson Pirie Scott & Co. (Schlesinger & Mayer Department Store)
1 S. State St.
1899; 1903, Louis H. Sullivan
State St. addition (five bays)
1906, D. H. Burnham & Co.
State St. addition (three bays)
1961, Holabird & Root
Restored 1980, Office of
John Vinci

One of the first large department stores to be erected entirely with fireproof steel-frame construction, Carson Pirie Scott served American and European architects as a model for this modern building type. Designers perceived it as a representation of its architect's axiom, "Form follows function," for in it Louis Henri Sullivan had ingeniously extended the technology of skyscraper construction to the department store. However, as he had in his office buildings, Sullivan took artistic license with the expression of practical forms and their functions.

On his skyscrapers, Sullivan modified the expression of the grid of steel construction by emphasizing the vertical dimension with unbroken lines of piers and recessed spandrels. The main portion of the Carson Pirie Scott Store comprises a corner entrance pavilion and tower, flanked by twelve-story elevations. In the tower Sullivan reproduced the skyscraper effect, but on the elevations he emphasized the horizontal dimension by using unbroken stringcourses to unite expanses of Chicago windows.

Sullivan's emphasis on horizontality was initially determined by the lighting and spatial requirements of modern merchandising practices. Steel framing required minimal internal support, allowed the maximum amount of daylight for merchandise display, and increased open space for easy movement around display cases and between floors. This post-and-lintel construction is exhibited on the exterior as a thin white-tiled grid that frames recessed windows and defines layered floors. Its clearest expression

Carson Pirie Scott & Co.

Carson Pirie Scott & Co. detail

is in the plate-glass show windows, which are as wide as the vertical supports allow.

The base of ornamented display windows were to attract customers. Equally important, they served Sullivan's artistic purpose: to show the originality of his style of ornament close up. Sullivan used ornament as an artistic finish or, in his words, as "a garment of poetic imagery." He wrote extensively about architecture as a kind of poetic representation of nature capable of offsetting the materialist culture of an industrialized modern city. The intertwining geometric forms and botanical motifs (and his initials, LHS, above the corner entrance) are cast in iron and painted green over a red undercoat, emulating both oxidized bronze and dappled sunlit foliage. Sullivan's metaphor of the natural landscape is made manifest by strolling along the base and walking through the entrance. To-

gether with the mahogany-paneled vestibule and foliate column capitals, the experience recalls a treelined forest walk.

Sullivan's store was built in two sections for the retail firm of Schlesinger & Mayer. The first section (1899), three bays wide on Madison St., has nine stories. The twelve-story corner section (1903) extended the frontage through the seven northernmost State St. bays. The building lease and business were sold to Carson Pirie Scott & Co. virtually upon completion. The building has twice been sympathetically extended southward and has been subjected to numerous external and internal alterations, including the unfortunate removal of original ornamentation in metal, wood, and mosaics. Major restoration work was done on the facades and the main entrance in 1978–1980.
—Lauren S. Weingarden

84 Chicago Building
(Chicago Savings Bank Building)
7 W. Madison St.
1904, Holabird & Roche

Highly visible on State St. from the north because of an eastern shift in the roadway is this Holabird & Roche archetype. Large Chicago windows—flat on State St., alternately projecting and flat on Madison St.—dominate the facades. The emphasized corners and the rare intact cornice are also noteworthy.

Chicago Building

85 Mentor Building
39 S. State St.
1906, Howard Van Doren Shaw

Shaw's only skyscraper presents an unusual amalgam of styles, with windows grouped in horizontal bands between a four-level base of large showroom windows and a classically inspired top. The details are typically robust and idiosyncratic, retaining the character of their classical sources but used as large-scale, conspicuous motifs.

86 Palmer House
17 E. Monroe St.
1927, Holabird & Roche

Built by the same architects and at the same time as the Stevens (Hilton) Hotel and only slightly smaller, the Palmer House shares its massing of narrow towers grouped around light courts. Below the palatial second-floor lobby is an elegant commercial arcade.

87 Singer Building
120 S. State St.
1926, Mundie & Jensen

The Singer Sewing Machine Co. wanted a distinctive building but had only twenty-five feet of frontage. The white glazed terracotta molded into Gothic tracery and the polygonal top floor are

arresting, and the exceptionally tall lower floors provide maximum street exposure and daylight.

88 Baskin Building
137 S. State St.
1947, Holabird & Root

Four floors of ribbon windows turn the corner in a sharp-edged International Style manner.

89 The Berghoff
15 W. Adams St.
1872, architect unknown
27 W. Adams St.
1872, Charles M. Palmer

The Berghoff is housed in the Loop's only surviving public-hall building; the top-floor meeting room is indicated by the larger-scaled windows. One of two remaining cast-iron facades in the Loop is at 27 (the other is the Page Brothers Building).

90 F. W. Woolworth & Co.
211 S. State St.
1949, Shaw, Metz & Dolio

The holdover Moderne facade has strong vertical strips of windows and dark spandrels to counteract the boxy horizontality.

91 Maurice L. Rothschild Building
300 S. State St.
1906, Holabird & Roche
Three-bay south addition 1910, Holabird & Roche
Four-story addition 1928, Alfred S. Alschuler

The original, eight-story building had foundations and walls that would accommodate an additional four floors; but when they were added, the building lost its cornice to a simple parapet. The chamfered corner was designed to admit extra daylight to the selling floors.

92 DePaul Center
(formerly Goldblatt's, originally Rothschild & Co. Store)
333 S. State St.
1912, Holabird & Roche
Renovated 1993, Daniel P. Coffey & Assocs.

On the remarkably intact facade, the deep, bracketed cornice is especially noteworthy. Converted to a multiuse structure, it has shopping and food courts on the lower levels, rental offices in the middle, and academic floors on top.

93 Pritzker Park
West side of State St. at Van Buren St.
1992, Patrick Shaw, arch.; Ronald Jones, artist

When this land was cleared as part of the Harold Washington Library project, the City created a green haven with a five-year lease on life. The stand of trees beyond a stone wall with an urn re-creates a scene depicted in René Magritte's painting *The Banquet* at the Art Institute of Chicago. The circular seating areas were inspired by the council rings designed by landscape artist Jens Jensen.

94 Harold Washington Library Center
400 S. State St.
1991, Hammond, Beeby & Babka; A. Epstein & Sons International, assoc. archs.

It is wonderful that Chicago's most important new public building in many years should be a free public library. That kind of library is by far the most important monument that any city can build to itself and its people. From the deep entrance portals, through the wide reading floors, through the humanely small studios in the depth of its walls, to the blooming open space and dappled light of the winter garden under its roof, the Library works as that kind of living monument, a free and dignified place for every citizen to work and delight in.

It is also wonderfully appropriate that the building should be an embodiment of the urban environment of Chicago and of its physical structure. Indeed, the Library is one of the most wholly contextual of modern buildings. Its forms grew directly out of those elements which characterize Chicago's history, especially the skyscraper blocks of the Loop and the Great White City of 1893, along with the ghost of Daniel H. Burnham's 1909 Plan of Chicago.

The early skyscrapers were the three-dimensional projection of Chicago's grid plan, blocks built right up to the property line and strongly defining the Loop's packed and teeming streets. The Library is like H. H. Richardson's great lost Marshall Field

Harold Washington Library Center

Wholesale Store, reflecting the full volume of its whole block, and it is one of that building's finest successors. But its west side is inflected toward the elongated half-block slabs that bound it on that side; it is all glass, as if sliced through by Plymouth Ct. Its north end adjoins the elevated railroad, itself a major shaper of the Loop; the south end faces Congress Pkwy., which is effectively the Loop's southern boundary and was the intended east–west axis of Burnham's classic plan. The Library commemorates and uses that vision by exploiting Congress Pkwy. as a southern facade for the Loop and as an artery opening the way inland.

The building blocks with which Burnham intended to flank his boulevard are clearly recalled by the Library's shape and scale, but its details evoke those of the World's Columbian Exposition of 1893. In that tradition, they are the most boldly and inventively classical of all; the enormous acroteria frame the vast pediments at a scale never before attempted. This is a classicism that, in a sense, is all Chicago's: big and brutal like the city itself but specifically metallic and fluid like the interlocking ironwork of Louis H. Sullivan's Carson Pirie Scott store. Also thoroughly Chicago are the heavy rusticated arches of the ground floor and the high arcuated piers that rise above them. These ultimately derive from Henri Labrouste's Bibliothèque Ste. Geneviève of the 1840s and passed through Richardson's hands to culminate in Sullivan's Auditorium.

The Harold Washington Library manages to condense all of these elements into one powerful mass, built of the very bones and blood of Chicago, of the tough body of the Loop, and the ancient urban gesture of its classical facade.
—Vincent Scully

95 Second Leiter Building (formerly Sears, Roebuck & Co. Store, originally Siegel, Cooper & Co. Store)
403 S. State St.
1891, William Le Baron Jenney

In the Second Leiter Building what seems to support *does* support. Cornices and colonnettes articulate the underlying skeleton, with piers and spandrels resolving themselves into magnificent ranks of glass-filled grids. The exterior reflects an interior extraordinarily spacious, especially for its time. Each of the eight stories is an open composition of broad avenues and slender iron columns 16 feet high. Contemporaries saw the building as a manifestation of a new age.

The building constitutes the response of William Le Baron Jenney, who must be considered one of the century's most significant architects, to the demands of its developer, Levi Z. Leiter, Marshall Field's partner from 1867 to 1881. Leiter wanted a "complete and perfect" building to house a single major retail establishment, but not without the ability to subdivide if required. In the diminutive First Leiter Building (1879) which stood at Monroe and Wells Sts. until 1972, Jenney had given Leiter a predominantly glass envelope by supporting timber joists and girders on cast-iron columns. For Leiter's second

Second Leiter Building

commission all of the beams and girders were steel; supports remained cast iron. The steel's high tensile strength enabled Jenney to open the exterior walls to glass to an unprecedented extent. The system, introduced by Jenney with wrought-iron horizontals on the demolished Home Insurance Building (1884), obviated the need for supporting partitions, permitting Leiter to arrange the interior as he saw fit. The extensive exterior glazing made space-consuming light courts unnecessary.

For most of its history the building functioned as a store for a single retailer, originally Siegel, Cooper & Co., and later Sears, Roebuck & Co. Until the building was subdivided in 1981, the open qualities of its steel framing were instantly obvious.

Striking in its formal ex-cellence, the Second Leiter Building recalls Jenney's training in the early 1850s at the École Centrale des Arts et Manufactures in Paris: the school's architectural curriculum taught that purpose and structure determine form. Leiter was the rare client who made the fullest use of Jenney's training, permitting the most modern materials and their expression in the building's design. The forward-looking qualities of the building's functionalism have fascinated historians such as Sigfried Giedion, who described it as "the first high building to exhibit the trend toward pure forms." And so it does. With a little imagination, one can see the Second Leiter Building as a modern composition of the mid-twentieth century.
—Theodore Turak

96 Manhattan Building
431 S. Dearborn St.
1891, William Le Baron Jenney
Renovated 1982,
Hasbrouck Hunderman

Viewed with awe by visitors to the 1893 World's Columbian Exposition, who called it Hercules, the Manhattan earned a long line of firsts: the first tall building to use skeleton construction throughout; the first sixteen-story building in the United States and briefly the world's tallest building; and the first building with a structurally sophisticated wind-bracing system. The north

Manhattan Building

and south bays are cantilevered to avoid overloading the footings of adjacent buildings.

97 Plymouth Building
417 S. Dearborn St.
1899, Simeon B. Eisendrath
West facade remodeled 1945,
W. Scott Armstrong

The Gothic face-lift was intended to give a collegiate image to a correspondence school. Eisendrath's design remains visible on Plymouth Ct. with Sullivanesque ironwork executed by Winslow Bros. Inside is a newel post identical to those executed by Winslow for the Schlesinger & Mayer (Carson Pirie Scott & Co.) store—not surprising, since Eisendrath had worked for Adler & Sullivan.

98 Old Colony Building
407 S. Dearborn St.
1894, Holabird & Roche

Here is the Loop's sole survivor of a group of Chicago School skyscrapers with gracefully rounded corner bays. To offset its narrowness, continuous piers and recessed spandrels visually contract the long sides, while enhanced spandrels on the narrow elevations attempt to emphasize the horizontal. This was the first American structure to use portal arches (fillets joining column and girder) for wind bracing. Phoenix columns are wrought iron, and the girders and floor beams are steel.

99 Chicago Bar Association Building
321 S. Plymouth Ct.
1990, Tigerman McCurry

Gothicism à la Eliel Saarinen imbues this small building with a vivid presence. Emphasis is on the decorative facade at street level and at the pinnacled top. The cast-aluminum figure above the entry is *Themis* by Mary Block.

Old Colony Building

100 Fisher Building
343 S. Dearborn St.
1896, D. H. Burnham & Co.
Northern addition 1907, Peter J.
Weber

Fisher Building

Terra-cotta fish, salamanders, crabs, snakes, and shells celebrate the name of the developer, Lucius G. Fisher. The building resembles the Reliance Building in heavier Gothic garb. The original building has a steel frame with spread footings on piles to compress the soil. The system proved inadequate; the south half leans into the taller, northern addition, which was built on caissons. The second floor retains its original mosaic flooring and veined Carrara marble walls; the elevator gates are original.

101 Monadnock Building
53 W. Jackson Blvd.
1889–1891, Burnham & Root
Addition
54 W. Van Buren St.
1893, Holabird & Roche

Monadnock Building

The Monadnock Building was erected in two parts along Dearborn St. for Peter C. and Shepherd Brooks, Boston developers who commissioned many prominent Chicago buildings. The northern section was designed with exterior masonry walls; the southern addition has a steel frame clad in terra-cotta. At sixteen stories it was briefly the world's tallest office building.

The northern half has always been the subject of attention and wonder. It was constructed as a thick-walled brick tower, 66 feet wide, 200 feet long, and 200 feet high. The *American Architect* in 1892 described it as a chimney. Two cross walls divide the interior space into three fluelike cavities, the centers of which are open from street to roof. A freestanding staircase spirals down from the brilliance of the skylit sixteenth floor to the dark lobby cut lengthwise through the ground floor. Around this open stairwell a light structural grid sustains stacks of rental floors. From these extend the modular alcoves pushing through the facade to become bay windows.

The thick, perforated exterior wall is an expansion of the series of thick wall slabs that Burnham & Root origi-nally proposed to divide the building vertically, like bookends, into a series of steel-framed cells. This is a modification of the steel system first decisively demonstrated in Holabird & Roche's demolished Tacoma Building (1889), where two such thick walls were set at right angles to discipline the grid and achieve stability. In the Rookery (1888) Burnham & Root themselves used two perforated masonry facade walls and four elevator and stair stacks to stabilize the iron skeleton. There is a nice play of hard and soft, enclosure and exposure in each of these designs. Steel and masonry are in balance. The old material has not yet been abandoned; the new material has not yet supervened.

It was not the Monadnock's remarkable constructive organization that contemporaries particularly remarked but, rather, the lack of exterior ornament. Burn-ham & Root shaped it as a single massive unit: a plinthlike base below a curved brick plane moving inward and up-ward, transformed into a sub-tle batter for fourteen floors before returning outward to overhang in a cavetto cornice, giving the whole a shape sug-gestive of an Egyptian pylon. As the walls retreat, the win-dow alcoves emerge as bays. Bevels at each corner expand and pace the rise of the fa-cade.

The windows are not out-lined with decoration but re-main mere holes cut in this huge shape. Contemporary critics saw this as rational, honest, and exemplary of the starkness that a commercial building should accept; the Monadnock came to be cited as a model for steel-framed buildings of entirely different structure. But, as Sigfried Gied-ion observed in *Space, Time and Architecture* (1941), the nature of steel construction is a grid of panels, as in the Re-liance Building (1895). The Monadnock was exceptional. Its sense of upward thrust and the contrast of thick ma-sonry and fragile steel look back to the traditional craft of building brick by brick and are appropriate to its fiercely ar-chaic Egyptoid form.
—David Van Zanten

102 Chicago Federal Center
Dearborn St. between Adams St. & Jackson Blvd.
1959–1974, Ludwig Mies van der Rohe; Schmidt, Garden & Erikson; C. F. Murphy Assocs.; A. Epstein & Sons, assoc. archs.
103 Everett McKinley Dirksen Building
(1959–1964)
219 S. Dearborn St.
104 John C. Kluczynski Building *(1966–1974)*
230 S. Dearborn St.
105 U.S. Post Office—Loop Station *(1966–1974)*
219 S. Clark St.

By accident rather than de-sign, the axial siting of three great plazas forms a rhythmic pattern that adds a discernibly urbanistic unity to the Loop. The outermost spaces, at the Richard J. Daley Center to the north and the Federal Center to the south, are ori-ented inward, as if addressing the intervening First National Bank plaza. The symbolism of government bowing to fi-nance, while fortuitous in this instance, is not without poetic appropriateness to Chicago's history. Such a metaphor, however, would have meant little to the chief architect of the Federal Center, Ludwig Mies van der Rohe, whose design is notable as much for its indifference to a traditional iconography of government as for the evidence it offers of his lifelong search for a universal order and grammar of the building art.

Outwardly, the Chicago Federal Center "reads" as many of Mies's residential and commercial works do: as ab-stract and nonallusive, rather than as representational, ar-chitecture. It has been criti-cized for this. Even so, Mies's uncompromising devotion to principle, together with his vaunted sensitivity to propor-tion and structural detail, and, in this case, the organizational scale, combine to give the complex a monumental ur-ban presence.

Three buildings occupy a space divided by Dearborn St. The thirty-story Dirksen courtroom building takes up

Chicago Federal Center

a half-square block to the east. The forty-two-story Kluczynski office building and a one-story postal facility are sited on the full block to the west. This ensemble encloses a large space at the southwest corner of Adams and Dearborn Sts., where in 1974 Alexander Calder's vermilion-painted steel construction *Flamingo* was installed. Its color and organic contours serve as a counterfoil to the matteblack geometries of Mies's buildings.

Both towers are curtainwall structures characteristic of the high-rise designs of Mies's American period. Their steel frames, suppressed behind uniform walls of glass and steel, are marked off by projecting steel I-beam mullions. The Post Office, a unitary space with a central core, is similarly typical of Mies's reductivist concept of the single-story pavilion. Externally thin yet powerful structural columns of steel brace enormous panes of tinted glass.

Commissioned by the U.S. General Services Administration, the Federal Center was part of a 1950s plan to modernize the federal government's administrative and judiciary buildings. Begun in 1959, the center had been fully designed by 1964, the first of Mies's urban, mixed land use projects. Budgetary problems delayed completion until 1974.
—Franz Schulze

106 Marquette Building
140 S. Dearborn St.
1893–1895 Holabird & Roche;
Westernmost Adams St. bay
1906, Holabird & Roche;
Renovation and restoration
1980, Holabird & Root

The Marquette Building is an exemplar of the Chicago style: the rectangular grid of its structural steel skeleton is clearly articulated by its brick and terra-cotta cladding. The decorative treatment establishes the organization of the elevation, with its hierarchy of base, shaft, and capital, and gives it a sense of verticality that is expressed through the greater sculptural depth of the piers in comparison to the spandrels. The arms of the E-shaped building

Marquette Building

embrace a large light well with the elevator and service shafts in the central projection. All of the offices, which line the arms of the plan, have a window either to the street or the light well. This design, combined with the structural and aesthetic treatment of the wall, guaranteed the maximum amount of natural light for the interior spaces.

The architects, William Holabird and Martin Roche, would become recognized as among the most prolific working in the Chicago commercial style. They had met as draftsmen in the office of pioneer skyscraper designer William Le Baron Jenney and founded their own firm in the early 1880s. The prominent structural engineer Corydon T. Purdy collaborated on this design.

The building was named in honor of Jacques Marquette, a Jesuit priest and explorer. His journal, in which he recorded his expedition through the Illinois Country in 1674–1675, included the first description by a European of the site of Chicago. Owen F. Aldis, a real estate developer, amateur historian, and one of the building's original owners, had translated Marquette's journal in 1891, providing the inspiration for the structure's name and decorative program. Relief sculptures over the main portal by Hermon A. MacNeil depict events associated with Marquette's expedition. The two-story lobby is sumptuously decorated with marble trim and mosaic scenes of Marquette's trek designed by J. A. Holzer and executed by the Tiffany Glass and Decorating Co. Bronze reliefs above the elevator doors by Edward Kemeys depict French explorers and Native Americans.

Alterations include the removal of the original Ionic columns from the main portal and the replacement of the cornice by the top floor (1950).

—Timothy Wittman

107 Xerox Centre
55 W. Monroe St.
1980, C. F. Murphy Assocs.

Taut and streamlined, the curtain wall slides around the corner, while diagonals in the sidewalk, on the lobby floor, and on the roof slice across it. To cut energy costs, the proportion of glass to aluminum paneling changes from 75 percent on the north elevation, which receives little direct sun, to 50 percent elsewhere.

108 33 W. Monroe St.
1980, Skidmore, Owings & Merrill

The three stacked atriums were a first in office design, but the colors, materials, and lighting are unusually dreary.

109 Shubert Theater & Majestic Building
16–22 W. Monroe St.
1905, Edmund R. Krause

Here is a celebration of the terra-cotta modeler's skills at imitating heavy stonework.

110 Inland Steel Building
30 W. Monroe St.
1954–1958, Skidmore, Owings & Merrill

Chicago has always been a city where measurable superlatives like "largest," "tallest" and "busiest" have been the cornerstones of civic pride. It is indeed ironic that the Inland Steel Building, an office tower of modest scale and limited visual prominence, has achieved celebrity status, while its taller, larger, and significantly more conspicuous contemporary, the Prudential Building, is now virtually ignored.

Inland Steel Building

Inland Steel's pioneering attributes are well known. Its unobstructed floor plate (177 × 58 feet) was unprecedented. This was accomplished by placing core services in the adjacent tower to the east. For the first time, steel pilings, driven eighty-five feet through mud and clay into bedrock, were used to support a high-rise structure. Inland Steel was Chicago's first fully air-conditioned building, the first with dual glazing, and the first to provide indoor below-grade parking. It pioneered the use of stainless steel as a cladding material. Critics and scholars have consistently praised its graceful proportions, the elegance of its detailing, and the sophistication of its public art.

But the Inland Steel Building has not been adequately cited for one of its most praiseworthy attributes, the civic benefit of its presence on the streetscape. Avant-garde for its time, the building has become increasingly engaging, compatible, and understated as the character of the surrounding area has evolved. This is attributable in large measure to the excellence of its site plan and to the civility of its scale. The placement of its principal mass respects and reinforces the established building lines of the fronting streets. The longer dimension, along the line of Dearborn St., is interestingly maintained by seven projecting columns encased in stainless steel. The alignment of the shorter Monroe St. dimension not only enhances the sculptural quality of the services tower but also imparts a personal scale and orientation to the entrance, which is recessed at grade, glazed on three sides, and flooded by natural light. A substantial single-story annex houses loading docks, mail rooms, and the garage entrance. Its skillful placement on the site's northeastern corner makes it all but invisible to the public.

The economics of modern urban development and current code standards have secured the uniqueness of the Inland Steel Building and have qualified it to be a protected architectural landmark. It survives as an enduring reminder of an optimistic period when the future was a beacon and long-restrained architectural skill and creativity blossomed once again. While its designers could not possibly have anticipated the adjacent construction, especially of the plaza on the west side of Dearborn St., they could not have prepared for it more effectively.
—Lawrence Okrent

⚅ First National Bank of Chicago
Block bounded by S. Dearborn, W. Madison, S. Clark, & W. Monroe Sts.
1969, Perkins & Will; C. F. Murphy Assocs., assoc. archs.

Because of state laws prohibiting branch banking, the building had to accommodate tens of thousands of daily transactions on a single site. Departments with public access required large spaces at or near street level; tenants needed traditional office-building floors and access outside of banking hours. The graceful solution was this tapering shape and a pair of end cores that hold all services. The spread base and the cores combine to achieve stability and efficient load-carrying; they also create the landmark profile. The multilevel, sunken plaza combines services with spaces around a fountain and Marc Chagall's mosaic mural *The Four Seasons*. The ancillary building at 20 S. Clark St., known as the Two First National Building (1973, C. F. Murphy Assocs.), includes the entrance ramp for service vehicles to the site's lower levels.

⚄ Three First National Plaza
W. Madison St. at N. Dearborn St.
1981, Skidmore, Owings & Merrill

SOM broke their own mold with this carnelian granite-clad companion to the First National Bank. Two towers are connected by a nine-story atrium with exposed steel truss supports. The sawtooth, setback configuration provides many corner offices and greenhouses at the top, which is lower than the First National Bank in order to

First National Bank of Chicago

leave the views from the bank's boardroom unobscured.

ⅢⒷ 10 N. Dearborn St. (Covenant Club)
1923, Walter S. Ahlschlager
Facade restored and interior remodeled 1987, Eckenhoff Saunders

Designed for a Jewish men's social and service club, this Renaissance Revival structure was completely gutted and rebuilt for office and retail uses.

ⅢⒸ 69 W. Washington St. (Brunswick Building)
1965, Skidmore, Owings & Merrill

The weight is carried by the innovative tube-in-a-tube system—a concrete elevator core at the center and concrete exterior walls—that allows flexible, column-free floors. To provide a visually open base, a massive ring girder (behind the thick windowless line at the second floor) transfers and distributes the weight of over five dozen vertical members to the perimeter first-floor columns. Above the girder, the walls curve gracefully inward, recalling the profile of the nearby Monadnock Building. In the plaza to the west is Joan Miró's *Miss Chicago* (1981).

ⅢⒹ 33 N. Dearborn St. (Connecticut Mutual Life Building)
1967, Skidmore, Owings & Merrill

On this masonry-clad Miesian steel frame, visual enhancement is limited to subtle emphasis around the window openings. The first floor was originally arcaded, a configuration favored by Chicago's zoning ordinance, but later filled in to provide better retail spaces.

ⅢⒺ Richard J. Daley Center (Chicago Civic Center)
Block bounded by W. Washington, W. Randolph, N. Dearborn & N. Clark Sts.
1965, C. F. Murphy Assocs.; Loebl, Schlossman & Bennett and Skidmore, Owings & Merrill, assoc. archs.

Sternly elegant in its skin of rusting steel, the Daley Center is an outstanding example of Chicago's love for Miesian architecture. The scale is remarkable: at 648 feet it is immensely tall for only 31 stories, and its structural bays are an unprecedented 87' wide and 47'8" deep. Warren trusses frame each floor, stiffening the overall structure and allowing ample room between floors for service ducts and conduits. In its logic and execution, the resulting structure resembles a beautifully detailed bridge.

A framework of such scale and precision was deemed

Richard J. Daley Center

necessary to allow varied interior spaces. The structure was built to house more than 120 court and hearing rooms, a law library, and office space. Offices were accommodated by normal floor-to-ceiling heights of twelve feet, while twenty-six-foot-high courtrooms extended through two floors. Future space needs were taken into consideration; courtrooms can be converted into office space—and vice versa—with minimal structural rearrangement.

In its interior flexibility the Daley Center is truly Miesian in spirit. The ruggedly handsome exterior reflects the underlying structure in its refined detailing. Cruciform columns stand outside the exterior wall plane, which is composed of six-foot-high spandrel panels and twelve-foot-high bronze-tinted windows. Both the spandrels and columns are clad in Cor-Ten, a self-weathering steel developed in the 1930s for use in railway hopper cars and not previously used in building construction. The building's bronzed coloring and hefty proportions give it a Promethean character, conjuring images of the foundry infernos of WPA murals.

The Daley Center brought a building of immense visual power to the Loop but at a heavy price—the destruction of an entire block of shops and restaurants that encouraged downtown pedestrian traffic day and night. Yet something wonderful was gained; the plaza has become Chicago's Forum. As the locus of activities as diverse as concerts, farmers' markets, and peace rallies, the Daley Center fulfills a civic purpose consistent with its architectural dignity.
—Terry Tatum

117 Untitled Sculpture ("The Picasso")
Daley Center Plaza, W. Washington St. between N. Dearborn and N. Clark Sts.
1967, Pablo Picasso, artist

Though many hated it at first, locals and visitors alike have come to love this enigmatic Cor-Ten head, which resembles the artist's drawings both of his wife and his afghan hound, Kaboul. The frontal view looks more like the dog; walk around toward the rear to see how in profile it resembles a woman.

118 Commonwealth Edison Company—Dearborn St. Substation
117–121 N. Dearborn St.
1931, Holabird & Root

Despite such changes as filled-in windows, elegance prevails in this Art Deco shell, which houses electrical equipment. In a canted panel above the window is a low-relief panel by Sylvia Shaw Judson.

119 Delaware Building
(Bryant Building)
36 W. Randolph St.
1874, Wheelock & Thomas
Two-story addition 1888, Julius H. Huber
Renovated 1982, Wilbert R. Hasbrouck

A rare survivor from the early post-Fire years demonstrates High Victorian variety: bays of differing widths, rectangular and segmental arches, dissimilar stringcourses, and competing horizontal and vertical emphases. Added to the mix are a variety of materials: glass and cast iron on the first two floors, cast stone (an early form of precast concrete) on the next four levels, and pressed metal on the top two floors. Step into the lobby from Randolph St. to see the interior court. The beveled glass blocks, which allow light to filter down from the skylight, are also a product of Huber's addition.

120 Oliver Building
159 N. Dearborn St.
1908, Holabird & Roche
Addition 1920, Holabird & Roche

The cast-iron window spandrels include images of typewriters, which the Oliver Co. manufactured from 1896 to 1940.

121 Selwyn Theater
186 N. Dearborn St.
122 Harris Theater
170 N. Dearborn St.
1923, Crane & Franzheim

Richly detailed and clad in terracotta, these theaters are identical in plan and elevation except for the Selwyn's English-inspired ornament, which contrasts with the Harris's Italian derivation. The original interiors had walnut walls and considerable gilding.

123 Theatre District Self Park
181 N. Dearborn St.
1987, Hammond, Beeby & Babka

The precast concrete base of this early "theme" garage reflects the neo-Classical styling of nearby theaters. Music and posters from Broadway shows are assigned to each floor to help customers find their cars.

124 Leo Burnett Building
35 W. Wacker Dr.
1989, Kevin Roche–John Dinkeloo & Assocs.; Shaw & Assocs., assoc. archs.

Roche's Chicago debut is an overly detailed and dreary interpretation of the columnar skyscraper; rows of columns and pilasters constitute the base and capital as well as a midpoint break for a mechanical floor. Stainless steel bullnose mullions, which have been compared to pencils, add sparkle but do not make a brilliant design.

125 55 W. Wacker Dr. (Blue Cross–Blue Shield Building)
1968, C. F. Murphy Assocs.

Concrete is both the major structural material and the primary design element. Eight huge pylons act as structural members; duct enclosures are counterbalanced by concrete spandrels and cornices. Perpendicular surfaces have bush-hammered corrugations; horizontal ones are smooth, with exposed tie holes.

126 Marina City
300 N. State St.
1959–1967, Bertrand Goldberg Assocs.

Few Chicago buildings were as innovative in design or had as great an impact on their environment as Marina City. Marina City stood out immediately among Chicago's many architectural highlights and was for a long time one of the most photographed buildings in the city. The two round apartment towers with their semicircular balconies— for many people they resembled corncobs—were especially intriguing, as were the spiraling garages that occupy the lower half of each tower.
Marina City was designed for the yuppie *avant-la-lettre.* Goldberg and his client, the Building Service Employees International Union, decided that despite the exodus to the suburbs, many of those employed in the Loop were single or childless and wanted an apartment close to their

Marina City under construction

work. They were right. The complex was a success from the start and a prototype for many others on the edge of the Loop.
In the absence of facilities that would glamorize living in an area previously devoted to railroading, Goldberg incorporated stores, a restaurant, a health center, a swimming pool, a skating rink, an exhibi-

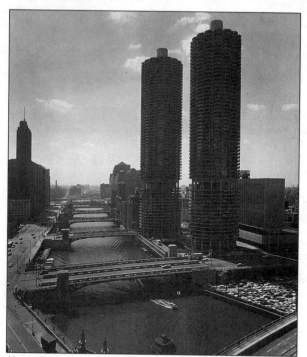
Marina City

tion space, a theater, a marina, a bowling alley, and an office tower. The complex was advertised as a "city within a city," a place for "24-hour urban living," both clearly commentaries on the suburbs, in which commuters spent only their nights.

Goldberg's masterful design imparts an open feeling to the small, packed complex, every part of which seems to defy gravity and move upward; the plaza, for example, is lifted above the water and dematerialized by the windows of the restaurant. It is experienced as a thin slab, very different from the heavy box beneath its neighbor, Mies van der Rohe's IBM Building. Because of the spiraling garage floors, the apartment towers seem to grow out of the plaza. Indeed, the towers appear virtually transparent, with the garage floors and balconies cantilevering from the perimeter columns. The office tower is also lifted off the plaza, to stand on columns above a windowless

slab containing the bowling alley. This structure, in turn, is separated from the plaza by a glass-enclosed floor housing the lobby of the office tower and spaces for a bank and stores. The irregularly shaped theater is the only structure that seems to rest on the plaza instead of taking off from it.

The apartments themselves are also designed to create feelings of openness. Not only are they placed above the garages and the warehouses formerly in the vicinity, but also their pie shapes allow for ever-expanding views of the city. More than in any other high-rise apartments, in Marina City one has the feeling of having the whole city at one's feet.

Although modernistic in design, Marina City's round, cast-concrete forms were a clear reaction against the glass and steel towers of Mies van der Rohe, whose style was prevailing in Chicago at the time.

—Wim de Wit

127 Hotel Nikko Chicago
320 N. Dearborn St.
1987, Hellmuth, Obata &
Kassabaum; Takayama & Assocs.,
assoc. archs.

The Japan Air Lines hotel chain placed on the riverfront a simple design of light masonry and dark trapezoidal bays. The small meditation park (1988) on the southern riverbank, designed by Kenzo Tange, is visible from the Dearborn St. bridge.

128 Quaker Tower
321 N. Clark St.
1987, Skidmore, Owings & Merrill

This late example of flat-topped, rectangular modernism includes a transparent ground floor, designed to the client's taste. Semicircular stainless-steel mullions stress verticality. Sleek and crisp from a distance, the look is shattered closer up by a hodgepodge of product displays in the lobby.

129 R. R. Donnelley Center
77 W. Wacker Dr.
1992, Ricardo Bofill Arquitectura,
design arch.; DeStefano & Partners,
supervising archs.

For his first American skyscraper, the Spanish proponent of modern classicism supplied a square, silver-tinted glass column, under four pedimented roofs. At night, theatrical lighting downplays the inglorious mismatch between the glazing and the white granite exoskeleton.

130 Chicago Title & Trust Center
161–171 N. Clark St.
1992, Kohn Pedersen Fox

Lacking the prominent unobstructed sites of their 225 and 333 W. Wacker Dr. buildings, the designers created an intriguing top to make the building leap out of the skyline. An identical tower is intended for the site's northern half.

131 State of Illinois Center
100 W. Randolph St.
1979–1985, Murphy/Jahn; Lester
B. Knight & Assocs., assoc. archs.

It's either breathtaking or exhausting, depending on your

State of Illinois Center

threshold for retinal fatigue, but it draws crowds of tourists and ennobles such humble tasks as renewing a driver's license and picking up tax forms. A series of dazzling concepts traveled a rocky road in translation to actual buildable materials. Helmut Jahn's original design called for silicone glazing, which would have produced a mullionless skin, but it scared off contractors fearful of liability problems. Salmon, silver, and blue were already in Jahn's palette and fit the standard governmental red, white, and blue but as executed look tawdry and ill chosen. But the central "people place," the massive atrium that rises a full seventeen floors and is expressed by a sliced-off cylindrical crown, is a resounding success. The plaza placement of Jean Dubuffet's fiberglass sculpture, *Monument with Standing Beast*, was resented by the champions of Illinois artists and has been uncharitably compared to piles of dirty, melting snow.

132 Garrick Garage
60 W. Randolph St.
1961, William M. Horowitz

In a textbook example of civic barbarity, terra-cotta panels of ornament from the demolished Schiller Building, an 1892 Adler & Sullivan masterpiece, were incorporated into and duplicated in the concrete grille of the parking structure that replaced it.

133 County Building/Chicago City Hall
118 N. Clark St. (County Building)
121 N. La Salle St. (City Hall)
1911, Holabird & Roche

This is in essence an office building—or, rather, two office buildings built around light wells—one of which has its offices interrupted for two stories to accommodate the City Council. The goal was to erect a building of eleven very high stories that would not look like a skyscraper. It was accomplished by doubling the scale of the exterior mask, minimizing fenestration, and introducing what were at construction (and probably still are) Chicago's biggest columns, seventy-five feet high, hollow, and comprising fifteen arc-shaped granite segments. The Corinthian capitals are the height of an entire floor. To support these purely decorative elements required caissons ten feet in diameter.

134 Chicago Title & Trust Building (Conway Building)
111 W. Washington St.
1913, D. H. Burnham & Co. and Graham Burnham & Co. Renovated 1986, Jack Train Assocs.

Burnham's version of the Chicago skyscraper (this was the firm's last before his death in 1912) continued to use the open light well introduced in the Rookery. Designed by Frederick P. Dinkelberg, the Conway Building eschewed the expression of its skeleton frame in favor of the image (but not the low scale) of the Beaux Arts city that permeated the pages of the 1909 Plan of Chicago.

135 Chicago Temple (First Methodist Episcopal Church)
77 W. Washington St.
1923, Holabird & Roche

A twenty-one-story office tower is crowned by an eight-story spire, the Loop's only church spire, which tops the world's tallest church (568 feet), according to the *Guinness Book of Records*. The shaft uses the vertical styling, small windows, and Gothic detailing that characterize the Tribune Tower; the spire, however, is more accurately executed. Officially, this is the home of the First United Methodist Church of Chicago, which has a ground-floor sanctuary and a chapel in the spire.

136 Chicago Loop Synagogue
16 S. Clark St.
1957, Loebl, Schlossman & Bennett

This congregation began in a hotel room where travelers and businessmen could assemble a daily minyan. The building now serves that function in a ground-level chapel and an upper sanctuary. Reached by a ramp, the sanctuary is dominated by an eastern wall of Abraham Rattner's stained glass, *Let There Be Light.*

137 Harris Trust & Savings Bank
111 W. Monroe St.
1911, Shepley, Rutan & Coolidge
East Tower 1960, Skidmore, Owings & Merrill
West Tower, 115 S. La Salle St.
1974, Skidmore, Owings & Merrill

Stainless steel Miesian towers are fitted around a neo-Classical, red granite and brick "traditional" bank in a way that affords each its own identity. The centerpiece features a five-story base in which three stories are deeply recessed behind Ionic columns. The East Tower uses thin window mullions to obtain a lively vitality and to avoid the surface distortion characteristic of large flat surfaces. It also makes a virtue of a mid-height mechanical floor, recessing it to fully expose the columns. The West Tower's wide bays and huge spandrels add horizontality to the mix.

138 Bankers Building
105 W. Adams St.
1927, Burnham Bros.

A tower building with a U-shaped base employs Classical detailing with a hint of Art Deco.

139 Ralph H. Metcalf Federal Building
77 W. Jackson Blvd.
1991, Fujikawa, Johnson & Assocs.

Tall, rectangular, flat-topped (rare in 1991), and designed to blend with Mies's Federal Center buildings, this concrete structure is finished in granite (not painted steel). A day-care center on the Van Buren St. side was part of the program.

140 Chicago Metropolitan Correctional Center
(William J. Campbell U.S. Courthouse Annex)
71 W. Van Buren St.
1975, Harry Weese & Assocs.

Chicago Metropolitan Correctional Center

More people ask "What the hell is that?" about the Chicago Metropolitan Correctional Center than about any other building in the Loop. And well they should, for there are few buildings like this twenty-seven-story, triangular federal detention center. However, a simple analysis of the concrete, slit-windowed exterior reveals much about the prison's interior, which houses indicted criminals awaiting trial in nearby federal courts.

The shape is a response to the U.S. Bureau of Prisons's then-new approach to incarceration. In an attempt to reform prisons, the Bureau had Weese's office experiment with placing cells around a loungelike common area supervised by an unarmed officer. Weese found that a triangular floor plan allowed the maximum number of cells to be most efficiently centered around the lounge. The triangular plan was not intended to symbolize the three branches of government, although some members of those branches have been guests at the facility.

The first nine floors contain administrative facilities. The windows in this section are ten inches wide, to provide ample light and views for the staff. Above the tenth-floor mechanical room, identifiable by its angled air intakes, are five-inch-wide windows for the inmates' rooms. The long, thin windows were meant to symbolize an opening that people could not pass through. Not caring much about symbolism, some architecturally disrespectful inmates discovered a way around this design feature and escaped. Lights now wash the exterior, and bars have been added to the interiors of the cells.

The eight two-level housing units have recreation and private meeting rooms. These secured areas are represented by the long strips of horizontal windows at the upper floors. A rooftop basketball and volleyball court, covered by wire mesh, tops the building. Attempted helicopter escapes necessitated the installation of struts, which support cables that deter unauthorized aerial exits.

Although the Metropolitan Correctional Center can be

seen as a straightforward solution to a building program,
it is not without its architectural precedents. It owes a
great deal to Le Corbusier,
whose mixed-use Unité
d'Habitation in Marseilles
(1952) includes two-level
housing units, a rooftop garden, and smooth concrete
finishes. Although Le Corbusier hoped to create designs that would inspire
worldwide imitation, it is
Weese's building that has
been widely copied.

The direct-supervision
method of running correc-
tional facilities has been
successful, and Weese's triangular plan has been the
basis for many of the housing
units. His provocative but
graceful building form, however, has not been matched.
—Michael Bordenaro

141 One Financial Place
440 S. La Salle St.
1985, Skidmore, Owings & Merrill

Built on the site of the La Salle
St. Station's shed and tracks are
an unadorned, flat-roofed office
tower with forty bay windows
per floor—a recollection of a
Chicago School characteristic—
and the five-story Midwest Stock
Exchange straddling the Eisenhower Expressway approach.
The Stock Exchange's two
arched windows (lighting a fitness center, not the trading area)
are meant to honor Adler & Sullivan's demolished Chicago Stock
Exchange Building. Access to the
present La Salle St. commuters'
station is through these buildings.
The plaza, a gentle element in
an otherwise hard environment,
contains a bronze horse created
by Ludovico de Luigi in homage
to the horses of St. Mark's, Ven-
ice.

142 Chicago Board Options
Exchange
141 W. Van Buren St.
1985, Skidmore, Owings & Merrill

This virtually windowless box occupies the site of the La Salle St.
Station's headhouse and turns
its back on Van Buren St. It features a 44,000-square-foot trading floor.

143 Traders Building
(Fort Dearborn Hotel)
401 S. La Salle St.
1914, Holabird & Roche
Renovated 1985, Booth/Hansen &
Assocs.

Strategically positioned next to
the La Salle St. Station, this relatively modest former hotel has a
symmetrical Georgian facade, a
luxurious lobby sheathed in Cir-
cassian walnut and Rookwood
tile, and a mezzanine adorned
with murals depicting early Chicago. These elements were refurbished, retained, or replicated
when the hotel was converted
into offices. This was accomplished by closing the south end
of the original U-shape with an
elevator bank and adding skylights at the second floor and
roof.

144 Chicago Board of
Trade Building
141 W. Jackson Blvd.
1930, Holabird & Root
Addition 1980, Murphy/Jahn;
Shaw & Assocs. and Swanke,
Hayden, Connell, assoc. archs.

The Chicago Board of Trade
is that rare hybrid in American architecture that successfully combines designs
from two periods. The main
portion, which faces north
from the foot of La Salle St.,
Chicago's main financial artery, is a striking forty-five-
story tower whose facade
features the jagged, sawtooth

profile often associated with Art Deco skyscrapers. The twenty-four-story steel and glass postmodern addition to the south is entered on Van Buren St. Although its black and silver exterior contrasts sharply with the gray limestone cladding of the original, the new is visually linked to the old through a skillful updating of the Art Deco building's vocabulary of setbacks and symmetry and a recapitulation of its pyramidal roof.

Likewise, the lobbies throughout the building complement each other, with the abstracted sculptural forms of the 1930 entry inspiring two equally intriguing spaces in the 1980 structure. The original building's three-story lobby features streamlined cascades of buff-colored marble that alternate with massive black marble piers. Its sculptural volumes are further articulated by dramatic lighting, particularly through a panel that cuts a wide swath across the ceiling and down the wall.

Chicago Board of Trade addition

In the addition the first-floor lobby is a compact, two-story variation of its antecedent executed in shades of jade and turquoise. On the twelfth floor is a second lobby—actually a spectacular atrium—another twelve stories high, made up of cascading walls of gleaming steel and reflective glass. The north wall is the limestone exterior of the original building, a skillful combination of contemporary and historic structures.

Sculpture and painting were important in both building campaigns. The carved figures holding wheat and corn on the La Salle St. facade were designed by Illinois artist Alvin Meyer; the pyramidal roof is topped by an aluminum statue of Ceres, the Roman goddess of agriculture, by the renowned American sculptor John Storrs. The similarly shaped skylight on the addition features an ornamental abstraction of a trading pit. Finally, reinstalled in the addition's atrium is a monumental mural of Ceres by Chicago artist John Warner Norton, removed years before from the original trading room.
—Pauline A. Saliga

Chicago Board of Trade Building

145 Federal Reserve Bank Building
230 S. La Salle St.
1922, Graham, Anderson, Probst & White
Southwest addition 1957, Naess & Murphy
Renovation and northwest addition 1989, Holabird & Root

146 Continental Illinois National Bank & Trust Company (Illinois Merchants Bank Building)
231 S. La Salle St.
1924, Graham, Anderson, Probst & White
Renovated 1990, Skidmore, Owings & Merrill

Continental Bank

The southern end of La Salle St. is flanked by a pair of virtually identical buildings with Classical columns and cornices neatly lined up. The Federal Reserve Building has Corinthian columns; Continental's are Ionic. On the interiors, similarity ends. Continental's second-level banking floor is a richly appointed recreation writ large of a Roman temple, lacking only the god's statue. It prompted Louis H. Sullivan to suggest that bankers here wear togas and speak Latin. Jules Guerin's murals adorning the frieze are allegorical references to international commerce. The Federal Reserve's dictate to avoid extravagance left the corresponding space dressed in white limestone under a restrained coffered ceiling. Continental is largely unchanged except for the introduction of escalators; most of the Federal Reserve has been reworked.

147 The Rookery
209 S. La Salle St.
1885–1888, Burnham & Root
Lobbies and light court renovated 1907, Frank Lloyd Wright
Lobbies renovated 1931, William Drummond
Restored and rehabilitated 1992, McClier Corp.

After the Fire of 1871 a temporary city hall stood at the southeast corner of La Salle and Adams Sts. The site and nearby stables attracted pigeons and these—together with roosting politicians— gave the building the name the Rookery. When a new city hall was completed in 1885 and a group of investors acquired the lot, the name stayed with the new structure to be designed by Daniel H. Burnham and John W. Root.

More than two dozen Burnham & Root designs for commercial buildings were under construction in downtown Chicago in the 1880s and 1890s. Of these only the Rookery remains. To support the building on Chicago's notorious clay soils, Root utilized a rail-grillage foundation. The street facades are entirely load-bearing masonry construction, while the lower floors on the alleys are supported by cast-iron columns and wrought-iron beams. The floor system and the walls of the light well are supported by iron framing, allowing large expanses of glazing. The design took advantage of other innovations: fireproof clay tile, plate glass, improved mechanical systems, and that remarkable invention, the hydraulic passenger elevator.

The Rookery exterior

In 1905 Frank Lloyd Wright was commissioned to redesign the lobbies and light court, and he replaced Root's iron railings and terra-cotta cladding with those of his own more geometric design. Wright's former student William Drummond later altered the lobbies into one-story spaces and replaced the open-grille elevator cages with solid doors ornamented with rook motifs designed by Annette Byrne. During the following decades the skylight was covered over, the mosaic floor was removed, and the interior surfaces grew dim.

The nearly square Rookery is organized around a central court surmounted by a skylight above the second story. A cast-iron oriel stair extends the height of the light well above. A walkway encircles the court at the mezzanine level, with grand stairways leading to that pre-eminent rental floor from two light-filled lobbies.

The bold facades feature a red granite base, pressed brick facades, terra-cotta ornament, and turrets. The light court is faced with light-colored glazed brick and terra-cotta. All public spaces are clad in incised and gilded marble and copper-plated and Bower-Barff ironwork. Contemporaries extolled the Rookery as "the most modern of office buildings" and "a thing of light."

A comprehensive program completed in 1992 revitalized the offices and public spaces and restored the Rookery's historic features. The exterior was returned to its original ruddy hues, the public lobbies were re-created to approximate the 1907 renovation, and Drummond's elevator lobbies were retained. The skylight over the light court was reopened, with a second skylight added at the top of the light well. The court's 1905 marble and ironwork were restored. Because of this remarkable commitment to preservation, the Rookery offers a rare glimpse of downtown Chicago at the turn of the twentieth century.
—Deborah Slaton

The Rookery interior

148 208 S. La Salle St.
(formerly City National Bank, originally Continental & Commercial Bank Building)
1914, Graham, Burnham & Co.

The street-level colonnade establishes the "financial" look of La Salle St. in many minds. The granite Doric columns have steel cores to support the block-filling structure. The colonnade reappears atop the building, where loss of the cornice destroys the "temple" effect.

149 190 S. La Salle St.
1987, John Burgee Architects with Philip Johnson; Shaw Assocs., assoc. archs.

Philip Johnson's only Chicago building is postmodernism at its most serious and successful, responding strongly to its context and proclaiming its deep roots in Chicago's architectural history. The granite base is topped by a many-gabled summit that echoes similar elements on neighboring buildings. Its arched windows and doors parallel those on the Rookery; its overall design is drawn from John W. Root's demolished Masonic Temple (1892); the upper elevations alternate the punched-window limestone facades of the 1920s with contemporary curtain walls. The overscaled, barrel-vaulted lobby features rich marble and a gold-leaf ceiling.

150 135 S. La Salle St.
(formerly La Salle Bank Building, originally Field Building)
1934, Graham, Anderson, Probst & White

Conceived as the Loop's largest office building, the Field Building was one of the city's last sizable buildings under construction as the Depression deepened. It is an H-plan building with a central rectangular tower rising from a base with four lower corner towers. The limestone exterior creates strong verticals alternating with window tiers of similar size. Embellishment consists only of a dark granite base and incised lines at the summits of the

135 S. La Salle St.

five shafts. The marble lobby is lush by contrast, offsetting beige walls with white pilasters and metalwork of nickel silver bronze. Mirrored Art Deco bridges connect the north and south balconies.

151 120 S. La Salle St. (State Bank of Chicago Building)
1928, Graham, Anderson, Probst & White

The overall lines are slimmer and the colonnade is reduced to a four-column entrance, but the outline is similar to the firm's bank at 208. What's more, the second-floor banking space is intact.

152 Northern Trust Company Building
50 S. La Salle St.
1905, Frost & Granger
Two-story penthouse addition
1928, Frost & Henderson

This banking house *without* an office tower above it is singular on a street that is a virtual canyon.

153 39 S. La Salle St.
(formerly La Salle–Monroe Building, originally New York Life Building)
1894, Jenney & Mundie
Eastern half 1898, Jenney & Mundie
One-story addition 1903, architect unknown

This early steel-frame building is allegedly the first whose walls were built simultaneously at several stories instead of from the ground up.

154 19 S. La Salle St. (Association Building, known as Central YMCA Building)
1893, Jenney & Mundie

The heavy banding and the shifting design characterized much of Jenney's work at this time.

155 11 S. La Salle St. (formerly Lumber Exchange Building, originally Roanoke Building)
1915, Holabird & Roche
Five-story addition 1922, Holabird & Roche
Tower 1926, Holabird & Roche; Rebori, Wentworth, Dewey & McCormick, assoc. archs.
Renovated 1984, Hammond, Beeby & Babka

This building with an unusual number of changes and additions began as the Lumber Exchange, a sixteen-story late Chicago School commercial building with windows under arches at the fourth and top floors. The top rank of arches disappeared in 1922, when five floors were added under a re-creation of the original cornice. The vertical ranks of paired windows were later adapted to a tower addition at the eastern end of the Madison St. frontage. The tower, one of the first to incorporate setbacks, was primarily the design of Andrew N. Rebori. The 1984 renovation replaced a 1950s modernization with a postmodern evocation of the original, profusely ornamented features.

156 Chemical Plaza
10 S. La Salle St.
1989, Moriyama & Teshima; Holabird & Root, assoc. archs.

The exterior walls of the base of the Otis Building (1912, Holabird & Roche) were reused in order to retain the scale of La Salle St., while building a sleek tower. No attempt was made to disguise either the old or the new: the stone base is contrasted by the facade, whose grid it sets. The new elevations are of matching blue-painted aluminum and glass

with details picked out in bright green. The surface is interrupted for a seven-story semicircular entry and for a single strip of bay windows from the nineteenth floor to the roof.

157 1 N. La Salle St.
1930, Vitzthum & Burns

Slim strips of windows and limestone alternate to assert the tower's verticality. Virtually the only break is at the fifth floor, where sculptured panels commemorate the explorations of Robert Cavalier, Sieur de La Salle, who allegedly camped on this site in 1679.

158 2 N. La Salle St.
1979, Perkins & Will

Ribbons of windows, set flush in alternating bands with structural aluminum wall panels, stress the smoothness of this building's skin; rounded corners emphasize its continuity. The unglazed corners at the second level identify the mezzanine of transfer beams that allowed the building to reuse the foundations of the demolished La Salle Hotel.

159 American National Bank Building (Foreman State National Bank Building)
33 N. La Salle St.
1930, Graham, Anderson, Probst & White

The upward thrust is enhanced by facing the recessed spandrels on the central portion of each facade in a darker terra-cotta than the piers. The gradual tapering of the peak and the sculpted relief on the rose granite base, which includes suggestions of pediments at the fourth floor, are forms of stripped eclecticism. The Art Deco interiors were destroyed in 1971 in favor of a colonial Williamsburg look deemed more appropriate to the bank's name and image.

160 Savings of America Tower
120 N. La Salle St.
1991, Murphy/Jahn

Through carefully executed, elegant detail the building enriches

Savings of America Tower

the La Salle St. corridor with a vigorous three-dimensionality. East and west facades feature a gently curving, gray-tinted, butt-glazed window wall, bordered by a contrasting, deeply suppressed vertical bank of windows. Both facades are crowned by a glazed three-story half-vault. A cantilevered trellis on the north wall extends the length of Court Pl. Curving over the entrance is artist Roger Brown's *Flight of Daedalus and Icarus,* executed in a colorful mosaic. Above the entrance loggia, all masonry is coursed in alternating bands of light and dark gray flame-cut granite. Dividing the facade into two unequal parts, a vertical granite-clad plane pulls the window wall out over the sidewalk and separates the office spaces from the service and mechanical areas. Polished granite clads the horizontally banded, deeply rusticated lobby walls; at the height of the door lintels, a brass strip lines the horizontal joint in the granite.

161 160 N. La Salle St. (Burnham Building)
1924, Burnham Bros.
Renovation and addition 1992, Holabird & Root

A U-shaped office building with a traditional tripartite facade was retrofitted to create courtrooms and offices for the State of Illinois. A mechanicals floor was added, sheathed in limestone and fitted with a cornice and

belt courses that resemble the original summit. The walls of the light well were opened up behind a reflective glass curtain wall. The single arched entry was expanded into a new lobby resembling a walled Italian courtyard.

162 200 N. La Salle St.
1984, Perkins & Will

This "extruded ice cube" is clad in a curtain wall of green-tinted glass, half of which has been sprayed from behind to make it opaque. The perimeter is serrated to create ten corner offices per floor. The taller windows at these corners help to emphasize verticality.

163 203 N. La Salle St.
1985, Skidmore, Owings & Merrill

This is an unusual example of a garage topped by an office tower. The horizontal slits ventilate the parking levels and are repeated for unity above. The massive glass column on Clark St. houses the elevator; slanting skylights above it cover two interior atriums.

164 La Salle–Wacker Building
221 N. La Salle St.
1930, Holabird & Root; Rebori, Wentworth, Dewey & McCormick, assoc. archs.

Dramatically sited at the "gateway to finance" on La Salle St., this building allows a clear reading of the H-shaped plan devised in response to the 1917 ordinance restricting buildings to floor areas one-quarter of their site above a certain height. Stripped-down classicism and setbacks mark the changes. The three-story base shifts to an H configuration with north and south light courts. At the twenty-third-story cross of the H, the tower ascends uninterrupted for another eighteen floors.

165 222 N. La Salle St. (Builders Building)
1927, Graham, Anderson, Probst & White
Renovation and additions 1986, Skidmore, Owings & Merrill

City of Chicago Central Office Building

This is a late appearance of Daniel H. Burnham's tripartite, limestone-clad, flat-roofed office block around a light court. Don't miss the central atrium, which the building trades that developed the building used as an indoor fair.

166 City of Chicago— Central Office Building
(Reid, Murdoch & Co. Building)
320 N. Clark St./321 N. La Salle St.
1914, George C. Nimmons

The most visible of Nimmons's warehouse designs, this is regarded as perhaps his best work. The building lost its rigid symmetry with the removal of the westernmost bay in 1930, when La Salle St. was widened.

167 Helene Curtis Building
325 N. Wells St.
1912, L. Gustav Hallberg
Renovated 1984, Booth/Hansen & Assocs.

An old riverfront warehouse was transformed into a distinctive office building by inserting green glass topped by a terraced crystalline addition housing the company boardroom.

168 Engineering Building
205 W. Wacker Dr.
1928, Burnham Bros.
Renovated 1982, Himmel Bonner

This U-shaped building had its original entrance below an open court on Wells St. The windows are uniform except at the corners; ornament is restricted to the base and top, where it projects slightly in the manner of Art Deco skyscrapers. Traces of the original lobby were retained in a renovation that moved the entrance to the Wacker Dr. side.

201 N. Wells St.

169 201 N. Wells St.
(Trustees System Service Building)
1930, Thielbar & Fugard

This was Chicago's last skyscraper begun before the stock market crash of October 1929. It introduced to the city an Art Deco device used elsewhere: above the fourth floor the brick is purple, shading lighter to the top, which is buff to match the sunburst terra-cotta ornament. It is topped by a ziggurat and lantern. Around the original banking entrance on Lake St. are panels depicting finance through the ages by Eugene van Breeman Lux, who also designed the allegorical figures at the second-floor level. The lead panels of workingmen are by Edgar Miller.

170 188 W. Randolph St.
(Steuben Club Building)
1929, Vitzthum & Burns
Renovation 1993, Stenbro Ltd.

This is possibly the last of the historicist limestone tower buildings whose shapes were conditioned by the 1923 zoning ordinance. The silhouette of telescoping "towers" also characterizes the firm's later design for 1 N. La Salle St.

171 180 W. Washington St.
(Equitable Building)
1929, Hyland & Corse
172 "I Am" Temple
(Elks Club Building)
176 W. Washington St.
1916, Ottenheimer, Stern & Reichert

Two narrow eccentric structures: 180 is a veritable terra-cotta catalog, while the Temple's unusual character is ascribed to the fact that the Viennese-born Rudolph Schindler was working for this firm. It was his first American job, after his studies with Otto Wagner and before joining the office of Frank Lloyd Wright.

173 175 W. Washington St.
(Chicago Federation of Musicians)
1933, N. Max Dunning
Addition 1949, architect unknown

The added third story of this tiny Bedford limestone gem carefully respects the original facade.

174 Washington Block
40 N. Wells St.
1874, Frederick & Edward Baumann

This rare survivor from the immediate post-Fire years has survived virtually intact. It is singularly well conceived, with a facade of alternating wide

and narrow stone courses and windows clearly outlined and topped with a variety of Italianate crowns. Frederick Baumann advocated isolated-pier foundations as more suitable than continuous perimeter ones to Chicago's compressible soil. This building is assumed to have them, since it was designed just after he published a pamphlet on the subject.

175 Hotel La Salle Public Garage
219 W. Washington St.
1919, Holabird & Roche
Additional five bays 1923, Holabird & Roche

The aesthetics of the multilevel parking structure were resolved in this early uncelebrated gem by mimicking a conventional office building. However, there is nothing conventional about the way the fifteen narrow bays with their sash windows alternate with the vigorous uninterrupted piers. The wonderful rhythm is enhanced by the use of black Roman brick as striping in the red facade and by crisply detailed spandrel panels. A stringcourse above the shops and a well-proportioned cornice contain the design. Unlike most later garages, this one has flat, not sloped, floors and a single elliptical ramp in the center of the rear wall, with an elevator to move cars in the low-traffic direction.

176 Madison Plaza
200 W. Madison St.
1982, Skidmore, Owings & Merrill

The serrated front creates a distinctive plaza and a setting for Louise Nevelson's steel sculpture *Dawn Shadows;* the stepped-back top allows views to the east from the top floors. A partially prefabricated, steel framing system limited on-site welding, resulting in high-speed erection of the exterior tube.

177 PaineWebber Tower
181 W. Madison St.
1990, Cesar Pelli & Assocs.

Frankly echoing Eliel Saarinen's second-prize design in the 1922 Chicago Tribune Tower Competition, this symmetrical tower has truncated setbacks to enhance the strongly expressed—even exaggerated—verticality. The cladding is white granite, reflective metal mullions are set forward from the windows, and the finials are nickel-plated. A five-story lobby with a vaulted, coffered ceiling is meant to echo an entrance of the Uffizi Gallery in Florence, Italy. Each end wall of the lobby displays a large sculpture by Frank Stella.

178 Williams Building
205 W. Monroe St.
1898, Holabird & Roche

This wholesale building clearly reveals its metal framing on its upper floors and its low cost in the sparse ornament around the doorways.

CTA—Quincy Station

179 Chicago Transit Authority—Quincy Station
W. Quincy and S. Wells Sts.
1897, Alfred M. Hedley
Restored 1988, City of Chicago, Dept. of Public Works, Bureau of Architecture

Lightweight and inexpensive materials were used in elevated stations. This one had its wood framing and decorative, pressed sheet-metal cladding restored to the original design and what paint analysis indicated was the original color. After completion, a 1902 article came to light revealing that the original finish coat was gray; the station's "restored" color was a primer.

180 Insurance Exchange Building
175 W. Jackson Blvd.

1912, D. H. Burnham & Co.
South addition 1928, Graham, Anderson, Probst & White

Finished in enameled brick and terra-cotta trim, it has the styling of the first-quality buildings by the Burnham firm and its successors. Architect Ernest R. Graham was part owner of this project; its success enabled him to endow the Graham Foundation for Advanced Studies in the Fine Arts.

181 Dixon Building
411 S. Wells St.
1908, Nimmons & Fellows

This loft design is easily identified by the firm's characteristic ahistorical capitals, the banding of the piers near the summit, and the portions blocked out in light limestone against the dark brick.

182 Van Buren Building
212 W. Van Buren St.
1893, Flanders & Zimmerman

A second-floor Romanesque oriel adds a graceful touch to this midblock building.

183 Brooks Building
223 W. Jackson Blvd.
1910, Holabird & Roche

Gothic shafts and moldings in beige terra-cotta articulate the columns, presaging the Gothic office towers of the coming decades. But the walls are as clear and precise an articulation of their skeleton frame as the Chicago School could produce. The clasplike ornament atop the piers recalls its use a decade earlier by Louis H. Sullivan on the Gage Building.

184 City Colleges Building
(Chicago & North Western Railway Office)
226 W. Jackson Blvd.
1904, Frost & Granger
Renovated 1978, Altman-Saichek Assocs.

As sons-in-law of Marvin Hughitt, the railroad's president, Charles S. Frost and Alfred H. Granger received many commissions, including the demolished Chicago & North Western Railway Terminal; they were not known for their office buildings. This one, like their railway stations, stresses structural sufficiency: strong corners, larger-than-necessary piers, a heavy base tapering into the wall above, and an entrance marked by sturdy columns.

185 AT&T Corporate Center and USG Building
227 W. Monroe St. and 125 S. Franklin St.
1988, 1992, Skidmore, Owings & Merrill

This blocklong complex of two high rises with a connecting base represents a reinterpretation of the conventions of the late 1920s setback office tower. Pronounced vertical lines, granite cladding, spiky pinnacles at the roof and setbacks, and lavish lobbies characterize this Adrian Smith design. The materials and general approach are the same for both buildings, but the details vary. The centers of the main facades are set-in vertical curtain walls; elsewhere windows are punched into the granite sheathing. On the AT&T Building the granite shades from deep red at the base to a light rose-beige at the top. Sporting a hipped roof, the USG Building has a much less soaring appearance. The lobby is a sequence of spaces of varying ceiling heights.

186 303 W. Madison St.
1988, Skidmore, Owings & Merrill

Designer Joseph Gonzalez integrated references to the work of Frank Lloyd Wright, Otto Wagner, and the Chicago School in a design that emerges as distinctly his own. The debt to Wright is in the interlocking right-angle geometries; Wagner is quoted in the glass-block storefronts; and the facade's tripartite composition and Chicago windows evoke the Chicago School. The relatively small building is clad in granite and tinted glass in white-painted aluminum frames. The horizontal banding of contrasting-colored granite serves to broaden the narrow facades. The general scale, treatment of the Washington St. entrance, and arcading at the top are reminiscent

of Wright's unbuilt 1912 Press Building project in San Francisco.

187 I N. Franklin St.
1991, Skidmore, Owings & Merrill

Sheathed in cast stone, the primary facade has various window types arranged in vertical rows; in sharp contrast the south facade has uniform ranks of Chicago windows. Two cylindrical glass towers set within square railings suggest the Art Moderne of the 1930s. The notched corners at the base are filled with glassy bays cantilevered over the sidewalk.

I N. Franklin St.

188 225 W. Washington St.
1986, Skidmore, Owings & Merrill

This slablike building makes several references to the Chicago School. Within its tripartite facade, the shaft is articulated with full-bay variations of the Chicago window, drawing attention to the underlying frame. The glassy corner bays are another reference to the first Chicago School. The top floors on Franklin St. have a three-bay-wide recessed arcade. Prominent arches signal the entrances on both streets, but the arch on Washington St. leads to a blank stone wall.

189 Building for the Alexander White Estate
227–229 W. Lake St./177 N. Franklin St.
1872, Burling & Adler

190 Building for Samuel Cole
233 W. Lake St./185 N. Franklin St.
1873, Burling & Adler
191 Building for William Rowney
235 W. Lake St.
1873, architect unknown
192 Building for Albert E. Kent
175 N. Franklin St.
*1875, George H. Edbrooke
Renovated 1983, Stuart Cohen & Anders Nereim*

Known informally as the Lake-Franklin Group, this quartet constitutes the Loop's largest concentration of 1870s commercial buildings. They are typical of construction before the general use of passenger elevators and steel framing. All have load-bearing walls and relatively narrow Italianate windows.

193 225 W. Wacker Dr.
1989, Kohn Pedersen Fox; Perkins & Will, assoc. archs.

175 N. Franklin St.

The skillfully combined glass-and-granite cladding lightens considerably near the top, crowned by corner lanterns that pierce the skyline without dominating it. As a companion to the same firm's 333 Wacker Dr., its glass is green, but gray cladding and a lean profile give it its own identity.

194 333 Wacker Dr.
1979–1983, Kohn Pedersen Fox; Perkins & Will, assoc. archs.

Sited at the bend of the Chicago River, this green glass tower has been called Chicago's first postmodern skyscraper. But William E. Pedersen, the design partner of Kohn Pedersen Fox, would never use that term to describe his buildings. He does, however, use such phrases as "a strategy of assemblage or collage—pieces, each of which has references to its context."

Indeed a "collage" of contextual "references," 333 is a quintessentially Chicago building in its tripartite structure of base, shaft, and clearly defined top. But base and shaft are strikingly different: a modern tower rests on a classi-

cally inspired base. These disparate forms are united by their color, utilized uniformly for the curtain wall and as a strong accent in the base, where bands of dark green polished marble alternate with gray granite. The same verde antique marble, combined with black granite, sheathes octagonal entrance columns that take their shape from the towers on the Merchandise Mart, which dominates the opposite bank of the river.

Above all, 333 is site-specific, its form adapted to its triangular lot. The Wacker Dr. facade is a graceful arc that follows the river's curve. The taut skin of mirrored glass reflects water, sky, and buildings in a constantly changing montage and, in an unmodern fashion, conceals

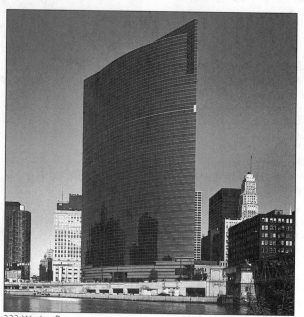

333 Wacker Dr.

the cross-braced steel supporting skeleton. The entrance is flush with the street, elegantly detailed and exactly centered.

The opposite facade, facing the gritty edge of the Loop at the junction of Franklin and Lake Sts., is sliced and notched. To defy the neighborhood's generally dilapidated state in the late 1970s, Pedersen gave this side a splendid center entrance that invites passersby to ascend its curving steps. Such attention to the street level is part of his belief that "the connective fabric which was the hallmark of the traditional city has been eroded" and that the tall urban office building should be brought into a "more social state of existence."

This thirty-six-story tower established the seven-year-old firm as award-winning skyscraper designers. Worldwide commissions followed, including 333's immediate neighbor at 225. An element of contextualism in that masonry tower is porthole medallions that recall the ventilation covers for 333's third-story mechanicals. This circular motif has become almost a signature of Pedersen's designs. It appears, for example, on the firm's Procter & Gamble complex in Cincinnati and as blind medallions on 900 N. Michigan Ave.
—Jane H. Clarke

195 Merchandise Mart
North bank of the Chicago River between Wells and Franklin Sts.
1930, Graham, Anderson, Probst & White
Renovated 1992, Beyer Blinder Belle; Jack Train Assocs., assoc. archs.

The Merchandise Mart's significance lies more in its history and dimensions than in its design.

Built as a wholesale store by Marshall Field & Co., it now serves as a display center for furniture and furnishings dealers as well as an office building. Field's wholesale operations declined in the 1930s, and in 1945 the building was sold to Joseph P. Kennedy, whose family still owns it. With some 4.1 million square feet of rentable space, it remains

Merchandise Mart

the world's largest commercial building.

The design is typical of the late 1920s: prominent piers, recessed spandrels of darker color, and modest, geometric ornament. Jules Guerin's lobby murals depict worldwide trade and commerce. The pedestrian bridge (1991, Murphy/Jahn) that links the Mart with the Apparel Center echoes the deco geometry.

196 Apparel Center and Holiday Inn Mart Plaza
350 N. Orleans St.
1977, Skidmore, Owings & Merrill

One of the central city's dreariest high rises assaults the eye from one of Chicago's most prominent sites.

197 150 N. Wacker Dr.
1975, Joel Hillman

Concrete haunches at either end support column-free interiors, which include five floors of parking behind a screen.

198 123 N. Wacker Dr.
1988, Perkins & Will

An arcade repeats the one on the Civic Opera Building; both the opera house and the Merchandise Mart are echoed in the pyramidal roof, the granite skin with punched windows, and the tripartite organization.

199 Morton Building
110 N. Wacker Dr.
1961, Graham, Anderson, Probst & White

The Wacker Dr. elevation of this International Style building is balanced with a central limestone wall, flanked by matched, three-story curtain-wall segments with fluted stainless-steel panels above and below paired windows.

200 101 N. Wacker Dr.
1980, Perkins & Will
Arcade altered 1990, Kober/Belluschi

A cool, comfortable effect pervades this modernist block, in which energy efficiency was a major aim. Monitors behind the white aluminum curtain wall adjust to shifting sunlight, and vision and spandrel glass reflect or absorb light and heat as needed.

201 Civic Opera Building
20 N. Wacker Dr.
1929, Graham, Anderson, Probst & White

The last big real estate venture of Chicago's traction and utilities mogul Samuel Insull is an office building wrapped around a 3,500-seat opera house and a 900-seat theater. Art Deco and French Renaissance styling pervade the building, along with musical motifs. An arcade runs the entire length of the east facade, in which the entrances to the theaters are marked with pediments. The Grand Foyer of the opera theater is forty feet high, with colors chosen by Jules Guerin, the designer of the theater's fire curtain.

202 1 S. Wacker Dr.
1982, C. F. Murphy Assocs.

Designer Helmut Jahn speaks of such buildings as a synthesis of Sullivanian and Miesian Chicago architecture with 1980s technology. Here he faced a concrete stepped-back structure with a curtain wall of black, silver, and coral tones in which the dark glass defines grouped vertical bands of "windows." The "draped curtain" entrance leads to a streamlined, well-ordered lobby.

203 Chicago Mercantile Exchange Center
10 & 30 S. Wacker Dr.
1983 (30 S. Wacker Dr.), 1988 (10 S. Wacker Dr.), Fujikawa, Johnson & Assocs.

To get a pair of office buildings and two large trading floors onto the site required cantilevering substantial portions of the towers over the trading rooms in the intervening base pavilion. To do this—while keeping trading floors column-free—required diverting loads to the ground via a system of thickened walls, wide columns, and huge trusses. The serrations boost the number of corner offices to sixteen per floor.

204 Hartford Plaza (Hartford Fire Insurance Building)
100 S. Wacker Dr.
1961, Skidmore, Owings & Merrill

"Simple technique uncelebrated" marks this column-and-slab concrete frame, later covered in polished gray granite.

205 101 S. Wacker Dr. (U.S. Gypsum Building)
1963, Perkins & Will

Using masonry when most other buildings were not, this cruciform tower is set at a 45° angle to the street. The verticality is strongly asserted by the contrast of the triangular white marble exterior columns against the recessed slate spandrels and gray glass curtain walls. The steel frame permits column-free floors; the cruciform shape offers eight corner offices per floor, a feature that became common in the 1980s.

206 200 S. Wacker Dr.
1981, Harry Weese & Assocs.

Responding to an irregularly shaped riverfront site, Weese experimented with triangular geometries, as he had in the Metropolitan Correctional Center, designing a building composed of two triangles joined at the hypotenuse. One segment is seven stories taller than the other, making the scheme most apparent at the top of the building. The perimeter columns of the concrete frame are rotated 45° to present a slim edge on a taut curtain wall of white-painted aluminum and tinted glass.

207 Sears Tower
233 S. Wacker Dr.
1968–1974, Skidmore, Owings & Merrill
Ground-floor renovation and Wacker St. atrium addition 1985, Skidmore, Owings & Merrill
Renovation and lower-level remodeling 1992, DeStefano & Partners

Stand back . . . waaaaaay back . . . and look at the 110-story Sears Tower. Its modernist rendition of base, middle, and top clearly illustrates the goals of client Sears, Roebuck & Co. and architect Bruce Graham: housing 5,000 Sears employees in the base, leasing the middle to tenants, and using the top to establish the world's tallest building for the world's largest retailer.

By creating the massive, 50,000-square-foot floor plates in the first fifty floors, Sears was able to consolidate its merchandising group employees from seven Chicago locations. The large floors allowed the greatest amount of employee interaction without

Sears Tower

moving up and down elevators. By stepping the building back above the fiftieth floor, Graham created prestige leasable space that helped Sears pay for—and profit from—the $186 million project.

Of that amount, one third was used for the superstructure. Structural engineer Fazlur R. Khan skillfully carried out his duties by designing a "bundled tube" consisting of nine squares, seventy-five feet each. These squares, formed by I-beams spaced fifteen feet apart, are anchored in a deep concrete slab below the three subbasements. The slab rests on 114 steel and concrete caissons embedded in bedrock sixty-five feet below.

Two of the nine tubes stop at the 50th floor, two more end at the 66th floor, and the last three terminate at the 90th, leaving two tubes to rise the full 1,454 feet. The termination of the tubes was determined as much by the lateral stiffness required to resist wind loads as by spatial considerations or aesthetic needs.

The daily movement of 25,000 tenants and visitors in and around the building has been problematic. The windswept plaza was difficult to access and rarely used. A redesign of the entry and lower levels in 1985 improved the original circulation design, which was confusing. Following Sears's move to Hoffman Estates in 1992, another lower-level renovation sorted out circulation for the building's new post-Sears life.

Sears Tower has always been more of a structural engineering triumph than an architectural accomplishment. While Graham and Khan were like a well-oiled, twin-cam engine firing on all cylinders when they designed the elegant John Hancock Center, the architectural manifold was slightly backfiring when they were running the Sears 500.
—Michael Bordenaro

208 311 S. Wacker Dr.
*1990, Kohn Pedersen Fox;
Harwood K. Smith & Partners,
assoc. archs.*

The world's tallest concrete-
framed building (a title it took
away from Water Tower Place)
will have two companions, presumably with their own back
walls and tower projections; the
winter garden, which serves as
an open space, will thus be
blocked off from sunlight. The
summit, a seventy-foot drum surrounded by four smaller ones,
now looks overdone at any
hour. At night, lit by nearly 2,000
fluorescent tubes, it is a visual
poke in the eye. Three of them
are unthinkable.

209 Gateway Center IV
300 S. Riverside Plaza
1983, Skidmore, Owings & Merrill

This ungainly addition to the
riverfront has an odd curve
meant to echo the bend in the
river.

210 Gateway Center III
222 S. Riverside Plaza
211 MidAmerica Commodity Exchange
444 W. Jackson Blvd.
1971, Skidmore, Owings & Merrill

The complex that replaced
Union Station's vaulted concourse comprises a bland tower
and a low building designed
to accommodate a trading-
exchange floor. Enormous black
aluminum trusses makes the latter look like a supine version of
the John Hancock Center.

Union Station

212 Union Station
210 S. Canal St.
*1913–1925, Graham, Anderson,
Probst & White
Renovated 1992, Lucien Lagrange
Assocs.*

One of the last of the grand
American railroad stations, Union Station was intended as the
major element in West Loop
development under Burnham's
1909 Plan of Chicago. The austere facade encloses a huge
travertine-clad waiting room. The
eight-story office tower above,
set well back from the base and
virtually invisible from the sidewalk, was meant to be twenty
stories high. The double "stub
end" tracks are the only ones in
the United States where north-
bound and southbound tracks
for different railroads end at the
same point.

213 Florsheim Shoe Company
130 S. Canal St.

Florsheim Shoe Company

1949, Shaw, Metz & Dolio
Two-story infill addition 1977,
Shaw & Assocs.

With its emphasis on flat planar surfaces, its continuous steel-sash ribbon windows, and its uniform cladding of light-colored glazed brick, the Florsheim building was the first major Chicago structure to emphatically embrace the design elements of European modernism. It was also Alfred P. Shaw's first major independent design after leaving Graham, Anderson, Probst & White. Above the base, which housed administrative functions, the shallow U-shaped plan of the production floors provided maximum natural illumination. The tower concealed mechanical equipment and was also an effective backdrop for the company's name.

214 Gateway Center I
10 S. Riverside Plaza
1965, Skidmore, Owings & Merrill
215 Gateway Center II
120 S. Riverside Plaza
1968, Skidmore, Owings & Merrill
Esplanade renovated 1986,
Skidmore, Owings & Merrill

This pair of Miesian office buildings is carried over active rail yards by columns. "Riverside Plaza" is used by virtually all of the new waterfront buildings east of Canal St.—although no such street exists.

216 525 W. Monroe St.
1983, Skidmore, Owings & Merrill

This pedestrian office building was overshadowed soon after construction when developers expanded the West Loop glitz zone from Franklin St. and Wacker Dr., bringing taller, more dramatic "signature" buildings.

217 Heller International Tower
500 W. Monroe St.
1992, Skidmore, Owings & Merrill

This granite-clad skyscraper stands in contrast to the firm's glassy modernism as seen at its Gateway Center buildings. A tower marks the southeastern

corner, where the structure is built to the street edge; the building steps down to the west.

218 Riverside Plaza (Daily News Building)
2 N. Riverside Plaza
1929, Holabird & Root

For evidence of the continuing cheapening of the urban vista, just compare the grand civic enhancement of this former newspaper building with Freedom Center, the *Chicago Tribune*'s modern printing plant. The interlocking vertical masses of the office block rise from the public plaza, Chicago's first to be planned as part of an office building. Step inside the narrow concourse to see elegant detailing and the ceiling mural by John W. Norton.

Riverside Plaza

219 Northwestern Atrium Center
500 W. Madison St.
1987, Murphy/Jahn

Designer Helmut Jahn's sinuous curtain wall reads like a waterfall that cascades in precise sheets down the southern facade. Enter through the receding arch at the base or via the walkway from Riverside Plaza to a dazzling multilevel space where steel structure is articulated, exposed, and celebrated.

220 River Center & One North Western Center (Butler Bros. Warehouses)
111 N. Canal St.

1913, D. H. Burnham & Co.
Renovation begun 1982,
Balsamo/Olson Group
165 N. Canal St.
1922, Graham, Anderson, Probst
& White
Renovated 1992,
Graham-Thomas Architects

Detailed like a nineteenth-century armory, complete with machicolations, the design of these warehouses was *retardataire* by 1913 but greatly admired by Andrew Rebori, who found remarkable the "very noble largeness and simplicity." 111 stands in its original spot; its twin originally stood on its eastern side but was demolished and reincarnated at 165.

221 Morton International Building
100 N. Riverside Plaza
1990, Perkins & Will

Located atop active train tracks, the building accommodates lower floors with large uninterrupted spaces for computer operations. With much smaller floor plates for offices, the tower rises from a long base, an entire corner of which is suspended over the tracks from an exposed truss on the roof.

Morton International Building

222 Metra/C&NW/Chicago Passenger Concourses
(Chicago & North Western Station Yards)
Bounded by N. Canal, W. Lake, and N. Clinton Sts. and Northwestern Atrium Center
1911, Frost & Granger

The station yards were kept long (over two blocks) and low by covering sixteen tracks with Bush sheds, developed in 1906 by civil engineer Lincoln Bush. Steel beams carry concrete roofs that span two tracks and a half platform; a continuous open slot over each track allows exhaust to escape, avoiding the necessity of a higher roof.

223 North Western Terminal Powerhouse
N. Clinton St. between Milwaukee Ave. & W. Lake St.
1911, Frost & Granger

A 226-foot chimney is the exclamation point of the complex, which began four blocks to the south. The powerhouse's nine arches along Clinton St. recall the Beaux Arts styling of the demolished station.

224 E. W. Blatchford & Co. Buildings
212–230 N. Clinton St.
1883–1889, Frederick W. Waescher; Adler & Sullivan

The genealogy of this sequence of substantial brick buildings is confusing. We know for certain that Blatchford, trustee of the Newberry estate, used its architect, Waescher, to design one of these buildings for his own business, which manufactured lead pipe and linseed oil. After a fire Adler & Sullivan rebuilt the interiors; they may (or may not) have received the commission for another Blatchford building.

225 Burlington Building
547 W. Jackson Blvd.
1911, Marshall & Fox

Gleaming terra-cotta celebrates steel construction in the former headquarters of the Chicago, Burlington & Quincy Railroad. The arched arcades of the base are repeated at the top.

226 Illinois Institute of Technology—Chicago-Kent College of Law
565 W. Adams St.
1992, Holabird & Root

With security a paramount planning issue, public spaces such as

St. Patrick's Church

classrooms and auditoriums were located on low floors; more private areas such as faculty offices and the library are on higher ones. The reading room, atop the building, features a ceiling with an exposed lamella truss.

227 Glessner Center
(Warder, Bushnell & Glessner Co. Office and Warehouse)
130 S. Jefferson St.
1883, Jaffray & Scott; William W. Boyington
Converted to offices 1985, Booth/Hansen & Assocs.

Comprising a southern office and a northern warehouse, the building was completed by Boyington after a series of construction disasters. The firm made farm machinery; partner John J. Glessner

commissioned Glessner House, H. H. Richardson's masterpiece.

228 Presidential Towers
555, 575, 605 & 625 W. Madison St.
1986, Solomon Cordwell Buenz & Assocs.

These four enormous and mundane apartment towers are noteworthy for the neighborhood change they hastened—the eradication of several blocks of seamy, colorful, and "underdeveloped" Skid Row.

229 Harold Washington Social Security Administration—Great Lakes Program Service Center
600 W. Madison St.
1976, Lester B. Knight & Assocs.

The design of this dull office building has one saving grace— the reflective curtain wall which is a beautiful backdrop to Claes Oldenburg's strong and structural, yet totally whimsical *Bat Column.*

230 St. Patrick's Roman Catholic Church
140 S. Desplaines St.
1852, 1856, Carter & Bauer

Chicago's oldest church has a simple facade of Milwaukee common brick above a Joliet limestone base. The onion dome symbolizes the Church in the East; the spire, the Church in the West.

Bat Column

NORTH MICHIGAN AVENUE/STREETERVILLE

MICHIGAN

12 Woman's
   Athletic Club
13 Crate & Barrel
14 664 N Michigan
15 Terra Museum
16 663 N Michigan
17 669-675 N Michigan
18 City Place
19 Chicago Place
20 Allerton Hotel
21 Neiman Marcus
22 Olympia Centre
23 Banana Republic
24 Arby's
25 Water Tower and
   Pumping Station
26 Wally Findlay Galleries
27 Loyola Lewis Towers
28 840 N Michigan
29 Water Tower Place
30 Hancock Center
31 Fourth Presbyterian
32 900 N Michigan
33 919 N Michigan
   (Palmolive Bldg)

49 Rubloff Bldg
50 Mayer Hall
51 Wieboldt Hall
52 Ward Bldg
53 Tarry Bldg
54 Chicago Fire Dept
55 Wesley Pavilion
56 Olson & McGaw
   Pavilions
57 Passavant Pavilion
58 Prentice Center
59 Rehabilitation
   Institute

65 Museum of
   Contemporary
   Art
66 633 St Clair Place
67 230 E Ohio
68 232 E Ohio
69 541 N Fairbanks
   (Time & Life Bldg)

James Jardine
Water Filtration
Plant

70

OLIVE
PARK

North
Pier
Apts

Lake
Point
Tower

72

71 Navy
   Pier

75

Lake Shore Dr

In a city notable for dramatic transformations, the story of North Michigan Avenue/Streeterville deserves a special place. It is amazing to contrast a picture of today's densely built-up neighborhood with an aerial photograph taken in 1926. Then, apart from a handful of scattered buildings, the roughly square-mile area was a gigantic vacant lot, awaiting development. More remarkably, forty years earlier there had been little land there at all. Lake Michigan then covered virtually all of Streeterville, from the east side of N. Michigan Ave. (then Pine St.) reaching from Chicago Ave. north to Oak St. The scruffy land south of Chicago Ave. was mostly uninhabited sand dunes.

Now one of Chicago's most valuable real estate parcels, the area was created almost by accident. A breakwater, constructed to the north of the mouth of the Chicago River in the early 1830s, was extended eastward during the following decades, creating sand dunes along the shoreline to the north. By the 1880s there was a considerable accumulation up to about Chicago Ave.

In July 1886 George Wellington ("Cap") Streeter arrived on the scene. A show and circus promoter, and surely one of Chicago's most memorable mavericks, the eponymous Streeter ran aground with his rickety ship on a sandbar near today's John Hancock Center. As the weeks went by and the water failed to rise and free his ship, the wily captain built a crude causeway to the land and encouraged builders who were developing the nearby Gold Coast residential area to dump their excavated materials around his ship. Since the land thus created stood outside the official boundaries of the State of Illinois as depicted in the 1821 shoreline survey, he declared it a free "federal district" answerable only to the national government—and set himself up as its governor. He was soon selling off the land to gullible investors.

The rapid development of the Near North Side increased the size of the "District of Lake Michigan," and Chicago's initial indifference to Streeter's claim turned to indignation. Repeated attempts to evict him met with no success until 1918, when the enormous clout arrayed against him proved overwhelming, and his claim was rejected by the courts. He was finally evicted for selling whiskey on Sundays.

The southern part of Streeterville, along with Ogden Slip and the Chicago River, burgeoned in the 1890s with warehouses and dock facilities. After 1900, additional factories, lofts, and offices appeared to the north and west; the Pugh warehouses (now North Pier) date from this period. The other area of early development lay to the north, when the elegant Gold Coast residential district spread south of Oak St., beginning with the construction of 999 N. Lake Shore Dr. in 1911–1912.

Between these industrial and residential areas lay an extensive tract of land that remained largely undeveloped until 1920, when Northwestern University purchased a large parcel along E. Chicago Ave. as a campus for its professional schools. The university soon expanded to the west and south, primarily to accommodate a large hospital complex.

Michigan Ave. experienced as rapid and dramatic a transformation as Streeterville itself. A new and Europeanized "grand" boulevard for Pine St., proposed in the 1909 Plan of Chicago, became a reality with the opening of the monumental Michigan Ave. Bridge in 1920. The great building boom of the Soaring Twenties left its distinctive mark on the new avenue in the modestly scaled, limestone-clad, neo-Classical and Art Deco buildings that made this street unique in Chicago.

Although comparative "skyscrapers" anchored its northern and southern ends, Michigan Ave. retained its human scale until the erection in 1969 of the 100-story John Hancock Center. This behemoth amply demonstrated the truth of the real estate adage that giants attract giants, for five more towers only slightly less titanic now cluster around it. What the astute real estate developer Arthur Rubloff dubbed the Magnificent Mile in 1947 has become, alas, the Manhattanized Mile.

The Gold Coast has gradually expanded southward east of Michigan Ave. to Pearson St. Postwar development has generally followed the pattern set by Mies van der Rohe's pathbreaking steel-and-glass towers at 860–880 Lake Shore Dr.

That old visionary scoundrel "Cap" Streeter must be saying I told you so. Only a stone's throw from where he ran aground a century ago, twenty million people come every year to shop, dine, see, and be seen at this shopping mall Mecca of the Middle West.
—William B. Hinchliff

▊ Michigan Ave. Bridge
Chicago River at
E. Wacker Dr.
1920, Edward H. Bennett; Thomas G. Pihlfeldt, city bridge eng.; Hugh Young, eng. of bridge design

Chicago has more movable bridges than any other city in the world, and most, like this one, are trunnion bascules. Ideal for this visible and busy location, it spans the river gracefully and economically with no protruding superstructure, while leaving a wide, navigable channel. Construction of this bridge was a top priority in the 1909 Plan of Chicago, and it led the way to the rapid redevelopment of real estate on N. Michigan Ave. The exemplar for its design was Paris' Alexander III Bridge (1900), with

Michigan Ave. Bridge Pylon

four corner pylons, ornamental abutments, a graceful flat arch profile, and integrated embankments. The forty-foot pylons are functional operator houses. Each is embellished with sculptural reliefs depicting events in Chicago's history: *Defense* and *Regeneration* by Henry Hering grace the south pylons, while the north pylons feature *The Discovers* and *The Pioneers* by James Earle Fraser.

▣ William Wrigley, Jr. Building
400 & 410 N. Michigan Ave. *1919–1924, Graham, Anderson, Probst & White* **Plaza** *1957, L.R. Solomon, J.D. Cordwell & Assocs.*

Wrigley Building

London has Big Ben, Paris has the Eiffel Tower, and Chicago has the Wrigley Building. With its towering form, its lively white cladding, and its incomparable setting on the Chicago River, the Wrigley symbolizes the city in the hearts of its citizens. Because of the bend in Michigan Ave. at the river, the building is also the glittering climax of the Magnificent Mile's southern end. From the east and west its impact is doubled by its watery reflection.

But the Wrigley is not just a popular emblem: it embodies the essentials of the history of Chicago architecture up to the 1920s as transformed into a new synthesis by the gifted young architect Charles G. Beersman of Graham, Anderson, Probst & White, one of the city's most prolific firms. Beersman gave the building a tripartite base, borrowing from the European tradition, as Chicago commercial architects had done since the rebuilding after the Fire of 1871. The dazzling effects of the 1893 White City inspired the sparkling terracotta cladding, and Beersman further specified six shades of tiles, ranging from creamy white at the bottom to blue-white at the top, so that the brightness increases as the building rises. At night, banks of floodlights mounted on adjacent buildings illuminate the building in ever-increasing intensity upward. At noon or at midnight it stands out in a brilliant blaze against the sky.

The Wrigley Building is actually two structures conceived consecutively, but the parts stand side by side almost like fraternal twins. The taller, southern building with its tower seems stately; the shorter, northern building, constructed later, seems monumental. The seeming subservience of the "annex" is all the more noteworthy given the area of its site: 21,000 square feet, compared to 11,000 of the "original." The pleasantly proportioned offices have large windows and handsome moldings, but there are no great public rooms. The tower soars to 398 feet, where an observation room in the round, templed "Lysicrates" cupola once allowed visitors to view the city from its highest peak.

Ernest R. Graham and

Beersman, the architects, and William Wrigley, Jr., their client, were keenly aware of the soaring verticality in the Manhattan skyline. They must have admired Cass Gilbert's Woolworth Building (1913), but it was more likely McKim, Mead & White's Municipal Building (1913), with its combination of classicism and a tower, that inspired the Chicagoans. They hoped their new building would have the dignity of the traditional architecture of Daniel H. Burnham's day and the great heights of the modern age, the best of both worlds, a synthesis of aspiring monumentality.

—Sally A. Kitt Chappell

3 Equitable Building
401 N. Michigan Ave.
1965, Skidmore, Owings & Merrill

The height and setback were dictated by the Tribune Company when they sold the land, to ensure the prominence of their own building. The Tribune also mandated the development of an intervening plaza, christened Pioneer Court. In 1992 it received a welcome SOM-designed face-lift to harmonize with the pedestrian spaces of Cityfront Center to the east. In a gracious urbanistic gesture that was twenty years ahead of its time (although it had been recommended in Burnham's 1909 plan), the plaza continues down to the riverfront via a curving staircase. The building itself is a strong Miesian statement, with an articulated facade that emphasizes the underlying steel frame.

Equitable Building

Behind the Equitable, a sliver of land just west of Columbus Dr. is the site of the planned University of Chicago Graduate School of Business Downtown Center (scheduled for completion in 1994, Lohan Assocs.).

4 Tribune Tower
435 N. Michigan Ave.
1923–1925, Howells & Hood
Addition
441–445 N. Michigan Ave.
1934, John Mead Howells; Hood & Fouilhoux and Leo J. Weissenborn, assoc. archs.

To observe its seventy-fifth anniversary, the *Chicago Tribune* in 1922 announced an international competition for the design of "the most beautiful office building in the world." Hyperbole notwithstanding, the competition was a major event: the 264 entries constituted a compendium of skyscraper design and sparked considerable debate about the proper form of the modern office building.

Approximately 90 percent of the entries relied on the historical precedents that had dominated American architecture at the beginning of the decade: Beaux Arts ideals inspired nearly 40 percent of them, and another 20 percent employed the neo-Gothic style popularized by Cass Gilbert's Woolworth

Tribune Tower

above the setback, creating a spidery crowning silhouette that recalls the thirteenth-century Butter Tower of the Rouen Cathedral.

The three-story arched entryway contains a richly detailed stone screen depicting characters from Aesop's fables. Note the howling dog and Robin Hood figures at the midpoint of the arch's curve, visual allusions to the architects' names. Embedded in the exterior walls are stones from well-known structures throughout the world. Some were gifts to Colonel Robert R. McCormick, the *Tribune*'s publisher; others were secured at his request by the paper's foreign correspondents.

The Tribune Tower, together with the Wrigley Building to the west and the 333 and 360 N. Michigan

Building (1913) in New York, then the tallest and one of the best-known American office buildings. Other entries reflected an emerging modernism: Walter Gropius submitted an exercise in the International Style, and Eliel Saarinen's second-prize entry, with its abstract and insistent verticality and graduated setbacks, pointed toward the skyscrapers of the late 1920s.

The first prize was awarded to the studied Gothic design of New York architects John Mead Howells & Raymond M. Hood. Rising thirty-six stories (460 feet), its structural steel frame is sheathed in Indiana limestone elaborately carved at the base and top in Gothic forms. At its base the structure covers a rectangle that extends 100 feet along Michigan Ave. and 326 feet eastward to adjoin the newspaper's former printing plant (1920, Jarvis Hunt). At the twenty-first floor the easternmost portion ends, and the tower becomes square in plan. Above the twenty-fourth floor the building steps back and rises as an octagonal tower. Two prominent piers from each of the four sides continue in the form of flying buttresses

Eliel Saarinen's design

Ave. buildings across the Chicago River, frames the monumental Michigan Avenue Bridge (1920), a major gateway to the North Side. Each of these office towers represents a facet of 1920s architecture documented by the contest entries; as a group they define one of Chicago's most dramatic spaces.
—Roy Forrey

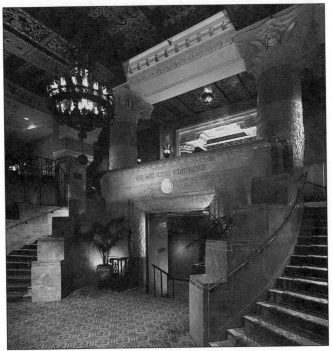

Hotel Inter-Continental

5 **Hotel Inter-Continental Chicago** (Medinah Athletic Club)
505 N. Michigan Ave.
1929, Walter W. Ahlschlager
Restoration 1989, Harry Weese & Assocs.

The decorative program and the idiosyncratic gold-leafed dome hint at the feast of illusion and artifice within. Neo-Egyptian low-reliefs designed by George Unger are carved into three sides of the facade, depicting masons on the south, builders on the north, and architects presenting a model of the building to the pharaoh on the west. The interior spaces are modest in scale but grandiose in spirit, infused throughout with a romantic historicism.

6 **520 N. Michigan Ave.** (McGraw-Hill Building)
1929, Thielbar & Fugard

This Art Deco triumph is a classic of its genre. The smooth limestone facade is graced with shallowly incised ornament that includes fluted piers and a mythologically inspired sculptural program. The stone sheathing is carried across part of the south side, in contrast to many other buildings of the era whose ugly brick side walls anticipated construction that was often decades in coming.

7 **Chicago Marriott Hotel**
540 N. Michigan Ave.
1978, Harry Weese & Assocs.

This faceless, graceless clunk has a large multilevel lobby in a token gesture to big-city glamour.

520 N. Michigan Ave.

543–545 N. Michigan Ave.

and artists' studios on the top floor. It was built by restaurateur John R. Thompson ("Thompson's Restaurants Must Be a Good Place To Eat") as speculative office space and an anchor for his chain of eateries.

Ⅲ 612–620 N. Michigan Ave. (Decorative Arts Building)
Remodeled 1928, Philip B. Maher

During the Avenue's boom decade, residential and industrial buildings were frequently remodeled for retail use rather than replaced. This brick and limestone building was transformed from a four-story coffee warehouse into a furniture store. The second-floor Palladian windows have broad central panes to create large display areas. Maher probably chose the Georgian style over his preferred French idiom to reflect the nationality of the furniture displayed within.

8 543–545 N. Michigan Ave. (Jacques Building)
1929, Philip B. Maher

Maher had studied in France in 1925–1926, and his supremely elegant buildings lent credibility to the appellation "Boul Mich." Easily overlooked among its larger, more strident neighbors, this narrow retail building combines classical proportions and a mansard roof with the flattened ornamentation of Art Deco. The female figures in panels above the doors recall the building's origins as a luxury dress shop.

9 Lake Shore Bank (Lake Shore Trust Building)
605 N. Michigan Ave.
1922, Marshall & Fox
Renovation and addition 1982, Perkins & Will

The original windows were replaced with large, undivided panes of dark-tinted glass, drastically altering the bank's character and making the wall vanish between the colossal engaged Corinthian columns. The monumental, freestanding bank modeled on a temple, though common in many cities, is relatively rare in Chicago.

10 Michigan-Ohio Building
612 N. Michigan Ave.
1925, Alfred S. Alschuler

The classical facade, ironed flat, is divided according to the building's original uses: shops on the first two floors, offices above,

Woman's Athletic Club

12 Woman's Athletic Club
626 N. Michigan Ave.
1928, Philip B. Maher

This unusually well preserved reminder of the Avenue's gentility has a sober elegance typical of Maher's French-influenced work. Tall windows at the second and seventh floors indicate the important public spaces.

13 Crate & Barrel
646 N. Michigan Ave.
1990, Solomon Cordwell Buenz & Assocs.

Crate & Barrel

Wearing summer whites to a black-tie affair, Crate & Barrel's flagship store issues a brazen challenge to the architectural conventions of Michigan Ave. Unlike its masonry-clad neighbors, the building is bright, shiny, and shamelessly transparent; a glass-enclosed, crisp corner cylinder nestles slightly inward from the outer walls. The smooth, white skin and continuous bands of windows pay homage to Le Corbusier, while the continuation of the specially finished sidewalk through to the building's interior flooring is a favorite Miesian device. Nothing constructed on the avenue since the Hancock Center has made such a strong modernist statement.

City Place

14 664 N. Michigan Ave. (Farwell Building)
1927, Philip B. Maher

The success of this prominent commission led Maher to five more Michigan Ave. projects in rapid succession. Despite the round-arched entrances and mansard roof, the strong vertical lines of the piers and window-spandrel combination impart a strong Art Deco feeling. The building was saved from destruction when it found a new function as gallery space for the Terra Museum.

15 Terra Museum of American Art
666 N. Michigan Ave.
1987, Booth/Hansen & Assocs.

The glassy central portion reveals that this small building is devoted primarily to circulation space for the galleries, which occupy renovated space next door at 664.

16 663 N. Michigan Ave.
1966, Holabird & Root
17 669–675 N. Michigan Ave. (Blackstone Shops, later expanded for Saks Fifth Avenue)
1925, Philip B. Maher
Renovated 1966, Holabird & Root

The verticality of the first two buildings was re-created surprisingly well in all of the subsequent work.

18 City Place
676 N. Michigan Ave.
1990, Loebl, Schlossman & Hackl

One of the trio of mixed-use behemoths that invaded Michigan Ave. in the late 1980s, this building presents its slimmest profile to the Avenue but commands attention from the side, with its garish pink-red palette and potpourri of window patterns. In an inversion of the typical formula, the hotel is located on the middle floors, giving offices the best views.

19 Chicago Place
700 N. Michigan Ave.
1990, Skidmore, Owings & Merrill (retail base); Solomon Cordwell Buenz & Assocs. (condominium tower)

The Chicago theme crops up everywhere in this overdesigned temple to commerce. The exterior of the base is meant to recall the great emporiums of State St.—Marshall Field & Co. (classical columns) and Carson Pirie Scott (curved corners)—but the result is ersatz. In a formula firmly established by Water Tower Place, the skyscraper tower is set well back from the mid-rise base. The eight-level atrium offers the acrophobe's usual nightmare of freestanding escalators and glass-enclosed elevators, but with a dizzying distraction of color and pattern.

Allerton Hotel

20 Allerton Hotel (Allerton House)
140 E. Huron St.
1924, Murgatroyd & Ogden; Fugard & Knapp, assoc. archs.

Built as part of a New York City–based chain of residential "club hotels" for single men and women, the Allerton has a northern Italian Renaissance style that proved popular as a model for other hotels and apartments. The thronelike massing reflects Chicago's 1923 zoning ordinance, which required setbacks on large buildings that covered their entire lot.

21 Neiman Marcus
737 N. Michigan Ave.
1983, Skidmore, Owings & Merrill
22 Olympia Centre
161 E. Chicago Ave.
1986, Skidmore, Owings & Merrill

Postmodernism was slow to penetrate the citadels of Chicago orthodoxy; Neiman Marcus, in design since 1978, was one of the first examples. The large glass arch evokes the work of H. H. Richardson and Louis H. Sullivan, but with an obligatory wink: the glass slit in place of a keystone underscores the arch's structural irrelevance. The high-rise Olympia Centre tapers on two sides as it rises. The changes in fenestration reflect reduced structural loads, with larger windows where the function shifts from office to residential.

23 Banana Republic
744 N. Michigan Ave.
Remodeled 1991, Robert A. M. Stern

The modest scale of the building, Stern's first in Chicago, makes it an anomaly among its gargantuan contemporaries and may reflect the scaled-down ambitions of the 1990s. Stern transformed a nondescript two-story store into a building out of a Disney World South Pacific/Main Street.

24 Arby's
115 E. Chicago Ave.
Remodeled 1977, Stanley Tigerman & Assocs.

To the south of the Water Tower is another example of the Magnificent Mile's metamorphosis. The infill facade of stucco and glass gave a curving, partially transparent skin to a narrow, four-story building. The "non-architecture" of the facade calls attention to the exposed ducts and piping within.

25 Chicago Water Tower & Pumping Station
806 & 811 N. Michigan Ave.
1866, Pumping Station, and 1869, Tower, William W. Boyington

One of only a few buildings to survive the Great Fire, the Water Tower is a potent symbol of Chicago's "I Will" spirit. In three days in October 1871, the city's commercial center and a third of its residences were leveled by fire. But the tower stood, holding out the promise that Chicago would rise from the ruins and ashes around it. Within months the city was rebuilding, resuming its role as the nineteenth century's fastest-growing city.

The famous 154-foot tower was actually a secondary structure. It was built to house a 138-foot standpipe that stabilized the pressure of the water distributed from the adjacent pumping station. Both buildings were built in the "castellated Gothic" style of locally quarried Joliet-Lemont limestone, widely used in Chicago before it was replaced by Indiana graystone in the 1890s. The stone is recognized by its distinctive yellow patina.

The Pumping Station and Tower are two of only a few surviving buildings by William W. Boyington, one of the city's most prominent early architects who gave shape to the Chicago that burned as well as to the phoenix that replaced it. Working in the popular revival styles, Boyington designed major hotels, commercial structures, churches, and other institutions from the 1850s to the 1890s.

The four facades of the Water Tower are identical and feature a massive arched door flanked by pointed-arch windows surmounted by drip moldings. Small towers with lancet windows, castellated crowns, and tourelles frame each level as the base rises to the tower itself, which is surmounted by a crown of eight tourelles and a copper cupola. The overall effect led Oscar Wilde to call it "a castellated monstrosity with salt and pepper boxes stuck all over it." Boyington used the same styling not only on the pumping station but also on the first University of Chicago (demolished), the prison at Joliet, Illinois (1858), and the entrance to Rosehill Cemetery (1864).

Chicago Water Tower & Pumping Station

A Chicago landmark of great visceral magnitude, the Water Tower has nonetheless battled three times for its life. In 1906 the standpipe became obsolete, and only a public outcry saved the tower from demolition. In 1918 the tower obstructed the northward progress of the new Michigan Ave., but preservationists prevailed over planners. A 1948 plan for an art center on the site was also defeated, and the first restoration of the tower began in 1962. Today the Water Tower is a focus of Michigan Avenue, whose buildings have come to dwarf the structure that once stood tall amid smoldering ruins.
—Vincent Michael

26 Wally Findlay Galleries (Perkins, Fellows & Hamilton Studio & Office)
814 N. Michigan Ave.
1917, Perkins, Fellows & Hamilton

This is a rare example of an originally freestanding building designed by architects for their own offices. The red brick facade, with Gothic details and extensive sculpture by Emil R. Zettler, has been terribly obscured by paint and extensive signage.

27 Loyola University—Lewis Towers (Illinois Women's Athletic Club)
820 N. Michigan Ave.
1927, Richard E. Schmidt, Garden & Martin

This Gothic skyscraper had shops on the first two floors, offices to the ninth floor, and club facilities above. A relief of Diana with her dog guards the entrance.

28 840 N. Michigan Ave.
1992, Lucien Lagrange & Assocs.

This dignified low-key addition to the Avenue extends the human scale that reigns on its western side between Superior St. and Delaware Pl. The corner tower and mansard roof evoke earlier retail establishments, and the six shades of limestone harmonize with the masonry of the streetscape.

29 Water Tower Place
845 N. Michigan Ave.
1976, Loebl, Schlossman & Hackl

This marble-clad monument to mammon forever changed the Avenue's character—for better or worse. It moved the retail center of gravity north from State St. in the Loop (which has yet to recover) and heralded the arrival of a more international and luxurious marketplace. Despite the setback of the building's tallest part, great violence was done to the streetscape with its blank walls and recessed storefronts, a mistake avoided by its imitators. The bland marble walls cover a reinforced-concrete frame that was the world's tallest until the construction of 311 S. Wacker Dr.

30 John Hancock Center
875 N. Michigan Ave.
1969, Skidmore, Owings & Merrill

Of the three giants that dominate the late 20th-century Chicago skyline, Sears Tower and the Amoco Building are taller, but the John Hancock Center best exemplifies the Chicago tradition of combining bold structural advances with brawny architectural form.

Despite its gigantism, the 1,127-foot, 100-story, 2.8-million-square-foot Hancock is a beloved urban icon. Nicknamed "Big John" soon after

John Hancock Center

its completion, it features a distinctive tapering profile and exterior cross bracing that have inspired countless schoolchildren to portray it as a cartoonlike series of stacked Xs. So deeply is the building ingrained in the Chicago psyche that in 1989 Mayor Richard M. Daley attacked the owner's plan to fill in the tower's sunken plaza and add a three-story retail atrium to its base. In 1992 a new scheme was announced to reconfigure the rectangular plaza into an elliptical form. The happy result is that the Hancock tower remains undefiled, a high-water mark for Skidmore, Owings & Merrill and a triumph of modern architecture.

Designed by SOM architect Bruce Graham and engineer Fazlur R. Khan, the Hancock exemplifies another Chicago tradition, the multipurpose building. Floors 1–5 are devoted to retail space; 6–12 to parking; 13–41 to offices; 42–43 to mechanical equipment; and 44–93 to residences. The 94th floor houses a public observatory; a bar and restaurant occupy floors 95 and 96, with television and communications equipment housed on 97 and mechanical equipment on 98–100. Supporting it all, as well as the television and radio antennas that bring the building's total height to 1,476 feet, are 46,000 tons of steel. Exterior columns, horizontal beams, and cross braces form a highly efficient structural system comparable to a rigid box; the tower was erected for the cost of a conventional forty-five-story office building.

The tapering form provides large floor areas for retail and office use and smaller spaces for the condominiums. The form also evokes the permanence and monumentality associated with the obelisks of ancient Egypt or the Washington Monument.

Monumental presence is both a blessing and a curse. For all its swaggering presence on the skyline, the Hancock stumbles as it meets the street. The tower, which is clad in black aluminum with travertine marble covering the base, has been compared to a man in a tuxedo wearing white socks. Before the Hancock Center was built, N. Michigan Ave. largely resembled a Parisian boulevard of elegant low- and mid-rise Classical buildings. After the tower shattered that fragile scale, the Avenue became an urban canyon of hulking blockbusters, making the open space of the Hancock's sunken plaza all the more valuable, even if it somewhat dims the tower's brilliant synthesis of architecture and engineering.

—Blair Kamin

31 Fourth Presbyterian Church

866 N. Michigan Ave.
1914, Ralph Adams Cram; Howard Van Doren Shaw, assoc. arch.
Cloister 1914, Howard Van Doren Shaw
Manse, Parish House, Blair Chapel 1925, Howard Van Doren Shaw

One of Chicago's wealthiest congregations turned to a nationally renowned practitioner of the Gothic Revival for their church. Parishioner Shaw collaborated with Cram on the interior and designed the much more informal buildings that create a peaceful courtyard, or garth. The stained glass is by Charles J. Connick of Boston; local artist Frederick C. Bartlett designed the illuminated ceiling and the wooden statuary.

32 900 N. Michigan Ave.

1989, Kohn Pedersen Fox; Perkins & Will, assoc. archs.

Known as the Bloomingdale's Building, this mixed-use structure by the developers of Water Tower Place builds on that project's commercial success and corrects some of its errors. The eight-story shopping block extends to the lot line with a welcoming entrance and plenty of large display windows. The spacious, understated neo-Deco atrium has the anchor store at the back, so that shoppers pass the boutiques first. The hotel, office, and condominium floors have entrances on the side streets. Like Water Tower Place, the exterior is a stack of embellished boxes, but with a more ambitious decorative program. Though it does not all hang

Fourth Presbyterian

together, the four huge lanterns atop the building are a visual delight.

33 919 N. Michigan Ave.
(Playboy Building, originally Palmolive Building)
1929, Holabird & Root
Storefront renovated 1982,
Skidmore, Owings & Merrill

Like New York, Chicago enacted a zoning law for skyscrapers (in 1923) that would work perfectly for the Art Deco buildings soon in vogue. This building, like the Chicago Board of Trade by the same architects, is a shining example of the style, with setbacks making it a powerful sculptural object.

919 N. Michigan Ave.

34 One Magnificent Mile
940–980 N. Michigan Ave.
1983, Skidmore, Owings & Merrill

Although it uses the bundled tube structure of the Sears Tower, this pink granite triad is clad in 1980s garb. The window patterns express the familiar divisions of retail, office, and residential use.

35 Drake Hotel
140 E. Walton St.
1920, Marshall & Fox

This luxurious hotel anchors both the north end of Michigan Ave. and the west end of the E. Lake Shore Dr. Historic District, combining the public splendor of the Avenue with the residential elegance of the Drive. The H-shaped plan maximizes lake views. The Italian Renaissance–inspired facades effectively incorporate a *piano nobile* treatment for the public spaces on the lower floors.

East Lake Shore Drive Historic District
From Michigan Ave. east through 999 N. Lake Shore Dr.

36 Drake Tower Apartments
179 E. Lake Shore Dr.
1929, Benjamin H. Marshall

37 Mayfair Regent Hotel
(Lake Shore Drive Hotel)
181 E. Lake Shore Dr.
1924, Fugard & Knapp

38 199 E. Lake Shore Dr.
(The Breakers)
1915, Marshall & Fox

39 209 E. Lake Shore Dr.
1924, Marshall & Fox

40 219 E. Lake Shore Dr.
1922, Fugard & Knapp

41 229 E. Lake Shore Dr.
1919, Fugard & Knapp

42 999 N. Lake Shore Dr.
1912, Marshall & Fox

This remarkable group creates a harmonious streetwall that is one of the few lakefront stretches with no recent structures interrupting its cohesiveness. It also provides an intriguing glimpse of Benjamin H. Marshall's design evolution, from the Second Empire exuberance adorning the corner at 999 to the sober ahistoricism of the Drake Tower Apts.

999 N. Lake Shore Dr.

43 227 E. Walton St.
1956, Harry Weese & Assocs.

While Mies was refining and simplifying the glass-and-steel curtain wall that would become de rigueur for high-rise facades, Weese was moving toward greater variety and plasticity. Inspired by the multibayed facades of the early Chicago School, he used a warm palette of red brick with concrete trim here.

44 860–880 N. Lake Shore Dr.
1949–1951, Ludwig Mies van der Rohe; Pace Assocs. and Holsman, Holsman, Klekamp & Taylor, assoc. archs.

860–880 N. Lake Shore Dr.

These towers constitute the first and most forceful demonstration of Ludwig Mies van der Rohe's ideas for tall buildings. No other building by Mies had as immediate or strong an impact on his American contemporaries, and the influence of these structures was to pervade much of modern architecture.

Mies had come to Chicago from Germany in 1938 to become director of the school of architecture at what would later become the Illinois Institute of Technology. He also established an architecture practice and in 1948 designed the concrete-framed Promontory Apartments in Hyde Park, the first of many projects for developer Herbert Greenwald. Mies had prepared two versions of the Promontory. One was the form actually used; the other had a steel-and-glass exterior on the long elevations, his first use of the curtain wall that came to be his hallmark.

While the Promontory was under construction, Greenwald commissioned these apartments. The plan was developed from the alternative version for the Promontory and from sketches that Mies had drawn between 1919 and 1921 for two radically innovative glass towers, which had brought him to the forefront of the modern movement. The unexecuted designs re-emerged here and in 1968, through the hands of Mies's former students, in Lake Point Tower.

The buildings acquire their strong verticality from the narrow I-beams welded to the columns and mullions, a feature necessitated in part by the building code's requirement that steel-framed buildings be fireproofed with concrete. Mies satisfied the code and achieved the appearance he desired by finishing the framing elements with steel plate, which served as formwork for poured concrete, and by welding I-beams onto the plate.

Questioned on his use of a structural material as applied ornament, Mies gave a good reason and then the real reason. He noted that the I-beams functioned well as mullions. "But why weld them onto the column plates?" he was asked. "It strengthens the plates," Mies replied. "Do the plates need strengthening?" "Well, no," he confessed, "but if you leave out the I-beams there, it breaks the rhythm!"

The "Glass Houses" were startling not only in terms of form but also as habitation; critics wondered at the psychological impact of transparent homes. The apartments were a financial success, however. The buildings became the international prototype for steel-and-glass structures and engendered an architecture now so commonplace that it is almost impossible to appreciate their initial impact, when it was "as if steel and glass [were] seen for the first time."

—Joan Pomaranc

45 900–910 N. Lake Shore Dr. (Esplanade Apartments)
1953–1956, Ludwig Mies van der Rohe; Pace Assocs. and Holsman, Holsman, Klekamp & Taylor, assoc. archs.

The success of 860–880 led Greenwald to commission another pair. They have a sleeker version of the expressive curtain wall, with dark-tinted glass and without the contrasting aluminum window frames. The structural system is not a steel skeleton but a flat-slab concrete frame, resulting in complete independence of skin and structure.

46 Northwestern University—Lake Shore Center (Lake Shore Athletic Club)
850 N. Lake Shore Dr.
1924, Jarvis Hunt

This student residence was built as a combination clubhouse and apartment building. The hulking mass consists of a large neo-Classical base topped by rather plain upper floors.

47 860 DeWitt Apartments (DeWitt–Chestnut Apartments)
860 N. DeWitt Pl.
1963, Skidmore, Owings & Merrill

This was Chicago's first building with a tubular structural system, in which closely spaced exterior columns create a load-bearing screen-wall. The reinforced-concrete frame is sheathed in marble. It was the first collaboration of SOM architect Bruce Graham and engineer Fazlur R. Khan, the team that created the Hancock Center and Sears Tower.

48 200 E. Pearson St.
1916, Robert S. DeGolyer

This vintage palazzo was home to Ludwig Mies van der Rohe, who moved out of his free apartment at 860–880 N. Lake Shore Dr., the story goes, because the tenants treated him like the maintenance man.

The block bounded by Chicago Ave., Mies van der Rohe Way (Seneca St.), Pearson St., and Lake Shore Park is the site of a new building planned for the Museum of Contemporary Art. The design, by German architect Josef Paul Kleihues, was unveiled in 1992 and is scheduled for completion in 1995.

Northwestern University—Chicago Campus
This campus houses law, business, medical, and dental schools and is concentrated between Chicago Ave. and Huron St., from the lake west to St. Clair St. James Gamble Rogers created a campus plan in 1924 and designed a row of buildings in his signature Collegiate Gothic style. The original group marched west from the lake along Chicago Ave., with the buildings increasing in height. This pattern has been broken by recent construction, but Rogers's Gothic precedent has proved amazingly durable. Fallen from grace and superseded by bland modernist buildings, the style was strongly evoked in two major additions of the 1980s: the Law School's Rubloff Building and the Medical School's Tarry Building.

49 Northwestern University School of Law—Arthur Rubloff Building
375 E. Chicago Ave.
American Bar Center
750 N. Lake Shore Dr.
1984, Holabird & Root

This handsome addition to the campus has a finely detailed curtain wall, the base of which

Northwestern Law School

gestures to its Gothic neighbors with abstracted buttresses. A glazed atrium links it with the Gary Law Library building.

50 Northwestern University School of Law—Levy Mayer Hall
357 E. Chicago Ave.
1927, James Gamble Rogers; Childs & Smith, assoc. archs.

The Law School quadrangle surrounds a leafy courtyard and includes Rogers's Albert H. Gary Library (1927; note the owls perched atop the buttresses) on Chicago Ave. and Robert R. McCormick Hall (1960, Holabird & Root) at 350 E. Superior St., executed in a self-effacing and harmonious non-style.

51 Wieboldt Hall of Commerce
339 E. Chicago Ave.
52 Montgomery Ward Memorial Building
303–311 E. Chicago Ave.
1926, James Gamble Rogers; Childs & Smith, assoc. archs.

An attractive arcade links these two buildings (a twin links Wieboldt to the Law School complex) and creates a peaceful courtyard, a hallmark of Rogers's campus designs. The Ward Building was the nation's first Collegiate Gothic skyscraper. Although stylistically dull in comparison with the architect's better-known buildings at Yale University, the planning makes the most of the cramped urban site.

53 Tarry Medical Research & Education Building
300 E. Superior St.
1990, Perkins & Will

Collegiate Gothic returns in 1990s materials in this addition, which completes the block begun by the Montgomery Ward Building and continued in the Morton (1955) and Searle (1956) Medical Research Buildings (310 & 320 E. Superior St.) Method Atrium (part of Tarry), an elegant glassy lobby, links all four buildings.

Tarry Building

54 Chicago Fire Department
202 E. Chicago Ave.
1902, Charles F. Hermann, Chicago city arch.

This tiny fire station repeats in miniature the castellated Gothic of the Water Tower & Pumping Station.

55 Northwestern Memorial Hospital—Wesley Pavilion (Wesley Memorial Hospital—George Herbert Jones Hospital Center)
250 E. Superior St.
1937–1941, Thielbar & Fugard

This virtually featureless building would be almost invisible if not for its bulk. A pier in the simplified Gothic lobby is inscribed FREDERICK THIELBAR • SI MONUMENTUM REQUIRIS CIRCUMSPICE, an epitaph used with considerably more justification for Sir Christopher Wren's tomb in St. Paul's Cathedral (If you seek his monument, look around you).

In 1992 Northwestern Memorial Hospital announced plans for a new complex (on a site bounded by Huron, Erie, and St. Clair Sts. and Fairbanks Ct.) that call for the demolition of Wesley and Passavant Pavilions.

56 Northwestern Memorial Hospital—Northwestern University Health Sciences Building/Olson & McGaw Pavilions
233 E. Superior St.
1979, Holabird & Root

This unabashedly high-tech building lost some of its edge when its gleaming white metal panels were painted buff to blend in with the surrounding limestone and concrete. Pedestrian bridges with exposed trusses make connections to buildings across both streets.

57 Northwestern Memorial Hospital—Passavant Pavilion (Passavant Hospital—Floyd E. Patterson Memorial Building)
303 E. Superior St.
1928, Holabird & Root

Many of the hospital's buildings were originally independent hospitals acquired by Northwestern. Holabird & Root's Gothic style fits in perfectly with the buildings that Rogers had designed during the same decade.

Prentice Women's Hospital

58 Northwestern Memorial Hospital—Prentice Women's Hospital and Maternity Center
333 E. Superior St.
Northwestern University Institute of Psychiatry
330 E. Huron St.
1975, Bertrand Goldberg & Assocs.

At street level, this is just another modern hospital building, but above the fifth story is a curving concrete shell that seems to have landed like a spaceship on the steel-and-glass podium. The split personality reflects split functions. The conventional base contains generic space adaptable to the constant remodelings that hospital treatment facilities undergo, while the curving portion is a "bed tower" with separate nursing stations for each of the four wings. The oval windows enhance energy efficiency and construction economy. Goldberg repeated this curving plan in many hospital designs.

59 Rehabilitation Institute of Chicago
345 E. Superior St.
1974, C. F. Murphy & Assocs.

The campus's most purely Miesian hospital building has a bronze-tinted skin that clearly expresses the steel frame.

60 Abbott Hall
710 N. Lake Shore Dr.
1939, Holabird & Root

Built as a student residence, this unadorned limestone structure has more bulk than style. The ornamental wrought-iron gate, designed for the original 1920s campus, sits uselessly on the site's southeast corner.

61 Lake Shore Place
(American Furniture Mart)
680 N. Lake Shore Dr.
East End: 1924, Henry Raeder Assocs.; George C. Nimmons & Co. and N. Max Dunning, assoc. archs. West End: 1926, George C. Nimmons and N. Max Dunning Converted 1984, Lohan Assocs.

This lavishly ornamented monument to the wholesale furniture trade was built when Chicago was at the industry's center. Although the exterior seems all of a piece, a closer look reveals a difference between the sixteen-story east end, which has a reinforced-concrete structure, and the twenty-story western section, which is a steel-framed skyscraper. The Gothicism of the exterior reaches its apogee in the thirty-story tower, which was inspired by the Houses of Parliament. The interior carries out the theme in the lavish Whiting Hall lobby, which runs the length of the building. The Furniture Mart declined with the industry's decentralization and the move of many showrooms to the Merchandise Mart. It is now a mixed-use building of apartments, offices, parking, and stores.

Lake Shore Place

62 Onterie Center
446–448 E. Ontario St./441 E. Erie St.
1979–1986, Skidmore, Owings & Merrill

This building was the final collaboration between architect Bruce Graham and engineer Fazlur R. Khan, who died in 1982 after completing the structural design. A pair of reinforced-concrete tubes, their cross bracing expressed by concrete infill panels, embrace a central core. This system combines the cross bracing of the Hancock Center with the tubular structure of the Sears Tower, though it lacks their elegance. Retail and office space occupy the lower floors, with apartments in the tower.

63 CBS Building (Chicago Riding Club)
630 N. McClurg Ct. (William S. Paley Pl.)
1924, Rebori, Wentworth, Dewey & McCormick

The unusual roof, with sloped planes designed to provide light and ventilation, was more often found on industrial buildings.

64 McClurg Court Center
333 E. Ontario St.
1971, Solomon Cordwell Buenz & Assocs.

This apartment complex offers the kind of self-contained, multi-use environment popular since the 1970s. Although some shops face the street, it presents a forbidding presence. The curved corner towers are placed at right angles to each other in order to maximize views.

65 Museum of Contemporary Art
(Messinger's Lunch Rooms Building)
237 E. Ontario St.
1915, architect unknown Remodeled 1967, Brenner-Danforth-Rockwell Remodeled 1979, Booth, Nagle & Hartray

Seen from the alley, the high-tech treatment is only skin-deep. The building's fate is uncertain with the museum's planned move to larger quarters.

66 633 St. Clair Pl.
1991, Loebl, Schlossman & Hackl

Spidery superstructures perch incongruously atop a granite-and-glass office tower.

67 230 E. Ohio St. (Pelouze Building)
1916, Alfred S. Alschuler
68 232 E. Ohio St. (Pelouze Scale & Manufacturing Co. Factory)
1916, Hill & Woltersdorf

These are among the few remaining loft buildings in this former industrial area.

Time and Life Building

69 541 N. Fairbanks Ct. Building (Time and Life Building)
1968, Harry Weese & Assocs.
Renovated 1989, Perkins & Will

This brawny building of Cor-Ten steel with bronze-tinted mirror glass is a foray by Weese into the Miesian realm. The reflective glass, unusual at the time, conserves energy. Double-deck elevators are programmed to stop at two floors at the same time during rush hours and to provide regular service at other times.

70 James Jardine Water Filtration Plant (Central District Filtration Plant)
1000 E. Ohio St.
1952–1964, C. F. Murphy Assocs.

On this long finger of landfill is a campus of buildings that filter and purify water for the metropolitan area. The low buildings are of steel-frame construction with metal-and-glass curtain walls.

71 Navy Pier (Municipal Pier No. 2)
600 E. Grand Ave. at Lake Michigan
1916, Charles S. Frost
Renovated 1976, Jerome R. Butler, Jr., Chicago city arch.
Renovated 1990–1994, Benjamin Thompson & Assocs; VOA Assocs., assoc. archs.

A 1910 plan called for the construction of five municipal piers, of which only Navy Pier was built. Its 3,000-foot length, set on 20,000 wooden piles, made it then the world's largest pier. During its golden age (1918–1930) it was an important terminal for freight and passenger traffic, as well as a site of public entertainment. The rise of trucking combined with the Depression to curtail both uses; it became a naval training facility during World War II and served as the Chicago branch of the University of Illinois from 1946 until 1965. When the east buildings were restored in 1976, the pier was again host to civic and cultural events.

In 1989 the city and state created the Metropolitan Pier & Exposition Authority to oversee both McCormick Place and Navy Pier and committed $150 million to reconstructing the latter as a public recreational and cultural center. The plan calls for the restoration of the headhouse and the ballroom structure that anchor the west and east ends. A long linking building will serve as a huge enclosed pleasure ground, with museums, shops, and entertainment and recreational facilities.

72 Lake Point Tower
505 N. Lake Shore Dr.
1968, Schipporeit-Heinrich; Graham, Anderson, Probst & White, assoc. archs.

Inspired by a 1919–1921 visionary project of Mies van der Rohe, two of his former students and employees designed this undulating glass tower as their

Lake Point Tower

urban planning that resulted in bleak landscapes of isolated towers. Its pleasant river orientation could be possible only in this postindustrial era, when waterways are more important as pleasure grounds than as transportation arteries. Development has been carried out separately, with land ownership divided between the Chicago Dock & Canal Trust (east of Columbus Dr.), and the Equitable Life Assurance Society (between Columbus Dr. and Michigan Ave.).

firm's first commission. The first skyscraper with curving glass walls, it still outshines its imitators. The Y-shaped plan (which differs from Mies's asymmetrical model) provides the optimal combination of density, views, and privacy. The tower sits on a large podium that contains parking and commercial space and is topped with a private park. The base presents a bleak brick wall to those few pedestrians who traverse this isolated, formerly industrial area.

73 Police Department Building (Kraft-Phenix Cheese Co. Building)
510 Peshtigo Ct.
1938, Mundie, Jensen, Bourke & Havens

One of the last manufacturers to abandon the area, Kraft left behind an Art Deco warehouse with a gold stripe running from the base to the top, where the ledge once supported the company's logo.

Cityfront Center
Bounded by the Chicago River, N. Lake Shore Dr., E. Grand Ave., and N. Michigan Ave.
Master plan: 1985, Cooper, Eckstut Assocs.; Skidmore, Owings & Merrill
Ongoing planning: Lohan Assocs. (east of Columbus Dr.); Skidmore, Owings & Merrill (west of Columbus Dr.)

Cityfront Center is rapidly becoming Chicago's most successful planned urban landscape. Scaled to the pedestrian but convenient for traffic, it consciously repudiates the kind of

North Pier Chicago

74 North Pier Chicago (Pugh Terminal)
435 E. Illinois St.
1905–1920, Christian A. Eckstorm
Renovated 1990, Booth/Hansen & Assocs.; Austin Co., assoc. archs.

Constructed as an exhibition center for wholesale products, this sprawling building capitalized on Chicago's emerging role in American merchandising to locate numerous manufacturers and product lines under one roof. It was originally more than twice as long and stretched east across the path of Lake Shore Dr. The conversion to a three-story retail mall with four office floors was the first completed project at Cityfront Center.

Fan-shaped steel canopies punctuate the ground floor on Illinois St. between windows that were originally loading docks. This facade is of face brick and, although simple, presents a more finished appearance than the common-brick river and side walls, which are now more prominent. Inside, a three-story rotunda introduces the inventive combination of materials that evoke the area's nautical and industrial past in a 1990s vocabulary. The Ogden Slip facade has been extended with two neo-Miesian glass-and-steel gallerias.

75 North Pier Apartment Tower

474 N. Lake Shore Dr.
1991, Dubin, Dubin & Moutoussamy; Florian-Wierzbowski, design consultants

This grim box is sorry evidence that the level of design quality will vary widely in the Cityfront development, despite guidelines. The sixty-one-story tower, Cityfront's first major residential project, is crudely detailed and faced with precast concrete panels in dissonant shades of rust and brown. Worst of all, it occupies one of the development's most prominent sites.

76 Cityfront Place

400, 440, & 480 N. McClurg Ct.
1991, Gelick Foran Assocs.

A mid-rise tower of thirty stories and a pair of linked twelve-story structures are Cityfront's second major residential development, and a welcome improvement on their predecessor. Although the tower-on-a-podium composition of the mid-rise is a faux pas in this pedestrian-friendly context, the public plaza formed by the lower buildings more than compensates for it. A grand staircase leads to a terrace whose west section features a long, low fountain and glorious views of the skyline. To the east, a curving section like the prow of a boat provides a good perch for people-watching at North Pier.

77 Centennial Fountain

McClurg Ct. at the Chicago River
1989, Lohan Assocs.

This monument honors the centennial of the Metropolitan Water Reclamation District, the agency charged with ensuring a constant supply of healthy drinking water. The summit of the stepped granite pavilion represents the eastern continental divide (located just southwest of Chicago), with water flowing east

to the Atlantic Ocean and west to the Gulf of Mexico. During the day, in season, a water cannon shoots an eighty-foot arc of water across the river every hour.

78 Sheraton Chicago Hotel & Towers

301 E. North Water St.
1992, Solomon Cordwell Buenz & Assocs.

This enormous but well-articulated convention hotel anchors the southwest corner of the Chicago Dock & Canal property. Automobile access is from the north; to the south the hotel opens onto a river esplanade linking it with the rest of Cityfront Center. The public spaces, which include the city's largest ballroom, are surprisingly warm and welcoming, with large windows taking advantage of the river views.

NBC Tower

79 NBC Tower at Cityfront Center

454 N. Columbus Dr.
1989, Skidmore, Owings & Merrill

Chicago's most unabashedly derivative postmodern skyscraper is redolent of New York's Rockefeller Center in its streamlined verticality and of the Tribune Tower in its borrowed buttresses. It is probably Chicago's most popular postwar building—except among those architects who see it as the ultimate betrayal of the modernism once so vigorously championed by SOM.

RIVER NORTH

Blue Thistle Flower Market
May
Fry
St John Cantius
Carpenter
81
82
83
Empire Cooler Service
84
Chicago
River West Plaza
77
Chicago Academy for the Arts
Superior
78
700 N Green
Ogden
Aberdeen
Morgan
Huron
Sangamon
River West 2
80
79
River West Lofts
Milwaukee
CTA O'Hare (Blue) line
Peoria
Green
Halsted
Huron
Erie
Kennedy Expwy I-90/94

JOINS MAIN MAP

El...
72
Sewa... Pa...
Cabrini Extension
69
St M...
70 **William Green H...**
north of Division...
west of Larrabe...

Sedgwick

74
Larrabee
Cambridge
Cabrini Homes
Hudson
68
Chicago

Chicago Tribune Freedom Center
76
75
73
Montgomery Ward & Co

NORTH BRANCH OF

JOINS INSET MAP

Urban West Associates Bldg
← To I-90/94
THE
Wallace Computer Services
86
85
Salvation Army
67
Halsted
Grand

CHICAGO RIVER

Kingsbury
66
John Sexton & Co

6 **Driehaus Financial Services**
7 **R.H. Love Galleries**
8 **American College of Surgeons**
9 **Chez Paul**
10 **Episcopal Church Center**
11 **National Congress of Parents & Teachers**

37 **802-812 N Dearborn**
38 **Fewkes Tower**
39 **Houses for Newberry Estate**
40 **Newberry House**
41 **Tooker House**
42 **Washington Square**
43 **Scottish Rite Bodies**
44 **Taylor House**
45 **Carpenter House**
46 **Scottish Rite Cathedral**

River Cottages
89
87 Kinzie St Bridge

Fulton House
88

River North is one of Chicago's newest neighborhoods, created from one of its oldest. It covers the territory west of N. Michigan Ave. and north of the towers that bank the riverfront. The area has the city's most numerous and prominent examples of the conversion of underutilized industrial property to commercial, recreational, and residential use.

The poorest part of the city when incorporated in 1837, River North was the site of Chicago's first industries; of the city's first railroad line, which ran down Kinzie St.; and of its first slum, an Irish ghetto near the fork of the north branch. In the late 1850s three bridges—at Rush St., Erie St., and Grand Ave.—established the first stable links between the North Side and the rest of the city. From then on the area's role as the city's industrial district expanded, with the river and the rail lines attracting more factories, warehouses, and lumber and brick yards. Miles of frame cottages soon appeared to house the neighborhood's laborers.

In an exception to this pattern of land use, an exclusive residential enclave emerged north of Grand Ave. along Rush and adjacent streets. Leading citizens, including many members of the McCormick reaper clan, established estates here on quarter-block parcels. The city's oldest park, Washington Square, was a developer's creation to stimulate upscale residential expansion north of Chicago Ave.; a legacy of this venture is the deviation of the city's grid in the surrounding blocks.

The 1871 Fire devastated the residential portions but left the lumber yards and industries untouched. Rebuilding followed the old patterns, with luxury neighborhoods east of La Salle St. and ethnic enclaves—first Irish and Swedish, later Italian—to the west. After 1900, however, factory construction spread northward and eastward from the river edges and gradually turned poor neighborhoods into slums.

The opening of the Michigan Avenue Bridge in 1920 was the coup de grace that sent everything west of the Magnificent Mile into a decline. As grand mansions were subdivided into rooming houses, the residential area near the Water Tower briefly became a Left Bank bohemia known as Tower Town. Washington Square, dubbed Bughouse Square, became a lively forum for free speech. The slums to the west were razed beginning in the 1940s for the enormous public housing complex now known as Cabrini-Green. Industries in the southwest corner gradually closed or moved their operations elsewhere.

The transformation of the area began in the late 1970s, when artists and gallery owners converted former warehouses into inexpensive, light-filled living and working spaces. As in other cities, the artists' settlement raised real estate values and made the area decreasingly affordable for the occupants. Boutiques, trendy restaurants, and luxury apartments have edged out studios and galleries as the main attraction. Offices and hotels followed, especially in the southeast corner of the area, expanding the Loop northward and Michigan Ave. westward. The former residential enclave around Rush and Dearborn streets has kept its small scale with conversion of houses to small office buildings. Much undeveloped land remains just north of the riverfront skyscrapers, mostly in the form of surface parking lots. The area west of the north branch of the Chicago River has recently been dubbed River West and is a popular, less-expensive location for galleries and lofts.

The character of River North is still most strongly shaped by the long ranks of former industrial buildings. Imaginative conversions have kept the structures viable for new uses, and much new construction has retained the low scale and simple materials of these old buildings.
—Mary Alice Molloy

Buildings north of the river are included in the Loop chapter.

◼ 420 N. Wabash Ave.
Converted 1983, Pappageorge Haymes

One of the city's best-designed loft conversions creatively uses negative space by inserting a second skin of glass and metal behind the partially hollowed-out brick facade.

◼ IBM Self Park
401 N. State St.
1974, George Schipporeit

A delicate screen of vertical, self-weathering Cor-Ten fins conceals intricate scissor ramps and space for 800 cars. The gentle curve of the Wabash Ave. elevation has a sculptural quality.

◼ 515 N. State St.
1990, Kenzo Tange; Shaw & Assocs., coordinating archs.

Modernism is alive and well in this strong opening statement in the redevelopment of almost twelve acres controlled by the American Medical Association. The sculptural glass-and-aluminum curtain wall building creates a distinctive top with a four-story cutout near its summit. The leftover wedge of space houses mechanical equipment.

◼ Medinah Temple
600 N. Wabash Ave.
1913, Huehl & Schmid

Built for the Shriners to host conventions, circuses, and concerts, it displays the Arabic motifs that lent exoticism to the organization's rituals. The textured brickwork is laid in an unusual variety of Flemish bond, with clustered stretchers forming both stretchers and headers. Huehl & Schmid created scores of fanciful Shriners auditoriums; this is one of their largest and best-preserved.

◼ Steve Foley Cadillac (Cadillac Building)
630 N. Rush St.
1948, Victor L. Cham

Just off the Magnificent Mile (which prohibited auto dealerships), this showroom pays streamlined respects to its product and location. Note the chevron-patterned spandrels on Rush St.

◼ Driehaus Financial Services (Ransom R. Cable House)
25 E. Erie St.
1886, Cobb & Frost
Renovated 1992, John Victor Frega Assocs.

This house introduced to Chicago such Richardsonian design elements as rock-faced ashlar (here of Kasota stone), the slightly battered foundation, the low-sprung triple arches of the corner entry, and encrustations of neo-Byzantine carving. The medieval coach house is a superb complement.

Medinah Temple

R. H. Love Galleries

7 R. H. Love Galleries (Samuel M. Nickerson House)
40 E. Erie St.
1883, Burling & Whitehouse

The sedate sandstone facade conceals an opulent palace with alabaster, onyx, and twenty-seven varieties of marble. The excessive weight required a perfectly level parquet base set into hardpan, or compacted clay, and four parallel brick walls, each about two feet thick.

8 American College of Surgeons—John B. Murphy Memorial Auditorium
50 E. Erie St.
1922–1926, Marshall & Fox

This auditorium-library was intended as the center of a complex devoted to postgraduate medical education. It is modeled remarkably closely on the Chapelle de Notre-Dame de Consolation in Paris (1900, Albert Guilbert), including the central street-level door and the curving stairs to the pillared and porticoed upper entrance, with its bronze doors by Tiffany Studios.

9 Chez Paul (Robert Hall McCormick House)
660 N. Rush St.
1875, architect unknown

Built for the brother of the reaper's inventor, Cyrus H. McCormick, this was once at the heart of McCormickville, a neighborhood dominated by massive homes of family members. L. Hamilton McCormick's Renaissance palazzo at 631 N. Rush is visible above the roofline of a 1950 addition to what is now Lawry's Restaurant.

10 St. James Cathedral—Episcopal Church Center
65 E. Huron St.
1969, James W. Hammond & Peter Roesch

This scaled-down version of a steel-and-glass skyscraper has forty-five-foot clear spans within.

11 National Congress of Parents & Teachers
700 N. Rush St.
1954, Holabird & Root & Burgee

Rich materials and spare lines mark this incredibly well preserved 1950s classic. The facade sculptures by Milton Horn (now inside the large window on Rush St.) represent the Teacher, the Mother, and the Father.

12 Episcopal Cathedral of St. James
N. Wabash Ave. at E. Huron St.
*1857, Edward J. Burling
Rebuilt 1875, Burling & Adler*

Cathedral of St. James

*Chapel of St. Andrew 1913,
Bertram Grosvenor Goodhue
Memorial narthex 1928, Goodhue
Assocs.
Restored 1985, Holabird & Root*

The stenciled nave, a chorus of color, is one of the nation's finest Victorian interiors. It was designed by Edward Neville Stent, a student of William Morris, in 1888. The church tower still bears the scars of the Great Fire.

13 La Casita Court Apartments
747 N. Wabash Ave.
1929, Richard E. Schmidt, Garden & Erickson

A rare reminder of the area's Left Bank atmosphere, this urbane limestone building with Art Deco–patterned spandrels features French doors opening onto balconettes. The entry on Wabash Ave. appears unaltered.

14 Hotel St. Benedict Flats
42–50 E. Chicago Ave./801 N. Wabash Ave.
1882, James J. Egan

This is a rare and prominent example of the early years of the "flat craze" (1881–1893), when apartments were marketed to the upper middle class as "French flats." It uses Second Empire elements to resemble attached houses.

Hotel St. Benedict Flats

Chapel of St. James

🔢 The Chicagoan
750 N. Rush St.
1990, Solomon Cordwell Buenz & Assocs.

This "lipstick building" is oval with octagonal bays at opposite comers, allowing six "comer" apartments per floor and living rooms with 180° views.

🔢 Archbishop Quigley Preparatory Seminary & Chapel of St. James
831 N. Rush St.
1919, Zachary T. Davis

The seminary building on Rush and Chestnut Sts. is Flamboyant Gothic, with energetic stonework throughout; the chapel on the southwest comer is modeled after the mid-thirteenth-century Sainte-Chapelle in Paris. Like that building, the chapel was conceived as an armature for a dazzling display of stained glass, executed in thousands of pieces of antique English glass by Robert T. Giles.

🔢 Barneys New York
25 E. Oak St.
1992, Peter Marino & Assocs.

This is an elegant, understated backdrop for the unusual window displays for which the flagship store in New York is famous.

🔢 Esquire Theatre
58 E. Oak St.
1938, Pereira & Pereira

Renovated 1990, Gelick Foran Assocs.

This streamlined and gracious cinema once served matinee tea and offered art exhibits. Now, chopped, diced, shopping-malled, and multiplexed, it shows six flicks at once and contains a bank and two-story commercial space.

🔢 Green Bay Triangle Shelter/Mariano Park
Rush St., State St., and Bellevue Pl.
1900, Birch Burdette Long

In delicately colored polychrome terra-cotta the hardy, humble morning glory climbs the columns and blooms on the capitals of this simple Prairie School park shelter.

🔢 Newberry Plaza
1030–1050 N. State St.
1975, Ezra Gordon–Jack M. Levin & Assocs.

Paired "stilts" support a concrete apartment tower above a three-level brick base for commercial space and parking. Town houses perch high above the Oak St. side.

🔢 10 W. Elm St.
1928, B. Leo Steif

With chevrons, zigzags, and fancifully imagined plant and animal forms, a group of French terra-cotta modelers brought a vivid new decorative vocabulary to

10 W. Elm St.

Chicago. This high-rise apartment is clothed at top and bottom in the pastel decorative essays of Edouard Chassaing and his colleagues at the Northwestern Terra Cotta Company. He was one of six sculptors imported by the company in 1927 after the Exposition Internationale des Arts Décoratifs et Industriels Modernes (1925) in Paris. In contrast to the magisterial streamlining of Holabird & Root and Graham, Anderson, Probst & White, here is the brash side of the late 1920s.

22 Biggs Restaurant (John DeKoven House)
1150 N. Dearborn St.
1874, Edward J. Burling

This imposing Second Empire house has elaborate window surrounds and the original wrought-iron roof cresting and stoop railing.

23 Palette & Chisel Academy of Fine Art (William Waller House)
1012 N. Dearborn St.
1874, architect unknown

A relic of post-Fire residential grandeur, this Italianate mansion retains its principal features under the care of the academy, founded in 1895 under the sponsorship of sculptor Lorado Taft.

24 Chestnut Place Apartments
850 N. State St.
1982, Weese, Seegers, Hickey, Weese

A vicarious trip to Florence awaits tenants in their private lobby, whose painted walls (by Richard Haas) evoke San Miniato al Monte. Bands of brick, dark at street level and lighter above, delineate each floor.

25 Edwin S. Hartwell Houses
14–16 E. Pearson St.
1885, Julius H. Huber
Renovated 1980, Bauhs & Dring

Mirror-image town houses feature terra-cotta portrait rondelles of Hartwell's son and daughter, for whom these houses were built.

26 Frank Schofield House
18–20 E. Pearson St.
1934, Flora Schofield; Eugene B. Reiner, supervising arch.

Designed by an artist, this simple but lively building has garages and an exhibition room on the ground floor, her studio and family's living quarters on the second floor, and a top-floor studio for her son. The facade has the handcrafted charm of Sol Kogen's work on W. Burton Pl., with mottled bricks, multicolored tiles, and a copper parapet.

27 Holy Name Cathedral
735 N. State St.
1875, Patrick C. Keeley
Renovated 1890–1893, Willett & Pashley
Addition 1914, Henry J. Schlacks
Remodeled 1969, C. F. Murphy Assocs.

Although not the archdiocese's most beautiful building, it is one of the hardiest and most embellished. Brooklyn architect Keeley was a very successful if unimaginative church specialist who usually relied on formula,

Tree Studios

which is Gothic here. Schlacks's ambitious changes moved the apse and inserted an additional fifteen feet of nave.

28 Lambert Tree Studios
601–623 N. State St.
1894, Parfitt Bros.; Bauer & Hill; and Hill & Woltersdorf
Addition 1912, 12–16 E. Ohio St., Hill & Woltersdorf
Addition 1913, 7 E. Ontario St., Hill & Woltersdorf

Built to entice out-of-town artists working at the Columbian Exposition to remain in Chicago, the Studios comprise ground-floor shops with large windowed studios above. The atmosphere is a cross between a college dormitory and a commercial studio. Hidden from view is a charming rear court created by the two additions and the rear wall of the Medinah Temple. The State St. storefronts are remarkably well preserved.

29 Harry Weese & Associates
10–20 W. Hubbard St.
1883, Stephen V. Shipman
Converted 1975, Harry Weese & Assocs.

These quintessential examples of investor-built industrial lofts have interior brick walls twenty feet apart spanned by wood floors and plain, non-loadbearing facades. Weese, an early and strong Chicago preservationist, adapted the building for his own and other architects' offices.

30 Harry Caray's (Chicago Varnish Co.)
33 W. Kinzie St.
1900, Henry Ives Cobb

This "quoin bank" is filled with Dutch Renaissance exuberance.

31 Courthouse Place (Cook County Criminal Courts Building)
54 W. Hubbard St.
1892, Otto H. Matz
Renovated 1986, Solomon Cordwell Buenz & Assocs.

The Romanesque Revival mass, with more history than artistry, has a lavish if less than authentic lobby.

32 Hard Rock Cafe
63 W. Ontario St.
1985, Tigerman, Fugman, McCurry
Commonwealth Edison Substation
Southwest corner, Dearborn and Ontario Sts.
1989, Tigerman, Fugman, McCurry

It's the T-shirts and the decor that draw the tourists, not the Tuscan proportions and neo-Palladian windows. These elements were meant to identify the building with an adjacent Commonwealth Edison substation that proved to be scheduled for demolition. The replacement substation was then designed to respond to the Hard Rock Cafe, reusing the original's medallions, plaque, and wrought-iron fence.

33 Excalibur (Chicago Historical Society)
632 N. Dearborn St.
1892, Henry Ives Cobb

Vigorous and picturesque, this fine Richardsonian Romanesque edifice housed the city's oldest cultural institution for over thirty-five years before sheltering a Moose lodge, a school of design, a recording studio, and several nightclubs. Admiringly called a "pyramidal pile of brownstone" by an 1890s critic, this behemoth conveys a stability that belies its checkered past.

Excalibur

34 The Raleigh
650 N. Dearborn St.
1891, architect unknown
Top-floor remodeling 1912,
architect unknown
Renovated 1990, Berger & Assocs.

With its serpentine stone skin, this was one of the more colorful hotels to open in anticipation of the World's Columbian Exposition.

35 Asbury Plaza
750 N. Dearborn St.
1981, George Schipporeit

The intriguing geometry, which gives this concrete high rise a different massing from every angle, also serves to reduce its bulk and maximize the lake views.

36 Victor F. Lawson YMCA House
30 W. Chicago Ave.
1930–1934, Perkins, Chatten & Hammond

Intact if timeworn, this limestone-and-brick skyscraper emulates more lavish office buildings of the period. The Art Deco ornament includes spandrels with low-relief athletes above the main entrance. A second-floor drawing room preserves its Deco fireplace, paneling, and etched-glass doors.

37 802–812 N. Dearborn St.
early 1870s, architects unknown

These well-preserved Italianate row houses have neo-Grec ornament on the low buildings to the south and lavish Second Empire trim on the four-story north buildings.

38 John Fewkes Tower
55 W. Chestnut St.
1967, Harry Weese & Assocs.

Fenestration is everything here. Eight-inch masonry walls alternate with thirty-story strips of trapezoidal bay windows and corners chamfered with slim windows. The windows even prompted a trapezoidal silhouette for interior partitions.

39 Houses for the Newberry Estate
827–833 N. Dearborn St.
40 Newberry House (Grant's Seminary for Young Ladies)
839 N. Dearborn St.
1878, Frederick H. Waescher

Although constructed as a set, the row houses have incised ornament that only hints at the Frank Furness–style detailing evident on the corner building's compressed columns and angled bay. The wall in front of 827–831 includes portrait rondelles from Adler & Sullivan's demolished Schiller Building. Waescher was the Newberry estate's architect for over a decade, specializing in heavy structures such as warehouses and factories.

41 Robert N. Tooker House
863 N. Dearborn St.
1886, Jenney & Otis

One of the few remnants of the two-year Jenney-Otis partnership has a two-tone rosy granite

Newberry House (see description on page 129)

facade. Tooker Place, the adjacent alley, was the site of the Dill Pickle Club, a 1920s hangout for local bohemians and denizens of Bughouse Square.

42 Washington Square

Chicago's oldest park was donated to the city in 1842 by Orsamus Bushnell as the centerpiece of his subdivision of the blocks bounded by State, Chicago, Division, and La Salle streets. By the 1890s it was a genteel place of crossing walks, benches, and a central fountain. After 1900, as the buildings to the east were acquired by the Masonic Oriental Consistory, and as other homes in the area were divided into rooming houses, the square became "the outdoor forum of garrulous hobohemia" known as Bughouse Square. The city now leases it to the Chicago Park District with the stipulation that the square remain usable as a public forum. Accordingly, in 1985 the dilapidated fountain was replaced by a raised concrete platform used for concerts and annual debates sponsored by the Newberry Library.

43 Scottish Rite Bodies (John Howland Thompson House)
915 N. Dearborn St.
1888, Cobb & Frost

Superb masonry design, second only to that on H. H. Richardson's Glessner House, patterns the reddish brown Lake Superior sandstone, which provides rich texture but never overwhelms with massiveness. The balanced but asymmetrical bays on the Delaware Pl. elevation, the steeply pitched slate roof of gables and turrets exuberantly outlined in copper, and the tripartite entrance separated by bundled columns with rock-faced lintels below a handsome panel of foliate diaperwork all combine to demonstrate what can happen in an inspired partnership.

44 George H. Taylor House
919 N. Dearborn St.
1895, Treat & Foltz
45 George B. Carpenter House
925 N. Dearborn St.
1891, Treat & Foltz

These neighboring houses are a lesson in shifting tastes. The rough stonework on portions of the Carpenter House seems to be peeled away to reveal Georgian Revival forms like those of the Taylor House.

46 Scottish Rite Cathedral
(Unity Church)
929 N. Dearborn St.
1867, Theodore Vigo Wadskier
Rebuilt 1873, Burling & Adler
South Tower 1882, Frederick B. Townsend

The original structure with a matched set of towers, touted as one of the grandest of the city's Joliet limestone churches, lost all of its wooden portions in the 1871 Fire. Rebuilding within

Newberry Library

the original walls gave Dankmar Adler his first experience with acoustical design by installing raked seating. The light color of the entry is a sprayed-on attempt to thwart melting stone.

47 Newberry Library
60 W. Walton St.
1890–1893, Henry Ives Cobb
Addition 1981, Harry Weese & Assocs.

The "uncommon collection of uncommon collections" provided for in the will of Walter Loomis Newberry (1804–1868) has an impressive housing whose original building is only half as deep as what Cobb intended. The jagged lines where the addition was to have picked up are visible on the side elevations. Cobb was asked to abandon his partnership with Charles S. Frost to devote full attention to this commission. The facade, which centers on a triple-arched entrance inspired by the twelfth-century church of Saint-Gilles-du-Gard, is attributed to Cobb's employee Louis C. Mullgardt. The interior plan was conceived by the Newberry's first librarian, William F. Poole.

In the addition, whose brickwork hints at the arches of the original, even the walls and their plenum spaces are part of the mechanical system, which provides climate-controlled storage for twenty-one miles of books, maps, and manuscripts. The replicated chandelier in the restored lobby has bulbs that point down-

ward to prove that this was one of Chicago's first electrified buildings.

48 Burlingham Building
1000 N. Clark St.
1883, Alfred Smith
Two-story addition 1897, Alfred Smith

A cast-iron corner turret, bays that feature cast-iron piers, slate spandrels, and colored window glass constitute an elaborate array of Queen Anne details. The bays have unusual proportions, with the central window narrower than those to the side.

49 Cosmopolitan National Bank of Chicago
(Cosmopolitan State Bank)
801 N. Clark St.
1920, Richard E. Schmidt, Garden & Martin

In 1921 *American Architect* called it "a fine example of unfashionable bank designing" in notable contrast to the Classical temples being erected everywhere else. Especially praiseworthy were the large, unbroken wall surfaces, simple and severe lines, and rich and neutral colors.

50 Chicago-Clark Building
(Bush Temple of Music)
100 W. Chicago Ave.
1901, J. E. O. Pridmore

Unashamedly overblown and retardataire, it originally contained studios, practice rooms, rehearsal halls, and a large theater used by German performers.

51 516 N. Clark St./101 W. Grand Ave.
1872, 1873, architect unknown
1883, 1884, Cyrus P. Thomas
Renovated 1985, Swanke Hayden Connell

Beginning as a four-story grocery with lofts, it grew additions and extra stories until it became The Albany, an 1880s first-class apartment building with hardly a seam visible.

52 430 N. Clark St.
1872, architect unknown
53 432 N. Clark St.
Facade 1988, Florian-Wierzbowski
54 436 N. Clark St.
1872, William W. Boyington

A clever copy filled in a gap between two of the city's oldest business buildings.

55 John R. Thompson Building
350 N. Clark St.
1912, Alfred S. Alschuler

Renovated 1983, Metz, Train & Youngren

Known for years as the Commissary Building, it housed the general offices of the Thompson restaurant chain. Its creamy terra-cotta facade bespeaks good hygiene as well as Chicago School proportions.

North La Salle Blvd. Renovations

From the river north to its terminus at Lincoln Park, La Salle was an Avenue in the post-Fire years, when it was lined with elms and some of the city's finest residences. In 1930—already a little seedy and with commercial structures encroaching on its southern end—it became a Street, as trees, lawns, porches, and often entire facades were sliced off to widen the roadway by fourteen feet on each side. The project had been proposed as part of the 1909 Plan of Chi-

La Salle before widening

La Salle after widening

cago, to provide fast motor access to the Loop. Evidence of the widening can be seen along the length of the street, with the best examples of Art Deco facades on the east side between Chestnut and Delaware streets. An estimated $13 million in private funds was spent in 1978–1979 to revitalize the street after decades of unbenign neglect. The move led to another name change to indicate its upscale image: La Salle Boulevard.

Grommes & Ullrich

56 350 N. La Salle Blvd.
1990, Loebl, Schlossman & Hackl in consultation with Wojciech Lesnikowski

A conscious reuse of Chicago School elements articulates the skeleton frame with red brick and fills the bays with green glass. The curved and towered corners create internal variety in a very slim building.

57 442–444 N. La Salle Blvd.
Remodeled 1930, George F. Lovdall

The street widening cost this old warehouse its front, but in the remodeling it gained a dazzling polychrome Art Deco terracotta facade.

58 108–114 W. Illinois St. (Grommes & Ullrich Warehouse)
1901, Richard E. Schmidt

This former liquor distribution center, designed by Hugh M. G. Garden, expresses its structure boldly. Horizontality is emphasized by discontinuous recessed

piers and unusually broad Chicago windows.

59 Anti-Cruelty Society
157 W. Grand Ave.
1935, Leon Stanhope
Addition on La Salle Blvd. 1982, Stanley Tigerman Assocs.

The original sleek Art Moderne building displays its purpose with low-relief carvings of pet owners on either side of the door. The cheeky addition has a "doggie in the window" storefront.

60 Ohio House Motel
600 N. La Salle Blvd.
1960, Shayman & Salk

This may be the city's best-preserved expression of the colorful, angular, space-age design of the Sputnik era.

61 Moody Bible Institute
820 N. La Salle Blvd.
1937–1939, Thielbar & Fugard
62 Moody Bible Auditorium
840 N. La Salle Blvd.
1954, Fugard, Burt, Wilkinson & Orth

English Gothic styling gives a quasi-religious look to this high-

Anti-Cruelty Society

rise school. The auditorium was completed after a fifteen-year hiatus.

63 160 W. Wendell St. (James A. Sexton Public School)
1882, architect unknown

This typical Italianate school is remarkable for its age and unusual cornice.

64 North Branch Center (J. P. Smith Shoe Co.)
223 W. Erie St.
ca. 1896, architect unknown
Addition 1899, John H. Wagner
Renovated 1980, Jerome Brown

This large industrial building uses exposed metal mullions to open up the facade, a technique unpopular after miles of cast-iron facades melted in 1871.

65 430–440 N. Wells St. (Liquid Carbonic Acid Manufacturing Co.)
1903, Holabird & Roche
Renovated 1982, Hammond, Beeby & Babka

This loft building has the large windows, high ceilings, and open-beam construction that made this type of structure so popular for office conversions in the 1980s. The facade is unusually well detailed, with terra-cotta ornament and recessed courses of brick.

66 John Sexton & Co.
500 N. Orleans St.
1916, 1919, Alfred S. Alschuler

Built by a grocery and food-processing company for use as its office, manufacturing plant, and warehouse, this building represents the final stage in Chicago loft construction. Unlike the previous generation of lofts, the elevations not only reflect the various uses of the interior space but also identify stairwells, light shafts, and elevators. Appearance and image were so important that the addition, which added the easternmost 150 feet, matched the original building's load-bearing walls, even though the structural system was now reinforced concrete.

67 Wallace Computer Services—Factory (Railway Terminal and Warehouse Co.)
444 W. Grand Ave.
1909, Nimmons & Fellows

The self-banding at the base and top, also reflected in the stone capitals, is tantamount to this firm's signature.

This stretch of Orleans St. north to Division is best seen from the elevated train or a car.

68 Chicago Housing Authority—Frances Cabrini Homes
Chicago Ave., Larrabee St., Oak St., and Hudson Ave.
1942, Henry Holsman, George Burmeister, Maurice B. Rissman, Ernest A. Grunsfeld, Jr., Louis R. Solomon, George M. Jones, Karl M. Vitzthum, I. S. Loewenberg and Frank A. McNally

69 Cabrini Extension
Division, Larrabee, Oak, and Orleans Sts.
1958, A. Epstein & Sons

John Sexton & Co.

Montgomery Ward Warehouse

⁊⁰ William Green Homes
Division and Larrabee Sts.,
Clybourn and Ogden Aves.
1962, Pace Assocs.

One of Chicago's largest and
most notorious public housing
complexes, now comprising
3,600 apartments, began with
two- and three-story buildings
that are little more than unadorned loaf-shaped masses
tightly packed onto sixteen acres.
Fifteen buildings of seven, ten,
and nineteen stories were added,
followed by eight buildings north
of the previous site. Boarded
windows in the upper stories of
the high rises attest to the use-
lessness of units that cannot be
reached by stairs when elevators
are not maintained.

⁊¹ St. Matthew United Methodist Church
1000 N. Orleans St.
1969, Skidmore, Owings & Merrill

A pastor seeking to expand
community programs in a very
depressed area admired the University of Illinois at Chicago, and
so engaged Walter Netsch to
apply his field theory to this
church. A series of rotated
squares constitutes the church,
fellowship hall, classrooms, and
two suites for day care. Sculptor
Richard Hunt's Cor-Ten cross
marks the church end of the site.

⁊² Seward Park Field House
375 W. Elm St.
1908, Dwight H. Perkins

The Prairie School tradition is
manifest in the clear, logical
expression and use of materials.
Sloping brick piers with metal
capitals support the wood knee
brackets, which in turn support
the overhanging eaves with their
exposed wooden rafters.

*Return to Chicago Ave. via Wells
St. rather than Larrabee St.*

⁊³ Montgomery Ward & Co.—Corporate Offices
535 W. Chicago Ave.
1974, Minoru Yamasaki & Assocs.
⁊⁴ Warehouse
604 W. Chicago Ave./800 N.
Larrabee St.
*1906–1908, Richard E. Schmidt,
Garden & Martin*
⁊⁵ Warehouse and Offices
619 W. Chicago Ave.
1930, Willis J. McCauley

Richard E. Schmidt was a master
of concrete construction, and
this warehouse is his most impressive achievement. It is best
seen from the river, whose contours it follows. The facades are
mostly the exposed edges of the
concrete frame and are unmis-
takably horizontal, celebrating the
building's 717-foot length. Details
are lost in the monochromatic
palette, but their quality and skillfully spare usage reward close
examination.

⁊⁶ Chicago Tribune Freedom Center
777 W. Chicago Ave. at North
Branch of Chicago River
1982, Skidmore, Owings & Merrill

Built on a site that includes railroad air rights, this sprawling structure houses the nation's largest newspaper printing and distribution facility.

77 River West Plaza (Devoe & Raynolds Co.)
770 N. Halsted St.
1902, Hill & Woltersdorf
Converted to offices 1989, Berger & Assocs.

A four-building office complex was made from former paint-making business buildings. The frontispiece, the two buildings at the Halsted-Chicago corner, acquired a glass link and an atrium inserted around the old elevator tower.

700 N. Green St.

78 700 N. Green St. (Koenig, Henning & Gaber Co.)
1877, architect unknown

Common brick walls set off with small windows, tie rods, and occasional touches of red brick characterize this furniture factory. John Koenig moved his mechanized operations here after having been burned out in the 1871 Fire, in order to be near riverfront lumber yards and railroads.

79 River West Loft Apartments (J. P. Smith Shoe Co.)
915–925 W. Huron St.
1912, Horatio R. Wilson & Co.
Huron St. addition 1919, Shankland & Pingrey
Converted 1987, Berger & Assocs.

This factory was built within three years of Albert Kahn's demonstration of the advantages of metal sash windows in Ford's Highland Park plant. The introduction of metal sash windows, covering fourteen-foot-wide areas in this case, changed the configuration of mullions and fenestration and the overall composition of factory facades. Vertical wall surfaces are merely thin piers rising from sidewalk to cornice; walls are embellished with very simple patterns of projecting and recessed brickwork. The building was dilapidated and underutilized when its conversion to apartment units sparked the revitalization of an area designated a slum.

80 River West 2 Condominiums
939 W. Huron St.
1991, Berger & Assocs.

This poured-in-place concrete building is a modern application of the old loft concept: concrete ceilings and columns, heating and air-conditioning ducts, and other industrial finishes are exposed. Stylistically the elevations call upon contemporary German and Japanese sources.

81 Blue Thistle Flower Market (White Tower Restaurant)
1060 W. Chicago Ave.
1930, L. J. Coleman

This was a local outpost of a chain that began in Milwaukee in 1926 selling two-inch hamburgers for five cents ("Buy a Bagful"). The shining white walls, tower over the door, and green trim are standard fare. The tile roof and clock are specialties of this house.

St. John Cantius

82 St. John Cantius Roman Catholic Church
813–817 N. Carpenter St.
1893–1898, Adolphus Druiding
Rectory *1901, architect unknown*
83 Chicago Academy for the Arts (St. John Cantius Parish School)
1010 W. Chicago Ave.
1903, Theodore Ostrowski, mason

These three buildings exhibit very different styles. The church is described in parish publications as "Romanesque Baroque"— perhaps meaning that the main elevation spans the history of round-arch styles. The Rectory's high mansard roof with gabled dormers shows the influence of S. S. Beman's Kimball House. The Parish School is a heavy-handed rendition of northern European Baroque.

84 Empire Cooler Service
(Paepcke-Leicht Lumber Co.)
940 W. Chicago Ave.
1906, Louis Guenzel

This small industrial building makes a bold statement with nontraditional stone ornament on a textured brick facade. Look above the roofline to see the tower of the Italianate house that it enveloped.

85 Salvation Army Thrift Store (Braun & Fitts Butterine Factory)
509 N. Union Ave.
1891, Furst & Rudolph
Addition and alterations 1917, Postle & Fischer
Alterations and remodeling 1947, Albert C. Fehlow
86 Urban West Associates Building
685 W. Ohio St.
Remodeling 1992, Keith Talbert & Jay Keller, Urban West Assocs.

These side-by-side examples of adaptive reuse were done forty-five years apart. The Salvation Army, as the client converting a margarine factory to institutional use, employed an Art Moderne seam of an elevator core and light well to wed the seven-story and five-story pieces of the Braun & Fitts structure. Talbert & Keller, as owner-architects of a

THE FAR SIDE   By GARY LARSON

In a tunnel under the Chicago River, a descendent of Mrs. O'Leary's cow follows her calling.

"The Official Explanation"

two-story heavy timber structure, slathered multicolored Dryvit on masonry bearing walls that had been wrecked by permanent imitation brick.

87 Kinzie Street Bridge
W. Kinzie St. at North Branch of Chicago River
1908, John E. Ericson, city eng.; Thomas G. Pihlfeldt, city bridge eng.

This bridge was known locally as a mild irritant, because of its low clearance for navigation and its narrow roadway. But it gained international notoriety on April 13, 1992, when a piece of the abandoned freight tunnel system below its protective pilings sprang a major leak, flooding Loop basements.

88 Fulton House (North American Cold Storage Co.)
345 N. Canal St.
1908, architect unknown
Converted 1981, Harry Weese & Assocs.
89 River Cottages
357–365 N. Canal St.
1988, Harry Weese & Assocs.

Sailor Weese's enthusiasm for riverfront living manifested itself in these very different projects. Fulton House's windows are carved out of the thick walls of an insulated warehouse. At the opposite end of the scale—and style—spectrum are River Cottages' futuristic facades adorned with porthole windows.

SOUTH LOOP

Post Office

Van Buren

Wacker

Franklin

60

CTA Congress/Douglas (Blue)

61

Greyhound Bus Terminal

Harrison

59

US Customs House

SOUTH BRANCH OF THE CHICAGO RIVER

Wells

Polk

Continental Bank Technical Center

River City

58

53

57

Canal Center

Taylor

56

Chicago Fire Academy

DeKoven

South Loop Marketplace

Roosevelt

United Parcel Service

54

55

Maxwell

Jefferson

Clinton

Canal

14th Pl

25 Columbia College
   Wabash Campus
26 Harrison Hotel
27 Jones Commercial
   High School
28 South Loop Club

39 Lakeside Loft Apts
40 Dearborn Station Galleria
41 Donohue Bldg
42 Donohue Annex
43 Second Franklin Bldg
44 Printers Square
45 Grace Place
46 Transportation Bldg
47 Pontiac Bldg
48 Terminals Bldg
49 Mergenthaler Lofts
50 Old Franklin Bldg
51 Hyatt on Printer's Row

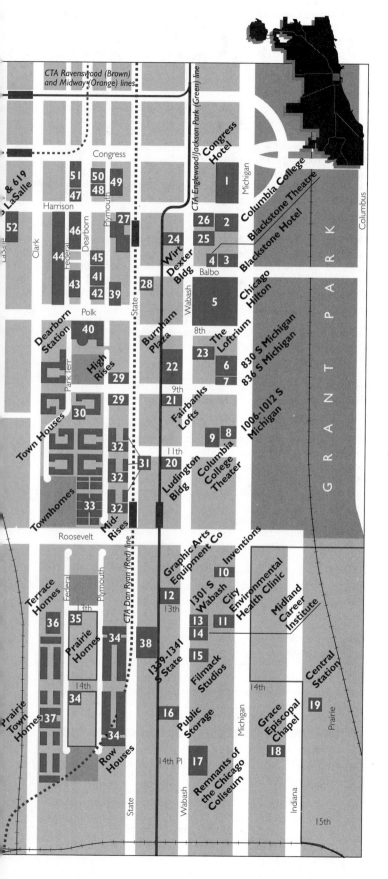

F ashionable apartments fill the shells of former industrial buildings, luxurious single-family houses cover abandoned railroad land, and a mixed-use complex with a marina hugs the banks of the Chicago River's south branch. Commercial uses thrive in computerized back-office operations for downtown businesses. The South Loop offers wonderfully diverse examples of changing land-use patterns on the fringes of the central city.

For decades the area was dominated and divided by miles of railway trackage. Along the lakefront, the Illinois Central Gulf Railroad tracks stretched as far north as the mouth of the Chicago River at what is now Illinois Center. Other tracks converged at the four depots clustered at the Loop's south edge. They carried freight as well as passengers, and printing industries sprang up just north of the Dearborn Station to take advantage of this proximity.

As trucks and planes superseded trains after World War II, vast tracts of land became available for development, but the question of by whom and for what purpose was subject to continuing debate. Municipal government skirted the issue by drawing up master plans for every area except the central city. Concerned about the Loop's economic and cultural decline, a group of business leaders formed the Chicago Central Area Committee and, in 1973, proposed that the abandoned South Loop railyards be used for mixed-use development that would include abundant middle-class housing.

Dearborn Park, developed on that land, has been a success as a residential neighborhood but never met expectations for other uses. To the north, restaurants and shops were filling the ground floors of the former printers' buildings, which were gradually being converted to apartments starting in the late 1970s. Dearborn Park and the adjacent Printers Row offer contrasting models of urban living. The former is a self-contained residential enclave; the latter is very much part of the urban fabric.

In the early 1990s an ambitious scheme was announced for another self-contained urban environment on abandoned railway land. Central Station's first step is to extend the residential popularity of Dearborn Park to the east, forming a nucleus from which commercial and residential development will presumably radiate. This community is intended to link the lakefront attractions with the built-up city to the west.

Michigan and Wabash avenues are the missing links in the South Loop's redevelopment. The restoration of the enormous Hilton Hotel to its originally luxurious status was a powerful show of confidence in the area, but most buildings along Wabash Ave. continue to deteriorate. The success of Dearborn Park I led to the creation of another self-contained neighborhood, more affluent than the first, to the immediate south, but it has had little impact on the streets to the east. As living close to the central city becomes increasingly attractive to the middle and upper class, the South Loop seems likely to continue its metamorphosis from an industrial and transportation center to a fashionable residential neighborhood. It remains to be seen whether development will be confined to a series of enclaves gated and locked against the hazards of a dilapidated neighborhood, or whether Printers Row will serve as the model for imaginative restoration.
—Laurie McGovern Petersen

■ Congress Hotel
(Auditorium Annex)
520 S. Michigan Ave.
1893, Clinton J. Warren
1902, 1907, Holabird & Roche

Built as an extension of the Auditorium Hotel, the "Annex" was designed to harmonize with it, even though its steel frame made the arcaded windows anachronisms more appropriate to the Auditorium's load-bearing walls. The additions respected the original section, including the generous bay windows overlooking the lake, but without the arcades.

2 Columbia College
(Harvester Building)
600 S. Michigan Ave.
1907, Christian A. Eckstorm

Here is one of the most colossal cornices remaining on a Chicago high rise.

3 Blackstone Hotel
636 S. Michigan Ave.
1908, Marshall & Fox
4 Blackstone Theatre
60 E. Balbo Dr.
1910, Marshall & Fox

The elegance of this opulently roofed palace is shared by the adjacent theater.

Chicago Hilton

5 Chicago Hilton & Towers Hotel (Stevens Hotel)
720 S. Michigan Ave.
1922–1927, Holabird & Roche
Renovated 1986, Solomon Cordwell Buenz & Assocs.

Built to be the world's "largest and most sumptuous" hotel and designed in a "modification of the style of Louis 16th," this twenty-five-story behemoth contained 3,000 rooms—all of them outside rooms with private baths—plus a convention hall seating 4,000, an exhibition hall "equal in dimensions to the Coliseum," and a rooftop golf course. Because the number and size of the public rooms on the lower floors required the frequent displacement of loads throughout the steel framing system, fewer than half of the 300 columns on a typical floor extended from the basement to the attic. In some cases trusses ran through several stories and required that corridors be threaded through them.

Purchased by the War Department for use as a barracks in 1942, the Stevens changed hands several times until it was acquired in 1945 by Conrad Hilton, who renamed it in 1951. The renovated building now has 1,600 rooms as well as new parking and fitness facilities.

6 830 S. Michigan Ave.
(YWCA Hotel)
1894, John M. Van Osdel II

Despite considerable abuse, poor paint choices, and "modernization," it still has a delicate air, especially in its top-floor bays.

7 836 S. Michigan Ave.
(Crane Company Building)
1912, Holabird & Roche

This virtually intact Classical Revival version of the tripartite highrise formula lacks the Chicago School's vertically emphasized central shaft.

8 1006–1012 S. Michigan Ave.
1904, Edmund R. Krause

This highly refined office building features large amounts of glass set in Chicago windows as well as columns and beams that have been reduced to the minimum.

Columbia College—Theater Music Center

9 Columbia College— Theater Music Center
(Chicago Women's Club Building)
72 E. 11th St.
1929, Holabird & Roche

The building for the city's premier women's service club included a recital room, various clubrooms, and three floors of hotel rooms. The so-called "contemporary"—i.e., Art Deco—style was chosen to affirm the fifty-year-old club's youthful outlook.

Film Row
Wabash and Michigan Aves. from Roosevelt Rd. to W. 16th St.

For almost fifty years exhibitors who ran Chicago's 1,100 movie theaters came here for everything they needed: feature films, cartoons, short subjects, and coming-attractions trailers; movie projectors and sound heads; lobby posters, billboards, and still photographs; numbered tickets, popcorn, and candy; seats, canopies, carpeting, light bulbs for marquees—even dishes for premium nights. By the 1930s more than two dozen studios and independents were operating film exchanges here, mostly near 13th St. In the 1960s television changed the movie world, and neighborhood squalor began driving the exchanges elsewhere.

⑩ Inventions (Universal Pictures Film Exchange)
1234 S. Michigan Ave.
1947, architect unknown

This late film exchange replicates the Art Deco style of the earlier exchanges on Wabash Ave.

1306 S. Michigan Ave.

⑪ City of Chicago Environmental Health Clinic (Paramount Pictures Film Exchange)
1306 S. Michigan Ave.
1930, Anker S. Graven

A calm, sedate limestone skin serves as a backdrop to Art Deco ornament highlighting flowers—with no suggestion of things cinematic.

⑫ Graphic Arts Equipment Co. (Twentieth Century–Fox Film Exchange)
1260 S. Wabash Ave.
1939, Loebl & Schlossman

This brick-and-limestone exchange with a curved, recessed entrance was built simultaneously with its northern neighbor, which supplied Monogram Films.

⑬ 1301 S. Wabash Ave. (Universal Studios Film Exchange)
1937, Olsen & Urbain

This yellow brick structure features an intact, curving glass-block corner.

⑭ Midland Career Institute (Warner Brothers Film Exchange)
1307 S. Wabash Ave.
1929, Zimmerman, Saxe & Zimmerman

Integral zigzag brickwork rather than applied ornament lends interest to this Art Deco exchange.

⑮ Filmack Studios (Famous Players–Lasky Corporation Film Exchange)
1327 S. Wabash Ave.
1923, Rapp & Rapp

Despite filled-in windows, the glistening terra-cotta triumphal doorway conveys some of the exuberance of Rapp & Rapp's cinema palaces. Paramount Pictures' logo remains in one corner of the cornice.

⑯ Public Storage Rental Spaces (Central Market Furniture Building)
1414 S. Wabash Ave.
1912, Peter J. Weber

Pharaohs' heads and lotus flowers lend an Egyptian flavor to this otherwise straightforward exposition center built by paper bag manufacturer Lucius G.

Fisher. The carp in the shield above the central first-floor windows had already appeared on his Fisher Building.

17 Remnants of the Chicago Coliseum (Libby Prison Museum)
East side of S. Wabash Ave. at 14th Pl.
1889, Charles M. Palmer

Two walls of Lemont limestone and a "No Souvenir Hunting" sign are the remains of several profit-seeking schemes on this site. In 1888 Libby Prison, a Richmond, Virginia, warehouse that had held Union prisoners of war, was dismantled, reassembled in Chicago, encased in castellated stone walls, and opened as a Civil War museum. When interest waned, the prison was demolished, and some of its limestone casing was reused as the east facade of the Chicago Coliseum, site of prizefights, horse shows, and Republican nominating conventions. Except for these fragments, the Coliseum was demolished in 1983.

18 Grace Episcopal Church Chapel
1448 S. Indiana Ave.
1928–1931, Tallmadge & Watson

The chapel for the old St. Luke's Hospital (whose buildings include 1435–1447 S. Michigan Ave., 1908, Frost & Granger; and 1440 S. Indiana Ave., 1925, Charles S. Frost) is a diminutive version of the Gothic churches that became a mainstay of this firm after the demise of the Prairie School.

19 Central Station
S. Michigan Ave./S. Indiana Ave. east to Lake Shore Dr., between E. Roosevelt Rd. and E. 21st St.
Begun 1992

This $3 billion mixed-use project is to be built on land and air rights over existing railroad tracks. Burnham Place, the first phase of development, includes Park Row town houses (Fitzgerald Assocs.) along S. Michigan Ave. between Roosevelt Rd. and 13th St., and Harbor Square condominiums (Roy H. Kruse & Assocs.) along S. Michigan Ave. between 13th and 14th Sts.

20 Ludington Building
1104 S. Wabash Ave.
1891, Jenney & Mundie

This unusually well preserved high rise is one of the first all-steel structures, built at the same time as the Second Leiter Building, which has a steel-and-wrought-iron frame. In both, the exterior exactly reflects the form of the skeleton frame, and the demand for light is well satisfied.

21 Fairbanks Lofts (Fairbanks, Morse & Co. Building)
900 S. Wabash Ave.
1907, Christian A. Eckstorm

Ludington Building

This completely intact loft building has showrooms that are outlined in ornamental cast-iron trim and separated from the rest of the facade by a molded limestone sill.

Burnham Plaza

22 Burnham Plaza (YMCA Hotel)
828 S. Wabash Ave.
1916, Robert C. Berlin; James Gamble Rogers, consulting arch. Converted 1988, Schroeder Murchie Laya

The hotel provided simple and wholesome quarters at moderate cost. The small rooms, placed around two light wells, were completely gutted in the conversion to apartments. A penthouse and roof-deck and a new building containing theaters, commercial space, and a garage were constructed.

23 The Loftrium (Munn Building)
819 S. Wabash Ave.
1909, Christian A. Eckstorm

The cast-iron storefront is framed by handsome Sullivan-esque ornament. Above, the brick-sheathed frame is fully expressed, and wide windows light the interior.

24 Wirt Dexter Building
630 S. Wabash Ave.
1887, Adler & Sullivan

Fire damage and two added floors have somewhat obscured the intent, but you can still see how the firm was seeking to open up a facade and light the interiors. The central unit's cast-iron frame makes large windows possible on the main facade. Look to the rear, where perforated cast-iron braces were used for the same purpose.

25 Columbia College— Wabash Campus (Second Studebaker Building)
623 S. Wabash Ave.
1896, Solon S. Beman

Look past the added story (1941) and main-floor alterations to the strikingly modern structural expression and Gothic detailing.

26 Harrison Hotel
65 E. Harrison St.
1930, Alfred S. Alschuler

High-style Art Deco embellishments include voluptuous figures and stylized foliage.

27 William Jones Commercial High School
606 S. State St.
1965–1968, Perkins & Will

A skyscraper to house this secretarial and office training school was first suggested in 1909 by Dwight H. Perkins. The reinforced-concrete tower is connected by covered passageways with two-story auditorium and gymnasium buildings.

28 South Loop Club (East 7th Street Hotel)
1 E. Balbo Ave.
1930, Michaelsen & Rognstad

Behind the fire escapes is an Art Deco building with an intact entry floor and window surrounds of terra-cotta.

Enter the Dearborn Park community at 9th and State Sts. (the only vehicular access point) to tour the self-contained streets of Plymouth Ct. and S. Park Terr./Federal St.

Dearborn Park I
State to Clark Sts., Polk St. to Roosevelt Rd.
Master Plan *1974–1977, Skidmore, Owings & Merrill*
1979–1987, various architects

Dearborn Park grew out of SOM's comprehensive blueprint for the central city, drafted in 1973 for the Chicago Central Area Committee and exploiting the abandoned railyards immediately south of downtown.

The site was split into two parcels, with the twenty acres

north of Roosevelt Rd. to be developed first. The original scheme of high-density super-blocks was scaled down to a mixture of town houses, mid rises and high rises—a "suburb in the city"—with parks and heavily landscaped open space but no offices or entertainment complexes. Internal roads end in cul-de-sacs. In 1977 the design was parceled out to several architecture firms, with the first occupancies in 1979. Phase I was substantially complete by 1985, with just over 1,200 units, about half of them in mid-rise buildings.

Design guidelines specified white brick for the two-story town houses and red brick for all other buildings. Such cohesiveness as there may be relies on the abundant landscaping rather than a shared aesthetic. The tallest buildings, sited on the street perimeter, are centered on the landscaped spaces surrounding the town house clusters. The two **29 High Rises** (Ezra Gordon–Jack M. Levin & Assocs.) flank the 9th St. access road but fail to provide a significant gateway, serving only to create an inward-focused enclave. The **30 Two-Story Town Houses** (Hammond, Beeby & Babka) cluster around parking areas and are oriented toward private gardens that overlook shared green spaces. Stepped corner entrances and exterior corner columns are the main design

elements. The **31 Three-Story Town Houses** in turn enclose the courtyards formed by the **32 Mid-Rise Buildings** (Booth/Hansen & Assocs.). The **33 Townhomes of Dearborn Park** (Michael J. Realmuto), developed last, were intended as luxury housing, presaging the low-density, upmarket development of Phase II.

Dearborn Park II
State to Clark Sts., Roosevelt Rd. to W. 15th St.
Begun 1988

Phase II proceeded very differently from its predecessor. There is more parking, and buildings are no more than four stories high, with an abundance of luxury housing. The parcel lacks even minimal cohesiveness, with the variety of building types and architects making for something of a hodgepodge.

34 Row Houses, Metropolitan Mews, & Park Homes
1300 & 1400 blocks of S. State St.
1989–1992, Booth/Hansen & Assocs.

The properties east of Plymouth Ct. are organized formally in long rows around central green spaces, while the freestanding Park Homes are far more suburban and seem out of place.

Dearborn Park II Row Houses

35 Prairie Homes
1300 to 1356 S. Plymouth Ct.,
1301 to 1357 S. Federal St.
1992, Fitzgerald & Assocs.

Prairie School elements like brackets under hipped roofs and horizontal divisions of the facades make these the liveliest buildings, but the crowded siting and essentially vertical massing detract.

36 Terrace Homes
1328 & 1338 S. Federal St.
1993, Barton Assocs.

37 Prairie Town Homes
1342–1442 S. Federal St.,
1341–1443 S. Clark St.
1992, Roy H. Kruse

The Terrace Homes offer the unusual combination of two- or three-story town houses built over single-story flats, made possible by the twenty-two-foot width.

38 1339–1341 S. State St.
(Arthur Dixon Transfer Co. Truck Garage)
1921, Holabird & Roche

Making an admirable virtue of spareness, this handsome, flat brick facade adorned only with stepped detailing conceals a single wood-framed space lit from rooftop monitor windows.

Printing House District
The Dearborn St. Station was a source for paper and supplies and an easy route for outgoing publications, making Dearborn St. south from Jackson Blvd. a convenient center for the printing trades from the 1880s through the 1950s. Plymouth Ct. and Federal St. provided back doors for Dearborn St. buildings and were direct routes to the depot's loading docks. The widening of Congress St., called for in the 1909 Plan of Chicago, was finally accomplished (1945–1955) to create an expressway link. Construction destroyed twelve buildings on Dearborn St. and many others on adjacent streets, effectively separating everything south of Congress St. from the Loop. Rejuvenation began in the late 1970s, spurred by the development of the former railyards as Dearborn Park.

39 Lakeside Loft Apartments
(Lakeside Press Building)
731 S. Plymouth Ct.
*1897, 1902 (four north bays),
Howard Van Doren Shaw; Samuel A. Treat, assoc. arch.
Renovated 1986, Lisec & Biederman*

This exceptionally creative amalgam of traditional and nontraditional architectural detailing was Shaw's first nonresidential commission. It established his and owner R. R. Donnelley & Sons Co.'s reputations as creators of printing plants that are a joy to behold.

40 Dearborn Station Galleria
(Polk St. Station, also known as Dearborn St. Station)

Dearborn Station Galleria

47 W. Polk St.
1885, Cyrus L. W. Eidlitz
Reconstructed after fire, 1923,
architect unknown
Converted 1983, Kaplan/
McLaughlin/Diaz and Hasbrouck
Hunderman

Chicago's oldest train station is a U-shaped Romanesque building whose Italian brick tower closes the Dearborn St. vista. The tower is a replacement of a Flemish one, destroyed in a 1922 fire, which also took the building's hipped roofs. The reworked station, comprising a cleaned-up but historic north facade and a modern galleria to the south, acts as a transition between the renovated printing district and the new Dearborn Park development.

41 Donohue Building
711 S. Dearborn St.
1883, Julius Speyer
42 Donohue Annex
727 S. Dearborn St.
1913, Alfred S. Alschuler

This was the first major printers' structure in the district. The main portion exhibits the basic masonry construction system with punched window openings, one window per opening. It utilizes both Romanesque rustication and incised designs, and its slightly enhanced round-arched sandstone and granite entrance bay was originally topped with a tower. The simple and functional annex harmonizes with the original.

43 Second Franklin Building
720 S. Dearborn St.
1912, George C. Nimmons
Converted to apartments 1987,
Lisec & Biederman

Using the modified Prairie School style that characterized his factory and warehouse work, Nimmons incorporated colorful tilework designed by Oskar Gross depicting the history of printing. The sloped roofline, a frequent feature on factories of this era, permitted a very high top floor under an enormous skylight—helpful for hand binding.

Second Franklin Building

44 Printers Square (Borland Manufacturing Buildings)
700, 740, & 780 S. Federal St.
1909, 1912, and 1928, Frost &
Granger and successor firms
Converted to apartments 1983,
Louis Weiss

This series of simply detailed loft buildings was constructed in sections from the designs of one architect. It now has 356 apartments and underground parking.

45 Grace Place
637 S. Dearborn St.
1915, architect unknown
Renovated 1985, Booth/Hansen &
Assocs.

The second floor of this renovated printers' building contains a worship space encircled by an internal wall with pointed-arch windows. A skylight floods the altar with natural light.

46 Transportation Building
600 S. Dearborn St.
1911, Fred Prather
Rehabilitated 1980, Booth/Hansen
& Assocs.

Twenty bays wide but only four bays deep, this was designed to be built in sections and to have its great breadth broken regularly by vertical bands of roughened brickwork. The contrast is not enough to do the job. The rehabilitation of this building was crucial to the area's rejuvenation.

Pontiac Building

47 Pontiac Building
542 S. Dearborn St.
1891, Holabird & Roche
Renovated 1985, Booth/Hansen & Assocs.

An air of substance and repose emerges from this earliest extant Holabird & Roche skyscraper. The heavy corner piers rise from base to cornice, interrupted only by the shelf angles supporting each floor of brick sheathing; the windows are small and double-hung. The gently projecting oriels that span two bays are unique in the firm's work.

48 Terminals Building
(Ellsworth Building)
537 S. Dearborn St.
1892, John M. Van Osdel & Co.

Renovated 1986, Community Resources Corp.

A heavily rusticated rock-faced limestone base is balanced by the crisp modeling of the brick into vertical elements above.

49 Mergenthaler Loft Condominiums
(Mergenthaler Linotype Building)
531 S. Plymouth Ct.
1886, architect unknown
Renovated 1917, Richard E. Schmidt, Garden & Martin
Rehabilitated 1980, Kenneth A. Schroeder & Assocs.

This early example of a loft building converted to stylish apartments is also one of the best. The new work included the introduction of windows in colorful framing on the south wall and the incorporation of the shell of Tom's Grill, a former adjacent eatery, as a sculptural *objet trouvé*.

50 Old Franklin Building
525 S. Dearborn St.
1887, Baumann & Lotz

This printers' building demonstrates how, in an effort to provide light for detail work, architects began to group windows by using iron spandrels between brick piers and supporting them with cast-iron mullions. The lobby shows the beamed ceilings found in the loft apartments.

Mergenthaler Lofts

River City

51 Hyatt on Printers Row
(Morton Hotel)
500 S. Dearborn St.
Renovation and addition 1987,
Booth/Hansen & Assocs.
Duplicator Building
530 S. Dearborn St.
1886, Edward P. Baumann
Morton Building
538 S. Dearborn St.
1896, Jenney & Mundie

This hotel combined new construction with two old buildings. The Duplicator is a traditional loft structure; the Morton shows how classical elements, in the form of atlantes supporting the projecting bay, were supplanting the vigorous expression of skeleton construction that had characterized that firm's earlier commercial work.

52 601 & 619 S. La Salle St.
(Brock & Rankin Building)
North portion, 1901–1902;
Two-story addition, 1903; South
addition, 1909; Holabird & Roche

What looks like two attached buildings is one loft built during two phases of Holabird & Roche's work. The northern part has colored tiles set on angle; the southern part relies on brickwork, especially the "zippered" window surrounds.

53 River City
800 S. Wells St.
1986, Bertrand Goldberg Assocs.

The curves for which Goldberg's buildings are famous result here

in a complex form, a four-story base for a pair of S-shaped apartment buildings supported on concrete piers with penthouse towers above the rooflines. River Road, the combination corridor and atrium, has an array of monumental and undulating shapes softly lit from above. The stone wall at the east end is a remnant of a bridge built over the Baltimore & Ohio Railroad's tracks; south of Polk St. is Goldberg's copy of the original wall to the north.

54 South Loop Marketplace
(Soo Line Terminal, also known as Chicago Tunnel Co. Universal Freight Station No. 4)
501 W. Roosevelt Rd.
1913, H. Hauslinger

One of the few above-ground remnants of the Loop's freight tunnel system, this vast concrete depot was one of the four original stations that accepted small shipments for delivery throughout nearly sixty miles of the underground network. The facility operated as a standard railroad siding on its second level, where trains pulled up, and it received packages at sheltered docks at street grade. The tunnel company ceased operations entirely in 1959, and the building now accommodates a weekend flea market and acres of parking topside, where trains once pulled in.

55 United Parcel Service—
Distribution Center
1400 S. Jefferson St.
1965, Edward D. Dart

By the mid-1960s highly auto-
mated package handling had
helped the trucking industry to
supersede the archaic operations
of the Chicago tunnel system.
This center uses two conveyer
assemblies to sort parcels and
has a mid-floor control center
that employs a carousel with
giant pigeonholes. Separate loading docks and marshaling areas,
each with its own traffic control
station, are sheltered under second-floor office space and steel
sheds.

56 Chicago Fire Academy
558 W. DeKoven St.
*1960, Loebl, Schlossman &
Bennett*

Fire fighters are trained on the
site of the Patrick O'Leary barn,
where a cow allegedly kicked
over a lantern, setting off the
holocaust of 1871. The tall building is the drill hall, where train-
ees learn to operate snorkels,
manuever on fire escapes, and
open windows. The red glazed
brick is a backdrop for the
flame-shaped sculpture by Egon
Weiner.

57 Continental Bank
Technical Center
840 S. Canal St.
*Remodeled 1973, Metz, Train,
Olsen & Youngren*

A new skin, an atrium, and a
heliport were added to an old
distribution center to create a
heavy-duty computer and check-
processing facility with swift access to O'Hare Airport.

58 Canal Center (Northern
Trust Company Operations
Center)
801 S. Canal St.
*1990, Eckenhoff Saunders
Architects*

The length of the precast concrete facade is mitigated by a recessed glass-walled entrance on
Canal St. and by the terraces of
a cafeteria and a day-care center
on the eastern side.

59 United States Customs
House
610 S. Canal St.
*1932, James A. Wetmore, acting
supervising arch; Burnham Bros.
and Nimmons, Carr & Wright,
assoc. archs.*

Eagles hover on the parapets of
this sleekly massed, pristine government facility.

Central Post Office

Greyhound Bus Terminal

60 Central Post Office
433 W. Van Buren St.
1921, 1932, Graham, Anderson, Probst & White

It was designed to straddle the broad Congress St. projected in the 1909 Plan but not realized until decades after the building's completion. When opened this was the world's largest post office. With four large corner towers, the rectangular mass is further subdivided into base, shaft, and top; the verticality of uninterrupted piers and narrow windows somewhat mitigates the length. The Van Buren St. lobby is clad in cream marble with French glass and tile reliefs. Multistory postal operations require the heavy use of elevators and are regarded as inefficient; a new post office to the south by Knight Architects Engineers Planners will be completed in 1994.

61 Greyhound Bus Terminal
630 W. Harrison St.
1991, Nagle, Hartray & Assocs.

Drivers zooming past on the Eisenhower Expressway get an elevated view of this elegant essay in architectural engineering (structural design by Cohen-Barreto-Marchertas). The striking roof is suspended by steel supporting stays connected to ten slim vertical masts, whose upward sweep creates a taut, graceful contrast.

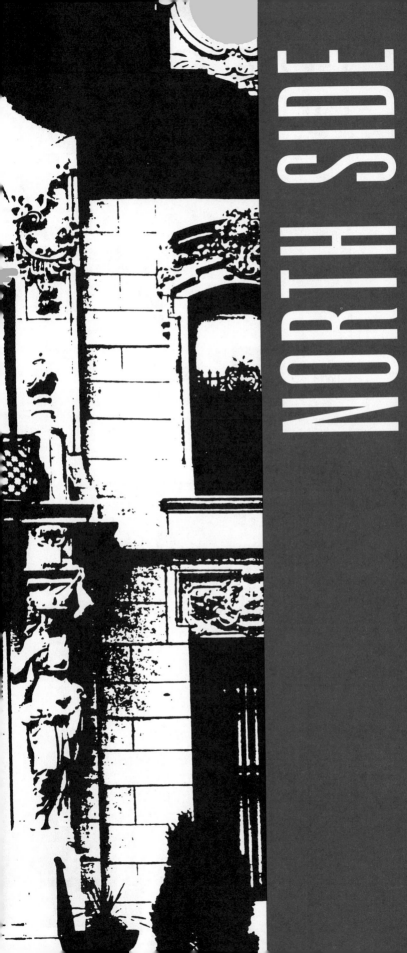

NORTH SIDE

GOLD COAST/ OLD TOWN

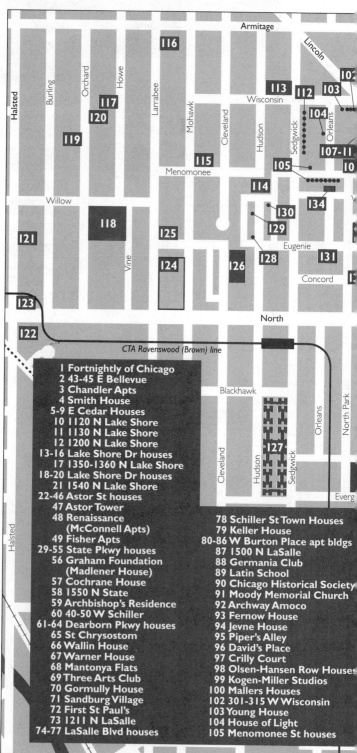

1 Fortnightly of Chicago
2 43-45 E Bellevue
3 Chandler Apts
4 Smith House
5-9 E Cedar Houses
10 1120 N Lake Shore
11 1130 N Lake Shore
12 1200 N Lake Shore
13-16 Lake Shore Dr houses
17 1350-1360 N Lake Shore
18-20 Lake Shore Dr houses
21 1540 N Lake Shore
22-46 Astor St houses
47 Astor Tower
48 Renaissance
    (McConnell Apts)
49 Fisher Apts
29-55 State Pkwy houses
56 Graham Foundation
    (Madlener House)
57 Cochrane House
58 1550 N State
59 Archbishop's Residence
60 40-50 W Schiller
61-64 Dearborn Pkwy houses
65 St Chrysostom
66 Wallin House
67 Warner House
68 Mantonya Flats
69 Three Arts Club
70 Gormully House
71 Sandburg Village
72 First St Paul's
73 1211 N LaSalle
74-77 LaSalle Blvd houses

78 Schiller St Town Houses
79 Keller House
80-86 W Burton Place apt bldgs
87 1500 N LaSalle
88 Germania Club
89 Latin School
90 Chicago Historical Society
91 Moody Memorial Church
92 Archway Amoco
93 Fernow House
94 Jevne House
95 Piper's Alley
96 David's Place
97 Crilly Court
98 Olsen-Hansen Row Houses
99 Kogen-Miller Studios
100 Mallers Houses
102 301-315 W Wisconsin
103 Young House
104 House of Light
105 Menomonee St houses

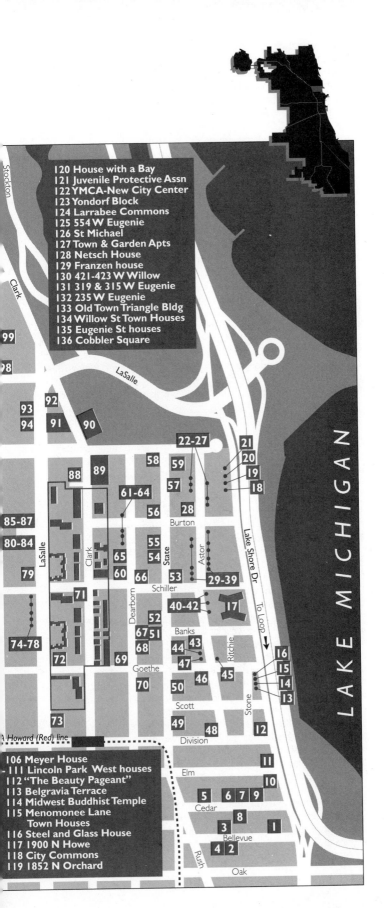

120 House with a Bay
121 Juvenile Protective Assn
122 YMCA-New City Center
123 Yondorf Block
124 Larrabee Commons
125 554 W Eugenie
126 St Michael
127 Town & Garden Apts
128 Netsch House
129 Franzen house
130 421-423 W Willow
131 319 & 315 W Eugenie
132 235 W Eugenie
133 Old Town Triangle Bldg
134 Willow St Town Houses
135 Eugenie St houses
136 Cobbler Square

Stockton

Clark

99
98

LaSalle

93
94
92
91
90

88
89
58
59
22-27
21
20
19
18

61-64
57
56
28
Burton

85-87
80-84
79
LaSalle
Clark
65
60
66
55
54
State
53
29-39
Astor

71
Schiller
40-42
17

52
67 51
68
Banks
Dearborn
44
43
47
Ritchie
16
15
14
13

74-78
72
69
Goethe
46
45
70
50

73
Scott
49
48
12

A Howard (Red) line
Division

106 Meyer House
- 111 Lincoln Park West houses
112 "The Beauty Pageant"
113 Belgravia Terrace
114 Midwest Buddhist Temple
115 Menomonee Lane
     Town Houses
116 Steel and Glass House
117 1900 N Howe
118 City Commons
119 1852 N Orchard

Elm
11
10

5
6 7 9
Cedar
8
3
Bellevue
1
4 2

Rush

Oak

Lake Shore Dr
To Loop
Stone

LAKE MICHIGAN

Throughout most of their history, the neighborhoods of the Gold Coast and Old Town presented a sharp contrast between rich and poor, elegance and squalor. Today, however, their demographics are surprisingly similar. While many Gold Coast mansions have been replaced by high rises or subdivided into smaller but still desirable apartments, a tidal wave of money has swept over the workers' cottages and flats of Old Town, many of which have been converted into expensive single-family residences or sold as "tear downs."

The streetscapes of the two communities are still worlds apart. Old Town is filled with charmingly restored cottages, row houses, and small flats as well as coach houses, many of which were built for Gold Coast residents. The Gold Coast, apart from its many modern high rises, has an abundance of mansions and large row houses. Along the Clark St./LaSalle Blvd. boundary between the two neighborhoods is that exemplar of 1960s redevelopment, Carl Sandburg Village, constructed as the Gold Coast's Maginot Line against the creeping disintegration of Old Town and points west.

Old Town, as one might guess, is the earlier community, although the entire area was not included in the city's 1837 charter. It was settled by German produce farmers, who were numerous enough to form St. Michael's parish in 1852. After the devastation of the Fire of 1871, wooden cottages sprang up to house the homeless. Most of the tiny, crudely built "relief shanties" are long gone, but many wooden cottages remain from the short period between the Fire and the northward extension of the city's strict building code in the 1874 fire ordinance. The area remained heavily Germanic throughout the following decades, and by 1900 North Ave. as far west as Halsted St. was known as German Broadway.

Industry, which located in the heart of the area as well as along the river, provided employment for many. Housing west of LaSalle Blvd., built for the working class and new immigrants, deteriorated in the twentieth century. By the 1940s most of the Germans had moved away, replaced by Italians, African-Americans, Asians, and, later, Hispanics.

Artists took advantage of depressed real estate values. In the 1920s Sol Kogen and Edgar Miller turned decrepit housing on Burton Pl. into masterpieces of folk art, and in the 1960s artists began buying and rehabilitating many of Old Town's small houses. Wells St. became the center of Chicago's counterculture, with head shops selling drug paraphernalia and psychedelic posters and record stores catering to flower children and the inevitable gawking tourists.

The massive urban renewal that resulted in the 1960s construction of Sandburg Village, together with the pioneering efforts of artists and architects, bolstered the area's reputation and effectively extended the Gold Coast west of its traditional boundaries. Apart from the Sandburg complex and a few tall buildings near the lake, the area has retained its low scale. Scattered urban renewal and private projects in the 1960s and 1970s were confined mostly to town houses and three- to four-story apartment buildings that respect the street's scale, although many critics find fault with the ubiquitous private garden that presents a blank brick wall to the street.

Rising land values in the 1980s resulted in the replacement of many early cottages by postmodern multibathroom extravaganzas whose overblown character or scale—if not both—is frequently jarring. But the area also has much exemplary new construction: town houses that extend welcoming stairways to the sidewalk, freestanding houses that echo the materials and styles of their more modest neighbors, and renovations that return buildings to their original character after decades of concealment beneath ugly siding materials. Old Town's projects span the careers of such well-known residential architects as Stanley Tigerman, Ben and Harry Weese, Larry Booth and Jim Nagle, from early town houses and renovations to large new houses.

The Gold Coast was created almost single-handedly by State St.

retail mogul Potter Palmer and his wife, Bertha, Chicago's reigning socialite. When they built their Henry Ives Cobb–designed castle (demolished) at 1350 N. Lake Shore Dr. in 1882, the locus of social power began an inexorable shift north from S. Prairie Ave. to this area. Palmer also bought land for speculative development in order to profit from his self-created gold rush, in which land values soared 400 percent within a decade.

Early development concentrated on the Drive itself and on adjacent streets from Bellevue Pl. north to Burton Pl. The north half was developed after the turn of the century, when the Catholic archbishop subdivided property on Dearborn, State, and Astor Sts. just south of his North Ave. mansion. Modest 1870s Italianate row houses further west were joined in the 1880s by flashier Queen Anne and Romanesque residences. Commissions for houses from New York architects McKim, Mead & White in the 1890s started a trend toward neo-Classical and Georgian Revival styles; the latter was particularly well suited to the town house format and proliferated after 1900.

Apartment buildings had appeared in the Gold Coast as early as the 1890s, but their construction was concentrated in two great eras. The boom of the 1920s brought large revival style towers, mostly on Lake Shore Dr. In the 1950s and 1960s many mansions were replaced by behemoths that changed the area's character forever. Even the narrow streets further west have almost all had their scale disrupted by high-rise apartment buildings. Yet the Gold Coast remains a fashionable address, if somewhat less exclusive than in its heyday as home to the city's "Four Hundred." Its enduring appeal is remarkable in a city where many neighborhoods have experienced dramatic change.
—Patricia Marks Lurie with Laurie McGovern Petersen

**1 Fortnightly of Chicago
(Bryan Lathrop House)**
120 E. Bellevue Pl.
*1892, McKim, Mead & White
Restored 1972, Perkins & Will*

New Yorker Charles F. McKim, a leading architect of the 1893 World's Columbian Exposition, designed this elegant Georgian Revival trendsetter when Romanesque was still the dominant residential style. By 1900, Georgian was the favorite Gold Coast style. This exceptionally graceful essay has gently curving bays at each end of the unusually wide house. The symmetry is broken only by the off-center placement of the door. Occupied by a women's club since 1922, the building is in excellent condition, with a new fiberglass cornice that replicates the original.

Fortnightly of Chicago

2 43–45 E. Bellevue Pl.
1892, Charles M. Palmer

This Romanesque double house, built by Potter Palmer as an investment, is on a much larger scale than many he built in the area. The rustication diminishes with each floor. Unfortunately, the cornice is gone.

3 Chandler Apartments
33 E. Bellevue Pl.
1911, Richard E. Schmidt, Garden & Martin

This Georgian Revival apartment building has lavish Classical detail. Some of it is treated rather originally, such as the keystone-and-lintel arrangement on the fifth-floor projecting bays.

4 Lot P. Smith House
32 E. Bellevue Pl.
1887, Burnham & Root

One of John Wellborn Root's few extant residential designs displays his flair for decorative detail in the unusual dormer with its knobby finials, and in the pattern of circles in the pediment and above the entry door.

5 20 E. Cedar St.
1924, Fugard & Knapp

Splendid Gothic terra-cotta frames huge windows that illuminate two-story living spaces. The deep fourteenth-floor setback creates a large terrace and a "castle in the air" crown.

6 42–48 E. Cedar St.
1896, Charles M. Palmer
7 50–54 E. Cedar St.
1892, L. Gustav Hallberg

Rusticated stone, roundheaded windows, and foliate capitals mark these Romanesque town houses. Each group was designed as a unit, with gabled ends flanking a flat-topped central section. The symmetry breaks down for the group at 42–48 (built by Potter Palmer), because 42 has a fourth floor with a ballroom.

8 49 E. Cedar St.
1908, Marshall & Fox

The elegant semicircular bay of this small apartment building (built as an investment by the architects) recalls their larger buildings nearby, such as 1200 N. Lake Shore Dr. and 1550 N. State Pkwy. By contrast, this structure is Georgian, with its Flemish bond brickwork alternating red stretchers with dark brownish-black headers.

9 60 E. Cedar St.
1890, Curd H. Gottig

Flamboyant even in this ritzy neighborhood, a gable and three turrets squeeze onto the roofline, while six squat columns support ground-floor arches. The facade is of rusticated Georgia marble, with abundant copper trim above the cornice line.

10 1120 N. Lake Shore Dr.
1926, Robert S. DeGolyer

The prosperous 1920s produced a variety of residential high rises in this neighborhood. This one offered smaller, customized apartments rather than the floor-throughs of nearby luxury buildings.

11 1130 N. Lake Shore Dr.
(90 E. Elm St.)
1911, Howard Van Doren Shaw

One of the first tall apartment buildings to invade the line of mansions along the Drive was also a pioneer cooperative apartment, where occupants were shareholders in a corporation. Each apartment occupied an entire floor; Shaw was among the first owners. Tudor Revival, his favorite domestic style, gives the building the appeal and character of his country houses. The facade is dotted with medieval motifs and carved panels of fruit. Like many apartments with corner sites on the Drive, its entrance is on the side street, but the address has been changed to emphasize the lakefront location.

12 1200 N. Lake Shore Dr.
(Stewart Apartments)
1913, Marshall & Fox

The architects' trademarks include the graceful Adamesque detailing, the rounded bays, and the spacious plan, which places living room and dining room on either side of a sun parlor with a generous bay.

13 Carl C. Heisen House
1250 N. Lake Shore Dr.
1890, Frank B. Abbott

14 Mason Brayman Starring House
1254 N. Lake Shore Dr.
1889, L. Gustav Hallberg
Renovated 1990, Marvin Herman & Assocs.

This pair of single-family houses offers a fragmentary glimpse of the Drive's early appearance. The arched entries, squat towers, and deeply recessed porches are hallmarks of the Richardsonian Romanesque. 1250 is rough and rugged, even down to the small columns and piers. 1254 has smoothly polished columns with elaborately carved capitals, one of which includes a grinning face. In 1990 the buildings were joined and the interiors were gutted to create four new residences.

Heisen House

15 Arthur T. Aldis House
1258 N. Lake Shore Dr.
1896, Holabird & Roche

Even no-nonsense architects had occasional flights of fancy. While designing this Venetian Gothic palazzo, they were also working for Aldis's brother Owen (agent for Boston developers Peter and Shepherd Brooks) on the Marquette Building.

16 Lawrence D. Rockwell House
1260 N. Lake Shore Dr.
1911, Holabird & Roche

This is far more characteristic of the firm than the Aldis House. With its simple rectangular massing, minimal Classical details, restrained surfaces, and overall symmetry it is typical of houses built just after the turn of the century.

1350–1360 N. Lake Shore Dr.

17 1350–1360 N. Lake Shore Dr.
1949–1951, Loebl, Schlossman & Bennett

Just as the construction of Potter Palmer's crenellated castle on this site in 1882 spurred a local boom in mansion building, its replacement by this pair of twenty-two-story towers led a new generation of high-rise development on the Drive. Richard M. Bennett's overriding concern was to give every unit a view of the lake. The brick walls, with their windows set flush, bend like paper around the irregular plan. The angled bay windows and the mid-building bends create a multitude of planes on the long facades.

18 International College of Surgeons (Edward T. Blair House)
1516 N. Lake Shore Dr.
1914, McKim, Mead & White

19 International College of Surgeons Museum (Eleanor Robinson Countiss House)
1524 N. Lake Shore Dr.
1917, Howard Van Doren Shaw

20 Polish Consulate (Bernard A. Eckhart House)
1530 N. Lake Shore Dr.
1916, Benjamin H. Marshall

This trio's austere neo-Classicism belies their separate authorship. The Blair House's setback and restrained use of classical ornament on a smoothly polished facade set the standard for the others. The Countiss House is a rare Shaw essay in French architecture. His strong-minded clients insisted on a copy of the Petit Trianon at Versailles but with four stories instead of three. Go inside to see the many intact interior features, including the stone staircase with partially gilded iron balustrade and a lovely paneled library on the second floor.

21 1540 N. Lake Shore Dr.
1925, Huszagh & Hill

Mundane at ground level, it has a top inspired by medieval French châteaus. The expensive upper floors are best seen from the Drive.

22 1524 N. Astor St.
1968, I. W. Colburn & Assocs.

This 1960s essay in contextualism almost pulls a vanishing act by continuing the brick wall of its neighbors to the south. Look at the north wall to see the U-shaped plan that brings light to the interior.

23 1520 N. Astor St.
1911, Jeremiah K. Cady
24 1518 N. Astor St.
1911, Jenney, Mundie & Jensen
25 1525 N. Astor St.
1916, architect unknown

26 1511 N. Astor St.
1911, Arthur Heun
27 1505 N. Astor St.
1911, Jenney, Mundie & Jensen

These variations on the popular Georgian row house theme have a ground floor of stone, usually with banded rustication, and upper floors of brick trimmed with limestone. Each floor has three window openings stacked above those of the floor below, usually decreasing in height above the tall windows of the second-floor *piano nobile*. The parapet is frequently crowned by a balustrade whose openings align with those of the windows below. The few details present are usually classically inspired (pediments above windows or doors, etc.), as is the rigid system of proportions.

28 1500 Astor (Elinor Patterson–Cyrus H. McCormick Mansion)
20 E. Burton Pl.
1893, McKim, Mead & White Addition 1927, David Adler Converted to condominiums 1978, Nagle, Hartray & Assocs.; Wilbert R. Hasbrouck, consultant

Together with the nearby Lathrop House of a year earlier, this Stanford White design is an early and influential example of a neo-Classical residence. Closer to an Italian palazzo than its predecessor, the materials here are orange Roman brick with terra-cotta trim. McCormick bought the house in 1914, and

1500 Astor

in 1927 David Adler doubled its size to the north.

29 John L. Fortune House
1451 N. Astor St.
1910, Howard Van Doren Shaw

By 1910 Jacobethan was a close competitor of Georgian Revival, although better suited to expansive country properties than narrow city lots. The corner site makes this an only slightly scaled-down version of the country houses that Shaw was designing so prolifically at the time. His favored motif of carved fruit baskets tops the strapwork panels flanking the Astor St. entrance.

30 1449 N. Astor St.
1899, architect unknown

The massive château, made fashionable by Solon S. Beman's Kimball House, was even more difficult to adapt to narrow city lots than the Tudor Revival. The large bay and massive entry porch dominate the facade, which has an unusual frieze pattern of shells under the cornice and rather odd, twisted half-columns at each end.

31 Edward P. Russell House
1444 N. Astor St.
1929, Holabird & Root

Sleek, urbane, sophisticated, and very French, this elegant Art Deco town house is timeless and unique. The poised and polished facade is of stone from Lens, France, with gleaming granite trim, a barely suggested three-story bay, and incised ornament.

32 C. Vallette Kasson House
1442 N. Astor
1891, Pond & Pond

The doorway's pointed stone arch is echoed in tracings of arches in brick above the windows.

33 Horatio N. May House
1443 N. Astor St.
1891, Joseph Lyman Silsbee

The quarry-faced granite blocks of the rigidly symmetrical facade are on a colossal scale.

May House

34 George W. Meeker House
1431 N. Astor St.
1894, Holabird & Roche

Although reminiscent of Boston's Federal-style houses, it has suffered from the unsympathetic additions of a pedimented porch, disproportionate shutters, and a discordant paint scheme. The best original feature is the metal cornice with its garlands of balls.

35 Eugene R. Hutchins House
1429 N. Astor St.
1891, Pond & Pond

This quirky design combines rough Romanesque masonry with such Gothic details as the pointed arch above the door and the crocketed dormers with small-paned windows.

36 Rensselaer W. Cox House
1427 N. Astor St.
1889, William Le Baron Jenney

The rock-faced brick is an unusual feature of this otherwise mundane design.

37 Thomas W. Hinde House
1412 N. Astor St.
1892, Douglas S. Pentecost

Much of the ornate stonework has been removed, but this unusually decorated facade still evokes the English Renaissance, mixing classical elements with diamond-paned windows and medieval motifs.

Charnley House

38 Joseph T. Ryerson, Jr. House
1406 N. Astor St.
1922, David Adler
Addition 1931, David Adler

Adler fluidly adapted French style to the Chicago town house formula. His mansarded fourth-floor addition accommodated a large collection of Chicago memorabilia later donated to the Chicago Historical Society. Note the owner's initials in the decorative ironwork over the entrance.

39 Perry H. Smith House
1400 N. Astor St.
1887, Cobb & Frost
Addition 1991, Hammond, Beeby & Babka

The Astor St. side is handsome but underplayed; it is along Schiller St. that the house sprawls, punctuated by a magnificent Romanesque arch. So beautifully matched that it is almost indistinguishable from the original is the 3,000-square-foot rear addition, which contains the kitchen and a master bedroom suite.

40 James Charnley House
1365 N. Astor St.
1892, Adler & Sullivan
Restored 1988, Skidmore, Owings & Merrill

This is a landmark in the early career of Frank Lloyd Wright, who as an Adler & Sullivan employee was chiefly responsible for its design. The interplay of planes shows Wright beginning to break down the solidity of the mass, and the flattened Sullivanesque ornament is deemphasized. A central light well runs the full height of the house, which despite its size has only eleven well-proportioned rooms.

41 Astor Court (William O. Goodman House)
1355 N. Astor St.
1914, Howard Van Doren Shaw

In this very formal exercise in neo-Classical/Georgian Revival composition, the details are alternately robust (the second-floor window surrounds) and delicate (the design of stacked urns around the central window, the feathery pilaster capitals, and animal heads and skulls topped with fruit baskets forming keystones). The entrance on the south, originally a drive, leads to a landscaped court and entries to several units.

42 Edwin J. Gardiner House
1345 N. Astor St.
1887, Treat & Foltz

Astor Court

Houghteling Houses

The sandstone from Dunreath quarry, Ohio, in a mélange of fruit sherbet colors, is one of the street's most vivid materials—and the only notable element of this otherwise ordinary Romanesque town house.

43 Houses for Potter Palmer
1316–1322 N. Astor St. and 25 E. Banks St.
1889, Charles M. Palmer

Four of this group are textbook examples of rustication, especially the striated or banded variety on 1316 and 1320.

44 James L. Houghteling Houses
1308–1312 N. Astor St.
1887–1888, Burnham & Root

Root designed four town houses (1306 was demolished) for Houghteling and moved into 1310. The large second-floor bay is not part of his original design, which had a series of three arched windows. The group of houses shows a remarkably coherent combination of stylistic influences.

45 1301 N. Astor St.
1932, Philip B. Maher
46 1260 N. Astor St.
1931, Philip B. Maher

These severe, decorous Art Moderne apartment buildings were among the first Gold Coast high rises west of Lake Shore Dr.

47 Astor Tower (Astor Tower Hotel)
1300 N. Astor St.
1963, Bertrand Goldberg

Concrete columns raise the lowest floors above the rooflines of surrounding houses, and permanent metal jalousies screen the glass windows in this design experiment, which is less felicitous than Goldberg's contemporaneous Marina City.

48 Renaissance Condominiums (McConnell Apartments)
1200 N. Astor St.
1897, Holabird & Roche

Perhaps the ultimate Chicago School apartment building, this is

1301 N. Astor St.

a forthright composition in red brick with strong bays that echo the firm's Old Colony Building and many demolished hotels.

49 Frank F. Fisher Apartments
1209 N. State Pkwy.
1937, Andrew N. Rebori; Edgar Miller, design assoc.

Ignoring the street's parade of Revival styles, Rebori wrote a new chapter with this coolly masterful Art Moderne block. Onto a long, narrow, unpromising lot, he shoehorned thirteen duplex apartments oriented around a sliver of private space. The terra-cotta plaques (some are missing) are by Edgar Miller.

Fisher Apartments

50 Charles Henry Hulburd & Charles C. Yoe Double House
1243–1245 N. State Pkwy.
1880, architect unknown

This Second Empire design uses a contrasting stone to join window heads and sills. The abstract foliate ornament in the keystones has a neo-Grec crispness.

51 1328 N. State Pkwy.
*1938, Andrew N. Rebori
Remodeled 1956, Bertrand Goldberg*

A simple brick zigzag unites the facade and leads the eye to the small entry sculpted from the severe front. Two houses were built on opposite ends of this narrow lot, each with the main second-floor living space designated a "studio." Goldberg made

the houses into a home and studio for his mother-in-law, sculptor Lillian Florsheim. Look for Rebori's tiny initials in the wooden spandrel.

52 George S. Isham House
1340 N. State Pkwy.
1899, James Gamble Rogers

The leaden sobriety of this stiff, French-inspired mansion became an odd backdrop for later owner Hugh Hefner's 1960s Playboy excesses.

53 1411 N. State Pkwy./10 E. Schiller St.
1914, Andrew Sandegren

This unique Tudor-Craftsman hybrid smoothly incorporates generous balconies, not only enhancing the floor plans but also strengthening the facades.

54 George A. Weiss House
1428 N. State Pkwy.
1886, Harald M. Hansen

The deep pockets of Gold Coast clients enabled the use of highly worked, unusual materials such as this pink Georgia marble and the copper crockets, crests, and parapets.

55 Charles K. Miller House
1432 N. State Pkwy.
1884, A. M. F. Colton

Remarkable individual elements give the facade that vigorous incoherence so typical of the early Queen Anne style. Most peculiar is the terra-cotta plaque, where florid Sullivanesque ornament appears to spew from a flaming brazier.

Miller House

Graham Foundation

56 Graham Foundation for Advanced Studies in the Fine Arts (Albert F. Madlener House)
4 W. Burton Pl.
1902, Richard E. Schmidt
Restored 1963, Brenner, Danforth & Rockwell

Heaven's gate can be no more finely crafted than this doorway. The building's cubical massing and Teutonic severity owe a debt to the early nineteenth-century villas of Karl Friedrich Schinkel, but the precise ornament is pure Chicago. Schmidt's employee Hugh M. G. Garden is credited with the design. A collection of architectural fragments is on display in the rear court.

57 J. Lewis Cochrane House
1521 N. State Pkwy.
mid-1890s, George W. Maher

Developer Cochrane selected Maher from among the many architects who designed for his Edgewater subdivision and elsewhere. What he got is ordered, disciplined, and mainline—and a little dull.

58 1550 N. State Pkwy.
1912, Marshall & Fox

This was the ultimate in luxury when it was built, by architects who set the standards for early twentieth-century hotels and apartments. Each apartment originally had fifteen rooms and occupied an entire floor—over 9,000 square feet. From the bowed windows and metal balconies to the *orangerie*, it is the

dernier cri in French elegance. There is an ordered rhythm to the lively facade, with more dimension to the wall plane.

59 Residence of the Roman Catholic Archbishop of Chicago
1555 N. State Pkwy.
1880, Alfred F. Pashley

This early Queen Anne residence still has Italianate windows but is dominated by the busy, picturesque roofline typical of the style, punctuated by nineteen chimneys.

60 40–50 W. Schiller St.
1922, Rebori, Wentworth, Dewey & McCormick

To envision the original aspect of this elegant small apartment

1550 N. State Pkwy.

building, picture the garden opening onto the street where a low wall now partially fills the arches. The primary entrances used to face this garden, and the doors that now serve as street entrances were for servants and tradesmen.

61 George E. Rickcords House
1500 N. Dearborn Pkwy.
1889, William W. Clay

The Richardsonian Romanesque style frequently gives substance and street presence to a house squeezed onto a narrow lot. The entry is carved from the body of the house and is framed by low-springing arches. Look past the age-darkened patina on the granite to see the fine banded rustication.

62 Joseph C. Bullock House
1454 N. Dearborn St.
1877, Edbrooke & Burnham
63 John P. Wilson House
1450 N. Dearborn St.
1877, architect unknown
64 Philo R. King House
1434 N. Dearborn
1876, architect unknown

The Bullock House is a fine rare example of a full-blown Second Empire town house. In addition to the characteristic mansard roof (still shingled in slate), there is abundant Classical detail. A pavilion effect was created by setting back the entrance bay and emphasizing the north corner with pilasters and incised quoins. The Wilson and King houses share many of the details, with crisp incised ornament giving them even more of a French flavor.

65 St. Chrysostom's Episcopal Church
1424 N. Dearborn St.
1913, Brown & Walcott
Addition to church & parish house 1922, Clark & Walcott
One-story addition & belfry 1925, Chester H. Walcott
Remodeled 1925, Chester H. Walcott and Bennett, Parsons & Frost

The intimate church has the feeling of a campus chapel. The complex swallowed a house by William Le Baron Jenney to the south to create the parish house.

66 Thomas S. Wallin House
1401 N. Dearborn St.
1877, architect unknown

One of Chicago's oldest Queen Anne houses exhibits the style's characteristic variety. A rotated corner bay enlivens the irregular but not excessively polygonal facade. The severe planar surfaces are enriched with carved stone plaques—like the griffin crouched in a niche under the chimney.

67 Augustus Warner House
1337 N. Dearborn St.
1884, L. Gustav Hallberg

The deep overhanging bay is the major design element, making the house look as if it had been plucked from a narrow European street.

68 Lucius B. Mantonya Flats
1325 N. Dearborn St.
1887, Curd H. Gottig

The facade is bedecked with seventeen Moorish arches, many infilled with rich leaded glass.

69 Three Arts Club
1300 N. Dearborn St.
1914, Holabird & Roche

This residence for female art students was John A. Holabird's first design after he joined his father's firm on his return from Paris. The musical, dramatic, and pictorial arts have been expanded to include architecture, film, and fashion, but the club's mission is unchanged: to provide safe, inexpensive accommodations for women studying within.

The vaguely Mediterranean exterior hints at the lovely courtyard within. The ornament is highly eclectic, drawn from a variety of European sources. On the inside, note especially the stenciling in the dining hall and on the chandeliers. The sculptural panels on the east facade were inspired by Jean Goujon's Fontaine des Innocents (1549) in Paris.

Sandburg Village

70 R. Philip Gormully House
1245 N. Dearborn St.
1884, architect unknown

The pink slate is a foil to the magnificent copper work of the second-floor windows and third-floor dormer. It must have served as a billboard-size advertisement for Gormully's business, galvanized iron cornices and metalwork.

71 Carl Sandburg Village
Clark St. and LaSalle Blvd. between Division St. and North Ave.
1960–1975, Louis R. Solomon and John D. Cordwell & Assocs.

A blighted area of run-down housing was demolished for this new urban neighborhood, part of the Clark–LaSalle Redevelopment Project. Most prominent are the high rises, which do not match the charm of the low-rise apartments or town houses.

72 First St. Paul's Evangelical Lutheran Church
1301 N. LaSalle Blvd.
1970, Edward D. Dart

Severe on the outside but serene and comfortable inside, the church has an inward focus; north windows bring gentle, clear light to the extremely simple chancel.

73 1211 N. LaSalle Blvd.
1929, Oldefest & Williams
Renovated 1981, Weese Seegers Hickey Weese

An old apartment hotel with one decorated facade was converted to an apartment building whose walls became a canvas for artist Richard Haas. His *Homage to the Chicago School of Architecture* arranges the windows into trompe l'oeil bays on the eastern facade. On the south wall, Louis H.

1211 N. LaSalle Blvd.

Sullivan's round, terra-cotta–encrusted window from the Merchants' National Bank in Grinnell, Iowa, rises above the Golden Doorway of his Transportation Building at the 1893 World's Columbian Exposition. Between them, the Board of Trade Building two miles south is "reflected" in painted windows.

Here is a fragment of fashionable LaSalle Blvd., once the western fringe of the Gold Coast, walled off from old neighbors to the east by Carl Sandburg Village. Most of the houses were demolished or else converted to apartments or commercial use. Many survivors were badly remuddled, but several have been restored.

74 Anna A. Wolf House
1338 N. LaSalle Blvd.
1888, Frederick W. Wolf

The tiny copper turret has gusto, from its engaged column "leg" to its fish-scale panels to its belcast roof. In the gable is a wolf's head, a pictorial reference to the owners' name.

75 Double House for John McEwen
1340–1342 N. LaSalle Blvd.
1888, Burling & Whitehouse

Mirror images up to their mismatched gables, these chocolate brown sandstone houses are distinguished by fine craftsmanship on the bays and in the stonework.

76 John McEwen House
1346 N. LaSalle Blvd.
1872, architect unknown

Although altered, this grand mansard-roofed villa with its projecting central pavilion still reveals a French influence. In the late nineteenth and early twentieth centuries, the neighborhood was heavily Swedish; the house was both a Swedish Lutheran hospice and a home for the elderly before its 1986 rehabilitation as luxury housing.

77 John F. Jelke House
1352 N. LaSalle Blvd.
1895, Beers, Clay & Dutton
Renovated 1981, Marvin Ullman

This facade playfully exaggerates its classically derived elements. The Palladian window stretches to five panes across, while a low row of rolling swan's-neck pediments forms the parapet. The appendage to the north is a 1980s elevator.

78 Schiller Street Town Houses
141–149 W. Schiller St.
1988, Nagle, Hartray & Assocs.

Bulging exaggerated bays grab for the maximum north light.

79 Frederick Keller House
1406 N. LaSalle Blvd.
1882, architect unknown

Far from the spartan "octagon front" formula of the 1870s is this finely crafted fussbudget. It has a distinctly French flavor with its mansard roof, stringcourses, and colonnettes.

80 West Burton Place (Carl Street)

Across the street from the ordered universe of Carl Sandburg Village is a small, happily slapdash dreamworld, credited as the birthplace of Old Town as an artists' community. In 1927 a lively group of artists and craftspeople began to reinvent W. Burton Pl., then called Carl St. This neighborhood of "tumble-down old flats and cheap rooming houses," as the *Chicago Daily News* described it in 1940, became their urban canvas.

Entrepreneur and artist Sol Kogen and artist Edgar Miller had met at the School of the Art Institute in 1917. Chicagoan Kogen then worked several years in his family's yard goods business before moving to Paris. Miller grew up in Idaho, where he was influenced by Native American artists and developed a love for animals—including the antelopes, horses, and weasels that populate his work. After returning to Chicago, Kogen began his conversions by inviting Miller to join him in the work at 155 W. Burton Pl.

Kogen and the others began with Victorian houses like those still visible at 147 or 164–166

W. Burton Pl. (both built in 1881) and remade them in a richly decorative, freehand Art Deco style. Some were merely embellished; others were entirely slipcovered with brick and sported additions and new profiles.

Much was done without building permits, and when architects were retained, they apparently had only a minor influence on the designs, which were directed by the artist-owners and their artist-craftsmen friends. Andrew N. Rebori, for instance, who worked with Kogen on 155 W. Burton Pl., recalled, "Yes, I was the consulting architect, but only when I was consulted—which was damned little."

Low on capital but high on vision, the owners went scavenging in Maxwell St. flea markets for tiles, copper tubs, wooden doors, and hardware. Construction was often limited to one apartment at a time, using rents to capitalize slow unit-by-unit conversions. Some were never really finished, as their owners continued to add new art objects. Appreciative tenants and owners care for and continue to carefully embellish their buildings.

81 Theophil Studios
143 W. Burton Pl.
Renovated 1940, Frank J. LaPasso

With Kogen's advice, artist Theophil Reuther rebuilt an 1892 house to a Moderne look with stucco facades sporting red brick trim, porthole windows, and Milleresque decorative plaques. Note the leaded-glass windows.

82 151 W. Burton Pl.
Remodeled 1932–1935, architect unknown

Self-confident pizzazz transformed an 1887 house into this stylish apartment building. Kogen served as an advisor to owner and rehabber William Giuliani, a former opera singer. A front addition brought the house out to the street, while at the rear it grew to engulf the old coach house. The deliberately rough brick walls, set with flagstones and tiles, serve as artful foils to

151 W. Burton Pl.

three sets of rounded corner windows. Glass and tile scavenged from the 1933 World's Fair form the curving windows and line the stairway and halls.

83 155 W. Burton Pl. (Carl Street Studios)
Remodeled 1927, Sol Kogen, artist/contractor; Edgar Miller, artist; Andrew N. Rebori, consulting arch.

Lovingly detailed and devotedly maintained, this apartment complex is intriguing, beguiling, unpredictable, and visually bounteous. A mansarded Victorian was converted to seventeen (now sixteen) idiosyncratic studio apartments. Corridors and spaces open up in unanticipated directions, with a surprise around every corner. Miller's beloved

155 W. Burton Pl.

animals, especially weasels, enliven the stained-glass windows and wooden carvings, while Kogen's vigorous hand can be seen in the mosaic sidewalk.

84 161 W. Burton Pl.
Remodeled 1940, William Wendland

An 1879 Italianate house with a Joliet limestone front (the brick side wall is still visible on the alley) was rebuilt into a snazzy four-unit apartment building. The enclosed stair is lit by four slit windows that climb the facade. The two-story windows on the front and side lend the stylistic cachet of artists' studios, though the owner, Norman E. Johnson, intended the dwellings "for the average person in commercial life."

85 160 W. Burton Pl.
1887, architect unknown
Remodeled 1938, Lawrence Monberg

The original window locations on this 1887 house still show through the paint and the patching on the severe facade. Miller maintained that Kogen duplicated some existing sculptured plaques by Miller without his permission and installed them on several Burton Pl. buildings, including this one.

86 152–156 W. Burton Pl.
Remodeled 1933–1939, architects unknown; Sol Kogen, Clive Rickabaugh, and Carl Peter Koch, artists/contractors

The resident artists created a courtyard complex by combining two rooming houses and three coach houses. They bricked up old windows and added new ones, leaving a roundheaded third-floor dormer on 156 as a clue to the original, nineteenth-century look.

87 1500 N. LaSalle Blvd.
1892, Edmund R. Krause

Bays serve this apartment building as well as they did the sky-scrapers downtown, providing light, ventilation, and a pleasingly rhythmic facade.

Germania Club

88 Germania Club
1536 N. Clark St.
1888, August Fiedler

This ethnic meeting hall is a symbolic gateway to the Old Town Triangle, settled by German immigrants in the late 1840s. The club was built by the Germania Maennerchor, organized in 1865 to sing a requiem for President Lincoln when his bier rested in Chicago. The elaborate terracotta ornament includes lyres centered on the Ionic capitals. Step inside the bank lobby to see the stained-glass windows.

89 Latin School of Chicago
59 W. North Ave.
1969, Harry Weese & Assocs.

This concrete-and-brick structure houses the upper grades of the private Latin School, founded in 1888. Completely filling its limited site, the school uses the roof for a botanical laboratory and the playing fields of Lincoln Park for recreation.

90 Chicago Historical Society
Clark St. at North Ave.
1932, Graham, Anderson, Probst & White
Addition 1988, Holabird & Root

It's grown in all directions—but, happily, in the hands of skillful designers respectful of precious park space. The major remaining GAPW facade faces Lincoln Park in a sober Federal Revival Style. The plaza surmounts underground storage areas that accommodate growing collections without infringing on open space. The Clark St. addition, which

Chicago Historical Society

consumed a previous addition, blends with the original's massing, colors, and materials, but with a more open and welcoming appearance at the entry under its precisely gridded pediment and curtain wall. Sheila Klein's sculpture *Commemorative Ground Ring* (1989) honors Chicago's architectural past with suggestions of the Getty Tomb and a Prairie School roof. It invites inspection, but agressive southbound positioning seems to suggest that architecture is on the attack!

91 Moody Memorial Church
1609 N. LaSalle Blvd.
1925, Fugard & Knapp

Evangelist Dwight L. Moody came to Chicago in 1856 as a businessman but soon devoted his life to uplifting working people and the poor. According to the dedication-day program, the church design was inspired in part by the Byzantine Hagia Sophia in Istanbul; the offices and meeting rooms on the LaSalle Blvd. side were based on various Romanesque churches from Lombardy. A brick structure with sparing use of terracotta ornament, the building provided a large gathering place at limited cost.

92 Archway Amoco Gas Station
Clark St. and LaSalle Blvd.
1971, Standard Oil of Indiana (now Amoco Oil Co.); George W. Terp, Jr., supervising arch.

Standard Oil used the prominent location to make a bold corporate statement with a space-age gas station, while placating developer Arthur Rubloff, who did not want unattractive views from his planned high rise across the street. A shipyard welded steel beams into the desired curves, and an innovative white material—since replaced by the standard tar and gravel—covered the roof.

93 Emma Fernow House
1620 N. LaSalle Blvd.
1883, Frommann & Jebsen

While delighting modern eyes, this type of early Queen Anne eclecticism drove critics to exasperation: French Second Empire roof; an almost Gothic third-floor window; slate, brick, stone, and metal work; and a carved stone head commonly found on homes of this period designed or owned by Germans.

94 Christian Jevne House
1614 N. LaSalle Blvd.
1885, L. Gustav Hallberg

Originally one of the street's most expensive houses, it is the lone survivor of a group of nearby greenstone houses. This unusual variety of sandstone, its color due to chromium oxide, was quarried only in small pieces and weathered poorly.

The streets of Old Town are inviting but narrow and difficult to navigate by car. The area between Wells St. and Cleveland Ave. is best seen on foot or by bicycle.

95 Piper's Alley Commercial Mall
Wells St. north of North Ave.
1974–1977, Stanley Tigerman & Assocs.

The renovation of a bakery on the west side of Wells St. and new construction on the east created a retail complex around this busy intersection. While Tigerman's building for the Walgreen's drugstore chain has functioned successfully, the building to the west has been through many changes. One part that has remained constant is Second City, the popular theater company, which occupies space behind a terra-cotta frieze salvaged from Adler & Sullivan's demolished Schiller Theatre. Designed for the third-floor balcony, it features the heads of great German writers and philosophers and is the largest of several Schiller fragments scattered around the near North Side. At Walgreen's, the exterior light fixtures of crouching frogs supporting light globes are from Navy Pier.

96 David's Place
1656 N. Wells St.
1974, Booth & Nagle

The traditional combination of flats above stores, as seen in Crilly's building to the north, is quietly interpreted in a modern idiom, now somewhat compromised by signage. Residential units above and behind the commercial space are reached by a side-street entrance. The building virtually fills the lot, but roof terraces provide open space.

97 Crilly Court Development
North Park Ave. and Wells St., St. Paul Ave. and Eugenie St.

This late nineteenth-century mixed-use Queen Anne development offered many housing options and convenient retail space. Real estate developer Daniel F. Crilly purchased this block in 1885, cut a street (Crilly Ct.) through it, and built the row houses on the west side. Three years later 1717–1719 N. North Park was moved to its present site from Germania Pl., just south of North Avenue. The combination commercial and apartment building at 1700–1718 N. Wells St., designed by Flanders & Zimmerman (1888), was followed in 1893 by the three apartment buildings designed by that firm at 1701 to 1713 North Park Ave. Crilly's undertaking culminated in 1895 with four apartment buildings on the east side of Crilly Ct., named after his children, Isabelle, Oliver, Edgar, and Erminie.

98 Olsen-Hansen Row Houses
164–172 W. Eugenie St.
1886, Harald M. Hansen

Of the twelve houses that the Norwegian-born Hansen de-

Crilly Court Row Houses

signed for Adolph Olsen at this corner, only five survive; 164 was the architect's own residence. The fanciful facades of these Queen Anne structures, together with their irregular rooflines and combinations of materials and colors, typify the most exuberant Victorian design.

🄿 Kogen-Miller Studios
1734 N. Wells St.
Remodeled 1928–1932, Sol Kogen, contractor/artist; Edgar Miller, artist

As with their W. Burton Pl. collaborations, Kogen and Miller designed and built with great enthusiasm and imagination but little documentation. They built onto the front in 1928, raised the building in 1931, and put on a top addition in 1932. Their handiwork includes carved doors and windows, Miller's stained glass, small decorative plaques, and ceramic tiles from Kogen's scavenged collection.

🄸🄾🄾 Houses for John B. Mallers
1834–1836 N. Lincoln Ave.
1876, John J. Flanders
1838 N. Lincoln Ave.
1879, John J. Flanders

An Italianate variation popular in post-Fire Chicago is this triangular bayed type, usually executed—as it was here—in Joliet limestone.

🄸🄾🄸 Row Houses for Edwin B. Sheldon
1841–1849 N. Lincoln Ave.
1881–1882, architect unknown

These well-preserved Second Empire houses feature sunburst pedimented dormers and corbeled brick cornices.

🄸🄾🄸 301–315 W. Wisconsin St.
1878, architect unknown
🄸🄾🄸 John N. Young House
317 W. Wisconsin St.
1879, architect unknown

Here is a long row of the classic "octagon front" Italianates that sprang up all over Chicago after the Fire. The bays not only increase light and ventilation but also set up a lively rhythm. The

remodelings show the many approaches to altering the facade that result from changing the entrance from the very high first floor to the English-basement level.

House of Light

🄸🄾🄸 House of Light
1828 N. Orleans St.
1983, Booth/Hansen & Assocs.

The widely imitated plan overcomes the disadvantages of the narrow city lot with a central stairwell that floods the interior with daylight. The limestone facade has prominent joint lines, echoed by the window mullions, that describe its proportional elements and call attention to its Classical derivation.

🄸🄾🄸 325 through 345 & 348 W. Menomonee St.

These nine cottages, all in various states of remodeling, give a good idea of what the community looked like before the Fire of 1871. The tiny cottage at 348, on the edge of the alley, is a rare surviving example of a "fire relief cottage." Immediately after the Fire, the Relief & Aid Society supported the construction of these one-room dwellings, which could be moved by wagon to a burned-out lot. This one has been slightly enlarged and has new siding.

🄸🄾🄸 Henry Meyer House
1802 N. Lincoln Park West
1874, architect unknown

The narrow end, on Lincoln Park West, has window hoods with

carved wooden keystones that imitate those on more expensive masonry buildings.

107 1829 N. Lincoln Park West
1875, 1882, architect unknown
108 1835 N. Lincoln Park West
1874, architect unknown

These Italianate wood houses have very well preserved trim. 1829 has a pilaster and pediment surround on all the window and door openings, as well as incised scrolling designs. The trim on 1835 is mostly of the bull's-eye type found in many interiors, but it also has pierced work above the door and rope molding around the attic window.

109 Houses for Ann Halsted
1826–1830 N. Lincoln Park West
1884, Adler & Sullivan
1832–1834 N. Lincoln Park West
1885, Adler & Sullivan

Built as rental property, these houses are rare examples of the early Picturesque phase of the firm's work. The bold ornament shows the influence of Sullivan's early employer, Frank Furness of Philadelphia. The three original houses were designed as a symmetrical group.

110 Charles H. Wacker House
1836 N. Lincoln Park West
early 1870s; remodeled 1884, architect unknown

The Wackers' coach house, in which the family lived while 1838 was under construction, was relocated from the rear of the property to this position and remodeled by Frederick's son, Charles. The namesake of Wacker Dr., Charles was the youngest director of the World's Columbian Exposition of 1893 and a vigorous promoter of Daniel H. Burnham's 1909 Plan of Chicago.

111 Frederick Wacker House
1838 N. Lincoln Park West
1874, architect unknown

A Swiss-born brewer, Wacker built his frame house just before new regulations prohibited wood construction in that part of the city destroyed by the Great Fire of 1871. The form is typical of a Chicago cottage, but the ornament is unusually elaborate, with incised pilasters around the doors and windows and a large overhanging porch that recalls a Swiss chalet.

112 "The Beauty Pageant"
1811 to 1845 N. Sedgwick St.

In the early 1970s the Department of Urban Renewal closed Ogden Ave., a major southwest thoroughfare, from North Ave. at Larrabee St. to Armitage Ave. at Clark St. The former roadbed and some adjacent property was offered for development, including ten lots on the east side of Sedgwick St. that were sold in 1977. Efforts were made by the buyers to consider design

Halsted Houses

guidelines for their new houses, but each ultimately preferred to go his own way. Of the resulting diversity, Stanley Tigerman, who designed 1847, said, "This is an American street . . . It's quiet, dumb, Wild West, egocentric, and typically American. Americans have always seen themselves as individuals, and that individual imperative governs everything."

Booth/Hansen & Assocs. did 1843 and 1829, while Wilbert O. Rueter, a former protégé of Walter A. Netsch, Jr. at Skidmore, Owings & Merrill, designed 1841, whose angled bay looks southwest down the abandoned street. In one of several small parks aligned with the former street is a sculpture of two horses by Chicago artist John Kearney, who uses old car bumpers to create creatures with great character.

113 Belgravia Terrace
W. Wisconsin St. between Sedgwick St. and Hudson Ave.
1989, Gelick Foran Assocs.

In a gracious urbanistic gesture, these row houses come out to the lot line with split staircases designed to invite entry rather than repel intruders. The absence of high brick walls is a welcome change from the usual formula.

114 Midwest Buddhist Temple
435 W. Menomonee St.
1971, Hideaki Arao

The base contains classrooms and meeting rooms and also serves as a terrace for ceremonial processions. The temple's combination gable and hip roof is traditionally Japanese. A rectory stands to the west.

115 Menomonee Lane Town Houses
1801–1813 N. Mohawk St.
1986, Michael Lustig & Assocs.

English row houses were the inspiration for this fourteen-unit project. Lines of contrasting brick are laid over Flemish bond, uniting the windows and doors and enlivening the surfaces with a crisply articulated grid.

Steel and Glass House

116 Steel and Glass House
1949 N. Larrabee St.
1981, Krueck & Olsen Architects

It's aloof and mechanically pristine—but at night, when the light shines alluringly through the windows and steel grating, who'd turn down an invitation to step inside this beautiful cage? This 5,000-square-foot house is made of shop-fabricated steel angle frames joined to form structural bays. The U-shaped plan has two levels with a two-story living space. A central court and an informal garden provide private outdoor space.

1900 N. Howe St.

117 1900 N. Howe St.
1991, Max Gordon; Office of John Vinci, assoc. arch.

This 10,000-square-foot house meets the neighborhood standard of lavishness but is a quiet island of understatement and good taste. Executed in rosy brick, with long, taupe window frames divided into small panes, it was designed to accommodate the owners' art collection.

118 City Commons
W. Willow St. between N. Orchard and Vine Sts.
1986, Pappageorge Haymes

Trendsetting developers Horwitz-Matthews worked with the

architects to devise a project that organizes town houses around a private, secured courtyard. Walled gardens act as a buffer between the street and the unbroken perimeter wall and increase the fortresslike quality. But through the tinseltown entrance with its backlit glass block is a ring of row houses that honor their Italianate grandparents, complete with a long flight of stairs up to the stoop.

119 1852 N. Orchard St.
1985, Nagle, Hartray & Assocs.

It's Bauhaus Revival in boldface, with the facade shaped by a few large, precisely placed elements: the deep bay, the window grid, and the entry with glass-block sidelights.

House with a Bay

120 House with a Bay
1873 N. Orchard St.
1986, Nagle, Hartray & Assocs.

In Adler & Sullivan's work of a century earlier, several examples of which survive in Old Town and Lincoln Park, severe red brick facades serve as backdrops for bold, prominently placed, geometric or "organic" terra-cotta ornament. This modern interpretation of that historic precedent focuses attention on the bay window, whose ornamental casting in fiberglass is an enlargement of the design of the terra-cotta.

121 Juvenile Protective Association
1707 N. Halsted St.
1986, Tigerman, Fugman, McCurry

Modest materials are skillfully arranged in an ordered yet friendly facade, making the most of a low budget. A warm, skylit interior awaits the visitor.

122 YMCA—New City Center
1515 N. Halsted St.
1981, Metz, Train & Youngren

Glazed brick in bright colors covers the exterior, which has very few openings for security and functional reasons. The design is far from fortresslike, however, with the mass broken up by a varied roofline.

123 Yondorf Block and Hall
758 W. North Ave.
1887, Frederick Ahlschlager
Renovated 1989, Fitzgerald Assocs.; Office of John Vinci, assoc. arch.

This combination retail and hall building was constructed by the owners of a clothing business that occupied a nearby storefront on North Ave. In 1910 the storefronts were remodeled with a white terra-cotta facade for a bank, and roof cresting at the corner was removed. The largest of the six halls is complete with a stage and gallery. They were rented for social gatherings and meetings by unions and fraternal organizations. The building has stylistic elements of both the Victorian Gothic and the Romanesque Revival.

124 Larrabee Commons
North Ave., Eugenie St., Larrabee St., and Mohawk St.
1988, Pappageorge Haymes

The yellow stone and contrasting dark green trim set this complex apart from its neighbors. Small square rooms cantilevered off the corners enliven the facades. Like City Commons, the development is oriented inward, toward the center, surrounded by the attached row houses whose enclosed patios face the street.

125 554 W. Eugenie St.
1991, Banks/Eakin

The colossal scale of this PoMo palazzo makes it look more like a six-flat than a single-family house. The tower was intended to echo that of St. Michael's Church to the east.

126 St. Michael's Roman Catholic Church
447 W. Eugenie St.
1869, rebuilt 1872, August Wallbaum
Alterations and steeple 1888, Adam F. Boos
Clock 1889, Schwalbach Co.
Remodeling and brick facade 1913, Hermann J. Gaul

Generations of German architects, craftspeople, designers, and parishioners made St. Michael's a Romanesque monument with a Bavarian Baroque interior. The church was largely destroyed in the Fire; but the exterior walls survived, and the church was rebuilt within them. The grandest single element is the high altar, designed and installed along with four subsidiary altars by E. Hackner & Sons of La Crosse, Wisconsin. Within an arched niche, flanked by the archangels Gabriel and Raphael, St. Michael stands high above a defeated Lucifer. The stained-glass windows, by the Mayer Window Art Institute of Munich, were installed, as was the altar, in celebration of the parish's golden jubilee in 1902.

127 Town & Garden Apartments (Marshall Field Garden Apartments)
N. Sedgwick St., W. Evergreen Ave., N. Hudson Ave., and W. Blackhawk St.
1928–1929, Andrew J. Thomas; Graham, Anderson, Probst & White, assoc. arch.
Renovated 1993, Dubin, Dubin & Moutoussamy

Under the direction of Marshall Field III, the Marshall Field Estate built this low-income housing complex of ten buildings on two city blocks with a large central courtyard, communal interior spaces, and retail space on Sedgwick St. One of the nation's largest such efforts, it was an attempt to see if private initiatives could eliminate slum housing and become economic successes. A New York architect, Thomas was a preeminent designer of housing projects; his spartan, almost Art Deco complex was a success on aesthetic grounds. But it failed to provide housing to low-income tenants because costs proved greater than anticipated and required moderate, rather than low, rents.

128 Walter A. Netsch, Jr. House
1700 N. Hudson St.
1974, Walter A. Netsch, Jr.

This is a rare example of the domestic work of the former general partner at Skidmore, Owings & Merrill best known for his design of the Air Force Academy Chapel in Colorado Springs and the University of Illinois at

Town & Garden Apartments

Chicago. While ensuring privacy from the street, the interior offers a lofty, open central space, thirty-three feet high, under skylights covered with a passive solar collector.

129 Anton Franzen House
1726 N. Hudson Ave.
1880, architect unknown

The form of the Chicago cottage lent itself to brick construction, although it was more typically built of economical wood.

Franzen House

130 421–423 W. Willow St.
1982, Frederick F. Phillips & Assocs.

Two divided by three equals this pair of Siamese twins. The town houses are joined behind a white steel frame that suggests the shape of a third.

131 319 & 315 W. Eugenie St.
1874, architect unknown

These well-preserved frame cottages have lively woodwork, including dentils and paired brackets below the gabled cornices.

132 235 W. Eugenie St.
1962, Harry Weese & Assocs.

The varied layouts were intended to lure renters to this pioneering example of modern design in Old Town. Constructed of Chicago common brick, it maintains a nineteenth-century scale all the way up to its mansard roof.

235 W. Eugenie St.

133 Old Town Triangle Association Building
1728–1732 N. North Park Ave.
1922, Graham, Anderson, Probst & White

Throughout the Triangle are brick buildings designed as garages with apartments above. They were chauffeurs' quarters for employees of Gold Coast residents whose narrow lots could not accommodate cars. The garage space of this building was remodeled to house meeting rooms and classrooms.

134 Willow Street Town Houses
312–318 W. Willow St.
1974, Harry Weese & Assocs.

The architect and three friends built these row houses for themselves. Their inspiration was London's row house "terrace" altered to accommodate the automobile. Their plan has become standard: garage, en-

215 W. Eugenie St.

trance foyer, family room, and garden at street level; living room, dining room, and kitchen on the second floor; and bedrooms on the third and fourth floors.

[135] 225, 219, 217 & 215 W. Eugenie St.
1874, architects unknown

This unusual concentration of one- and two-story frame cottages was built just before the 1874 ordinance banning wooden construction. They all have high basements (in some cases a full story), gabled roofs with bracketed cornices, and simple trim that reflected the prevailing Italianate style.

[136] Cobbler Square
(Western Wheel Works)
1350 N. Wells St.
Block on W. Schiller St. at North Park Ave.: 1889, Henry Sierks
Block on W. Evergreen St. at North Park Ave.: 1891, Henry Sierks
Block on W. Evergreen St. at Wells St.: 1895, Julius H. Huber
Renovated 1985, Ken Schroeder & Assocs.

This residential and retail complex was created from some twenty buildings built from 1880 to 1959. The oldest structures, of heavy wooden-beam mill construction, belonged to the

Cobbler Square

Western Wheel Works, bicycle manufacturers, and reflect the vertical organization of the manufacturing process. In 1911 the company founded by Dr. William M. Scholl acquired the property for the manufacture of his foot care products, adding structures in the 1940s and 1950s. After the company vacated the site in 1981, some of the interior buildings were demolished, and a slice was cut out of a building on Wells St. to create an entry to the 295 residential units. An engaging series of courtyards, hollowed out of the center of the site, is ringed by steel walkways and entered through a three-story atrium.

LINCOLN PARK

Diversey

72 2780 N Lincoln

Southport
Wayne
Schubert
Magnolia
Racine
Lincoln
Wilton
Mildred

73

Embassy Club

Wrightwood

Lill

Altgeld

Montana

Fullerton

8 12

9 10 11

Belden

Janssen
Southport
Wayne
Lakewood
Magnolia
Racine
Clifton
Seminary
Kenmore
Sheffield
Bissell
Fremont

CTA Howard (Red) and Ravenswood (Brown) lines

16

19

15

16

13

7

Webster

2107 N Magnolia

6

Clybourn

Treasure Island Market Square

5

St Vincent de Paul

1 2100-214 N Fres

Dickens

4

Row Houses

Cortland St Bridge

74

Armitage

CTA Station

3

2

Old Town Sch of Folk Mus

8 University Hall
9 Stuart Center
10 Schmitt Center
11 O'Connell Center
12 Library
13 Thompson House
14 Sherlock House
15 DePaul East Campus
16 McCormick
   Row Houses
17 835 W Chalmers

18 834 W Chalmers
19 840-859 W Chalmers
20 Kaufmann Store
21 2225-2245 N Burling
22 Graham House
23 Mannheimer House
24 Guest House
25 Bellinger Cottage
26 Hudson Studios
27 Grant Place Portals
28 Halsted House

49 The Cobden
50 The Belden
51 Reebie Storage
52 McNally Row Houses
53 2236-2258 N Lincoln Park West
54 Belden-Stratford Apts
55 2344 N Lincoln Park West
56 2350 N Lincoln Park West
57 345 W Fullerton
58 2400 N Lakeview

39 Cenacle Retreat House
40 Staiger House
41 Church of Our Savior
42 Lincoln Park Presbyterian
43 Kohtz House
44 Austrian House
45 Kirchstein Houses
46 Ammon House
47 Peterson House
48 639 W Fullerton

No other Chicago neighborhood has witnessed as dramatic a resurgence as Lincoln Park. The 1950 *Local Community Fact Book*, the city's decennial oracle of sociological trends, predicted "the end of much of Lincoln Park as a residential community." Today it is for many people the most desirable neighborhood—with real estate prices to match. The density and congestion that constitute its chief drawbacks are the inevitable side effects of its popularity. Yet unlike the Gold Coast, the only neighborhood with higher median home values, high-rise construction has invaded only a small area, and the vast majority of streets retain their late nineteenth-century character.

Lincoln Park had distinctly inauspicious origins. Like the rest of the North Side, it was less accessible to the central city because of the intervening river. The lakefront just beyond North Ave. was considered remote enough for use as the city's cemetery, until the growth of the North Side population (still primarily farmers) led public health crusaders like Dr. John H. Rauch to demand the removal of the bodies to cemeteries farther north. This was accomplished in 1864, and the city established in its place Lake Park, renamed for the assassinated president the following year.

The Fire of 1871 destroyed the North Side as far as the city limits at Fullerton Ave., and an 1874 ordinance extended the fireproof building codes to the entire city. The growth of industry along the north branch of the river in the 1880s provided an impetus for the construction of workers' housing to the west. Cable cars arrived on Clark St. and Lincoln Ave. later in the decade, increasing middle-class settlement near those streets. The 1889 annexation of Lake View bumped the city boundary well north of Fullerton Ave., ending the construction of wooden houses, which had flourished just north of the former city limits. Construction of the Northwestern Elevated Railroad Company's tracks along Sheffield Ave. in the late 1890s spurred further commercial development.

By 1900 ethnic patterns were well established, with wealthy Germans living in large houses near the lake, and middle- and working-class Irish and Poles in modest flats further west. The 1920s and 1930s brought an extensive turnover, with poorer immigrants moving in and buildings subdivided to accommodate them. New construction was limited to the ever-desirable lakefront, while west of Halsted St. rooming houses were carved out of already modest dwellings.

After World War II most of Lincoln Park was considered a slum. The housing stock was similar to that of most other close-in neighborhoods: fifty-year-old buildings that were aging badly through neglect and subdivision into tenement-size units. But because the situation was less desperate than in other neighborhoods, such as the Near South Side, urban renewal arrived at a slower, more measured pace. Funds were not allocated until 1964, eight years after most of the community had been included in a 226-acre urban renewal area. By then there was less enthusiasm—and money—for the wholesale replacement of the housing stock with clusters of high rises. Private owners had already begun to renovate their property—if sometimes in a way that horrifies today's preservationists. An influx of Baby Boomers in the 1970s filled the rehabbed graystones, vintage apartments, and new high rises, bolstering the demand for shopping and entertainment. Restaurants, bars, theaters, and boutiques would quickly make this one of the city's liveliest neighborhoods.

Gentrification proceeded slowly westward, crossing Halsted St. in the early 1980s. Deconversion became the rage: not only were rooming houses returned to their original configuration of large apartments, but structures built as two- and three-flats were remodeled into luxurious single-family residences. The passion for preservation also led to the increasingly authentic restoration of facades, even where the interiors (whose original features were sometimes unsalvageable) have been redone in white-on-white modern.

Retail and entertainment establishments have followed the westward expansion, creating a new frontier along the formerly industrial

Clybourn Ave. The availability of large parcels of land hard by the Chicago River's north branch led to the creation of suburban-style strip malls that offer the abundant free parking that is in woefully short supply closer to the lake.

The demographic dip in the number of twenty- to thirty-five-year-olds and the white-collar recession of the late 1980s have chastened the area's gold rush mentality, but suburban empty-nesters returning to the city provide a whole new source of homeowners. Lincoln Park will no doubt enter the twenty-first century as one of the city's most vital residential communities.
—Patricia Marks Lurie with Laurie McGovern Petersen

■ 2100–2144 N. Fremont St.
1875, Edward J. Burling

Rebuilding after the Fire filled entire blocks with Italianate houses and flats. The ritzier dwellings were termed marble fronts, because they were built of Joliet limestone. For this more modest project, common brick walls and cast stone (concrete) sills and hood molds were used all around. An elaborate cornice unites this monolithic block with end houses set slightly forward. The porches closest to original are probably those with a simple bracketed canopy over the door.

Old Town School of Folk Music

■ Old Town School of Folk Music (The Aldine)
909 W. Armitage Ave.
1896, Joseph Bettinghofer
Renovation and storefront restoration 1987, Lisec & Biederman

In anticipation of the Northwestern Elevated Railroad Company's Center St. (Armitage Ave.) station, business blocks sprang up here during the mid-1890s; 917, 919, 921, and 925 all date from

1895–1897. Their Baroque embellishments—cherubs, figures, and banded pilasters—and elaborate corner bays compete for shoppers' attention.

■ Chicago Transit Authority—Armitage Avenue Station
944 W. Armitage Ave.
1900, William R. Gibb; J. A. L. Waddell, consulting eng.

This station of the Northwestern Elevated line from the Loop to Wilson Ave. is similar to five others by Gibb at Belmont, Fullerton, Diversey, Sedgwick, and Chicago. The brick walls are trimmed with cast stone tinted to look like terra-cotta.

■ 2100–2144 & 2101–2145 N. Bissell St.
1883, Iver C. Zarbell

John Davis developed these rental row houses, which are clustered in pairs and triplets to resemble grand homes. Second Empire mansard roofs and central pavilions blend with the Queen Anne's quirky variety of shapes, colors, and materials.

■ Treasure Island Market Square
Clybourn, Wayne, Lakewood, and Webster Aves.
1987, Booth/Hansen & Assocs.

This complex is notable less for its design, a serviceable post-modern composition of industrial materials, than for its site plan, which places shops on the periphery and parking in the middle. Regrettably, the other shopping centers lining Clybourn

2107 N. Magnolia St.

Ave. did not follow this pattern, offering instead the standard sea of surface parking between sidewalk and storefronts.

6 **2107 N. Magnolia St.** (Joel T. Headley Public School)
1875, architect unknown

Converted to apartments 1985, Bauhs & Dring

The city's oldest public school building now houses condominium lofts, but the Italianate exterior and spartan lobby are little changed.

7 **St. Vincent de Paul Roman Catholic Church**
1004 W. Webster Ave.
1897, James J. Egan

Egan's smooth and graceful interpretation of the Romanesque does not evoke the sense of shelter associated with the style's fortresslike Richardsonian version. The high altar (1903–1909), of Carrara marble, is inlaid with mother-of-pearl and mosaics.

DePaul University— Lincoln Park Campus
Webster Ave., Fullerton Ave., Halsted St., and Clifton Ave.

Founded as St. Vincent's College in 1898 and chartered under its current name in 1907, DePaul's small Lincoln Park campus was until recently dominated by a pair of megabuildings dating from a 1960s and 1970s expansion. The campus east of the elevated tracks originally belonged to the McCormick Theological Seminary, which sold it to DePaul in 1973. The most recent projects were charted in 1988, when Lohan Assocs. developed a new master plan to make the collection of buildings work more like a campus. Dormitories and athletic facilities were planned to attract residential students, and context-sensitive design will better integrate the school's buildings with the surrounding neighborhood. In 1992 the university closed the 2300 block of Seminary Ave. to traffic in order to create a landscaped quadrangle that would be the symbolic heart of a pedestrian-friendly campus.

8 **University Hall**
2345 N. Clifton Ave.
1986, Lohan Assocs.

Architect and client worked to create housing with massing and materials sympathetic to surrounding nineteenth-century houses and flats. The window hoods are inspired by the Italianate, although the openings that they top are almost square rather than tall and narrow.

9 **Harold L. Stuart Center** (University Center)
2324 N. Seminary Ave.
1978, C. F. Murphy Assocs.
10 **Arthur J. Schmitt Academic Center** .
2323 N. Seminary Ave.
1968, C. F. Murphy Assocs.

These brutalist concrete buildings rise above steeply bermed green spaces, epitomizing the "university as fortress" image that DePaul seeks to shed.

11 **Michael J. O'Connell Center** (Hall of Science)
1036 W. Belden Ave.
1938, Shaw, Naess & Murphy

This modest Art Moderne building denotes chemistry, biology, and physics in spandrel panels that depict laboratory beakers, splayed frogs (presumably awaiting dissection), and engines and gears.

DePaul Library

🛈 Library
2350 N. Kenmore Ave.
1992, Lohan Assocs.

The first major building designed in accordance with the 1988 master plan is this signature building. The red brick trimmed in pale masonry establishes a strong presence yet blends well with the neighborhood. Piers suggestive of buttresses lend a collegiate air, while the towers anchor the building. The eclectic vocabulary—Classical keystones, Gothic buttresses, and Chicago School towers—fails to speak with a clear voice, although it is too subdued to be cacophonous.

🛈 Hiram J. Thompson House
851 W. Belden Ave.
1885, Burling & Whitehouse

This Queen Anne house retains the flat-fronted sobriety of the Italianate style on the first two floors but explodes in scale at the top, where the huge dormer pierces an oversized cornice ornamented with giant shells between brackets. These bulky elements and the wide variety of materials (red brick trimmed in brownstone, hung with a metal bay) are typical of the uninhibited if awkward early Queen Anne style.

🛈 James P. Sherlock House
845 W. Belden Ave.
1895, Louis Brodhag

Sedate and cohesive compared to its next-door neighbor, it shows the relative quietness and monochromatic palette of the later Queen Anne style, here executed in the Romanesque mode. The once-popular variety of brown sandstone known as Lake Superior raindrop stone shows characteristic "spattering."

🛈 DePaul University— Lincoln Park Campus (East Portion) (McCormick Theological Seminary)
Halsted St., Belden Ave., Fullerton Ave., and the El tracks

The Presbyterian Theological Seminary was founded in Indiana in 1829, moved to Chicago in 1859, and relocated here in 1864. All of the original academic buildings, which faced Halsted St. and Belden Ave., were demolished, most of them during a 1960s building campaign. The most notable remnant is the collection of Queen Anne row houses, now a designated landmark district. Dissatisfied with the return produced by investing the endowment in bonds and mortgages, the seminary began constructing row houses in 1882 to produce rental income and create a comfortable island of Protestants in a sea of German Catholics.

The next building phase began in 1929, when architect Dwight G. Wallace created a grand plan to redesign the entire campus in the Collegiate Gothic style. What are now DePaul's Gymnasium (1929) and Commons Building (1932) are the sole offspring of Wallace's efforts. After moving to Hyde Park in 1973, the seminary sold its institutional buildings to DePaul University and the houses to private owners.

McCormick Row Houses on Chalmers Pl.

16 McCormick Row Houses
832–840, 844–858 W. Belden Ave.
833–841, 845–859, 901–913, 917–927 W. Fullerton Ave.
1884–1889, A. M. F. Colton

These modest Queen Anne dwellings have lively rooflines, a streetwall that steps in and out, and ornamental brick patterns. Construction proceeded from east to west, and the later buildings in the 900 block of Fullerton Ave. differ slightly.

17 835 W. Chalmers Pl.
1882, William Le Baron Jenney
18 834 W. Chalmers Pl.
1889, A. M. F. Colton & Son

These two freestanding houses were built for the seminary's faculty members; 835 was for high-rankers and was moved from its original location on Belden Ave. when a library (now demolished) was constructed there in 1894.

19 840–858 & 841–859 W. Chalmers Pl.
1889–1891, A. M. F. Colton & Son

The row houses surrounding the greensward on Chalmers Pl. are more subdued than their predecessors on the avenues. Each group shares a long gabled roof broken by a symmetrical pattern of round and triangular cross gables. They have smooth brick facades with recessed windows and deep arches sheltering the doorways. The dark color, arched entries, and corner tourelles convey a Victorian—or is it Presbyterian?—sobriety.

20 Ferdinand Kaufmann Store & Flat Building
2310–2312 N. Lincoln Ave.
1883, 1887, Adler & Sullivan

The south portion is earlier, although the design for the entire building was probably done at the same time. The only element distinguishing it as the firm's work is the robust ornament in the stone moldings and terra-cotta lunettes and the small lotus flowers topping the first-floor pilasters.

Kaufmann Store

21 2225–2245 N. Burling St.
1875, Edward J. Burling

These row houses are almost identical to those at 2100–2144 N. Fremont St. A large cornice joins an undifferentiated group of common brick Italianates, with the two houses at each end breaking forward only slightly.

22 Bruce Graham House
2215 N. Cleveland Ave.
1969, Bruce Graham

Unabashedly different and fiercely private is this SOM partner's home, which tries no harder to fit in here than does his Sears Tower in the Loop. Lacking streetside windows, it is oriented around a walled garden; the steel gate is the only opening on the street facade.

23 Leon Mannheimer House
2147 N. Cleveland Ave.
1884, Adler & Sullivan

The outsized chunks of lotuslike metal ornament are close to the scale of decoration on the firm's business buildings downtown. Along with the idiosyncratic semicircle topping the window and the triangular bay, they are the only clues to Sullivan's involvement.

Guest House

24 Walter Guest House
2150 N. Cleveland Ave.
Remodeled 1932, Edgar Miller, artist

The Art Deco streetside and topside additions of buff brick gave this old house a face-lift. The facade is dominated by large expanses of Miller's characteristic chevron-patterned leaded-glass windows. The screen on the front door displays another Miller favorite: animals from antelopes to sea horses.

25 Richard Bellinger Cottage
2121 N. Hudson Ave.
1869, William W. Boyington

Like Boyington's Water Tower, this house survived the Fire and became a legendary landmark. Located near the northernmost edge of the Fire's reach, it was saved when Bellinger allegedly soaked the roof with cider (his wife claimed it was water). This superb example of an 1860s Chicago cottage is clapboarded and shingled and was ultimately raised for a new foundation.

26 Hudson Studios
2134–2138 N. Hudson
Remodeling and additions, 1948–1952, Frank LaPasso

Attorney Lawrence S. Adler and commercial artist Clive Rickabaugh developed this courtyard complex with the bohemian, do-it-ourselves charm of W. Burton Pl., where Rickabaugh lived near his friend Sol Kogen. A long-vacant burned-out shell at 2138 was replaced by four apartments in 1948, with duplexes on the second and third levels. 2134 was converted next and still has the bricked-in windows of its earlier incarnation as a Victorian house. In 1952 additions were built on the back of each, with diamond-shaped bays and "Miami windows." The maple railings, doors, carvings, and fireplaces were scavenged from the La Salle St. Methodist Church, which had burned.

27 Grant Place Portals
415–443 W. Grant Pl.
1972, Booth & Nagle

These stacked town houses meet the street with the walled yards typical of others nearby, but within is a village atmosphere. Despite the density (fifty houses on less than an acre), the slice of landscaped space knits them together.

28 Ann Halsted House
440 W. Belden Ave.
1883, Adler & Sullivan

The lotus motif that decorates many Sullivan houses and business buildings of this era adorns the gable of this severely simple, early Queen Anne house.

The Cobden

29 The Cobden
418–424 W. Belden Ave.
1892, Charles S. Frost

On busy Clark St. it is a typical flats-above-storefronts building, while the facade on residential Belden Ave. derives its picturesque variety from its bays and the shaped gable that breaks the roofline.

30 The Belden
2300 N. Clark St.
1991, Solomon Cordwell Buenz & Assocs.

The architects tried to mitigate the height and massive bulk with an open plaza. Apartments are stacked on a retail base whose signage, like the building's palette, is out of control.

31 Reebie Storage & Moving Company
2325 N. Clark St.
1923, George S. Kingsley

"If Old King Tut were alive today, he'd store his goods the Reebie way!" Thus did the enterprising Reebie Brothers capitalize on the Egyptomania occasioned by the opening of King Tut's tomb in 1922. The well-preserved polychrome terra-cotta facade (missing only its cavetto cornice, similar in shape to those above the second-floor windows) is guarded by two statues of Ramses II, representing William C. and John C. Reebie. The hieroglyphics at the base say, "Forever I work for all of your regions in daylight and darkness" (left statue) and "I give protection to your furniture." Much of the elaborate sculptural program, which extends to the interior foyer and office lobby, was devised by Northwestern Terra Cotta Co. sculptor Fritz Albert.

Reebie Storage & Moving Company

32 Row Houses for Andrew McNally
2103–2117 N. Clark St./310–312 W. Dickens Ave.
1885, Joseph Lyman Silsbee

Queen Anne variety enlivens this corner block, designed by one of

2344 N. Lincoln Park West Penthouse

Frank Lloyd Wright's first employers.

33 2236–2258 N. Lincoln Park West
1910, Simeon B. Eisendrath

The influence of Eisendrath's former employer, Louis H. Sullivan, shows in the hearty foliate terracotta surrounding each entrance.

34 Belden-Stratford Apartments (Belden Hotel)
2300 N. Lincoln Park West
1922, Fridstein & Co.

This elegant apartment building seems almost to have been plucked from a Parisian boulevard and enlarged to Chicago scale. The mansard roof dominates the skyline, and the smooth limestone facade is embellished with quoins and Classical carving.

35 2344 N. Lincoln Park West
1917, Karl M. Vitzthum
Penthouse addition 1991,
Frederick Phillips & Assocs.

A small sixth-floor apartment was remodeled and a 2,000-square-foot seventh-floor added to create a dazzling penthouse that is still low enough to be seen from the street. With its twin limestone belvederes, it fits securely atop this Beaux Arts facade.

36 2350 N. Lincoln Park West/305 W. Fullerton Ave.
1916, Andrew Sandegren

A master of quiet elegance, Sandegren created signature sunrooms with million-dollar views of Lincoln Park.

37 345 W. Fullerton Ave.
1973, Harry Weese & Assocs.

The concrete frame surrounding the dark glass windows is made less severe by the gradual stepping-back of each facade. But beware of the fierce spikes of the needlessly hostile fence!

38 2400 N. Lakeview Ave.
1963, Ludwig Mies van der Rohe

This is the last residential high rise that Mies designed for Chicago.

39 Cenacle Retreat House
513 W. Fullerton Ave.
1967, Charles Pope

Siting the parking lot on Fullerton Ave. was unfortunate, but it lessens the impact of the tall buildings behind, which house sleeping rooms. The complex is a terrific example of the warm side of clean, quiet modernism in brick, with narrow brick piers forming strong verticals. Go inside the chapel to see the same sensibility, augmented with boldly abstract windows.

40 Carl M. Staiger House
520 W. Fullerton Pkwy.
1891, Lamson & Newman

All the bang is in the bay. With a swan's-neck pediment and large acroterion, it projects from the facade like a corsage.

41 Church of Our Savior (Episcopal)
530 W. Fullerton Pkwy.
1888, Clinton J. Warren

The tourelled Romanesque facade blends seamlessly with the rector's house on the west. The nave has walls of unglazed terra-cotta tiles and a beautifully trussed ceiling. Some of the original, geometrically patterned leaded-glass windows were replaced with figural stained glass, several by Tiffany Studios.

42 Lincoln Park Presbyterian Church (Fullerton Avenue Presbyterian Church)
600 W. Fullerton Pkwy.
1888, John S. Woollacott
Addition 1898, William G. Barfield

Every corner on this massive Richardsonian Romanesque church is soft and rounded. Fat disks of greenish sandstone are stacked to form giant tourelles, and blocks of many sizes are knit into a tall tower (minus its steeple since 1970.) This variety of green stone, called Michigan buff sandstone, was popular from the mid-1880s to the mid-1890s. From the pulpit on the west wall the aisles radiate in a semicircle on an ascending grade as in "all the first-water Presbyterian churches of the city," as the *Daily Inter Ocean* noted. Barfield's addition pushed the west wall back twenty-five feet but maintained this orientation.

43 Louis O. Kohtz House
620 W. Fullerton Ave.
1886, architect unknown

44 Leo Austrian House
624 W. Fullerton Ave.
1886, Theodore Karls

The Austrian House sets itself apart from its neighbor with a flattened Romanesque castle front that includes a corner tower, parapet, and shallow machicolations.

45 Herman Kirchstein Houses
621 & 627 W. Fullerton Ave.
1888, Julius H. Huber
623–625 W. Fullerton Ave.
1887, Julius H. Huber

Austrian House

Awkwardly massed but beautifully detailed, the two slightly later houses stiffly bookend the double house. All are enlivened by robust wooden porches whose comices feature disks that look like flying saucers impaled on spikes.

46 Ernest Ammon House
629 W. Fullerton Ave.
1889, Frommann & Jebsen
47 Peter Peterson House
631 W. Fullerton Ave.
1889, Julius H. Huber

Look closely at 629 for an extroverted Queen Anne palette; although begrimed, the red-and-green sandstone still peeks through.

639 W. Fullerton Ave.

48 639 W. Fullerton Ave.
early 1890s, architect unknown

This house is saved from formula by the fabulous acanthus-leaf symphony at the entry. The fingered leaves swirl and twist, framing jesters' faces at the bottom. At the top they become

Newman Brothers Houses

spiky collars that frame facing dog faces—or are they caricatures of humans?

49 Newman Brothers Houses
2424, 2430 & 2434 N. Orchard St.
1895, John M. Van Osdel II

S. S. Beman popularized the Châteauesque locally with his Kimball House of 1891; many elements of his design are squeezed here into a narrower, high-shouldered version. This trio was to have been done in shades of red stone, but the middle house was executed in limestone. Van Osdel was the nephew of John Mills Van Osdel, Chicago's first architect.

50 St. Clement Roman Catholic Church
646 W. Deming Pl.
*1918, Barnett, Haynes & Barnett
Restored 1989, Holabird & Root*

The architects of the St. Louis Cathedral produced a scaled-down version here, complete with a Byzantine dome inspired by Istanbul's Hagia Sophia. Trompe l'oeil mosaic, plaster-work, and marble make the interior a riot of colors and *faux* textures.

51 William A. Wieboldt House
639 W. Deming Pl.
1896, Robert C. Berlin

The plain but vaguely Italian facade is topped by a determinedly German Baroque third-floor gable.

52 Jacob Gross House
632 W. Deming Pl.
1892, Edmund R. Krause

Krause prized the massiveness and geometries of the Queen Anne style, while eschewing its fussiness. This facade is a balance of squares and rectangles, topped by triangles and cones. The monochromatic palette quiets the clamor.

53 William Schmidt House
618 W. Deming Pl.
1889, Frederick Foehringer

Tourelles on the third-floor dormer, a Classical cornice with modillions and brackets, a man-

St. Clement

sard roof, a rusticated stone facade, and Ionic porch columns create a house with an identity crisis.

54 Frederick J. Lange House
612 W. Deming Pl.
mid-1890s, Thomas W. Wing

The handsomest stone detailing on the street is on the porch parapet.

55 Chateau VI
546 W. Deming Pl.
1968, Jerome Soltan

Ranging from banal to bruising, the curse of city neighborhoods in the 1960s and 1970s was the infamous four-plus-one, invented by Soltan in 1960. Here twenty-four apartments on four floors are squeezed onto a space that originally accommodated a single-family home. The ground-level parking is partially screened by decorative concrete blocks. All but filling the lot, the four-plus-one not only provides little light to the units on the sides and back but also cuts off light to neighboring buildings. They were never built with sufficient parking, and streets were clogged with the overflow cars. The lack of parking was their ultimate downfall.

Groetzinger House

56 William C. Groetzinger House
526 W. Deming Pl.
1895, Frederick B. Townsend

Ponderous but comfortably cave-like and beautifully detailed, the Romanesque facade is Gothicized with pointed arches.

57 439 W. Arlington Pl.
1908, architect unknown

The owner of this Georgian house maintains the wooded lot to the west as a bird sanctuary, protected from development by an easement given to the Chicago Audubon Society.

O'Brien House

58 William V. O'Brien House
426 W. Arlington Pl.
1894, Flanders & Zimmerman

Built for an art dealer, this house is one of the city's most unusual for its era. The band of windows tucked under the eave was a favorite device of Frank Lloyd Wright, although it predates his use of the motif. The enormous dormer that continues the wall plane in an upward surge is also an anomaly, perhaps inspired by Adler & Sullivan's towered Victoria Hotel (1892) in Chicago Heights. The house is well preserved, although at some point (possibly in 1921) the front entrance was moved to the side, and the eastern arch was transformed from a door to a window.

59 2430 N. Lakeview Ave.
1927, Rebori, Wentworth, Dewey & McCormick

Although Rebori's most distinctive work is his interpretation of the Deco and Moderne styles, he was also a fluent translator of the Georgian idiom so beloved of his wealthy clients. The horizontal separation of living spaces and bedrooms is evident in the window arrangement.

2440 N. Lakeview Ave.

60 2440 N. Lakeview Ave. (Lake View Avenue Apartments)
1927, Rissman & Hirschfeld

Despite its frilly facade, six units per floor make for less luxury than in its more sober neighbors.

61 2450 N. Lakeview Ave.
1924, Howard Van Doren Shaw

Servants lived on the second floor of this simplified Georgian building, which was designed with only one unit per floor. Shaw was one of the original owners, but he died only two years later at the age of fifty-six, having just been awarded the gold medal of the American Institute of Architects.

62 Joseph Theurer/Philip K. Wrigley House
2466 N. Lakeview Ave.
1897, Richard E. Schmidt

The monochromatic scheme of orange brick and terra-cotta and the palazzo form have a kinship with Stanford White's Patterson–McCormick Mansion, but the asymmetrical bays and exaggerated quoins add a German neo-Classical flavor. This was Schmidt's first major commission.

63 2474 N. Lakeview Ave.
1993, Lohan Assocs.

The architects describe the elevation as "an abstract collage on which the spatial and constructive elements are realized." The most prominent element is a sinuous skylighted galleria that runs the length of the interior.

64 Marlborough Apartments
400 W. Deming Pl./2608 N. Lakeview Ave.
1923, Robert S. DeGolyer

The clever massing and delicate Adamesque ornament diminish the bulk. Apartments on the Lakeview Ave. side were for the building's investors; the much smaller units on Deming Pl. were rented to others.

65 Francis J. Dewes House
503 W. Wrightwood Ave.
1896, Cudell & Hercz

This Prussian confection can't decide whether to be neo-Classical, Baroque, or Rococo, but it does succeed in being impressive. The rich carving includes statues supporting a balcony above the entrance.

Dewes House

66 Mrs. Arthur Ryerson House
2700 N. Lakeview Ave.
1917, David Adler
67 Abram Poole House
2704 N. Lakeview Ave.
1917, David Adler
68 Henry C. Dangler House
2708 N. Lakeview Ave.
1917, Henry C. Dangler
69 Ambrose C. Cramer House
2710 N. Lakeview Ave.
1917, Ambrose C. Cramer

Although designed by different architects, this cohesive block seems straight out of Georgian London—up to the cornice line, at least. The houses share an Adamesque sensibility in the details as well. Dangler was Adler's partner, and he stamped all of the construction drawings because Adler had never passed the engineering test needed to obtain an architect's license.

70 Elks National Memorial Building
2750 N. Lakeview Ave.
1923–1926, Egerton Swartwout
Magazine Building *1967, Holabird & Root*

This memorial to fallen Elks of World War I (rededicated after subsequent conflicts to include latter-day heroes) contains one of the city's grandest public spaces. The Memorial Rotunda is a riot of colored marble and mural painting, dazzling in opulence if not taste. Eugene Savage painted the enormous and rather cryptic murals here and in the reception room (on axis with the main entrance); Edwin H. Blashfield was responsible for the more subdued wall paintings in the small lobby between the two rooms. Adolph A. Weinman sculpted the gesticulating figures in the niches; James Earle Fraser was responsible for the sculpture in the entry vestibule; and Laura Gardin Fraser designed the life-size elks that flank the steps where they meet the sidewalk on Lakeview Ave. Weinman also designed the monumental bronzes in the pair of exterior niches.

71 Urantia Foundation
(Sylvan Kunz Flats)
533 W. Diversey Pkwy.
1908, Frommann & Jebsen

Urantia Foundation

Light-years from the firm's turgid, tourelled stone-front houses on Fullerton Ave. is this grand flat, the star of this graceless south-side stretch of Diversey Pkwy. Lavish ornament grows out of the wall organically, recalling Art Nouveau and Jugendstil masters. The integration of the metal railing with the stone balcony is the jewel in the crown of this sculptured facade.

72 2780 N. Lincoln Ave.
(John E. Hufmeyer Building)
1888, Charles F. Hermann

The diagonal path of Lincoln Ave. creates dozens of six-point intersections that are a motorist's nightmare but provide high-visibility sites for storefronts. This mansard-roofed block is one of the city's most elaborate flatiron flats-above-shops buildings.

73 Embassy Club
Southport Ave., Greenview Ave., and Wrightwood Ave. just south of Diversey Pkwy.

Elks National Memorial Building

1989–1992, Pappageorge Haymes
2609 & 2613 N. Greenview Ave.
1992, Diamond Phillips

One of Chicago's grandest yup-scale developments has narrow row houses grouped around cobbled streets. The elaborate facades feature the bay windows and lively streetwall rhythms of their Queen Anne ancestors but with a Georgian formality. The resulting Queen George amalgam conveys a Disneyland ambience of virtual reality, with none of the quirks or messiness—or vitality—of a true cityscape.

74 Cortland St. Bridge
(Clybourn Place Drawbridge)
Cortland St. (1400 W.) at the Chicago River
1902, John E. Ericson, city eng.; Thomas G. Pihlfeldt, city bridge eng.

This was the nation's first trunnion bascule bridge. The leaves are hinged at the shore end on a trunnion, or shaft. Chicago's conception and execution of this type of bridge became a textbook example around the world.

Lincoln Park

Oak St. to Ardmore Ave.; Lake Michigan to N. Lake Shore Dr., N. Clark St., Lincoln Park West, Lakeview Ave., Lake Shore Dr., Marine Dr.
1865–1880s, Swain Nelson & Olaf Benson
1903–1921, Ossian C. Simonds
1920s–1960, Ernst G. Schroeder;
1936–1938, Alfred Caldwell

Chicago's largest and busiest park has more noteworthy features than any other and offers a variety of landscapes, buildings, and activities. It reflects more than a century of design and the work of many talents, but each succeeding designer knit his contributions into the existing fabric, resulting in an overall unity of appearance. The landscape also reflects a century of competing interests and ideas about how parkland should best be used.

Lincoln Park's history is unusually complex. Much of its 1,212 acres, which stretch along almost six miles of shoreline, were created from landfill. The southern section, from North to Webster Aves., comprised the municipal cemetery, established in 1837. The first area used as parkland was sixty vacant acres of the cemetery between Wisconsin St. and Webster Ave. As the population of surrounding neighborhoods increased, pressure grew to relocate the bodies for health reasons. In 1864 the Common Council prohibited the sale of burial plots and designated the land for a Lake Park, although reinterment in private cemeteries outside the city limits did not begin until 1871 and took three years to complete. In 1865 the park was renamed for the recently assassinated president, and three years later a zoo was established when New York City's Central Park donated two pairs of swans. In 1869 state legislation created the Lincoln Park Commission to manage the park and permitted its northward expansion.

Landscape gardener Swain Nelson drew up the first plan for the park in 1865. Its naturalistic style, derived from eighteenth-century French landscaping, featured small lawn areas outlined with winding pathways and interspersed with three ponds. The Waterfowl Lagoon in the Zoo is the principal surviving feature of his tenure. His colleague Olaf Benson took over as landscape gardener in 1870 and expanded on Nelson's plan to encompass the entire area from North Ave. to Diversey Pkwy., adding a few formal elements and the first park structures. The first landfills were created in the 1880s, including the narrow extension south of North Ave.

In 1903 Ossian C. Simonds began to promote a midwestern style of naturalistic landscaping inspired by the land forms, rock outcroppings, waterways, and native plants of the prairies.

LAKE

MICHIGAN

Irving Park
Sheridan
Grace
Waveland
Addison
Cornelia
Stratford
Hawthorne
Roscoe
Aldine
Melrose
Belmont
Briar
Barry
Wellington
Oakdale
Surf
Diversey
Drummond
Wrightwood
Wrightwood
Deming
Arlington
Fullerton
Belden
Grant
Webster
Dickens
Armitage
Wisconsin
Eugenie
North

Broadway
Clark
Lakeview
Sheridan
Commonwealth
Orchard
Geneva
Lincoln
Orchard
Howe
Larrabee
Mohawk
Cleveland
Hudson
Sedgwick
Vine
Clark
LaSalle Dr.

Lake Shore Dr.

LINCOLN PARK

Waveland Field House
91

Diversey Pkwy Facilities Bldg
90

Rustic Pavilion
89

I Will
87

Theatre on the Lake
88

Conservatory
85

Zoo Rookery
86

Storks at Play
84

Lincoln Park West
Stockton

Café Brauer
82

Zoo
83

Cultural Arts Center
80

Chicago Academy of Sciences
79

Comfort Station
81

Couch Mausoleum

Abraham Lincoln
75

76

Grant Memorial
78

North Avenue Beach House
77

To Loop

Simonds proposed extending the park all the way to Devon Ave., a mile past its present terminus, and during his tenure it grew north to Cornelia St.

Beginning in the 1920s engineer Ernst G. Schroeder directed the park's growth to its termination in 1957 at Ardmore Ave./Hollywood Beach. The newly created sections were laid out in a naturalistic style that incorporated interesting rockwork elements. The most important designer during this period was Alfred Caldwell, a disciple of landscape architect Jens Jensen. During his two-year tenure Caldwell brought the Prairie School spirit into the park, most dramatically in the Lily Pool (now the Zoo Rookery). His work can also be seen in the broad open spaces defined by groves of hawthorn trees in the Montrose Point area.

The most dramatic changes since the 1950s have been made to accommodate the ever-increasing demands of the automobile. Wheeled traffic has been an issue since 1873, when a speed limit was established for the park's roadways; two years later a separate speeding track was built. Encroachment on park land began in earnest in 1938, when La Salle Dr. was extended through the park's south end. Lake Shore Dr. now cuts a wide swath through its entire length, separating the lakefront from the rest of the city. The many issues concerned with the use of Lincoln Park—cars vs. pedestrians, passive vs. active recreation, buildings vs. open space—continue to generate lively dialogue and inspire strong passions.
—Joan Pomaranc

75 Couch Mausoleum
Northwest of *Abraham Lincoln*

The only tomb left from the park's early days as the municipal cemetery is here because the Illinois Supreme Court supported the family's refusal to move it. Construction excavations have uncovered other remains unknowingly left behind.

Abraham Lincoln

76 Abraham Lincoln ("The Standing Lincoln")
East of the Chicago Historical Society
1887, Augustus Saint-Gaudens; base and exedra McKim, Mead & White

One of America's greatest nineteenth-century sculptures and widely considered Saint-Gaudens's most significant work, this imposing statue commands its handsome setting. The face and hands are based on life casts by sculptor Leonard W. Volk, but Saint-Gaudens had also seen Lincoln, once in life and when his body lay in state. The great orator is portrayed in the penultimate moment before a speech, as he gathers his thoughts to step forward and address the crowd.

77 North Ave. Beach House
Lakefront at North Ave.
1939, E. V. Buchsbaum

Buchsbaum designed several beach houses in "early ocean liner" style.

78 Ulysses S. Grant Memorial
1891, Louis T. Rebisso; Francis M. Whitehouse, architect

The aesthetic quality of this ponderous monument has been the subject of debate since its unveiling. One early newspaper account called it suitable only for impressing country cousins.

79 Chicago Academy of Sciences
2001 N. Clark St.
1893, Patton & Fisher

MATTHEW LAFLIN MEMORIAL over the entrance recalls the pioneer businessman who provided this Renaissance Revival home for Chicago's oldest museum, founded in 1857 to promote knowledge of the region's natural history.

80 Lincoln Park Cultural Arts Center & Recreation Building (Lincoln Park Commission Headquarters)
2045 N. Lincoln Park West
1927, Edwin H. Clark

This Georgian Revival building recalls the architect's contemporaneous work for the Lincoln Park Zoo.

81 Comfort Station (Carlson Cottage)
Stockton Dr. southwest of Café Brauer
1888, Joseph Lyman Silsbee

One of the earliest park structures, it was first identified as Men's and Ladies' Cottage. Inappropriate alterations and loss of the berm into which its north side originally nestled have diminished the appearance of this picturesque structure.

82 Café Brauer (South Pond Refectory)
2021 N. Stockton Dr.
*1908, Perkins & Hamilton
Renovated 1989, Lawrence B. Berkley & Assocs.; Meisel & Assocs.; Wiss, Janney, Elstner Assocs.*

The Lincoln Park Commission constructed on the banks of the South Pond a new refectory financed by restaurateurs Paul and Caspar Brauer. The building would be a masterpiece of designer Dwight H. Perkins, one of the Prairie School's leaders.

The massing includes a large closed central pavilion flanked by two graciously curving loggias. A broad expanse of green tile roof with deep overhangs, combined with earthy red brick, subtle terra-cotta details, and polychromatic mortar, settles the building into the landscape. Viewed from Stockton Dr. to the west, the large block of the central pavilion dominates, while the curving loggias recede. But on the lagoon side the two loggias are seen to wrap around the end of the pond. Simultaneously the loggias contain the water, and the lagoon's form controls their curves. Also on this side, large expanses of glass open up the facade of the main pavilion.

The Great Hall occupies the second floor of the pavilion, rising thirty-four feet from the floor to the peak of the skylight. Two art-glass chandeliers hang from the

Café Brauer

Café Brauer

trusts. The walls are buff speckled brick, and Rookwood mosaics enhance recessed corner alcoves and a musicians' gallery. From the loggias, which open off the Great Hall, the skyline unfolds to the south.

The café was a favored establishment during its early years and throughout Prohibition. The dining room fell into decline, however, after repeal, because state law forbade the sale of liquor in the parks. The Great Hall closed in 1941, and throughout the late 1950s and 1960s the space was used as a winter theater.

Not until the sale of liquor was permitted on parkland could a viable plan for restoration be undertaken, and in 1989 a $4.2 million rehabilitation began. The clay tile roof and the skylight, which had been removed in the 1940s, were reinstalled; the original light fixtures were refabricated; all the original paint colors were re-created; and the electrical and mechanical systems were updated. The two chandeliers, which had hung throughout the hall's incarnations, required only cleaning and minor repairs. They are the centerpieces of that room, which has been restored to its original appearance.

Café Brauer reopened to the public in 1990, an outstanding example of the Prairie School style in a public building.

—William W. Tippens

83 Lincoln Park Zoo
Armitage to Fullerton Aves., Stockton to Cannon Drs.

Early zoo buildings, little more than decorative cages for the separation of species, evolved into settings designed to appropriately frame the animal for human eyes. Modern design stresses the re-creation of natural habitats with human intrusion kept to a minimum. The beasts in the beautifully detailed **A Lion House** *(1912, Perkins,* *Fellows & Hamilton; renovated 1986, Hammond, Beeby & Babka)* had indoor and outdoor quarters, not just for their own comfort but to increase their visibility. The Georgian Revival architecture popular in the 1920s is represented by the **B Reptile House** *(Aquarium & Fish Hatchery, 1923)* and **C Primate House** *(Small Animal House, 1927),* both by Edwin H. Clark and renovated by John Macsai & Assocs. in 1984 and 1992, respectively. The D McCormick Bird House *(1900, Jarvis Hunt)* has been completely renovated to house naturalistic habitats. The E Waterfowl Lagoon *(1865, Swain Nelson; renovated 1978, Chicago Park District)* recreates the naturalistic landscape planned by the park's original designer.

84 *Storks at Play* (The Bates Fountain)
1887, Augustus Saint-Gaudens and Frederick William MacMonnies

Saint-Gaudens received this commission together with that for the *Standing Lincoln,* which so absorbed him that he called upon a former student to work on the fountain. He later gave MacMonnies primary credit for this popular work.

85 Lincoln Park Conservatory
Stockton Dr. between Belden Ave. and Fullerton Pkwy.
1894, Joseph Lyman Silsbee

The Crystal Palace–inspired conservatory (its entrance was enlarged in the 1950s) overlooks a formal French garden to the south and an English-style peren-

nial garden on the west, across Stockton Dr. Both gardens have been in place at least since 1887.

86 Zoo Rookery (Lily Pool)
Fullerton Pkwy. between Stockton and Cannon Drs.
1937, Alfred Caldwell

Caldwell redesigned a Victorian lily pool to evoke the midwestern landscape by way of Japan and the Prairie School, with stratified stonework, a wooden pavilion, and native plants. Despite overuse and insensitive maintenance, it remains one of the city's most evocative landscapes.

87 *I Will*
Cannon Dr. at Fullerton Pkwy.
1981, Ellsworth Kelly

The park's first contemporary sculpture honors Chicago's unofficial motto of the 1890s, recalling the rebuilding after the Fire of 1871.

88 Theatre on the Lake
(*Chicago Daily News* Fresh Air Sanitarium)
Lakefront northeast of Lake Shore Dr. and Fullerton Pkwy.
1920, Perkins, Fellows & Hamilton

Zoo Rookery

Major changes to Lake Shore Dr. and Fullerton Pkwy. in 1937 necessitated significant alterations to this Prairie School structure, later remodeled into a theater.

89 Rustic Pavilion
Lakeview Ave. at St. James Pl.
1883, Mifflin E. Bell

An artesian well once briefly bubbled up nearby. The site's naturalness has been obscured, but the structure has been restored to its original color. The Adirondack twig detailing recalls a bygone era of pleasure grounds and picturesque vistas.

90 Diversey Parkway Facilities Building (Golf Course Shelter)
Diversey Pkwy. east of Lake Shore Dr. West
1916, 1919, Andrew N. Rebori

Originally open to the golf course, the north side was filled in by Rebori's expansion.

At the north end of Lincoln Park is one of Clark's finest park buildings.

91 Waveland Field House and Brett's Café (Refectory)
East of Lake Shore Dr. opposite Waveland Ave.
1932, Edwin H. Clark

The Collegiate Gothic field house includes a clock tower with the Wolford Memorial Chimes. In 1992 a dedicated group of volunteers finished restoring the long-silent chimes and the clock's immobile hands.

LAKEVIEW/
UPTOWN/
RAVENSWOOD

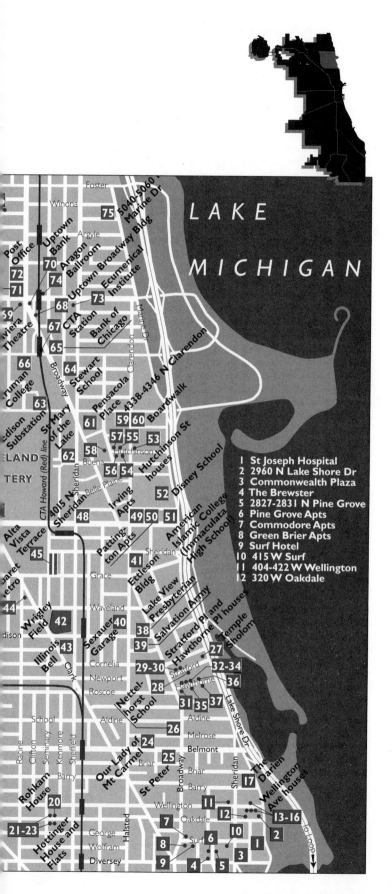

LAKE

MICHIGAN

Foster
Winona
75 5040-5060 Marine Dr
Post Office
72
71
Uptown Bank
70
74
Argyle
Aragon Ballroom
Uptown Broadway Bldg
Ecumenical Institute
69
Riviera Theatre
68
CTA Station
73
67
Bank of Chicago
66
65
Truman College
63
64
Stewart School
Edison Substation
St Mary of the Lake
Broadway
Pensacola place
4338-4346 N Clarendon
Boardwalk
Marine Dr
Clarendon
61
59 60
LAND TERY
62
58
57 55
53
Hutchinson St houses
56 54
Hutchinson
Buena
Belle Plaine
Irving Apts
52
Disney School
4015 N Sheridan
Sheridan
48
49 50 51
American Islamic College (Immaculata High School)
Alta Vista Terrace
45
Patting-ton Apts
41
Ettleson Bldg
Sheridan
garet
etro
Grace
44
Wrigley Field
42
Waveland
Sexauer Garage
40
38
39
Lake View Presbyterian
Salvation Army
Stratford Pl and Hawthorne Pl houses
Temple Sholom
dison
Illinois Bell
43
Cornelia
Newport
Roscoe
29-30
28
Nettel-horst School
27
Stratford
32-34
36
Hawthorne
Lake Shore Dr
Racine
Clifton
Seminary
Kenmore
Sheffield
Clark
School
Aldine
31 35 37
26
Aldine
Melrose
Our Lady of Mt Carmel
24
Belmont
Rohkam House
20
25
Briar
St Peter
Briar
Broadway
Barry
Sheridan
17
The Darien
Wellington Ave houses
21-23
Hottinger House and Flats
Barry
Wellington
11
12
13-16
Halsted
7
Oakdale
10
8
Surf
6
George
Wolfram
9
4
5
1
2
3
Diversey

1   St Joseph Hospital
2   2960 N Lake Shore Dr
3   Commonwealth Plaza
4   The Brewster
5   2827-2831 N Pine Grove
6   Pine Grove Apts
7   Commodore Apts
8   Green Brier Apts
9   Surf Hotel
10 415 W Surf
11 404-422 W Wellington
12 320 W Oakdale

Throughout the nineteenth century, this area resembled the garden in Chicago's motto, "Urbs in Horto," or "City in a Garden." Farms dominated the landscape to the west, and country estates lined the lakefront. Even the name of Lake View Township, organized in 1857, came from a resort hotel in the area. While annexation by Chicago brought increasing urbanization, outdoor entertainment remained a specialty, with beer gardens, Riverview Amusement Park, and Wrigley Field baseball stadium. Although the movie palaces and dance halls of the Roaring Twenties are now mostly dark, and poverty has overtaken many once-fashionable neighborhoods, the area continues to attract weekend crowds of the young and the restless.

Lake View Township extended north from Fullerton Ave. to Devon Ave. and from the lake to Western Ave., but the neighborhood now known as Lakeview goes only from Diversey to Addison. Communities to the north include Wrigleyville (Addison to Irving Park), Buena Park (to the west and east of Graceland Cemetery), Uptown (north of Montrose), and Ravenswood (Addison to Lawrence, Ashland to Western). Lakeview retains a high concentration of early frame houses to the west of Halsted St., with graystones and apartment buildings predominating to the east. Buena Park was developed as an affluent suburb, as pockets of spacious houses continue to bear witness. Uptown had the sharpest rise and the steepest fall in fortunes, going from 1920s entertainment mecca to 1970s magnet for the impoverished and mentally ill. The residential neighborhoods of Ravenswood are interrupted by small-scale commercial strips and an industrial corridor along the Chicago & North Western tracks.

In 1836 Conrad Sulzer established a farm near the present intersection of Clark St. and Montrose Ave., and the prosperous truck farmers who followed his lead enabled Lake View to become the center of the Midwest's greenhouse industry and the nation's largest shipper of celery. Along the lake shore, developers James B. Rees and Elisha E. Hundley acquired 225 acres of land between Belmont Ave. and Irving Park Rd. in 1852. Two years later they established a first-class lakefront hotel, the Lake View House, and subdivided the remaining land into spacious residential lots. Wealthy Chicagoans such as real estate investor Samuel H. Kerfoot laid out beautifully landscaped estates that attracted visitors from miles around. To the west, near the Chicago & North Western right-of-way in Ravenswood, developers built frame houses to attract working-class families displaced by the Chicago Fire of 1871.

When Lake View was annexed to Chicago in 1889, improved municipal services encouraged boom development. The pace accelerated after 1900, when elevated train service was extended north to Wilson Ave. By the 1920s the area around Wilson Ave. and Broadway had been christened Uptown, a name that reflected the glamour and urbanity of a vibrant commercial and entertainment district. Uptown never really recovered from the Depression and for years lagged ever farther behind adjacent neighborhoods. Private renewal began slowly in the 1980s, and the community now enjoys a new vitality as a "port of entry" neighborhood for immigrants.

Postwar development was initially concentrated along the ever-desirable lakefront, resulting in a canyon of concrete high rises and infill pockets of "four-plus-one" apartments. The loss of the lakefront single-family neighborhoods has spurred renewal of the older neighborhoods further west, where houses and apartments are being returned to their original charm.
—Mary Alice Molloy

St. Joseph Hospital Chapel

1 St. Joseph Hospital
2900 N. Lake Shore Dr.
1963, Belli & Belli

Forgive the blue walls with their diamond-shaped windows and the dark glass cylinder that hangs like a uvula from the front. The eleventh-floor Dan Ryan Memorial Chapel, open every day, is a great treat. It may be the city's most perfectly preserved 1960s interior, from the mosaic-lined, concrete baldachin to the pointy-legged altar furniture. Architects would like to think the 1960s looked like Mies's Federal Center, but this is what that era *really* looked like.

2 2960 N. Lake Shore Dr.
1990, John Macsai & Assocs.

Competing with St. Joseph Hospital in the aggressive-palette category is this red brick high rise banded in glossy blue and white. The sill line of this upscale Hyatt residence for the elderly dips down to twenty inches in the living room bays to provide views for those in a chair or wheelchair.

Walk this densely built lakefront neighborhood from Diversey Ave. to Wellington Ave. to see a variety of Chicago housing types from the 1890s to the 1990s.

3 Commonwealth Plaza
(Commonwealth Promenade Apartments)
330–340 W. Diversey Pkwy.
1953–1956, Ludwig Mies van der Rohe; Friedman, Alschuler & Sincere, assoc. archs.

This is curtain-wall modernism in full stride. The project was commissioned by developer Herbert S. Greenwald, Mies's early and influential client, whose death in 1959 halted development of two additional towers planned for the site. The glass-and-aluminum skin is suspended in front of the columns, which comprise two different structural systems (reinforced concrete on the lower floors and steel above). The space between the columns and the skin contains vertical ventilation shafts, allowing for more efficient heating and cooling than in Mies's previous buildings.

Commonwealth Plaza

4 The Brewster (Lincoln Park Palace)
2800 N. Pine Grove Ave.
*1893, Enoch Hill Turnock
Renovated 1972, Mieki Hayano*

The Brewster

It looks like a brooding high-rise armory from the outside, but beg your way indoors to see the "sky lobby," a fantasy in steel and glass block. Every apartment opens onto a gabled, skylighted court. Turnock's early years in the office of William Le Baron Jenney may account for the steel frame and the atrium design, which resembles bridge construction. The rugged "Jasper stone" (quartzite) walls set off an outstanding Sullivanesque terra-cotta frieze on the top floor. The polished granite entry on Pine Grove Ave. was originally the ladies' entrance.

5 2827–2831 N. Pine Grove Ave.
1891, Ostling Bros.

The use of a uniform building material increases the apparent size of the units, while variations on bay shapes and stone cuts provide individuality.

6 Pine Grove Apartments (Pine Grove Apartment Hotel)
2828 N. Pine Grove Ave.
1924, Loewenberg & Loewenberg

Upper-class vintage apartment buildings frequently have remarkably understated entrances, to downplay the communal nature of the accommodations. But apartment hotels, which offered dining, recreation, and other services, flaunted their congregate nature. Playing up the grand public spaces, an octagonal entry pavilion leads to an enormous lobby, and an ornate belt course separates the monumental and heavily detailed first floor (which contained the public spaces) from the private residential floors above.

7 Commodore Apartments
550–568 W. Surf St.
*1897, Edmund R. Krause
Renovated 1985, Nakawatase, Rutkowski, Wyns & Yi*

This exemplary Chicago School apartment building owes as much to the skyscrapers of Holabird & Roche as to the flats of the era. A massive building, it is broken into smaller blocks to increase ventilation and light. The Roman brick facade is crisply edged and sparingly ornamented, with oculi at the top story and an Ionic temple front entrance.

Commodore Apartments

8 Green Brier Apartments
559–561 W. Surf St.
*1904, Edmund R. Krause
Renovated 1985, Architects International—Chicago*

Familiar from the Commodore are the temple front entrance and the use of Roman brick, but the flat facades—with their pox of brackets—are trite and repetitious by comparison.

9 Surf Hotel
555 W. Surf St.
1925, Rissman & Hirschfeld

Behind the ornate terra-cotta facade is an apartment hotel shaped like a bowling alley: the footprint is 36 × 216!

10 415 W. Surf St.
1910, Samuel N. Crowen

Crowen was more successful than most in marrying Prairie School detailing to apartment-house formulas. This brick three-flat has Wrightian geometric decoration and an unusual stepped elevation ending in a large square bay.

11 404–422 W. Wellington Ave.
1939, Loebl & Schlossman

The enduring desirability of this lakefront community called for the successful reintroduction of a decades-old housing type, the row house. These ten stream-lined Lannon stone examples, each with from five to seven rooms, are densely packed on the site. The courtyard is an important amenity, made private by its half-story elevation from the street.

12 320 W. Oakdale Ave.
1953, Milton M. Schwartz

The concrete overhangs of this high rise, which make the building look like a stack of plates, were designed to control heat gain and prevent rain infiltration. Charitable observers call it a hybrid of Mies van der Rohe and Frank Lloyd Wright.

On this short block of Wellington Ave. are elegant single-family houses dating from the 1920s. This area developed later than the Gold Coast because much of the land east of Sheridan Rd. between Diversey and Belmont Aves. had been created by an ongoing pro-cess of filling in the shoreline. In the early twentieth century, Lincoln Park expanded north of Diversey, and the streets immediately to the west filled up with stately homes in fashionable revival styles.

13 Arthur H. Apfel House
341 W. Wellington Ave.
1925, E. H. Frommann
14 Oscar Mayer Houses
333 & 335 W. Wellington Ave.
1926, Rissman & Hirschfeld
15 Philip T. Starck House
330 W. Wellington Ave.
1925, Mayo & Mayo
16 Lester Armour House
325 W. Wellington Ave.
*1915, Howard Van Doren Shaw
Remodeled 1925, Howard Van Doren Shaw*

These houses are as substantial and bourgeois as their owners, bastions of the business community. Individual but not eccentric, they exude fine craftsmanship while blending nicely in the streetscape. Starck's French neo-Classical house is the most elegant; Apfel's Tudor Revival, the most charming.

17 Darien Condominiums
(Darien Apartment House)
3100 N. Lake Shore Dr.
1948–1951, Loebl, Schlossman & Bennett

Bennett folded the masonry curtain wall like paper, arranging the floor plans to maximize lake views. The metal-framed windows are laid almost flush with the brick, emphasizing the wall's thinness.

Apfel House

Starck House

Farther west in Lake View were more ethnic neighborhoods. Two reminders of the large German community still stand on Southport Ave.

18 Schuba's
3159 N. Southport Ave.
1903, Frommann & Jebsen

At the turn of the century, the Joseph Schlitz Brewing Company built dozens of its own saloons in order to increase its market share and ensure maximum distribution. A busy street in a German neighborhood was a prize location. Vice president Edward G. Uihlein purchased the properties and hired the architects. Although no emphasis was placed on unique design, the Schlitz trademark was always prominent on the facade.

19 St. Alphonsus Roman Catholic Church
2950 N. Southport Ave.
1889–1897, Adam Boos and Josef Bettinghofer; Schrader & Conradi

The unusual central placement of the large tower follows a German Gothic precedent that was later translated to a smaller scale in nineteenth-century English parish churches. The small lantern windows high atop the roof were a popular feature in nineteenth-century German neo-Gothic churches. In the nave, a steel support system with exposed rivets tops the ornate decor.

St. Alphonsus

From 1048 to 1059 W. Oakdale Ave. is "Terra-Cotta Row," a group of houses and flats built for executives of the Northwestern Terra Cotta Company. Established in 1877, the company opened a large plant at Clybourn and Wrightwood aves. in 1883 and became a leader in the booming industry of architectural ornament.

Rohkam House

20 Henry Rohkam House
1048 W. Oakdale Ave.
1887, Theodore Karls

Built for one of the founders of Northwestern Terra Cotta, this exuberant brick house and ornate fence display the company's products with great flair. A full range of wares is on display, from small geometric stock pieces to elaborately sculpted plaques, tympana, and chimney pots. The wild eclecticism of the ornament is held in check by a monochromatic color scheme. Don't miss the relief of a woman at a spinning wheel on the west side.

21 Gustav Hottinger House
1054 W. Oakdale Ave.
1886, Julius H. Huber

This more modest house, built for Northwestern's founder and president, has been substantially altered but retains a terra-cotta panel in the gable and volutes bracketing the east window.

22 Adolph Hottinger Flat
1057 W. Oakdale Ave.
1916, Moritz F. Strauch
23 Gustav Hottinger Flat
1059 W. Oakdale Ave.
1901, Theodore Andresen

Terra-cotta's ability to ape any material in any style made it equally appropriate for the banded Ionic columns at 1059 and the geometric ornament on 1057.

24 Our Lady of Mt. Carmel Roman Catholic Church
700 W. Belmont Ave.
1914, Egan & Prindeville

An imposing English Gothic edifice of Indiana limestone, this rib-vaulted Catholic church has two organs and frequently hosts concerts of sacred and modern music. The reredos behind the altar continues the Gothic vocabulary in a backdrop for statues of the four evangelists.

25 St. Peter's Episcopal Church
615 W. Belmont Ave.
1895, William A. Otis

This one-and-a-half-story structure of rusticated limestone was planned as the base of a larger church that was never built.

26 Louis Nettelhorst Public School
3252 N. Broadway
1892, John J. Flanders
1911, Arthur F. Hussander

The public schools' Queen Anne period was shaped by Flanders, who between 1884 and 1893 designed over fifty projects for the Board of Education. His earliest formula was gloomy and Flemish-gabled, but after William Carbys Zimmerman joined him in practice in 1886 his designs brightened, with lively ornament and larger, more varied windows. Flanders's portion faces Broadway; its polygonal forms and bands of ornament typify Chicago's public school of the early 1890s. Hussander's addition defers to the original.

27 Temple Sholom
3480 N. Lake Shore Dr.
1930, Loebl, Schlossman & Demuth and Coolidge & Hodgdon

Loebl, Schlossman & Demuth conceived this project while in graduate school at the Armour Institute. Byzantine in inspiration, the octagonal limestone synagogue is elaborately ornamented with friezes, ornate column capitals, and a portal with stained-glass windows over three-paneled doors. The sanctuary is illuminated with indirect light, and a movable wall doubles the seating capacity.

28 Albert B. Towers House
551 W. Stratford Pl.
1894, George W. Maher

A great gambrel roof and enormous boulders at ground level hint at the rustic grandeur of this much altered house.

29 George M. Harvey House
600 W. Stratford Pl.
1888, Adler & Sullivan

Though greatly altered, this is of interest as one of only two frame houses designed by Adler & Sullivan.

30 606 W. Stratford Pl.
1912, Huehl & Schmid

This is a two-flat masquerading as an urbane single-family house. The monochromatic color scheme suits the severity of the pared-down facade, which seems to anticipate the angular crispness of Art Deco architecture.

Hawthorne Place between Broadway and Lake Shore Drive

Subdivided in 1883 by John and Benjamin F. McConnell, this tree-lined street is a rare and cohesive remnant of the single-family-house district that once stretched for miles along the lakefront.

31 Nicholas J. Sheridan House
587 W. Hawthorne Pl.
1906, Borst & Hetherington

The battered sides, art glass, and balcony roof with exposed supports are all Craftsman touches.

32 Alfons Bacon House
580 W. Hawthorne Pl.
1937, Mayo & Mayo

This house presents an elegant Art Deco interpretation of the Georgian style.

33 George E. Marshall House

574 W. Hawthorne Pl.
1886, Burnham & Root
Addition 1896, architect unknown
Alterations 1938, architect
unknown

The original Queen Anne design is visible only in the half-timbered third-floor dormers. Subsequent alterations, such as the pedimented front door and Palladian window, were mostly Classical Revival.

Benjamin F. McConnell House

34 Benjamin F. McConnell House

568 W. Hawthorne Pl.
1884, Remodeled 1887, George Beaumont
Addition 1987, Schroeder Murchie Laya Assocs.

The oldest house on the block has been spectacularly transformed by the rear addition of a fun house for people and plants.

Inside this luxuriously modern version of a Victorian conservatory are a swimming pool and a hot tub.

35 Herman H. Hettler House

567 W. Hawthorne Pl.
1892, architect unknown
Addition and remodeling 1899, Julius H. Huber

This lavish Queen Anne, built by a wealthy lumber merchant, is pierced and anchored by a great round bay. A gigantic coach house and diminutive playhouse complete the complex, now owned by the Chicago City Day School, which uses the house for meeting rooms and offices.

36 John McConnell House

546 W. Hawthorne Pl.
1885, architect unknown

This brick and limestone villa with rotated corner bay seems like the city cousin of the rambling clapboard house at 568.

37 Chicago City Day School Addition

541 W. Hawthorne Pl.
1990, Weese Langley Weese

The clock tower and low canopy create a modest civic presence and an inviting entrance. An addition to a classroom facility built in 1969 and 1973, the building was sited on the rear of the property to lessen the impact on the residential streetscape.

Chicago City Day School Addition

38 Lake View Presbyterian Church

716 W. Addison St.
1888, Burnham & Root

This simple Shingle Style structure—now unfortunately sided—has a high pitched roof and octagonal tower with conical steeple. Built shortly before the annexation of Lake View, it features the wood frame construction that had been prohibited in Chicago after the Fire. In the 1890s the church was enlarged, shifting the axis to north–south.

39 Salvation Army School for Officers' Training
(Joseph E. Tilt House)
700 W. Brompton Ave.
1913, Holabird & Roche

This grand Tudor Revival mansion, built for the owner of a shoe company, has been almost obscured by later buildings and a brick wall.

40 Sexauer Garage

3640 N. Halsted St.
1924, David Saul Klafter

The winged wheel in polychrome terra-cotta is both advertising and decoration.

Ettleson Building

41 Isaac G. Ettleson Building

3837–3845 N. Broadway
1911, Harry Hale Waterman

Wingtip to wingtip, terra-cotta eagles flap in formation across the top of this otherwise typical retail and office building.

42 Wrigley Field (Weeghman Park)

1060 W. Addison St.
1914, Zachary Taylor Davis

Chicago's beloved "Cubs Park" is the oldest surviving National League ballpark and one of the few survivors of baseball's golden age (1910–1925). Key features from that era include the use of permanent materials (steel and concrete instead of wood); large seating capacity (usually over 10,000); post-and-beam construction, which allowed spectators to be close to the action; and an urban context that frequently determined the dimensions of the playing field (as was the case here). Davis had designed several other ballparks (including Chicago's now-demolished original Comiskey Park), and his knowledge and foresight facilitated the park's constant enlargements and remodelings. Little of the original structure remains visible, but Wrigley still has the ambience of an old-time ballpark, offering views of surrounding three-flats instead of parking lots.

43 Illinois Bell Telephone—Lakeview Office
(Chicago Telephone Company—Lakeview Office)
3532 N. Sheffield Ave.
1914, Holabird & Roche

In the early twentieth century Holabird & Roche developed a generic Georgian brick box to house telephone switching equipment throughout Chicago and its suburbs. This example is less altered than most, with a pedimented entrance and simple limestone lintels, cornice, and base.

44 Cabaret Metro
(Northside Auditorium Building)
3730 N. Clark St.
1928, Michaelsen & Rognstad

Spanish Baroque Revival, with its exotic connotations and exuberant ornament, was the style of choice for many Roaring Twenties entertainment halls.

Alta Vista Terrace

45 Alta Vista Terrace
3800 block of N. Alta Vista Terr.
1904, Joseph C. Brompton

This tiny street is well worth the circuitous route needed to reach it. Alta Vista Terrace was one of the last real estate developments of Samuel Eberly Gross, a prominent developer of working-class housing during the 1880s and 1890s. Inspired by a European sojourn, Gross re-created the character of London row houses on newly purchased land. As with Georgian terraces, the street wall is designed as a unit—but with a wealth of contrasts in color, rooflines, and stylistic detail. Twenty small row houses on each side of the narrow street create an intimate streetscape; the designs are mirrored diagonally across the block. All are two-story buildings of Roman brick except for a quartet of three-story graystones in the center. In 1971, Alta Vista Terrace was designated Chicago's first historic district.

46 Lakeview High School
4015 N. Ashland Ave.
1898, Normand S. Patton
1916, Arthur F. Hussander
1939, John C. Christensen

The influence of Oxford and Cambridge is evident in American college and university designs of the 1890s (see University of Chicago). This magnificent complex, intended to emulate the style and quality of a university building, was Chicago's first public high school in the Tudor style. Patton's design comprises the section running from the gatehouse tower (with 1898 carved above the entry) north to the center of the block; it was an addition to a building (now demolished) on Irving Park Rd. Patton's design was echoed by Hussander's quarter blocks to the north and south; note especially the fine doorway on Irving Park Rd. The extreme northern quarter came last. Gables, crenellated towers, ornamentation, and fenestration create a unified whole.

Lakeview High School

47 Graceland Cemetery
4001 N. Clark St.

These 121 acres were a rural area when the cemetery was founded in 1860 by Thomas B. Bryan, a lawyer and real estate investor who received a state charter in 1861 exempting the property from condemnation for public purposes. The first designers were William Saunders, who also worked at Rosehill, assisted by Swain Nelson and followed by Horace W. S. Cleveland, who may also have worked on the design for Oakwoods Cemetery.

Bryan's nephew, Bryan Lathrop, served for many years as president and was a self-taught naturalist. Under his influence, architects William Le Baron Jenney and Ossian Cole Simonds were brought in to improve the site in 1878. Simonds decided to devote his practice to landscape design and was superintendent from 1881 until his death in 1931. His harmonious settings using native flora presaged the Prairie School movement.
—Joan Pomaranc

Holabird & Roche designed the **A Entrance Gates and Fence,** along with the adjacent **B Office Building and Waiting Room** in 1896 (office building remodeled 1986, Frederick Phillips & Assocs.). The firm received many commissions at Graceland from Simonds, who had been a founding partner of the firm in 1880.

C Howard Van Doren Shaw designed his family plot with a tall central column and separate stones for the families of two of his daughters. A traditionalist in his architectural work, Shaw created a flat-sided column topped by a bronze ball, cast with the words of the Twenty-third Psalm.

The rusticated red granite **D Chapel and Mortuary Crypt** was designed by Holabird & Roche and constructed in 1888 (with several later additions).

E **William A. Hulbert** founded the National League of Professional Baseball Clubs in 1876. The names of the league's eight teams are carved into the giant baseball that marks his grave.

The columnar monument with an urnlike top, designed by Richard E. Schmidt for his parents, **F** **Ernst and Therese Schmidt,** is a handsome and personal example of his Prairie School style.

The grave of structural engineer **G** **Fazlur Rahman Khan,** whose work at Skidmore, Owings & Merrill included the John Hancock Center and the Sears Tower, is marked by a square stone of red granite, snugly surrounded by low, tight greenery.

Photographer **H** **Richard Nickel** was an early crusader for architectural preservation, renowned for his efforts to document and save the great works of Chicago architecture. While salvaging ornament from Adler & Sullivan's Stock Exchange Building during its demolition in 1972, he was killed by falling masonry. His black granite stone was designed by architects John Vinci and Lawrence Kenny.

The flat slab of black granite that marks the grave of **I** **Ludwig Mies van der Rohe** was designed by his grandson, architect Dirk Lohan. Mies came to Chicago from Germany in 1938 to direct the architecture department of the Armour Institute, which became the Illinois Institute of Technology. His designs for steel and glass buildings revolutionized modern architecture and established the International Style.

Architect Peter Weber designed the **J** **Lucius**

Fisher columbarium in 1916, and sculptor Richard W. Bock designed the hooded figure.

Architect Henry Bacon and sculptor Daniel Chester French designed the monument for **K** **Marshall Field,** which French titled *Memory.* On the base of the statue is the emblem of the caduceus, the staff of Mercury, Roman god of commerce. Bacon and French later collaborated on the design of the Lincoln Memorial in Washington, D.C.

Getty Tomb

Louis H. Sullivan designed the **L** **Getty Tomb** for lumber merchant Henry Harrison Getty after the death of his wife, Carrie Eliza, in 1890. Getty was a partner of Martin Ryerson, whose nearby tomb was also Sullivan's work. Freed from addressing the normal practical requirements of a working building, Sullivan gave free rein to his decorative talents in designing this monument, planning the ornament in full-scale drawings. The frilly acanthus leaf, a favorite plant form of Sullivan and his contemporaries, is lushly but delicately rendered in Bedford limestone and bronze. Look through the gates to the explosion of ornament on the massive door. Frank Lloyd Wright said of this work, "Outside the realm of music, what finer requiem?"

M **Ernest Robert Graham** was one of Daniel Burnham's partners who established the firm of Graham, Anderson, Probst & White in 1917, after Burnham's death.

Ryerson Tomb

N **Daniel Burnham** and his family are buried on an island in the lake, reached by a plain concrete footbridge; boulders mark the burial sites. As an architect, chief of construction for the 1893 World's Columbian Exposition, and author of the 1909 Plan of Chicago, Burnham was a central figure of the Chicago School.

New York architects McKim, Mead & White designed the **O** **Potter and Bertha Palmer** tomb, tall twin sarcophagi set within an open-air temple of Ionic columns.

Across the road from the Palmers, McKim, Mead & White designed a French Gothic tomb for Bertha's parents, **P** **Henry H. and Eliza Honoré.** Southeast of the Palmer tomb is an equally grandiose McKim, Mead & White monument to piano manufacturer **Q** **William Kimball.**

The **R** **Goodman Family** tomb, designed by Howard Van Doren Shaw in 1918, nestles into the lake shore, its top appearing as an overlook and its entrance reached by a flight of stairs leading to the water's edge.

The grave of **S** **Louis H. Sullivan** was designed by Thomas Tallmadge in 1929, five years after Sullivan's death. Upon a wide boulder Sullivan's profile is set in one of his own ornamental designs; Tallmadge wrote the tribute on the back of the stone. On the narrow sides, a setback skyscraper seems to be emerging, reflecting Sullivan's role in the development of the high rise. Tallmadge wrote a history of nineteenth-century Chicago architecture and coined the term "Chicago School."

Lumber merchant and real estate speculator **T** **Martin Ryerson** died in 1887; his son, Martin A. Ryerson, commissioned this mausoleum from Louis H. Sullivan, who had designed four downtown office buildings for the senior Ryerson. The polished black granite tomb is inspired by Egyptian funerary forms, the mastaba for the lower portion and the pyramid for the top. Unlike most Egyptian-style tombs, the design calls on Egyptian precedents not for detailing but for the dark and massive form, which seems as timeless as the concept of eternity itself.

Solon S. Beman, who was responsible for the design of the company town of Pullman, also designed the **U** **George M. Pullman** monument, a very tall Corinthian column placed in a terraced setting with an exedra on either side. Pullman died after a bitter and violent strike had disrupted his town. Fearing that his remains might be vandalized, the family had him interred below the monument inside a concrete block topped with railroad ties set in concrete.

Brewer **V** **Peter Schoenhofen** rests in a steep-sided pyramid, entered through an Egyptian portal with a sun disk. A sphinx and a rather out-of-place Victorian angel stand guard, the latter holding a key and gazing heavenward.

Root Monument

statue was erected in 1931, six years after the death of the philanthropic publisher of the *Chicago Daily News.*

a Peirce Anderson was one of Daniel Burnham's partners who became a founding member of Graham, Anderson, Probst & White. Anderson's profile is featured on a large pink granite monument, with his name and dates in very small letters near the lower edge.

Designer **b László Moholy-Nagy** came to Chicago in 1937, after the Bauhaus had been closed by the Nazis. Here he opened the New Bauhaus, renamed the Institute of Design and later merged with the Illinois Institute of Technology. His cremated remains are buried under a small, standardized granite square behind the chapel.

Along with her husband, Walter Burley Griffin, and her cousin, Dwight H. Perkins, **c Marion Mahony Griffin** was an architect of the Prairie School movement, known for her beautiful Japanese-influenced renderings of buildings. Her burial site near the chapel is unmarked.

The family plot of pioneer Chicagoan and hotel owner **d Dexter Graves** features a mysterious and haunting bronze sculpture, *Eternal Silence,* by Lorado Taft.

e Dwight H. Perkins played an important role in the Prairie School movement, designing innovative schools and park buildings. He also helped to establish the Cook County Forest Preserves.

Other architects buried at Graceland include: David Adler, Augustus Bauer, L. Gustav Hallberg, Richard G. Schmid, James J. Egan, Alfred Shaw, and Edward Burling.

Burnham's partner **W John Wellborn Root** died of pneumonia while their firm was planning the World's Columbian Exposition. Included among the abstract ornament on the Celtic cross that marks his grave is his last drawing, a design for the entrance to a building proposed for the fair. The cross was designed by Jules Wegman, a member of the firm.

X William Holabird, another central figure of the Chicago School, is buried in a family plot tucked into a low ridge.

The work of **Y George Grant Elmslie** is a highly personal interpretation of the Chicago and the Prairie schools. His name is engraved on a flat slab of black granite along with the names of members of his wife's family.

"Above All Things Truth Beareth Away the Victory" are the only words on this monument to **Z Victor F. Lawson.** Lorado Taft sculpted the larger-than-life, polished black granite figure of a medieval Crusader. The

Pattington Apartments

48 4015 N. Sheridan Rd. (Marmon Hupmobile Showroom)
1920, Paul Gerhardt

Things Egyptian were very popular in this era of archaeological marvels, which culminated in the opening of King Tut's tomb in 1922. Gerhardt was so enamored of Egyptian motifs that he incorporated them into two entries for the Chicago Tribune Competition.

49 Irving Apartments (Kellshore Apartment Hotel)
718–756 W. Irving Park Rd.
1915, E. Norman Brydges

In the description of this project, *The Book of the North Shore* said, "Much as one may regret the necessity of people living in apartments instead of in attractive vine-covered houses, the problem is with us and so has to be met in a manner which will insure the maximum of comfort, light, air, and pleasing composition." Although basking in the reflected glory of the grand Pattington Apartments, the units here are small studios and one-bedrooms designed to appeal to young marrieds and single office workers. Shallow urns that flank the courtyard entryways and top the corner piers provide a Prairie School touch.

50 Pattington Apartments
660–700 W. Irving Park Rd.
1903–1904, David E. Postle

Chicago's best turn-of-the-century courtyard building is the largest built to that time. All seventy-two units were capacious apartments with servants' quarters, marketed to upper-middle-class families as an alternative to single-family residences. The two courtyards each have five elaborate neo-Classical entrances. The design provides complete cross-ventilation for each apartment, enhanced by bay windows that flood the rooms with light and air.

American Islamic College
(Immaculata High School)

51 American Islamic College
(Immaculata High School)
640 W. Irving Park Rd.
Former Mary Hall
600–634 W. Irving Park Rd.
1922, Barry Byrne
Former Convent
4030 N. Marine Dr.
1955, Barry Byrne
Former St. Joseph's Hall
636 W. Irving Park Rd.
1956, Barry Byrne

This important early modern school displays Byrne's characteristic combination of Prairie School massing and forms with a very personal interpretation of Gothic detailing. Shared facilities such as the assembly hall and the gymnasium dominate the pavilion, which breaks out slightly from the southeast corner; the window treatment here reflects the scale of the interior spaces. Classroom windows are arranged in groups of three, enframed by slender pointed arches rising the building's full height. The spare ornament (which originally included sculpture by Alfonso Iannelli) is concentrated at the entrances.

52 Walt Disney Magnet School
4140 N. Marine Dr.
1973, Perkins & Will

Chicago's first magnet school draws students from large areas rather than just the surrounding neighborhood. Innovations include flexible classroom space organized into nine "pods."

Hutchinson Street Landmark District
Hutchinson St. between Marine Dr. and Hazel St.

This two-block area, a showcase for residential architecture of the late nineteenth and early twentieth centuries, is particularly rich in designs by George W. Maher, spanning two decades of his career.

53 Edwin J. Mosser House
750 W. Hutchinson St.
1902, George W. Maher

The cream-colored Roman brick walls flower with luxuriant Sullivanesque ornament, especially around the main entrance facing west. The south facade is domi-

nated by a one-story sun porch, with a projecting roof that forms a porte cochere.

54 Claude Seymour House
817 W. Hutchinson St.
1913, George W. Maher

Maher's last house on Hutchinson St. is broad, monumental, and dignified. It includes a favorite motif, the flanged segmental arch over the door, and features such Prairie Style characteristics as a hipped roof, pronounced horizontality, and bands of windows under deep eaves.

55 William H. Lake House
826 W. Hutchinson St.
1904, George W. Maher

Asymmetrical but formal and subtly balanced, the monumental facades are topped by great overhanging low-hipped roofs.

56 Grace Brackebush House
839 W. Hutchinson St.
1909, George W. Maher

This mature design combines the straightforwardness and severity that Maher admired in such English contemporaries as C. F. A. Voysey with the long horizontals of the Prairie School.

57 John C. Scales House
840 W. Hutchinson St.
1894, George W. Maher

This is the earliest house in the district, designed for the street's developer in the Queen Anne style of Maher's early career. Complex roof forms, beautifully reshingled, and high chimneys top heavily textured walls of boulders and half-timbering.

Seymour House

Pensacola Place Apartments

58 Louis Wolff House
4234 N. Hazel St.
1904, Richard E. Schmidt

Long attributed to Schmidt's chief designer, Hugh M. G. Garden, this house is now credited to another employee, William Drummond. The very closed facade, with small windows and large brick walls, has beautifully carved stone around the front door.

59 4338–4346 N. Clarendon Ave.
1905, Samuel N. Crowen

Crowen frequently blended Prairie Style elements with a dash of the Egyptian in his blocky apartment buildings. The delicate Sullivanesque frieze contrasts with robust entrance canopies.

60 Boardwalk Apartments
4343 N. Clarendon Ave.
1974, Stanley Tigerman & Assocs.

This pleasingly proportioned and economically successful complex of reinforced concrete and bronze-tinted glass was an early attempt to lure young middle-class tenants to a somewhat tattered neighborhood.

61 Pensacola Place Apartments
4334 N. Hazel St.
1981, Stanley Tigerman & Assocs. with Robert Fugman, assoc. arch.

The eastern facade of this "two-faced" structure mirrors the Boardwalk Apartments; the western facade is an essay in pop architecture. Semicircular balconies are intended to suggest the shafts of gigantic columns that culminate in huge Ionic volutes—a visual joke more clearly read in drawings than on the building. A ground floor of retail space and a mezzanine of aluminum-sided town houses form the base.

St. Mary of the Lake

62 St. Mary of the Lake Roman Catholic Church
4200 N. Sheridan Rd.
1913–1917, Henry J. Schlacks
School *1915, Joseph W. McCarthy*
Convent *1939, McCarthy, Smith & Eppig*

Unlike an earlier generation of church designers who knew historic architecture more through drawings and photos than direct experience, Schlacks traveled extensively in Europe in search of inspiration. This Renaissance design freely combines several major fourth- and fifth-century Roman churches: the freestanding campanile was patterned after that of St. Pudentiana, while the facade borrows from the Basilica of St. Paul Outside the Walls. The richly painted interior, decorated by Arthur Hercz, features fine stained-glass windows by F. X. Zettler.

63 Commonwealth Edison Electric Power Substation
4401 N. Clifton Ave.
1916, Hermann V. von Holst

Like many of von Holst's power stations, this strong, blocklike design is enriched with brickwork in geometric patterns.

64 Graeme Stewart Public School
4525 N. Kenmore Ave.
1907, Dwight H. Perkins

Pairs of enormous copper brackets support the massive hipped roof of this imposing brick and limestone structure. Features in common with Perkins's other schools include the robust consoles serving as keystones atop the large arched windows of the central block and, on the end pavilions, vertical pairs of windows with only the lower of the two pedimented.

65 Bank of Chicago Lakeshore (Standard Vaudeville Theater)
1050 W. Wilson Ave.
1909, William F. Behan
Renovated 1989, Mayes-Vostal Architects

A building with many lives, the original theater closed in 1922 and was replaced by a series of banks. Bank of Chicago arrived in 1947 and added a trompe l'oeil mural that hides a wall left bare by the demolition of an adjacent building in the 1980s. Through the "arch" is a southern Italian formal garden!

66 Truman College
1145 W. Wilson Ave.
1977, Dubin, Dubin, Black & Moutoussamy

This City College in a gritty neighborhood has an appropriately sturdy, hard-edged Miesian campus.

Because Northwestern University's original charter specified a "four-mile limit" banning liquor sales, for many years no alcohol could be served north of Devon Ave.—making Uptown the city's northernmost outpost for taverns and the first spot south of suburban Highwood to get a drink. With the advent of Prohibition, the booze just went underground, making this neighborhood a bootlegging and roadhouse center, filled with young people and entertainment complexes.

67 CTA—Wilson Avenue Elevated Station (Uptown Union Station)
4604–4634 N. Broadway
1923, A. W. Gerber

This small building served as a transfer point between suburban railroads and elevated trains that ran downtown. The Beaux Arts arcade (which replaced one designed by Frank Lloyd Wright) was designed for a glamorous era of train travel but now reflects the grimy reality of public transportation.

68 Uptown Broadway Building
4707 N. Broadway
1927, Walter W. Ahlschlager

Uptown boomed when terracotta was at its peak of popularity, and this commercial building is a visual encyclopedia, with human faces, animal heads, foliage, columns, and ribbons rendering in yellow and gray the Spanish Baroque style. A popular claim that the building was built by Al Capone is unsubstantiated.

69 Riviera Theatre
4746 N. Broadway
1918, Rapp & Rapp

This was the second theater built by Balaban & Katz and the first for which they used Rapp & Rapp. Its success led B & K to use Rapp & Rapp almost exclusively. Originally started by another owner, the project went broke during construction. The facade and adjacent commercial building were by another architect (unknown) and were probably left intact by the Rapps; the facade is tame by comparison with the firm's subsequent work.

Uptown National Bank

70 Uptown National Bank of Chicago (Uptown Bank Building)
4753 N. Broadway
1924, Marshall & Fox
Addition 1928, Huszagh & Hill

Originally constructed with only eight floors and later expanded, the building has two cornices. The base reflects the importance of the second and third floors, which contain the main banking spaces. Step inside to see original fixtures and ornamental work. The plaster ceiling was originally cast in Italy and shipped in pieces for installation.

Uptown Theatre

71 Uptown Theatre
4814 N. Broadway
1925, Rapp & Rapp

Eight stories tall and with 4,381 seats, it was the largest theater ever for both the architects and the developers, Balaban & Katz. The Uptown was an important addition to the entertainment district, which included the Aragon Ballroom and the Green Mill Lounge. The Spanish Baroque Revival style, with its emphasis on the grandly ornamented portal, was perfect for a movie palace. Through those doors lay a world much grander and more exotic than the neighborhood's cramped apartments and smoky bars.

72 U.S. Post Office— Uptown Station
4850 N. Broadway
1939, Howard L. Cheney

Polished granite eagles guard this small Moderne post office. Inside, murals (1943) by Henry Varnum Poor depict Carl Sandburg and Louis H. Sullivan, who holds a model of the Carson Pirie Scott store.

73 Ecumenical Institute (Mutual Insurance Building)
4750 N. Sheridan Rd.
1921, Fugard & Knapp
Addition and alterations 1926, B. Leo Steif

Handsomely clad in gleaming terra-cotta, this office building was originally a four-story retail building with an arcaded corridor; its facade was "stretched" to insert three more floors.

74 Aragon Ballroom
1106 W. Lawrence Ave.
1926, Huszagh & Hill

The golden age of ballroom dancing came to life in this Moorish dreamland. A grand entrance lobby, running the length of the building, culminated in a wide staircase flanked with plaster dragons. Double-tiered, ornate terra-cotta arches, mosaics, tiles, palm trees, and a promenade surrounded the dance floor. Lights from Spanish-style fixtures glowed under the twinkling stars in the cobalt blue dome. Ceilings that imitated the night sky were key features of 1920s "atmospheric" theaters and dance halls, transporting snowbound Midwesterners to warm Mediterranean landscapes. The Spanish or Moorish—or sometimes Oriental—decor enhanced the appealing exoticism.

When ballroom dancing faded after World War II, the Aragon was used for a series of unsuccessful ventures before becoming a concert hall in the 1970s.

75 5040–5060 N. Marine Dr.
(Marine Drive Apartments)
1939, Oman & Lilienthal

This development followed close on the heels of the Granville Gardens and Wolcott Gardens and shows the same simple Art Moderne detailing: corner windows (originally metal casements), multicolored stripes of brick, and a very thin wall plane, with windows set close to the surface. Six staggered blocks are arranged to take advantage of lake views and maximize ventilation.

76 Myron Bachman House
1244 W. Carmen Ave.
Remodeled 1948, Bruce Goff

If the Jetsons had remodeled a house after World War II, it might have looked like this. Goff had designed Quonset huts during the war and applied his interest in corrugated metal to this renovation of an old house, incorporating a recording-studio

Bachman House

control room in front. Though hardly contextual, it is fascinating—especially the combination of corrugated metal and weeping mortar.

77 Wolcott Gardens
4901–4959 N. Wolcott Ave.
1939, Michaelsen & Rognstad

A full block of twenty-one modest Art Moderne apartment buildings is arranged around open space, creating courtyards that are more private than those in traditional U-shaped flats of the 1920s. The detailing varies subtly, usually around the doorways. This was another project made possible by FHA mortgage insurance, and construction was not started until Granville Gardens on N. Hoyne Ave. had been successfully leased.

78 Carl Sandburg House
4646 N. Hermitage Ave.
early 1890s, architect unknown

Sandburg moved into the second-floor flat in 1912 with his wife and infant daughter and wrote "Chicago" while living here.

Wolcott Gardens

79 Wallace C. Abbott House
4605 N. Hermitage Ave.
1891, Dahlgren & Lievendahl

One of the finest Victorian homes lining Hermitage and Paulina aves. is this one built for the founder of Abbott Laboratories. Beautifully restored and maintained, it also retains a nineteenth-century stable.

All Saints Church

80 All Saints Episcopal Church
4550 N. Hermitage Ave.
1883, John C. Cochrane

This distinctive Stick Style structure may be the city's oldest frame church. The bell in the corner tower summoned the volunteer fire department and announced services, which Carl Sandburg attended here.

81 Ravenswood Place
4530–4554 N. Paulina Ave.
4541–4555 N. Hermitage Ave.
1988, Environ, Inc.

The stylistic free-for-all of the 1980s produced developments like this one, combining Prairie-influenced and Victorian-inspired houses. One prototype evolved into four models rotated and subtly varied.

82 Ravenswood United Methodist Church
(Ravenswood Methodist Episcopal Church)
4501 N. Hermitage Ave.
1890, John S. Woollacott

Behind the prim rusticated facade is a sculpted space inspired by H. H. Richardson and Louis H. Sullivan. A great roundheaded arch filled with organ pipes dominates the almost square worship space. A hammer-beam ceiling rises above gently curving amphitheatrical seating and a balcony. The church was designed to accommodate these leaded-glass windows, which were brought from an earlier church nearby.

83 Ravenswood Public School
4332 N. Paulina Ave.
1892, John J. Flanders
1912, Arthur F. Hussander

The broad-eaved Flanders design was echoed by copycat Hussander; cut-stone ornament is reproduced in terra-cotta on later sections.

84 Kelmscott Gallery (Krause Music Store)
4611 N. Lincoln Ave.
1922, William C. Presto with Louis H. Sullivan, assoc. arch.

Unlike his professional fortunes, Sullivan's talent never waned, as this, his final design, testifies. William Krause asked his neighbor, Presto, to design a building to house his music store showroom below and his family above. Presto, in turn, asked former employer Sullivan to design the facade, which he did while working out of an office of the American

Kelmscott Gallery (Krause Music Store)

Terra Cotta Company. With the help of their modeler Kristian Schneider, Sullivan's characteristic foliate ornament bloomed as beautifully on this modest project as it had on the magnificent Auditorium Theater over thirty years before. The elaborate system of ornament culminates in a large cartouche rising three feet above the parapet. The facade was restored by the current tenant.

85 Hild Performing and Visual Arts Center (Chicago Public Library—Frederick H. Hild Regional Branch)
4544 N. Lincoln Ave.
1931, Pierre Blouke

The restrained Art Deco facade on Lincoln Ave. is smooth and blocky, a discreet owl the only playful element. Around the corner, on the "residential" side, informality prevails. A semicircular bulge houses the library stacks. Another owl guards the entrance to what was the children's library, reached by stairs at the north end.

86 Chicago Public Library—Conrad Sulzer Regional Branch
4455 N. Lincoln Ave.
1985, Hammond Beeby & Babka with Joseph W. Casserly, city arch.

This friendly, whimsical, and inviting public building is worth exploring for its decorative delights. The long facade continues the street wall of Lincoln Ave. and ends in a graceful curve. The entrance is subtly indicated by a large gabled window that opens into the second-floor reading room. Inspired by neo-Classical architecture, the building is nonetheless modern in its revelation of metal structure with infills of glass or brick. The division of functions is logical, with noisy activities (circulation desk, audio and video materials, children's library) concentrated on the first floor. Whimsically painted furniture, originally intended for the children's area, now delights patrons throughout the building.

Sulzer Branch Library

87 St. Benedict's Roman Catholic Church
2201 W. Irving Park Rd.
1918, Hermann J. Gaul

The large German congregation built their church in a northern Italian version of the Romanesque style, exuberantly studded with short columns outside as well as inside. The interior is more Germanic and features artglass windows by F. X. Zettler.

88 Albert G. Lane Technical High School
2501 W. Addison Rd.
1934, Paul Gerhardt
Stadium *1940, John C. Christensen*

The Board of Education took technical education seriously, creating special facilities for these schools and endowing them with the dignity and focused purpose of a college campus. Lane Tech looks like an Industrial Gothic factory, with its large glazed areas, clock tower, and smokestack. A light court gives outside exposure to all classrooms and shops. The interior is worth a visit to see sculptures in the library by Peterpaul Ott and frescoes in the auditorium lobby glorifying *The Teaching of Art* (late 1930s, Mitchell Siporin). The concrete football stadium, a 1930s version of Gothic, was built by the WPA.

Lane Technical High School

89 DeVry Institute of Technology
3300 N. Campbell Ave.
1973, Caudill Rowlett Scott

Approaching from the south, you might mistake this for an appliance superstore, with its logo ornamenting a painted metal facade. Rounding the corner to the northwest, the building turns into a reflective glass structure, with metal framework projecting at each end. DeVry is part of a national chain of for-profit vocational schools owned by Bell & Howell. Round-the-clock shifts of instruction and changing technology made flexibility of classroom and lab sizes a key element, and the exposed-structure design expresses this capacity for flexibility and expansion. This site was part of the home of the Riverview Amusement Park from 1904 to 1967.

90 Friedrich Ludwig Jahn Public School
3149 N. Wolcott Ave.
1907, Dwight H. Perkins

This is a Prairie form with simplified Gothic details. The depth of the facade and the Secession-style entrance link it with Perkins's other powerfully modeled schools of this period.

91 Brundage Building
3325 N. Lincoln Ave.
1923, William G. Uffendell

The robust neo-Classical facade of this elegant flatiron building (note the four-foot-wide pilasters) looks like limestone but is entirely of terra-cotta. Brundage, famous as the longtime head of the International Olympic Committee, acquired properties that he had built as a contractor and that went under in the 1930s.

Jahn School

EDGEWATER/
ROGERS PARK

Jarvis
Sherwin
Chase
Jarlath
Touhy
Fitch
Estes
Greenleaf
Lunt
Coyle
Morse
Farwell
Pratt

Park
Gables
42

Casa Bonita
Apts **48**

7221
N Ridge
49

Park
Castle
43

Marshall
House
46

Ridge Ave
houses
50-52

53

Jackson-
Thomas House

Indian
Boundary
Park
41

44

47

Winter
House

45

Park
Crest Park
Manor

54

6901 N Ridge

Rogers

Clark

W A R R E N
P A R K

Richmond
Francisco
Mozart
California
Fairfield
Washtenaw
Talman
Rockwell
Maplewood
Campbell
Artesian
Western
Claremont
Oakley
Bell
Leavitt
Hamilton
Hoyne
Seeley
Damen

Ridge

Angel
Guardian
Church
55

Granville
Gardens

58

Unity
Church
56

57

Ravenswood

Winchester-
Hood
Garden
Homes

Winchester
Wolcott

Peterson

Lincoln

59

R O S E H I L L
C E M E T E R Y

Bowmanville

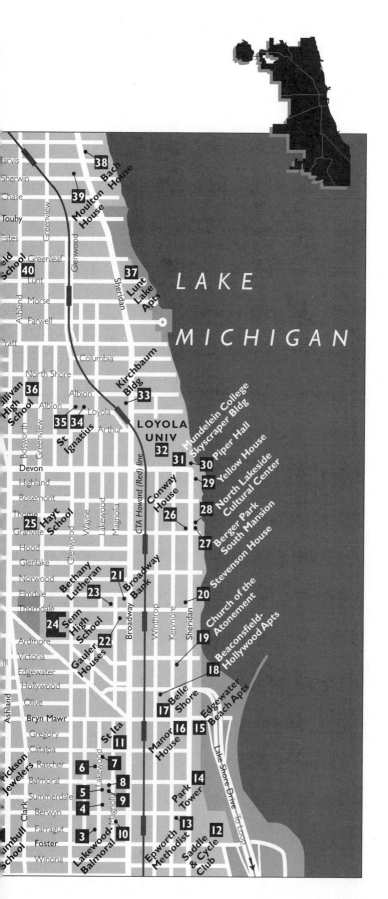

LAKE

MICHIGAN

38 Bach House

39 Moulton House

37 Lunt Lake Apts

40

Kirchbaum Bldg **33**

36 Sullivan High School

35 **34** St Ignatius

LOYOLA UNIV

32

31

Mundelein College Skyscraper Bldg

30 Piper Hall

29 Yellow House

North Lakeside Cultural Center **28**

Conway House

26

Berger Park South Mansion **27**

25 Hayt School

Stevenson House

21 Broadway Bank

Bethany Lutheran

23

20 Church of the Atonement

24 Senn High School

22 Gauler Houses

19 Beaconsfield-Hollywood Apts

18

17 Belle Shore

St Ita

11

Manor House **16** **15** Edgewater Beach Apts

6 **7**

8

5 **9**

4

14 Park Tower

3 **10**

13 Epworth Methodist

12 Saddle & Cycle Club

The history of Edgewater and Rogers Park tells of the metamorphosis from genteel suburb to urban neighborhood. As usual, the catalyst was the extension of a transit line, making the community more accessible to legions of Loop office workers. Highway construction brought further changes, turning quiet streets into congested thoroughfares. But behind the row of Sheridan Road's high rises are pockets of elegance that hint at the area's enduring appeal.

Edgewater and Rogers Park began as farming communities but originally belonged to different townships, separated at Devon Avenue. Edgewater joined the city as part of the Lake View annexation in 1889; four years later Rogers Park voted to secede from Evanston and become part of Chicago.

Edgewater's landscape of celery farms began its suburban transformation in 1885, when J. Lewis Cochran purchased lakefront property—the first of his many subdivisions—bounded by Foster Avenue, Broadway, and Bryn Mawr Avenue. Known as the "father of Edgewater," Cochran installed roads, sidewalks, drainage, and electricity; gave the area its name; and built about fifty "stylish mansions" on streets named for towns along the Main Line of his native Philadelphia. By 1910 Sheridan Road had become an exclusive stretch lined with mansions, while developments west of Broadway (such as Cochran's Lakewood-Balmoral) retained the suburban ambience on a more modest scale. Further west, working-class Swedes and Germans built single-family homes and two-flats near industries clustered along the Chicago & North Western tracks. The extension of the Northwestern Elevated Railroad (now the Howard El) through Edgewater in 1908 spurred further residential growth, and by the 1920s some of the original houses had yielded to high-rise hotels and apartments.

Rogers Park was incorporated as a village in 1878. It was named by its chief promoter, Patrick L. Touhy, for his father-in-law, Phillip Rogers, an early settler. Development took place first along the Ridge, a shelf of land left by the receding lake shore and the site of an Indian trail that was the area's only north–south road for decades. Farmers, especially Luxembourgers and Germans, built cottages here, and wealthier families like the Touhys built substantial homes in the picturesque styles. Even after the coming of two railroads, development was slow until the 1908 extension of the elevated line to Evanston. With stops every three blocks, the El set off a boom in apartment and hotel building adjacent to the lakefront.

In the southeastern corner of Rogers Park, Loyola University opened in 1922 on sand dunes acquired by the Jesuits in 1906, and Mundelein College opened its skyscraper campus in 1930. With less public transportation, West Rogers Park (west of Ridge Blvd.) was sparsely settled until after World War I, when brick bungalows and flats sprouted along its streets. For decades the site of nurseries, truck farms, and greenhouses, it was extensively developed after World War II.

—William B. Hinchliff

▮ Lyman Trumbull Public School

5200 N. Ashland Blvd.
1910, Dwight H. Perkins

Shorn of traditional ornament and showing the influence of the progressive Prairie School movement, this massive block has the power and purity of form that distinguishes Perkins's work as Chicago Board of Education architect. Towering and percussive, the walls roll from pier to pier, punctuated with deep vertical window reveals. The strong entrance pavilion rises above the busy intersection, marking the site as a community anchor. Innovations of this era include a ground-floor (rather than top-story) auditorium to facilitate community use of the space, generous corridors to improve

Trumbull School

circulation, washrooms on every floor instead of in the basement, and skylights. The grimy brick, once creamy, and the lunar landscape of the grassless playground now cast a pall.

2 Erickson Jewelers
5304 N. Clark St.
Remodeled early 1940s, architect unknown

In 1935 America's aging and dowdy retail areas were suffering from the effects of the Depression; for years merchants had put little money into remodeling. That year the Federal Housing Administration began insuring loans for store improvements up to $50,000, and in June *Architectural Record* announced a competition sponsored by the Libbey-Owens-Ford Glass Co. to "Modernize Main Street," with a jury that included Albert Kahn, William Lescaze, and John W. Root. Architects were directed to rethink the typical cluttered storefront as a merchandising device: "The store front with its plate glass show windows establishes the character of the store . . . It must serve to make the passer *buy,* inviting him or her to stop and shop." L-O-F sponsored the competition to promote Vitrolite, their opaque, pigmented structural glass (marketed under different names by other companies). Attached by adhesive to masonry, Vitrolite was a perfect modernizing material for storefronts: low maintenance, extremely durable, sleek and shiny. According to the *Record,* the properly "modernized"

storefront should feature a prominent sign or logo against an unadulterated surface. Fragments of these storefronts survive in many neighborhood shopping districts; few are as well preserved as this example. The black-glass background still sets off the brushed metal name and the diamond ring, almost two feet in diameter—enticing us to stop, look . . . and buy.

Erickson Jewelers

Lakewood-Balmoral Neighborhood
Lakewood, Magnolia, and Wayne Aves. from Foster to Bryn Mawr Aves.

Developer J. Lewis Cochran began energetically promoting his Edgewater subdivisions in the mid-1880s. The grandest houses, built on lots east of the railroad (now CTA) tracks, have almost all been replaced by apartments. These more modest dwellings, substantial yet often half the price of those closer to the lake, form a still-desirable neighborhood of single-family residences.

Cochran sold unimproved lots and also built houses on speculation, frequently five or ten at a time. Between 1885 and 1896 he commissioned designs from Joseph Lyman Silsbee, L. Gustav Hallberg, Henry H. Sprague, George W. Maher, J. N. Tilton, Joseph C. Brompton, Julius H. Huber, Church & Jobson, and Handy & Cady. Attributions are difficult because of the number of architects Cochran commissioned and the extensive remodeling that many houses have undergone. But even the unattributable Victorians are of interest, as they reemerge under the care of owners who remove artificial siding, repair the porches, and strip the woodwork.

3 Herman C. Lammers House
5222 N. Lakewood Ave.
1898, Julius H. Huber
Addition 1901; Remodeling 1911

The Hansel and Gretel remodeling was intended to make the house look more "European."

4 5313 N. Lakewood Ave.
1903, architect unknown

The pinched verticality of the dormers gives a piquant silhouette to Cochran's speculative house.

5 Angelica Holzaffel House
5347 N. Lakewood Ave.
1910, Leon E. Stanhope

Features typical of the Craftsman Style include diamond-paned windows and a pergola-like porch.

6 5426 N. Lakewood Ave.
1893, architect unknown

Cochran built this Queen Anne with an unusual lidded third-floor window surround.

7 Patrick H. McNulty House
5453 N. Lakewood Ave.
1898, Holabird & Roche

The centrally placed door and second-floor bay of this classically inspired house are a play on Palladian window composition.

McNulty House

8 Arthur Deppmann House
5356 N. Magnolia Ave.
1904, George W. Maher

Maher's simple, rectilinear design is firmly rooted in the twentieth century.

9 H. Mark Flat
5344 N. Magnolia Ave.
1913, Henry L. Newhouse

The huge two-story bay makes both floors equally grand, revealing this house's true nature as a two-flat. Corinthian columns as attenuated as toothpicks rise the full height of the bay.

10 5247 N. Magnolia Ave.
1899, Harvey L. Page & Co.

The classical language is bold and self-confident; Ionic columns support a double-height porch.

11 St. Ita's Church
1220 W. Catalpa Ave.
1927, Henry J. Schlacks

The M carved in the stone parapet honors the powerful Cardinal Mundelein, whose preference for French Gothic was not lost on Schlacks: he made it solidly thirteenth-century inside and out. The graceful, cohesive interior is warmed by wood wainscoting with Gothic detailing.

Lincoln Park and Lake Shore Drive ended at Foster Ave. until the early 1950s, when a huge landfill project extended them to Hollywood Ave. On the lake north of Foster Ave. were the private beach areas of the Saddle and Cycle Club and the Edgewater Beach Apartments and hotel complex.

12 Saddle and Cycle Club
900 W. Foster Ave.
1898, Jarvis Hunt
Additions 1904, 1909, Jarvis Hunt
Addition 1968, C. F. Murphy
Assocs.

You can catch a fleeting glimpse of this private club from Sheridan Rd. or Lake Shore Dr. In the mid-1890s the main club facilities were downtown; the Edgewater location was originally for cyclists and equestrians riding on the lakefront. The Shingle Style clubhouse and its first additions, designed by club member Hunt, are now barely visible; the tower with its bell-shaped cap is their most prominent remaining feature. The private beach was originally only 100 feet from the veranda and at the turn of the century had a boathouse and pier.

13 Epworth United Methodist Church (Epworth Methodist Episcopal Church)
5253 N. Kenmore Ave.
1890, Frederick B. Townsend
Addition and renovation 1930,
Thielbar & Fugard

The massive boulders that form the craggy, random-coursed stone walls were floated down Lake Michigan from Wisconsin to a shoreline slip. The composition is beautifully balanced by three towers: square, round, and octagonal. An early drawing shows entries in the square and octagonal towers; the current one dates from the 1930 addition and sanctuary renovation.

14 Park Tower Condominiums
5415 N. Sheridan Rd.
1974, Solomon, Cordwell, Buenz &
Assocs.

The beautifully detailed and proportioned curtain wall stands out among Edgewater's lakeside cliff of largely dreary high rises.

15 Edgewater Beach Apartments
5555 N. Sheridan Rd.
1928, Benjamin H. Marshall

This is the sole survivor of the Edgewater Beach Hotel complex,

Edgewater Beach Apartments

a sophisticated luxury resort and center of Roaring Twenties nightlife. A central octagonal tower and four Y-shaped wings rise from a rectangular base. When built, three out of four apartments had a view of the lake.

16 Manor House
1021–1029 W. Bryn Mawr Ave.
1908, J. E. O. Pridmore

British-born Pridmore designed this elegant Tudor Revival apartment building with only six units (later subdivided) of twelve to sixteen rooms—and two of the apartments had ballrooms. Once the home of the British consul and known as the Prince of Wales House, it bears the royal coat of arms in terra-cotta at the rear of the courtyard. Other upscale features were the rounded sun porch on the corner (the "Orangerie") and the private "family room" at the rear.

17 Belle Shore Apartment Hotel
1062 W. Bryn Mawr Ave.
1929, Koenigsberg & Weisfeld

Behind the Art Deco terra-cotta facade are 138 one-room/kitchenette apartments. Sculptural embellishments include an Egyptian frieze above the storefronts and Art Nouveau–influenced figures.

18 Beaconsfield-Hollywood Apartments
1055–1065 W. Hollywood Ave.
1913, J. E. O. Pridmore

This complex of connecting three-flats has fanciful terra-cotta ornament that culminates in an elaborate portal with diamond-patterned columns and a crest modeled on that of Castile, Spain.

Church of the Atonement

19 Church of the Atonement
5749 N. Kenmore Ave.
1919, 1924, J. E. O. Pridmore

The use of red sandstone ran counter to the tidal wave of Bedford limestone covering most Gothic churches of the era, but the overall design is conservative and elegant. The towering nave is a uniform vision, with pale colors and rich wood. Buried within the north transept is a piece of the original church, designed in 1890 by Henry Ives Cobb.

20 Harry M. Stevenson House
5940 N. Sheridan Rd.
1909, George W. Maher

Signature details include the dormer window, a complex play on a Palladian theme, and the second-floor window recessed behind colonnettes. At the rear, the broad cornice unites the garage, porte cochere, and house.

21 Broadway Bank
(Riviera-Burnstine Motor Sales)
5960 N. Broadway
1925, R. Bernard Kurzon

Terra-cotta is spun like sugar across a brick facade to form French Gothic lancets, finials, and drop-pendant window hoods. The interior is a fine example of a 1920s automobile showroom. The Mediterranean decor, with its stuccoed walls, columns, and grand staircase, was meant to suggest an outdoor setting such as a plaza or courtyard—which was considered the most appropriate backdrop for displaying cars.

22 John Gauler Houses
5917–5921 N. Magnolia Ave.
1908, Walter Burley Griffin

Griffin achieved maximum impact by carefully placing these twin Prairie School houses on their narrow lots. Framed by embracing porches, the intervening space—a gangway in less skillful hands—offers an additional architectural experience. The visitor is deep into this space before even seeing the very private front doors. Griffin's characteristic touches are the wood-mullioned windows and unbroken vertical piers.

23 Bethany Evangelical Lutheran Church
1244 W. Thorndale Ave.
1914, Grant C. Miller
Bible Chapel *1908, Patton & Miller*

Broadway Bank

Gauler Houses

Patton & Miller was among the few firms that designed churches in the informal, domestically scaled, simply but beautifully detailed Craftsman Style. The Tudor Revival–Craftsman Bible chapel (now a Montessori school), which served as the first church, blends well with the larger Craftsman church on the corner. Religious motifs are limited to the stone crosses on the bell tower and small medallions in the grapevine-patterned leaded-glass windows. Inside, an unsympathetic paint scheme obscures some of the original charm, but a few pieces of vintage Craftsman furniture remain.

24 Nicholas Senn High School
5900 N. Glenwood Ave.
1912, Arthur F. Hussander
Additions 1931, Paul Gerhardt

Grand but bland, it is greatly enhanced by the broad lawn, a rarity on Board of Education properties. Hussander's block, the north–south rectangle, contains a 2,000-seat auditorium. Gerhardt's perpendicular additions form a broad U-shaped court.

25 Stephen K. Hayt Public School
1518 W. Granville Ave.
1906, Dwight H. Perkins

Bold arches top vertical rows of windows in this school, which is closely related to the Francis Scott Key School in the Austin neighborhood.

26 Richard F. Conway House
6200 N. Sheridan Rd.
1906, William Carbys Zimmerman

27 Berger Park South Mansion (Joseph Downey House)
6205 N. Sheridan Rd.
1906, William Carbys Zimmerman
Renovated 1988, Chicago Park District

28 North Lakeside Cultural Center (Samuel H. Gunder House)
6219 N. Sheridan Rd.
1910, Myron H. Church
Renovated 1988, Roula Assocs. Architects and Simon & Co.

This prestigious residential area resembled neighboring North Shore suburbs until high rises replaced most of the mansions during the 1950s and 1960s. A hint of grandeur survives in the lavish, historically inspired detail of the Conway House, in contrast to the more sober Downey House.

On Sheridan Rd. are the buildings of Mundelein College, a women's school that merged with Loyola University in 1991.

29 Yellow House (Adolf Schmidt House)
6331 N. Sheridan Rd.
1917, George W. Maher

The decorative motif on this late work of Maher is the water lily, used on the capitals of the octagonal columns.

30 Piper Hall (Albert G. Wheeler House)
956 W. Sheridan Rd.
1909, William Carbys Zimmerman

Wheeler, chief engineer of the Chicago Tunnel Company, provided the architect with a lavish budget, enabling him to create

Classical, Romanesque, Tudor, and Prairie details from rough-textured white Vermont marble. Mundelein retained the interior detail and first-floor grandeur. A breathtaking art-glass window fills the wall behind the stair landing.

31 Skyscraper Building
(Mundelein College)
6363 N. Sheridan Rd.
1930, Naime W. Fisher and Joseph W. McCarthy

The first "skyscraper college," Mundelein's thoroughly modern school for women was head-quartered in this impressive fifteen-story tower. With its Art Deco massing and zigzags, curves, and stylized floral pat-terns, it could house the *Daily Planet*—were it not for the co-lossal archangels flanking the entrance. Uriel (Light of God) holds a book inscribed with a

Skyscraper Building

cross and points skyward; Jopiel (Beauty of God) holds aloft the torch of knowledge and grasps a celestial globe.

---

32 Loyola University Chicago Lake Shore Campus
6525 N. Sheridan Rd.

In 1906 the Jesuits of St. Ignatius College on Roosevelt Rd. pur-chased a twenty-acre site be-tween Devon and Loyola Aves. and Sheridan Rd. They estab-lished Loyola Academy, a high school, in 1909. The first college building followed in 1912; the university moved from Roosevelt Rd. in 1922. Several buildings of the 1930s are memorable, but those of the 1960s building boom are eminently forgettable. A long-standing plan for campus expansion on a landfill project was shelved in 1990 after envi-ronmentalists raised objections.

The Loyola campus occupies the lakefront north and east of Sheri-

dan's right-angle turn at Broadway and Devon. Major entries are on the north side of W. Sheridan Rd. at Winthrop Ave., on N. Sheridan Rd. just north of the elevated tracks, and on Loyola Ave. at Winthrop Ave. Street addresses are of little help in locating buildings, which are best found by checking the prominently posted campus maps.

Loyola's earliest years are best represented by

A Dumbach Hall (Loyola Academy)
1909, Worthmann & Steinbach

B Michael Cudahy Science Hall
1912, attrib. to Worthmann & Steinbach

These near-twins blend Spanish Mission Style with Renaissance details such as elaborately decorated arched windows. Dumbach was originally the high school, Cudahy the first college building.

C Madonna della Strada Chapel
6525 N. Sheridan Rd.
1939, Andrew N. Rebori

D Elizabeth M. Cudahy Memorial Library
1930, Rebori, Wentworth, Dewey & McCormick
Addition 1968, Barry & Kay

In vivid contrast to the historical styles of the early buildings, Loyola's Library and Chapel are fresh and bold. Facing each other across a broad lakefront lawn, they offer a striking display of Rebori's distinctive interpretation of modernism. Although designed as an ensemble in the late 1920s, the buildings were constructed nearly ten years apart due to the Depression.

The artless library addition, with its aluminum sculpture by Steven Urry—at one point titled *Erection* by the artist, later rechristened *Resurrection*—obscures most of Rebori's work. But walk around to the lake side to view the carved frieze with Latin names of subjects, the tower with its ziggurat, and the sundial. Go inside to see the main reading room with its large mural by John Warner Norton, who also painted the murals in the Board of Trade and Chicago Daily News Buildings. It celebrates the seventeenth-century French explorers of the region and re-creates Father Marquette's map of Illinois.

Rebori reworked his earlier design of the Chapel in the late 1930s. The curving Art Moderne form is reminiscent of a small dirigible or airplane hangar. The walls of the apse are "accordioned"—the folds filled with glass blocks, which admit slim

Madonna della Strada Chapel

slices of light. Names of famous Jesuits are crisply incised along the roofline; the tall tower is flat-topped and windowless. The Chapel has fared better than the Library with recent changes. The sanctuary was reoriented from the west to the north side of the church, creating a cozier and more intimate feeling and opening up a lake view through the glass doors on the east.

E Loyola University Living-Learning Center

6333 N. Winthrop Ave.
1991, Solomon Cordwell Buenz & Assocs.

Loyola may enter a new era of high-quality design if this opener is any sample. Their newest residence hall is a model of architectural collegiality, fitting well into this dense residential neighborhood. The varied roof heights of the interconnected buildings signal different functions, which include student housing as well as a conference and study center.

Living-Learning Center

33 Kirchbaum Building
6560 N. Sheridan Rd.
1922, Ronneberg, Pierce & Hauber

Look above the cluttered storefronts to see the Northwestern Terra Cotta Company's panorama of Chicago's growth. The long panel between Fort Dearborn, on the left, and the newly completed Wrigley Building, on the right, shows the contemporary skyline and features many of Northwestern's greatest hits, including the Railway Exchange Building and the Blackstone Hotel.

34 St. Ignatius Auditorium
1320 W. Loyola Ave.
1931, Rebori & Wentworth

Art Deco lettering over the entrance hints at Rebori's authorship.

35 St. Ignatius Roman Catholic Church
6559 N. Glenwood Ave.
1917, Henry J. Schlacks

Here is a monument to God and to Bedford limestone; the giant columns of the Roman Renaissance portico are each carved from a single block of stone. A six-story campanile anchors the eastern end.

36 Roger C. Sullivan High School
6631 N. Bosworth Ave.
1927, John C. Christensen

Low and laid out close to the sidewalk, Sullivan was designed to a residential scale. Take in the delightful Tudor details—finials, quoins, medallions, and gargoyles—in a trip around the block. Gothic-lettered panels identify various sections, from boiler room to assembly hall.

Sullivan High School

37 Lunt Lake Apartments
1122–1140 W. Lunt Ave.
1949, Holsman, Holsman, Klekamp & Taylor

The same issue of *Architectural Forum* (January 1950) that featured Mies van der Rohe's Promontory Apartments and his 860–880 Lake Shore Drive (for which Holsman's firm was consulting architect) gave equal space to this project and to the firm's Winchester-Hood Garden Homes. What most impressed the magazine were the innovative construction techniques, especially the use of "rowlock bond" brickwork, developed by structural engineer Frank Kornacker. Steel rods reinforce concrete poured in the cavity between outer and inner courses of brick, creating a very strong, very thin bearing wall.

38 Emil Bach House
7415 N. Sheridan Rd.
1915, Frank Lloyd Wright

One of the few Wright houses within Chicago, this is also one of the last small urban commissions of his Prairie Style period. It is a compact version of Wright's suburban residences, with a cantilevered second story. The floor plan is a condensed version of the open layouts pioneered by Wright.

39 J. Benjamin Moulton House
1328 W. Sherwin Ave.
1908, Walter Burley Griffin

The massing follows a scheme developed by Frank Lloyd Wright, Griffin's employer from 1901 to 1905: the first-floor living room wing projects from the main two-story block, creating a

Moulton House

Field School

tiered effect. Griffin preferred windows with thick wood mullions to the more delicate, leaded art glass favored by most Prairie School architects.

40 Eugene Field Public School
7019 N. Ashland Blvd.
1898, Normand S. Patton
Addition 1916, Arthur F. Hussander
Addition 1940, John C. Christensen

Many elementary schools in older neighborhoods were built over several decades, and until the 1960s the Board of Education's architects designed additions to match. The oldest part is the central section facing Ashland Ave.; it was built as an addition to Rogers Park's preannexation East Side School, which faced Greenleaf Ave. The proportions, the hipped roof, and the rusticated base were all respected when the complex was expanded to a harmonious blocklong campus.

41 Indian Boundary Park
2500 W. Lunt Ave.
Field House *1929, Clarence Hatzfeld*

Through this thirteen-acre park runs the northern boundary of an 1816 Indian treaty ceding the Chicago area to the federal government. In 1922, when the park opened, the surrounding area was almost completely undeveloped. The small zoo at the northwest corner is is the city's only remaining neighborhood zoo. A recent addition to the park is an elaborate playground designed by Robert Leathers and constructed by local residents. The field house combines Tudor and American Indian motifs. In the assembly hall, the beamed ceiling features chandeliers sporting peace pipes, drums, and arrowheads.

42 Park Gables
2438–2484 W. Estes Ave.
1927, James F. Denson

Park Gables

43 Park Castle
2416–2458 W. Greenleaf Ave.
1925, Jens E. Jensen
44 Park Manor
2415–2437 W. Greenleaf Ave.
1926, Melville Grossman
45 Park Crest
2420–2434 W. Lunt Ave.
1925, James F. Denson

This magnificent ensemble is crowned by Park Gables, a Tudor Revival double-courtyard complex with enormous projecting gables, slate roofs, tall casement windows, and ornamented chimney pots. Cathedral ceilings grace the upper floor apartments. Park Castle reaches back to the medieval castle for its machicolations, crenellations, and gargoyles. The two smaller buildings to the south are less flamboyant but reiterate the English theme.

46 Fred B. Marshall House
2238 W. Greenleaf Ave.
1915, Fred B. Prather
47 Fred Winter House
2246 W. Greenleaf Ave.
1928, Fred Winter

Marshall's house is monastically simple, honest, and unadorned, while down at the corner Winter pulled out all the stops when he designed his own massive bungalow. The red-tiled roof, Tudor half-timbering, battered walls, and Georgian windows are a raucous blend of colors, textures, and materials.

48 Casa Bonita Apartments
7340–7350 N. Ridge Ave.
1928, Alexander Capraro & Morris Komar
Renovated 1974, Warner, Brejcha, Evans & Assocs.

Glistening white terra-cotta facades define the deep courtyard.

49 7221 N. Ridge Ave.
Remodeled 1914, Niels Buck

Ridge Ave. follows the still-discernible contour of an ancient beach. Because the lower land to the east was frequently swampy, many of the first houses in Rogers Park were built on this street. A few cottages, some from

Casa Bonita Apartments

the 1870s, remain. This one was remodeled in the Craftsman Style popular before World War I. Characteristics include the exposed rafters under overhanging gables, bands of casement windows, and wood strips decorating stucco walls. Another Craftsman house is next door at 7215.

50 7114 N. Ridge Ave.
1913, Robert E. Seyfarth
51 7106 N. Ridge Ave.
1913, Robert M. Hyde
52 7100 N. Ridge Ave.
1916, A. J. Smith

Built during Ridge Ave.'s heyday as a fine residential street, 7100 has elaborate Craftsman Style brackets under a gabled roof. The house at 7106, similar to Hyde's Charles A. Carlson House in the Austin area, has an asymmetrical gabled roof that extends over the recessed entrance with battered piers. Other Craftsman features include decorative brickwork, exposed rafters, and floral-design leaded windows on the south wall. The Dutch Colonial house at 7114 presents an unusual treatment of a common style, with its gambrel roof exaggeratedly broadened to hold down the entire house, which is built at grade.

53 Jackson-Thomas House
7053 N. Ridge Ave.
early 1870s, architect unknown

Commissioned by Andrew B. Jackson, a founding trustee of

Jackson-Thomas House

Rogers Park, this was one of the first generation of grand houses on Ridge Ave. that rose above the modest cottages in bracketed splendor. The symmetrical facade with its central pavilion, the tall windows, and the bracketed hood molding and eaves make this a fine example of the Italianate style at its zenith.

54 6901 N. Ridge Ave.
1959, Donald E. Erickson

While many neighborhood apartment buildings were being built to a watered-down Georgian Revival formula, former Frank Lloyd Wright Foundation fellow Erickson curved this flagstone and curtain-wall building to give every apartment a view of open space. The steel-rod stairway gave the building its nickname, "the birdcage," and originally rose above a fish pond whose reflections doubled its pizzazz.

55 Angel Guardian Croatian Catholic Church (St. Henry's Roman Catholic Church)
6346 N. Ridge Ave.
1906, Henry J. Schlacks

This towered and gabled church is Schlacks's most folkloric design. St. Henry's parish was founded in the early 1850s by German-speaking Catholics, many from Luxembourg, who decided in 1904 to replace their church buildings with this brick and limestone Gothic edifice. Clocks fill in the tops of the tower's louvered arches, and in a niche above the round window on Ridge Ave. is a statue of St. Henry standing next to a model of Bamberg Cathedral, which he built.

56 Unity Church in Chicago (Chicago Town and Country Tennis and Swim Club)
1925 W. Thome Ave.
1925, George W. Maher & Son

The chimney of this grand Tudor manor house bears a limestone shield sporting the club's emblem: tennis racquets flanking intertwined initials. Though best known for his modern Prairie School–influenced work, Maher also did revivalist buildings between World War I and his death in 1926. Given the late date of this building, his son Philip may have been responsible for the design.

Winchester-Hood Garden Homes

57 Winchester-Hood Garden Homes
1823–1825 W. Granville Ave., 1908–1922 & 1940–1960 W. Hood Ave., 6149–6175 N. Wolcott Ave., 6113–6129 N. Winchester Ave., 1920–1922 W. Norwood Ave.
1949–1951, Holsman, Holsman, Klekamp & Taylor

This ambitious project encompasses twenty-two four- and five-story apartment buildings and contains some 800 units. Like the similar Lunt Lake Apartments by the same architect-developer-engineer team, Winchester-Hood combines innovative construction techniques—including concrete-reinforced brick walls and radiant-heated ceiling beams—with a "Scandinavian Modern" look that recalls the work of Eliel Saarinen and Alvar Aalto. Ornament is used sparingly but effectively. The stair halls rise behind walls punctuated by a series of three concrete panels depicting stylized signs of the zodiac, designed by architect Coder Taylor.

58 Granville Gardens
6200–6242 N. Hoyne Ave.
1938, Rissman & Hirschfeld

FHA mortgage insurance stimulated a slow resumption of residential construction in the few years before America's entry into World War II halted nonessential building. Several stripped-down Art Deco housing projects were built on the Far North Side, where undeveloped land was still available. Granville Gardens was Chicago's first large, privately financed housing complex since the onset of the Depression and the first built under direct government supervision. The carefully tailored design kept construction costs low enough to charge a monthly rent of no more than $15 per room. Fourteen buildings, each containing fourteen units, face two garden courts. To increase the sense of spaciousness, steel-framed casement windows were placed at the corners of each unit. The wall planes are very flat, with windows recessed only slightly. Decoration is limited to horizontal brickwork, which defines the ground floor and enhances the corners. Amazingly, the entire complex is in close to original condition.

59 Rosehill Cemetery
5800 N. Ravenswood Ave.

The Chicago area's largest nonsectarian cemetery was established in 1859 on a rural 350-acre site over four miles north of the existing city limits. The name came from an error in the charter documents that referred to Hiram Roe's tavern on a nearby hill as Roe's Hill. The cemetery's founders ensured the success of their investment by placing the entrance adjacent to the Chicago & North Western Railroad line. They also sought advice from John Jay Smith, founder of Philadelphia's Laurel Hill Cemetery. He recommended his associate, William Saunders, who provided the initial landscaping in a parklike setting of drives and walkways amid artificial lakes and well-tended grounds.

—Joan Pomaranc

Rosehill Entrance Gate

🅐 Entrance Gate and Office Building
1864, William W. Boyington

Built of Joliet limestone, these structures were designed in the "castellated Gothic" style, which employed the forms of medieval English architecture for picturesque effect.

Mid-nineteenth-century rural cemeteries were located on the outskirts of the city near rail lines. Railroads owned special funeral cars that could be rented to transport funeral parties to and from the city center. When the train tracks were elevated after 1900, a new Rosehill station and an elevator (for caskets) were designed to match the nearby entrance. The station has been demolished, although part of the platform remains. The elevator tower remains but is no longer in use.

Atop the hill is the 🅑 **Civil War Soldiers Memorial,** in the grassy center of a circular driveway ringed with other memorials to the Civil War. The columnar monument, designed by sculptor Leonard Volk and titled *Our Heroes,* is topped by a figure of a Union soldier. Four bronze plaques near the base represent the four service branches: army, navy, artillery, and cavalry.

🅒 **George S. Bangs** invented the railway mail car that made it possible to collect and sort mail on a moving train. His monument depicts a dead tree that represents the deceased; despite death, the trunk continues to support life in the form of plants and animals. A "fast mail" rail car emerges from a tunnel at the base of the trunk.

Bangs Monument

🅓 **"Long John" Wentworth,** one of twelve mayors buried at Rosehill, has a seventy-two-foot obelisk, the cemetery's tallest monument.

Around the lake, near the center of the cemetery, is an impressive row of mausoleums representing the popular styles of the late nineteenth century. The Egyptian temple for railroad president 🅔 **Darius Miller** reflects the popularity of a cultural style whose greatest monuments focused on death and eternity.

Miller Tomb

A Greek temple with Doric columns marks the resting place of **F Charles Gates Dawes,** the nation's vice president under Calvin Coolidge.

Look across the lake for the best view of banker **G Norman W. Harris's** mausoleum, with its Corinthian columns and copper-clad dome. The tomb is a perfect Classical tempietto in the eighteenth-century manner. The burial chambers lie below the floor of the structure.

H Charles M. Hewitt, a manufacturer and financier, has a rusticated Romanesque mausoleum.

Another very impressive temple form, for **I Adam Schaaf,** has two lions resting at the front steps.

May Chapel

J Horatio N. May Chapel
1899, Joseph L. Silsbee

The picturesque design combines Gothic and Romanesque elements. The chapel is generally kept locked, but walk through the porte cochere and note the handsome mosaic ceiling.

K William B. Mundie was William Le Baron Jenney's partner from 1891 to 1907 and worked on the design of the Manhattan Building.

The mausoleum of banker **L Oscar G. Foreman** is noteworthy for its unusual Art Nouveau architecture (designer unknown) and because it is empty; the Foremans are buried in Graceland Cemetery.

Sculptor **M Leonard W. Volk** carved the life-size statue of himself that marks his family plot. His wife's cousin, Senator Stephen A. Douglas, and his political opponent, Abraham Lincoln, were frequent and popular subjects for Volk's work.

N John M. Van Osdel, Chicago's first professional architect, was responsible for more than seventy commercial and public buildings in the Loop alone.

O William W. Boyington, an early Chicago architect, was a leading designer of Chicago railroad stations and other public buildings.

The grave of architect **P George W. Maher** is marked with a small unadorned block of granite. Maher's work is generally classified with that of the Prairie School, but his was a highly personal interpretation of ideas from various contemporary sources.

Q Rosehill Mausoleum
1914, Sidney Lovell

Within its marble-lined hallways, family crypts open off long corridors embellished with stained-glass windows; the most impressive is the Tiffany window in the John G. Shedd Memorial Room.

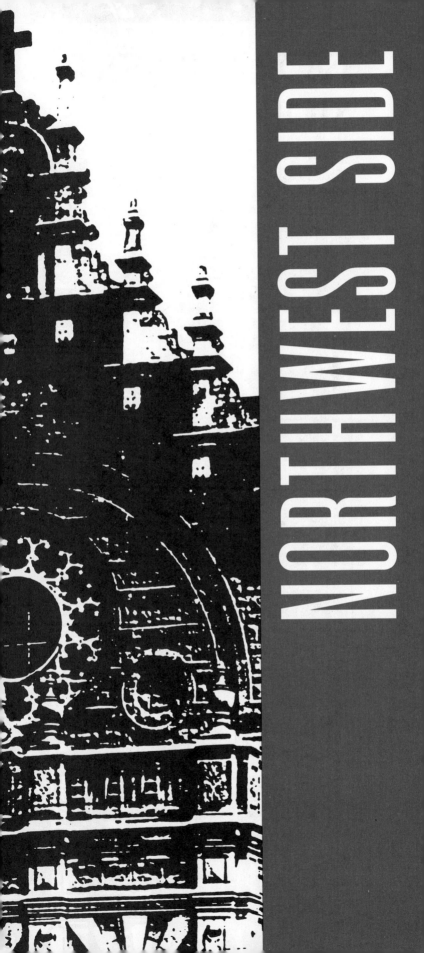

NORTHWEST SIDE

NORTHWEST
SIDE

Diversey

NORTH BRANCH OF CHICAGO RIVER

Logan Blvd
Elston
Damen
Ashland

Wrightwood

Clybourn

Fullerton
Medill
Belden
Lyndale
Palmer
33
Holstein Park
St Hedwig
31
30
Webster
Webster
34
Shakespeare
Charleston
Kamka Bldg
32
Dickens
McLean
Oakley
Leavitt
Hoyne
Armitage
Homer
Winchester
Wolcott
Damen
29
227-45 W Homer
Milwaukee
Wilmot
Winnebago
Moffat
Churchill
Cortland
St Mary of the Angels
28
Cortland
Bloomingdale
Willow
St Paul
Northwest Tower
Honore
Wood
Hermitage
Paulina
Marshfield
Wabansia
26
24
Caton
25
Concord
23
27
North
19-22
Pierce
Elk Grove
Wood
Pierce
LeMoyne
Julian
Beach
Wicker Park houses
18
17
LeMoyne
Wicker Park
12
Pulaski Park
16 **15**
Schiller
14
13
Elfen
Paulina
Blackhawk
Bosworth
Greenview
Cleaver
11
Evergreen
Clemente High School
St Mary of Nazareth Hospital
9
10
St Stanislaus Kostka
5
4
Potomac
Marion
Kennedy Expwy I-90/94
Elston
To Loop
Crystal
Division
6
Division St Baths
Haddon
Holy Trinity
3
Thomas
Damen
Winchester
Wolcott
Honore
Wood
Hermitage
Paulina
Marshfield
Ashland
Cortez
8
Holy Trinity
Cortez
Augusta
Augusta
Walton
Walton
Iowa
St Nicholas
7
Chestnut
Rice
2
Chicago
Superior
Huron
Sts Volodymyr & Olha
"It's What I Do"
Fry
Chicago
Armour
Bishop
Noble
1

The Northwest Side comprises disparate neighborhoods united by the important artery of Milwaukee Ave. Like many of Chicago's diagonal streets, it began as an Indian trail, was developed as a plank road and streetcar route, and remains a heavily traveled commercial thoroughfare. The many changes in neighborhood names and boundaries along the Milwaukee Ave. corridor reflect the area's shifting populations and their various motives of ethnic pride, historical interest, and real estate promotion.

The major community areas, which extend west from the north branch of the Chicago River for about two miles, are West Town, from Kinzie St. to about Bloomingdale Ave.; Logan Square, from Bloomingdale to Diversey avenues; Avondale, from Diversey Ave. to Addison St.; and Irving Park, from Addison St. to Montrose Ave. West Town includes the neighborhood of Wicker Park; the section of Logan Square east of Western Ave. is known as Bucktown.

In 1851 Chicago's boundaries were extended to Western and North avenues. The earliest housing in West Town was built by German Catholics who came after the 1848 revolutions in Europe and settled around Milwaukee Ave. and Division St. By the mid-1860s they were joined by large numbers of Polish immigrants, and animosities between nationalities caused conflicts. Germans and Poles both emphasized the establishment of "national" parishes and built large churches that served as both community and religious centers.

The boulevard system radiating from Humboldt Park is a major feature of the area. An 1869 act of the State Legislature established the West Park Commission, one of three municipal bodies responsible for creating a system of peripheral boulevards and pleasure grounds intended to ring the city. William Le Baron Jenney, better known as the father of the skyscraper, was hired in 1870 to design the West Side parks and boulevards. Conceived as an ensemble and originally named Upper, Central, and Lower parks, these landscapes are now known as Humboldt, Garfield, and Douglas parks and are linked by broad boulevards lined with stately houses and apartments.

The creation of Humboldt Park attracted real estate speculators, and the Fire of 1871 was another impetus to population growth, driving many workers from damaged areas to this expanding industrial and residential corridor. Much of what is now the Northwest Side lay beyond the city limits, with the housing stock consisting of inexpensive wooden buildings free from the ban on frame construction enacted within Chicago itself.

In 1870 Charles G. and Joel H. Wicker donated a small triangle of land at the center of their subdivision to become a city park. By the late 1880s and early 1890s the surrounding area had developed as fashionably middle- and upper-class. The construction of streetcar lines and the extension of the elevated line to Logan Square in 1895 fostered growth north along the boulevards. Many of the successful immigrants who ran businesses on Milwaukee Ave. and had lived there in "flats above the store" built elegant graystones, brick town houses, and two- and three-flats emulating single-family homes on Kedzie and Logan boulevards.

In the great annexation of 1889 Chicago added 125 square miles, and the extension of the city's north and west boundaries placed the boulevard system in the center of the city, rather than on its periphery. North along Milwaukee Ave. the annexation of part of Jefferson Township added the suburb of Irving Park. Evidence of this nineteenth-century community is still visible in the cluster of fine Victorian homes in the area of Irving Park Rd. and the Kennedy Expressway. Many of them have shed their siding to emerge as clapboard Cinderellas. Electric streetcar lines were established along Irving Park Rd. and Milwaukee and Elston avenues in the 1890s, and the neighborhood began to develop as part of the city. But even greater development occurred between 1910 and 1920, when Irving Park's population more than doubled.

Early settlers of West Town included not only Germans and Poles

Irving Park Area

but also Scandinavians and Italians. After World War I a tremendous influx of Russian Jews replaced some of the Poles and Germans. The newest wave of newcomers includes Hispanics as well as Polish immigrants. St. Stanislaus Kostka now offers masses in English, Polish, and Spanish, testifying to the area's continuing diversity.
—Julia Sniderman

1 Sts. Volodymyr & Olha Church
739 N. Oakley Blvd.
1975, Jaroslaw A. Korsunsky

2 St. Nicholas Ukrainian Catholic Cathedral
2238 W. Rice St.
1915, Worthmann, Steinbach & Piontek

Liturgical differences split St. Nicholas's congregation, leading the traditionalists to build their own church. The cathedral's thirteen domes represent Christ and the Apostles; the application of intricate mosaics derives from the Cathedral of St. Sophia in Kiev. The church has a simpler profile but still includes five domes and an enormous mosaic commemorating the conversion of Grand Duke Vladimir of Kiev to Christianity in 988, an occasion also marked by the sculpture of the two saints northwest of the church. The mosaics and paintings are dazzling.

3 Holy Trinity Russian Orthodox Cathedral & Rectory
1121 N. Leavitt St.
1899–1903, Louis H. Sullivan

Sullivan synthesized Orthodox iconography and Byzantine tradition with his own design ideals and the theories of the nineteenth-century Gothic Revival architect Eugène-Emmanuel Viollet-le-Duc. The portal's ogee-arched canopy derives from Russo-Byzantine precedent, while the decorative sheet metal under the canopy, though subsidiary, is as fine and fluid as Sullivan's contemporary work on the Carson Pirie Scott & Co. Building. The Eastern Orthodox central plan creates an intimate interior; the congregation stands in a square space surmounted by a painted octagonal dome. The sacred apse is screened from view by an elaborate iconostasis. Although most of the decoration is stenciled, it is not by Sullivan.

Holy Trinity Cathedral

4 St. Mary of Nazareth Hospital
2233 W. Division St.
1975, Perkins & Will

The fluted exterior resembles the AT&T Long Lines Building in New York and could have inspired the sets of the futuristic movie *Brazil.*

5 Roberto Clemente High School
1147 N. Western Ave.
1974, Fujikawa Conterato Lohan

To squeeze a large high school onto a limited site split by a major street, Clemente's instruction building rises nine stories and is connected to the athletic building by a steel bridge over Division St.

6 Division Street Russian & Turkish Baths (Kaplan Baths)
1916 W. Division St.
1907, Maurice Spitzer

Unlike the municipal baths, these provided more than just hygiene; behind the Classically derived limestone facade they were a luxurious retreat.

1544 W. Chestnut St.

7 "It's What I Do"
1544 W. Chestnut St.
Begun 1979, Edwin Szewczyk, artist

Despite the crosses, this bold, layered installation bespeaks the artist's devotions not to religion but to film stars. The artist says his work is not architectural or religious: "It's what I do."

8 Holy Trinity Roman Catholic Church
1120 N. Noble St.
1906, Herman Olszewski and William G. Krieg

The exuberant pilastered facade with its balustrades, urns, and obelisks is based on Roman Baroque models, with additional homage to the Pantheon's pedimented portico. Under the iron-vaulted ceiling, the column-free space is adorned with unusual ceiling paintings and windows by F. X. Zettler and Mayer & Co.

⑨ St. Stanislaus Kostka Roman Catholic Church
1327 N. Noble St.
1876–1881, Patrick C. Keeley
Towers 1892, Adolphus Druiding

The dazzling interior focuses on the apse, with richly embellished paintings of the life of St. Stanislaus by Thaddeus Zukotynski. In 1923 the brick walls were covered with stucco in an economical if gritty imitation of stone. The southern tower was destroyed by lightning in 1964.

St. Stanislaus Kostka

⑩ St. Stanislaus Kostka School
1255 N. Noble St.
1959, Belli & Belli

The John F. Kennedy Expressway was routed around the church but displaced many parishioners and destroyed the old school. The replacement is a slightly kitschy take on Corbusian modernism with a classroom block atop pilotis.

⑪ Pulaski Park
Blackhawk St., Potomac Ave., Noble St., and Cleaver St.
1912, Jens Jensen
Locker Building 1913 and Field House 1914, William Carbys Zimmerman

The West Park Commission carved this Progressive Reform movement park out of a densely populated neighborhood and programmed it to meet a wide range of needs. The bathing facilities of the Locker Building, intended for men and boys, served 500 patrons per hour. Dominated by a multiplaned, clipped gable roof, the Tudor Revival/Craftsman style field house is as grand as a manor house, its generous scale and high style contrasting sharply with the modest flats nearby. It housed men's and women's gyms (with separate entrances), an auditorium, and, originally, a branch of the Chicago Public Library, hinted at by the sculptured owl and open book in the western gable.

⑫ Wicker Park
Damen, Schiller, & Wicker Park Aves.

The only recognizable nineteenth-century element is the 1880s fountain, later converted into a spray pool. The field house (1985, Chicago Park District) is reminiscent of John S. Van Bergen's Oak Park playground shelters of the 1920s (now remodeled or demolished), built to a domestic scale with Prairie School lines.

Often called Chicago's ethnic Gold Coast, Wicker Park housed many prosperous Scandinavian and German immigrants who could have afforded to live farther east and south but chose to build here, alongside other successful compatriots.

⑬ Harris Cohn House
1941 W. Schiller St.
1891, Theodore Lewandowski

A standout among its more sedate Italianate neighbors, this costly Queen Anne has a rusticated and towered stone facade with granite columns—a fine display of the style's forms, materials, and window shapes.

⑭ Nels T. Quales House
1951 W. Schiller St.
ca. 1873, architect unknown
Addition and remodeling 1890
Thiel & Lang

The original, Italianate house was set far back from the street; its stone window hoods are still visible on the sides. The Queen Anne front addition, complete with Moorish arch, is a stylish update. It distinguished the house from adjacent properties such as 1955–1957 (1883, Charles O. Hansen), which Quales, a Norwegian immigrant who became Chicago city physician, developed.

15 1407 N. Hoyne Ave.
1879, architect unknown

This high-shouldered Second Empire house is tall and exuberantly French, with its curbed mansard roof, incised foliate detailing, sawtooth window hoods, and cast-iron porch details.

1407 N. Hoyne Ave.

16 Louis Hanson House
1417 N. Hoyne Ave.
1879, architect unknown

The side porch on this Italianate house has nothing to do with entry but was intended as a frame for viewing the garden.

17 Henry Grusendorf House
1520 N. Hoyne Ave.
1886, Gustav Bloedner
18 Adolph Borgmeier House
1521 N. Hoyne Ave.
1895, Henry T. Kley

Bloedner's Second Empire design is embellished with a carved portrait of a woman, of the type frequently seen on houses designed by or built for Germans. Kley's turreted Queen Anne has an intricately detailed stoop framed with wooden "lace."

Weinhardt House

19 Hermann Weinhardt House
2135 W. Pierce Ave.
1889, William Ohlhaber

Fancy houses in neighborhoods of successful immigrants often looked to Europe for inspiration and ingenuously used elements that had gone out of style elsewhere. The side porch with the garden view is a holdover; the rich and heavy metal bargeboards recall northern Europe.

20 John D. Runge House
2138 W. Pierce Ave.
1884, Frommann & Jebsen

The elaborate two-story porch beautifully frames the views through robust posts and finely worked motifs, such as the Masonic insignias under the eaves of the gabled dormer.

Runge House

21 Theodore Juergens House
2141 W. Pierce Ave.
1895, Henry T. Kley

22 **2146, 2150 & 2156 W. Pierce Ave.**
1890, Lutken & Thisslew

These fine examples of rusticated Romanesque show how the style was better adapted in the long run to the more durable limestone (2141 and 2150) than to the softer sandstone (2146 and 2156).

23 **Albin Greiner House**
1559 N. Hoyne
1876, architect unknown

This elaborate gabled brick cottage with Italianate window hood moldings is one of the area's oldest houses, featuring the side garden porch common in this neighborhood.

24 **Flats for Iver Christianson**
1658 N. Leavitt St.
1893, Charles F. Sorensen
25 **Flats for Gustaf Murbach**
1644 N. Leavitt St.
1896, Charles Thisslew

Using high-quality materials such as stone, cast iron, and art glass, owners built many handsome flats, such as these rusticated Romanesque graystones, in this prestigious area of single-family houses.

2156 W. Caton St.

26 **2138, 2142, 2146, 2152 & 2156 W. Caton St.**
1891, Faber & Pagels

"No two alike!" the architects could boast. When built, 2152 was described as Renaissance; 2146 was called Swiss.

Northwest Tower

27 **Northwest Tower**
1608 N. Milwaukee Ave.
1929, Perkins, Chatten & Hammond

The peaked tower of this neighborhood skyscraper was to have housed a revolving red, green, and white beacon across the northwest side. The first two floors were designed for retail, with medical offices on the middle floors.

28 **St. Mary of the Angels Roman Catholic Church**
1850 N. Hermitage Ave.
1914–1920, Worthmann & Steinbach
Rehabilitated 1992, Holabird & Root

An ambitious pastor's architectural ambitions, combined with a devout and generous congregation's funds, created this neo-Renaissance "Polish cathedral," where angels tread on the parapets and hover in the massive nave. The tile and terra-cotta dome recalls the silhouette of St. Peter's in Rome.

29 **2227 through 2245 W. Homer Ave.**
1888, Theodore N. Bell

Still remarkably well preserved, these tiny Queen Anne cottages miniaturized the style for the budget-conscious.

30 St. Hedwig Roman Catholic Church
2100 W. Webster Ave.
1899–1902, Adolphus Druiding

In this high-octane Renaissance Revival design for a Polish congregation, the geometric facade is anchored by square corner piers topped by robust cupolas. The aedicula above the entry is echoed by a pedimented reredos behind the altar.

31 St. Hedwig Rectory
2226 N. Hoyne Ave.
1892, Adolphus Druiding

This kind of Second Empire grandeur was already out of style in more fashionable neighborhoods. Essentially a boardinghouse, the rectory is masquerading as a mansion, its breadth visually diminished by setbacks.

32 Joseph Kamka Building
2121 W. Webster Ave.
1910, Worthmann & Steinbach
Remodeled 1940, architect unknown

The first-floor funeral parlor was modernized with a pigmented, structural glass facade that is sleek and elegant—and completely at odds with the prim slice of dull flats above it.

33 Holstein Park
Shakespeare Ave., Oakley Ave., and Lyndale St.
Field House *1912, William Carbys Zimmerman*

In 1854 three developers donated just under two acres of their Holstein District property in the hope that a city park would increase the value of their surrounding land. But development did not pick up until after the city had given the land in 1901 to the West Park Commission, which began improvements five years later. Clunky compared to the refined Pulaski Park field house, this blockwide recreation center contained many of the same elements: gymnasiums, a library, assembly rooms, showers, and lockers.

34 2100 Block of N. Oakley Ave.

Tall, narrow, and stiff, the gabled brick cottages and two- and three-flats ringing Holstein Park are curious anachronisms created between 1901 and 1908 by neighborhood architect Joseph A. Wilkowski and contractor John Konczik. Their monotonous uniformity is relieved only by slightly varying colors and setbacks. German names were originally given to the park and surrounding streets, but by 1901 many Germans had moved out, replaced by Poles.

35 Bernard Moos Public School
1711 N. California Ave.
1910, Dwight H. Perkins

Best described as castellated Chicago School, with crenellated parapets above the projecting stair towers, this is a close cousin of the architect's contemporaneous George M. Pullman School.

Humboldt Park
W. North Ave., N. Kedzie Ave., W. Augusta Blvd., N. Sacramento Blvd., W. Division St., N. California Ave.
Addition 1912: W. Augusta Blvd., N. Whipple St., W. Walton St., west of N. Sacramento Blvd.
1871–1877, William Le Baron Jenney
1877–1890s, Oscar F. Dubuis
1906–1909, Jens Jensen

The most impressive of the three great nineteenth-century West Side parks, Humboldt Park gives no hint of its originally flat and boggy site. As did his colleagues in the naturalistic landscape movement, such as Frederick Law Olmsted, Jenney strove to create man-made vistas that aspired to the beauty of the natural. His work is best seen in the section east of Humboldt Dr., where the irregularly shaped 36 **Lagoon & Islands** typify the picturesque ideal. The concrete bases of lamp standards

Receptory & Stables

marking Jenney's northeast entrance to the park still stand at the corner of California and North Aves. His southeast entrance, at Division St. and California Ave., marked by the *Miner and Child* sculpture (1908, Charles J. Mulligan) was eliminated during Jensen's era.

Humboldt Park played a significant role in the development of Jensen's style. Early in his career, he served here as park superintendent, returning to it after being named chief landscape architect of the West Park System in 1905. The area west of Humboldt Dr. shows his hand in the three large **37 Meadows,** sheltered from Kedzie Ave. by berms and heavy landscaping. He narrowed the western section of the **Lagoon** (called the "New Lake") to form a signature **38 Prairie River** that imitates one of his beloved native Illinois landscapes. Nearby he bermed and set below grade the formally designed **39 Rose Garden,** which in 1911 gained bronze castings of Edward Kemeys' **40** *Buffalo*

sculptures originally created for the 1893 World's Columbian Exposition.

Jensen also introduced Prairie School architecture into Humboldt Park, hiring Schmidt, Garden & Martin and William Carbys Zimmerman. The former firm's **41 Lanterns** (1907), identical to those in Columbus Park, have been virtually destroyed by vandals.

42 Receptory & Stables
South side of W. Division St. west of Humboldt Dr.
1896, Frommann & Jebsen

Domestically detailed but lavishly scaled, this was intended to resemble "the old German Style of country house architecture" according to the West Park Commission. Renovation to house a Hispanic Cultural Arts Museum was severely set back by a fire in 1992. The nearby Lily Pond (1897) is thought to be an early Jensen project.

43 Refectory & Boat Landing
East side of Humboldt Dr. north of Division St.

Refectory & Boat Landing

1907, Richard E. Schmidt, Garden & Martin

The hovering hipped roof and the three great arches are bounteously reflected in the lagoon to the north. This great Prairie School amenity encouraged visitors to stay outdoors, sheltering summer guests on the terraced open-air room and their rental boats below, and serving as a warming house for ice skaters in the winter. The parking lot to the south was once the Music Court.

44 Natatorium
W. Augusta Blvd. west of N. Sacramento Blvd.
1914, William Carbys Zimmerman

This simple Prairie School pool house provided other recreational opportunities as well.

45 Refectory & Field House
1400 N. Sacramento Blvd.
1928, Michaelsen & Rognstad

Georgian and Tudor details combine in this eclectic facility, grandly historic in derivation.

46 Illinois National Guard, Thirty-third Division— Northwest Armory
1551 N. Kedzie Ave.
1940, Chatten & Hammond

Late nineteenth-century armories were fortified like castles to preserve public order against possible workers' demonstrations and other civil unrest. By the 1930s the typical armory was more civil, with more entrances and windows, because its drill hall could also serve as a convention hall or sports arena. This strong Art Deco limestone block gives the reassurance of a fort—but with the modern styling of an office building or movie palace. The panels of men in uniform are by John J. Szaton.

Humboldt and Kedzie Boulevards and Logan Square

No part of the twenty-six-mile boulevard system offers more pleasure than the drive from Humboldt Park to Logan Square, a trip that would be even more pleasant at a nineteenth-century pace. The 250-foot-wide roadways were designed with central "carriage drives" and service roads framed by formal lines of elm and catalpa trees. The roadway widens to 400 feet at Palmer Square, a popular raceway for nineteenth-century carriage drivers and cyclists.

47 2224 N. Kedzie Blvd.
1915, Jean B. Rohm & Son

A stolid square facade is enlivened by inventive Art Nouveau stone trim, especially the cartoonish human face.

48 Peter M. Zuncker House
2312 N. Kedzie Blvd.
1911, Huehl & Schmid

Northwest Armory

The quirkiness of the unusual dormer, with its ski slope profile, ornaments a conservative Prairie School design.

Chicago Norske Club

49 Chicago Norske Club
2350 N. Kedzie Blvd.
1916, Giaver & Dinkelberg

The stylized dragons and heavy brackets are borrowed from Norwegian vernacular architecture.

50 William Nowaczewski House
2410 N. Kedzie Blvd.
1897, architect unknown

One can only wonder at the appetite for display that funded this virtuoso panorama of carved limestone. Flemish stepped gables, a medieval crenellated tower, Gothic crockets and window hood molds, and Classical capitals and modillions compete for attention on the ashlar front.

51 Illinois Centennial Monument
Logan Square
1918, Henry Bacon, architect; Evelyn Beatrice Longman, sculptor

Around the base range Native Americans, explorers, workers, and farmers, an honor roll of citizens from the state's first century of statehood. Longman frequently collaborated with Bacon, the designer of the Lincoln Memorial in Washington, D.C.

52 Logan Boulevard Graystones

After the Fire and through the early 1890s, architects experi-

mented with a variety of decorative sedimentary stones, from yellow Joliet-Lemont limestone to Minnesota's pink Kasota stone to the dark red sandstones of the northern Wisconsin shores of Lake Superior. But by the mid-1890s Chicago's proximity by rail to Indiana's limestone quarries and a shift to simpler styles had created a demand for Bedford limestone not only among developers of skyscrapers and mansions but also first-generation citizens building homes and flats.

The ace of sedimentary stones, limestone is hard and durable, takes carving beautifully, and holds its crisp lines even through Chicago's vicious freeze-thaw cycles. Smooth or rusticated, it weathers well, discoloring little and adapting to any style of masonry.

Logan Blvd. has the city's finest and most easily viewed collection of graystones. Classical detailing abounds, as at **2955** (1908, Douglas S. Pentecost) and **2947, 2949, and 2951** (1907, Albert J. Fisher). Groups are frequently built to a uniform height, usually with roofline emphasis above the bay. Checkerboard patterning, alternating solids and open spaces, is popular for balcony walls. Curious amalgams abound: at **2959** (1909, Herman

2959 W. Logan Blvd.

J. Gaul) the porch piers are embellished with stripes that are apparently Prairie School at the corners but become meander patterns on the central piers.

Classical and Gothic details combine at **2715** and **2741** (1905, Burtar & Gassmann), which bracket **2735** and its pronounced Richardsonian Romanesque porch arch. Even the grandest buildings are flats masquerading as houses, like the immense gabled and balconied examples at **2820** (1904, Fred & John Fred Ahlschlager) and **3024** (1908, John Ahlschlager).

3024 W. Logan Blvd.

Because of limestone's durability, there has been little replacement on these homes, which retain unusual integrity. The front porches and steps alone deserve landmark designation—perhaps as a historic Stoop District, to celebrate the

six-to eight-inch-wide railings and eight-foot-wide treads.

53 John Rath House
2701 W. Logan Blvd.
1907, George W. Maher

The low, Prairie School profile and characteristic Maher detailing, such as the flanged segmental arch shapes of the entrance bay and doorway, are resolutely individual. The floral-patterned art glass is remarkable, as is the carved wood and stone. Under the exaggeratedly deep eaves of the low, hipped roof, the curious boulevard facade features impressive second-floor art-glass windows across the immense porch opening.

Gerson Apartments

54 Apartments for John Gerson
2934–2936 W. Logan Blvd.
1909, Frederick R. Schock

The Art Nouveau doorway leads through a mosaic-lined hall to

F. W. Woolworth Co.

Craftsman Style apartments lavishly decorated with art glass and decorative tiles. The stacked porches make the facade rhythmic, while capturing the boulevard's beauty for outdoor living rooms.

55 F. W. Woolworth Co.
3401 W. Diversey Ave.
Remodeled 1938, architect unknown

The five-and-ten was created by Frank Winfield Woolworth in 1879 and, as late as 1932, still sold no merchandise over twenty cents. Removing that limit in 1935 led to a wave of new stores and modernizations, such as this stylish Art Deco one. The characteristic logo with its streamlined stripes bulges out into a small canopy over the corner entrance.

56 Grover Cleveland Public School
3850 N. Albany Ave.
1910, Dwight H. Perkins

The bold, almost intimidating massing is warmed by bands of subtly colored brick that run like a tapestry along the edges of the elevations.

57 The Villa District
Bounded by Addison St., Hamlin Ave., Avondale Ave., and alley east of Pulaski Rd.

In 1907 Albert Haentze & Charles M. Wheeler subdivided the land of this historic Villa District, stipulating single-family homes "of bungalow appearance." Two popular types appear here. The "Chicago" bungalow is narrow, long, and built of brick with a side entrance; it is represented at 3700 N. Avers Ave.

3740 N. Harding Ave. in The Villa

and on the west side of the 3600 block of N. Hamlin Ave. The "California" bungalow is usually wider and has a front entrance, an open front porch, wide eaves, and more varied materials; 3700 N. Springfield Ave. (1920, John C. Christensen) is a good example. Prairie School touches enliven 3646 N. Avers Ave. (1912, Hatzfeld & Knox); while generic Sullivanesque ornament, such as that on many Irving Park Rd. storefronts, graces the facade at 3608 N. Avers (1917, Harley & Aga).

58 Irving Park Public School
3815 N. Kedvale Ave.
1912, Dwight H. Perkins

Best viewed from the corner of Grace St., the assembly hall is treated like a separate block, with massing similar to a Louis H. Sullivan bank.

59 3800 N. Keeler Ave.
before 1870, architect unknown

The earliest houses on these blocks can be identified by their brick foundations. This delicate villa combines Gothic Revival (steeply pitched gabled roofs), Italianate (high corner tower), and Second Empire (mansard roof) elements.

60 Charles N. Loucks House
3926 N. Keeler Ave.
1889, Clarence H. Tabor

Despite alterations, this remains one of the area's finest Queen Annes, especially for its rich art glass and idiosyncratically capped turret.

61 Ropp-Grabill House
4132 N. Keeler Ave.
before 1871, architect unknown

This lovely Italianate house still has its cupola, an ornamental feature useful as a "chimney" for drawing fresh air up through the house.

62 Stephen A. Race House
3945 N. Tripp Ave.
ca. 1870, architect unknown

This Italianate house originally faced Irving Park Rd. but was turned on the lot in 1905.

63 Carl Schurz High School

3601 N. Milwaukee Ave.
1908–1910, Dwight H. Perkins
Addition 1915, Arthur F.
Hussander
Addition 1924, John C.
Christensen

Schurz High School is an ideal model for urban development and for its expression in architectural form.

Commissioned by a reform-minded school board headed by Jane Addams, the project was one highlight of a broad program for rescuing the immigrant poor from the ignorance and isolation engendered by the industrial city.

One revolutionary aspect of this program was the linking of the development of schools with the development of neighborhood parks. In 1904 Perkins, in partnership with landscape designer Jens Jensen, had written Chicago's first citywide park plan, promoting a network of "breathing holes" that would bring the social and health benefits of natural landscapes to the common citizen. Perkins was thus the ideal choice to bring these qualities to the expanding school system as architect of the Board of Education.

Chicago's typical Dickensian public school before 1905 was a poorly lighted and ventilated box, set into the city grid with no significant playgrounds. Toilet facilities were archaic and located in the basement. The forty-odd schools that Perkins designed between 1905 and 1910 changed all that, creating a building type with grass and trees, sunlight and fresh air, safety from fire, and good sanitation.

At the same time that these functional transformations were taking place, a similar revolution was developing in the art of architecture. A circle of young architects, including Perkins, Frank Lloyd Wright, Hugh M. G. Garden, Purcell & Elmslie, Walter Burley Griffin, Pond & Pond, Robert Spencer, and others, was transforming the concepts of the Arts and Crafts Movement into the indigenous Prairie School.

Schurz High School represents the translation of what was mainly a domestic vocabulary into an institutional one. A centralized composition that telescopes out from a dominant center, it sits astride its site. Its syncopation of horizontal sills and eaves with vertical piers, together with its hovering roofs and

Schurz High School

earth-toned brick and terracotta trim, place it squarely among the contemporaneous Prairie School explorations of Perkins's colleagues. The interiors and decoration are somewhat generic Prairie designs. Lighting fixtures, trim, and other details are highly geometric, often reflecting stylized natural forms; the auditorium, before alterations, was a cubic volume with spatial, planar, and linear transparencies similar to—if not as bold as—Frank Lloyd Wright's spectacular Unity Temple.

Carl Schurz High School asserted that the urban public school belongs much higher on the architectural hierarchy than had been allowed. Beyond its task of providing a safe, healthy, and beautiful place to learn, it towers over the trees, sheltering the entire community, an immense Prairie house for the new citizens of its immigrant, working-class neighborhood.
—Eric Emmett Davis

64 John Gray House
4362 W. Grace Ave.
Before 1870, architect unknown

The nearby Chicago, Milwaukee & St. Paul Railroad station was named Grayland after this early settler, as was the neighborhood created when his farm was subdivided in 1873 and this country villa became a suburban home.

65 Sears, Roebuck & Co.
4730 W. Irving Park Rd.
1938, Nimmons, Carr & Wright

In the early 1930s Sears established a department to design stores built around the presentation of merchandise; this was one of the first five constructed to their specifications. Windows, intended as a kind of transparent billboard, were for display, not illumination; products inside were better lit artificially. The plain, vaguely Art Moderne concrete facades are a backdrop to these windows and to a giant logo.

People's Gas Co.

66 People's Gas Co.—Irving Park Store
4839 W. Irving Park Rd.
1926, George Grant Elmslie and Hermann V. Von Holst

Elmslie was Louis H. Sullivan's chief draftsman, and this finely carved facade shows his mastery of the Sullivanesque ornamental style. Bedford limestone blooms in delicately embellished carvings atop the side piers and across the cornice. The vestigial display of gas appliances recalls the days when People's Gas sold and rented them at neighborhood stores.

Within a mile of this area are two unusual houses by a leading Prairie School architect.

67 Karl Stecher House
4840 W. Pensacola Ave.
1910, Walter Burley Griffin

The soaring roof seems poised for takeoff from its ground-hugging base. Horizontal board-and-batten siding, stucco, and corner windows with geometric mullions are prominent Prairie School motifs.

68 Harry V. Peters House
4731 N. Knox Ave.
1906, Walter Burley Griffin

A broad side-gabled roof dominates this small house, with eaves extending far beyond the wall plane. The front door is tucked into a tunnellike entry passage.

CHICAGO-O'HARE INTERNATIONAL AIRPORT

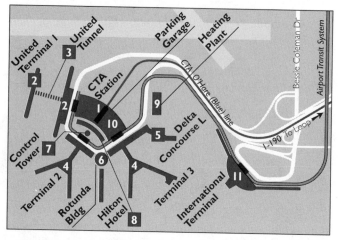

I n 1942 the federal government bought 1,000 acres surrounding the small Orchard Place Airport to establish the Douglas Aircraft Co. factory, which built C-54 transport planes there during World War II. In 1945 an urgent search to replace Midway Airport, then the world's busiest, led to this wartime factory site. Although fifteen miles northwest of the Loop, and burdened with an existing infrastructure of streets and railroads, it offered the best chance for rapid development. The federal government gave the site to the city, retaining 280 acres for the Army Air Force, and the first commercial flight left the following year. In 1948 City Engineer Ralph H. Burke published his phased master plan for a commercial airport that would cost the taxpayer nothing. The airport was renamed in 1949 to commemorate Edward H. ("Butch") O'Hare, a World War II flying ace lost over the Pacific in 1942. "Orchard" lives on, however, in ORD, the call letters appearing on all inbound luggage tags.

The introduction of commercial jet service in Europe in 1952 and the anticipated debut of American jets demanded a facility with different terminal and concourse configurations as well as longer runways. By 1955, city money had funded rerouting of railroads and highways and construction of a terminal building, runways, and a control tower; several airlines were operating regularly scheduled flights. In 1956 recently elected Mayor Richard J. Daley invited the architectural and engineering firm Naess & Murphy (which became C. F. Murphy Associates in 1957 and Murphy/Jahn in 1981) to examine the existing master plan for O'Hare's development. Most important, Daley persuaded the airlines to fund, from landing fees, revenue bonds for the construction of a series of connecting but separate terminals.

Naess & Murphy worked with several consultants, most notably airport specialists Landrum & Brown, focusing on design concepts of "concentration, consolidation, and connections." The original terminal was converted to the International Terminal (a building replaced by the current United Airlines Terminal). The location of the new terminals (now Terminals 2 and 3) was determined by the airlines' requirements for five two-story concourses, radiating like fingers, with covered "accordion" ramps to planes. The boarding functions would be on the terminals' upper levels, arrival functions on the lower levels, and administrative services on a mezzanine level. The three terminals would form a half-hexagon, with parking in the center.

In 1958, as the huge Air Force Academy project was completed in Colorado, many members of the Skidmore, Owings & Merrill design team left that firm to join this project. Among them was Stanislav A. Gladych, who became O'Hare's chief designer. The new terminals were Miesian in concept, exploiting concrete, steel, and specially fabricated glass as the principal exterior materials.

Construction of the $120 million airport, the largest public works project ever undertaken in Chicago, began in 1959. Most of the work was completed within thirty-three months, much of it under adverse weather conditions. In 1946 Ralph Burke had predicted an almost unbelievably high 12,000,000 passengers at O'Hare by 1960, but his estimate proved low; although the airport was still under construction, traffic that year topped 13,000,000.

As the airlines added jet aircraft, they shifted their operations from Midway to O'Hare, serving passengers from temporary facilities that were quickly demolished as the project progressed. Construction included two terminals and a restaurant pavilion, an underground utilities tunnel, a fire station, fuel farm, two new runways, a post office, telephone exchange, heating plant, and hangars. Existing runways were reinforced and lengthened, and the parking lot was enlarged. The design was unusually consistent throughout, from baggage handling to furnishings and signage, with high quality materials and craftsmanship.

At the dedication in March 1963, Mayor Daley hailed the "engineering and administrative wonder," and the terminals have proved durable and surprisingly flexible.

Although the distance from the central city provided needed opportunities for expansion, it also created problems of accessibility. Completion of the Northwest (now Kennedy) Expressway in 1960 facilitated automobile access; before that time, travelers joked that O'Hare could be reached only by plane. Rapid transit did not arrive until 1984, when the Jefferson Park line from the Loop was extended.

The introduction of ever bigger aircraft, combined with increasing traffic, have constantly challenged the terminal facilities. For many years it has been the world's busiest airport, with a 1990 passenger volume of 59.9 million. O'Hare's current configuration was forged in the $2 billion O'Hare Development Plan for 1982–1995, initiated by the city's Department of Aviation. Among its improvements are the United Airlines and International terminals. The expanded terminal areas will be linked to parking facilities by an automated, high-speed "people mover," operating on an elevated guideway 3.2 miles long with five stations at each of the terminals and the parking lot.

With its award-winning buildings spanning thirty years, Chicago O'Hare International Airport provides a unique "Design Gateway" to the city.

—Anne Royston

O'Hare is exciting on many levels, and is well integrated with connecting terminals, underground moving sidewalks, and the planned Airport Transit System. It is easier on Chicagoans, who never change flights here, than on out-of-towners, frequently seen sprinting across the great plains of terrazzo to make a connecting flight. But the airport is logical, well signed, and suitable for an indoor walking tour.

CTA—O'Hare Station

1 Chicago Transit Authority—O'Hare Station
1984, City of Chicago, Dept. of Public Works, Bureau of Architecture; Murphy/Jahn, assoc. arch.

If only air travel could live up to the glamour of this subway terminal! The backlit glass-block walls undulate softly to deaden sound and please the eye. The abrupt transition into the basement of the parking garage is eased by the Jahn-designed wall treatments.

2 United Airlines Terminal One Complex
1982–1988, Murphy/Jahn; A. Epstein & Sons, assoc. arch.

United's terminal is that rarest of species, an instant landmark: conspicuously, singularly, and clearly an expression of its time, place, and function.

Any terminal designed to serve 35 million passengers a year would have to be conspicuous, but designer Helmut Jahn and his colleagues confounded expectations by refusing to match the two handsome structures already in place around O'Hare's tight U-shaped core—a move that would have completed the three-part configuration as originally conceived. Far from being capricious, the new architectural expression derived from changes in air travel. In the early jet age terminal designers had used the logic of railroad and bus stations, with their large waiting rooms in which passengers arrived, bought tickets, and waited to depart. Such configurations proved unsatisfactory as air traffic grew and as greater distances between ticket counters and planes encouraged passengers to cluster at woefully underscaled gates.

One way out of the impasse, used by Eero Saarinen at Dulles International Airport outside Washington, D.C., was to reinforce the terminal's centrality and to provide access to aircraft with shuttle buses. Although this created a magnificent architectural space, it raised new functional problems and ducked the issue of using architectural form to express the linkage between automobile and airplane. The more common solution was to decentralize, pulling apart terminals so that cars could deliver passengers close to airplanes. At its extreme this produced Dallas–Fort Worth, one of the nation's newest and most impressive airports. But the enormous distances between terminals created functional problems, and the possibility of significant interior spaces was almost ruled out.

United's Terminal represents a cross between the two approaches. It is necessarily compact because of its position within the tight O'Hare horseshoe, but it is split into two main concourses connected by an underground tunnel to increase the interface with airplanes. Its longer, lower profile along the curb gives maximum access to automo- biles. The straightforward, steel-framed simplicity of the earlier terminals is brilliantly fused with a more elaborate development of the building's section and a richer palette of materials. The resulting monu- mentality is as grand as Dulles's but much lighter and more lu- minous. It also expresses more directly the reality of the con- temporary airport as the place where the automobile meets the plane.
—Robert Bruegmann

🔳 United Airlines Terminal Pedestrian Tunnel

Connecting Concourses B and C is an 860-ft.-long pedway sub- merged thirty-five feet below the apron with its parked and taxi- ing jets. An integral part of the United complex, it is a gigantic version of the undulating glass- walled tube of the CTA O'Hare Station. The colored walls ripple over white vertical bands sym- bolizing trees whose canopies cover the walkways. The passage compels forward motion with a four-lane moving sidewalk, a neon-on-Dexedrine ceiling sculp- ture entitled *Thinking Lightly* by Michael Hayden, and piped-in music that has improved from feloniously tuneless to mildly irritating.

🔳 Terminals 2 & 3; Concourses E, F, G, H, and K
1961, C. F. Murphy Assocs. American Airlines Concourses H & K Remodeled 1990, Kober/ Belluschi and Welton Becket Assocs.

🔳 Delta Airlines Concourse L
1982, Perkins & Will; Milton Pate & Assocs., assoc. arch.

The terminals' vintage "glass box" look is best seen on street sides;

United Airlines Terminal One

Heating Plant

concourse sides have been more altered with security gates, kiosks, and concession stands. Originally identical, the concrete-framed, column-free, 770-foot-long terminals spin off the Rotunda. Specially formulated tinted glass, terrazzo floors, and Charles Eames–designed waiting area chairs have worn exceptionally well, visually and practically. Because of changes in baggage handling, ticketing, and seat-assignment procedures, passengers now spend less time in the terminals and more time in the concourses. E, F, and G are no fun; they are still spartan 1960s in style. By comparison, the concourses stamped by a particular airline's signature (and money) look sybaritic; waiting travelers linger in a variety of bars, restaurants, stores, and spruced-up lounges. American Airlines' Concourses H and K, started by one architectural firm and finished by another, are pleasant but read as a weak echo of the stunning United Airlines Terminal. Delta Airlines' expansive steel-framed Concourse L was the first of the 1980s generation. Its greater width allows more spacious passage as well as more efficient baggage handling at the ground level. The glass-walled gate at the far end is popular with plane watchers.

6 Rotunda Building
1962, C. F. Murphy Assocs.

When O'Hare opened, jet travel was a spectator sport as well as a means of transportation. The Rotunda, with its bars, restaurants, and expansive views, was the airport's social center. The circular building, which links Terminals 2 and 3 and Concourse G, not only relieves the rectilinearity but is also a practical connecting shape. To enhance circulation, the building is column-free, with a precast-concrete slab roof suspended by steel cables from a central steel ring—Chicago's only such structural tour de force.

7 Control Tower
1970, I. M. Pei

O'Hare's central nervous system was built from Pei's prototype designed for the FAA. The glass bubble 200 feet in the air is the radome.

8 O'Hare Hilton Hotel
1972, C. F. Murphy Assocs.

The slight curve relieves its immense (720-foot) length.

9 Heating Plant
1961, C. F. Murphy Assocs.

Another Stanislav Gladych design, this is Chicago Modern at its best. Considered O'Hare's finest Miesian building, it undergoes a transformation at night, when the dark glass curtain wall vanishes and the mechanical equipment inside appears as if on a giant TV screen.

10 Parking Garage
1973, C. F. Murphy Assocs.

International Terminal

The largest construction contract ever awarded by the city and the world's largest garage when built, it has a total of seventy-nine acres of parking on six levels.

⊞ International Terminal
1993, Perkins & Will

Long underserved at O'Hare, the international airlines fill this gateway building. The gentle arc of the long curvilinear roof recalls old hangars while evoking an "architecture of movement." The transparency, intended to enhance the traveler's orientation and conserve energy, makes the terminal dazzling at night.

WEST SIDE

NEAR WEST SIDE

The Near West Side is a patchwork of historic pockets separated by vast stretches of urban renewal and blight. From a Civil War–era residence, to industrial districts, to modern institutional complexes, the area displays the cycles of growth, decline, and rebirth that characterize mature industrial centers. Exclusive Victorian residential districts have become blighted neighborhoods, while immigrant ghettos have yielded to brutally modern university buildings.

The area is split east–west by the Eisenhower Expressway (I-290), completed in 1960. To the south, the former immigrant area around Hull House continues to be replaced by the growing University of Illinois at Chicago, scheduled to displace even the historic Maxwell St.

Market by the end of the century. A pocket of an Italian neighborhood survives between this campus and the vast Medical Center, which runs from Ashland Blvd. west to Damen Ave. Modern residential construction circumscribes the Medical Center, while to the south is the rapidly gentrifying Tri-Taylor Historic District just east of Western Ave.

North of the Eisenhower Expressway, the expanding central business district grows toward Greek Town on Halsted St. and the Randolph St. Market area. Industrial loft buildings predominate, and while some have been converted to residences and offices, large wholesale markets and businesses extend west to Ashland. Historic pockets near Union Park and along Jackson Blvd. recall some of Chicago's premier addresses of the post–Civil War era. West of this narrow strip are large stretches of vacant land around the Chicago Stadium, some of which are intended for a new stadium to be surrounded by blocks of parking. The area's many churches represent a wide variety of faiths and provide much-needed stability.

The Near West Side is witness to the history of immigrant struggle at Hull House and immigrant success in the Tri-Taylor area, to Yankee prosperity along Ashland Ave. and 1960s racial strife and frustration along Madison St. It reflects the social engineering implicit in large-scale urban renewal at the University of Illinois campus, and it affirms Chicago's enduring commercial vitality in the Randolph St. and South Water markets. Eternally half-made and half-mad, the Near West Side is Chicago's private face, a thousand miles distant from its lakefront profile.
—Vincent Michael

Walsh Construction Co.

929 W. Adams St.
1992, Solomon Cordwell Buenz & Assocs.

Here's a miniature suburban office park in the city, with a low-rise structure surrounded by landscaping and surface parking. The lively, irregular profiles are unified by stolid brick walls with large windows reminiscent of nearby loft buildings. The wing with the high ceiling, on the north, houses not a corporate boardroom but the company gym.

Harpo Studios

1058 W. Washington Blvd.
Remodeled 1989, Nagle, Hartray & Assocs.

Pieces of this blocklong Art Deco Revival office and studio complex have served as a stable, a bowling alley, and a film studio. The remodeled whole is owned by the palindromic Oprah (read it backward) Winfrey, who tapes her popular talk show here.

Richter's Food Products

1040 W. Randolph St.
1933, H. Peter Henschien

This rare local example of an Art Deco factory produced sausages as well as smoked and boiled meats; Henschien's specialty was meat-packing facilities. The closely spaced piers frame striking geometric designs; the elegant entrances are framed in black terra-cotta flecked with gold.

Richter's Food Products

Chicago Florists' Center

1313 W. Randolph St.
1928, Fox & Fox

Large Art Deco posies grace this concrete loft structure, which concentrated the wholesale floral trade in the Randolph St. Market area of meat and produce distributors.

Union Park

Lake St., Randolph St., Ogden Ave., Warren Blvd.; Ashland Ave.
1853

The history of Union Park reflects the changing fortunes of its neighborhood. In 1853 local landowners seeking to increase the value of their property successfully lobbied the city to make this area a park. Named in honor of the Union cause, the park was the centerpiece of a wealthy residential area. Described as the "Bois de Boulogne of the West Side" in the 1870s, it included a band shell, gazebos, and a bridged lagoon. By the 1920s the surrounding streets were no longer fashionable, and many mansions on Ashland Ave. had become labor union headquarters—lending an ironic twist to the name Union Park.

6 Field House (West Park Commission Headquarters)
1888, William Le Baron Jenney
North addition 1909, William A. Otis

Jenney's original Shingle Style building has been defaced by subsequent remodelings; only the stair tower suggests his original design. Since 1934 brick facades have concealed the original wood structure. The West Park System was headquartered here from 1888 until it moved to Garfield Park in 1928.

7 Locker and Gym Building
1917, James B. Dibelka

Most notable is the large pergola of concrete columns.

8 Carter Henry Harrison Monument
1907, Frederick C. Hibbard

A relentless city booster, Harrison was the Richard J. Daley of his era, serving five terms as mayor (1879–1887, 1893) and fathering Carter H. Harrison II, who was elected in 1897. The quote on the monument's base, taken from Harrison's speech at the World's Columbian Exposition on October 28, 1893, captures the city's 1890s spirit: "Genius is but audacity, and the audacity of Chicago has chosen a star. It has looked upward to it

and knows nothing that it fears to attempt and thus far has found nothing that it cannot accomplish." Later that day, Harrison was assassinated in his home at the southwest corner of Ashland and Jackson boulevards. The statue's pose is mayoral but the rendition is naturalistic, especially the drape of the trousers and the soft felt hat clutched in the mayor's hand.

9 Chicago Transit Authority—Ashland Avenue Station
1601 W. Lake St.
1893, architect unknown

Look north as you cross Ashland Ave. to see a relic of the Metropolitan West Side Elevated Railroad's early days. The station is sided with stamped metal panels and crowned with an ornate metal cupola.

10 First Baptist Congregational Church (Union Park Congregational Church)
60 N. Ashland Ave.
1869–1871, Gurdon P. Randall

The attenuated spire and yellowed, rusticated Joliet limestone mark one of Chicago's oldest churches. But the prim and dignified Gothic facade won't prepare you for the warm and encircling interior, the oldest remaining amphitheatrical nave in Chicago. The speaker is surrounded by the congregation, in contrast to

First Baptist Congregational Church

the celebrant-worshiper division apparent in Catholic and Episcopalian churches. The enormous Kimball organ still joyfully rocks the trussed ceiling during services.

⑪ William Gilman House
1635 W. Washington Blvd.
1887, Louis J. Bourgeois

This essay in Gothic is smoothly finished and lavished with crocketed arches, a corner oriel, and an elaborate third-floor dormer.

⑫ Metropolitan Missionary Baptist Church (Third Church of Christ, Scientist)
2151 W. Washington Blvd.
1901, Hugh M. G. Garden

Garden combined the Greek Revival forms favored by Christian Scientists with his own Prairie Style details, especially the window surrounds on the west facade and the art glass. Gray granite columns have inverted capitals reminiscent of Secessionist architecture—and of Wright's Heller House in Hyde Park.

Metropolitan M. B. Church (Third Church of Christ, Scientist)

⑬ 220 to 230 S. Hoyne Ave.
1992, Landon Architects

Dubbed "the houses the Bulls built," this tidy row of capacious two-flats was built for homeowners displaced by construction of the new stadium. Each is pleasingly neo-Victorian, complete with a low stoop and an embellishing tickle of decoratively laid brick in the gable.

⑭ Chicago Stadium
1800 W. Madison St.
1929, Hall, Lawrence & Ratcliffe

Designer and Cook County architect Eric E. Hall emphasized the north and south limestone facades of this enormous box with Art Deco detail (note the athletes), while the east and west facades are of tan brick. It will be replaced as the home of the Bulls and the Blackhawks by a lavish new sports complex across the street designed by Hellmuth, Obata & Kassabaum Sports Facilities Group.

⑮ Isaac N. Camp Row Houses
1526–1528 W. Monroe St.
early 1870s, architect unknown

The height of each story diminishes as these exaggeratedly vertical town houses rise; large blocks of Joliet limestone are striated to appear as many stacked, smaller blocks. The robust bracketed cornice and window trim are currently overdone in "painted lady" colors.

⑯ Illinois Bell Telephone—Monroe Office
1340 W. Monroe St.
1932, Holabird & Root

This cool, severe, but lovely Art Deco switching office is trimmed with black granite and cast aluminum. Abstract bas-relief panels above the entrance and first-floor windows depict the transmission of sound.

⑰ Painters District Council 14
1456 W. Adams St.
1956, Vitzthum & Burns

A pristine echo of the Art Deco style, this blocky little corner building is one of thirty union headquarters in the neighborhood. It provides an artful show of the beauties of limestone and polished granite—with not a painted surface in sight.

⑱ Iram Nye House
1535 W. Adams St.
1874, architect unknown

The flat, crisp wall of large unbroken blocks of Joliet limestone is treated like a canvas on which incised ornament is stiffly embroidered. The ornament is a

Church of the Epiphany before completion of tower

miniaturized element adapted from more lavish, overtly "French" style homes; incised ornament was also cheaper than carved hood molds and keystones.

19 Walter M. Pond House
1537 W. Adams St.
1879, architect unknown

The profusion of pilasters and engaged columns, together with the mansard roof with its pedimented dormers, mark this as a rare surviving example of a full-blown Second Empire town house.

20 Church of the Epiphany
201 S. Ashland Blvd.
1885, Burling & Whitehouse

Here is one of Chicago's earliest and best examples of the Richardsonian Romanesque, a style known as "Norman" in the 1880s. The basic forms are simple and geometric—broad gables, a stocky tower, and roundheaded doors and windows—while the wall surfaces are complex. Rich, ruddy Lake Superior sandstone is carved into rectangles, squares, slivers, voussoirs, and colonnettes that fit together like an intricate jigsaw puzzle. Although the interior has taken some hard hits, including stained-glass theft and water infiltration, it remains a comfort-

able Victorian cave, punctuated by rows of deep-set windows. The wall treatment is most unusual: unglazed terra-cotta tiles in alternating squares of fluid ribbons and pods that seem to have been squeezed from a pastry tube. Against the dark backdrop of wood and terra-cotta, the remaining windows and the Venetian glass mosaic murals in the sanctuary glow softly, visual feasts of Victorian polychromy.

21 William J. Chalmers House
315 S. Ashland Blvd.
1885, Treat & Foltz

Uniform in material but richly varied in form, this house exhibits in stone many elements of the frame Queen Anne style: a turreted corner tower, windows (some mullioned) of many shapes and sizes, and a complex, irregular roof. Although only brownstone is used, it is carved, rusticated, planed smooth, and set in a checkerboard pattern for the stringcourse.

22 B. Dorr Colby House
1539 W. Jackson Blvd.
1894, Russell B. Powell

The robust Richardsonian Romanesque personality derives from the prominent turreted entry tower, with second-floor loggia.

23 Richard Norman Foster House
1532 W. Jackson Blvd.
1892, Patton & Fisher

The formula for this elegant limestone Romanesque town house includes a shallow facade, off-center entry, combination of smooth and rusticated stone, eaveless gable, and acanthus leaf carvings.

24 Mortimer & Tapper Houses
1533–1537 W. Jackson Blvd.
1881, architect unknown

The flat fronts and emphasized roofline of these Italianate row houses set the stylistic tone for the developing block.

25 Flora M. Chisholm House
1531 W. Jackson Blvd.
1886, John M. Van Osdel

Queen Anne breaks through the Italianate with a broadened bay and two-tone brickwork.

26 Norman Bridge House
1529 W. Jackson Blvd.
1883, architect unknown

27 William Messenger House
1527 W. Jackson Blvd.
1884, Alfred Smith

28 Mary J. Dodge Houses
1526–1530 W. Jackson Blvd.
1885, William Strippelman & Co.

These early Queen Anne designs retain the flat fronts and mansard roofs of slightly earlier styles.

29 William P. Henneberry House
1520 W. Jackson Blvd.
1883, Furst & Rudolph

The Second Empire facade is ironed almost flat, with shallow pilasters and incised ornament surrounding the door and windows. An aggressively overscaled dormer interrupts the mansarded tower.

30 Henry C. Morey House
1519 W. Jackson Blvd.
1884, John J. Flanders

Queen Anne exuberance bubbles up at the roofline, with a pink slate mansard and unusual semi-

Henneberry House

circular metal pediments filled with symmetrical flowering plants.

31 John C. Nicol House
1515 W. Jackson Blvd.
1879, architect unknown

The gargantuan blocks of Joliet limestone and the high level of the first floor are hallmarks of one of the block's oldest houses.

32 George Ross House
1514 W. Jackson Blvd.
1884, John M. Van Osdel
33 Andrew T. Merriman House
1516 W. Jackson Blvd.
1884, John M. Van Osdel

Unmatched but balanced, the slopes of the mansard roofs are the perfect foil for the robustly pedimented dormers.

34 Matilda Hale House
1513 W. Jackson Blvd.
1883, L. Gustav Hallberg

Even this three-story residence wears a shallow mansard lid.

35 1506 & 1508 W. Jackson Blvd.
1884, Edward Baumann

Designed by Baumann for himself, these are late examples of "marble front" (Joliet stone) Italianates.

36 1501–1509 W. Jackson Blvd.
1882, architect unknown

These Second Empire town houses are united by wide cornices and a broad stringcourse with grape leaf decoration. At 1501 was the home of lumber merchant Benjamin Franklin Ferguson, who left almost $1 million upon his death in 1905 to establish a fund for public sculpture to be administered by the Art Institute.

Apart from a brief spurt of public and semipublic construction in the late 1920s, there was very little development in the area north of Congress St. for decades. In the early 1970s three large government-funded projects in the Miesian style put a stamp of brawny modernism on these rough-edged precincts.

37 Whitney M. Young Magnet High School
211 S. Laflin St.
1971, Perkins & Will Partnership

This steel-framed trio has the cold efficiency of a factory for learning. The enclosed truss bridge spanning Jackson Blvd. links the fine arts building to the south with the academic and physical education buildings.

38 Timothy J. O'Connor Training Academy (Chicago Police Training Center)
1300 W. Jackson Blvd.
1976, Jerome R. Butler, Jr., Chicago city arch.

Haymarket Riot Monument
1889, John Gelert

The only tangible reminder of the 1886 disturbance is the sculpture now in the courtyard of this modernist training center. The police officer, his arm upraised, restrains an invisible mob, commanding peace "In the name of the people of Illinois." The controversy that surrounded the riot continued to plague this statue, which was erected near the site. The plaques at the base were stolen in 1903, and later a streetcar motorman rammed into the statue, claiming to be sick of looking at it every day. Moved to Union Park in 1928,

the statue remained unmolested until the civil unrest of the 1960s, when it was defaced with black paint and twice blown up by a bomb. The statue was placed under twenty-four-hour guard and moved to Central Police Headquarters, from which it was transferred to its present site in 1976.

39 Malcolm X College
1900 W. Van Buren St.
1971, C. F. Murphy Assocs.

This state-operated junior college was designed to serve a student population of 10,000 as well as the local community. The steel frame has brick and glass infill; in contrast with Whitney Young and the Training Academy, the building's structural expression is limited to the first-floor columns. The third floor has two open-air courtyards.

South of the Eisenhower Expressway (I-290), the steady growth of the University of Illinois and the Medical Center has spurred residential redevelopment since the mid-1980s. Historic buildings have been renovated, and clusters of town houses have sprouted. Of special note is the pocket between Polk St., Ogden Ave., and Western Ave., part of the Tri-Taylor Historic District. A "second settlement" community, it received upwardly mobile immigrants graduating from the Maxwell St. area on the Near West Side. Tri-Taylor contains many examples of 1880s working- and middle-class housing.

40 Campbell Flats
2168 W. Bowler St.
1886, Charles A. Weary

41 2125–2133 W. Bowler St. & 2135–2145 W. Bowler St.
1881, architect unknown

42 2147–2159 W. Bowler St. & 2136–2146 W. Bowler St.
1882, architect unknown

43 2148–2158 W. Bowler St.
1882, Edbrooke & Burnham

This remarkable ensemble was developed by James L. Campbell. With the exception of the red brick row houses with Gibbsian

2148–2154 W. Bowler St.

quoins framing the windows and doors at 2148–2158, all are Italianate with neo-Classical details. The Joliet limestone facades are of massive ashlar blocks, and each row shares a pressed-metal cornice with brackets and dentils.

44 801–811 S. Oakley Blvd.
late 1870s, architects unknown

The Italianate row houses at 801 and 811 were moved from a site two blocks north and now "bookend" similar neighbors.

45 Vietnam Survivors Memorial
815 S. Oakley Blvd.
1987, William S. Lavicka

One of the city's quirkiest pieces of folk art is this assemblage of ten cast-iron columns, taken from the interior of the Page Bros. Building and arranged around a granite marker. Structural engineer, Vietnam veteran, and preservationist Lavicka erected the memorial on his property with the help of other volunteer veterans.

46 Claremont Cottages
1000 block of S. Claremont Ave.
1884, architect unknown

Turn west on Grenshaw St. and north on Claremont Ave. for an unexpected delight: a block of small Queen Anne brick cottages. A speculative development by Turner & Bond, they feature projecting gables, dormers, and overhanging eaves with slightly recessed entrances—and, at 1016, 1024, 1042, and 1045, excellent integrity.

Claremont Cottages

47 700 Block of S. Claremont Ave.
1886–1887, architect unknown

This is an unusually cohesive streetscape of Queen Anne two-flats. Almost all of them were developed by George N. Hull and feature deep red face brick, stringcoursing, and pressed-metal cornices. Much rehabilitation took place on this block after 1983, when it was added to the National Register of Historic Places as part of the Tri-Taylor Historic District.

48 Chicago Medical Center
Ashland Ave. to Oakley Blvd.; Congress Pkwy. to Roosevelt Rd.

In 1941 the state legislature created the Chicago Medical Center Commission and empowered it to acquire land on a 305-acre tract surrounding existing medical buildings. The commission was charged with clearing blighted slum areas, allocating sites to medical institutions (five hospitals and ten professional schools), encouraging them to expand their facilities and create new housing for their employees, and relegating land for small parks. The scheme's promoters envisioned a "Garden of Health," a very different image from what confronts the visitor to this gritty urban complex.

Over a century of health-care architecture is represented here. Most of it is fairly undistinguished, burdened by the strained budgets and ever-changing needs that beat the beauty out of most hospital architecture. But there are a few gems—and several curiosities. Almost every facility has been expanded and remodeled, some of them many times. Only the original architects of major visible sections are noted here.

49 Cook County Hospital
1835 W. Harrison St.
1913, Paul Gerhardt
Addition 1914, Richard E. Schmidt
Additions 1916 & 1926, Eric E. Hall

The area's first hospital was located here by the county in 1874 as an anchor institution, in response to lobbying by West Side real estate interests. With its mansarded profile, it is like an aging dowager in straitened circumstances: presenting a grand facade to the world, while desperately battling a lack of resources.

50 Rush–Presbyterian–St. Luke's Medical Center Atrium Building
1653 W. Congress Pkwy.
1982, Hansen, Lind, Meyer;
Solomon Cordwell Buenz & Assocs.

51 Rush Medical College—Johnston R. Bowman Health Center
West side of S. Paulina St. between Harrison & Polk Sts.
1976, 1977, Metz, Train, Olson & Youngren

Presbyterian Hospital was established here in 1883 and merged with St. Luke's in 1956. Rush Medical College, the first of its kind in Illinois, was founded in 1837, deactivated in 1942, and revived in 1969 as part of Presbyterian–St. Luke's. Still visible on Congress Pkwy. are the 1888 Presbyterian Hospital (a mangled Queen Anne structure by Stephen V. Shipman) and the 1956 Presbyterian–St. Luke's. The constricted site led to dramatic solutions for the 1970s and 1980s expansions. Paulina St. was closed; the blocklong metal-paneled Rush Medical College and Bowman Health Center bestride Harrison St. and the elevated tracks. These are further enclosed by the Atrium Building, which emulates a modern hotel, with many patient rooms facing pleasant atria.

52 University of Illinois Medical Center Administration Building
1737 W. Polk St.
1971, Loebl, Schlossman, Bennett & Dart

Designer Edward D. Dart's hallmark, in small churches or a medical office building, was the readable, natural expression of structure rendered in sculpted but unadorned materials.

U. of I. College of Medicine Courtyard

53 University of Illinois College of Medicine Complex (Research & Educational Hospitals of the State of Illinois)
Bounded by Polk St., Wolcott Ave., Taylor St. and Wood St.

College of Medicine West (Medical & Dental College & Laboratories)
1853 W. Polk St.
1931, Granger & Bollenbacher

College of Medicine West (Research Laboratory & Library)
1819 W. Polk St.
1924, Richard E. Schmidt, Garden & Martin

Clinical Sciences North Building (General Hospital & Clinical Institute)
1819 W. Polk St., **inside courtyard**
1925, Richard E. Schmidt, Garden & Martin

College of Medicine East (Medical & Dental College Laboratories)
808 S. Wood St.
1937, Granger & Bollenbacher

Clinical Sciences Building (Hospital Addition)
820–840 S. Wood St.
1954, Holabird, Root & Burgee

Neuropsychiatric Institute
912 S. Wood St.
1941, C. Herrick Hammond

Biological Resources Laboratory (Medical Research Laboratory)
1840 W. Taylor St.
1959, Skidmore, Owings & Merrill

Institute for Juvenile Research
905–907 S. Wolcott Ave.
1929, C. Herrick Hammond

Medical Sciences—South Building (Surgical Institute for Crippled Children)
905 S. Wolcott Ave.
1925, Richard E. Schmidt, Garden & Martin

Medical Sciences Building (Medical Sciences Addition)
901 S. Wolcott Ave.
1964–1967, Richardson, Severns, Scheeler & Assocs. and Shaw, Metz & Assocs.

The original scheme for this two-square-block complex, developed in 1920 by Richard E. Schmidt, Garden & Martin, was followed closely for the northern half of the site, which was built out by later architects working in an Art Deco–influenced version of the 1920s English Gothic. The south half was to have contained one huge courtyard, but this plan was abandoned in 1930 with the construction of a nurses' residence; the 1954 Hospital Addition further injured the scheme. The hidden treasures among these red brick buildings are the secluded courtyards. On Polk St. near Wood St., enter the picturesque north courtyard through an arched entryway lined with WPA mosaics of astrological motifs. Sculptures of Aesculapius (the Greek god of medicine) and

Hygeia (his daughter, the goddess of health) by Edouard Chassaing grace the west end of the court. In the Neuropsychiatric Institute courtyard above the entrance, a bas-relief of a brain is surrounded by names of famous brain researchers.

54 Illinois Institute for the Visually Handicapped
1151 S. Wood St.
1965, Harry Weese & Assocs.

This small-scale village of linked brick buildings has a welcoming presence sorely lacking among its large institutional neighbors.

55 St. Basil Greek Orthodox Church (Temple Anshe Sholom)
733 S. Ashland Blvd.
1910, Alexander L. Levy

The Greek Revival temple front made the synagogue well suited for conversion to a Greek Orthodox church in 1927, after the original congregation had moved to Lawndale (now the Independence Boulevard Seventh-Day Adventist Church). The dome, originally ribbed but now asphalt-shingled, gives the building the height of a spired church, while maintaining the classical language of the ensemble.

56 Garibaldi Square
1400–1600 W. Harrison St., south side
1984–1988, Nagle, Hartray & Assocs.

An unfussy low-rise development fits eighty-six town houses, forty-two condominiums, and a hotel onto an irregular 7½-acre site. The red brick and Indiana limestone buildings fit the neighborhood well.

57 Thomas Jefferson Public School
1522 W. Fillmore St.
1884, John J. Flanders

As Board of Education architect, Flanders designed dozens of schools during the 1880s and early 1890s; only a handful from the era before his partnership with William Carbys Zimmerman

(1886–1898) are still in use. Tall and foreboding, most of them have even lost Flanders's signature Flemish gables, replaced with a flat parapet requiring lower maintenance.

58 Notre Dame de Chicago Church
1336 W. Flournoy St.
1887–1892, Gregory Vigeant
Renovated 1982, Historic Boulevard Services

French Catholics built this nearly circular church, whose transept walls are almost entirely filled with stained glass. The bronze Virgin Mary atop the dome replaced a lead-coated wooden version struck by lightning.

59 Académie de Notre Dame
1338 W. Flournoy St.
1885, architect unknown
One-story addition 1896, architect unknown

This charming Victorian Gothic school has inexpensive materials but fancy details, especially the pointed-arch windows, mansard roof, and incised crosses on the third floor. The parish's first building, it originally housed the church and convent as well. It is currently abandoned and faces an uncertain future.

60 James Foley Building
626 S. Racine Ave.
1889, Patrick J. Killeen

This Queen Anne "flats above the store" sports pressed-metal bays, terra-cotta panels, a cast-iron storefront, and a foliate cornice.

61 John Coughlan House
1246 W. Lexington St.
1871, architect unknown

62 William J. Onahan Row Houses
1254–1262 W. Lexington St.
mid-1870s, architect unknown

The street was an Irish stronghold named Macalister Pl. when these Italianate houses were built. The row houses' huge blocks of yellow Joliet limestone are scored to resemble smaller

Onahan Row Houses

blocks, a technique that enlivened the surface and saved on labor costs.

63 Holy Family Church
1080 W. Roosevelt Rd.
1857–1859, attributed to Dillenburg & Zucher
Interior and facade 1860, John M. Van Osdel
Upper steeple 1874, John Paul Huber
South addition 1886, architect unknown
Restoration begun 1991, Office of John Vinci and Wiss, Janney, Elstner Assocs.

A hardy survivor, the church is a tribute to the craftsmanship of neighborhood workers and to the leadership of Jesuits from the parish's founder, the Reverend Arnold J. Damen, to Father George Lane, head of a 1990s restoration campaign. The phlegmatic German Gothic structure is bent with age; some of the tall Gothic pillars are as much as eighteen inches out of plumb, displaced by the weight of the slate roof. But generations of embellishments crowd the nave and sanctuary. The spired and crocketed wooden reredos (1865), painted white to imitate marble, was created by nearby resident Anthony Buscher, a carver of cigar store Indians. The altar front features a folksy Last Supper—down to carved knives and forks.

64 St. Ignatius College Prep
(St. Ignatius College)
1076 W. Roosevelt Rd.
1866–1874, Toussaint Menard
Northwest addition 1895, architect unknown

St. Ignatius College Prep

Illinois Regional Library

The upstanding and disciplined facade is decidedly French, from the mansard roof to the projecting pavilion, to the stringcourses and quoining. The formal five-part facade features a columned entry atop a double-axial staircase. A typical feature of late nineteenth-century schools is the assembly room or library on the top floor, where a clear span space was structurally easier to include. The fourth floor here contains a fabulous example. Now known as the Brunswick Room, it was originally a natural history museum donated in 1873 by John M. Brunswick, a leading manufacturer of billiard tables and bowling equipment.

65 Illinois Regional Library for the Blind and Physically Handicapped
1055 W. Roosevelt Rd.
1975–1978, Stanley Tigerman & Assocs., in association with Jerome R. Butler, Jr., Chicago city arch.

Many visually impaired persons can perceive bold shapes and colors; this building reaches out to them with red metal facing panels, yellow structural mem-

bers, and blue mechanical and electrical elements. A 165-foot-long window snakes across the concrete wall of the Blue Island Ave. elevation, its strange shape representing the library's curving circulation plan. In a signature piece of whimsy, the parking lot contains a two-car garage, shaped like a giant automobile, for the librarians.

66 South Water Market
W. 14th Pl. and W. 15th St., between S. Morgan St. and S. Racine Ave.
1925, Fugard & Knapp

The sprawling open-air poultry and garden markets along the south bank of the Chicago River were displaced by the construction in 1925 of Wacker Dr., but they kept their name when they moved to this landlocked site served by trucks, not ships. The six neo-Classical terra-cotta buildings are virtually identical and share a continuous canopy above the first-floor loading docks. The overcrowded market's move to a new location, announced in 1992, leaves this complex to an unknown fate.

67 University of Illinois at Chicago (University of Illinois at Chicago Circle)
East Campus Eisenhower Expressway to Roosevelt Rd.; Halsted to Racine Sts.
1965, 1967, Skidmore, Owings & Merrill

Hailed as the college of the future when it opened in 1965, UIC is one of Chicago's strongest individual architectural statements—and one of the most violently disliked. The opening salvo was fired by architecture critic M. W. Newman, who shortly after its opening dubbed it "Fortress Illini."

UIC is an unmistakable product of an era proud of grand schemes and social engineering; few college campuses have been so strongly shaped by their original architect, designer Walter A. Netsch, Jr. Although many of the social and aesthetic principles that guided the design are now considered outdated, the university itself has prospered far beyond original expectations. Planned as an undergraduate branch of the well established University of Illinois, it is now a major research institution, with a third of its 25,000 students enrolled in graduate and professional programs.

The first and most lasting controversy surrounding the school was its location. In 1946 the university had opened a Chicago branch at Navy Pier to provide a two-year college course for returning servicemen. The predicted crush of Baby Boomers created a need for a perma-

Amphitheater and Lecture Center as originally built

nent site for a four-year college; the search began a decade later. Garfield Park, Meigs Field, and several suburban sites were considered and discarded. Mayor Richard J. Daley favored a South Loop location, in what is now Dearborn Park, but negotiations with the railroads that owned the land could not be concluded quickly enough; in 1959 Daley proposed a fifty-five-acre site at Harrison and Halsted streets. The densely populated neighborhood, already designated for urban renewal, was variously considered an expendable slum or a vibrant community—depending on the source. Community activists in the affected area tried to fight City Hall, but almost everyone else—including other West Siders—favored the site. The 1960 Democratic electoral landslide (President Kennedy was a grateful Daley supporter) gave the mayor the backing he needed to acquire the site and finance the project.

In 1961 Skidmore, Owings & Merrill presented a campus master plan, and construction began when the U.S. Supreme Court removed the last legal hurdle two years later. The university opened in February 1965, and five more buildings were added in Phase II by 1967. After this initial burst of construction,

the pace slowed somewhat but never stopped, and a 1990 master plan envisioned considerable growth.

Probably the only university named for a traffic interchange, the campus was originally known as the University of Illinois at Chicago Circle, for the "spaghetti bowl" freeway tangle just to the east. In 1982 this campus was merged with the university's long-established medical center to the west, and the combined institution was renamed the University of Illinois at Chicago. The earlier name was not inappropriate, however, as SOM designer Netsch had taken many cues from his own theories of transportation and movement.

The campus had two main organizing principles: a double-level system of walkways and a central hub consisting of a raised plaza surrounded by the most heavily used buildings. Netsch described the plan as "concentric rings with elements of most intense usage in the center; activity decreases and specialization increases with outward movement."

Grouping buildings by function rather than discipline gave great flexibility to the newly developing university but decreased teacher-student contact and increased the sense of anonymity.

This scheme was gradually abandoned as more specialized graduate divisions were added, but the core continues to function as planned, with a central area of lecture halls flanked by the library and student union.

The most controversial design element was the Lecture Center. This vast area (300 × 450 feet), with an amphitheater whose seats formed stairs to the lower level, was meant to be the spiritual heart of the campus. But the weather made it a windswept tundra or a broiling desert most of the time, and in 1992 it was slated for partial demolition and reconstruction.

The entire campus is built of exposed concrete, dark brick, and brown-tinted glass; granite was used for the walkway slabs. The reinforced-concrete structure is exposed on all the early buildings except Science & Engineering, and the decision to use concrete of uniform strength everywhere led to huge amounts of it in buildings with heavier structural loads. In an excessive refinement of the visible-structure principle, the concrete that carries heavier loads is sandblasted more to give it a coarser aggregate. The brutalism is extended inside the buildings: concrete ceilings support exposed mechanical and lighting elements, and tinted glass of varying intensities is intended to eliminate the need for window treatments.

The dual-level walkways were probably the least successful element. The upper level provided no shelter; the lower level was a hostile forest of concrete columns, with the cover too insubstantial to provide protection from the elements. Netsch conceived the upper walkway as a pedestrian "expressway," a large-scale, straight, hard-surfaced thoroughfare. The ground-level walkways were meant to be more intimate, with curves and softer textures, although the security concerns of an urban university call into question his stated goal that these paths be "secluded, devious, shaded." The walkways were also slated for demolition, in 1993.

Explore the campus on foot.

A University Hall
601 S. Morgan St.
1965, Skidmore, Owings & Merrill

Looming over the campus is its only skyscraper—the campanile, to use Netsch's metaphor—this twenty-eight-story office building for faculty and administration. In a paradoxical display of structuralism, the building becomes wider as it rises, with fewer columns creating bays of increasing width. The number of stories in each of the upper tiers—five, eight, and thirteen—was derived from another of Netsch's aesthetic principles: use of the golden section.

Continue south toward the center of campus. The blocky structure on the left is the Commonwealth Edison Vernon Park substation, a vivid reminder of the logistical difficulties of planning a new campus over a century-old grid of city utilities. Just past the substation is a cluster of classrooms around an informal court.

B Lecture Center & Court
821 S. Morgan St.
1965, Skidmore, Owings & Merrill

The plaza at the core of the campus was also the common roof of six lecture halls, which were reached by descending the stairs of the amphitheater. In 1992 funds were approved for the reconfiguration of the central space.

C University Library
801 S. Morgan St.
1965, Skidmore, Owings & Merrill

Part of the first phase of campus construction, and expanded soon afterward, the Library is accessible from both the plaza and the ground-level walkways.

D Chicago Circle Center
710 S. Halsted St.
1965, C. F. Murphy Assocs.

This is the only one of the original buildings designed by a firm other than SOM. Walk through it for a shortcut to Hull House.

Architecture & Art Laboratories

E Science & Engineering Laboratories
840 W. Taylor
*1965, Skidmore, Owings & Merrill
Addition 1990, Hansen Lind
Meyer*

This hulk forms the south wall of the campus core. The giant structural bays are divided by concrete columns five feet square at the base. The bricks are twice as large as those on other campus buildings, and the concrete aggregate is coarser.

F Architecture & Art Laboratories
845 W. Harrison St.
1967, Skidmore, Owings & Merrill

In contrast to the earlier buildings, Netsch developed his "field theory" of rotated squares here. In drawings, the plans look like lovely snowflakes, but in three dimensions, they are dark and confounding, with no perceptible spatial logic. The raw walls on the exterior indicate where a planned expansion never happened.

G Science & Engineering South
801 W. Taylor St.
1968, Skidmore, Owings & Merrill

The last of Netsch's "field theory" trio of buildings was based on a complex geometry that

Netsch developed while collecting op art paintings.

H Physical Education Building
901 W. Roosevelt Rd.
1967, Harry Weese & Assocs.

Remarkable chiefly for its enormous bulk, the building was reoriented by Weese from its north–south axis on the plan to close the campus off on the south.

I Jane Addams's Hull House Museum (Charles J. Hull House)
1856, architect unknown
J Hull House Dining Hall
*1905, Pond & Pond
Reconstruction of both 1967,
Frazier, Raftery, Orr & Fairbank*
800 S. Halsted St.

Representative more of Hull than of Addams is this rebuilding of a first-generation Italianate "cube and cupola." The Italianate reigned in Chicago from the 1850s to the 1880s. The symmetry, low foundations, arched windows, shallow sloped roof, and heavy bracketed eaves offer a rare view of a pleasing composition of the pre–Civil War era.

By the 1880s rapid expansion had overtaken the area, and the house was a furniture shop prior to its conversion to a settlement house by social reformers Jane Addams and Ellen Gates Starr in

Hull House

1889. During the 1890s and early 1900s thirteen buildings covering two city blocks were built around the house. The resulting complex, which offered social, cultural, and educational facilities for the urban poor and underprivileged, was inspired by the Progressive Reform movement and Toynbee Hall settlement house in London. The Dining Hall, a simple Craftsman Style building, is the sole survivor of this complex; its architect, Allen Pond, was a social activist and supporter of the settlement. The house was substantially altered prior to Addams's death in 1935, gaining a third story and losing its wide veranda.

In 1963 the property was acquired by the University of Illinois and dedicated to a museum of Jane Addams's good works. As the other buildings in the Hull House complex were demolished, the house itself reemerged and was reconstructed. Furnishings from Addams's era were restored, and others were gleaned from antique stores, creating an interior that is a comfortable Victorian mélange. The fireplaces and moldings are original; the chandeliers were reproduced from photos. The Dining Hall, relocated from its nearby site, is now used for exhibits and presentations.

K University Center Housing & Commons
700 S. Halsted St.
1988, Solomon Cordwell Buenz & Assocs.
West addition 1993, Solomon Cordwell Buenz & Assocs.; Loebl, Schlossman & Hackl, assoc. archs.

A marked departure for the campus in form and function, these buildings are the first undergraduate housing here, and the first complex to create a street wall and a grassy courtyard. They face the central city with a welcoming gateway, displaying a visual richness and logical form missing in much of the campus.

L Education, Communications & Social Work
1040 W. Harrison St.
1968, Harry Weese & Assocs.

This balconied bunker meets the standard of bleakness set by the first phase of campus construction.

M Behavioral Sciences Building
1007 W. Harrison St.
1967, Skidmore, Owings & Merrill

The tortuous floor plan of this "field theory" building is the butt of many jokes about rats in a maze.

68 Reliable Corporation Mural
1001 W. Van Buren St.
1984, Richard Haas

If Burnham's plan of 1909 had been realized, this area would have been the site of a grand civic center. It exists today in this trompe-l'oeil tour de force, best seen from the UIC campus. Haas illustrates both Burnham's visions and the actual skyline, complete with a peekaboo illusionist "cut-out" view of the Sears Tower, visible from the west. The medallions contain visual odes to Chicago's importance as a transportation center.

GARFIELD PARK/ AUSTIN

Garfield Park Area

Conservato

Flow
Hi

Fulton

CTA Lake St (Green) line

6

5

Maypole

Tilton School

20

West End

4000 Guyon Towers

St Martin de Porres

21

Washington

19

3800 W Madison

17

G A R F I E

P A R K

7

Field House

Legler Library

18

Pergolas and Benches

Springfield

12

Bandstand

10

Prov
St M
S

13

11

Golf Shelter

Kildare

Keeler

Karlov

Pulaski

Hamlin

Central Park

Jack

Van

Eisenhower Expwy   I-290

CTA Con

To those traveling from Western Ave. to the city limits—past
empty lots, crumbling six-flats, well-maintained graystones, battered retail areas, and sturdy churches—the suburban origins of these
neighborhoods may seem remote and invisible. But the area from
Western Ave. to Harlem Ave. in Oak Park, and from North Ave. to
Pershing Rd., was once Cicero Township, an independent political en-
tity founded in 1857. Its villages, which grew up along the train lines,
were coveted by Chicago politicians eager to add their public properties and tax assessments to the city's holdings.

In 1869, a seminal year for the West Side, Chicago annexed most
of the eastemmost two miles of Cicero Township, from Western
Ave. to what is now Pulaski Rd. That year also saw the establishment
of the West Park Commission, which immediately began acquiring
property for what are now Humboldt, Garfield, and Douglas parks.
Selection of the Garfield Park site spurred speculation in surrounding
properties, but construction accelerated only after transportation had
improved. A station on the Chicago & North Western Railroad at
Kedzie Ave. led in the early 1870s to residential development there;
but not until the 1890s, with the advent of the Metropolitan West

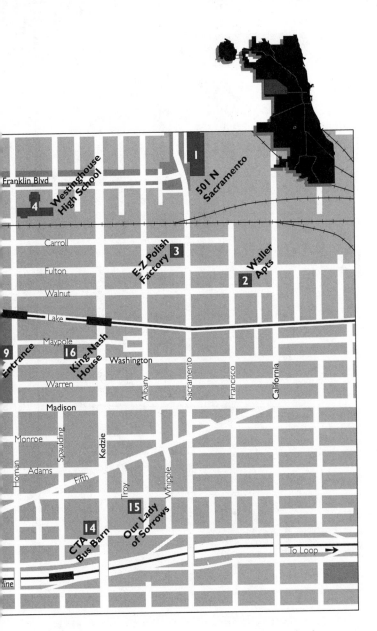

Franklin Blvd

Westinghouse High School

501 N Sacramento

1

4

Carroll

E-Z Polish Factory

3

Waller Apts

Fulton

Walnut

2

Lake

Maypole

King-Nash House

Entrance

9

16

Washington

Albany

Sacramento

Francisco

California

Warren

Madison

Monroe

Spaulding

Kedzie

Whipple

Homan

Adams

Fifth

Troy

15

Our Lady of Sorrows

14

CTA Bus Barn

To Loop ➡

line

Side Elevated and better streetcar service, did the area begin to
burgeon.

In the huge 1889 annexation that quadrupled Chicago's size, the
city bit off another chunk of Cicero Township: Central Park and
Moreland, the two communities immediately west of Garfield Park.
Pulaski Rd. (then 40th St.) was already a transportation center: at Kinzie were the carbarns for the Chicago & North Western Railroad
and, at Madison, the transfer point from city streetcars to suburban
lines such as the Cicero & Proviso Street Railway. The latter intersection grew into a vibrant urban center, a minidowntown halfway between the Loop and Oak Park shopping areas. In the 1920s developers put up high-rise hotels, apartments, dance halls, and clubs. But the
area was hard hit by the riots and fires that erupted after the 1968
assassination of Dr. Martin Luther King, Jr. Despite massive disinvest-
ment in the area, the intersection remains a retail hub, one of the
few shopping centers between the West Loop and the city limits.

Annexation's pro-and-cons were long debated in Austin, which
retained its autonomy as a village in Cicero Township until 1899.
Austin and Oak Park, the township's two largest villages, battled for

Austin Area

46

Drummond House

Chicago

47

5200 W Chicago

Superior

Huron

Erie

Race Ave and Midway Park houses

Hitchcock House

Warner House

Langford House

48
49

Key School

Gammon Methodist

39 40 41 42
43
44
45

St Martin

Ohio

Race

25
23

Austin Library

24
22

Austin Town Hall

Race

Ferdinand

38 36
30-34 29 27
28 26

Midway Park

37 35

Lake

CTA Lake (Green) line

Lake

Greater Holy Temple

Fire Station

Fulton

West End

Austin
Mason
Mayfield
Menard
Waller
Parkside
Central
Pine
Lotus
Long
Lorel
Lockwood
Latrobe
Laramie

Washington

50

Walser House

Madison

Monroe

Player's Hill

Adams

Quincy

Refectory and Boat Landing

58

Entrance Lanterns

51 Council Ring

Jackson

56

53

Gladys

Waterfalls

57

52 Play Area

Van Buren

COLUMBUS PARK

54 Recreation Bldg

Congress

55 Men's Gymnasium

Harrison

59 Golf Course

CTA Congress (Blue) line

Eisenhower Expwy I-290

To Loop →

decades over allocations of funds in a rivalry that came to a head in the 1890s. Although not in the majority, there was some sentiment in Austin for annexation, largely among developers and investors in the Metropolitan West Side Elevated. Anti-annexation fervor was much stronger in Oak Park, but seceding was difficult, with a majority of the entire township needed. When Austin thwarted Oak Park's efforts to secede in an 1895 election, bitterness increased and Oak Parkers redoubled their efforts to become independent. The *Oak Park Vindicator* editorialized, "the larger the municipality the greater are the opportunities for boodlers—vile men, who can no more appreciate the fine sentiments of patriotism than can Satan the sweet melodies of heaven. The Chicago boodler is the worst type in existence. The question before fair Cicero is, will she willfully put her head into his yoke?" The majority of Austin residents felt the same way. But in the decisive election of April 1899, Oak Park vanquished its rival, leading the township's villages in voting Austin into Chicago, despite Austin's 972-to-516 vote to remain.

Austin retains preannexation features such as Merrick and Town Hall parks, many churches and widely spaced homes, and the fire station on Waller Ave. During the 1920s apartment buildings and commercial buildings replaced single-family homes along major arteries such as Lake St., Central Ave., and Jackson and Washington Blvds. The 1920s also saw the completion of Jens Jensen's masterpiece, Columbus Park.

The West Side shows typical inner-city scars of age and blight. There is little new construction, and empty lots outnumber buildings on some blocks; the building stock is aging faster than money becomes available to save it. But the positive effects of dedicated institutions and strong individuals are seen in every neighborhood, from the well-tended church and school complexes of Garfield Park, to the rehabilitated homes of central Austin, to the restored sections of Columbus Park.

—Alice Sinkevitch

■ 501 N. Sacramento Blvd.
(Sprague, Warner & Co.)
1941, A. Epstein

The Art Deco tower anchors this stretch of the boulevard system, developed as an industrial area because of nearby railroads. Food processors Sprague, Warner brought in raw materials and shipped out finished goods via a railway siding directly connected to the first floor. The tower housed offices and concealed the water tank.

Two lesser-known works of Frank Lloyd Wright are nearby in an area east of Garfield Park that is difficult to navigate due to railroad embankments and street conditions.

■ Edward C. Waller
Apartments
2840–2858 W. Walnut St.
1895, Frank Lloyd Wright

Real estate developer Waller was interested in low-income housing; of his several schemes, these were among the few actually built. Four of the five units remain; all once backed up to Waller's more famous Wright-designed project, the Francisco Terrace Apartments, demolished in 1974 and partially re-created in Oak Park.

■ E-Z Polish Factory
3005 W. Carroll Ave.
*1905, Frank Lloyd Wright
Addition 1913, Harry H. Mahler*

This greatly altered factory is Wright's earliest essay in re-

inforced concrete. After commissioning him to design their homes, William E. Martin of Oak Park and his brother Darwin D. Martin of Buffalo hired him to design this stove- and shoe-polish factory. The windows have been bricked in and two floors have been added; the only exterior suggestion of Wright's involvement is the detailing around the entries and the ordered geometry of the facade.

Westinghouse High School

■ George Westinghouse
Vocational High School
(Bunte Brothers Candy Co.)
3301 W. Franklin Blvd.
*1921, Schmidt, Garden & Martin
Rehabilitated for Board of Education 1969, Saul Samuels*
Physical Education Building *1982, Kenneth Groggs*

One of the largest (400,000 sq. ft.) Chicago School buildings ever designed, this blunt and forthright factory/office building shuns the prettifying Industrial Gothic details popular for post–World War I factories. Horizontal bands of windows are rhythmically punctuated by powerful piers, whose verticality is echoed by the eight-story tower. The office wing faced the boulevard; the factory was the blocklong wing paralleling the tracks.

5 **Lucy L. Flower Vocational High School**

3545 W. Fulton Blvd.
1927, John C. Christensen

The structurally expressive facade has light touches of Gothic detailing, a favorite design type of Board of Education architect Christensen. "Flower Tech" first opened in 1911 on the South Side as an open-enrollment high school for girls. Technical education included sewing, millinery, the "home arts," and, later, business classes.

Some of the activities in Garfield Park might be termed "underground economies" and are hostile to strangers. The park is best explored by automobile.

Garfield Park (Central Park)
From the Chicago & North Western Railroad tracks to Fifth Ave. between Hamlin Blvd. and S. Central Park Blvd.; central section extends east to Trumbull Ave.

The middle of the West Park System's three great parks (see Humboldt and Douglas parks) still clearly shows the work of William Le Baron Jenney and Jens Jensen, two of the commission's major talents. Starting in 1869 with a 185-acre tabula rasa, Jenney began transforming the flat and treeless site into a picturesque landscape of winding lagoons and romantic vistas. Among the first improvements was the "pretty little inland sea," a fifteen-acre lagoon with excursion boats and flocks of ducks.

Although he resigned as West Park Commission chief engineer in 1874, Jenney was retained as a consultant until the 1890s.

From 1877 to 1893 Oscar F. DuBuis continued developing acreage, somewhat modifying Jenney's plans. When Jens Jensen became general superintendent and chief landscape architect in 1905, his vision of a prairie landscape shaped the park's unfinished southern portion and altered the central section. Jensen also introduced Prairie School architecture into the park, hiring William Carbys Zimmerman and Schmidt, Garden & Martin for major improvements.

Only a portion of Garfield Park's structures remain, but several—such as the Bandstand, Conservatory, and West Park Commission Headquarters—are prime examples of their styles. Vandalism and theft have taken a heavy toll on the rich sculpture collection; only **Robert Burns** (1906, W. Grant Stevenson; Washington Blvd. between

---

6 **Conservatory**
300 N. Central Park Blvd.
1906–1907, Jens Jensen and Schmidt, Garden & Martin; Hitchings & Co., eng.; Renovated 1958, Chicago Park District

Considered revolutionary when it opened, the Conservatory was conceived by Jensen as a work of landscape

art under glass and was designed in collaboration with a New York engineering firm that specialized in greenhouse design. Unlike Victorian hothouses—which had showy floral displays that often included potted plants, benches, and exposed pipes—this conservatory was designed as a series of internal landscapes of tropical

Garfield Park Conservatory

plantings, stonework, and water features.

Those who know Jensen as the dean of the Prairie landscape style might conclude that this work strayed from his usual efforts to convey symbolically the Midwest's indigenous landscape. Some of the gardens, however, were meant to emulate poetically the tropical appearance of the Chicago region during prehistoric times. In addition, according to Jensen, the structure's form was inspired by "the great haystacks which are so eloquent of the richness of prairie soil." Jensen, who was the West Park System's chief landscape architect from 1905 to 1921, had recommended replacing small greenhouses in Humboldt, Douglas, and Garfield parks with one economical, centrally located facility, which is thought to be one of the world's largest. Its size also allowed for a fuller expression of Jensen's art.

The Conservatory plan consists of a large rectangular palm house and several small square rooms configured around the structure's premier space, the fern room. In the center of this compelling landscape is a small naturalistic lagoon framed by lush ferns on stratified stonework meant to emulate the outcroppings found along Illinois's Rock River. A path winds past the lagoon to the far end of the room, where stepping-stones cross a rocky brook fed by a "prairie waterfall." In a 1930 interview Jensen explained that when the waterfall was being constructed he was consistently dissatisfied with the stonework and required the mason to dismantle and rebuild it several times. When the workman became frustrated, Jensen suggested that he listen to Mendelssohn's "Spring Song." After hearing the music, the mason constructed the waterfall perfectly, so that the "water tinkled gently from ledge to ledge, as it should in a prairie country."

The Conservatory's original vestibule and decorative art glass features in the palm house were designed by Schmidt, Garden & Martin. Unfortunately, they were lost in 1958, when the palm room's elegant, lacy truss system was demolished and replaced with a bolder structure of I-beam construction. Despite these changes, the Conservatory retains a strong feeling of Jensen's original intent and still offers special refuge from the city's severe winters.

—Julia Sniderman

Central Park and Hamlin Blvds.) remains.

The park's most interesting historic landscape features are between Lake St. and Jackson Blvd. The area north of Lake St. was intended by Jenney as an open green meadow for "croquet parties, military parades, and baseball games." It became the site of several of the park's largest buildings, housing the Conservatory and a cluster of much altered service buildings that are difficult to see and in varying states of repair. The **Power Plant** (West Park Light Plant, 1896, Solon S. Beman) was designed to serve a large part of the West Park system but became obsolete only a decade later, when it proved cheaper to purchase power from a utility than to generate it. The pair of ventilators atop the roof of the **Garage** (Stable, 1890, William Le Baron Jenney, with a 1915 addition) is a clue to its initial use.

Health Center/Field House

7 District Health Center and Field House (West Park Commission Administration Building)
100 N. Central Park Ave.
1928, Michaelsen & Rognstad

Bertram Goodhue's Spanish Baroque Revival creations for the 1915 Panama-California Exposition in San Diego were cream-hued, grand, and bristling with sculpture. Their popularity changed the direction of architecture in southern California and filtered east to inspire a new decorative vocabulary. Goodhue's California State Building from the exposition was the inspiration for this headquarters of the politically powerful West Park Commission; it housed their administrative offices, engineering department, and police force.

The facade is exuberantly if rather breathlessly punctuated with a Churrigueresque entry pavilion of spiral Corinthian columns, cartouches, and portrait sculptures. The gold terra-cotta dome shelters a rotunda with a geometric terrazzo floor. Four panels sculpted by Richard W. Bock pay homage to Art and Architecture (figures hold a model of this building), Chicago's parks and playgrounds, and the Illinois highway system. After the 1934 consolidation of the city's park districts, the building served as a field house and now includes the District Health Center, which occupies the south wing; the meeting room to the north was the commissioners' boardroom.

From the front of the District Health Center are excellent views of the eastern Lagoon and Suspension Bridge, the park's oldest elements.

8 Lagoons and Island
1870, William Le Baron Jenney
Suspension Bridge
1874, William Le Baron Jenney

The lagoons are the most notable remnants of Jenney's landscape design, and the area east of Central Park Blvd. is the oldest preserved landscaped space in a Chicago park. Done on an intimate, romantically miniaturized scale, the very irregular shoreline creates many inlets and changing vistas. Here one can imagine Chicagoans escaping to the city's edge to promenade, view the landscape, and partake of such amenities as the healthful water from the artesian well (which ran dry and was later removed by Jensen.) Jenney's Suspension Bridge, the sole survivor of a group of ornamental bridges, is a miniature display of his engineering talents and an elegant adornment. Steel cables support a wooden deck hung from concrete piers, which have replaced the stone originals.

Look across the Lagoon to see the park's eastern entrance, at Washington Blvd.

9 Washington Boulevard Entrance
Washington Blvd. at Homan Ave.
1907, William Carbys Zimmerman

Originally laid out in a semicircle by Jenney, the entrance was reemphasized by Jensen, who hired Zimmerman to design the architectural enhancement. In their current deteriorated condition, the short concrete bollards arranged in a semicircle appear more Druidic than Prairie School, although they are still sheltered by hawthorns, a tree favored by Jensen for its horizontal branching.

10 Bandstand
Music Ct. east of Hamlin Ave.
1896, Joseph Lyman Silsbee

Nineteenth-century park planners chose the site for this white marble octagon, part of a never-completed scheme for the park's southern portion. A 100-piece orchestra could fit on its broad platform, sheltered by the fantastic copper roof. The inspiration was Arabian for the trefoil arches and the calligraphic mosaic panels. No longer host to music lovers, it is frequently surrounded by jitney cabs and idling

chartered buses waiting to pick up Conservatory visitors.

11 Golf Shelter
1907, attrib. to Hugh M. G. Garden

While greatly altered, the area south of Madison St. shows Jensen's contribution to the landscape. He placed a semicircular earth berm south of the Bandstand to create a gently sloped amphitheater and a spot from which to view the golf course (now eradicated) that he created to the south. The now vacant Golf Shelter that served the course had a full-width pergola across its southern facade.

12 Pergolas and Benches
1907, attrib. to Hugh M. G. Garden

Jensen linked the Bandstand to the western Lagoon by the siting of a large formal garden with reflecting pools running north. They were on axis with the Boathouse (burned in 1981; a fragment of the stair remains on Washington Blvd.), which stood on the southern edge of the western Lagoon. A second formal garden paralleled Madison St. to the south, flanked by Pergolas and Benches. The Pergolas are now fragmentary and merely suggest their original role as pleasant walkways and frames for the pedestrian's views of the park.

13 Providence–St. Mel School (Providence High School)
119 S. Central Park Blvd.
1929, Morrison & Wallace

The Tudor style, particularly that of Oxford and Cambridge universities, was a popular model for Chicago public high schools from 1898 through the 1930s. The Central Park Blvd. entrance, derived from a fifteenth-century Gothic gatehouse, features carved reliefs of young scholars. One peers at a plant through a magnifying glass; the other, her hair in a fashionable 1920s bob, studies in a library.

14 Chicago Transit Authority Bus Barn
358 S. Kedzie Ave.
1984, Lester B. Knight & Assocs.

Patterned brickwork breaks up the immense wall surfaces of this maintenance facility.

15 Our Lady of Sorrows Basilica
3121 W. Jackson Blvd.
1890–1902, Henry Engelbert, John F. Pope, and William J. Brinkmann

It's Bramante on the Boulevard—with a coffered, barrel-vaulted ceiling rising above the

Our Lady of Sorrows

long nave. The stolid Classical façade is enlivened by an English Baroque steeple (its mate was destroyed by lightning).

16 King-Nash House (Patrick J. King House)
3234 W. Washington Blvd.
1901, George W. Maher

An interesting counterpoint to Maher's smooth, finely finished, Roman brick and stucco houses is the occasional appearance of a megalithic work. The influence is Richardsonian in this husky limestone city house, with its exquisitely carved columns, capitals, and urns. The rhythmically recurring motif is the thistle, seen in the capitals and dormer and used extensively inside. The monochromatic palette originally offset jewel-like glass mosaic panels, fragments of which remain beneath the second-floor window. Elongated Roman tray shapes, a favorite Maher motif, form the tall fence. Patrick Nash,

a later owner, was a prominent politician.

To tour west of the park, continue along Washington Blvd., noting the Washington Blvd. Entrance, and turn south at the west edge of the park (Hamlin Blvd.).

17 3800 W. Madison St.
(Midwest Athletic Club)
1926, Michaelsen & Rognstad

The Spanish Baroque Revival palette and decorative vocabulary translated beautifully into terracotta. The fifth-floor shields commemorate the short-lived athletic club, which offered West Side businessmen all the amenities of a Loop club—including two ballrooms, an Olympic-size pool, a gym with a running track, plus a fabulous view across the park to the city skyline—before sinking into receivership in 1930.

18 Chicago Public Library—Henry E. Legler Regional Branch
115 S. Pulaski Rd.
1919, Alfred S. Alschuler

This dignified Beaux Arts building, with its elegant raked brickwork, was Chicago's first regional library. The seventeenth-century priest/explorer Father Marquette is portrayed on the wall of the study room in a WPA mural by R. Fayerweather Babcock.

19 4000 Guyon Towers
(Guyon Hotel)
4000 W. Washington Blvd.
*1928, Jens J. Jensen
Rehabilitated 1988, Heard & Assocs., Ltd.*

Legler Branch Library

4000 Guyon Towers

"The Land of the Moors" was the inspiration for this pleasure palace guarded by avian gargoyles. The poured-concrete structure is faced with cream and red brick and ornamented with flora and fauna in terra-cotta and tile. West Side dance hall entrepreneur J. Louis Guyon developed this stretch of Pulaski Rd. as an entertainment center and occupied the hotel's southernmost penthouse.

20 George W. Tilton Public School
4152 W. West End Ave.
1908, Dwight H. Perkins
Addition 1965, Saul Samuels

It was "the most successful of all Mr. Perkins's designs" in the opinion of *Architectural Record* (1910). The architect's bold hand sculpted a strong, geometric facade deriving drama from the articulate layering of planes, from windows to walls to towering piers. The virtuoso masonry is in unusually rich tones of mustard and burnt orange brick.

21 St. Martin de Porres Roman Catholic Church
(St. Thomas Aquinas Church)
4301 W. Washington Blvd.
1923–1925, Karl M. Vitzthum

Austinite Vitzthum's grandest local project is Gothic Moderne, a house of worship yearning to be a soaring skyscraper. The Celtic cross atop the tower is the clue that this church was built for a predominantly Irish congregation. Inside, extensive gold mosaic work and opalescent grisaille glass make the nave worth a visit.

22 Austin Town Hall Park Field House
5626 W. Lake St.
1929, Michaelsen & Rognstad
Renovated 1992, Chicago Park District

From 1871 to 1928 the Cicero Town Hall stood on this site, which was donated by Henry W. Austin. When the West Park System took over the property in 1927, planning began for a "patriotic memorial hall for Austin organizations." This Georgian Revival recreational facility, with a tower modeled on Independence Hall in Philadelphia, once contained a swimming pool, auditorium, and shooting range.

23 Gammon United Methodist Church (Austin Methodist Church)
502 N. Central Ave.
1900, Sidney R. Badgley
1909, Badgley & Nicklas

A staid facade in plain-Jane Gothic hides an unusual rotated plan with the altar in the northwest corner. The west wall of the nave could be raised to increase the size of the worship space. When the church burned in 1909, the congregation again hired Cleveland architect Badgley and rebuilt to his original design.

24 Chicago Public Library—Henry W. Austin Branch
5615 W. Race Ave.
1928, Alfred S. Alschuler

This Beaux Arts library subtly integrates Egyptian forms in the papyriform capitals.

25 Francis Scott Key Public School
517 N. Parkside Ave.
1906, Dwight H. Perkins

Here is a handsome project from Perkins's early years as Board of Education architect.

Fire Station

26 **Fire Station** (Cicero Township Fire and Police Station)
439 N. Waller Ave.
1899, Frederick R. Schock

The last municipal building erected before Austin's annexation to Chicago is now one of the West Side's oldest firehouses. The eclectic facade is dominated by the very flat, vaguely Gothic stone trim around doors and windows.

Begin a tour of Austin's finest residential area on the other side of the cul-de-sac of Midway Park at Waller Ave., where the Congregationalists and the Episcopalians had a stylistic face-off. The Episcopalians clung more tightly to tradition, while the Congregationalists threw caution to the winds.

27 **St. Martin's Episcopal Church** (St. Paul's Methodist Episcopal Church)
5700 W. Midway Park
1901, Allan M. Barrows

The interior of this simplified Tudor Revival church is a small glory, with a beautiful timbered ceiling and rich stained glass. In the chapel are five stained-glass windows saved from the wooden church (1880) that originally occupied this site. The rectory, at 5710, echoes the Gothic church in the pointed-arch forms of the side entry, the dormer windows, and the porch piers.

28 **Greater Holy Temple, Church of God in Christ** (First Congregational Church of Austin)
5701 W. Midway Park
1908, William E. Drummond

Greater Holy Temple (First Congregational Church)

Drummond's first independent commission owes much in plan and massing to employer Frank Lloyd Wright's design for Unity Temple in Oak Park. After you enter through a small, low-ceilinged vestibule, the worship space at the top of the stairs seems very spacious. A central nave with an ornamental colored-glass skylight is flanked by lower side aisles. Unlike Wright's design, the social hall and kitchen here are underneath the raised worship space, in a variation of the typical "church basement" style.

29 5744 W. Midway Park
1988, John Kraii

Donated materials and services made possible this unique home built by West Side Habitat for Humanity and the Home Builders Association of Greater Chicago. It was designed for a quadriplegic child and her family; ease of access was a prime consideration. The simple gable and the veranda enable it to slip unobtrusively into the nineteenth-century streetscape.

30 Frederick R. Schock House
5804 W. Midway Park
1886, Frederick R. Schock

The empress of Queen Annes, this richly inventive design was Schock's home for almost fifty years. Schock purchased the property just when central Austin was beginning to boom as a desirable residential location. The house was his architectural calling card, announcing his talents to new residents buying lots in the area, and it remains a traffic stopper. The rusticated stone base supports a riot of materials and forms, from slate shingles to arched window surrounds that look like wood but are actually pressed metal. The extremely varied roofline is topped by a large crest shaped like a handle—an invitation, perhaps, to carry this dollhouse away. Inside, the architect finished or re-modeled rooms during different eras; there is a Queen Anne entry hall, a French parlor, and a Craftsman dining room.

31 Frederick Beeson House (2)
5810 W. Midway Park
1892, Frederick R. Schock

Manneristic excesses abound in this Queen Anne house—from the wooden "keystone" piercing the Palladian window form, to the cartoonish broken pediments atop the second-floor bay windows, to the stable's peculiar gable. The lavish budget was a step up from Beeson's modest Schock-designed first house in South Austin, and it paid for the stone and leaded colored glass, as well as interior finishes such as African mahogany and walnut.

Schock House

Beeson House (2)

32 Frederick Beeson House (4)
5830 W. Midway Park
1922, Frederick R. Schock

With the construction of this amiable Georgian residence, the peripatetic Beeson ceased his restless architectural wandering of Midway Park.

33 Frederick Beeson House (3)
5840 W. Midway Park
1901, Frederick R. Schock

The rounded second-floor bay and the Baroque gable whisper nineteenth-century eclecticism, while the hipped roof, deep eaves, urns, and Roman brick herald the emerging Prairie Style.

34 Edward Funk House
5848 W. Midway Park
1886, Holabird & Roche

Originally a shingled, turreted counterweight to Schock's extravaganza on the eastern end of the block, this house is now greatly altered.

35 Alvin F. Davis Flats
5849 W. Midway Park
1912, Frederick R. Schock

Austinites favored the suburban look even after annexation to the city in 1899. Although the depth of the building bespeaks a multifamily residence, the facade—with its geometric detailing popularized in nearby Oak Park—could pass for that of a single-family home.

36 William Ford House
5928 W. Midway Park
1893, James Bevins

Some embellishments on this Queen Anne are of recent vintage, but all are in the spirit of the original style.

37 Frank Barrett House
5945 W. Midway Park
mid-1890s, architect unknown

Almost every kind of window appears on this Queen Anne, most notably the circular series atop the turret.

38 Charles A. Carlson House
5964 W. Midway Park
1910, Robert M. Hyde

This lovely Craftsman house is enriched by leaded-glass doors and windows, arched corner entry, and battered dining room bay at the rear. The chimney bisects the facade, an indication of the importance of the fireplace, a key element in the Craftsman style.

39 Benjamin Wikoff House
5939 W. Race Ave.
1894, Oliver C. Smith

The picturesque tower and gambreled dormer pierce the gambrel roof of this large but snug Queen Anne.

40 Elwood Riggs House
5929 W. Race Ave.
1895, architect unknown

Although neo-Classical on the front, with a curiously dissected Palladian dormer, the sides are more stubbornly irregular and eclectic. With its billowing wall plane, the third-floor dormer on the east side could have been plucked from a Shingle Style house.

41 5850 W. Race Ave.
1901, John D. Chubb

Builder Henry Hogan and owner Henry W. Austin, Jr., developed the property with this very late Queen Anne style house.

Schlecht House

42 Francis Pray House
5837 W. Race Ave.
1904, architect unknown

This fine example of a transitional style is still Queen Anne in plan and overall proportions but simpler and more rectilinear. Across the street at 5824 and 5830 are two more of the same era.

43 Catherine Schlecht House
5804 W. Race Ave.
1887, Frederick R. Schock

It could have been assembled from two different kits—it has two prominent entries, sides flat and sides rounded, and porches on several levels. The best element is on the west side: the high and hooded third-floor balcony flanked by shingled tourelles.

44 Marie Schock House
5749 W. Race Ave.
1888, Frederick R. Schock

Schock designed it for his mother, then had it published in *Building Budget* as "A Cheap Suburban Residence." All wall surfaces and roofs were originally covered in stained shingles.

45 Charles Hitchcock House
5704 W. Ohio St.
1871, architect unknown

This archetypal suburban Italianate house is strongly vertical and frosted with elaborate paired brackets and a fretsawn porch balustrade. Most suburban Italianates were built in wood, and many mimic grander masonry homes. Here the wooden window molding imitates incised keystones.

Hitchcock House

46 Eugene Drummond House
813 N. Central Ave.
1888, architect unknown
Post-1900 remodeling, William Drummond

Contractor Drummond's house was reworked in the Prairie Style by his son William, an employee at Frank Lloyd Wright's Oak Park studio.

5200 W. Chicago Ave.

Before continuing south on Central Ave., a detour east to Laramie Ave. will take you to one of the city's finest terra-cotta neighborhood business blocks.

47 5200 W. Chicago Ave.
(Laramie State Bank)
Remodeled 1928, Meyer & Cook

What started out as a one-story addition and remodeling of a modest 1909 building grew into a major overhaul. The celery, mustard, and off-white facades are terrific examples of the craftsmanship of the Northwestern Terra Cotta Company. Decorative panels portray men at work, clouds of gigantic coins, and bees and squirrels—familiar symbols of industry and thrift.

48 Seth P. Warner House
631 N. Central Ave.
1869, architect unknown

Compare this symmetrical Italianate with the Charles J. Hull House (1856) on S. Halsted St. to see how slowly architectural styles changed in the mid-nineteenth century. The projecting central pavilion, pediment, central stair-hall plan, and cupola typify this phase of the style.

49 Thomas J. Langford House
621 N. Central Ave.
1895, architect unknown

Warner House

Langford House

echo the cupola of the Seth P. Warner House to the north. To the south stands The Langford, an English Gothic six-flat developed by Langford in the 1920s.

50 Joseph J. Walser House
42 N. Central Ave.
1903, Frank Lloyd Wright

One of the last single-family houses built on Central Ave. during its heyday as a fine residential street, it has been altered by the removal of leaded-glass windows and by the addition of side porches.

On their property the Langfords spanned the architectural generations. The roundheaded windows in the Queen Anne turret

---

Columbus Park
W. Adams Blvd., S. Central Ave., Eisenhower Expressway, and S. Austin Blvd.
1920, Jens Jensen
Restored 1992, Chicago Park District

Jensen's prairie vision for Chicago's parks was most completely realized here, and the spirit lives on. The landscape, natural and man-made, was filled with emotional content for Jensen, who wrote of this work, "Looking west from the river bluffs at sundown across a quiet bit of meadow, one sees the prairie melt away into the stratified clouds above . . . this gives a feeling of breadth and freedom that only the prairie landscape can give to the human soul."

Concerns that nearby Oak Parkers would use a park on their border argued against a city park at this location. The West Park Commission explored the expansion of its tax district to include the neighboring village but was defeated by the Oak Park lobby. Because it was the last large piece of land in the area, the property was acquired anyway; the Knights of Columbus suggested the name. Noting the lingering resentment toward Oak Park, sociologist W. R. Ireland commented, "Memorializing the great explorer and the patron saint of travelers, the park's name links to one another the

Italian and Irish co-religionists of nearby populations and looks across the city limit to the Protestant 'Indians' of Oak Park who failed in their part of a projected bargain."

A shared public space that portrayed the beauties of the country was of great spiritual value to city dwellers, Jensen felt. Although largely man-made, the lines of the park feel natural and informal. When Jensen began work, the land was almost flat, rising only seven feet from east to west, an elevation he interpreted as an ancient glacial beach. Drawing inspiration from the landscape of northern Illinois, Jensen created a symbolic "prairie river": the Lagoon that flows south and east from the Refectory and features two rock-ledge Waterfalls. Dirt excavated to form the river was used to create a ridge shielding the body of the park from the city to the east and, originally, from the railroad to the south. Jackson Blvd. was rerouted slightly to flow through the park's north end. North of Jackson Blvd. is an area intended by Jensen for casual strolling and tennis courts.

The sheltering ridge and lagoon were truncated when the park's southern end was destroyed during construction of the Eisenhower Expressway in the 1950s. The extreme tip of the original lagoon still exists as a small pond just behind the athletic fields north of the expressway. A parking lot and bus turnaround have also been carved from the park's southeastern corner.

Though heavily used for swimming, golf, and other sports, the park also harbors less healthful activities. Major buildings are heavily programmed and welcome visitors; the paths around the Lagoon should be explored in groups.

Columbus Park Entrance Lantern

51 Entrance Lanterns
Jackson Blvd. at Central Ave.
1918, Schmidt, Garden & Martin

Hipped-roof copper lanterns hover atop the concrete bases of these massive light fixtures, which are identical to those designed for Humboldt Park.

52 Children's Play Area
S. Central Ave. near Gladys Ave.
early 1920s

The playlot shelter (with modern metal roof), wading pool edge, and Council Ring are all built from stratified limestone, one of Jensen's favorite materials.

53 Council Ring
early 1920s

The council ring, one of Jensen's trademarks, was a large circular bench intended to inspire fel-

lowship and storytelling in the Native American tradition of gathering around a campfire. Most are circles of layered flagstone; this one is built of flagstone piers, originally topped by solid slabs of stone.

54 Recreation Building
(Locker and Shower Building)
S. Central Ave. south of Van Buren St.
1918, John C. Christensen

An eclectic, vaguely English brick building with a spreading U plan, it originally contained changing facilities for Jensen's rock-ledged swimming pool (since replaced by a modern pool).

55 Men's Gymnasium
(Stable)
West of Recreation Building
1917, James B. Dibelka
Converted to Gymnasium 1936

One of the handsomest remaining stable buildings in the Chicago Park District reveals its intended function on the west wall, where outlines of the original doors are visible. Built on Central Ave. at Lexington St., it was moved here from the path of the expressway in 1953, when it was connected to the Fieldhouse. Columbus Park's bridle paths were the only ones on the West Side; visitors rented horses at the Stable.

56 Refectory and Boat Landing
South of Jackson Blvd. between Waller and Menard Aves.
1922, Chatten & Hammond
Restored 1992, Chicago Park District

Jensen envisioned Prairie School architecture in his park and was dismayed at the commissioners' insistence on more traditional styles. He may have been disappointed by the revivalist design chosen for the Refectory, but the rolling arches are romantic and rhythmic. The Refectory and the "prairie river" are each a beautiful vista for the other. The primary space is a light-filled dining room/meeting hall, where the Columbus theme is evoked by a

Columbus Park Refectory

mural on the west wall depicting his three ships. On the Refectory's eastern end is a concrete boat landing and dining terrace. On the lower level, forty boats were available for rental in the summer—and 1,000 pairs of ice skates in the winter.

57 Waterfalls
early 1920s

The sources of Jensen's "prairie river" are two waterfalls built of stratified limestone and designed to resemble an Illinois river bluff in miniature.

58 Player's Hill
early 1920s

Jensen was committed to the idea of education through community theater, with open-air performances heightening communication with nature. The grassy slope between the two Waterfalls was the stage, which the audience looked up to from the meadow to the southeast. Originally the hill was much more heavily planted; clearings provided natural dressing rooms shielded from the audience by greenery.

59 Golf Course
early 1920s

Under Jensen's hand the nine-hole golf course occupying the park's western half became a miniaturized prairie—broad and expansive, dotted with clusters of vegetation. The starter shed, first tee, and concession stand were moved to their present locations in 1953.

Columbus Park Waterfall

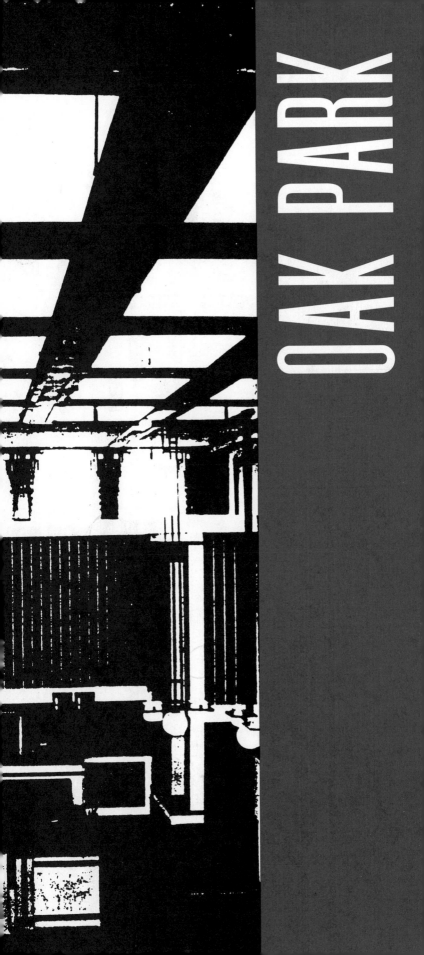

OAK PARK

OAK PARK

Arriving in waves after the Chicago Fire, settlers came by the thousands to build homes: freestanding, sun-filled, hygienic, secure. Fleeing the city's crowded, combustible flats and row houses, cholera epidemics, and corruption, they sought to create a community in harmony with God and with the help of like-minded souls.

Today, tens of thousands come to tour their houses, for it was in Oak Park that the modern American home was born. Twenty-seven designs by Frank Lloyd Wright still stand, from the fanciful experiments of his early years, through his own Home and Studio, to mature Prairie School masterpieces. The geometric lines, the nature-inspired ornament, the hovering deep-eaved roofs, and the artful plans reflected a cohesive aesthetic vision and were Wright's heartfelt response to the need for shelter.

The twenty-two-year-old Wright moved here in 1889, brought by his mother, who distrusted "the raw winds of the lake." Oak Park was a borderland community, separated from similar settlements by stretches of prairie, connected to the city and to other suburbs by train lines. Realtors extolled the artesian wells, the many churches, and the public library, but the streets were largely unpaved and houses were just being numbered. Wright chose for his homesite an overgrown lot on the edge of an undeveloped prairie where he often went for nature walks.

During Wright's formative years in Oak Park, the community was dominated by hard-nosed British immigrants and transplanted Yankees. Disciplined, resourceful, and inventive problem-solvers, they sought to shape their own environment and to have local control of taxes, schools, transportation, and development. Threatened by annexation to Chicago, which had already swallowed up townships such as Lake View and Hyde Park, determined Oak Parkers stopped the city's westward movement. They created and pushed through the state legislature a law enabling towns to withdraw from townships and set up independent village governments. The new village of Oak Park was incorporated in 1902.

Up to 1880 settlers had built cottages and small villas with Greek Revival, Italianate, or Gothic detailing. As the population boomed, the prairie filled with subdivisions of wooden houses, from the structurally expressive Stick Style to the heavily ornamented Queen Anne and Classical Revival. No one style prevailed; unschooled architects and builders delighted in miniaturizing elements from grand houses and uninhibitedly combining them for maximum picturesque effect.

Later in his career Wright would blast such designs: "These over-dressed wood house walls had cut in them, or cut out of them to be precise, big holes for the big cat and little holes for the little cat . . . The whole exterior was be-deviled, that is to say, mixed to puzzle-pieces with corner-boards, panel-boards, window-frames, corner-blocks, plinth-blocks, rosettes, fantails, and jiggerwork in general . . . Simplicity was as far from this scrap-pile as the pandemonium of the barnyard is far from music." But the designs themselves stimulated him, and he himself in the 1890s worked with some of their forms before synthesizing his own ideas.

Like most middle-class suburbs of its era, Oak Park was a conservative community, a temperance town nicknamed Saint's Rest for its many churches. But the young architect thrived in this atmosphere—nourished by the town's rapid growth, emphasis on the home, and respect for resourceful individualists. His neighbors became his friends and clients; their commissions constitute the nation's most amazing open-air museum of houses. Their freshness of concept and beauty of form, their modernity and originality, are strikingly set amidst not only their Victorian predecessors but also their offspring designed by Wright's employees and contemporaries.

Wright entered a new phase of his life when he broke the bonds of Oak Park propriety with his 1909 trip to Germany. He had gone there to oversee the preparation of the Wasmuth edition of his work, taking with him his lover, Mamah Borthwick Cheney, wife of his Oak Park client Edwin H. Cheney. It was a turning point in many respects. Now in midlife, with a new love, he was seeking fresh challenges and an international profile. In the two decades of his residence the population of 4,500 had quadrupled. No longer a suburban frontier, Oak Park had become an established center of its own, concerned less with innovation than with the status quo. Along the streets of his village, Wright could see his own ideas interpreted and rehashed not only by younger architects who had worked in his studio but also by speculative builders cashing in on "the look."

The frontier had disappeared; locally, his aesthetic was mainstream. Seeking new horizons, he moved on to Taliesin, his home in Wisconsin, leaving behind his family, his friends, and a dazzling body of built work.

—Alice Sinkevitch

Curtis House

From the second-floor row of miniature Moorish arches, to the Tudor half-timbering, to the profusion of window shapes and styles, this picturesque snapshot captures the uninhibited freedom of the Queen Anne style. How fresh, lively, and inventive the robust porch and well-broken skyline and wall surfaces still appear! The shingles were originally stained, making the roof and walls read like a uniformly fuzzy fabric.

■ John Farson House (1)
237 S. Oak Park Ave.
1888, architect unknown

Farson's Queen Anne was a comfortable, commodious, and picturesque home for an up-and-coming young investment banker. After rapid financial success, he sought something more avant-garde, and in 1897 commissioned the modern "Pleasant Home" a few blocks to the west.

❷ Edward P. Curtis House
231 S. Oak Park Ave.
1889, Frank Ellis

Considered Oak Park's first architect, Ellis was actually a builder with a certain flair. This rectilinear Queen Anne house differs from his slightly earlier Stick Style houses only in the addition of a rounded corner bay with an exotic onion-shaped cap.

❸ John I. Jones House
209 S. Grove Ave.
1887, Cicero Hine

Seaman House (1)

❹ John A. Seaman House (1)
139 S. Grove Ave.
1894, Fiddelke & Ellis

The Columbian Exposition of 1893, a gleaming White City built to an awesome scale, created an enormous appetite for the Classical Revival style; this grand wedding cake was one of the first homes in Oak Park to reflect the fair's influence. Profusions of garlands decorate porch and dormer pediments. A plainer sibling, also designed by Fiddelke, was built diagonally across the corner in 1899.

5 Asa W. Burrows House
142 S. Kenilworth Ave.
1887, Frank Ellis

Devoid of historical references, geometrically paneled frame houses like this were in their era called modern and are now called Stick Style. The exterior cladding suggests the underlying balloon frame, with bands of wood dividing all wall planes into a series of clapboard and shingle rectangles. The wooden porch echoes the house's structure, framing the view of the world outside. The banded, rotated corner bay is a rectilinear version of the rounded Queen Anne tower.

Arnold House

6 Wesley A. Arnold House
130 S. Kenilworth Ave.
1888, Wesley A. Arnold

Many homes of the 1880s that became "painted ladies" in the 1980s have been bedecked in colors that would have been chemically impossible and aesthetically undesirable at the time of construction. Here is a rare opportunity to study a true Victorian color palette. Built with unusually expensive materials, such as Darlington sandstone and slate, Arnold's own home promoted his talents. The pleasing but sober colors of nature favored in the late 1880s are displayed in the hard materials, which Arnold bent to his will, rounding off every corner. The richest element is the doorway, framed by beveled-glass sidelights and a Moorish arch.

7 Edmund F. Burton Row Houses
200–208 S. Clinton Ave.
1892, Willett & Pashley

Five Queen Anne dwellings with Romanesque details are shoe-horned into a space that could have accommodated only two freestanding houses. The most elaborate occupies the eye-catching corner plot; its first tenant was Wright's future client Arthur Heurtley. A disastrous fire in 1979 destroyed 202 and damaged the others; sensitive rebuilding has brought them back.

8 Henry B. Waterman House
309 S. Clinton Ave.
1894, William J. Van Keuren

Oak Parkers were fond of the no-nonsense Stick Style, with clapboards and rotated corner bay, which persisted here well into the era of Queen Anne and Classical Revival.

9 Isaac N. Conrad House
321 S. Clinton Ave.
1902, Eben E. Roberts

Roberts created dozens of versions of this classic Oak Park house. Typical elements include the exaggerated breadth, the very low hipped roof and deep eaves, the manneristic brackets scrolling down the walls, and the disproportionately large abacus between the porch roof and columns.

10 George D. Webb House
329 S. Clinton Ave.
1896, architect unknown

Showing the increasing East Coast influence that followed the Columbian Exposition, this high-shouldered house features a New England curbed gambrel roof, dentils, and decorative columns.

11 George W. Smith House
404 S. Home Ave.
1898, Frank Lloyd Wright

Designed in 1895, this house of contrasts looks forward and backward. The walls are subtly broken into rectangular planes like a Stick Style house but are covered in shingles rather than clapboard. Although as tall as its Queen Anne and Classical Revival neighbors, the house has proto–Prairie School elements: the entry is hidden from view and the house hugs the ground. Originally shingled like the walls, the steep double-pitched roof is now covered with pink asphalt, making the house look like a crazed pagoda.

12 Garland House
241 S. Home Ave.
early 1850s, architect unknown

Beneath the stucco, which dates from around 1910, is one of Oak Park's oldest houses. According to local lore, it was moved from Lake St. in the mid-1880s. The symmetry, the rows of modillions, and the cornice return on the sides hint at the Greek Revival design.

13 Richard S. Thain House
210 S. Home Ave.
1892, Patton & Fisher

The tall roof with the eaveless edge, and the combination of robust forms with thin, crisp, clapboard siding, are hallmarks of this firm's version of the Queen Anne style. Every room on the first two floors, except the kitchen, was designed with a bay, providing expansive views and a charmingly irregular form.

Thain House

14 "Pleasant Home" (John Farson House 2)
217 S. Home Ave.
1897–1899, George W. Maher

Designed in 1897 for investment banker John Farson, "Pleasant Home" was named for the streets that bound it. Maher considered it a "type for an American style," representative of the indigenous architecture that he and other Prairie School architects were creating. It would become a prototype for many of Maher's houses.

"Pleasant Home" is approached by a formally landscaped, raised garden that emphasizes the facade's symmetry. The original ornamental fence and garden urns are preserved; the stable and greenhouse are not. Many aspects of the house relate to the William H. Winslow House in River Forest (1893) by Frank Lloyd Wright, with whom Maher had appren-

"Pleasant Home"

"Pleasant Home" Dining Room (historic photo)

ticed in the office of Joseph Lyman Silsbee. Its low-pitched roof, horizontality, buff-colored Roman brick, and simple stone enframements for the windows respond to Wright's work. Maher introduced the emphasis on symmetry, the broad front porch, the elaborate centralized dormer, and the use of a floral motif in the decoration.

The house's decoration introduced a personal design philosophy that Maher later called motif-rhythm theory. Selecting three decorative motifs—the American honeysuckle, the lion's head, and the shield—Maher unified the exterior details with art glass, mosaics, woodwork, light fixtures, and furniture. The art-glass door and windows at the entry repeat the honeysuckle pattern and shield of the porch medallions; lion's heads appear on the porch and are carved into the hall's oak mantel. Maher designed

the dining room table, chairs and sideboard that are on view.

Maher developed a highly successful residential practice in the Chicago suburbs, especially in Kenilworth; his Chicago work is best represented on Hutchinson St. He developed his motif-rhythm theory to create visual unity in later commissions, exploiting the thistle in the James Patten House (Evanston, Illinois, 1901), the coral lily at Rockledge (Homer, Minnesota, 1911), both demolished, and the poppy in the Ernest Magerstadt House (Chicago, 1908).

His subsequent furniture and interior decorations link his work to modern European design after 1900.

Herbert S. Mills, the house's second owner, sold the house to the Park District of Oak Park in 1939.
—Kathleen Cummings

15 Samuel A. Rothermel Houses
100–110 S. Home Ave.
1891, William J. Van Keuren

South and North Blvds. were originally the Boulevard, a broad street split by train tracks at grade and one of the village's earliest residential streets. With

increasing traffic on the train lines, lots on the Boulevard became less desirable for fine homes and were developed as rental properties. Miniaturizing a variety of Queen Anne fronts, the design maximizes the number of units and features a style whose "stage set" quality is literally only skin-deep.

16 William J. Van Keuren Houses
100 & 102 S. Clinton Ave.
1896, William J. Van Keuren

Oak Park architect Van Keuren built these late Queen Anne houses himself as an investment.

106 S. Grove Ave.

17 106 S. Grove Ave.
1914, John S. Van Bergen

A former Wright employee, Van Bergen excelled at designing small houses with flowing plans and horizontal lines, for deep but narrow lots. Tucked into the side, the entry brings the visitor directly into the heart of the house.

18 115 N. Oak Park Ave. (Cicero Gas Company Building)
1893, Patton & Fisher

This narrow business block springs from a base of beautifully detailed Roman brick. An upstairs hall was available for rental to local fraternal organizations.

19 Scoville Block (1)
116–132 N. Oak Park Ave.
1899, Patton, Fisher & Miller
North addition 1901, Eben E. Roberts
Ground-floor remodeled 1929, Roy J. Hotchkiss

With this project, developer Charles B. Scoville accelerated the change of the Oak Park Ave./Lake St. district from single-family residential to commercial. Unusual for Oak Park are the Flemish stepped gables and the rich burnt-orange Roman brick and terra-cotta. Scoville is memorialized in medallions under the bays on the south wall. The original design was echoed beautifully in Roberts's Lake St. addition. The building remains a "flats above, stores below" complex.

20 Scoville Square (Scoville Block 2)
137 N. Oak Park Ave.
1908, Eben E. Roberts
Restored 1982, Office of John Vinci

This business block contained offices and a Masonic hall above shops. Bands of windows are divided by piers and topped by a row of roundheaded windows, a Sullivanesque organization of the wall popular with Oak Park architects Roberts and Normand S. Patton. The hipped roof and overhanging eaves are distinctly Prairie Style. Step inside to see a bright and breezy arcade.

Scoville Square

21 Horse Show Association Fountain

Lake St. at Oak Park Ave.
1969 replica of 1909 original
Richard W. Bock, sculptor

Man's relationship to his four-legged friends was a favorite sentimental theme of the period; this sculptured fountain symbolically and practically united them. People were to drink from the highest level, horses and dogs from the lower two. Bock showed a preliminary design to his friend and professional associate Frank Lloyd Wright, whose buildings frequently featured Bock's sculpture. Wright suggested the opening in the middle, a contribution that grew into the apocryphal story that Wright had designed the fountain.

22 Medical Arts Building

715 W. Lake St.
1929, Roy J. Hotchkiss

If Raymond Chandler's private eye Philip Marlowe had prowled the streets of Oak Park, his office would have been in this Art Deco miniskyscraper. In contrast to the overgrown domesticity of much suburban commercial architecture of the 1920s, the unrestrained verticality and geometric decorative panels suggest that Oak Parker Hotchkiss looked to Loop high rises for inspiration. The simple interior has been altered very little and is worth a look, especially for the light fixtures.

Prairie Courts

23 Prairie Courts

675 W. Lake St.
1987, Nagle, Hartray & Assocs.

This handsome, modern interpretation of the Prairie School idiom privatizes as much open space as possible, creating a tranquil spot that turns its back on the noises of Lake St. and the train tracks. Careful massing and choice of materials visually diminish the bulk. The lobby continues the look, featuring a fireplace with inglenook and Prairie Style light fixtures and leaded glass.

24 Francisco Terrace

W. Lake St. at N. Linden Ave.
1978, Harry Weese & Assocs.

This was among the first—and remains one of the best—Prairie School Revival projects in Oak Park. In 1973, as Frank Lloyd Wright's Francisco Terrace apartments in Chicago were about to be demolished, quick action on the part of realtor John Baird, attorney and historian Devereux Bowly, and architect Ben Weese salvaged the terra-cotta arch, cornice, decorative panels, and other ornamentation. Adapting Wright's plan, Weese created a courtyard complex of seventeen town houses, replicating the original massing and details. The entry arch forms a beautiful terminus to Linden Ave.

25 Pilgrim Congregational Church (Second Congregational Church)

460 W. Lake St.
South half 1889, Patton & Fisher
North half 1899, Patton, Fisher & Miller

The design bends a knee not to God but to H. H. Richardson, emulating his materials, polychromatic palette, bold forms, and confident vision. The rock-faced walls are trimmed in red brick, an inexpensive stand-in for Richardson's favored reddish Longmeadow stone. The Lake St. facade is unaltered; the remodeled office and chapel retain only the leaded-glass windows and fireplace. The addition to the north blends seamlessly, the stone base supporting a tall, rectilinear tower and an immense gable filled with a roundheaded window. Over 1,100 worshipers could be seated by raising the wall between the body of the church and the galleried Sunday school rooms to the east.

26 Oak Park and River Forest High School
201 N. Scoville Ave.
1906, Normand S. Patton and Robert C. Spencer; 1908, 1911, Patton & Miller; Erie St. addition 1913, Eben E. Roberts; 1921, Holmes & Flinn; 1924, Perkins, Fellows & Hamilton; Field House and Gymnasium 1928, Childs & Smith; Ontario St. infill addition 1968, Everett I. Brown & Assocs.

The clumsy Baby Boom era addition linking the field house and gym to the original school north of Ontario St. obscures the design, best seen from the Scoville and East aves. sides. This project was a political marriage for Oak Parker Patton and River Forest resident Spencer: the school board split the design commission between them. Sometimes described as Italian Renaissance, the school actually descends directly from Richardson's and Sullivan's organization of a large building block and strongly resembles Patton's best work as Chicago Board of Education architect in 1897–1898. A school designer with twenty years' experience, Patton had favored roundheaded windows since the 1880s; combined with the deep eaves and hipped roofs, the whole has a Prairie spirit. The additions filling out the block from Ontario St. north to Erie St. emulate the original design.

O.P.R.F. High School (Erie St. addition)

27 Torrie S. Estabrook House
200 N. Scoville Ave.
1909, Tallmadge & Watson

The gabled roofs and projecting vertical piers are typical of this firm's work. Like many bungalows of the era, it has a large footprint; the cruciform plan included not only kitchen, living, and dining rooms on the first floor but also a den, a music room, and two bedrooms. This house was considered noteworthy in its time for the basement garage, entered from the rear of the property.

28 Houses for Flori Blondeel
426, 432 & 436 N. Elmwood Ave.
1913–1914, John S. Van Bergen

This pleasing trio of Prairie School houses is symmetrical and simply detailed. The center house is one of Van Bergen's many versions of Frank Lloyd

Blondeel Houses

Wright's "Fireproof House for $5,000," an economical design published in the *Ladies' Home Journal* in April 1907 and imitated by Van Bergen and others for years.

29 Rollin Furbeck House
511 N. Fair Oaks Ave.
1897, Frank Lloyd Wright

Wright's first emphatically forward-looking design in Oak Park excites with its remarkable experimentation. The variety and broken roofline of the Queen Anne style would have been comfortably familiar to any nineteenth-century viewer, while the dynamic composition and geometric detailing catapult boldly into the twentieth century. With its towering central pavilion, the design was an odd choice for this already elevated lot, which rolls over the remnants of an ancient glacial beach. Despite the placement of the first floor low on a water table, and the horizontal banding of materials, the house reads as very tall—getting shyer as it rises. The very open "picture window" on the first floor contrasts sharply with the recessed diamond-paned windows above.

30 William G. Fricke House
540 N. Fair Oaks Ave.
1902, Frank Lloyd Wright
Garage (for Emma Martin)
1907, Frank Lloyd Wright

This dazzling and dynamic arrangement of planes was origi-

nally anchored by a loggia and porch that ran to the south. Without them, the massive tower pulls the composition vertically. Even so, the interplay of wall and roof planes and the diamond-shaped entry bay on the north are the work of a rapidly maturing visionary.

31 Charles F. Lorenzen House
635 N. Fair Oaks Ave.
1906, Eben E. Roberts
32 Charles Schwerin House
639 N. Fair Oaks Ave.
1908, Eben E. Roberts

These typical Four-Square houses are refracted through the Oak Park prism, their exaggerated breadth and horizontality adorned with geometric Prairie School details from the front porch to the chimneys. Roberts frequently inflated the third-floor dormers on hip-roofed houses to give them maximum flair. The dormer at 639 owes a debt to George W. Maher, particularly to his nearby house for Charles R. Erwin.

33 Vernon S. Watson House
643 N. Fair Oaks Ave.
1904, Vernon S. Watson

Watson designed this modest house before he joined Thomas Tallmadge in practice. Built for $2,000, it is sided with horizontal board-and-batten and clapboard. Watson later added bays at front and rear.

Lorenzen House

Martin House

34 Otto H. McFeely House
645 N. Fair Oaks Ave.
1905, Vernon S. Watson

Architects and owners valued concrete's fireproof qualities, especially after Chicago's disastrous Iroquois Theater fire of 1903. But the cost of constructing the forms was high, necessitating simple repetitive shapes and little or no ornament. This severe little experiment in concrete is softened somewhat by the porch and the Prairie-influenced string-course and wide eaves.

35 William E. Martin House
636 N. East Ave.
1903, Frank Lloyd Wright

"Here entered the important new element of Plasticity . . . The windows would sometimes be wrapped around the building corners as inside emphasis of plasticity and to increase the sense of interior space. I fought for outswinging windows because the casement window associated house with the out-of-doors, gave free openings outward."

This mature Prairie School design offsets its great height by three layers of hipped roofs, which emphasize the horizontal and shield sparkling ribbons of leaded glass.

36 Harry C. Goodrich House
534 N. East Ave.
1896, Frank Lloyd Wright

The steeply pitched fedora roof with flared edges and the off-center porch are in the same vein as the George W. Smith House. The thin, crisp clap-board that covers so many Queen Anne houses in Oak Park reaches its true rectilinear potential here.

37 Edwin H. Cheney House
520 N. East Ave.
1904, Frank Lloyd Wright

Eye-catching in its dramatic horizontality, yet guarding the path to penetration, this house protects as it entices. Even the location of the front door (in the middle of the south wall) is difficult to guess; the route to entry is circuitous and engaging. The lot slopes down to the east; the house snuggles into the same slight ridge that Wright's nearby Rollin Furbeck House (1897) surmounts. From the street, the terrace walls and the massive, low hipped roof hide most of the facade with its dazzling art glass. No wonder Cheney's wife, Mamah Borthwick, fell in love with Wright! Their trip to Europe in 1909 was the beginning of the end for their marriages and for Wright's Oak Park life and Chicago practice; they moved together to Spring Green, Wisconsin, in 1911. She is buried there at Wright's home, Taliesin East, where she and her two children were among those murdered by an insane servant in 1914.

38 Dale Bumstead House
504 N. East Ave.
1909, Tallmadge & Watson

This successful design, with its signature narrow vertical piers and emphasized entry bay, became a formula for the firm.

39 Gustavus Babson House
415 N. Linden Ave.
1913, Tallmadge & Watson

By the time this split-level house was built, the Prairie School had become mainstream Oak Park, mingling with massive Georgians on Linden Ave.

40 Salem E. Munyer Apartments
175–181 N. Linden Ave./
643–645 W. Ontario St.
1916, John S. Van Bergen

Stripped and spare, this Prairie School building has a severity that looks ahead ten years to the International Style. It gracefully rounds the corner, balancing the horizontals of roof, raked mortar joints, and stone lintels with piers, chimneys, and stacks of sun porches.

41 Cheney Mansion (C. A. Sharpe House)
208 N. Euclid Ave.
1913, Charles E. White, Jr.

This mansion, now owned by the Park District of Oak Park, is distinguished chiefly for its size and craftsmanship.

42 George W. Furbeck House
223 N. Euclid Ave.
1897, Frank Lloyd Wright

This snug exercise in symmetry has a prominently placed door (in an enclosed porch, altered in the 1920s) but gives little indication of the interior layout. Wright loved to play with the viewer's sense of anticipation by giving false clues. A favorite subtly confusing device used here is the visual "stretching" of the first floor and shortening of the second by placing the stringcourse very high on the facade, directly under the second-floor windows. The textured surface, complex but well ordered, features Chicago common brick that interlocks and projects at the corners. Diagonal piers projecting from the sides of the bays resemble those on the front of the Rollin Furbeck House, done the same year for his brother. The house was a wedding present from the resident's father, investor Warren Furbeck.

43 Edward W. McCready House
231 N. Euclid Ave.
1907, Spencer & Powers

This work—perhaps the firm's greatest—derives its grace from a subtle balancing of details: low urns, the high stringcourse, the deep-set door framed by glittering art-glass windows. The palette is simple but rich, the raked masonry joints of the orange brick emphasizing horizontality. It's a practical plan for a corner, often compared to H. H. Richardson's plan for the John J. Glessner House on Prairie Ave. The north wall continues straight back to the garage, shielding the yard from the street.

44 Herman W. Mallen House
300 N. Euclid Ave.
1905, George W. Maher

McCready House

Damaged by fire and greatly altered, the house was originally stuccoed and sported open porches on the east and west. But beautiful art glass still adorns the second-floor bays of the Euclid Ave. facade.

45 Calvin H. Hill House
312 N. Euclid Ave.
1904, Patton & Miller

The style is Colonial Revival, but the massiveness is characteristic of the firm's Queen Anne work.

46 Thomas S. Rattle House
315 N. Euclid Ave.
1885, George O. Garnsey

As editor of the monthly *National Builder*, a pattern-book magazine, Garnsey was one of Chicago's influential architects. This simple Queen Anne house has Stick Style details.

47 Charles E. Roberts House
321 N. Euclid Ave.
1883, Burnham & Root
Remodeled 1896, Frank Lloyd Wright

Most of Wright's work was on the interior; some of his leaded glass can be glimpsed from the alley. Roberts was a great champion of the young architect and a prominent member of the Building Committee for Unity Temple.

48 Charles E. Roberts Stable
317 N. Euclid Ave.
1896, Frank Lloyd Wright
Converted to a house 1929, White & Weber

Perhaps Wright remodeled an existing stable; if so, it was a complete remodeling. From the front, it reads as stacked volumes; from the sides, as decorated planes.

49 Unity Church (James Hall Taylor House)
405 N. Euclid Ave.
1912, George W. Maher

This formal house resembles Maher's grand designs for Hutchinson St. in Chicago. The colossal flanged segmental arch over the door was one of his favorite details of this period. The deep, unusually detailed roofline features wide soffits and fascia.

50 Charles R. Erwin House
530 N. Euclid Ave.
1905, George W. Maher

Look at the tall narrow windows above the scalloped door arch to see the pattern in the art glass that once graced all the windows. It was echoed in a beautiful wrought-iron gate and fence.

51 George G. Page House
637 N. Euclid Ave.
1896, Harvey L. Page

The grandeur and formality of this Federal Revival residence contrast sharply with other Oak Park houses of the era. Page had recently moved from Washington, D.C., and his academically correct cornice, pilasters, dentils, and Palladian windows have a measured and almost exotic beauty amid the efforts of Wright and Maher.

Page House

52 Harry S. Adams House
710 W. Augusta St.
1914, Frank Lloyd Wright

The unusual width of the lot allowed Wright to sprawl beyond his usual limits in this, his last Oak Park house. The breadth of the low chimney echoes the sweeping lines of the roof, stringcourse, and porte cochere. The sheltered entry features one of Wright's loveliest front doors.

53 Oscar B. Balch House
611 N. Kenilworth Ave.
1911, Frank Lloyd Wright

Wright had remodeled a store on Lake St. for decorator Balch and his partner Frank Pebbles in 1907. The music, living, and dining rooms flow straight across the front of the house, which is similar in first-floor plan to the Edwin H. Cheney House.

54 Clarence E. and Grace Hall Hemingway House
600 N. Kenilworth Ave.
1906, Henry G. Fiddelke

Mrs. Hemingway collaborated with the architect on the design, which included offices for Dr. Hemingway and a large music room. Ernest Hemingway lived here from the age of six until he left home at eighteen.

55 Walter Thomas Mills House
601 N. Kenilworth Ave.
1897, Patton & Fisher

The simplicity and lack of fuss, the reliance on powerful forms already characteristic of the firm's Queen Anne style work, are edging here toward something more modern and rectilinear. Note the symmetrically placed corner windows on the second floor.

56 Charles E. Cessna House
524 N. Oak Park Ave.
1905, Eben E. Roberts

Roberts indulged in rich materials: clay tile for the roof, a brick base, stone trim and brackets, and dazzling art glass. The emphasis on the horizontal is greatly exaggerated by the ponderous hipped roofs. The dormers are so deep that they subvert their function of admitting light into the attic space, much as the cavelike porch darkens the living room.

57 William M. Luff House
520 N. Oak Park Ave.
1886, Theodore V. Wadskier

Even on this street of excessive architectural personality, this rare, well-preserved Swiss chalet version of the Stick Style holds its own. The wooden members that frame the rectangular panels of shingles and clapboard break through the plane of the wall, forming picturesque balconies. These, in turn, increase the complexity of the surface as the sun moves across the house, casting bars of shadow across its face.

Luff House

58 Walter C. Hill House
516 N. Oak Park Ave.
1897, Harvey L. Page

As strict an exercise in Federal Revival as can be seen in Oak Park, it is rigidly symmetrical and well proportioned.

59 Burton F. Hales House
509 N. Oak Park Ave.
1904, Henry G. Fiddelke

Oak Park's grandest mansion is this sober brick and Bedford limestone Gothic house.

60 Ernest Hemingway Birthplace (Ernest Hall House)
339 N. Oak Park Ave.
1890, Wesley A. Arnold

Ernest Hemingway was born in the second-floor turret bedroom in 1899. Hall was his maternal grandfather.

61 Oak Park Club Condominiums
721 W. Ontario St. (Oak Park Club)
1923, Miller, Holmes & Flinn
156 N. Oak Park Ave. (YMCA)
1904, Pond & Pond
Converted to condominiums 1991, Bauhs & Dring

The Georgian YMCA and the Renaissance/Prairie Oak Park Club served diverse social needs for decades. The club is the last major local descendant of the handsome building blocks seen in Oak Park and River Forest High School and Scoville Square. Designed by Normand S. Patton's successor firm, it shifts to a more overtly revival style with Palladian detailing.

62 Parkview Apartments
173–181 N. Grove Ave.
1922, Eben E. Roberts

As developer of this quality apartment house, Roberts billed it as "late English Gothic" and marketed it as "owner-occupied." Included were maid's rooms in the basement, a vacuum-cleaning system, "sound deafening" between floors, and "radio-receiving apparatus" on the roof with outlets in each unit. Note the looming faces at the parapet, styled on the north side as an iceman and a deliveryman to identify the service entrances.

63 Oak Park Public Library
834 W. Lake St.
1966, Holabird & Root
Second-floor addition 1976, Hammond, Beeby & Babka

This low-key modern design is aging well, due largely to the choice and quality of materials; also pleasing is the horizontality, an overt reference to the village's Prairie School heritage.

64 Unity Temple
875 W. Lake St.
1905–1908, Frank Lloyd Wright
Throughout his life, Wright was absorbed with pathways of discovery. At Unity Temple, the experience is both physical and spiritual. The route from the radical and uncompromising Lake St. facade to the warm and intimate Temple is a sequence of spaces as compelling as any Wright ever created.

After their Gothic Revival church burned in June 1905, Oak Park's Universalists asked Wright to design a new building for four hundred members. The chosen site was prominent but small and close to noisy streetcar and train tracks. The budget was a modest $45,000.

These limitations, and a deep understanding of the principles of the Universalist faith, stimulated Wright's creativity. For reasons of economy, the architect selected reinforced concrete, usually used for important buildings only if covered with another material or molded to resemble stone. Construction technology and economics dictat-

Unity Temple

ed broad, unornamented expanses and repetitive shapes. High walls and side entries set far back would shield worshipers from as much noise as possible.

Two similar but unequal blocks—"Unity Temple" for worship and "Unity House" for social-service functions—are joined by a low entry link. The deep overhang of the slab roof covers the walkway; the monumentally scaled planter cuts off the view of the street as one ascends the short flight of stairs. The visitor is sheltered and then encircled by the building before ever crossing the threshold. Facing the doors, the sheer walls of the two blocks and the entry parapet dramatically emphasize the sky, presaging the Temple space. The inscription above each entry, "For the Worship of God and the Service of Man," reflects the Universalist belief that a house of worship must serve both sacred and secular needs.

Inside, the low-ceilinged entry area leads circuitously to even more confining cloisters from which one enters the dramatic Temple space. Only 30' from the clamor of Lake St. is another world, flooded with light from amber-colored skylights which create the impression of what Wright called a "happy cloudless day." Three sets of galleries for the congregation and an alcove for the choir create a Greek cross within the square, with the corners occupied by square stair towers. No seat is more than 45' from the pulpit, and most seats are just barely above or below the speaker's eye level. There are no religious symbols; the Universalists chose to focus all attention on the speaker. Wright placed doors to either side of the pulpit so the congregants would exit toward the minister.

Even before it gained worldwide renown, Unity Temple was widely praised both by the congregation and by local newspapers. Despite the unorthodox form and materials, they recognized that Wright had given form to a deeply rooted spirituality. It remains a transcendent work, bound to the earth and open to the heavens.
—Alice Sinkevitch

Unity Temple

65 U.S. Post Office—Oak Park Station
901 W. Lake St.
1933, White & Weber

Here sober Art Moderne is enlivened with amusing details, like the sculptured panels over the entries documenting the world of mail delivery: birds carrying letters, a mail bag and cap, the Pony Express, a mail truck, a covered wagon, a train and plane. Studded with patriotic stars, Art Deco sconces and chandeliers light the pale interior.

66 William J. MacDonald House
300 N. Kenilworth Ave.
1890, Wesley A. Arnold

Although added in 1911, the porch with its rock foundation complements the Queen Anne house.

67 George B. Pratt House
308 N. Kenilworth Ave.
1886, architect unknown

This fine Stick Style house is modest in scale but boldly articulated on both front and sides.

68 John Rankin House
245 N. Kenilworth Ave.
1891, Patton & Fisher

A great parade of Kenilworth Ave. Queen Annes begins with this behemoth. The massive bays are tightly wrapped in thin clapboards. The octagonal corner turret appears to bulge from the effort of containing the great spaces within.

69 Walter H. Gale House (2)
312 N. Kenilworth Ave.
1905, Henry G. Fiddelke

This symmetrical Colonial Revival work has a detailed cornice and front door with sidelights.

70 David J. Kennedy House
309 N. Kenilworth Ave.
1888, Patton & Fisher

Kennedy was a real estate investor and part owner of the Cicero & Proviso Street Railway. His barnlike Queen Anne features a layered gable front with flared edges.

71 William A. Douglas House
317 N. Kenilworth Ave.
1893, Patton & Fisher
Addition 1908, Patton & Miller

Capacious, rambling, and generously scaled, the Douglas house has one of Oak Park's best porches. As in the John Rankin House, shingled, rolled edges frame the third-floor dormer.

72 Harrison P. Young House (W. E. Coman House)
334 N. Kenilworth Ave.
1870s, architect unknown
Remodeled 1895, Frank Lloyd Wright

The porch and the leaded diamond-paned windows are the most visible part of Wright's work.

73 John Schmidt House
400 N. Kenilworth Ave.
early 1870s, architect unknown

This early Oak Park cottage has Italianate detailing. The wood molding around the exaggeratedly vertical windows imitates masonry.

74 Joseph K. Dunlop House
407 N. Kenilworth Ave.
1897, Eben E. Roberts
75 Simpson Dunlop House
417 N. Kenilworth Ave.
1896, Eben E. Roberts

The Dunlop Brothers were real estate developers and capitalists who established a bank in Oak Park in 1886. These magnificent houses are often labeled Rectilinear Queen Anne, because although quite geometric on the outside, the plans still open out from the Queen Anne "great hall."

76 Charles E. Matthews House
432 N. Kenilworth Ave.
1909, Tallmadge & Watson

The facade is sedate and formal, focusing on the entry, with its art-glass windows that illuminate the stair hall.

Melville House

77 Americus B. Melville House
437 N. Kenilworth Ave.
1904, Eben E. Roberts

Roberts abandoned the box for this free-flowing stucco house, which is complex in elevation and sophisticated in plan. His characteristic brackets don't really support anything but have grown to gigantic proportions, dripping down the walls and porch piers.

78 Anna L. Wright House (John Blair House)
931 W. Chicago Ave.
before 1873, architect unknown

Wright bought the steeply gabled Gothic Revival house and large lot from Blair, a landscaper. On the Forest Ave. side of Blair's property Wright built his own house; Wright's mother continued to live in "Grandmother's Cottage."

79 Frank Lloyd Wright Home and Studio
951 W. Chicago Ave.
1889–1911, Frank Lloyd Wright
Restored 1976–1986, Restoration Committee of the Frank Lloyd Wright Home and Studio Foundation

Wright's love was designing houses, and in seventy-two years of architectural life he created over 270 of them.

This was his earliest—and also the first that he called home. Containing the seeds of all the rest, it was built on a corner lot acquired in 1889. The shingle-clad houses that Wright saw in architectural magazines gave aspect to the Forest Ave. facade; but the forms are sharply cut, crystal-clear products of the childhood training in geometric shapes that infused his entire career.

Wright Home and Studio

Wright Studio

In keeping with the Shingle Style tradition, Wright's house is divided into three horizontal bands of base, walls, and roof. The base of Chicago common brick not only provides a protective wainscot but also roots the house in the suburban prairie. With what would be characteristic care for the setting, Wright retained most of the lot's tangle of native and exotic plants as a nest for his cottage. The wood-shingled middle zone almost disappears in the undulations of its wings and octagonal bays and in the transparency of its wide casement windows—a hint at the dissolution of the wall that characterized the Prairie School. The great gabled roof dominates the composition with proclamations of "shelter" and "home," as it always would for Wright. A dining room addition to the south and a kitchen/playroom addition to the rear

completed the home about 1895.

Wright's studio addition (1898), facing Chicago Ave., shows a bold massing that came out of his love for pure geometric grammar. The exterior is a direct expression of the octagonal spaces within—a cubic two-story drafting room to the east of the entry and a library to the west. Commercial in scale, as befits an architectural office, the studio is nonetheless visually coupled to the house by its use of the same materials. Decorative elements by Wright and sculptor Richard W. Bock highlight the studio's elevations.

The organic, flowing, harmonious, and reposeful qualities that pervaded Wright's interiors can be found throughout, especially in the dining room, playroom, drafting room, and library. The heating and lighting as well as the furnishings are everywhere integrated into the architectural environment.

After leaving Oak Park, Wright remodeled the studio as living quarters for his family, and the home was rented out; the complex was later remodeled into six apartments. The property was acquired by the National Trust for Historic Preservation in 1974. A National Historic Landmark, restored by the Frank Lloyd Wright Home and Studio Foundation to its 1905–1909 appearance, it offers an intriguing look at the early home life and workplace of a master architect.
—Donald G. Kalec

80 Robert P. Parker House
1019 W. Chicago Ave.
81 Thomas H. Gale House
1027 W. Chicago Ave.
1892, Frank Lloyd Wright

These "bootlegged" houses were designed by the moonlighting Wright while he was still employed by Adler & Sullivan; local realtor Thomas Gale knew Wright through the Unity Church. Both houses are a slight variation on a popular Queen Anne style, with a two-story corner bay topped by a turret. Wright's version is more geometric; the octagonal bay is a prominent element on both front and back, and the windows are massed in a band.

Walter H. Gale House (1)

82 Walter H. Gale House (1)
1031 W. Chicago Ave.
1893–1894, Frank Lloyd Wright

Construction of a cottage by architect L. D. Beman began in the spring of 1893 but apparently had not gotten far when Gale bought the lot later that year. This Queen Anne with its sweeping roof offers a rare example of Wright's skillful handling of spindles, an element frequently used to define interior spaces. Unusually tall and thin, they are so closely spaced that they appear as a solid wall as you approach. Not until you are directly in front does the view of the wall behind suddenly emerge.

83 Andrew J. Redmond House
422 N. Forest Ave.
1900, Eben E. Roberts

A giant step past the Victorianism of the Dunlop Houses, this is the first of a fifteen-year series of low, broad, beautifully detailed boxes. Maher's influence emerges in the urns, the emphasized third-floor dormer, the broad porch, and the formal symmetry.

84 William H. Copeland House (William Harman House)
400 N. Forest Ave.
early 1870s, architect unknown
Remodeled 1909, Frank Lloyd Wright
Garage *1908, Frank Lloyd Wright*

Known in Wright literature for later owner Copeland, this was originally an Italianate home in a yellowish "Milwaukee brick." An earlier renovation had already raised the roof when Wright remodeled the entry and interior, adding wood-mullioned windows and sidelights.

85 Sampson Rogers House
401 N. Forest Ave.
1890, Frank Ellis

This immense Queen Anne is made even larger by layers of porches, at least some of which were additions.

Moore House

86 Eben E. Roberts House and Studio
1019 W. Superior St.
Remodeled 1911, Eben E. Roberts

It has a cozy, hand-built look; most of the interest is in the interior, which is filled with detailed woodwork, art glass, and a built-in grandfather clock.

87 Francis J. Woolley House
1030 W. Superior St.
1893–1894, Frank Lloyd Wright

A curiosity in Wright's development, it bears a greater resemblance to Oak Park builders' houses of 1910 than to Wright's later work.

88 Nathan G. Moore House
333 N. Forest Ave.
1895, Frank Lloyd Wright
Remodeled 1923, Frank Lloyd Wright

This generously scaled and lovingly detailed house is the product of two stages of Wright's career. Moore came to him in 1894 for a remodeling of his frame house on this site, then decided it would be too small

and directed Wright to give him something "Elizabethan." The bold and impressive Tudor Revival house was imitated by local architects for the next twenty years. Wright wrote in his autobiography, "Anyone could get a rise out of me by admiring that essay in English half-timber. 'They' all liked it and I could have gone on unnaturally building them for the rest of my natural life."

In December 1922, the house burned down to the top of the first floor. Wright, who happened to be in Chicago, contacted Moore and received the commission to rebuild. This opulent hybrid, with touches of Gothic, Sullivanesque, and Mayan design, was the result. Charles E. White, Jr. was Wright's local coordinator for the project and is credited with the very traditional interior.

89 Arthur Heurtley House
318 N. Forest Ave.
1902, Frank Lloyd Wright

Rich, challenging, and satisfying, open yet mysterious, firmly

Heurtley House

rooted to the ground yet removed from prying eyes, this is one of Wright's most magnificent homes. The raised living rooms enable occupants to look out through uncurtained art-glass windows without fear of being seen. An overscaled brick half-wall shields the roundheaded portal, rendering the front door invisible. The great hipped roof, utterly simplified, hovers over bands of richly leaded casement windows and a variegated battered brick wall laid in a complex, textured pattern.

90 Edward R. Hills–Thomas DeCaro House
313 N. Forest Ave.
1883, Charles C. Miller
Remodeled 1900–1906, Frank Lloyd Wright
Reconstructed (for Thomas DeCaro) 1976, John Tilton Assocs.

After several reincarnations, this gift from Nathan Moore to his daughter, Mary, is in excellent condition. The original Stick Style frame house stood just to the north with its narrow end facing Forest Ave. Wright and Moore moved it, turned it ninety degrees, and overhauled it so dramatically that they might as well have started from scratch. Although built in 1906, it had apparently been designed in 1900, which partially accounts for the roofline with its flared eaves. The restored shingled roof is one of its most interesting features. Even here Wright emphasizes the horizontal, with every fifth row of shingles a double layer.

91 Charles A. Purcell House
300 N. Forest Ave.
1893, architect unknown

This sober Queen Anne was built by architect William Gray Purcell's father, who once commented to his family, "If that Wright don't quit, he'll have our street ruined."

92 Laura Gale House
6 Elizabeth Ct.
1909, Frank Lloyd Wright

A stylistic step beyond even the boldest of Wright's Forest Ave. homes, this cantilevered composition looks forward twenty-five years to Fallingwater in Pennsylvania. Wright wrote, "In integral architecture the room-space itself must come through. The room must be seen as architecture or we have no architecture." Here the porches are not applied appendages but "room-spaces" thrust through the wall, uniting exterior and interior. The leaded windows are screens, not barriers, protecting from the weather while enhancing the view.

93 Edgar Cook House
231 N. Forest Ave.
1870s, architect unknown

One of the first generation of Forest Ave. houses, this simple cottage is vertically oriented, with jigsawed bargeboards under the eaves. Most of the other cottages from this era were either remodeled beyond recognition or moved after 1885 to other, less expensive sites.

94 Peter A. Beachy House
238 N. Forest Ave.
1906, Frank Lloyd Wright

The original commission was to remodel a modest cottage, which was ultimately obliterated by this grand Prairie Style work. The thick lines of the eaves, lintels, and corner piers and the wood-mullioned windows have led to speculation that the talented hand of Wright's employee Walter Burley Griffin contributed much to the design.

Everett House

95 Joseph D. Everett House
228 N. Forest Ave.
1888, Wilson, Marble & Lamson

Thomas House

An overriding preference for the rectilinear once again harnesses the Queen Anne style.

96 Henderson Judd House
219 N. Forest Ave.
1881, architect unknown

The Italianate was in its final years of popularity when this house was built. In plan it resembles the emerging Stick Style, with an entry and stair hall pushed to the side. A very similar house was built at the same time at 223; remodeled after 1900, it is now unrecognizable as Italianate.

97 George T. Hayden House
209 N. Forest Ave.
1893, W. K. Johnston

The riot of materials includes brick, stone, and shingles. The turret, porch, and shingled colonnettes display more round forms than most Queen Annes in Oak Park.

98 R. K. Bickford House
203 N. Forest Ave.
1885, architect unknown

This Stick Style house retains a feature long lost on most houses of the era: the scrolling open brackets that enhance the second-floor porch and corners and cast moving shadows on the clapboard.

99 Frank W. Thomas House
210 N. Forest Ave.
1901, Frank Lloyd Wright

Rear addition 1922, Tallmadge & Watson
Restored 1975

Turning a blind eye to the Victorian timidity on its flanks, the Thomas House is considered Wright's first constructed Prairie School house. "First thing in building the new house, get rid of the attic, therefore the dormer," Wright wrote in *An Autobiography*. "Get rid of the useless false heights below it. Next, get rid of the unwholesome basement, yes absolutely—in any house built on the prairie. Instead of lean, brick chimneys bristling up everywhere to hint at Judgment, I could see necessity for one chimney only." This house meets the ground with a simple water table above which the walls rise unbroken to the line of dazzling art glass. The entry sequence is complex and unpredictable. The roundheaded portal appears to shield a door but actually conceals a stair leading up and back to the real front door.

100 Emerson Ingalls Row Houses
200–208 N. Forest Ave.
1892, William J. Van Keuren

Looking like an overgrown Queen Anne house, this symmetrical composition is interesting mainly for its sharp contrast with the Prairie Style, which emerged on the lot next door in 1901.

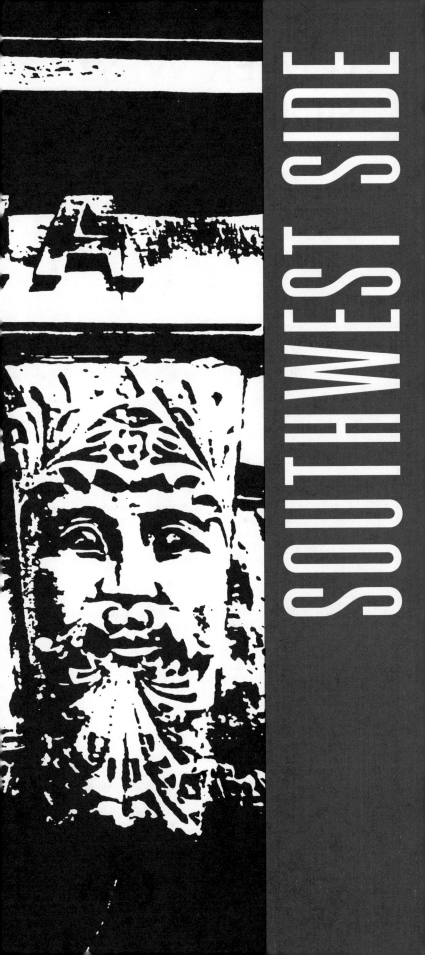

SOUTHWEST SIDE

LOWER WEST SIDE

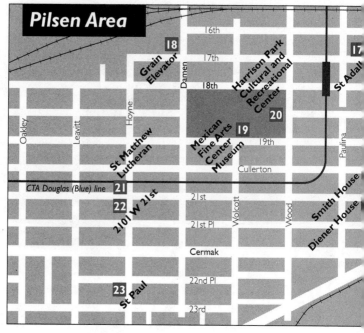

Pilsen Area

16th

18

17th

Grain Elevator

Damen

18th

Harrison Park Cultural and Recreational Center

St Adal

17

Hoyne

20

Oakley

Leavitt

St Matthew Lutheran

Mexican Fine Arts Center Museum

19

19th

Paulina

Cullerton

CTA Douglas (Blue) line

21

2101 W 21st

21st

Wolcott

Wood

Smith House

22

21st Pl

Diener House

Cermak

22nd Pl

23

St Paul

23rd

The Lower West Side grew up with Chicago's industry, thriving in the 1870s when the city was becoming an industrial power-house, and declining a century later as the manufacturing base withered away. The flats, cottages, and commercial buildings that met the needs of generations of factory workers suffer from decay and neglect, but lively areas persist in the immigrant neighborhoods, which continue to attract the newly arrived.

The Lower West Side comprises Pilsen, Heart of Chicago, Little Village, and Lawndale. Pilsen, the oldest community, is bounded on the south by the Illinois & Michigan Canal (1848) and was developed with lumber yards and breweries; on the north it ends at railroad tracks laid in the 1860s. Its major development occurred after the Great Fire of 1871, when burned-out industries and workers moved west. Immigrants from Bohemia were the earliest settlers, and they named the community for their homeland's second-largest city. Polish and Yugoslavian immigrants arrived in the early twentieth century and were replaced beginning in the 1950s by Mexicans and Puerto Ricans. Pilsen's early role as a "port of entry" called for flats, apartments, and combination retail-residential buildings, built mostly by investors for rental. Its continued status as a "first-stop" immigrant neighborhood has restricted development. The area has a concentration of buildings from the 1870s and 1880s, many of which feature the mansard roof characteristic of those decades. In 1875 the city's ongoing sewer project reached the Pilsen area. This process of raising streets and sidewalks above new sewer and drainage systems left many buildings with their first floors eight to ten feet below street level.

Heart of Chicago, which is west of Ashland Ave., also boomed after the 1871 fire, when industries began to cluster along the river. Germans, Poles, and northern Italians were the major ethnic groups. The leading industry was the McCormick Reaper (later International Harvester) works at Western and Blue Island avenues; like other large employers, it is long gone. The southern stretches of both Pilsen and Heart of Chicago contain many barren former industrial sites, but the residential portions remain vital.

Little Village, or Pueblo Pequeño, was originally known as South Lawndale and was renamed in the mid-1970s by its Mexican-American majority. Both Lawndales were primarily open swamplands west of the city limits at Western Ave. in 1863, when the Chicago, Burlington & Quincy Railroad was laid out on a southwesterly course that became the boundary between the two areas. Annexed by Chicago in 1869, South Lawndale witnessed residential development around 1885, with the general westward expansion of the built-up city, but it was contained on the south and west by the accelerating development of industry. Immigrants from Bohemian Pilsen were among the first occupants of the area's small brick houses, followed in the 1930s by Poles and, since 1960, by increasing numbers of Hispanics. By 1980 the community had the city's largest concentration of Mexicans.

Lawndale (originally North Lawndale) is crossed diagonally by Ogden Ave., built in the 1850s as a plank road along the portage trail linking Lake Michigan to the Des Plaines River. Residential development progressed westward along Roosevelt Rd., the commercial street at Lawndale's northern edge, after 1895, when the Garfield Park elevated train inaugurated service to Cicero Ave. The bulk of the residential construction—primarily rental apartments and two-flats—took place between 1910 and 1925. The earliest occupants were Russian Jews moving from the Near West Side; in the 1920s the area had seventy synagogues. After World War II African-Americans began following the same westward route and constituted 90 percent of the population by 1960. The West Side riots following the 1968 assassination of Dr. Martin Luther King, Jr., closed some businesses, and the refusal of insurance companies to extend their

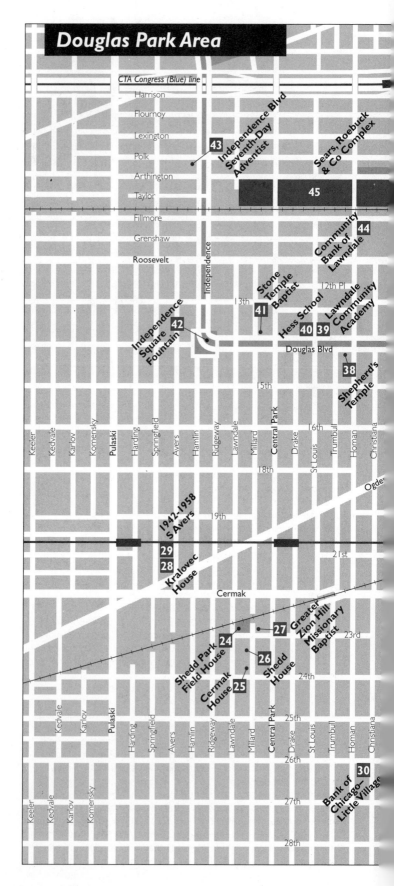

Douglas Park Area

CTA Congress (Blue) line

Harrison
Flournoy
Lexington
Polk
Arthington
Taylor
Fillmore
Grenshaw
Roosevelt

43 Independence Blvd Seventh-Day Adventist

45 Sears, Roebuck & Co Complex

44 Community Bank of Lawndale

41 Stone Temple Baptist

12th Pl

40 Hess School

39 Lawndale Community Academy

42 Independence Square Fountain

Independence

13th

Douglas Blvd

38 Shepherd's Temple

15th

Keeler
Kedvale
Karlov
Komensky
Pulaski
Harding
Springfield
Avers
Hamlin
Ridgeway
Lawndale
Millard
Central Park
Drake
St Louis
Trumbull
Homan
Christiana

16th

18th

Ogden

1942-1958 S Avers

19th

29
28 Kralovec House

21st

Cermak

27 Greater Zion Hill Missionary Baptist

23rd

24 Shedd Park Field House

26 Shedd House

25 Cermak House

24th

Kedvale
Karlov
Pulaski
Harding
Springfield
Avers
Hamlin
Ridgeway
Lawndale
Millard
Central Park
Drake
St Louis
Trumbull
Homan
Christiana

25th

26th

30 Bank of Chicago–Little Village

27th

Keeler
Kedvale
Karlov
Komensky

28th

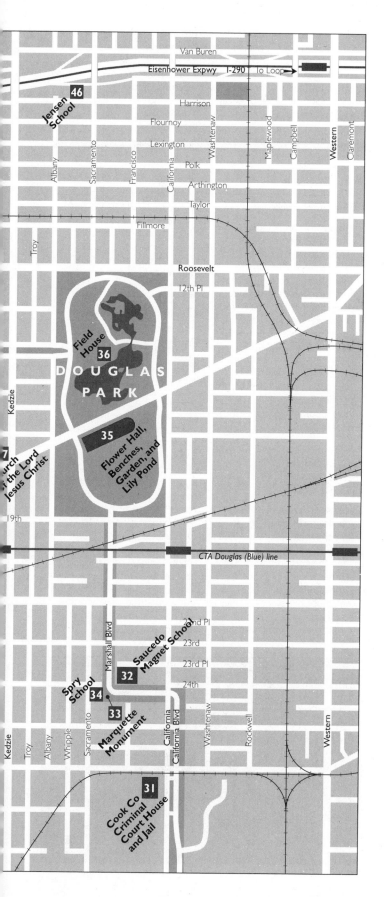

policies closed many more. Industrial properties have been vacated as the city shifted from a manufacturing to a service orientation. Lawndale's landscape is now characterized by aging housing stock, with blocks of neat graystones interspersed with vacant lots and crumbling buildings. Infill housing projects have begun to appear but have not kept pace with the rate of decay.
—Vincent Michael

■ St. Procopius Church
18th St. at Allport St.
1883, Julius H. Huber

The design of this "mother church" of Chicago's Bohemian parishes was inspired by the Romanesque Revival of early to mid-nineteenth-century Germany and eastern Europe, translated into inexpensive local materials. As in nearby flats and commercial buildings, walls of common brick are trimmed with Joliet limestone, sparely embellished with incised ornament. The leaded-glass windows are filled with plant forms and fleurs-de-lis, with religious imagery limited to small medallions.

■ Thalia Hall
1807 S. Allport St.
1893, Faber & Pagels

This husky Romanesque mixed-use building served Pilsen's Bohemian community as a social and political center and hosted musical and theatrical productions. Apartments and stores helped support the Hall, named for the Greek muse of comedy. Above the entry hovers a "green man," with hair, beard, and mustache

of acanthus. A popular pagan figure co-opted by Christians, he can be traced to the head-hunting and -worshiping Celts. He enjoyed a revival on turn-of-the-century buildings, particularly those faced with limestone, along with other elements borrowed from the Romanesque.

■ Iglesia Presbiteriana Emmanuel (Emmanuel Presbyterian Church)
1850 S. Racine Ave.
1965, Loebl, Schlossman, Bennett & Dart

Although small, modestly towered, and set back from the street, this church has a powerful, intriguing presence. The thin, angular, brick wall planes appear idiosyncratic until you step inside to see how their careful placement catches the light. Inspired rather than hamstrung by the small budget, designer Edward D. Dart made morning light the most powerful architectural element, casting it across the angled chancel wall to create a sense of shelter and spirituality. Pews fan out around the altar, and the angled ceiling focuses attention on the chancel.

Thalia Hall

4 Dvorak Park

Cullerton to 21st Sts.; Carpenter to May Sts.
1908, William Carbys Zimmerman and Richard E. Schmidt, Garden & Martin

Surviving features of this Progressive Reform movement park—used by 2,500 people a day during its first decade—include Zimmerman's original field house and fence posts; Schmidt, Garden & Martin's iron lamp standards; and 1920s fencing. Zimmerman's pool building has been heavily altered.

5 Benito Juarez High School

2150 S. Laflin St.
1977, Bernheim, Kahn & Lozano

Built for Pilsen's growing Mexican-American community, this school was designed in consultation with Pedro Ramírez Vázquez, a Mexican architect. The geometry of the elevations was meant to evoke pre-Columbian temples but unfortunately has none of their drama or rich narrative details.

6 St. Pius V Roman Catholic Church

1901 S. Ashland Ave.
1885–1892, James J. Egan

Egan brought a light touch to the Romanesque Revival style, preferring smooth masonry to the rough ashlar favored by other Chicago church architects such as Burling & Whitehouse and Edbrooke & Burnham. The finely detailed arched entrances and windows are echoed on the interior, which although modernized retains a powerful trio of roundheaded arches in the sanctuary, embellished with Norman carving and stencils. On the facade, the flowing geometric designs of the impost blocks and the band connecting the upper windows are in the vein of Frank Furness and Louis H. Sullivan.

7 U.S. Post Office—Pilsen Station

1859 S. Ashland Ave.
1935, John C. Bollenbacher

The Pony Express goes Moderne in the reliefs above the windows of this blocky post office, one of the finest of its WPA era.

Both sides of 18th St. from Ashland Ave. west to Damen Ave. are lined with well-worn but still heavily used retail, recreational, and residential buildings. Although many of them are remuddled and hung with modern signs, they are still vividly eclectic.

8 Francis D. Nemecek Studio

1439 W. 18th St.
1907, Frank Randak

This tiny Baroque storefront for a photographer had a well-lit studio space above a metal and leaded-glass storefront, which has been well preserved.

9 John Novak Store and Flats

1501 W. 18th St.
1887, architect unknown

This deep tenement (with a fourth floor squeezed under the mansard roof) above a storefront grabs for glory with an effusively ornamented pressed-metal corner tower.

Lozano Branch Library

10 Chicago Public Library—Rudy Lozano Branch

1805 S. Loomis St.
1990, Jay Carow Architects

Bands of red and blue terra-cotta ornament pierce the curved glass facade to run through the library's interior. The motif of the decorative tile is derived from pre-Columbian structures at Mitla, in Oaxaca.

On S. Blue Island Ave. between 19th and 20th Sts. are a cluster of three decades of typical Chicago "flats above the stores" buildings.

⓫ Store and Flats
1870 S. Blue Island Ave.
1899, Frommann & Jebsen

For Schlitz agent Edward G. Uih-lein, the architects bent their Germanic Queen Anne taproom formula around this oblique corner to visually command the intersection.

⓬ Jan Kralovec Stores and Flats
1923–1929 S. Blue Island Ave.
1886, architect unknown

Note the cast-iron columns with foliate capitals and the ornate spandrels between the second and third floors. The cornice, which is of pressed metal with paired brackets on Blue Island Ave., changes to a simpler brick corbel table around the corner on Cullerton St.

⓭ 2004–2006 S. Blue Island Ave.
1872, architect unknown

Still visible—despite the metal siding—are bracketed cornices above the first and second floors, as well as large arched window hoods that mimic in wood the stone details of nearby buildings.

⓮ George Van Dolen Stores and Flats
2008–2010 S. Blue Island Ave.
1879, architect unknown

Half of the storefront of this Italianate building is relatively unaltered, with cast-iron pillars carrying elaborate capitals and stone window hoods bearing prominent keystones.

⓯ Gustave Diener House
1529 W. Cullerton St.
1886, architect unknown

⓰ Frank Smith House
1530 W. Cullerton St.
1887, architect unknown

This street of late Italianate two- and three-flats is notable for the "boomtown" fronts (straight cornices disguising gable fronts) with straight or arched pediments projecting from the center. Here the cornice line leaps over an attic window, forming a semi-circle, a characteristic of Pilsen two-flats.

⓱ St. Adalbert Roman Catholic Church
1656 W. 17th St.
1914, Henry J. Schlacks

On a street so narrow that the 185-foot towers reach almost out of sight stands Schlacks's basilica-plan masterpiece. Grand and formal, intended to inspire awe rather than familiarity, the facade and worship space are Renaissance Revival, typical of Chicago's Polish churches. The imposing colonnaded porch combines granite columns and door surrounds with terra-cotta capitals and pediment. Inside, the long nave is filled with golden light from tall clerestory windows. The sanctuary wall, painted with scenes from Polish history, frames a fabulous Baroque baldachin over the marble altar. Polish saints including Casimir and Stanislaus Kostka are commemorated in the rich stained-glass windows, made by F. X. Zettler.

⓲ Grain Elevator of J. J. Badenoch Co.
2000 W. 17th St.
1915, Stephens Engineering Co.

This long-abandoned elevator is a vestige of Chicago's past as "stacker of wheat." A terminal elevator, it abuts the railway embankment that forms Pilsen's northern wall. The city's first grain elevators were adjacent to the waterways; in 1860 more than 90 percent of the grain shipped from Chicago went via Lake Michigan. By 1900 grain shipment was controlled by the railroads.

The elevator is a pure response of form to function. Grain acts like a liquid, exerting enormous pressure on the walls of a storage building. Early frame elevators were susceptible to collapse and explosion from the highly flammable dust. Concrete, in the familiar form of bundled tubes, came into use after 1900, and insurance costs soon dictated its adoption. Here, a large I-beam arm extended over the tracks to load grain directly into railcars. The six-story central section of the complex contained extensive ductwork for the drying system, which served eighteen concrete silos.

19 Mexican Fine Arts Center Museum (Harrison Park Natatorium)
1852 W. 19th St.
1914, William Carbys Zimmerman
Renovation 1978, Adrian Lozano

Brick, concrete, and glass block transformed an aging natatorium into a museum.

20 Harrison Park Cultural and Recreational Center
S. Wood St. at W. 18th Pl.
1992, Chicago Park District

The facade is bent like an exedra to welcome visitors, while respecting the park's original grid plan and maximizing the green space.

21 St. Matthew Lutheran Church (Evangelische Lutherische St. Matthäus Kirche)
2100 W. 21st St.
1888, Frederick Ahlschlager

The *Chicago Inter-Ocean* noted in 1888 that Ahlschlager "is getting the retainer for about everything Lutheran." His church is a rare surviving example of the off-the-shelf late nineteenth-century Gothic Revival that so many congregations replaced with larger, more academically correct buildings. Common brick and Lemont limestone are joined by pressed metal that pinch-hits for stone in places like the arcaded corbel table. The three entrances are topped by the original tympana of colored leaded glass, and the main door is surrounded by eight cast-iron columns.

22 2101 W. 21st St. (Evangelische Lutherische Schule)
1882, architect unknown

A very early private school is rendered in the Italianate style of the neighborhood's flats and storefronts. Look up at the roof to see a pressed-metal cupola with delicate cresting.

St. Paul Church

23 St. Paul Roman Catholic Church (St. Paulus Kirche)
2234 S. Hoyne Ave.
1897–1899, Henry J. Schlacks

The parish dreamed beyond reason, the architect designed beyond budget—and St. Paul's became Chicago's greatest Gothic leap of faith. In a working-class neighborhood of modest homes and flats, the 245-foot towers soared higher than the Loop's Reliance and Monadnock buildings. Thrillingly out of scale in both size and expense, the construction left the parish deeply in debt and led Archbishop Quigley to replace the pastor. The church was completed in just two years by an architect acting as contractor and by parishioners donating their skilled labor. Its strength lies in the boldness of scale, the integration of interior and exterior, and the selective embellishment that achieves maximum drama. Most of the building (and the surrounding parish complex) is modest common brick; the east facade and interior are a light brown face brick. Molded brick is used where Schlacks would have used stone on a more expensive design, such as the colonnettes and rib vaulting; only where absolutely necessary did he resort to terra-cotta.

St. Paul's held Schlacks's interest for several decades. He designed the main altar (1910), communion railing (1912), and side altars and pulpit (1916) in a complementary Gothic style in white marble. The luminous Venetian mosaics that decorate the interior and facade were the final major element. Installed in 1930, they combine natural forms with symbolic and pictorial content. Completing the lush but harmonious decoration are stained-glass windows. The transept windows, which depict six scenes in the life of Christ, are particularly fine, with unusually well detailed architectural backdrops and plant forms. Across the street to the north is St. Paul Parochial School (1892), also designed by Schlacks and connected by a second-story bridge to Casa Claret, once St. Paul's convent.

Subdivided in 1870 by Alden C. Millard & Edwin J. Decker, Millard Ave. south of the Chicago, Burlington & Quincy Railroad tracks was fashionable in the late nineteenth century. It retains a whisper of elegance in a sampling of Gothic Revival, Italianate, and Queen Anne houses, most of which have been greatly remodeled. The railroad had a station at what is now Shedd Park.

Shedd Park Field House

❷❹ Shedd Park Field House
(Recreation Building)
3660 W. 23rd St.
*1917, William Drummond
Gymnasium addition 1928,
Michaelsen & Rognstad*

By 1885 John G. Shedd had resubdivided part of Millard & Decker's subdivision and set aside just over an acre for a private park. After unsuccessful efforts to assess local homeowners for improvements, the land was transferred to the city in 1888 and to the Chicago Board of Park Commissioners ten years later. Although nothing remains of Jens Jensen's landscape (1917), the field house is one of the best examples of Prairie School architecture in the Chicago Park District. Above the south entrance, a large but delicately detailed wood pediment contains a fine tympanum with thin glass windows between vertical wooden slats. The sensitively realized gymnasium is recessed forty feet behind the main entrance and repeats the horizontal massing and stringcoursing of Drummond's original.

❷❺ Anton J. Cermak House
2348 S. Millard Ave.
1920, Randak & Rezny

This stolid essay in Bohemian Bourgeois was built by a solid citizen, a state senator, chairman of the Cook County Board, and Chicago's mayor from 1931 until an assassin's bullet intended for president-elect Roosevelt felled him in 1933.

❷❻ John G. Shedd House
2316 S. Millard Ave.
1888, architect unknown
Stable *1886, Charles A. Weary*

Shedd rose from stockboy to partner to president of Marshall Field & Co. His robust Queen Anne house is remarkably intact, retaining its original porch with simple turned columns.

❷❼ Greater Zion Hill Missionary Baptist Church
(Fowler Methodist Episcopal Church)
2255 S. Millard Ave.
1891, Wesley A. Arnold

Whether designing a bank, a house, or a church, Arnold favored highly textured surfaces and picturesque styling. This church evokes a castle, with a Romanesque voussoired rose window and conical-roofed towers capped by copper finials. Pink sandstone and granite accent the gray stone facade, which changes to brick at the rear half of the building.

1952 S. Avers Ave.

Just a few blocks northwest of Shedd Park, somewhat isolated by Ogden Ave. and one-way streets, is a cluster of unusually fine rusticated limestone homes.

28 Jan Kralovec House
2102 S. Avers Ave.
1892, Frederick B. Townsend
29 1942 through 1958 S. Avers Ave.
1893–1894, attributed to Frederick B. Townsend

In anticipation of a new streetcar line on Cermak Rd., the Czech-born Kralovec began developing homes nearby. His own house is an imposing example of the Richardsonian Romanesque style and has a matching coach house. The four adjacent houses he built are also of rusticated limestone, although only two of them continue the Romanesque style;

those at 1942 and 1950 are classically inspired.

30 Bank of Chicago—Little Village (Lawndale National Bank)
3341 W. 26th St.
1913, Frank Randak
Addition 1931, Rezny, Rezny & Liska

The snazzy Art Deco addition preserves the boxlike formality of the original bank, while adding big-city pizzazz. A stone eagle perches menacingly on the roof.

31 Cook County Criminal Court House and Jail
2600 S. California Blvd.
1927, Hall, Lawrence & Ratcliffe

Although far from the Loop's Cook County headquarters, this site was chosen because it adjoined the Bridewell House of Correction and offered room for expansion. This severe monument to criminal justice is realized in a brand of flat Classicism most notable for its rich sculptural program, which is largely the work of Peter Toneman of Joseph Dux Studios in conjunction with the Indiana Limestone Co. Above each of the giant Doric columns rises an allegorical figure: Law, Justice, Liberty, Truth, Might, Love, Wisdom, and Peace. S.P.Q.C., inscribed under the adjacent eagle panels, is Chicago's variant of the classical S.P.Q.R. (the Senate and People of Rome). The bisons above the doors grow their pelts in a Greek meander pattern.

Cook County Criminal Court House

32 Maria Saucedo Magnet School (Carter H. Harrison Technical High School)
2850 W. 24th Blvd.
1912, Arthur F. Hussander

Ponderous classicist Hussander succeeded Prairie School designer Dwight H. Perkins as architect for the Chicago Board of Education in 1910. The roofline of this heavily ornamented structure bristles with acroteria, the shell-shaped protrusions generally found only at the apex and corners of a pediment.

33 Jacques Marquette Monument
S. Marshall Blvd. at W. 24th Blvd.
Base 1925, Holabird & Roche
1926, Hermon A. MacNeil, sculptor

Explorers Marquette and Louis Jolliet are accompanied by an Algonquin Indian. Chicago's first known European inhabitant, Father Marquette spent the winter of 1674–1675 near what is now the intersection of Damen Ave. and 26th St. Bronze tablets at the bridge's northeast corner commemorate his stay.

34 John Spry Public School
2400 S. Marshall Blvd.
1899, Normand S. Patton
Addition 1919, Arthur F. Hussander

Patton's gently Romanesque central section was the Board of Education's first fireproof school.

Douglas Park
California Ave., Roosevelt Rd., Albany Ave., W. 19th St.
1871, William Le Baron Jenney
1885, Oscar F. DuBuis
1906, Jens Jensen

The saddest and shabbiest fragment of the three great West Side parks originally laid out by Jenney, Douglas Park is best seen by car from its inner drive and along Ogden Ave. Created along with Humboldt and Garfield parks by the West Park Commission in 1869, Douglas Park was developed and redesigned over the next forty years. The most glaring of many subsequent alterations was the intrusive siting of George W. Collins High School (1968, Andrew Heard & Assocs.), just north of the Douglas Blvd. entrance. Jenney was starting from scratch; the park had to be raised to grade level by filling it in with manure and sand. The *Land Owner* reported on progress in 1874: "To enhance the beauties of the place, there have been 40,000 yards of Stock Yards' manure deposited there in an imposing mass, not to speak of the thousands of yards of the same romantic material scattered broadcast over the other parks . . . The manure is magnificent soil medicine and

its effects can be plainly traced in the improved vegetation and general fertility of a region that two years ago was not much removed from 'a howling wilderness.' "

The most important surviving element of Jenney's design is the northernmost portion of the Lagoon, framed by the Iron Bridge (1893, Adolph Gottlieb) to the south and by the Stone Bridge (1897, designer unknown) to the north. Later neighborhood residents put this lagoon to good use; the Federal Writers Project *Illinois Guide* (1939) noted that annually "in early autumn, orthodox Jews gather at the lagoon for a ritualistic casting away of their sins."

Jensen's work is visible in the southern half of the park. At the Marshall Blvd. entrance at 19th St., the semicircular concrete foundation and bulkhead once sported a wooden pergola and reflecting pools. The other surviving features of his design are the bermed Prairie Meadow, with its hawthorn trees, and the formal flower garden ensemble that parallels Ogden Ave. The Stable & Shop Building (1892, Jenney & Mundie; alterations 1897 and 1907) is a rare surviving structure by Jenney in the West Parks, although changes have rendered his hand all but invisible.

Douglas Park Flower Hall

35 Flower Hall, Benches, Garden, and Lily Pond
ca. 1907

The reinforced-concrete Flower Hall (covered walkway) is Classical in form but Prairie Style in its integrated execution, with copper coping, extended cornice lines, and linear benches reinforcing the horizontality. The rectangular lily pond was designed to reflect the Hall and enhance the structure by serving as an entrance to Jensen's long, linear formal garden. Benches and lantern standards mark the east end of the garden, which is now planted with species similar to but less invasive than Jensen's original choices.

36 Field House
1928, Michaelsen & Rognstad

The southern half of the lagoon was made into a beach area with the construction of the field house, a virtual twin to the Humboldt Park field house in both Georgian style and siting.

37 Church of the Lord Jesus Christ of the Apostolic Faith
(Douglas Park Auditorium)
3202 W. Ogden Ave.
1910, Rusy & Rezny

Stores, offices, clubrooms, and a dance hall filled this massive, retardataire Second Empire structure lavished with terracotta.

Douglas Blvd. is lined with former synagogues and other remnants of the area's past as a Jewish community. Jews began moving here just before World War I, and between the wars Lawndale and Garfield Park were known as "Chicago's Jerusalem." Most of Chicago's synagogues built during the 1910s and 1920s were classically inspired, but Byzantine motifs surfaced with increasing frequency.

38 Shepherd's Temple Missionary Baptist Church
(Anshe Kenesseth Israel)
3411 W. Douglas Blvd.
1913, Aroner & Somers

The unusual organization of the facade, with a Byzantine semicircular pediment flanked by chunky wings, was derived from mid- to late nineteenth-century European synagogues. Above the doors are marble spandrels and the original stained-glass windows with geometric borders.

Shepherd's Temple M. B. Church

39 Lawndale Community Academy (Hebrew Theological College)
3450–3458 W. Douglas Blvd.
1923, Loewenberg & Loewenberg

In the 1920s Greek Revival styles became more popular than Renaissance designs for synagogues. The entrance features classical Greek decorative patterns, stylized in an angular, almost Art Deco fashion. Papyrus leaves below the Corinthian capitals add an Egyptian motif to the eclectic mix.

40 Julius Hess School/ Lawndale Community Academy (Jewish People's Institute)
3500 W. Douglas Blvd.
1927, Klaber & Grunsfeld

The Moorish capitals, religious symbols, glazed polychrome terra-cotta tile, abstract medallions, and ornamental brickwork evoke Judaism's Middle Eastern origins.

41 Stone Temple Baptist Church (Congregation Anshe Roumania)
3622 W. Douglas Blvd.
1926, J. W. Cohn & Co.

Classical facades lent themselves to discreet ornamental clues about a building's use and purpose. Here the Star of David is included on the modified Composite capitals, and a menorah and the Torah are depicted on stone medallions below the blind arcade.

42 Independence Square Fountain (American Youth and Independence Day Fountain)
Independence Sq. at Douglas and Independence Blvds.
1902, Charles J. Mulligan

Bronze children joyously celebrate Independence Day with Roman candles (the fountain's original waterspouts), musical instruments, and a flag.

43 Independence Boulevard Seventh-Day Adventist Church (Anshe Sholom Synagogue)
3803 W. Polk St.
1926, Newhouse & Bernham

The congregation's history vividly illustrates the rapid westward migration of the neighborhood's Jewish community. This synagogue replaced one built only sixteen years earlier on Polk St. at Ashland Ave. (now St. Basil Greek Orthodox Church). Here the austere Classical style of its predecessor continues, with a stone entablature bearing a Hebrew inscription.

44 Community Bank of Lawndale
1111 S. Homan Ave.
1982, Weese Hickey Weese

Louis H. Sullivan's National Farmers' Bank (1906–1908) in Owatonna, Minnesota, inspired this crisp, blocky bank, one of the few new buildings in this eroded neighborhood.

45 Sears, Roebuck & Co. Complex
900–930 S. Homan Ave.
1905–1906, Nimmons & Fellows

In 1906 the world's largest mail-order company moved into the world's largest commercial building. Founded in 1886, Sears sent out its first large general catalog ten years later and within another ten years was mailing catalogs and orders to 35,000 customers a day. The business was then conducted exclusively with a rural clientele; according to *Architectural Record,* "No business is solicited with people living in large cities, and, in fact, this firm refuses to fill any order from a citizen of Chicago." Two hundred carloads of freight went out each day; all goods were shipped within twenty-four hours after the order was received.

The centerpiece of this monument to efficiency and speed was the Merchandise Building, with 1.7 million square feet of optimally planned space. The second floor of the nine-story (plus tower) building was the central shipping location. Pneumatic tubes carried orders from the Administration Building to the upper floors, where workers

Sears, Roebuck & Co.

sent goods down to the second floor on spiral conveyors controlled by gravity and centrifugal force. Orders were loaded onto freight cars waiting in a train shed that spanned the space between the building's west wings. Completing the complex are the five-story (originally two-story) Administration Building, the four-story Printing Building to the east, and the Power Plant to the south. All are of brown brick trimmed in white terra-cotta with blue accents. The only elaboration is at the pedimented entrance to the Administration Building and at the entrance and top of the tower—the original "Sears Tower," in fact, with an observation room for visitors. The large arcades and red-tiled roof were inspired by the Tuscan style that the architects thought most appropriate to the simple materials.

In 1925 Sears expanded into retail operations and opened their first store in this complex. They maintained their dominance as the nation's largest retailer and in 1974 moved to the world's tallest building, the Sears Tower. Their 1992 move to suburban Hoffman Estates will, in a sense, bring them full circle— back to a sprawling low-rise complex in a residential area.

46 Jens Jensen Public School
3030 W. Harrison St.
1961–1963, Harry Weese & Assocs.

Built of warm, natural materials and on a human scale, the hexagonal classrooms establish the unusual geometry of this village-like school complex rendered in brick.

CHICAGO-MIDWAY AIRPORT

C hicago's 1922 airport plan called for several flying fields on the
city's fringes. Only one of them was actually built, at S. Cicero
Ave. and W. 63rd St., on the site of the private Chicago Aero Park.
In 1926 the city leased this land from the Board of Education, which
owned the square mile between 55th St., Cicero Ave., 63rd St., and
Central Ave. The Kelly Act of 1925 had turned over the transportation of airmail from the U.S. Post Office to private contractors, stimu-
lating commercial airline and airport development. The City Council
voted $10,000 in improvements for Chicago Municipal Airport, which
was dedicated in December 1927. Four cinder runways and twelve
hangars were in operation by 1928, when it became the nation's
busiest airport. Passenger service soon followed airmail, and expansion was necessary to accommodate larger aircraft. A 1930 bond
issue financed expansion west almost to Central Ave., including a runway extension, taxiways, and a terminal. By 1932 Chicago Municipal
was the world's busiest airport.

In 1940 a massive expansion was announced, necessitated by
ever-increasing traffic and by the introduction of the DC-4, the
world's largest commercial aircraft. The railroad tracks bisecting the
site were relocated, and the airport was expanded north to 55th St.
Parallel runways, now a standard pattern, appeared for the first time,
allowing simultaneous arrivals and departures. World War II interrupted construction but kept the airport busy; by 1946, when the
new terminal was under construction, Chicago Municipal Airport
handled 1.3 million passengers annually.

Renamed Midway in 1949 in honor of the famous World War II
battle in which planes had a key role, the airport grew from fifteen
gates in 1947 to twenty-eight in 1953 and handled 9 million passengers in 1956. But projections of increasing traffic and the growth of
commercial jet service demanded expansion on a scale that was not
feasible in this heavily built-up neighborhood. Chicago had acquired
the Orchard Place Airport northwest of the city in 1946 and had
begun the long task of financing and building a jet age airport.

While it would soon lose most of its commercial travelers to the new airport, Midway continued to serve as a nonscheduled-flight terminal for corporate aircraft and as a center for aviation training and technology. Within a few years a revival had begun, stimulated by increasing congestion at O'Hare. Some second-generation jets, such as the Boeing 727 and 737 and the McDonnell Douglas DC-9, could use Midway's shorter runways, to which airlines returned with limited schedules, joining longtime tenants such as fixed-base operator Monarch Air Service.
—John Tomassi

Terminal

1 Terminal
5700 S. Cicero Ave.
1947, Paul Gerhardt, Jr., Chicago city arch.
Remodeled 1968, C. F. Murphy Assocs.

Built when Midway was the crossroads of America, the streamlined concrete terminal is now gutted and largely obscured by Miesian remodelings. Visitors could sit in Marshall Field & Co.'s second-floor Cloud Room restaurant or climb to the rooftop observation deck and watch the steady stream of Lockheed Constellations and DC-6s take off and land.

2 5959 S. Cicero Ave.
(United Airlines Building)
1938, Albert Kahn

An uglifying entrance remodeling and window replacements mask the severe elegance of this corporate office building, originally topped by a backlit glass-block crown with huge letters that spelled out United Airlines. One of Chicago's oldest modernist buildings, it was designed by the Detroit architect famous for his bold, structurally expressive industrial facilities.

3 5035 W. 55th St. (Trans World Airlines Hangar)
1953, Ammann & Whitney, engineers

Midway's most powerful building is best seen from the terminal's passenger concourses. The great overlapping doors slid open wide to admit aircraft. This hangar and office building is of reinforced concrete covered by two thin-shell vaulted roofs; a similar structure at 5245 was built for American Airlines. Among structural engineer Othmar H. Ammann's most famous works are New York's George Washington Bridge, Verrazano–Narrows Bridge, and a large part of the Lincoln Tunnel; his partner Charles S. Whitney was an expert in thin-shell concrete structures.

5035 W. 55th St.

SOUTH SIDE

NEAR SOUTH
SIDE

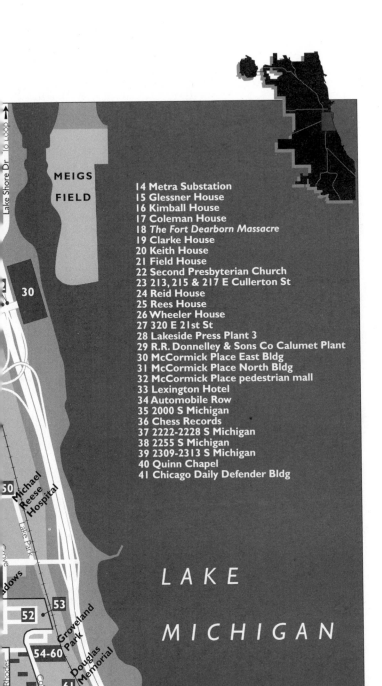

MEIGS
FIELD

14 Metra Substation
15 Glessner House
16 Kimball House
17 Coleman House
18 *The Fort Dearborn Massacre*
19 Clarke House
20 Keith House
21 Field House
22 Second Presbyterian Church
23 213, 215 & 217 E Cullerton St
24 Reid House
25 Rees House
26 Wheeler House
27 320 E 21st St
28 Lakeside Press Plant 3
29 R.R. Donnelley & Sons Co Calumet Plant
30 McCormick Place East Bldg
31 McCormick Place North Bldg
32 McCormick Place pedestrian mall
33 Lexington Hotel
34 Automobile Row
35 2000 S Michigan
36 Chess Records
37 2222-2228 S Michigan
38 2255 S Michigan
39 2309-2313 S Michigan
40 Quinn Chapel
41 Chicago Daily Defender Bldg

LAKE

MICHIGAN

As one of Chicago's earliest settlements, the Near South Side was one of the first areas to experience the typical urban cycles of prosperity, decay, and renewal, and it now contains the city's most intensely polyglot collection of buildings and neighborhoods. Beyond the conventioneers' mecca that is McCormick Place, and the tourist magnet of Chinatown, lies a mix of rehabbed mansions, glassy lakefront high rises, decaying residential areas, and thriving institutions.

When the City of Chicago was incorporated in 1837, its southern boundary was at Cermak Rd. (22nd St.), but the area south of the original riverfront settlement was still a wilderness. Small encampments were scattered along the two Indian trails now traced in part by Vincennes and Cottage Grove avenues, and Henry B. Clarke's house stood at what is now 16th St. and Michigan Ave. But the area remained undeveloped countryside for over a decade.

The arrival of the railroads in the 1850s brought the first major change to the area, with industry and working-class houses clustering near the train tracks. In 1853 the city limits were extended a mile south to 31st St.; a decade later they moved another eight blocks farther south, where they remained until the 1889 annexation of Hyde Park township. Politician and real estate speculator Stephen A. Douglas created the area's first planned residential development. He bought sixty acres of lakefront property between 33rd and 35th streets in 1852 and recorded his Oakenwald subdivision, three years later, with lots fronting on two private parks. Two short-lived institutions helped attract attention to the area: the first University of Chicago, whose Baptist founders accepted Douglas's donation of ten acres and had a small campus here from 1859 until going bankrupt in 1886; and Camp Douglas, which opened as an army training camp in 1861 and housed prisoners of the Civil War.

Because the north and west sides were separated from the central city by the Chicago River, the south side was the most accessible and quickly became the neighborhood of choice for wealthy homeowners. After the Fire of 1871 burned virtually everything to the north and west, businesses rebuilt in or near their original locations, but displaced residents moved south. Prairie Ave. between 16th and 22nd streets was soon lined with mansions, and Michigan Ave., designated a boulevard in 1880, also became a very fashionable address; meanwhile, the area west of State St. filled up with working-class housing. The abundance of transportation brought many new residents, with the Illinois Central Railroad along the lakefront, horsecars on Cottage Grove Ave. and State St., and in 1892 the city's first elevated line.

By the late 1890s the area had already peaked as a residential community and was beginning a long process of decay. The city's growth and the concentration of railroad terminals on the Loop's southern flank pushed industry and commerce (including the thriving vice business) farther south. The process accelerated after the turn of the century; by 1910 Michigan Ave. was known as Automobile Row, and the lakefront was crowded with railroad tracks, breweries, and industrial complexes.

As the city's social elite created a new Gold Coast on the North Side, upwardly mobile German Jews, Irish, and Norwegians moved farther south and west. They were replaced by Chinese and African-Americans moving from the south edge of the Loop. There had been a black community centered at 22nd and State streets since the 1870s, and the building frenzy that preceded the 1893 World's Columbian Exposition resulted in increased housing opportunities for middle- and upper-class blacks. The neighborhoods remained integrated until the great influx of African-Americans during the two world wars. Restricted from settling in other areas, the newcomers were forced into increasingly crowded and dilapidated housing, accelerating the transformation of once-fashionable houses into slum dwellings.

In the 1940s two of the area's major institutions, Michael Reese Hospital and the Illinois Institute of Technology, joined forces to plan a program of urban renewal, eventually redeveloping seven square miles. Dilapidated housing was razed, and shiny new Modernist buildings rose like beacons from the rubble. The Chicago School of Architecture Foundation (now the Chicago Architecture Foundation) was founded in 1966 to save Richardson's John J. Glessner House, sparking a movement that led to the creation of the Prairie Avenue Historic District in the 1970s. In the 1980s restoration of historic housing began around Calumet Ave. and 32nd St., including the only extant row houses designed by Frank Lloyd Wright. From the Prairie Avenue District, with the city's two most important house museums, to the bastion of Miesian modernism that is IIT, this area has a diversity of landmarks that suits its varied character.

—Joseph D. La Rue with Laurie McGovern Petersen

Schoenhofen Powerhouse-Warehouse

■ Peter Schoenhofen Brewing Co.

Administration Building
Northwest Corner W. 18th St. at S. Normal Ave.
1886, Adolph A. Cudell

■ Powerhouse-Warehouse
1770 S. Canalport Ave.
1902, Richard E. Schmidt
Renovated 1992, Norman Koglin & Assocs.

Beermaking was a thriving industry in Chicago, with over fifty breweries in operation by 1890; the proximity of rail lines and the river made this a logical spot for industry. These surviving buildings sum up the startling leap made by Chicago architects between the mid-1880s and 1900. The fussy Administration Building has Renaissance and Baroque detailing, with an elaborate cornice, terra-cotta keystones, and medallions sporting sheaves of grain. In contrast, the Powerhouse is a spare, strong statement in brick that fully exploits the expressive potential of masonry. On the west facade the dual functions of the building are clearly visible in the organization of the wall. The north half of this rectilinear trapezoid housed the boiler rooms; the Canalport Ave. side was the hops warehouse. Shooting through the roof is the tower, which hid the water tanks and surmounted the stairs and elevator. Although longer than it is tall, the Canalport Ave. facade appears proudly vertical with full-height brick panels on the ends and recessed windows divided by thin brick piers. The powerful Bedford limestone arch, with voussoirs up to seven feet long, is gracefully beribboned with the company name, sheltering what was surely the city's most graphically blessed loading dock.

3 Baltimore & Ohio Chicago Terminal Railroad Bridge
S. Branch Chicago River at 1500 south
1930, B&O Railroad and Strauss Bascule Bridge Co.

4 St. Charles Air Line Railroad Bridge
S. Branch Chicago River at 1500 south
1919, Illinois Central Railroad, A. S. Baldwin, chief eng.; relocated 1931

After 1900 the obstructive center-pier swing bridge was replaced by the trunnion bascule type, whose leaves swing up like one end of a seesaw. The "seam" in the middle of a double-leaf bridge is a potential pivot point as a heavy train begins to cross; movable railway bridges are usually single spans, which also require only one set of machinery.

On these single-leaf Strauss trunnion bascules, the trunnions are very high and balanced by concrete counterweights that slip in underneath. The St. Charles Air Line bridge was originally 260 feet, the longest of its type in the world, and weighed 3,500 tons. When built, the straightening of the south branch of the river was already anticipated. The bridge was designed to pivot to its new position but instead was dismantled, shortened (to 220 feet), and rebuilt in 1931. The B&O Bridge led to a large train yard on the east side of the river and to Grand Central Station at Wells and Harrison streets, demolished in 1971.

5 Pennsylvania Railroad—South Branch Chicago River Bridge
S. Branch Chicago River east of Canal St. at 2000 south
1915, Waddell & Harrington; fabricated by the Pennsylvania Steel Co.

Pennsylvania Railroad Bridge

With a pair of 195-foot towers, it's the kinetic cathedral of this railyard area, carrying south-bound freight and passenger traffic out of the city. Engineers J. A. L. Waddell and J. L. Harrington of Kansas City were the masters of the vertical lift bridge, designing two dozen between 1907 and 1914. Because of its dominating profile, this type was never popular downtown; remaining examples are in industrial areas. The entire center span lifts straight up and is balanced by heavy counterweights, visible here on the sides of the towers. A vertical-lift configuration was chosen for this site because it was more economical than a bascule for this long span. Because the tracks cross the river at an angle, the towers are trapezoidal to hug the shoreline and make the movable span no longer or heavier than necessary. The span is a 1,500-ton riveted steel Pratt through truss, which is 272 feet long and lifts to a height of 130 feet over the river. The original tenders' cabin on the upper chord of the lift span now houses only the electric drive motors that operate the span. Attendants in a control tower five blocks away at 14th and Lumber streets operate the span via television monitors.

6 Cermak Road Bridge
Cermak Rd. and the Chicago River
1906, Scherzer Rolling Lift Bridge Co.

Designed by William Scherzer, the rolling lift bridge was the first of the two bascule types to replace the cumbersome nineteenth-century center-pier swing bridges. The bridge was patented in 1893; the Chicago-based Scherzer Co. designed bridges constructed around the world. The Scherzer bridge works like a rocking chair, utilizing overhead counterweights to balance its truss double leaves, which roll into place on large steel girder rockers at their bases. The counterweights slide into the slots between roadway and sidewalk, as the teeth on the rounded tracks engage holes in the rockers. Despite its global success, the Scherzer type was soon surpassed locally by the trunnion bascule bridge. The Cermak Rd. Bridge is the last Scherzer-type owned and operated by the city.

7 Premium Plastics (William M. Hoyt Co.)
465 W. Cermak Rd.
1909, Nimmons & Fellows

Chicago's premier designers of industrial buildings created this sturdy but elegant concrete-frame office and warehouse for a wholesale grocer. The long facade on Cermak Rd. and the lovely chamfered corner (shades of the Schoenhofen Powerhouse) turn a civilized, corporate face to customers and guests. It's one of the firm's liveliest facades, with pronounced vertical piers that rise to Prairie Style "capitals." The warehouse functions are more visible on the river side and the south facade (which now faces an urban no-man's-land), where two railroad tracks enter the building. Wedged between the tracks and the river, the site was perfect for the easy shipment of goods.

8 Chinatown

Just a half mile to the east is densely built Chinatown. In 1912 a large group of Chinese were displaced from the South Loop by new construction. The On Leong tong (benevolent association) was responsible for the establishment of this Chinatown, arranging for their members fifty leases in the 22nd St. and Wentworth Ave. area, a neighborhood of modest stores and flats. Wentworth Ave. south of 22nd St. is lined with typical nineteenth-century buildings remodeled to look more Chinese. Many of the buildings constructed after 1912 are inspired by traditional Chinese architecture, in which the wall is not load-bearing. Instead, columns ascend toward the roof to support elaborately cantilevered brackets below wide eaves that extend far beyond the building's envelope. The wall is treated as a screen, and attention is focused on the brackets, which are often highly painted. The wall of the top floor is often recessed behind the columns to create a loggia.

9 Chinatown Square
Archer Ave., Cermak Rd., Chicago River, 18th St., and Wentworth Ave.
Begun 1992, Harry Weese Assocs.

Hemmed in for years by highways and railroad tracks, Chinatown was finally unleashed when the Santa Fe Railroad abandoned its yards north of Archer Ave. The first buildings to rise on the thirty-acre site are brick retail strips. Three-story town houses, mid-rise condominiums and apartments, and subsidized senior housing will follow.

On Leong Building

10 On Leong Chinese Merchants' Association Building
2216 S. Wentworth Ave.
1928, Michaelsen & Rognstad

After relocating from downtown, the On Leong tong carried on their activities—a hostel for immigrants, a Chinese-language school, business, job-placement, and dating services—in various nearby locations. For their new building they turned to Michaelsen & Rognstad, who had done restaurant remodelings for a prominent member. Although unfamiliar with Chinese architecture, they were willing students. Rognstad was responsible for the sculptural program, executed in terra-cotta, a very good substitute for the *liu li* glazed ceramic of traditional Chinese architecture. Polychrome terra-cotta flowers, vases, and moths cover the walls. Lions guard the doorway, their heads twisted so they face us but do not turn their backs on each other, which would be bad luck.

⓫ Won Kow Restaurant
2233 S. Wentworth Ave.
1928, Michaelsen & Rognstad

Look up at the top two stories, with recessed balconies supported by brick piers. Decorative roundels display herons and parrots; again, stylized lions guard the doorway. The building's central portion is flanked by square towers that symbolize the pagoda form but are flat-topped, with enameled urns at the corners.

⓬ Emperor's Choice Restaurant
2238 S. Wentworth Ave.
1928, Michaelsen & Rognstad

Two-story addition 1932, Michaelsen & Rognstad

Graceful terra-cotta herons fold sinuously around the door frame, while snakes encircle a pair of columns. More Chinese details appear at the top, which has a traditional Chinese profile.

⓭ Chicago Housing Authority—Raymond M. Hilliard Center
2030 S. State St.
1966, Bertrand Goldberg & Assocs.

The revolutionary design theories that Goldberg developed for Marina City were applied here to the problem of public housing, creating what is still regarded as one of the city's best examples of humane high-rise living for low-income families. In a parklike setting, a pair of twenty-two-story curving slabs accommodate families, and two sixteen-story cylindrical towers are devoted to seniors. The curved walls and windows express the character of poured concrete, while providing structural stability; curved windows also distribute stress in the building's "skin." The floor plan of the round towers, with wedge-shaped apartments ringing the elevator core, minimizes the corridor distances for the elderly occupants.

⓮ Metra (Metropolitan Rail) Substation (Commonwealth Edison E. 16th St. Substation)
1620 S. Prairie Ave.
1925, Hermann V. von Holst

CHA—Hilliard Center

Many substations are found near the Chicago Transit Authority's elevated tracks or Metra electrified rail lines. They were built by Commonwealth Edison between about 1900 and 1930 to supply power to the traction conglomerate of Samuel Insull, who also controlled Commonwealth Edison. They are usually of brick, with details that run the gamut of styles; many exhibit Prairie School massing and were designed by von Holst. This delightful polychromatic substation has whimsical limestone trim with reliefs of a 1920s electric locomotive and other traction devices.

15 John J. Glessner House
1800 S. Prairie Ave.
1885–1887, Henry Hobson Richardson

Glessner House is the finest urban residence of Henry Hobson Richardson. Richardson used a corner site to create a dwelling of extraordinary distinction, one eloquently expressing his desire for a modern American architecture. The house has two powerful facades. The primary, Prairie Ave. one calls upon American Colonial design; the subsidiary 18th St. one has an English prototype. Two striking arched doorways were derived from the Romanesque sources that Richardson favored. The seemingly symmetrical main facade includes a porte cochere leading to a walled courtyard. Norcross Bros. constructed the building with facade walls of pink-gray granite and courtyard elevations of rosy brick with limestone trim.

John Jacob Glessner, the vice president of a company that manufactured farm implements, and his wife, Frances Macbeth Glessner, commissioned the house in 1885 for use primarily as a winter residence. Richardson finished the design before his death in 1886, and his successors, Charles A. Coolidge and George F. Shepley, carefully carried it to completion in 1887. The functional plan is one of Richardson's best: principal living spaces face the southern courtyard and have large windows to capture the winter sun, while a service passage to the north mitigates Chicago's chilliest winds. The house served the Glessners perfectly for the next half century. Daniel H. Burnham, one of their earliest dinner guests, observed that it was in Chicago that the great Boston architect took new departures and did his most successful work.

The settings, furniture, and decorative objects assembled

Glessner House

Glessner House

within Glessner House are a cohesive grouping of items designed by architects or designers with architectural training. These include masterpieces of Modern Gothic case goods by Isaac E. Scott; a library double desk, dining room chairs, and a grand piano by Charles A. Coolidge and Francis Bacon, both designing for the A. H. Davenport firm; and wallpapers, upholstery and hanging fabrics, chairs, lamps, carpets, and ceramic tiles and vases from the British workshops of William Morris and William De Morgan, both known and admired by Richardson. Woodwork for paneling, doors, and mantels is primarily quarter-sawn oak. Wall colors were terra-cotta red, gold, and green, while gold leaf highlighted the dining room ceiling.

Understanding of the Glessners' uniquely close relationship with their architect, their home, and their lives is enhanced by extensive documentation, much of it utilized by restoration architects such as John Thorpe, Wilbert R. Hasbrouck, and John Vinci who have worked on the house.

Glessner House is now a house museum owned by the Chicago Architecture Foundation, formed in 1966 to preserve it.
—Elaine Harrington

16 William W. Kimball House
1801 S. Prairie Ave.
1890–1892, Solon S. Beman

As the Second Empire's influence faded in the 1880s, wealthy clients increasingly abandoned the eccentricities of the Queen Anne style in favor of more historically correct designs, such as those imitating the great French châteaus of the reign of Francis I (1515–1547). The "châteauesque" was an ideal choice for an era of pastiche. Its prototype was a polyglot style that had applied classical motifs newly introduced from Renaissance

Kimball House

Italy onto the irregularly massed forms of the medieval castle. Following the lead of New York

Clarke House

architect Richard Morris Hunt on the Vanderbilt châteaus, Beman here recalled picturesque, fragmented sixteenth-century French facades with pavilions and windows of varied shapes and sizes. His immediate inspiration was the design of the sixteenth-century dormers of the Château de Josselin in Brittany, the model for the massing for the three-story bay on the main facade.

17 Joseph G. Coleman House (Miner T. Ames House)
1811 S. Prairie Ave.
1885, Cobb & Frost

The entrance is a superb example of contrasting surfaces. Huge sandstone blocks form round-headed arches atop squat, clustered, smooth columns with Romanesque capitals, while in the second story a window-filled bay of smooth stone stands out against the rusticated walls.

18 The Fort Dearborn Massacre, or the Potawatomi Rescue
W. side of Prairie Ave., south of the Glessner House
1893, Carl Rohl-Smith

This statue has been giving children nightmares for years. Potawatomi chief Black Partridge interrupts a tomahawk chop intended for Margaret Helm, one of a group of settlers ambushed after fleeing Fort Dearborn on August 15, 1812. Legend has it that the attack occurred near what is now the corner of Prairie Ave. and 18th St.

19 Henry B. Clarke House
1855 S. Indiana Ave.
1836, architect unknown
Restored 1981, Joseph W. Casserly, Chicago city arch.; Wilbert R. Hasbrouck, restoration arch.

Chicago's only visibly Greek Revival building is very possibly the city's oldest structure (a contender for the title has emerged in Norwood Park). Originally built at 1700 S. Michigan Ave., it was moved twice, returning in 1977 to this, its original neighborhood. Its colonnaded grandeur still projects an aura of the civilizing influence that pioneers attempted to bring to frontier Chicago. The ancient forms of pedimented porticoes, Doric columns, and pilasters (although Roman, not Greek), and the "entablature" were considered most appropriate for a growing democracy. Greek Revival buildings were invariably white, regular, and symmetrical, with a central-hall plan. The Greek Revival style reigned from 1820 to 1860, and rebellion against its ordered predictability stimulated the development of the picturesque and irregular Gothic Revival and Italianate styles.

20 Elbridge G. Keith House
1900 S. Prairie Ave.
early 1870s, architect unknown
Mansard additions ca. 1880, architect unknown

This is the quintessential "marble front" of the 1870s, a brick house whose main facade is faced with Joliet limestone, then known as "Athens marble." This type almost universally has a single projecting bay running the full three-story height. The stable at the rear of the property may hint at the house's original roofline.

21 Marshall Field, Jr., House
(William H. Murray House)
1919 S. Prairie Ave.
1884, Solon S. Beman

This example of Beman's Queen Anne work is so heavily altered that, in novelist Arthur Meeker's words, "it's impossible to say any longer what it thought it was originally trying to be."

Second Presbyterian Church

22 Second Presbyterian Church
1936 S. Michigan Ave.
1874, James Renwick
Rebuilt 1900, Howard Van Doren Shaw

Renwick, architect of the Smithsonian Institution and St. Patrick's Cathedral in New York City, had in 1849 designed for this congregation the city's first Gothic Revival church, destroyed in the Fire of 1871. This replacement was built of a local limestone with bituminous mottling accented with strong horizontal bands of black rock from the same quarry. The strongest elements of Renwick's Gothic vocabulary, a steeply pitched roof and rose window, were altered after a fire in 1900. The interior is imbued with the Arts & Crafts and Pre-Raphaelite influences introduced in Shaw's rebuilding and by muralist Frederick Clay Bartlett. A tree of life mural on the rear wall, a screen with four heralding angels, the strapwork ceiling, and a palette of muted red, blue, green, and gold against buff and dark oak are a backdrop for an unrivaled collection of nineteenth-century stained glass, with examples from every phase of Louis C. Tiffany's career. There are also works by the British Pre-Raphaelite painter Edward Burne-Jones and the nineteenth-century American muralist John La Farge.

23 213, 215 & 217 E. Cullerton St.
Late 1860s, architects unknown

Insurance atlases show the smallest and earliest of this curious trio, the Italianate home at 215, in the center of three identical buildings. They probably date from after the 1865 closing of nearby stockyards, which increased the area's appeal. The two flanking houses are either replacements or enveloping additions built between 1886 and 1892.

24 William H. Reid III House
2013 S. Prairie Ave.
1894, Beers, Clay & Dutton

This lonely slice of a vanished block has a central, first-floor skylit room in an open plan made possible by the building's steel frame.

25 Harriet F. Rees House
2110 S. Prairie Ave.
1888, Cobb & Frost

The twenty-five-foot Richardsonian facade formula is polished and emboldened by the team that introduced it to Chicago. The smooth facade features an elegantly controlled use of ornamentation.

26 Calvin T. Wheeler House
(Joseph A. Kohn House)
2018 S. Calumet Ave.
Mid-1860s, architect unknown

Style sleuths will delight in Second Empire details and the mansard roof. The incised hood moldings around the windows are typical of the Italianate style; the matching incised pilasters are unusual.

27 **320 E. 21st St.**
(Columbian Colortype Co.)
1920, Alfred S. Alschuler

A pivotal building in the career of a prolific factory designer features innovations that became standard. Entrance, docks, stairwells, and all services were pushed to the west wall to minimize interference with clear floor spaces and natural lighting. Economical flat-slab concrete construction reduced vibration. The concrete columns were exposed on the main elevations so that—when used in combination with terra-cotta detailing at the base, entry, and cornice—the effect of a totally brick and terra-cotta facade was achieved without its expense.

28 **Lakeside Press Plant 3**
(American Book Company)
330 E. Cermak Rd.
1912, N. Max Dunning

This company shared with the other South Side presses the notion that books deserved to be made and stored more artistically than other goods. This red brick and terra-cotta warehouse features excellent surface-shadow effects accomplished by slight vertical and strong horizontal projections. Rooftop tanks and sprinkler equipment assume the usual tower disguise.

29 **R. R. Donnelley & Sons Co. Calumet Plant**
350 E. Cermak Rd.
1912–1924, Howard Van Doren Shaw

West-Central and South Sections (including tower) 1929, Charles Z. Klauder

The Donnelleys had commissioned Shaw to design their Lakeside Press Building on S. Plymouth Ct., and they returned to him for a master plan and design for a new printing facility, to be built in stages over two decades. Shaw took the opportunity to create one of the city's—perhaps the nation's—finest essays in Industrial Gothic. Buttresslike piers separate large vertical bands of windows capped by limestone arches. Stone medallions and terra-cotta plaques depict stylized marks and devices of early printers like Johannes Gutenberg, William Caxton, and John Baskerville. At the main entry are six seals, three with the initials of the architect and owners, and carved relief panels of a Prairie Indian and a frontiersman. The taller tower, designed after Shaw's death by collegiate Gothicist Klauder, contains a two-story Gothic library.

30 **McCormick Place on the Lake, East Building**
2301 S. Lake Shore Dr.
1971, C. F. Murphy Assocs.

This structural tour de force, which brutally interrupts the sweep of the lakefront, is one of Chicago's biggest planning gaffes. As early as 1954 the South Side Planning Board had proposed an exposition hall, to be designed by Mies van der Rohe, for a site on the south side of Cermak Rd.

Donnelley Calumet Plant

between King Dr. and Michigan Ave. The Metropolitan Fair and Exposition Authority, established in 1955 by the state, instead accepted the city's offer of a Burnham Park site east of the 23rd St. viaduct. Howls of protest, ignored by City Hall, greeted this proposal, which violated the dreams of city visionaries from A. Montgomery Ward to Daniel H. Burnham to keep the lakefront "forever open, clear and free." When the first McCormick Place (1960) burned in 1967, civic groups mounted a campaign to relocate it, but the economic pressures of getting the lucrative convention hall back in operation as quickly as possible dictated remaining on this site, where the foundations could be reused.

Designer Gene R. Summers, who had worked for Mies from 1950 to 1966, brought to life an airy, powerful hall. The statistics are staggering. The 1,360-foot roof, which cantilevers so gracefully seventy-five feet beyond supporting columns, covers nineteen acres and weighs 10,000 tons. Yet the 300,000-square-foot main exhibit space contains only eight columns. The cross-shaped columns of reinforced concrete poured into steel shells form a superstructure of 150 × 150-foot bays of unencumbered space and carry the roof fifty feet above the floor level. It's an impressive engineering feat and a keystone of the city's convention business—but neither built to nor intended for human scale.

31 McCormick Place on the Lake, North Building
450 E. 23rd St.
1986, Skidmore, Owings & Merrill

The diamond patterning symbolizes the hidden truss system and is a faint echo of Mies's convention hall project of the 1950s. As in the East Building, the roof is the dramatic focal point, using a fifteen-foot-deep truss system, supported by seventy-two four-inch, 450-strand cables hung from twelve concrete pylons. The system is designed to withstand abrupt changes in temperature, high winds, or broken cables. The pylons contain conduits for air-conditioning and heating, making ceiling vents unnecessary. The fixed vertical pipes on the long sides are designed to help stabilize the roof when it moves (normally up or down an inch or so) in certain kinds of weather.

32 Covered Pedestrian Mall, McCormick Place on the Lake
E. 23rd St. over S. Lake Shore Dr.
1986, Skidmore, Owings & Merrill

As close to whimsical as SOM can get, this amenity protects conventioneers from the lake's icy blasts while delighting motorists with its cupolas.

33 Lexington Hotel
2135 S. Michigan Ave.
1892, Clinton J. Warren

This Columbian Exposition–era hotel has clung tenaciously to life, surviving decay, dashed dreams for redevelopment, and Geraldo Rivera's fruitless televised search for onetime tenant Al Capone's lost treasures. Warren was the premier hotel designer of the Chicago School; of his other major works, only the Congress Hotel remains. The brick and terra-cotta curtain wall is hung from a steel frame and is

McCormick Place, North Building

organized into disciplined stacks of round and angular bays. Guest rooms (originally 370) are arranged around a light court.

34 Automobile Row
S. Michigan Ave., originally Roosevelt Rd. to 29th St.

In the 1880s the fashionable residential area of S. Michigan Ave. acquired a "magnificent stretch" of asphalt pavement "as level as a billiard table." After 1900 car dealers were eyeing the wide, deep (180 feet) lots for showrooms and by 1910 had created what *Architectural Record* called "the longest and best automobile course in any city of this country," with at least forty new buildings selling or servicing cars.

The earliest showroom buildings were only slightly more elaborate than factories, typically three stories high, on corner lots, and almost invariably three bays wide. Spans of up to thirty feet permitted windows low and wide enough to show an entire car. Construction methods varied from semi-mill to steel and reinforced-concrete framing. Interior finishes were kept close to utilitarian even in the salesrooms, which had easily maintained red terrazzo floors and inexpensive wood wainscotings. Exteriors were initially brick with terra-cotta trim and logos.

In the 1920s designers began addressing the problem of how to effectively display indoors an item meant to be seen outdoors. Interiors, often with offices tucked away on mezzanines, were made to look like exteriors, with walls of stucco or stone. Mediterranean and California Spanish styling were deemed highly suitable.

Since the 1960s most Automobile Row buildings have been converted to other uses, many of which are associated with activities at McCormick Place. Most buildings between 22nd St. and the Adlai E. Stevenson Expressway are vacant and ripe for redevelopment. Ground-floor remuddlings have dimmed most of the facades; look up to see the broad windows and fanciful terra-cotta logos.

35 2000 S. Michigan Ave.
(Locomobile Showroom)
1909, Jenney, Mundie & Jensen

Here is a quintessential early auto facility: a three-story corner building of reinforced concrete, trimmed in brick and terra-cotta.

36 Chess Records (McNaull Tire Co.)
2120 S. Michigan Ave.
1911, Horatio R. Wilson
Remodeled 1957, John S. Townsend, Jr.

This is Chicago's only building to inspire a Rolling Stones song, which was named for the building and recorded here in 1964 as a tribute to Chess Records. The company's headquarters from 1957 to 1967 were in this building, which—like its neighbors—began life "in the motor trade."

2222–2228 S. Michigan Ave.

37 2222–2228 S. Michigan Ave. (Hudson Motor Co. of Illinois)
1922, Alfred S. Alschuler

H (for Hudson) medallions sit above the Palladian window in the central bay. Exuberant terra-cotta imitates stone in twisted columns and rope moldings.

38 2255 S. Michigan Ave. (Thomas Flyer Garage & Service Building)
1910, Holabird & Roche
Addition 1916, Alfred S. Alschuler

Although two stories have been added, the base still reveals its origins as a classic auto-sales facility; varieties of brickwork and multicolored terra-cotta panels articulate the structural system.

39 2309–2313 S. Michigan Ave. (Automobile Buildings for Alfred Cowles)
1915, Holabird & Roche

Two small automotive buildings reveal lively uses of terra-cotta, in the jagged blind arcade of the northern building and in the three-dimensional geometric patterning entirely covering the southern one.

40 Quinn Chapel (African Methodist Episcopal)
2401 S. Wabash Ave.
1891–1894, architect unknown

Named for William P. Quinn, bishop of the Midwest diocese of the African Methodist Episcopal Church in the 1840s, the Chapel houses the city's oldest black congregation. Brick walls are faced with gray stone; the Victorian Gothic facade is distinguished by the north tower, with its belfry and tourelle. The church proper is a second-floor amphitheater, with seating arranged in a fan pattern and a balcony wrapping around three sides. The William H. Delle pipe organ was purchased from the German Pavilion at the Columbian Exposition.

41 *Chicago Daily Defender* Building (Illinois Automobile Club)
2400 S. Michigan Ave.
1936, Philip B. Maher

Built on the site of Adler & Sullivan's Standard Club (1887) and using the abandoned foundations of a predecessor organization's planned clubhouse, this two-story brick building with its lantern-topped clock tower employs a simplified Spanish Mission styling. Many of the social aspects of automobile clubs vanished after World War II, when cars became more readily available to the average person. This building has housed one of the nation's leading African-American newspapers since the 1950s.

42 City of Chicago Bureau of Comprehensive Environmental and Public Health (South Division High School)
27 E. 26th St.
1882, James R. Willett

Chicago's oldest surviving public high school building is battered with remodelings and poor maintenance.

43 East Lake Management Development Co. (Vista Accumulator Co.)
2850 S. Michigan Ave.
1919, Puckey & Jenkins

This was initially a deep, one-story sales and service building that housed a shock absorber business. A shallow second floor is now hidden behind a blind facade. The elaborate terra-cotta, which includes tympana of paired griffins, demonstrates the exu-

Chicago Daily Defender

Urban Renewal Area east of S. King Dr., from Stevenson Expy. to 35th St.

berance that enlivened auto-
related architecture in the 1910s.

44 Sidney A. Kent House
2944 S. Michigan Ave.
1883, Burnham & Root
Converted to apartments 1982,
Swann & Weiskopf

"Subdued richness" aptly describes this mansion. The ornamentation and styling, including
the enhanced central pavilion
carried above the cornice line,
were consciously drawn from
the châteaus of Francis I. But the
essentially cubic massing, the
unusual expanses of plate glass,
the wide undecorated Philadelphia pressed-brick wall surfaces,
and the uniform color all provide
repose. Built when its neighbors
were similar in size (60 × 100
feet), this house is now a rare
example of the residential work
of a major Chicago firm, surviving as five luxury apartments.
The wrought-iron fence is truly
French, having been purchased
by Kent from a Columbian Exposition display.

45 Near South Side Urban Renewal

The character of the area between 26th and 35th streets is
the result of decisions made in
the 1940s, when the area's anchor institutions considered

moving but instead stayed and
exercised their influence on
the neighborhood. The newly
created Illinois Institute of Technology (formed in 1940 by a
merger of two schools) was
building a new campus, and Michael Reese Hospital needed
room to expand. In 1945 the
hospital created a planning staff
with a mandate to devise a campus plan and also to improve the
character of its urban surround-
ings. The director was Reginald
R. Isaacs, and Walter Gropius
was architectural consultant. In
what was perhaps the most
comprehensive and ambitious
essay in urban planning since
Daniel H. Burnham's 1909
scheme for the entire city, the
final report envisioned the complete redevelopment of seven
square miles, from the lake west
to the Pennsylvania Railroad
tracks, and from 12th St. south
to 47th St. Taking a cue from Le
Corbusier's model cities of the
1920s and 1930s, the planners
advocated the abandonment of
the urban grid in favor of towers
set in open expanses of greenery. It was also during this decade that local, state, and federal
governments resolved to address
the lack of affordable urban
housing. The housing shortage of
the 1930s and 1940s, combined
with a large influx of blacks from

the South whose areas of settlement were restricted by prejudice and covenant, had resulted in intolerable slum conditions on the South Side. In 1947, when Reese completed its two-year study, the city had just established a land-clearance program that made possible many of the study's recommendations. Lake Meadows became the city's first racially integrated, middle-income housing, and Prairie Shores continued the success story. However, the "towers in a park" concept proved disastrous when governmental housing authorities applied it to low-income units. West of the lakefront, the State St. slum was demolished only to make way for a more vicious reincarnation, the high-rise projects of Stateway Gardens (State St. from 35th St. to Pershing Rd.) and the Robert Taylor Homes (State St. from Pershing Rd. to 54th St.).

46 South Commons
26th to 31st Sts., Michigan to Prairie Aves.
1966–1970, Ezra Gordon–Jack M. Levin & Assocs.; L. R. Solomon, J. D. Cordwell & Assocs.

Planned as a small village with ambitious goals of racial and economic balance, this was one of the final building blocks in the grand plan of postwar urban renewal on the Near South Side. The town houses turn their backs on cars and streets, clustering around quiet, neighborly open courts, playgrounds, and stores.

47 Chicago Housing Authority—Prairie Courts
26th St. and S. Prairie Ave. and King Dr.
1951–1956, George Fred Keck and William Keck

The combination of design talent, a good tenant mix of families and seniors, and city and state funding that freed the architects from bureaucratic federal guidelines created one of the CHA's more successful projects. The design features well-proportioned concrete frames with yellow brick infill. Elevator

buildings of exposed concrete framing are balanced with two-story apartment blocks and row houses. The elevator buildings' "sidewalks in the sky"—the outdoor hallways so popular on CHA buildings in the 1950s—were intended to improve ventilation and provide a "porch" for every apartment.

48 George Ellery Wood House
2801 S. Prairie Ave.
1885, John C. Cochrane

The sole reminder of elegant "Lower Prairie Avenue," this Queen Anne house survives because its 1950s owners fought orders for the wholesale demolition of what was regarded as one of the city's worst slums.

49 Prairie Shores
2801–3001 S. Martin Luther King, Jr., Dr.
1958–1962, Loebl, Schlossman & Bennett

This was Michael Reese Hospital's own contribution to the plan they advocated. Comprising five apartment towers, with a total of 1,677 units, the complex was intended primarily for hospital employees who wanted to live nearby. The narrow buildings are oriented north–south to maximize daylight, and each is massed as a pair of overlapping slabs. The curtain walls have ribbon windows and louvered spandrels of a different color on each building.

50 Humana–Michael Reese Hospital and Medical Center
S. Lake Shore Dr. and E. 31st St.
Begun 1907, various architects

Established at this site in 1881, the nonsectarian institution replaced the city's old Jewish hospital, destroyed in the fire a decade earlier. The campus, which has thirty buildings surrounding four parks, owes its look to the modernist design influence of Walter Gropius. There are no individual masterpieces, but they form a pleasing group; **2929 S. Ellis Ave.** (1907, Richard E. Schmidt, Garden & Martin) is the oldest, and its fate is uncer-

Prairie Shores

tain. Schmidt gave the building a Prairie Style look, with strong verticals balanced by continuous moldings at the sill and lintel lines. The unusual massing repeats that of the prior Michael Reese building at this corner site: two wings at right angles are joined by a pavilion that cuts across the corner. The hospital has converted the mechanical top floor to two floors for offices and research, and has removed the projecting cornice. The **Psychosomatic and Psychiatric Institute** (1951, Loebl, Schlossman & Bennett) has distinctive continuous slatted canopies over each window—clean, handsome detailing with good energy sense, reducing heat gain through the wide windows.

51 Lake Meadows
S. Martin Luther King, Jr., Dr. between 31st and 35th Sts.
1950–1960, Skidmore, Owings & Merrill

The overwhelming impression is of green, open space; the buildings cover only 9 percent of the land. The first housing constructed under the aegis of the Michael Reese plan, it was built on land assembled by the Chicago Land Clearance Commission and sold to New York Life Insurance Co. for about one-sixth of what the city paid for it. In 1946 *Architectural Forum* claimed that it would be "one of the first private housing projects to allow mixed Negro and white occupancy," an important advance in an area where as late as the 1930s properties carried covenants excluding sales to

nonwhites. The 70-acre, 2,033-unit complex includes ten apartment buildings, an office building, a small shopping center, and a community club.

52 Lake Meadows, 600 Building
600 E. 32nd St.
1960, Skidmore, Owings & Merrill

The last and most luxurious building of the complex is the only one with floor-to-ceiling windows. Miesian influence is evident in the columns set behind the glass-and-steel curtain wall, the recessed brick or tile infill panels between the piers, and the inset wall on the ends.

Lake Meadows Tennis Club

53 Lake Meadows Tennis Club
3211 S. Ellis Ave.
1960, Skidmore, Owings & Merrill

The second floor is the primary social space. The delightfully graceful pyramidal roof admits light through louvered corners and hangs far beyond the completely glazed exterior wall.

54 Groveland Park
S. Cottage Grove Ave. at
E. 33d Pl.

In 1847 Senator Stephen A. Douglas moved to Chicago and began acquiring property, including a sixty-acre tract spreading from Lake Michigan west to King Dr. between 33rd and 35th streets. His shrewd investment was made all the more valuable in the early 1850s, when the Illinois Central Railroad—whose right-of-way Douglas had encouraged politically—built its tracks along the lake shore. Douglas recorded the subdivision, Oakenwald, in 1855, setting aside the portion east of Cottage Grove Ave. for his own home and for two residential parks, Groveland and Woodland, with fifty-foot lots facing central open spaces. The depression of 1857 reduced the value of his holdings, which he mortgaged in order to finance his political campaigns. He was unable to redeem them before his death in 1861.

The property was developed only after years of lawsuits had been settled in favor of Douglas's sons in 1873, when a Groveland Park homeowner's association could finally be formed to oversee the maintenance of the common parklands. The first houses, clustered along the northern side of the park, have all been destroyed. Many of the others are altered, but all enjoy frontage on this small, quiet park. The drives are a graveyard of demolished homes, lined with slabs and blocks of limestone, sandstone, and terra-cotta.

Groveland Park Gardener's Lodge

55 Groveland Park Gardener's Lodge
601 E. Groveland Park Ave.
Early 1870s, architect unknown

This Gothic Revival dollhouse was originally trimmed with fancy bargeboards.

56 Charles W. and Edwin Pardridge Houses
607, 609 & 611 E. Groveland Park Ave.
late 1870s, architect unknown

Three houses remain of the five built on lots subdivided in 1878. The "Athens marble" fronts, heavy pressed-metal cornices, and incised neo-Grec carving proved attractive to professors at the first University of Chicago, which was located on the west side of Cottage Grove Ave. from 1859 to 1886.

57 Hamilton Borden and William E. Selleck Houses
613 & 615 E. Groveland Park Ave.
1882, architect unknown

Built by partners in a scales business, these rusticated sandstone houses have brownstone panels with robust leaf-and-tendril designs.

58 Frank N. Gage House
637 E. Groveland Park Ave.
1879, architect unknown

Gothic details, such as the trefoil carved over the entrance and the pointed relieving arches in the windows, enliven an otherwise Italianate facade.

59 Edward S. Hunter and John B. Mallers Houses
639 & 641 E. Groveland Park Ave.
1886, Flanders & Zimmerman

Mallers developed this double house with its brown sandstone facade; one half still has the original slate roof.

60 John M. Gartside House
663 E. Groveland Park Ave.
1885, Willett L. Carroll

This brick two-story and attic residence has a Euclid stone front.

61 Stephen A. Douglas Tomb & Memorial
636 E. 35th St.
1863–1881, Leonard W. Volk

St. Joseph Carondelet (Soldiers' Home)

This is a monument as much to its era as to its subject, the Little Giant, Stephen A. Douglas. A larger-than-life bronze figure perches ninety-six feet in the air surveying Lake Michigan—or preparing to dive in, according to more than one critic. To offset the height, sculptor Volk placed four allegorical figures on freestanding plinths around the vault that contains Douglas's sarcophagus. The grounds were intended for Douglas's own elegant home. Lack of funds delayed the statue's completion.

62 St. Joseph Carondelet Child Care Center

(Soldiers' Home)
739 E. 35th St.
North half of East Building 1864, attributed to William W. Boyington
Main Building (35th St.) 1866, William W. Boyington

South half of East Building 1873, architect unknown
Northwest Building 1878, architect unknown
Southwest Building 1923, architect unknown
South Building 1957, architect unknown

A rare example of a surviving Civil War–era building in Chicago, this home was intended to serve soldiers who were sick, wounded, or merely in transit. Its intended function as a permanent home for disabled soldiers was made obsolete when Congress established national veterans' care in 1869, and it has been operated since 1872 as a Catholic child-care facility. The simple Italianate style of Boyington's first buildings set the tone for all subsequent construction. The Northwest Building, which contains the entrance, has a second-floor chapel.

63 Illinois Institute of Technology (IIT)

S. Michigan Ave. to the Illinois Central Railroad tracks, 31st to 35th Sts.

IIT presents a remarkable example of a university campus that continues to be shaped by a single architectural sensibility. It may be one of the nation's last bastions of modernism in both its design and teaching philoso-

phy. Mies van der Rohe's original plan (as well as the buildings) has continued to serve the campus well, especially in his choice of steel, brick, and glass materials; additions vanish seamlessly into the fabric of the original buildings. The design of the campus was his first American commission, and his buildings here develop ideas that he and his many students would apply throughout the world.

In the late 1930s, as the Nazis tightened their grip on Germany's cultural life, many of the most talented artists fled to the United States. One of the most prominent of the Bauhaus architects, Ludwig Mies van der Rohe, was persuaded by Chicago architect John A. Holabird (son of William Holabird) to accept the directorship of the architecture school of the Armour Institute of Technology. Mies immigrated in 1938 and began his American career as a teacher and architect, a potent combination that exerted lasting influence. In 1940 Armour merged with Lewis Institute, a West Side technical school, to form the Illinois Institute of Technology.

Mies's campus plan for the new institution consisted of twenty buildings arranged symmetrically around 33rd St. between State St. and the railroad tracks (now the Dan Ryan Expressway) to the west. Mies chose a module of 24 feet × 24

feet bays, 12 feet high, to determine both the bay size of individual buildings and the distances between them. The uniformity of the twenty-four-foot length, a standard dimension for American classrooms at the time, allowed economies of construction and ensured a certain uniformity in campus design over time. The buildings are sited to form open spaces that are implied rather than defined. The buildings provided Mies with the opportunity to explore and elaborate on a new architectural vocabulary of skeletal steel construction. Welded steel frames, painted black, have infill panels of glass or tan brick. Guiding principles for all buildings are clarity of structure, appropriate use of materials, and sensitivity to proportions. Of his greatest achievement, Crown Hall, he said, "I think this is the clearest structure we have done, the best to express our philosophy."

After Mies retired as professor in 1958, he was replaced as campus architect by Skidmore, Owings & Merrill, one of the firms that had adopted his tenets most completely. Mies's twenty-two buildings were joined by others in the same vein, although many lacked the subtlety and refinement that had characterized his work.

A Main Building (Armour Institute of Technology)
3300 S. Federal St.
1891–1893, Patton & Fisher

IIT's roots as a no-frills working-man's school began here, when Philip D. Armour commissioned this manual training school. Designed as a companion piece to Bumham & Root's Armour Mission, a now-demolished settlement house across the street, it is rock-solid and Romanesque. The rhythmic wall composition with its round-arched windows owes, along with many of this firm's masonry buildings, a great debt to Louis H. Sullivan. The fourth story, served by its own elevator, housed the "girls' department," with cooking and dressmaking workshops. Walk inside to see the Philip Danforth Armour memorial window by Edwin P. Sperry on the stair landing.

B Machinery Hall
100 W. 33rd St.
1901, Patton, Fisher & Miller

This simplified version of the Main Building segregated noise-generating activities behind its Romanesque walls.

C IITRI Materials Technology Building
3350 S. Federal St.
1943, 1958, Ludwig Mies van der Rohe; Holabird & Root, assoc. archs.

This was the first campus building designed by Mies, and it established the basic concepts of subsequent classroom buildings. Stripped down and startlingly severe, the glassy east side is now the only original piece easily seen.

D Boiler Plant & Steam Generating Plant
3430 S. Federal St.
1945–1950, Ludwig Mies van der Rohe; Alschuler & Sincere, assoc. archs.; Frank J. Kornacker, struct. eng.; Sargent & Lundy, mech. eng. North addition 1964, Sargent & Lundy

The six north bays follow Mies's original specifications. Steam is generated in the 1990 Co-Generational Building, a smaller version of the original.

E IIT Research Institute Tower
10 W. 35th St.
1963–1964, Schmidt, Garden & Erikson

The tallest building on campus is the least sympathetic to earlier buildings.

Main Building

F S. R. Crown Hall

(College of Architecture, Illinois Institute of Technology)
3360 S. State St.
1956, Ludwig Mies van der Rohe; Pace Assocs. and C. F. Murphy Assocs., assoc. archs.

During his American career, Mies came to believe that structure and space were the essential elements of architecture; as a result, his American reputation has centered on the expression of those concepts. In Crown Hall he exposed the structure and enclosed the space with a powerful balance of steel, glass, and light.

Mies's building for the College of Architecture was in design as early as 1950 and was completed in 1956. It is dominated by the steel frame and glass pavilion of its upper level. Effectively a one-room school, the space is 120 by 220 feet and 18 feet high.

Crown Hall's greatness derives from both its clarity and its comprehensive solution of all the problems it set out to solve. The building reads as a largely transparent glass box floating between its translucent podium and its roof, which is suspended from the four plate girders that punctuate its silhouette. The podium is actually a concrete frame on a twenty-by-thirty-foot module, set with eight feet below grade and with four feet above grade glazed with translucent glass.

During the day Crown Hall seems a precisely defined, translucent, and transparent volume in perfect repose. At night it becomes a reliquary of light, as its interior illumination appears to make the building seem almost to float on a cushion of light. The travertine main entrance stairs, centered on a long side of the building, also seem to float, serving to invite the visitor inside, through entrances marked by floor-to-ceiling glass. Upon entering, one faces a central space defined by eight-foot-high oak partitions; the cross axis that divides this core into two parts helps orient the visitor to the richly developed spaces of a building that seems initially to be without a plan. One could easily locate the physical center of the building only to discover that much of the greatness of the space comes from its devel-

Crown Hall

opment whereby no single place is seen to have priority.

Crown Hall departs from the module that Mies established for the campus in his master plan. As a result, it—rather than a more traditional campus structure, such as a library, administration building, or student union—becomes what Mies called representa-tional. Such a building, Mies had maintained, must declare the highest purposes and ideals of the institution. At the dedication of Crown Hall he said, "Let this building be the home of ideas and ad-venture" that would be "in the end a real contribution to our civilization."
—Kevin Harrington

G Wishnick Hall (Chemistry Building)
3255 S. Dearborn St.
1946, Ludwig Mies van der Rohe; Alfred S. Alschuler and R. N. Friedman, assoc. archs.

Using the same materials and structure as Alumni Memorial Hall, but with smaller windows (four per bay), this building became the standard for subsequent classroom buildings.

H Grover M. Hermann Hall
3241 S. Federal St.
1962, Skidmore, Owings & Merrill

This is the student union building; together with the Library to the south it follows Mies's plan for two large buildings on this site. But both are done with a heavier hand; beams lie across the roof like logs, instead of being gracefully integrated with the wall as at Crown Hall. The original precast concrete porch, similar to that of Crown Hall, has been replaced with granite. Unlike that building, the structure here is hidden behind the glassy skin. To the north is Morton Park, landscaped by faculty member Alfred Caldwell.

I Alumni Memorial Hall (Navy Building)
3201 S. Dearborn St.
1946, Ludwig Mies van der Rohe; Holabird & Root, assoc. archs.
Addition 1972, Mittelbusher & Tourtelot

The first building completed after the war, this is also the first in which the glass panes fill the width of an entire twenty-four-foot bay. It was an archetype, with a primary structural frame of steel beams and a secondary structure of I-beams attached to the exterior to support brick infill and window frames. The hidden structural system is expressed in the reentrant corners, showing the secondary I-beam welded to the primary column.

J Arthur S. Keating Sports Center
3040 S. Wabash Ave.
1966, Skidmore, Owings & Merrill

Here is another SOM building that hides the structure behind the walls, although nighttime illumination reveals the steel columns. The first floor is raised, and windows below it provide clerestory lights for the lower level.

Keating Sports Center

K Carman Hall Apartments
60 E. 32nd St.
1951–1953, Ludwig Mies van der Rohe; Pace Assocs., assoc. archs.

Although primarily a commuter campus, IIT built these apartments for faculty and married students. Rare for this campus, the concrete-frame buildings show Mies's signature receding columns, which carry less weight as they rise.

L St. Saviour's Chapel
65 E. 32nd St.
1952, Ludwig Mies van der Rohe

Known on campus as the "God box," this is the only church that Mies ever designed. A non-denominational, meditational chapel, it is all glass on the east facade and enclosed by brick walls on the others.

M Commons Building
3200 S. Wabash Ave.
1953, Ludwig Mies van der Rohe; Friedman, Alschuler & Sincere, assoc. archs.

This is probably the world's only Mies building with a 7-Eleven store, whose prominent signage certainly compromises the architectural purity. The single-story height eliminated the need for fireproofing the steel columns. The immediate predecessor to Crown Hall, the building has large areas of glass above brick panels.

64 Single-Family Houses
3326, 3328 & 3337 S. Indiana Ave.
Two-Flats
3312, 3320, 3335, 3347, 3349, 3357, 3359, 3403 & 3405 S. Indiana Ave.
1989, Phillip Kupritz & Assocs. with Johnson & Lee, Roula Assocs. and Ray/Dawson Architects

Twelve of the houses built for those displaced by the new Comiskey Park are clustered near 34th St. and Indiana Ave. Owners were offered a choice of two building types and four designs. Common to all are red brick facades with white wood trim and concrete block sides. Because sites of varying sizes were chosen by lottery, some of the two-flats had to be adjusted to fit on cramped lots.

65 Pilgrim Baptist Church (Kehilath Anshe Ma'ariv Synagogue)
3301 S. Indiana Ave.
1890–1891, Adler & Sullivan

Pilgrim Baptist Church (KAM Synagogue)

Interior restoration 1986, Office of John Vinci

KAM (Congregation of the Men of the West) was Chicago's oldest Jewish congregation, founded in 1847; Adler's father had been rabbi from 1861 to 1883. The architects responded to programmatic needs by designing an auditorium (their specialty) expressed as two stacked rectangles—one for the worship space and the other for the clerestory necessary for good acoustics. Terra-cotta panels hint at the richness of the interior. The original design for an entirely limestone-clad building was over budget; economy made necessary a pressed-metal cladding for the top cube, now sided. The wide entrance of broad expanding arches gives a sense of the grandeur originally envisioned. But there is no skimping visible on the interior, a thrilling worship space. A balcony completely surrounding the seating space required a tunnel vault overhead, rather than the firm's usual ceiling of expanding curves. The lower walls are russet, and the upper ones are cream. Colorist Louis Millet combined both tones in a rubbed effect on the gallery face, blended cream and the ceiling's oak on the clerestory frieze, and incorporated all of these tones in the Healy & Millet art glass windows. The discovery during restoration of the precision of this coloration inspired scholars to reexamine the Sullivan-Millet palette on other buildings.

66 Ira A. Heath House
3132 S. Prairie Ave.
1889, Adler & Sullivan

The long-standing attribution of this house to Adler & Sullivan has been called into question ever since Frank Lloyd Wright asserted that the house Heath built was not the one Adler & Sullivan designed.

67 Samuel B. Steele House
3123 S. Calumet Ave.
Isaac Wedeles House
3127 S. Calumet Ave.
1890, Charles S. Frost

Carefully controlled Romanesque houses for partners in a wholesale grocery business, these stone-front dwellings feature two-story, gently projecting bays and strong stringcourses above their battered bases.

68 Thomas D. Stimson House
3132 S. Calumet Ave.
1886, George H. Edbrooke

A scalloped roofline distinguishes this Romanesque house, a virtual duplicate of the one the architect had designed for himself up the block at 3314–3316.

69 Carl D. Bradley House
3140 S. Calumet Ave.
1884, Charles M. Palmer

On the cusp of stylistic change, here is an Italianate house breaking out in a Queen Anne pox. This hybrid has the flat front, tall narrow windows, and bracketed cornice of the older style—but with the rounded elements, decorative roof peak, and varied materials of the new fashion.

70 Joseph Deimel House
3141 S. Calumet Ave.
1887, Adler & Sullivan

This is the lone survivor of over twenty residential commissions for Adler & Sullivan's Jewish clientele in this part of town. Like many of their residences, it lacks the flair of their larger commissions.

71 3144–3148 S. Calumet Ave.
1881, architect unknown

Investors John J. Curran and Maximillian and Isaac Wolff were partners in a lumber-drying business and invested in several row house developments along Calumet Ave. This set, in which three of the eight units survive, was home to the Wolffs; it features angular neo-Grec styling, incised ornament on Joliet limestone facing, and strong metal cornices.

72 3154 S. Calumet Ave./320 E. 32nd St.
1988, Joseph J. Hoendervoogt & Assocs.

Roloson Houses

This complex attempts to blend with its Victorian neighbors by assuming a single-family-house disguise, with towerlike corners and a pedimental roofline.

73 Robert W. Roloson Houses
3213–3219 S. Calumet Ave.
1894, Frank Lloyd Wright
Renovated 1980, Fitch/Larocca Assocs.

The only Wright row houses ever built date from the early years of his independent practice. In them he reduced the Jacobean gable to a simple geometric form. The Roman brick wall is a severe but lovely backdrop for Sullivanesque terra-cotta panels.

74 Thomas Brown Houses
3221–3223 S. Calumet Ave.
1885, Julius H. Huber

Terra-cotta spandrel panels featuring putti, masks, and foliage enliven this mansarded brick double house.

75 George H. Edbrooke Houses
3314–3316 S. Calumet Ave.
1884, George H. Edbrooke

A Romanesque facade with a Flemish roofline marks Edbrooke's own home at 3316. The attached house is smaller, simpler, and set back in deference to its showier neighbor.

76 Morris Cohn House
3321 S. Calumet Ave.
1891, Kley & Lang

A gently rounded second-floor bow window and arched first-floor openings compose a nicely varied facade, disturbed by a pedimented dormer and a turret above the roofline.

Knight House

77 Clarence A. Knight House
3322 S. Calumet Ave.
1891, Flanders & Zimmerman

The unusual palette and materials—pink-veined rusticated orange Kasota stone and orange rock-faced Roman brick—contribute to a very lively design

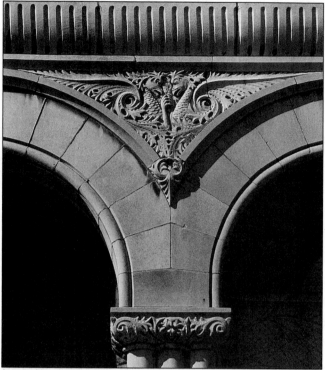

Seaton House

by architects known for their picturesque work. The combination of burly Romanesque corner towers and fine Gothic detailing in the ogee arches is skillfully handled.

78 John B. Cohrs, Albert R. Southard, and Chauncey E. Seaton Houses
3356–3360 S. Calumet Ave.
ca. 1890, architect unknown

A trio of Richardsonian Romanesque town houses strike a harmonic chord in sandstone, greenstone, and limestone. The elaborate carving on 3360 portrays dragons and enigmatic men.

79 Wendell Phillips High School
244 E. Pershing Rd.
1902, William B. Mundie for Jenney & Mundie

Hailed as one of Chicago's first modern high schools, Wendell Phillips was intended to grace an affluent neighborhood with a "stately presence" of red brick and a colossal Ionic order and to provide "everything that can vitalize and energize the school

work." Initially it had forty-eight classrooms fully equipped for the manual and academic training of 1,700 students, a gymnasium, a lunchroom, spaces for extracurricular activities, and—recognizing the new notion that schoolhouses should be civic centers open day- and year-round—a large auditorium.

Dr. Martin Luther King, Jr., Drive (Grand Blvd.)

In 1869 Frederick Law Olmsted and Calvert Vaux were commissioned to survey and plan two boulevards, eventually named Drexel and Grand. They were intended to link a park to be created in the township of Hyde Park with the city of Chicago, whose southern boundary was then at 39th St. As built, only Grand Blvd. was a continuation of an actual Chicago street. It ran from 35th St. to 51st St., curving gently into Washington Park for an impressive view of the huge meadow. Extensions to the north and south of the boulevard segment were named South Pkwy., and in 1968 the entire eleven-mile thoroughfare was renamed Dr. Martin Luther King, Jr., Drive. Unlike the other boulevards that converge on Washington Park, King Dr. has no central planted median. Its six wide central lanes are flanked by slim grassy strips, which are in turn bordered by local drives.

80 *Victory*
S. King Dr. at 35th St.
1928, 1936, Leonard Crunelle

Three life-size figures—a soldier, a mother, and Columbia—carved in high relief around a shaft honor the dead of the U.S. Army 370th Infantry, 93rd Division, a black World War I unit. Unveiled in 1928, it was topped by the three-dimensional doughboy in 1936.

81 Double House for Albert Mendel and James S. Toppan
3558–3560 S. King Dr.
1889, Wilson, Marble & Lamson
82 Double House for John F. Finerty and Edward J. Mendel
3562–3564 S. King Dr.
1888, Wilson, Marble & Lamson

Four rusticated limestone facades combine Gothic and Romanesque motifs.

83 John F. Whiting House
3568 S. King Dr.
1888, Thomas W. Wing

The great Queen Anne bay is robust and highly detailed, studded and pointed, serving as a signpost for this narrow house.

84 John J. Hill House
3608 S. King Dr.
1889, E. Clarke Johnson

This dignified Romanesque house has a beautiful entry, with a curving wall of small beveled windows, whose squares are echoed in the paneled wooden door.

85 John Tait House
3614 S. King Dr.
1888, Holabird & Roche

The simple facade is made interesting by the lively use of a single material, a variegated brownstone. This house was an excellent advertisement for its owner, a stone contractor, as well as for its architect, Tait's brother-in-law, Martin Roche. Both men lived here. Roche documented the construction in his diary.

86 John McCormick House
3616 S. King Dr.
1886, Charles E. Kauffmann

Hammer House

An idiosyncratic stone house, it has the tall, narrow proportions of the much earlier Gothic Revival.

87 Ida B. Wells House
(Martin Meyer House)
3624 S. King Dr.
1889, Joseph A. Thain

This house is noteworthy for its 1920s owners. Wells was a black-rights activist and a crusading journalist who exposed the ugly reality of lynching. Her husband was the lawyer and journalist Ferdinand Lee Barnett. This was the earliest and largest of a succession of somewhat fussy Romanesque houses on this stretch of the boulevard by a prolific but little-known architect.

88 Charles H. Nichols House
3630 S. King Dr.
1886, Rae & Wheelock

Queen Anne exuberance is manifested in rich detailing in pressed metal, an elaborate iron porch rail, carved brownstone animal masks and terra-cotta panels, a foundation of novel Hummelstown striated brownstone, two very different oriels, and a high picturesque roof.

89 D. Harry Hammer House
3656 S. King Dr.
1885, William W. Clay

It's the king of King Dr., a rare surviving example of the large houses that anchored many corners of the South Side boulevards by the 1890s. Striking color—orange brick, brownstone, and copper trim—enhances the more usual corner features of two impressively gabled sides and an angled tower element. Terra-cotta detailing, wrought-iron grilles, and art glass abound on this design, by one of the era's most flamboyant architects.

90 South Park Baptist Church
3722 S. King Dr.
1953, Homer G. Sailor

Here is a lingering postwar blast of Art Moderne styling. A broad expanse of narrow bright orange brick, broken only by the vertical thrust of a limestone tower, dips inward at the street-level portal and outward as ribbon windows are introduced to light the office wing.

BRIDGEPORT/ CANARYVILLE/ McKINLEY PARK/ BACK OF THE YARDS

Bridgeport/McKinley Park Area

OF THE CHICAGO RIVER

Stevenson Expwy I-55

Archer

Fillock

Budget
(factory
demolished)

Quinn
Poplar

1 2731 S
Archer

Farrell
Keeley
Throop
Bonfield
Eleanor
Loomis
Lyman

Immaculate
Conception

Bridgeport
Community
Center

3-4

5

31st

iary of
erpetual
Help

31st Pl

6

32nd

32nd Pl

Racine
May
Aberdeen
Carpenter
Morgan
Lithuanica

Halsted

32nd

Emerald
Union
Lowe
Wallace
Parnell
Normal
Canal

Stewart
Shields
Princeton
Wells
Wentworth

26th
27th
28th
28th Pl

29th

30th

31st

32nd

33rd St

33rd

33rd Pl

34th

Boys &
Girls Club

11

34th Pl

35th

35th Pl

36th

37th

37th Pl

38th

38th Pl

Sangamon
Lithuanica

9 McClellan
School

10 Richard J.
Daley
House

36th

37th

38th

Dan Ryan Expwy I-90/94

To LOOP ➔

7
Armour
Square
Park

Comiskey
Park

8

CTA Dan Ryan (Red) line

Pershing

ck
ard
District

40th

Exchange

Peoria

Stock
Yards
Bank

15

Union Stock
Yards Gate

16

Post
Office

14

International
Amphitheater

17

Bridgeport/Canaryville/McKinley Park/Back of the Yards   385

Canaryville/Back of the Yards Area

"They were left standing upon the corner, staring; down a side street there were two rows of brick houses, and between them a vista: half a dozen chimneys, tall as the tallest of buildings, touching the very sky—and leaping from them half a dozen columns of smoke, thick, oily, and black as night . . . stretching a black pall as far as the eye could reach."

The great smoking chimneys that so awed and ultimately over-whelmed the young Lithuanian immigrants in Upton Sinclair's *The Jungle* (1906) no longer blacken the sky over this industrial neighborhood. But church spires still rise above modest homes and apartments, commemorating the waves of immigrants that poured into the South Side beginning in the 1830s, pursuing the American Dream. The Lithuanians were only the most recent group in Sinclair's time. Canal construction and railroads, stockyards and slaughterhouses, steel mills and breweries had already brought the Irish, then the Germans, followed by Slavs and Balts in the 1880s and 1890s and, after World War II, Hispanics and African-Americans. These waves of newcomers flowed into an area rigidly divided by the physical barriers of the river

branches, the canal, railroad tracks and embankments, and, later, highways, creating a series of neighborhoods whose boundaries are more
visibly defined than in many other parts of Chicago.

Bridgeport, the first community to be settled, is one of the city's
oldest. The Illinois & Michigan Canal, begun in 1836 to connect the
Chicago and Illinois rivers, offered construction jobs to Irish and later
German immigrants, who settled along the Chicago River's south
branch at the northern terminus of the canal. Originally referred to as
Hardscrabble, Bridgeport was named for the port area created by a
bridge near Ashland Ave. built so low that it obstructed river traffic
and made it necessary to unload and reload cargo. The narrow diagonal streets perpendicular to Archer Ave. still retain the atmosphere
of this workers' community; though not the original shanties and
frame houses, many are quite old and little changed. After the
canal opened in 1848, Bridgeport attracted many new industries,
primarily slaughterhouses and supporting businesses. The area east of
Halsted St. and north of 31st St. was incorporated into the City of
Chicago in 1853; the area from 31st to 39th streets was annexed in
1863.

The opening of the Union Stock Yards in 1865 consolidated Chicago's livestock trade between 39th and 47th streets, Halsted St. and Racine Ave. The Union Stock Yard & Transit Company (backed largely by the railroads' investors) purchased 345 acres and laid the Chicago Junction Railway to link the yards with all major lines entering the city: "as far as the eye can reach," Sinclair wrote, "there stretches a sea of pens. And they were all filled—so many cattle no one had ever dreamed existed in the world . . . The sound of them here was as of all the barnyards of the universe." The stockyards and train lines that served them created physical barriers that still mark the divisions between ethnic and racial groups.

To the east of the yards' entrance at Halsted St. and Exchange Ave., Canaryville was originally middle-class. The Swifts, Libbys, and Hutchinsons settled on Emerald Ave., and the Irish community gradually expanded south from Bridgeport to be closer to the stockyards. St. Gabriel's parish was established in 1880 to serve them. In the 1890s the upwardly mobile began to move south, with many of them building large houses on Garfield Blvd., still within easy distance of the stockyards.

West of Bridgeport lies McKinley Park, also settled by Irish canal workers. Originating as a farming community in the 1840s, it grew into an industrial center incorporated as the Town of Brighton in 1851. Samuel E. Gross created several developments of small-scale workers' cottages that still exist.

By the 1870s, after the introduction of the refrigerated railroad car, packing plants had moved to the area immediately west of the yards, creating Packingtown, isolated by industrial sites, garbage dumps, and railroads. Living conditions in Back of the Yards epitomized the worst of industrialization. The noxious stench of Bubbly Creek, a stagnant fork of the river's south branch, permeated the area. Essentially an open sewer, it carried offal from the slaughterhouses and packinghouses. There were few or no services in these congested neighborhoods.

It was to these inhumane working and living conditions that progressive reformers turned their attention. Their emphasis on open areas or "breathing spaces" led to the development of a significant type of public space, the neighborhood park, which combined recreational and social facilities. Not surprisingly, due to the severity of local conditions, the South Park Commission led the way. After their first success with McKinley Park, the Commission hired D. H. Burnham & Co. and the Olmsted Brothers to design a series of small parks, of which Sherman and Fuller are perhaps the finest examples.

By 1900 another industry was contributing to the area's development. In 1890 a group of investors headed by Frederick H. Prince had purchased the Union Stock Yard & Transit Co. and the Chicago Junction Railway and, in 1902, began to acquire land north of the yards. In 1905 they announced the Central Manufacturing District (CMD), a planned industrial site that housed manufacturing and warehousing operations and employed thousands of local residents.

Since the 1950s, there has been little new construction. The Union Stock Yards closed in August 1971, after years of declining trade. The eclipse of related industries and the replacement of most of the International Amphitheater's uses by McCormick Place effectively curbed the area's growth. The stockyards' land was turned over to the CMD for development into the Donovan Industrial District. Low warehouse and light industrial buildings now sprawl out behind the old Stock Yards Gate, a sanitized relic of a pungent past. The neighborhood retains the varied ethnic character established throughout its development.
—Kathleen Nagle

Archer Ave. began as a path along the Illinois & Michigan Canal, named for canal commission member Colonel William B. Archer. Bridgeport's oldest neighborhoods are nearby and still contain early cottages and flats. Through Bridgeport, the Adlai E. Stevenson Expressway (I-55) runs along the site of the canal.

2731 S. Archer Ave.

■ 2731 S. Archer Ave.
1872, architect unknown

This "Dodge City" storefront (now a storage facility) is a rare survivor of a frame commercial building from the era when the canal was one of the nation's maritime Main Streets. The false front covering the gable could have been transplanted from a Wild West movie set.

■ St. Bridget Rectory (The Industrial School)
2932 S. Archer Ave.
before 1865, architect unknown

St. Bridget's was founded in 1850 to serve the burgeoning Irish community. The Industrial School doubled as an orphanage and was converted in 1883 to a rectory. The church was demolished in 1992.

■ Immaculate Conception Rectory
3109 S. Aberdeen St.
1901, Albert J. Fischer

■ Immaculate Conception Roman Catholic Church
3101 S. Aberdeen St.
1909, Hermann J. Gaul and Albert J. Fischer

The charming rectory creates a pleasing Gothic ensemble with the slightly later church, founded to serve a German parish.

■ Bridgeport Community Center (Immanuel Presbyterian Church)
1035 W. 31st St.
1892, Burnham & Root

Eye-catching in its simplicity, this brick church is probably one of Root's last designs.

■ St. Mary of Perpetual Help Roman Catholic Church
1035 W. 32nd St.
1889–1892, Henry Englebert

The dull brick Romanesque exterior gives no hint of the lavishly shaped and decorated nave enriched with stations of the cross and stained-glass windows with Polish inscriptions. Three domes sail high above, the central one lit by a ring of lantern windows and sheathed in a copper roof. The nave is further decorated with fine scagliola work, three elaborate marble altars, and a suspended pulpit topped by a wedding-cake cupola.

■ Armour Square Park
33rd to 34th Sts., from S. Wells St. to S. Shields Ave.
1904–1905, Olmsted Bros.
Field House 1905, D. H. Burnham & Co.

Of the parks proposed by the South Park Commission in 1903, eight were to be "small parks" of up to 100 acres, and six were to be "squares" of ten acres or less. The site plan is unusual for its placement of the field house across one corner; the park was designed symmetrically along this diagonal axis. Unfortunately, subsequent alterations have diminished the visual impact of this plan, and the poured-in-place concrete field house is unremarkable.

■ Comiskey Park
333 W. 35th St.
1991, Hellmuth, Obata & Kassabaum

This 43,000-seat stadium, built strictly for White Sox baseball, bows to tradition but responds chiefly to modern sports realities. With eighty-four skyboxes, broad walkways, and assorted clubs and restaurants it seems more like a suburban mall than a city ballpark. All the seats are blue, to achieve what the stadium architects call a "subtle womb of color," like the "great old stadiums." Each seat was positioned by computer and is free from visual obstructions to the playing field. To keep the sight lines clear, supporting columns were placed outside the lower deck. This, plus the need to make room for skyboxes, resulted in a steep upper-deck pitch of 34 degrees (compared to 14 degrees in the lower deck).

The designers were mindful of their directive, "Don't turn your back on old Comiskey," the beloved home of the White Sox since 1910. The most obvious tribute to the old park is the series of broad, reddish-brown concrete arches (filled with colored glass) that form the exterior structure. Unfortunately, they are often obstructed from view by large ramps. With its self-conscious regard for both baseball history and modern economics, new Comiskey Park may have tried too hard, but its heart is in the right place—when it can be glimpsed.

9 George B. McClellan Public School
3505 S. Wallace St.
1881, architect unknown
South addition 1896, August Fiedler

One of Chicago's oldest remaining public schools is in the popular, all-purpose, pedimented Italianate style.

10 Richard J. Daley House
3536 S. Lowe Ave.
1939, Eric E. Hall

Although built after the 1920s vogue for bungalows had peaked in Chicago, this is a modest continuation of the formula. Daley was born at 3602 and was a lifelong resident of S. Lowe Ave.

His son Richard M. Daley, elected mayor in 1989, lives nearby.

11 Boys & Girls Clubs of Chicago—Louis L. Valentine Unit (Valentine Chicago Boys' Club)
3400 S. Emerald Ave.
1938, Childs & Smith

The entrance to this Art Moderne temple to boyhood adventure is flanked by replicas of Alaskan Coastal Indian totem poles and is topped by a terracotta overhang suggesting a cliff cave entrance. The apparently romantic name is actually that of the donor, a retired furniture manufacturer.

Valentine Boys & Girls Club

12 Central Manufacturing District, East District
35th St. to Pershing Rd., Morgan St. to Ashland Ave.
1905–1915

The first American industrial park was established here in 1905 by a group of investors headed by Frederick H. Prince. They began acquiring land, mostly vacant except for three established industries, in 1902. By 1908 the 265 acres were serviced by individual switchtracks from the Chicago Junction Railways, and utilities, services, and street improvements were in place. The CMD built manufacturing buildings and warehouses designed by their own staff architects and engineers (until 1921 by S. Scott Joy, then A. Epstein) and financed the lease or purchase by tenant companies. The CMD's architectural standards dictated design basics, whether companies used Joy's services or another architect's. Among the companies that located here were William Wrigley, Jr., Co., American Luxfer Prism Co., Westinghouse Electric & Manufacturing Co., and Spiegel, May, Stern & Co. (later Spiegel, Inc.)

13 Stock Yard District

Clustered around the intersection of Halsted St. and Exchange Ave. are only a few structures recalling the days when Chicago was "hog butcher to the world." The city's location made it a natural trading hub and, after the invention of the refrigerated car, a processing center for many forms of livestock—a position further consolidated by the opening in 1865 of the Union Stock Yards. The stockyards attracted not only workers and livestock traders but also tourists, who marveled at the scale and efficiency of the operation. But by the mid-twentieth century, business was declining as trucking supplanted rail for transporting livestock products, and modern, decentralized packinghouses sprang up farther west. When the stockyards closed in 1971, the CMD began development of Donovan Industrial Park, a series of single-story, light-industrial buildings.

14 U.S. Post Office—Stock Yards Station
4101 S. Halsted St.
1936, Howard L. Cheney

The U.S. eagle meets the stockyards cow on reliefs ornamenting this small Art Moderne post office.

15 Stock Yards Bank Building
W. Exchange Ave. and S. Halsted St.
1924, A. Epstein

Philadelphia's Independence Hall inspired this anchor of the business district.

16 Union Stock Yards Gate
850 W. Exchange Ave.
1879, attributed to Burnham & Root

A lonely symbol of the vanished stockyards, the Stone Gate is almost certainly the work of Burnham & Root, who did other projects for the stockyards' owners (including a house for its organizer, John B. Sherman, Burnham's father-in-law). This tripartite gate marked the entrance to the animal pens, providing a large central arch for livestock and wagons flanked by pedestrian arches. The great copper roof concealed an iron grille that was lowered each night over the main arch; the southern arch has its original, hinged iron gate. Above the central arch is a relief head of another Sherman, the steer that won the American Fat Stock show in 1878.

17 International Amphitheater
4220 S. Halsted St.
1934, A. Epstein

On May 19, 1934, an enormous fire destroyed an eight-block area of the Stock Yards and consumed the exposition hall. Epstein set up an on-site office, and contractors worked around the clock to have this replacement facility ready for the annual livestock show in December. Now little-used, it gained international notoriety as a stand-in for the fire-damaged first McCormick Place, serving as the site of the infamous 1968 Democratic National Convention.

18 St. Gabriel Roman Catholic Church
4501 S. Lowe Ave.
1887, Burnham & Root

St. Gabriel's parish was organized by the Reverend Maurice J. Dorney in 1880 to serve Irish immigrant stockyard workers. According to Harriet Monroe, Root's biographer and sister-in-law, Root felt that "people too often attempted to build 'little cathedrals,' instead of being content with parish churches . . . the Romanesque was more suitable

St. Gabriel Church

[than the Gothic style] to a simple home of the people." Monroe considered the church one of Root's most characteristic works, "as personal as the clasp of his hand."

The preliminary design was for a centrally planned stone church with a low, massive tower over the crossing. For cost reasons the material was changed to brick, and the tower was moved to the side but made much higher. The north facade was altered in 1914 by the addition of a portico and vestibule; it originally had a taller arch in the middle, as seen in the window arrangement on the west transept. In 1944 the 160-foot tower was shortened by fourteen feet and lost its high pyramidal roof. The interior of the church has been substantially altered.

19 Fuller Park
45th St. to 46th Pl., S. Princeton Ave. to S. Stewart Ave.
1905, Olmsted Bros.
Buildings 1910, D. H. Burnham & Co.

The creative plan fits many recreational amenities onto a tight site, even making use of the railway embankment for spectators' seating. The buildings are of poured-in-place concrete with integrally cast ornament, an eco-

Fuller Park Field House

nomical alternative to cut stone known as "marblecrete" or "popcorn concrete" due to the roughness of the aggregate. Two open loggias connect the field house to the U-shaped gymnasium to the north. The wading pool to the east of the buildings, a common feature in Olmsted parks, is more intact than most.

20 718 W. Garfield Blvd. (Chicago Bicycle Club)
1898, Anders G. Lund

Club members departed from this late Queen Anne house on velocipede tours and other jaunts.

O'Leary House

21 James J. O'Leary House
726 W. Garfield Blvd.
1901, Zachary T. Davis

O'Leary, whose mother owned Chicago's most famous cow, was a gambling king who operated from his saloon across from the Stock Yards. His busy, château-esque house has Renaissance details such as the dormers and balustrades.

22 Sherman Park
W. 52nd St. to Garfield Blvd., S. Racine Ave. to S. Loomis St.
1904, Olmsted Bros.
Buildings *1904–1905, D. H. Burnham & Co.*

This sixty-acre oasis achieves the pastoral qualities of much larger parks by the gentle berming of its perimeter, which creates a tranquil spot focusing on a large lagoon. The extensive use of water is unusual in the South Parks but was suitable for this poorly drained site. Unlike Jenney's picturesque, frilly-edged lagoons in the great West Side parks, the landscape here is tranquil, broad, and modern. The island encircled by the lagoon accommodates playing fields, reached by four bridges at the corners of the park. The buildings at the north end create a strong axis and an impressive view from the south. The field house contains an auditorium, meeting rooms, and a refectory.

23 St. John of God Roman Catholic Church
1234 W. 52nd St.
1920, Henry J. Schlacks

The park's green foreground beautifully sets off the grand balance of the Renaissance facade, a Schlacks masterpiece. Although dimly lit, the barrel-vaulted nave is worth a look. Trompe-l'oeil painting imitates mosaics and marble.

St. John of God and Sherman Park Field House

24 Arthur A. Libby Public School

5300 S. Loomis St.
1901, William B. Mundie
Annex *1991, Roger Margerum*

The Annex, small-scale and intimate compared to its ponderous predecessor, is a rare example of new construction in this area.

25 Gage Park

W. 54th to W. 56th Sts.,
Claremont to Artesian and
Maplewood Aves.
1905, South Park Commission
Field House and Pool House
1928, South Park Commission

At the southwest corner of the original plan for the South Park System, Gage Park anchors the corner of Garfield and Western boulevards. The field house follows the earlier pattern established by D. H. Burnham & Co. Tom Lea's interior mural (1931) depicts a pioneer scene.

26 Western Blvd. Pumping Station

4919–4943 S. Western Blvd.
1927, Charles Kallal, Chicago city arch.; G. Dwight Tompkins, asst. eng., Dept. of Public Works

This dignified little box, encrusted with shells and crabs, is a decorative cap on a large node of Chicago's vast water system. At an intake crib three miles out into the lake, fresh water enters a tunnel running to the South District Filtration Plant. The purified water flows west through tunnels to this station (and others), where steam engines pump it to the area between Pershing Rd., Indiana Ave., 79th St., and the city limits, as well as to some southwestern suburbs. This station is one of the city's largest, with a capacity of 320 million gallons a day.

27 Sts. Cyril and Methodius Roman Catholic Church

5001 S. Hermitage Ave.
1913, Joseph Molitor

28 St. Joseph Roman Catholic Church

1729 W. 48th St.
1914, Joseph Molitor

29 Holy Cross Roman Catholic Church

1736 W. 46th St.
1913–1915, Joseph Molitor

Molitor, an immigrant from Bohemia, shaped the Back of the Yards skyline with this trio of towered Catholic churches. The Renaissance-style Sts. Cyril and Methodius, a Bohemian church now closed, is anchored by an Italian bell tower. The Romanesque St. Joseph, which still houses a Polish congregation, has twin Baroque towers and an exquisitely lit interior with rings of brass sconces and a leaded-glass chandelier. The Renaissance Revival Holy Cross features Lithuanian religious iconography, including facade sculptures of favorite saints George and Isidore, and rises to twin Baroque towers.

The Damen Ave. Viaduct (1962) runs from 47th St. almost to 37th St. over the old Chicago Junction Railways yards, offering dramatic views to the east of the stockyards site and, to the north, of the second major development of the Central Manufacturing District.

30 Central Manufacturing District, Pershing Road Development

Pershing Rd. between Ashland and Western Aves.

The brick and terra-cotta water tower at Damen Ave., flanked by massive warehouses, stands as a powerful signpost for this early industrial park. By 1915 the original East District was full, and the CMD purchased the entire south frontage of 39th St. from Ashland Ave. to Western Ave., extending 700 feet south to the Chicago Junction Railways' classification yards. The site included the infamous Bubbly Creek, which the CMD and the Sanitary District filled in and replaced with a sewer in the early 1920s.

The Pershing Rd. Development extended the industrial-park concept to include such comprehensive services as a central power plant and sprinkler plant, central union freight stations, comprehensive railroad

CMD—Pershing Rd. Development

CMD—Clock Tower

track arrangements, concrete traffic and utility tunnels connecting all buildings, brick paved streets with water and sewer systems, sidewalks and grass parkways, and street lighting. The standardized buildings were constructed of concrete or heavy timber, with pressed brick and terra-cotta exteriors. Most of them had six stories and basement, with uniform floor areas of about 30,000 square feet. They epitomize the multistory "gravity" system of manufacturing, which lost favor to the "straight line production" system, which called for single-story buildings.

The first four units of the Union Freight Station and Loft Buildings (A, B, C, D) were built between March and October 1917, faster than any other buildings of their kind. The CMD architect for almost all of the work up to 1921 was S. Scott

Joy, who was replaced by engineer A. Epstein in July 1921.

The view down Pershing Rd. is impressive, with the water tower dominating the mile of cohesive development. The terracotta logos (Goodyear Tire & Rubber Co., Montgomery Ward, Albert Pick & Co., L. Fish Furniture Co.) identify the original tenants.

31 McKinley Park
Damen Ave. to Western Ave., 37th St. to Pershing Rd.
1902–1906, South Park Commission
Field House *1916, South Park Commission*

The lovely foreground to the Pershing Rd. Development is idyllic McKinley Park, the first of the South Park Commission's neighborhood parks and a model for the progressive park movement. Designed by the commissioners and staff, the park was a laboratory for testing new ideas, with a swimming pool and changing rooms equipped with showers—an important amenity for occupants of cold-water buildings. When the commission retained the Olmsted Brothers and D. H. Burnham & Co. to design the next series of parks and park buildings, their designs were partially a result of experiments here.

Planning began in 1900 under South Park Commission General Superintendent J. Frank Foster. The park was enlarged in 1906 to include a lagoon, bath house, wading pool, and music pavilion (demolished); the old swimming pool building is currently a service building. The field house was designed by staff architects, who adapted models originated by D. H. Burnham & Co. The Damen Ave. Viaduct truncated the park's eastern end. President McKinley, assassinated in 1901, is commemorated with a statue by Charles J. Mulligan.

32 Illinois Bell Telephone—McKinley Office (Chicago Telephone Company)
2240 W. 37th St.
1917, Holabird & Roche

Addition 1938, Holabird & Root

Eschewing their "Phone Company Georgian" formula, the architects delivered a Renaissance Revival building with rusticated base and Venetian windows. When first built, the building was only three stories tall and three bays (the easternmost) wide.

🖽 DuPont–Whitehouse House
3558 S. Artesian Ave.
1876, Oscar Cobb & Co.

This unusually well documented house is a relic of the era when manufacturers stored explosives and gunpowder in what was then a sparsely populated area. E. I. DuPont de Nemours & Co.'s local agent, Junot J. Whitehouse, commissioned Cobb to design this residence, moved from 3616 S. Western Ave. in 1920. Gray cement parging now conceals the original brick, but the incised stone hood moldings and the pedimented pavilion mark the house as a rare example of the Italianate country-house style that reigned from the 1850s through the 1870s.

🖾 Samuel E. Gross's Archer Avenue Cottages
3200–3300 S. Hoyne Ave.
1887, architect unknown

The P. T. Barnum of working-class housing, developer Gross boasted that these houses, "for the price, are the handsomest, best built brick cottages in the city, with stone and brick trimmings, seven-foot basement, lake water and large lot." But, he admonished, "you must be quick if you want one at these prices and terms. They go fast. Go and see them and take your wife with you." He was right: they sold out. But fortunately there was almost always another one under construction; his annual catalog for 1889 cites five developments in the Bridgeport/Back of the Yards area alone.

The uniformity of the long rows of rooflines hints at the development's original cohesiveness. The plain facades have served as blank canvases for widely varied remodelings. In this modest subdivision, Gross not only provided the lot and infrastructure but built the house as well, selling it for $1,050–$1,200, payable on "easy terms" of $50–$100 down and $8 a month (equivalent to the cost of renting). To save excavation and drainage costs, houses had basements above ground; exterior stairs led to the main level, comprising a parlor, kitchen, two bedrooms, and a small pantry. The street level was later raised, placing the first floor virtually at grade. Many are now reached by a small footbridge between the sidewalk and the front door.

Gross's Archer Avenue Cottages

35 Edward Everett Public School

3419 S. Bell Ave.
1891, John J. Flanders
1914, Arthur F. Hussander

The corner towers of this archetypal Queen Anne school are visible from many nearby bridges and viaducts.

A worthwhile side trip lies west along the Adlai E. Stevenson Expressway (I-55) from Western Ave., where a textbook collection of bridges spans the Sanitary & Ship Canal north of the highway. These are of special note.

36 "Eight Track" Railroad Bridge

Chicago Sanitary & Ship Canal, west of Western Ave.
1901, 1909–1910, Scherzer Rolling Lift Bridge Co.

The inclined top chords of these parallel single-leaf bridges and their alternating orientations create a dramatic sculptural profile. The bridges, no longer movable, alternated north-south to better distribute the weight and allow room for each span's operating machinery.

37 Illinois Central Gulf Railroad Bridge

Chicago Sanitary & Ship Canal, east of Kedzie Ave.
1899

This is the easternmost of the canal's seven remaining center-pivot swing bridges, rare examples of Chicago's first generation of movable-bridge design. They opened and closed to river traffic by rotating around a central pier. Although now fixed, the stone pivot and its turntable are clearly visible. The drawbacks of this bridge type were the narrowing of the navigable space and the danger that vehicles, pedestrians, or trains would fall off the road edge after the bridge had swung open.

OAKLAND/
KENWOOD

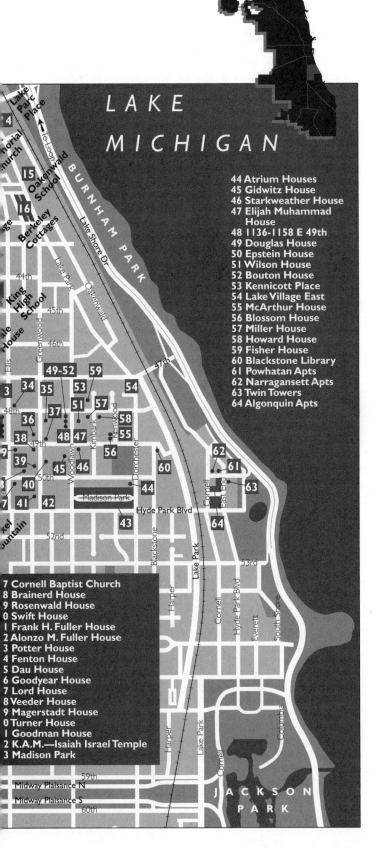

LAKE

MICHIGAN

44 Atrium Houses
45 Gidwitz House
46 Starkweather House
47 Elijah Muhammad
   House
48 1136-1158 E 49th
49 Douglas House
50 Epstein House
51 Wilson House
52 Bouton House
53 Kennicott Place
54 Lake Village East
55 McArthur House
56 Blossom House
57 Miller House
58 Howard House
59 Fisher House
60 Blackstone Library
61 Powhatan Apts
62 Narragansett Apts
63 Twin Towers
64 Algonquin Apts

7 Cornell Baptist Church
8 Brainerd House
9 Rosenwald House
0 Swift House
1 Frank H. Fuller House
2 Alonzo M. Fuller House
3 Potter House
4 Fenton House
5 Dau House
6 Goodyear House
7 Lord House
8 Veeder House
9 Magerstadt House
0 Turner House
1 Goodman House
2 K.A.M.—Isaiah Israel Temple
3 Madison Park

The residential development of this area reflects two contrasting ideals: the urban boulevard house and the country retreat. Chicago's earliest boulevards were established just north of Washington Park, and their popularity with wealthy homeowners set the pattern for other areas. Along the lake, Kenwood's large wooded lots created a secluded suburban setting that contrasted with the see-and-be-seen urbanity of the broad streets to the north and west. The fate of these neighborhoods began to diverge sharply as early as 1900, and today they have little in common. While the boulevards offer examples of past grandeur in decayed circumstances, the enclave of Kenwood south of 47th St. has retained its affluent character to a remarkable degree.

West of the lakefront communities of Oakland and Kenwood are the neighborhoods of Grand Boulevard, which lies north of 51st St., and Washington Park, which includes the park itself and the streets to its west. Kenwood was the first to develop and closely followed Paul Cornell's establishment in 1853 of the village of Hyde Park. In 1856 Jonathan A. Kennicott, a dentist and horticulture enthusiast, bought eight acres of countryside near the Illinois Central Railroad tracks south of 43rd St. and named his estate Kenwood after his mother's ancestral home in Scotland. A few wealthy families joined him in the area, and when the railroad added a station at 47th St. in 1859, it was named Kenwood.

In 1861 the area east of State St. from 39th to 63rd streets was incorporated as the township of Hyde Park. Separated by 43rd St. and sharing a western boundary at Cottage Grove Ave., Oakland and Kenwood grew as desirable lakefront suburbs throughout the next three decades. Kenwood outshone all its competitors, however, and was already known by 1874 as the Lake Forest of the South Side.

The neighborhoods west of Cottage Grove Ave. developed slightly later, receiving their impetus from the establishment of the boulevard and park system. Frederick Law Olmsted's 1870 plan for the South Park Commission, established in 1869, included a grand circuit of boulevards. Garfield Blvd. was planned as a link to the West Parks, and to the north Grand (now Martin Luther King, Jr. Dr.) and Drexel boulevards were connected by Oakwood Blvd. to form a four-mile circuit popular for fashionable carriage promenades. In 1874 improvements began on Grand Blvd., which soon became lined with mansions whose styles were emulated by the more modest houses on the side streets. The area north of 51st St. was built up by the 1890s, when development spread south to the Washington Park neighborhood.

The 1890s witnessed the decline in fashionableness of the mature neighborhoods. The City of Chicago had swallowed the township of Hyde Park in 1889, and the elevated train line was extended to Jackson Park in time for the 1893 World's Columbian Exposition. Apartment construction began to exceed that of single-family houses, and the original Protestant residents moved on to other neighborhoods. By 1900 Grand Blvd. had become a second settlement area for German Jews, and large houses in Oakland were being subdivided to provide apartments for Irish stockyard workers. The establishment of a streetcar line on 47th St. created a commercial strip that forms the present boundary between Oakland and Kenwood. To the south, Kenwood remained an exclusive neighborhood of single-family houses, and its status became more closely tied to that of Hyde Park.

In the 1920s middle-class African-Americans began to move into the Grand Boulevard and Washington Park neighborhoods, creating a thriving city within a city. Known variously as Black Metropolis or Bronzeville (the latter commemorated in the title of a 1945 collection of poems by Gwendolyn Brooks), the original community centered on 35th and State streets. Later in the decade it moved to 47th St., where the old Regal Theatre hosted nationally famous entertainers. In the wake of the African-American influx that occurred during World War II, overcrowding spilled into this neighborhood from the north, and middle-class residents fled. Decay overtook the area in the 1950s, and the absence of large institutions left a vacuum filled by the Chicago Housing Authority, which constructed the Federal St. corridor, a vast strip of high rises west of State St. The sad result is that these two neighborhoods have among the highest concentrations of public housing in Chicago while privately owned buildings continue to succumb to abandonment and decay. On the positive side, local institutions such as churches and community groups are fighting back with subsidized housing of their own. A public-private initiative has been established to provide funds for the repair and renovation of boulevard properties.

Oakland has shared the fate of its impoverished neighbors to the north and west. Success stories include the upgrading of a pair of Chicago Housing Authority lakefront properties and a smattering of new construction. South of 47th St., Kenwood has benefited from its proximity to Hyde Park and the stabilizing influence of the University of Chicago, which spurred extensive redevelopment in the 1950s and 1960s. Kenwood is now one of the city's most racially integrated and economically stable neighborhoods.

—Joseph D. La Rue with Laurie McGovern Petersen

■ Washington Park Court

S. Washington Park Ct. from 49th to 50th Sts.
1895–1905, Henry L. Newhouse, Andrew Sandegren, and others

The T. G. Dickinson real estate company created this one-block subdivision in 1892, specifying a ten-foot setback and selling the lots in clusters of two or three. Andrew and John M. Dubach developed at least twenty-five of the fifty-one lots, and Henry L. Newhouse was their architect for at least twelve designs. They set the tone of the street as an enclave of brick and limestone houses with common porch and cornice lines (third stories are often mansarded or recessed) and, almost invariably, with bay fronts.

■ Houses for the Hart & Frank Co.

4941–4959 S. Martin Luther King, Jr. Dr.
1901, Peabody & Beauley

The subdivision that created Washington Park Court allowed Robert & Emil Hart and their partner in a mortgage-loan business, David L. Frank, to create an unusually harmonious streetscape. Details are drawn from Gothic and Châteauesque idioms in three cases and from Classical and Renaissance Revival in the other four.

■ Corpus Christi Roman Catholic Church

4920 S. Martin Luther King, Jr. Dr.
1916, Joseph W. McCarthy Restoration 1976, Paul J. Straka

Built by affluent Irish Catholics just before racial change swept the South Side boulevards, this twin-spired Renaissance Revival church has support buildings grouped around an adjacent cloister. The church features a magnificent coffered ceiling, a main altar that is a mosaic replica of that in Leonardo da Vinci's *The Last Supper,* and windows by F. X. Zettler depicting the church's members in procession with Pope Pius X. This was McCarthy's first major commission; as Cardinal Mundelein's favorite architect, he went on to build twenty-eight churches, most of them during the 1930s.

Near King Dr. are several generations of subsidized housing, some more successful than others, many among Chicago's most eroded and notoriously dangerous. The Michigan Blvd. Garden Apartments, and especially the CHA housing projects that run like a long scar along S. State, Federal, and Dearborn streets from 35th to 54th streets, are best experienced in print—not in person.

Michigan Boulevard Garden Apartments

4 Michigan Boulevard Garden Apartments
4610–4646 S. Michigan Ave. and 40–78 E. 47th St.
1929, Ernest A. Grunsfeld, Jr.

Sears, Roebuck & Co. president Julius Rosenwald, one of Chicago's greatest philanthropists, planned the project to provide sound housing within the black community and a small return on investment. His inspiration was post–World War I municipal housing in Vienna (for example, the Metzleinstaler-Hof, 1921–1923; the more famous Karl-Marx-Hof, 1927–1930, was contemporaneous with Rosenwald's effort). The architect was his nephew, who shared the design of numerous subsequent housing developments; his son-in-law, Alfred K. Stern, was in charge of the plan. For decades the apartments were extremely attractive to working-class renters, but the profit was only 2.4 percent over seven years on a $2.7 million investment. After Rosenwald's death in 1932, Stern conceded that low-income housing required government support.

Five-story walls of cream brick are relieved with red brick banding. Storefronts line the base along 47th St., and eight Art Moderne terra-cotta doorways lead into a spacious inner court of gardens and playgrounds that provides access to the 421 walk-up apartments.

5 Robert Taylor Homes
S. State St. from 39th to 54th Sts.
1960–1963, Shaw, Metz & Assocs.

The world's largest public housing project is seen by millions each day from the Dan Ryan Expressway to the west. Twenty-eight identical, completely undistinguished sixteen-story buildings contain a total of 4,312 units. They line up mostly in U-shaped clusters of three on a half-mile-wide strip for two of the longest miles in the city. To the north, from 35th to 39th Sts., is the smaller Stateway Gardens (1955–1958, Holabird & Root & Burgee).

6 Ludwig van Beethoven Public School
25 W. 47th St.
1962, Perkins & Will

Public schools were planned as part of the housing projects and were usually more imaginatively designed. This one has a strong horizontal orientation, with projecting concrete floor slabs and a cheerful color scheme of yellow, blue, and white.

7 Mount Pisgah Missionary Baptist Church (Sinai Temple)
4622 S. Martin Luther King, Jr. Dr.
1909–1912, Alfred S. Alschuler

Alschuler capitalized on lessons learned as a tyro on Adler's Isaiah Temple to establish a widely copied formula for Reform synagogues: separate but linked community and worship buildings isolated daily activities from formal weekly ones. The freely adapted Classical styling was regarded as expressing the broad views of the congregation. The temple proper is a wide, shallow space, cross-axial to a broad lobby and entrances. Alschuler conceded that they were modeled on those of the Auditorium Theater, emulating the ease of ingress and egress.

8 Ebenezer Missionary Baptist Church (Isaiah Temple)
4501 S. Vincennes Ave.
1899, Dankmar Adler

Adler's last commission was an auditorium-style synagogue featuring a vaulted ceiling to create the "very nearly perfect" acoustics for which he was famous. Although the building sold out stylistically to the Georgian Revival, it was innovative in elevating school and community services from the basement to a separate but connected annex.

9 Metropolitan Community Church (41st Street Presbyterian Church)
4100 S. Martin Luther King, Jr. Dr.
1891, John T. Long
South gable remodeled 1913, Charles S. Frost

A Romanesque church, with a Greek-cross plan to accommodate semicircular seating, presents gable end walls with round arched openings that get smaller as they move up the variegated red sandstone faces.

Oakwood Blvd. provides a short, spacious link between Grand Blvd. (now King Dr.) and Drexel Blvd. that allowed carriages and riders to make a four-mile grand circuit to Washington Park without backtracking. As a major thoroughfare, it was a natural location for neighborhood churches.

10 Isaac N. W. Sherman House
442 E. Oakwood Blvd.
1889, Burnham & Root

The severity of John Wellborn Root's Monadnock Building imbues this large house, which is dominated by a huge front gable.

11 Holy Angels Roman Catholic Church
607 E. Oakwood Blvd.
1991, Skidmore, Owings & Merrill

When fire destroyed his 1896 church, Father George Clements recruited SOM to donate this design for the nation's first church heated and cooled by solar energy. Simplicity, flexibility, and energy efficiency characterize this concrete basilica with a pitched roof supported by exposed steel trusses. Stucco covers virtually all of the street elevations, while the south side has a glass-filled wall and a roof of solar collectors. The architects, the artists (Engelbert Nveng, Richard Hunt, and Roy Lichtenstein), and most of the contractors worked pro bono.

Center for Inner City Studies

12 Northeastern Illinois University—Center for Inner City Studies (Abraham Lincoln Center)
700 E. Oakwood Blvd.
1898–1903, Frank Lloyd Wright and Dwight H. Perkins; 1903–1905, Dwight H. Perkins
Renovated 1971–1976, Heard & Assocs.

A crusty client with a broad agenda of social reform had a major hand in shaping this high-rise settlement house. Jenkin Lloyd-Jones, Wright's uncle, was pastor of nearby All Souls Unitarian Church (demolished) and conceived the idea for this religious social center. Wright lived nearby when he first arrived in Chicago in 1887; it was at his uncle's church that he met his first wife, Catherine Tobin.

Pastor Jones' interests ranged far beyond Unitarianism; his desire for a nonsectarian facility led him to shun historic styles for his church center. The high basement behind dark cladding housed activity rooms and a library. The second and third floors, the site of the galleried auditorium-church, were identified by groups of windows united vertically. The three upper floors, devoted to meeting rooms, the pastor's quarters and a top-floor gymnasium and domestic science rooms, were marked by decreasing window heights. Strong corner piers strengthen the elevations; the dark floorline bandings cross the piers only four times. The 1970s renovation made extensive internal changes to suit the university's needs.

🔢 Monumental Baptist Church (Memorial Baptist Church)
729 E. Oakwood Blvd.
1899, Patton, Fisher & Miller

This is one of Chicago's finest surviving examples of the central lantern church, a type popularized by H. H. Richardson's Trinity Church in Boston.

🔢 Lake Parc Place (Victor A. Olander Homes and Olander Homes Extension)
3939 & 3989 S. Lake Park Ave.
1953 and 1956, Shaw, Metz & Dolio
Renovated 1991, David A. Sauer

In a remarkable demonstration of how the Chicago Housing Authority can redevelop its dreary 1950s properties, two fifteen-story Y-shaped public housing blocks, distinguished only by their views of Lake Michigan, were meticulously rehabbed, imaginatively landscaped, and secured with attractive fencing that emblazons their trendy new name.

🔢 Oakenwald Public School
4017 S. Lake Park Ave.
1935, John C. Christensen

Chicago's first Art Deco public school, and a model for others, uses reentrant corners on projecting brick piers, metal grilles, and corbeled arches to accentuate verticality. The massing is basically horizontal: a central two-story block with gymnasium and assembly hall pavilions.

🔢 Berkeley Cottages
4119 through 4169 S. Berkeley Ave.
4130 through 4162 S. Lake Park Ave.
1886–1887, Cicero Hine

Sited back to back are twenty-six freestanding cottages with wood "simple work" and detailed with Queen Anne elements. They are the survivors of a development that was entirely the work of the English-born Hine, who had a brief solo practice before becoming staff architect for the Brunswick, Balke, Collender Co., where he designed pool halls and bowling alleys.

🔢 Drexel Boulevard

The most elegant of the South Boulevards, Drexel was planned by Olmsted & Vaux in 1871 as a drive with traffic lanes on either side of a 100-foot-wide median, landscaped by H. W. S. Cleveland in 1873–1874 with winding walks and formal plantings. The land was donated by the Drexel banking family of Philadelphia, which reaped the benefits of greatly increased value for their South Side holdings.

🔢 New Testament Missionary Baptist Church (South Congregational Church)
3986 S. Drexel Blvd.
1886, George H. Edbrooke

The wonderfully bombastic tower juts out, immodestly trumpeting the church's presence on the corner and sticking out a big foot to visually trip boulevardiers.

New Testament M. B. Church
(South Congregational Church)

19 Grant Memorial African Methodist Episcopal Church
(First Church of Christ, Scientist)
4017 S. Drexel Blvd.
1897, Solon S. Beman

The first of Beman's Christian Scientist churches, this set the Classical Greek pattern followed for decades. The architect of Pullman was invited to submit plans for a 1,500-seat church with a "large vestibule hall" on a long, narrow site. He modeled his main elevation on the Ionic facade of the Erechtheion, on the Acropolis in Athens. A foyer is wrapped around three sides of the building, providing stairways to a column-free auditorium fitted with theater seats under a low Tiffany "fish scale" dome. The plan and styling were hailed for creating a distinctive architecture for the young religion.

20 Grant Village
4161 S. Drexel Blvd.
1991, Johnson & Lee

Grant Church developed this housing for senior citizens, one of the area's few new residential projects. To downplay the vertical block formula dictated by government guidelines while suiting the boulevard context, this eighty-unit, six-story development has two-tone horizontal brick banding and a third color on the windows, doors, grilles, and entrance canopy.

21 Martin Luther King, Jr., High School
4445 S. Drexel Blvd.
1971, Caudill, Rowlett & Scott

The concrete-framed school has its main entrance at the rear of an inner courtyard that flows toward the street, around the slab columns and beneath the second floor at the school's southwest corner. Glazing in blue metal frames is placed behind the deep columns as well as flush with their front planes.

22 William E. Hale House
4545 S. Drexel Blvd.
1885–1886, Burnham & Root
***School addition** 1925, E. Norman Brydges*

This vigorous house gets bigger as it rises, with ledges and corbels thrusting successive floors beyond the planes of lower ones.

23 Moses Born House
4801 S. Drexel Blvd.
1901, Frost & Granger

This smooth-faced limestone house demonstrates Charles S. Frost's masterly adaptation of historic styles.

24 Martin A. Ryerson House
4851 S. Drexel Blvd.
1887, Treat & Foltz

This Richardsonian mansion was built shortly after the marriage of the lumber-fortune heir. The stern massiveness was at odds with the qualities of the French Impressionist masterworks that once hung here.

25 McGill Parc Apartments
(John A. McGill House)
4938 S. Drexel Blvd.
1890, Henry Ives Cobb
***Annex for Carrie McGill Memorial YWCA** 1928, Berlin & Swern*
Converted to apartments 1982, Carl R. Klimek & Assocs.

Cobb's penchant for picturesque styles led him to a medieval French model for this limestone-clad mansion. McGill left the land, house, and funding to the YWCA, which added the annex of concrete and stucco with limestone details. After decades of

McGill Parc Apartments

use as a nursing home and cultist hangout, its derelict hulk was adapted to hold thirty-four apartments, some duplexed.

26 John H. Nolan House
4941 S. Drexel Blvd.
1887, Burnham & Root

This simply massed house of variegated brick dates from the last phase of Root's career, when strong gable facades characterized much of his work. The satisfied client wrote, "You not only can make a good picture of a house, but . . . when it comes to delivering up the keys make a man happier . . . than he expected he would be."

27 Cornell Baptist Church
(William M. Crilly House)
5001 S. Ellis Ave.
1908, William Carbys Zimmerman

In partnership with John J. Flanders or on his own, Zimmerman designed houses in various styles for the Crilly family of developers and contractors. This one, in the mode of Richard E. Schmidt's Madlener House, might best be called Chicago School Residential.

28 Ezra S. Brainerd House
1030 E. 50th St.
1867, architect unknown

Built with his mustering-out money by a Civil War soldier, this back-lot frame house with an extensive veranda evokes

Kenwood's era as a community of lakefront cottages.

29 Julius Rosenwald House
4901 S. Ellis Ave.
1903, Nimmons & Fellows

The head of Sears, Roebuck gave the commission for his house to the pair of masterful designers who became Sears's virtual house architects. Perhaps they had some trouble ratcheting down to the domestic scale; apart from such Prairie School elements as the hipped roof and Roman brick, it's otherwise a grand styleless galoot.

Swift House

30 Gustavus F. Swift House
4848 S. Ellis Ave.
1898, Flanders & Zimmerman

This meat-packer's palazzo features sweeping verandas, Palladian windows, and at each corner of the third floor, a terracotta lion bearing a shield emblazoned with a huge S.

31 Frank H. Fuller House
4840 S. Ellis Ave.
1891, Frederick W. Perkins

32 Alonzo M. Fuller House
4832 S. Ellis Ave.
1890, Frederick W. Perkins

A society architect who had been trained in Paris at the Ecole des Beaux-Arts, Perkins combined rock-faced stone and steep roofs here for different effects. Alonzo's imposing house works tan stone into towers, gabled pavilions, and verandas wrapped around a hip-roofed core. Frank's uses a version of the gambrel roof, a battered rubblestone tower, and varied window shapes in a most pleasing, relaxed manner.

33 Edward C. Potter House
4800 S. Ellis Ave.
1892, Charles S. Frost

This brick house has the double-tower facade popularized by Charles F. McKim at East Coast resorts.

34 William T. Fenton House
1000 E. 48th St.
1899, Wilson & Marshall

All of the exuberance and care that were to characterize Benjamin H. Marshall's flamboyant career appear in this Georgian Revival study—from the enormous portico to the faceted glass in the oval pediment window.

35 J. J. Dau House
4807 S. Greenwood Ave.
1897, George W. Maher

Designed while Maher was working on his innovative "Pleasant Home" in Oak Park, this house demonstrates that the style, drawn from Colonial American themes, was better served by a full-width veranda than by this hulking extended porch. The reddest of Roman brick is offset by limestone details, some of which introduce Maher's signature "motif rhythm"—in this case a round shield and berry-laden leaves.

36 Charles A. Goodyear House
4840 S. Greenwood Ave.
1902, William Carbys Zimmerman

An elaborate stone facade, which invokes such Tudor details as a broad arched entryway and a sort of strapwork on the second-story balustrade, also pairs lions within the tympanum and angels beside the arch.

37 John B. Lord House
4857 S. Greenwood Ave.
1896, Charles S. Frost

Frost again proves his deftness at picking up on McKim, Mead & White's free handling of historical styles. In this case, it's their Colonial Revival work in Newport.

38 Henry Veeder House
4900 S. Greenwood Ave.
1907, Howard Van Doren Shaw

The site allowed Shaw to place the entrance on the long 49th St. facade. It is organized symmetrically, with full-height bays at each end, but the door is off-center, occupying a space between four engaged columns. Shaw's free use of the Classical vocabulary comes through in the Lego-like metope blocks on the cornices.

Magerstadt House

39 Ernest J. Magerstadt House
4930 S. Greenwood Ave.
1908, George W. Maher

This is one of Maher's finest designs, sympathetic to the demands of a house whose narrow lot requires a side entrance. The carved poppies on the porch columns introduce the selected "motif rhythm," repeated inside in moldings, mosaics, and leaded glass.

Atrium Houses

40 Edward H. Turner House
4935 S. Greenwood Ave.
1888, Solon S. Beman

This Queen Anne house, built
entirely of masonry, has the
style's characteristic solidity but
little of its picturesque variety.

41 William O. Goodman House
5026 S. Greenwood Ave.
1892, Treat & Foltz

The heavy hand of Fritz Foltz
robs all possible grace from the
Italian palazzo form.

42 Kehilath Anshe Ma'ariv–Isaiah Israel Temple
(Temple Isaiah Israel)
1100 E. Hyde Park Blvd.
1924, Alfred S. Alschuler
Addition 1973, John H. Alschuler

To be "distinctive in style, majestic in appearance, and Jewish by
suggestion," the architect chose
"Byzantine lines" for this synagogue. The walls are polychromatic brick in various shapes laid
up randomly to suggest old, sun-
baked walls, while the smokestack is disguised as a minaret.
The acoustically perfect auditorium has a spherical Guastavino dome and a stone
treatment also intended to suggest age. The addition, designed
by the architect's son, adds a
chapel and social facilities around
a courtyard, one wall of which
is the old building. Brick is again
the main material, but in a single
shape.

43 Madison Park
Entrances on S. Woodlawn and
Dorchester Aves. between 50th
and 51st Sts.

In December 1883 John H.
Dunham, a sugar merchant and
banker who had acquired considerable property in Kenwood
shortly after the Civil War, filed
a subdivision of his holdings.
Mostly he provided spacious
lots for suburban homes but—
apparently emulating Stephen A.
Douglas's Woodland Park and
Groveland Park—he also set out
very small city-size lots around
an open common ground in
Madison Park and along 50th St.,
which backs up against the park's
lots. In no hurry to develop the
tracts, he built a few rental
houses along 50th St. but specified in his will that his holdings
could not be sold until his last
surviving heir had died. His heirs
supplied a number of single and
duplex rental houses, but major
development was not possible
until the 1920s, after the death
of Dunham's daughters. Lots
were then combined for the
apartment construction that had
become the norm in Hyde Park–
Kenwood.

44 Atrium Houses
1366–1380 E. Madison Park
1961, Y. C. Wong

The windowless street facades
give no clue to the light-filled interiors of these Modernist town
houses. Each is oriented to a
glass-walled atrium deep within.

Kehilath Anshe Ma'ariv–Isaiah Israel Temple

With their severe tan brick walls, beams for cornices, and simple doors, they have been praised as "the ultimate in reticence." Wong also designed the town house complex at 1239–1243 in 1966.

45 Willard Gidwitz House
4912 S. Woodlawn Ave.
1947, Ralph Rapson and John Van der Meulen

In the immediate postwar years, young architects wishing to build in the Modernist manner of Walter Gropius and Marcel Breuer sometimes chose traditional materials to ensure acceptance. Here the architects used the stone and wood of the existing house on the site—but completely transformed them. The rubblestone of the recessed base came from the porch; stones from its huge piers were reused in the chimney. Other materials on the new elevations are wood panels (originally light gray), steel supports, and a glass-enclosed cantilevered steel stair. The Crayola tones were added by a later owner.

46 Charles H. Starkweather House
4901 S. Woodlawn Ave.
1902, Howard Van Doren Shaw

As with Shaw's Veeder House one block to the west, this house faces 49th St. and offsets the symmetrical composition of the main block with an off-center entrance. The entrance contrasts with the house's

Georgian vocabulary with a pier-and-slab frame topped by a half-round window, creating a forced perspective that dramatizes the entrance.

47 Elijah Muhammad House
4855 S. Woodlawn Ave.
48 1136–1158 E. 49th St.
1971, MEESI

The leader of the Nation of Islam, his children, and his chief aides occupied this complex, a mix of Mediterranean and Modernist elements. The stained-glass windows incorporate Muslim emblems.

Douglas House

49 James Douglas House
4830 S. Woodlawn Ave.
1907, Howard Van Doren Shaw

This is an archetype of the formal, symmetrical Georgian Revival house that set the pattern for countless thousands of center-entry Colonials. A balustrade originally ran the length of the roof ridge from chimney to chimney.

50 Richard Epstein House
4824 S. Woodlawn Ave.
1980, Nagle, Hartray & Assocs.

The street side is a good neighbor, recalling the red brick and fanlight door of the Colonial Revival home it replaced. The private side is a sculptural facade of stucco and large window openings.

51 Thomas E. Wilson House
4815 S. Woodlawn Ave.
1910, Howard Van Doren Shaw

By 1910 Shaw was better known for palatial suburban estates than for city houses in Kenwood and Hyde Park. Despite its urban location, this house has much in common with those rambling, artfully asymmetrical Tudor-inspired country houses.

52 Christopher B. Bouton House
4812 S. Woodlawn Ave.
1873, architect unknown

Built as a substantial country villa on a large tract, this is regarded as the least altered 1870s house in Kenwood–Hyde Park. While the window shapes suit the Italianate roofline, their framing suggests another, indeterminate, era.

53 Kennicott Place
4701 and 4721 S. Woodlawn Ave.
1991, David Swan

These eighteen single-family and duplex "cottage style" town houses have either high stoops or English basement entries (slightly below grade). The Queen Anne houses on Kimbark Ave. near 48th St. were their prototypes.

54 Lake Village East
4700 S. Lake Park Ave.
1971, Harry Weese & Assocs.; Ezra Gordon–Jack M. Levin Assocs., assoc. arch.

The slim silhouette changes constantly as you move around its thirty-eight brick-and-glass facets. The twenty-five-story tower with eight units per floor is one of several Weese designs from the early 1970s that used "minimum perimeter" floor planning in re-

Lake Village East

sponse to demands for short corridors, interesting layouts, and structural economy. The multifaceted shape tends toward the circular—the most economical ratio of perimeter to floor area—but it also permits rectangular rooms. Window tiers were placed to capture the best lake and Loop views. The brick sections provide interior walls that welcome the large furniture that Modernist apartment design generally found anathema and did not accommodate. The additional cost of the irregular (rather than rectangular) concrete structural system was offset by the lower cost of enclosing a reduced perimeter.

55 Warren McArthur House
4852 S. Kenwood Ave.
56 George W. Blossom House
4858 S. Kenwood Ave.
1892, Frank Lloyd Wright

The most important of the "bootlegged" commissions done while he was working for Adler & Sullivan prove that the highly inventive Wright could create successful traditional designs. On the McArthur House, the gambrel roof and the porch with arched corner sections are Colonial motifs; the bay windows nestle under the eaves and gable as they do on Wright's own Oak Park home; and the molding dividing the brick base from the stucco wall becomes part of the entrance arch.

Blossom House

The Blossom House appears coldly symmetrical on the front, with three Palladian openings on each street facade, but its plan is not the traditional central hall. A living room and hall combination spans the midsection from north to south; the first floor ends in a glassy, sunlit, half-circular dining area in the southwest corner. Note the coach houses; McArthur's is a miniature of the main house set at an angle while Blossom's is a 1907 design exhibiting Wright's Prairie School themes.

57 George L. Miller House
4800 S. Kimbark Ave.
1888, George O. Garnsey

Garnsey unabashedly appropriated and miniaturized H. H. Richardson's William Watts Sherman House (1874–1876) in Newport, Rhode Island, almost detail for detail; he also advertised the plans for a double-house version of it in his magazine, *National Builder.*

58 Joseph H. Howard House
4801 S. Kimbark Ave.
1891, Patton & Fisher

Every peak, plane, dormer, and turret above the stone base is sheathed in the pink slate tiles found on numerous Queen Anne houses in Hyde Park and Kenwood but in few other places locally.

59 Reynolds Fisher House
4734 S. Kimbark Ave.
1890, Patton & Fisher

Miller House

The thin, tight clapboarding, high gables, and eaveless roof edges of the architect's own house are all typical Patton & Fisher elements.

60 Chicago Public Library—Blackstone Branch (T. B. Blackstone Memorial Library)
4904 S. Lake Park Ave.
1902, Solon S. Beman

Executed in Concord granite, this Beaux Arts cupcake was modeled after Beman's Merchant Tailors Building. That miniature domed temple, facing the lagoon at the 1893 World's Columbian Exhibition, had pleased both Blackstone and a critic who found it "one of the beauty spots of that grand architectural display."

61 Powhatan Apartments
1648 E. 50th St.
1928, Robert S. DeGolyer and Charles L. Morgan

62 Narragansett Apartments
1640 E. 50th St.
1929, Leichenko & Esser with Charles L. Morgan

In the late 1920s developers attempted a South Side version of the North Side's fashionable Streeterville on landfill holdings of the Chicago Beach Hotel (demolished), a longtime resort at the foot of Hyde Park Blvd. (51st St.). Five apartment buildings were begun before the stock market crash, the jewels of which are the Powhatan and the Narragansett; both were developed by the Garard Trust, with Morgan in charge of aesthetics. Native American names and themes were chosen, primarily because they were untapped sources for the Art Deco designs that embellish the black bas-relief spandrels in the limestone bases and the earth-toned tile panels inserted in the upper elevations. The Narragansett also features goofy, flat-faced pachyderms solemnly gazing down on visitors

Powhatan Apartments

and residents. The Powhatan is a reinforced-concrete structure with outer walls that could have been flat surfaces but are instead composed of a rhythmic pattern of projecting piers and mullions. It is the only large-scale Chicago apartment building that fully exhibits the "stripped architecture" of recessed spandrels and continuous piers introduced by Eliel Saarinen's entry for the Chicago Tribune Tower Competition of 1922.

63 Twin Towers
1645 and 1649 E. 50th St.
1951, A. Epstein

The recessed spandrels, finished in horizontally striated metal, stretch the entire distance between strongly expressed corner piers, contrasting with their earlier neighbors' vertical orientation.

64 Algonquin Apartments
Hyde Park Blvd., E. 50th St., Cornell Ave., and East End Ave.
1950–1952, Pace Assocs. and Holsman, Klekamp and Taylor

These spartan, fourteen-story concrete-frame units perpetuate the Native American theme of 1920s Chicago Beach development properties in name only. Ludwig Mies van der Rohe was associated with this complex—but removed his name when plans were altered to include first-floor residences.

65 Francis M. Drexel Fountain
Drexel Sq. (Drexel Blvd. and E. 51st St.)
1881–1882, Henry Manger, sculptor

Drexel Sq. serves as a transition space between Drexel Blvd. and Washington Park, a truncated version of the sweeping approach envisioned by Frederick Law Olmsted. The family of the Philadelphia financier donated the land and the fountain.

66 Walter H. Dyett Middle School
555 E. 51st St.
1972, David N. Haid

Between 1968 and 1973 the Public Buildings Commission, headed by architect Jacques C. Brownson, hired private architects to build twenty-six inner-city schools according to careful guidelines seeking universal modules and flexible plans. Park sites were sought to give underprivileged children the advantages of landscaped suburban schools, provoking protests from open-land advocates. The courts upheld the controversial invasion, but only three schools were eventually built on Chicago Park District property.

Sensitive to arguments against the site, Haid designed two large-span steel structures with identical modules and dark, fully glazed skins with the transparency to fit into their green setting; the front building is below grade. The instructional building accommodates four "learning houses" for team teaching around two open courts. It is connected underground to the sports facility, which is spanned by four plate girders.

67 George Washington Memorial
S. Martin Luther King, Jr. Dr. at E. 51st St.
1904, Daniel Chester French and Edward Clark Potter

French's rather stolid figure, in contrast to Potter's spirited horse, is meant to indicate Washington's rocklike support of freedom. The work is a second casting of a Paris monument.

68 International Brands Corporation (Schulze Baking Company)
40 E. Garfield Blvd.
1914, John Ahlschlager & Son

Paul Schulze planned his bakery as part of an aggressive campaign to sell his "better than home-made" bread to tradition-bound, cleanliness-conscious housewives. Five-story walls of glazed cream terra-cotta suggest hygienic conditions. Blue lettering, string-courses of rosettes, and foliated cornice ornament all carry associations of sunlight, fresh air, and purity, as do the 700 windows

Washington Park (South Park)

grouped in unified ranges. The ornamentation is abstract, Sullivanesque, and modern, not overtly classical and old, because Schulze's product relied on modern technology.

69 Washington Park
(South Park)
E. 51st St., S. Martin Luther King, Jr. Dr., E. 60th St., and S. Cottage Grove Ave.
1871 plan, Olmsted & Vaux, landscape architects; executed by H. W. S. Cleveland

Washington Park was designed in 1871 by Olmsted & Vaux as the Upper Division of a great "South Park" that also included a Lower Division (now Jackson Park) and a connecting strip, the Midway Plaisance. In contrast to Jackson Park's swampy lakefront site, Washington Park was flat prairie, which would not "elsewhere be recognized as well adapted to the purpose." It was also to be the terminus of three boulevards, Garfield from the west and Drexel and Grand (now Martin Luther King, Jr. Dr.) from the north.

Making an advantage of what they had, Olmsted & Vaux established in the park's northern half a "large meadowy ground," 100 acres of open space perceptible without break from all three approaches. The southern end was to be more verdant, with a pond that would connect—via

a canal down the Midway—with the lagoon in Jackson Park. In 1872 park commissioners entrusted the plan's execution to an Olmsted associate, H. W. S. Cleveland, stipulating that he avoid "extensive alterations of the natural surface," thereby putting an end to the Midway's waterway linkage.

Washington Park today retains its naturalistic character, with buildings restricted to the perimeter and with the main traffic lanes raised slightly, so that visitors must descend into the park proper. The casting pond and the islanded lagoon are the sole reminders of the intended emphasis on water.

70 Pool and Locker Building
(Refectory)
Pool and Russell Drs.
1891, D. H. Burnham & Co. Exterior restored 1992, A. Epstein & Sons with Dubin, Dubin & Moutoussamy and Hasbrouck Peterson Assocs.

This elegant, Classically derived refectory was built near the site chosen by Olmsted for a pavilion to overlook his "Southopen Ground." It features a deep ground-level colonnade and four open rooftop corner towers. The much-needed restoration was done in conjunction with the creation of adjacent pool facilities.

71 General Richard L. Jones Armory
5206–5310 S. Cottage Grove Ave.
1928, Perkins, Chatten & Hammond

The cubic, hard-edged profile of one of the nation's largest urban armories is softened by a crisply detailed bas-relief frieze of soldiers, vertical fluting, giant pilasters every fourth bay, and towers marking the entrances on the north and east sides. Ancient and modern (World War I) sentries emerge from the stone to guard the vehicular entrance.

72 Du Sable Museum of African-American History
(South Park Commission—Administration Building)
740 E. 56th Pl.
1910, D. H. Burnham & Co.
Addition 1992, Wendell Campbell Assocs.

The most elaborate of the firm's concrete buildings designed for the South Parks shows how a poured material can be manipulated to imitate a carved one; only the terra-cotta Ionic capitals at the main entrance are added on. The lightly sanded precast-concrete addition duplicates the original's color and fenestration, adding galleries, a theater, and exhibit space.

73 Drama and Rigger Shops
(Stable)
Payne Dr. south of 57th St.
1880, Burnham & Root

This rare roundhouse stable and its attendant buildings, all built of random ashlar Joliet limestone, survive as the scenery shops for Chicago Park District theaters.

HYDE PARK/ SOUTH SHORE

Madison Park

Hyde Park Blvd

102 Heller House

52nd

01 Tomlinson House

53rd

Woodlawn

University

Kimbark

103 Work Cottage

Harper Court

104

Lutheran School of Theology

93 **94** Chicago Child Care Society **96** **95** St Thomas the Apostle Church and School

Kenwood

Ridgewood

Dorchester

Blackstone

Harper

54th Pl

Lake Park

55th University Apts **69** University Bank **67**

44 **97** Augustana Church

68 **66** Hyde Park Historical Society

92 **90** Row Houses **81**

56th

89 Ray School Row Houses **80** **79** Hyde Park Redevelopment Project **78**

88 **87** **82**

41 **91** **86**

57th

30 **32** **85** **84** Hillel Foundation Hoyt House **70** **77** **65** **63** **64**

31 **21** 5748-56 S Kimbark Botsford House **71** **76** **75** **62** **61**

33 **40** **83** **72** **59** **60**

19 **34** **74** **73** **58** Rosalie Villas

5 **39** **38**

35 **36** **37** Cornell To Loop

59th

7-18 Midway Plaisance N

Jackson Park **3**

W A Y   P L A I S A N C E

Midway Plaisance S

60th

Baird Bell Law Quadrangle

61st

72 Chicago Theological Seminary Faculty Quadrangle	75 5757-5759 S Blackstone
73 5825 S Blackstone	76 Thompson House
74 Helstein House	77 5701 & 5707 S Blackstone
	78 St Stephen
	79 5621 & 5611 S Blackstone

Hyde Park/South Shore   417

The World's Columbian Exposition of 1893 had a powerful and lasting impact on Chicago's urban development, and nowhere was this felt as strongly as in Hyde Park. The enormous annexation of 1889, in which the city swallowed up huge townships like Lake View, Jefferson, and Hyde Park, was prompted in part by the theory that the larger the city's population, the better its chances of being named the site of the fair. Once Chicago had won this prize, in April 1890, civic pride demanded the creation of institutions befitting the nation's second most populous city. One of these was the University of Chicago, founded in 1890. Other preparations for the exposition included the long-postponed landscaping of Jackson Park (chosen as the site of the fair), the extension and expansion of public transportation from the Loop, and massive construction of hotels and apartments. Hyde Park would never again be the quiet suburb envisioned by its founder.

In 1853 Paul Cornell, a Chicago lawyer newly arrived from New York, bought 300 acres of lakefront land between 51st and 55th streets and deeded sixty of those acres to the Illinois Central Railroad in return for a train station located in his new community of Hyde Park. He knew that his hopes for a prosperous residential development would depend in equal measure on perceived seclusion from urban woes and easy access to the city's commercial and cultural institutions. Hyde Park was incorporated as a township in 1861 (its boundaries vastly exceeding those of the small settlement by that name) and as a village in 1872. Originally concentrated around 53rd St. and Hyde Park Blvd. (near the train station at 53rd St. and Lake Park Ave.), commercial development continued to follow the train's southward path, with districts emerging along Stony Island Ave. and East 71st, 75th, and 79th streets.

Local businesses were the only nonresidential users of land in Hyde Park; industry was deliberately excluded. Cornell hoped that a large institution would become an anchor for the area, but this did not come to pass until after his death, when the University of Chicago was founded. The lakefront location, although swampy and not very attractive in its unimproved state, gave the area great potential as both a resort location and a year-round suburban community. Hotels were among the earliest large buildings, and housing ranged from villas and cottages to row houses and apartment buildings.

The area's most ambitious landscape improvements resulted from the 1869 creation of the South Park Commission, of which Cornell was a member. The commission established an extensive system of connected parks and landscaped boulevards, and hired Frederick Law Olmsted and Calvert Vaux to design the enormous South Park (now Washington and Jackson parks and the connecting Midway Plaisance). Although several features of the original plan were altered or omitted, the overall character of these parks is remarkably close to Olmsted's pastoral vision.

The slow pace of land acquisition and a lack of money delayed the landscaping of Jackson Park. Not until it was chosen in 1890 as the site for the World's Columbian Exposition did work progress— but then at a breakneck pace that made up for two decades of neglect. The White City created here was intended to show how parks, boulevards, and buildings could be planned in a unified manner that would bring harmony and order to the chaos of the industrial city. It sowed the seeds of the City Beautiful movement, which culminated in Daniel H. Burnham's 1909 Plan of Chicago. Two of the plan's features that had the greatest impact on this area were the dedication of all lakefront land to public use and the creation of wide thoroughfares to facilitate access to and from the central city.

The increasing ease of transportation to the Loop—frequent train service would be supplemented in the twentieth century by automobile and bus access—brought greater density to Hyde Park and also spurred development to the south. The South Shore became a fashionable middle-class area, with an elegant country club and a planned subdivision called Jackson Park Highlands.

The diverse architecture of Hyde Park comprises excellent examples of almost every urban building type and style, from modest frame cottages to luxurious lakefront high rises. The area is particularly rich in houses from the 1890s, the era of its most feverish development. Many of them were designed by architects later grouped as the Chicago School, a term that includes both the Prairie School and less radical colleagues such as Pond & Pond and Howard Van Doren Shaw. All were experimenting with new forms and rethinking what the house should be. Frank Lloyd Wright's Robie House is the most outstanding example.

Some of Hyde Park's finest houses were designed for faculty members of the university, which has continued to play a pivotal role in the community and was instrumental in the large-scale redevelopment of the 1950s. Its reassuring presence has helped to maintain the desirability of the Hyde Park neighborhood for the last century. It will, no doubt, continue to do so for at least the next hundred years.
—R. Stephen Sennott

▌ Midway Plaisance
Between E. 59th & 60th Sts.
from Washington Park east to
Jackson Park

Although its name is a contradictory mix of the tawdry and the elegant, the Midway Plaisance is actually a broad boulevard with a vast sunken grassy median. The first half of its name resulted simply from its location midway between the two large parks that it connected. Its use as a grounds for the Ferris wheel and other amusements during the 1893 World's Columbian Exposition—in contrast to the high-minded, educational quality of the exhibits further east—made "Midway" synonymous with carnival grounds everywhere. A plaisance was one of Frederick Law Olmsted's landscape types and referred to a pleasure grounds with winding, shrub-lined paths for strolling and picnicking. Ironically, the Midway was never developed with such a landscape. Nor did it ever become the great water link between parks that Olmsted had envisioned, with its median canal planned to unite Jackson Park's lagoons to a lake in Washington Park. Today it serves as a broad greensward that sets off the neo-Gothic grandeur of the University of Chicago campus.

▌ Fountain of Time
Midway Plaisance at entrance
to Washington Park
1922, Lorado Taft
Base design, Howard Van Doren Shaw

Fountain of Time

One of Chicago's most impressive monuments anchors the west end of the Midway, which Taft wanted balanced by a Fountain of Creation at the east end. Inspired by lines from an Austin Dobson poem:

Time goes, you say? Ah no!
Alas, Time stays, we go. . . .

Taft depicts a hooded figure leaning on a staff and observing a panorama of humanity that rises and falls in a great wave. The statue's ambitious theme, size, and scope overshadow its original purpose, which was to commemorate a century of peace between England and the United States that resulted from an 1814 treaty resolving Canadian border conflicts. Taft envisioned the group sculpted from marble, but the material's high cost and vulnerability to Chicago's weather made it impractical. Bronze, his second choice, was also prohibitively expensive, leading to the selection of a pebbly concrete aggregate. The hollow-cast concrete form reinforced with steel was cast in an enormous, 4,500-piece mold. Taft himself appears among the figures that line the west side of the monument; he is wearing a smock, head bowed and hands clasped behind him.

---

3 Jackson Park (South Park)
E. 56th–67th Sts., S. Stony Island
Ave. to Lake Michigan
1871, Olmsted & Vaux
1895, Olmsted, Olmsted & Eliot

Although Olmsted & Vaux had prepared a comprehensive plan for the South Parks in 1871, Jackson Park did not receive major improvements for two decades. The primary features of the plan were aquatic: a channel cut through the beach would link a 200-foot pier with a series of lagoons that would lead to canals along the Midway and eventually to a small lake in Washington Park. During the 1870s dredging of the swampy land began, and in the 1880s a permanent beach was completed from 56th to 59th streets and later paved with granite blocks down to 63rd St. When planning began in 1890 for the World's Columbian Exposition, it finally

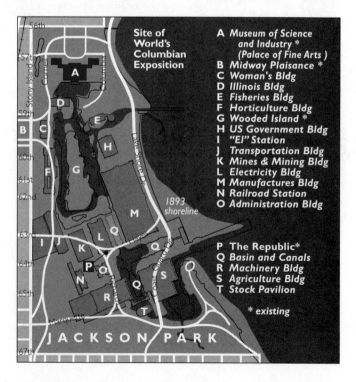

Site of
World's
Columbian
Exposition

A   Museum of Science
    and Industry *
    (Palace of Fine Arts)
B   Midway Plaisance *
C   Woman's Bldg
D   Illinois Bldg
E   Fisheries Bldg
F   Horticulture Bldg
G   Wooded Island *
H   US Government Bldg
I   "El" Station
J   Transportation Bldg
K   Mines & Mining Bldg
L   Electricity Bldg
M   Manufactures Bldg
N   Railroad Station
O   Administration Bldg

P   The Republic*
Q   Basin and Canals
R   Machinery Bldg
S   Agriculture Bldg
T   Stock Pavilion

* existing

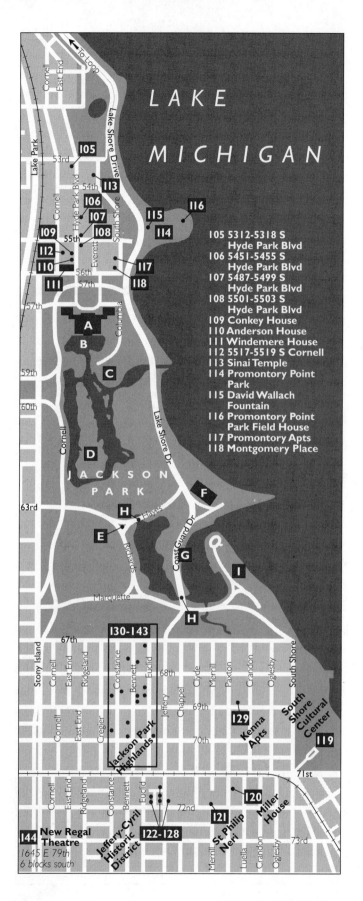

LAKE

MICHIGAN

105 5312-5318 S
    Hyde Park Blvd
106 5451-5455 S
    Hyde Park Blvd
107 5487-5499 S
    Hyde Park Blvd
108 5501-5503 S
    Hyde Park Blvd
109 Conkey House
110 Anderson House
111 Windemere House
112 5517-5519 S Cornell
113 Sinai Temple
114 Promontory Point
    Park
115 David Wallach
    Fountain
116 Promontory Point
    Park Field House
117 Promontory Apts
118 Montgomery Place

created an impetus to complete work on Jackson Park, the main site of the fair. Frederick Law Olmsted designed the fair-grounds, and his vision of a watery paradise was fulfilled with a ceremonial basin called the Court of Honor, canals, a lagoon with a wooded island, and a pond. The only tangible reminders of the fair's glory are the Museum of Science and Industry, the Lagoon and Wooded Island with its Japanese garden, and Daniel Chester French's statue *The Republic*.

The third and most influential plan for the park was drawn up by Olmsted, Olmsted & Eliot in 1895. The theme of water was central to the plan and can still be seen despite the loss of several links between ponds and lagoons. Improvements were made on a grand scale, so that by 1904 Jackson Park contained beautifully scenic greens, shrubbery, trees, walks, bridges, and driveways. The encroachment of the automobile has destroyed much parkland, but the essential character remains.

Museum of Science and Industry

A Museum of Science and Industry (Palace of Fine Arts)

S. Lake Shore Dr. at E. 57th St.
1893, D. H. Burnham & Co. Reconstruction 1929–1940, Graham, Anderson, Probst & White

Built as the Palace of Fine Arts of the World's Columbian Exposition, this is the sole remnant of the great 1893 fair and its only fire-proof structure. It was designed by Charles B. Atwood

Museum of Science and Industry

(1849–1895) to display paintings and sculpture assembled from all over the world. Following the fair, the building housed the Field Museum of Natural History until 1920. It then stood empty and deteriorating while architect George W. Maher, who called its neo-Classical architecture "unequaled since the Age of Pericles," spearheaded an effort by the AIA to save it. In 1930 Julius Rosenwald, philanthropist and president of Sears, Roebuck & Co., contributed $5 million to rehabilitate the structure and to establish a world-class museum. The rebuilding, completed in 1940, produced a stylistic anomaly. The original exterior of staff, a hemp-and-plaster compound, was replaced exactly in marble and limestone, while the interior received Art Moderne streamlining.

With its Ionic colonnades, caryatid porches, and domed roofs, the Palace of Fine Arts represented the acme of the classicism that made the fair a White City of marble temples. After Chicago won out over New York in a fierce rivalry to host the fair, Frederick Law Olmsted was hired to plan the grounds on a 700-acre site in Jackson Park. John Wellborn Root was selected the architect in charge of design; and his partner, Daniel H. Burnham, was to be chief of construction. Buildings of "high architectural importance" were to be designed by East Coast establishment architects, some of whom had been educated at the École des Beaux-Arts in Paris. These men included Richard Morris Hunt, third president and a founder of the AIA; Atwood; and the firm of McKim, Mead & White.

Root's sudden death in January 1891, however, left the architects free to agree among themselves that classical motifs would be stressed throughout. This choice not only secured the reputation of academically trained architects for decades to come but also ensured that classicism would become the standard dress for practically every city's major cultural, commercial, and municipal institutions virtually until the Depression. Burnham's role, as coordinator left totally in charge of the exposition, launched him as the nation's top city planner.

The Palace of Fine Arts was the greatest of Atwood's structures at the fair. It gained him such respect that he replaced Root as head designer in Burnham's office, where he completed the Reliance Building, a steel-and-glass marvel totally unlike the fair buildings. Deteriorating health led to Atwood's untimely death in 1895.

—Susan S. Benjamin

B Columbian Basin

This reflective pool, designed as part of the 1895 plan, replaced an informal pond but conveys the character of the fair's Court of Honor, which had been further south in the park. At the south end of the basin is the Clarence S. Darrow bridge, named for the lawyer who lived nearby and had his ashes scattered over the bridge into the lagoon.

C Music Court

Decorative lampposts are the only clue that this parking lot was once a Music Court, built to the 1895 plan.

D Wooded Island and Lagoon, Japanese Garden

A survivor of the 1893 Exposition, the island was the site of the Ho-o-den, a group of three Japanese pavilions that strongly impressed Frank Lloyd Wright with their inventive organization of space. In 1981 the gardens were restored and a new Japanese tea house built. The island is now a nature sanctuary, and its plantings of native midwestern foliage framed by the lagoon strongly evoke Olmsted's turn-of-the-century vision for the park.

E *The Republic*
1893, Daniel Chester French (cast 1918)
Restored 1992, Chicago Park District

The "Golden Lady" is, surprisingly, Jackson Park's only sculpture.

The Republic

It was cast from a plaster model of the original, which was almost three times as big and graced the eastern end of the fair's Court of Honor. Now located on the site of the fair's Administration Building, which terminated the western end of the Court of Honor, the statue symbolized the advanced state of civilization on the 400th anniversary of Columbus's landing.

F 64th St. Beach Pavilion
1919, South Park Commission

This enormous, classically inspired concrete bathhouse was modeled on the many buildings of this type designed by D. H. Burnham & Co. It included a covered promenade and an infirmary in addition to the lockers and showers.

G Former U.S. Coast Guard Station
1906, architect unknown
Restored 1992, Chicago Park District

This was commissioned by the federal government to serve the crowds of bathers and boaters flocking to the park. The shingled surfaces and roof terrace are like those of other, more remote Great Lakes Coast Guard stations.

H Hayes Dr. and Coast Guard Dr. Bridges

These are two of the four rusticated stone bridges erected in Jackson Park around 1904, when walkways, boulevards, meadows, and other landscape features were being completed. Part of the 1895 plan, the bridges are decorated with figures and reptiles meant to evoke the theme of wind and water.

I La Rabida Children's Hospital & Research Center
65th St. and Lake Michigan
1931, Graham, Anderson, Probst & White; Additions 1952–1959, Friedman, Alschuler & Sincere, and Pace Assocs.; Addition 1992, VOA Assocs.

The name comes from the Spanish pavilion at the 1893 exposition, which replicated the convent where Columbus awaited Queen Isabella's decision about his voyage to the New World. Converted to a children's hospital, it was later replaced by the present structure.

University of Chicago Campus

Because campus buildings are organized around landscaped quadrangles with little or no automobile access, the campus is best seen on foot. This walking tour begins at the southwest quadrangle of the central campus, where the earliest buildings are located.

4 University of Chicago Quadrangles
Bounded by Ellis and University Aves. and E. 57th and E. 59th (Midway Plaisance) Sts.
1891–1930
Plan and buildings to 1900: Henry Ives Cobb
Landscape design: Olmsted Bros., Beatrix Farrand, and others

The Gothic quadrangles of the University of Chicago were built on land donated by or purchased from Marshall Field in 1890, the year of the university's charter. With three exceptions the site's thirty-four buildings employ various interpretations of the Gothic that are faithful to the spirit of the initial plan and to the trustees' dream

The University of Chicago Quadrangles

of a unified, organic, self-contained campus that would nurture and sustain the ideal of a great research university.

Henry Ives Cobb, creator of the Fisheries Building at the 1893 World's Columbian Exposition, as well as structures for the Chicago Historical Society and the Newberry Library, designed the original scheme and its early modifications. It consists today of six broken quadrangles, three on the north side, three on the south, paralleling a larger, less defined central rectangle that runs between University and Ellis avenues. (Other academic buildings and complexes, many also wearing Gothic dress, are on adjacent streets.) Most of the structures built during the university's first ten years were designed by Cobb, including complexes running along the west and east sides of the southern half of the quadrangles and in the center on the northern half. Cobb also designed the university's Yerkes Observatory in Wisconsin and its President's House on University Ave. He was succeeded as master designer in 1901 by Shepley, Rutan & Coolidge, whose more elegant and elaborate structures include the Hutchinson Court complex in the northeast corner and Harper Memorial Library to the south. Other contributors of variations of campus Gothic included Dwight H. Perkins, Charles Z. Klauder, and Coolidge & Hodgdon.

Adorned with carved references to history, ancient and modern, to classical mythology, Christianity and folklore, featuring lancet windows, hammer-beam ceilings, loggias, corbels, gargoyles, and all the other elements of the Gothic, the picturesquely assertive buildings define a symmetrical plan whose scale and clarity recall the Beaux Arts vision of the Columbian Exposition. The beauty of these structures has also been enhanced by the work of an important series of landscape designers.

Derided by modernists for their archaic conceits, the quadrangles survive as one of the country's most remarkable expressions of commitment to a scholarly or priestly dream, one containing great stylistic variety within the larger Gothic vocabulary. The forty years of construction now seem all of one piece, the only jarring elements projected by three structures put up after World War II. By then, fortunately, this central campus was almost complete, and modern designers could build only in surrounding areas.
—Neil Harris

5 Cobb Lecture Hall
5811–5827 S. Ellis Ave.
1892, Henry Ives Cobb

This was the university's first building, one of eighteen designed by Cobb during his tenure (1891–1901) as campus architect. Named for donor Silas B. Cobb (no relation to the architect), it established the Gothic style that would be adhered to for the next four decades—but with a chunky, robust character that hints at Cobb's attraction to the Romanesque (as do the red tile roofs). Cobb, in fact, had to be persuaded to adopt the Gothic instead of the Romanesque style of his Newberry Library. The trustees felt strongly that the ecclesiastical and educational associations of the Gothic made it more appropriate to a university than the Romanesque, which was then so popular for commercial structures. Despite his initial hesitancy, Cobb executed a masterful rendition of the Gothic style, with gables and dormers piercing steeply pitched roofs and crowned with vigorous crockets. Oriels, bays, and pavillion-like projections break the wall planes and give a suitably medieval impression of picturesque irregularity despite the buildings' essential symmetry.

The fourth floor contains the Bergman Gallery, where for many decades the Renaissance Society has exhibited important modern art.

6 Blake, Gates, and Goodspeed Halls (Graduate, Middle Divinity, and South Divinity Halls)
5845 S. Ellis Ave.
1892, Henry Ives Cobb

Originally dormitories for fifty men each, they contained suites of two bedrooms on either side of a study. They continue the style of Cobb Hall, with an extra story added to Gates Hall to break up the roofline. A former reading room is now a recital hall and features its original windows and wood-trussed ceiling.

7 Classics Building
1010 E. 59th St.
1915, Shepley, Rutan & Coolidge

After the initial flurry of the 1890s, campus construction was heavily concentrated within three periods: 1901–1904 (see the Tower Group), 1912–1916, and 1926–1932. The second of these building booms, heralded by the long-awaited completion of Harper Memorial Library, was a period of increasing attention to architectural symbolism. No longer content with crockets and gargoyles, the university requested carved ornament indicative of activities inside the buildings, in an obsession that would culminate a decade later. The Classics Building is ornamented on the south with the heads of Homer, Cicero, Socrates, and Plato; characters from Aesop's fables; and depictions of the labors of Hercules.

8 William Wieboldt Hall
1050 E. 59th St.
1928, Coolidge & Hodgdon

Dating from the last efflorescence of campus Gothic, Wieboldt is similar to its earlier neighbor, the Classics Building. The west wall of the archway linking them has embedded in it a stone from the old University of Chicago, which went bankrupt in 1886. The authors represented on this building for the study of modern languages are Lessing, Goethe, Schiller, Ibsen, Dante, Molière, Hugo, Cervantes, Chaucer, Shakespeare, Milton, and Emerson.

9 Frederick Haskell Hall (Haskell Oriental Museum)
5836–5846 S. Greenwood Ave.
1896, Henry Ives Cobb

The building's original purpose as a museum is signaled by the unusual roof, which had skylights to illuminate the galleries. The university's collection of ancient Near Eastern art and artifacts was displayed here until the completion of the Oriental Institute in 1931. Note the trilingual cornerstone, with inscriptions in Hebrew, Latin, and Greek.

10 Swift Hall
1025–1035 E. 58th St.
1926, Coolidge & Hodgdon

Its central campus location, planned long before construction or even design of the buildings began, was meant to symbolize the centrality of religious belief to all fields of study at the university. The richly decorated interior includes a carved, hammer-beam ceiling in a third-floor lecture hall, which was a reading room for the Divinity School library.

ⅠⅠ Joseph Bond Chapel
1926, Coolidge & Hodgdon

The intimate interior is a jewel; if it is dark, look for light switches to the left of the front door. Appropriately connected to Swift Hall by a cloister, this small and beautifully ornamented chapel narrates a wide range of Christian doctrine on the exterior as well as interior. Adam and Eve flank a window on the west, while angelic and devilish figures play tag across the roofline and cornices. An orchestra of angels plays above a pierced inscription of the Beatitudes that scrolls across the walls. The designers (including Charles J. Connick, whose Boston firm executed the windows) had expert iconographical guidance from the Divinity School faculty, especially Edgar J. Goodspeed, chairman of the Department of New Testament and Early Christian Literature.

ⅠⅡ William Rainey Harper Memorial Library
1116 E. 59th St.
1912, Shepley, Rutan & Coolidge
Renovated 1972, Metz, Train, Olson & Youngren

Punctuating the skyline with two massive towers, this library formed the first important component in the southern wall of buildings oriented toward the Midway. Its location resulted from a comprehensive campus plan formulated in 1902 that called for concentrating the humanities and social sciences buildings in the southern part of the quadrangles, which would henceforth be academic and not residential. As other buildings in the plan were completed (the last one in 1929), second-story

Harper Memorial Library

bridges linked the library to reading rooms and departmental libraries in Haskell and Stuart halls. Visit the third-floor reading room, a grand space marked on the exterior by the long row of arched, double-height windows. Look for the university's coat of arms, devised during this time so that it could be included in the room's iconography along with those of other distinguished institutions. Cross the bridge into another reading room, modernized but retaining an elaborate ceiling, that is actually part of Stuart Hall.

ⅠⅢ Harold Leonard Stuart Hall (Law School)
5835 S. Greenwood Ave.
1904, Shepley, Rutan & Coolidge

The building is carved with figures of kings and magistrates (pre-democratic dispensers of justice) and features Moses and the Ten Commandments atop the roof.

ⅠⅣ Julius Rosenwald Hall
1101–1111 E. 58th St.
1915, Holabird & Roche
Renovated 1972, Samuel A. Lichtmann

The shield next to the door proclaims "Dig and Discover." Better yet, look up and discover; take out your binoculars and telephoto lens to capture all the beasts on this building. This was the home of the geology and geography departments, and the carvings reflect the interests of these disciplines and honor the donor, Sears, Roebuck magnate Julius Rosenwald, with a frieze of

Rosenwald Hall

roses around the entrance. The octagonal tower originally held meteorological instruments, and its gargoyles represent the four winds and four birds of the air. The square tower has four symbols of continents, with the buffalo, bull, elephant, and lion representing North America, Europe, Asia, and Africa.

⓯ George C. Walker Museum
1115–1125 E. 58th St.
1893, Henry Ives Cobb
Renovated 1980, Nagle, Hartray & Assocs.

Cobb designed this to be a natural history museum, pushing the stair tower out the south wall to allow space in the exhibition hall for prehistoric skeletons. It was used instead for desperately needed classrooms, laboratories, and offices; the prehistoric collection was eventually given to the Field Museum of Natural History. When the Graduate School of Business moved into the building, they took advantage of the generous ceiling heights to squeeze five floors of space into the three-story structure.

⓰ Social Science Research Building
1126 E. 59th St.
1929, Coolidge & Hodgdon

When this building completed the south wall of buildings in 1929, it represented the fulfillment of the 1902 plan for the original campus quadrangles. It was designed to bring together the departments of history, sociology, economics, and political science in order to foster the in-

terdisciplinary study of society. The elaborate program of ornament, which by this era of campus design was less concerned with historicism than with representational imagery, includes measuring devices such as calculators and calipers.

⓱ Beecher, Green, and Kelly Halls
5848 S. University Ave.
1893 and 1899 (Green Hall), Henry Ives Cobb
⓲ Foster Hall
1130 E. 59th St.
1893, Henry Ives Cobb

Coeducational since its founding, the university provided women's dormitories on the southeastern edge of the main quadrangle, mirroring the original four buildings to the west. Green Hall, which was completed later for financial reasons, is a story higher than its neighbors, just as Gates Hall stands out on the opposite side. Cobb emphasized the prominent Midway corner of Foster Hall with a profusion of crockets and gargoyles on the corner turret. Marion Talbot, dean of women from 1892 to 1925, influenced Cobb's plans for the so-called Women's Quadrangle. She recommended four smaller buildings rather than one large one, and single rooms rather than the two-bedroom-and-study arrangement used for the men. She also assured that there would be parlors and dining rooms for socializing; the men's dormitories had woefully inadequate public spaces.

⓳ Albert Pick Hall for International Studies
5820 S. University Ave.
1971, Ralph Rapson & Assocs.; Burnham & Hammond; J. Lee Jones

A modern attempt to evoke the Gothic tradition, this limestone building shares the materials, vertical proportions, and irregular profile of its earlier neighbors. Unfortunately, the prominent caulk lines make it look like a suit with the tailor's chalk marks still showing.

⁒ Administration Building
5801 S. Ellis Ave.
1948, Holabird & Root & Burgee

Cobb originally envisioned a library and "university hall" for this prominent site, and later plans called for a Gothic administration building. When final planning for this building began in earnest in 1945, the Gothic style was not considered aesthetically or economically appropriate, and so this utilitarian structure was erected. Truly a wallflower, it modestly directs attention to its more elaborate neighbors.

⁒ Bernard Albert Eckhart Hall
1118–1132 E. 58th St.
1930, Charles Z. Klauder

A late Gothic addition to the main quad, Eckhart Hall offers further proof of the style's power to unify the work of different architects. Klauder was nationally known for his Collegiate Gothic buildings at Princeton, the University of Pennsylvania, and the University of Pittsburgh. During the 1926–1932 campus construction boom, each building design was assisted by a faculty committee on symbolism. The ornament of this building related to the physics, astronomy, and mathematics departments housed within.

⁒ Ryerson Physical Laboratory
1110–1114 E. 58th St.
1894, Henry Ives Cobb
North Annex 1913, Shepley, Rutan & Coolidge

⁒ Kent Chemical Laboratory
1020–1024 E. 58th St.
1894, Henry Ives Cobb

This pair of ornate science buildings had complex interior requirements that combined with the lavishness of architectural ornament to drive the cost way over budget. Inside is a bronze relief of the donor, Sidney A. Kent, designed by Lorado Taft. The octagonal Kent Theatre to the north was the university's assembly hall until the completion in 1903 of Mandel Hall.

⁒ George Herbert Jones Laboratory
5747 S. Ellis Ave.
1929, Coolidge & Hodgdon

Room 405 is a National Historic Landmark, because it was where plutonium, the first man-made element, was first isolated and weighed.

⁒ Hull Court & Biological Laboratories
1025–1103 E. 57th St.
1897, Henry Ives Cobb

Entered from the south through the wrought-iron Hull Gate, this courtyard contains four laboratory buildings (anatomy, botany, physiology, and zoology) designed as a group in a simpler and less costly style than Kent and Ryerson laboratories. Joined by loggias and arcades, the buildings surround but do not actually face Hull Court and Botany Pond, both planned by landscape architect John C. Olmsted, as was the nearby Hutchinson Court.

⁒ Charles Hitchcock Hall
1009 E. 57th St.
1902, Dwight H. Perkins

Here is the university's most original interpretation of the Gothic style prior to World War II. Perkins's application of Prairie School principles can be seen in the low pitched roof, low dormers, and generally horizontal character of the building. The ornament was also a departure, with geometric stained-glass windows and corncobs and other prairie vegetation substituting for abstracted English flora. Perkins was a family friend of the donor, Mrs. Charles Hitchcock, and was one of the few outside architects brought in to design a campus building.

⁒ Snell Hall
5709 S. Ellis Ave.
1893, Henry Ives Cobb

The only undergraduate dormitory for men until 1901, Snell is one of just two central-campus residence halls still used as such.

28 Searle Chemistry Laboratory
5735 S. Ellis Ave.
1967, Smith, Smith, Haines, Lundberg & Waehler

Elements that relate to the existing campus include limestone, window and spandrel size, and building height.

Cobb Gate

29 Cobb Gate
South side of E. 57th St. between Ellis and University Aves.
1900, Henry Ives Cobb

After budgetary constraints had curbed his use of ornament on campus buildings, Cobb let his decorative impulses run wild on this fanciful ornamental gate, which he donated to the university. It ended up being his swan song, as he was replaced as campus architect the following year. The trustees felt that his attention was being diverted by efforts to build a national practice out of his newly opened office in Washington, D.C. Ironically, the successor firm of Shepley, Rutan & Coolidge was based in Boston.

Hutchinson Court and the Tower Group:
30 John J. Mitchell Tower, Charles L. Hutchinson Hall, Joseph Reynolds Student Clubhouse
31 Leon Mandel Assembly Hall
Southwest corner of E. 57th St. and University Ave.
1903, Shepley, Rutan & Coolidge Mandel Hall renovation 1981, Skidmore, Owings & Merrill with the Office of John Vinci

Shepley, Rutan & Coolidge made a significant campus debut with this monumental group of buildings, which anchors the northeast corner of the main quadrangle. It marks an increasing emphasis on historicism, including an effort to make the interiors correspond with the style of the facades. SRC's buildings generally have more elaborate wall planes than Cobb's, with arched and traceried windows. The rooflines, however, are simpler, with rows

Hutchinson Hall

of crenellations replacing the profusion of gables and dormers.

Seeking early on to associate their fledgling institution with significant historic European (especially English) universities, donor Charles L. Hutchinson and architect Charles A. Coolidge traveled to Oxford to study its collegiate architectural tradition. The design of Mitchell Tower, the first purely ornamental building on campus, was derived from the bell tower of Magdalen College. The ten Palmer chimes, named for the first dean of women, Alice Freeman Palmer (see the Daniel Chester French plaque in the lobby), are still used for change ringing, a traditional English style of play that some find cacophonous. Originally a men's dining hall, Hutchinson Commons was modeled after Oxford's Christ Church Hall. Enjoy a modestly priced meal in the grand dining room, remarkable for the hammer-beam ceiling and the many oil portraits of trustees and benefactors, including John D. Rockefeller and Martin Ryerson.

Reynolds Club was derived from St. John's College at Oxford, and its domestic feeling is enhanced by a stair hall that could have come straight out of an English manor house.

32 Quadrangle Club
1155 E. 57th St.
1922, Howard Van Doren Shaw

Shaw deliberately designed this faculty club in red brick with a multicolored slate roof to contrast with the surrounding gray limestone buildings.

33 Chicago Theological Seminary
5757 S. University Ave.
1926, Riddle & Riddle

Two wings are connected by a second-story arched corridor that spans the alley. The east wing contains residential quarters; the west wing houses two chapels, a library, and classrooms. Step inside to bask in the cloistered ambiance, and visit the Hilton Memorial Chapel, a tiny gem built a few years before the rest of the complex was constructed.

The Chicago newspaper publisher Victor F. Lawson financed the tower that bears his name.

34 Oriental Institute
1155 E. 58th St.
1931, Mayers, Murray & Phillip

This building was designed by the successor firm to Bertram Grosvenor Goodhue Assocs. (architects of Rockefeller Memorial Chapel) with an Art Deco simplicity that tempers the Gothic gables, bays, and buttresses. Egyptologist James H. Breasted, director of the institute from 1919 to 1935, designed the symbolic bas-relief over the north entrance. It illustrates elements of civilization from the ancient Near East and the Western World, including the Sphinx and architect Goodhue's Nebraska State Capitol.

35 University President's House
5855 S. University Ave.
1895, Henry Ives Cobb

The pale Roman brick, less expensive than limestone, blends with the surrounding buildings, as does the peaked tile roof with dormers. Many alterations have been made over the years.

36 Rockefeller Memorial Chapel (University Chapel)
1156–1180 E. 59th St.
1925–1928, Bertram Grosvenor Goodhue Assocs.

Towering over the Midway, this massive limestone church of load-bearing masonry employs traditional Gothic structural devices of arches and buttresses. Goodhue was a nationally famous proponent of the Gothic Revival and the Arts & Crafts movements, and this design is his interpretation of Modern Gothic. The university administration was heavily involved in the design process, and its president, Ernest DeWitt Burton, toured famous English cathedrals to satisfy himself that the design was appropriate. The greatest departure from medieval Gothic is in the proportions, with unusually wide bays and tall clerestory windows over low side aisles, and in the abundance of smooth, flat surfaces. Lee Lawrie designed the facade sculpture up to 30 feet from the ground; Ulric H. Ellerhusen was responsible for the higher designs. The interior has a cool, restful palette (except for some unfortunate brightly colored modern windows) and an unusual example of Guastavino tile vaulting, a technique in which the tile is actually structural rather than merely ornamental. The sculpture includes religious as well as allegorical and historical figures, along with coats of arms and inscriptions. A statue of Goodhue on the east transept wall personifies architecture (opposite him is Bach representing music), with Rockefeller Chapel in his hands and West Point Chapel behind him.

Lavishly decorated in a domestic Tudor Revival style, it was designed to offer women the kind of social and recreational facilities provided to men in the Tower Group buildings. It became a general student center in 1955, when women were no longer excluded from those premises. The lounge, library, and Cloister Club contain rich ornament and fixtures. Climb the elaborately carved staircase to see a third-floor student theater with an early mural by Jessie Arms Botke, *The Masque of Youth,* depicting a performance given at the building's dedication.

Noyes Hall

38 International House
1414 E. 59th St.
1932, Holabird & Root

With the completion of this building and the Henry Crown Field House, Holabird & Root ended the first era of Collegiate Gothic with a stripped-down, Art Deco interpretation. Campus building would not resume for over fifteen years—and then in a strictly utilitarian style. "I-House" rises elegantly on its long, shallow site and has an attractively landscaped interior courtyard.

39 Woodward Court
5825 S. Woodlawn Ave.
1958, Eero Saarinen; J. Lee Jones

In the mid-1950s the university was once again sufficiently confident of expansion to hire Saarinen to devise a new master plan for the campus. This was his first built project, a women's residence hall and dining commons.

Statue of Goodhue in Rockefeller Chapel

37 Ida Noyes Hall
1212 E. 59th St.
1916, Shepley, Rutan & Coolidge
Max Palevsky Cinema *1986,
Vickrey, Ovresat, Awsumb Assocs.*

Robie House

⑩ Frederick C. Robie House
5757 S. Woodlawn Ave.
1906–1909, Frank Lloyd Wright

This house, which Frank Lloyd Wright designed in 1906 for a bicycle and motorcycle manufacturer, is one of the world's most famous buildings. Magnificently poised, like a great steamship at anchor, it is the distilled essence of Wright's Prairie School style and the culmination of his search for a new architecture. It is also among the last of his Prairie houses; during construction Wright abandoned both his Oak Park practice and his family to embark on a new phase of his long career.

The Robie House faces west and south on a lot measuring 60 by 180 feet. Its basic form consists of two parallel, rectangular two-story masses at the meeting of which rises a smaller, square third story. The massive chimney effectively anchors these separate parts. The main living quarters occupy the second floor, with three bedrooms above. There is no basement. The exterior formulation of base, wall, and cornice, common to all of Wright's Prairie houses, is repeated in every part of the elevations. Here it is expressed by thin, long Roman bricks and limestone trim. Floors and balconies are reinforced concrete, while the great overhangs are made possible by numerous concealed steel girders, some as long as sixty feet.

Space is defined not by walls, in the conventional sense, but by a series of horizontal planes intercepted by

Robie House Living Room

vertical wall fragments and rectangular piers. These horizontals extend far beyond the enclosures, defining exterior space as well and echoing the flat midwestern landscape that so inspired the architect. The chief embellishments are the exquisite leaded- and stained-glass doors and windows, which not only provide accents of color and ornament but also screen interior from exterior space while preserving the unity between outside and inside.

The Robie House's calculated asymmetry, irregular form, and striking silhouette excite our curiosity and invite us to explore its carefully arranged sequences of spaces. This Picturesque manner of composition can ultimately be traced to the freely experimental buildings of the Shingle Style that Wright had learned in the 1880s from his first significant employer, Joseph L. Silsbee. The beautiful abstraction of the building's surfaces, clean geometry of form, and personal manner of decoration—its emphatic style—as well as the strong central axis that orders its raised living and dining rooms, are the legacy of Wright's "Lieber Meister," Louis H. Sullivan. Only by uniting these seemingly opposing traditions was Wright able to create a personal modern style in 1900 and give it its perfect expression six years later in the Robie House.
—Paul Kruty

41 Frank Dickinson Bartlett Gymnasium
5640 S. University Ave.
1904, Shepley, Rutan & Coolidge

Go to the second floor to see the romantic medieval-style mural and stained-glass window, which features a scene from *Ivanhoe*. The gym was donated by university trustee and hardware merchant Adolphus C. Bartlett in memory of his son. The mural was painted by another son, Frederic Clay, who also executed designs in the Tower Group. The first Heisman Trophy for outstanding college football players was awarded in 1935 to University of Chicago halfback Jay Berwanger and is exhibited in the trophy room that bears his name.

42 Joseph Regenstein Library
1100 E. 57th St.
1970, Skidmore, Owings & Merrill

Walter A. Netsch, Jr. brought the concrete brutalism of his University of Illinois at Chicago to this traditional campus, where it landed with a thud on the site of Stagg Field. The irregular massing and profile, slit windows, and vertically grooved facade are meant to allude to the surrounding Gothic buildings but are more a product of Netsch's own idiosyncratic design concepts. Fortunately, two of the seven floors are underground.

43 Henry Crown Field House (Field House)
5550 S. University Ave.
1932, Holabird & Root

Designed and redesigned over a five-year period, the building reflects the lines of its Gothic predecessors only in the vestigial buttresses and tall, arched windows. Earlier, more elaborate designs had proved too costly, and the winds of modernism had penetrated even the ivy walls of this august institution.

44 Stanley R. Pierce Hall
5514 S. University Ave.
1960, Harry Weese & Assocs.

Heralded by *Architectural Record* as a "Major Break-through on the Anti-Slab Front," this complex was designed by Weese at about the same time as the Hyde Park Redevelopment Project. In the unique interior configuration, groups of student rooms surround two-story interior lounges. The two-story pavil-

Kersten Physics Teaching Center

ion contains dining and lounge facilities and was intended to link the tower to a nearby twin, never built.

45 Cochrane–Woods Art Center
5550 S. Greenwood Ave.
1974, Edward Larrabee Barnes
46 Court Theatre
5535 S. Ellis Ave.
1981, Harry Weese & Assocs.

Planned as the nucleus of a never-completed Arts Quadrangle, Barnes's simple limestone buildings house the Art Department and the Smart Gallery of Art. They enclose the Vera and A. D. Elden Sculpture Garden, which includes a reclining figure by Henry Moore.

47 *Nuclear Energy*
East side of Ellis Ave. between E. 56th & 57th Sts.
1967, Henry Moore

Intended to suggest a human skull and a mushroom cloud, this abstract bronze form commemorates the moment on December 2, 1942, when Enrico Fermi and his colleagues created the first self-sustaining, controlled nuclear chain reaction. This initiation into the atomic age took place in a squash court under the bleachers of the now-demolished Stagg Field, site of the Regenstein Library.

The Science Quadrangle is the newest campus quad and features several modern interpretations of the Gothic style.

48 Samuel Kersten, Jr., Physics Teaching Center
5720 S. Ellis Ave.
1985, Holabird & Root; Harold H. Hellman, university arch.

The Ellis Ave. facade presents the most subtle and distinguished modern contribution to the Collegiate Gothic tradition on this campus. The Science Quadrangle facade reflects the brash modernity of its neighbors with a glass curtain wall that steps back to form a series of terraces. From a narrow stair hall, designer Gerald Horn forged a dynamic atrium, a pedestrian highway that shoots across 57th St. to the physicists' offices and research facilities.

49 Henry Hinds Laboratory for the Geophysical Sciences
5734 S. Ellis Ave.
1969, I. W. Colburn & Assocs.; J. Lee Jones

Colburn was a consulting architect to the university from 1964 to 1973, and his quirky, expressionistic Esperanto Gothic style dominates the Science Quadrangle. Bay windows and an irregular, sculptural facade loom above surrounding buildings.

50 John Crerar Library
5730 S. Ellis Ave.
1984, Hugh Stubbins Assocs.; Loebl, Schlossman & Hackl, assoc. arch.

The use of limestone, the window proportions, and the emphasis on the entry attempt to relate to the Gothic; while the projecting third floor provides cover, as in Gothic arcades and loggias.

51 Cummings Life Science Center
920 E. 58th St.
1973, I. W. Colburn & Assocs.;
Schmidt, Garden & Erikson

The tallest building on campus has forty red brick towers—exhaust ducts aspiring to be medieval chimney stacks.

52 Ingleside Hall (Quadrangle Club)
956–960 E. 58th St.
1896, Charles B. Atwood

Moved here in 1929 from its original location on the site of the Oriental Institute, the vaguely neo-Classical building is the only one designed for the campus in the 1890s by an architect other than Cobb.

53 University Bookstore (University Press Building)
5750 S. Ellis Ave.
1902, Shepley, Rutan & Coolidge

Another red brick building in a sea of gray, this one sports a variety of gabled forms. The unusually open first-floor facade has rows of tall arched windows.

A few of the university's buildings are located on E. 60th St., south of the Midway, and are easily seen by car. Those exploring on foot are advised not to wander to the south, where the neighborhood becomes distinctly uncollegiate.

54 Midway Studios
6016 S. Ingleside Ave.
1906, Pond & Pond
1929, Otis F. Johnson
Painting studio 1965, Loebl,
Schlossman, Bennett & Dart

Sculptor Lorado Taft and a group of fellow artists lived and worked in this cluster of studios and living quarters, which expanded gradually from the original converted carriage house. This is where Taft created *The Fountain of Time,* located at the west end of the Midway, and *The Fountain of the Great Lakes,* outside the Art Institute. The setting now provides studio and gallery space for the university's studio art program.

55 School of Social Service Administration
969 E. 60th St.
1965, Ludwig Mies van der Rohe

The purest example of modernism on campus was designed by the master himself. Inside the black steel and glass box is a large lobby that is an exercise in Miesian "universal space"—rather like his U.S. Post Office in the Loop.

56 Burton–Judson Courts
1005 E. 60th St.
1931, Zantzinger, Borie & Medary

The university jumped the Midway in constructing this pair of dormitories. Plans formulated in the 1920s called for the creation of a self-contained undergraduate campus south of the Midway, but they were scrapped in favor

School of Social Service Administration

of continued northward expansion. This remains the plan's only built component. The small landscaped quadrangles are worth a peek.

57 Laird Bell Law Quadrangle
1111 E. 60th St.
1959, Eero Saarinen & Assocs.

This complex is Saarinen's most significant contribution to the campus that resulted from his 1950s master plan. Following the tradition of clustering buildings of similar disciplines around a central court, Saarinen designed a group of four buildings (Constitution Hall, a classroom building, the law library, and the administration building) around a reflecting pool and fountain. Saarinen was quoted in *Architectural Record* in November 1960 that "By stressing a small, broken scale, a lively silhouette, and especially verticality in the library design, we intended to make it a good neighbor with the neo-Gothic dormitories." The bronze sculpture, *Construction in Space in the 3rd and 4th Dimension,* was designed for this space by Antoine Pevsner, a Russian-born sculptor who worked in the cubist and constructivist styles.

Rosalie Villas

The 5700 and 5800 blocks of S. Harper Ave. (originally called Rosalie Ct.) contain many of the houses built as part of Rosalie Villas, the area's first planned community. Rosalie Buckingham bought this land in 1883 and subdivided it into lots for forty-two freestanding houses. She hired Solon S. Beman, fresh from his planning of Pullman, to supervise the design and construction of the houses and of the commercial buildings planned for the corner of 57th St. At that time the Illinois Central Railroad's tracks ran at grade, giving the houses on the east side of the street views of open land and the lake beyond. By the end of the decade, several of the lots had been subdivided for smaller frontages, and an apartment building anchored 57th St., giving the development a less rural character than originally planned. The houses are currently in various states of repair, ranging from pristine to tumbledown.

58 5832–5834 S. Harper Ave.
1884, Solon S. Beman

Beman himself was one of the first to create an exception to the detached-residence rule when he designed this double house for John A. Jackman, Jr. It is composed as a unified facade, however, with a shared chimney creating a focal point at ground level with a large terra-cotta panel. A manager at the Pullman Co., Jackman also commissioned Beman to design the house at 5824.

59 William Waterman House
5810 S. Harper Ave.
1884, Henry F. Starbuck

One of the few brick houses in this clapboard and shingle enclave, it has an especially fine terra-cotta cornice and the rotated corner bay frequently seen in Stick Style homes.

60 5809 S. Harper Ave.
1888, E. Clarke Johnson

This Queen Anne town house was turned on its side to fit an unusual site: broad and shallow rather than long and narrow.

61 5759 S. Harper Ave.
1884, Solon S. Beman

The details of this frame Queen Anne, especially on the well preserved porch, are typically robust, showing an emphasis on cutouts and screens.

62 Charles Bonner House
5752 S. Harper Ave.
1889, William W. Boyington

This greatly altered frame house offers tantalizing glimpses of original details like the inset second-floor balcony.

63 Ernest W. Heath House
5744 S. Harper
1886, W. Irving Beman

This greatly altered house is difficult to piece together. W. Irving Beman was Solon's brother and worked in the Pullman architectural offices.

64 5719 through 5745 S. Harper Ave.
1888, Robert Rae, Jr.

Their similarity is obscured by varying states of integrity and upkeep. The three southernmost houses (5739–5745) are from 1888, which seems a likely date for the others as well. They all offer noteworthy examples of the vigorous punched ornament popular on late nineteenth-century frame houses. Unfortunately, it is often removed or replaced by spidery 1980s mass-produced spindle work.

Armour House

65 M. Cochran Armour House
5736 S. Harper Ave.
pre-1888, architect unknown

Then as now, this is one of the most lavish houses on the block. The exuberant forms include a

two-story elliptical bay, curved corner windows, and inset balconies. Fish-scale shingles, carved plaques, and half-timbering provide a potpourri of textures.

66 Hyde Park Historical Society (Chicago Street Railway Co. Station)
5529 S. Lake Park Ave.
1893, architect unknown
Renovated 1981, John Vinci

This small station once served passengers at the southern terminus of a cable car line, completed in anticipation of the 1893 World's Columbian Exposition. When the Illinois Central trains were elevated in the late 1920s, this building was tucked into their embankment.

University National Bank

67 University National Bank (Ritz 55th Garage)
1354 E. 55th St.
1929, M. Louis Kroman

This is an Art Deco paean to the glamour of the roadster. The terra-cotta facade cruises from one automotive image to the next: engines, stoplights, tires, gearshifts—and of course a flivver itself, with jauntily clad driver. The first floor, now altered, once included a chauffeur's lounge.

68 Hyde Park Redevelopment Project
From 53rd to 57th Sts., west of the Illinois Central Railroad
1957–1959, I. M. Pei; Harry Weese & Assocs.; Barton Aschman, civil & landscaping consultant

69 University Apartments
1400 & 1450 W. 55th St.
1961, I. M. Pei and Loewenberg & Loewenberg

The lush gardens and well-kept public spaces that mark the Hyde Park Redevelop-

Hyde Park Redevelopment Project Townhouses

ment Project testify to the continuing success of a pioneering effort to combat middle-class flight from this distinguished Chicago neighborhood. They belie, however, the controversy that surrounded the project in the mid-1950s. Flight to the newly burgeoning suburbs was in full force, and the University of Chicago was threatened by the increasing decay of the once substantial neighborhood that surrounded it. In 1957 a large area of blighted buildings was torn down; they were replaced by some 150 two- and three-story town houses and two ten-story apartment buildings. The project was financed by a combination of federal, city, and private monies and was strongly backed by the university.

This effort was different from other 1950s urban renewal schemes, which cut great swaths in the existing city fabric that seldom were artfully replaced. Such projects were often like ocean liners moored in the middle of the city—separate, apart, and a world unto themselves, with little direct relationship to surrounding street patterns or building types. Here in Hyde Park great care was taken to relate the new construction to the existing neighborhood, which comprised a mixture of single-family homes from the 1880s and small pre–World War I apartment buildings.

The project was guided by an overriding concern to preserve the urban neighborhood spirit. The master plan emphasized low buildings in

University Apartments

order to provide the strong relationship to the street characteristic of healthy and safe neighborhoods. Parklike public spaces were created, and town houses were built around inner squares. These are now filled with greenery and animated by playgrounds and basketball courts. The inclusion of a shopping center recognized that traditional neighborhoods have necessary goods and services close at hand.

Probably the most radical urban planning move was placing the mid-rise University Apartments in the middle of 55th St. and splitting traffic lanes on either side, thereby creating an island to discourage high-speed traffic. This was directly inspired by planning principles of the Modern movement as espoused by Le Corbusier in *La Ville Radieuse* (1935). The island has not had its intended effect; traffic speeds up on the split street, and pedestrians are discouraged from crossing.

Within the strong traditional forms of the overall plan, the architecture asserts a modernist design ethic. University Apartments saw the early use of fiberglass forms for poured-in-place concrete as well as a convenience unique at the time, a closed-circuit television entry system.

The two- and three-story town houses scattered throughout the area were the work of the New York office of I. M. Pei and the Chicago firm of Harry Weese & Assocs. Town houses had not been constructed in Chicago since the early 1900s and were a new element in this neighborhood. Pale brick sets them apart from their predominantly red-brick antecedents. Inspired by eighteenth-century English town house rows, or "terraces," Pei and Weese reinterpreted Georgian regularity and harmony. The strong horizontals of ground-floor recesses and third-floor clerestories unify the rows, while evenly placed door and window elements maintain symmetry throughout the project.

This project not only succeeded in combating middle-class flight but also spurred private renovation in the surrounding area. In addition, the town house form reintroduced here has been used in smaller infill sites throughout the city. The Hyde Park Redevelopment Project is notable as an outstanding example in Chicago of rebuilding a large urban area without creating a "project."
—Cynthia and Catharine Weese

70 William H. Hoyt House
5704 S. Dorchester Ave.
1869, architect unknown
71 Charles H. Botsford House
5714 S. Dorchester Ave.
1860, architect unknown

These Italianates are the granddaddies of the block, dating from the settlement of this area. Their form is typical of the suburban or country villa of the period, with symmetrical facades, tall, narrow windows, and bracketed cornices. The cupola (originally larger) of the Botsford House once provided a view of the

lake and aided in ventilation by drawing hot air up the central stairwell.

72 Chicago Theological Seminary Faculty Quadrangle
E. 58th St. and Dorchester Ave.
1963, Loebl, Schlossman, Bennett & Dart

This cluster of three- and four-bedroom units was designed by Edward D. Dart as rental faculty housing for the seminary. Set on diagonals at the perimeter of the lot, with heights varied to increase privacy, they surround a central common intended as a

Chicago Theological Seminary Faculty Quadrangle

children's play area. The village-like enclave recalls the work of Finnish architect Alvar Aalto.

73 5825 S. Blackstone Ave.
1909, Marshall & Fox

A building inspired by nineteenth-century Paris stands out among its Anglophile neighbors. This elegant four-flat has tall, narrow proportions (note the triple-sash windows), which had not been a prominent feature in this neighborhood since the Italianate boom of the 1860s and 1870s.

74 Helstein House
5806 S. Blackstone Ave.
1951, Bertrand Goldberg

Goldberg used his favored materials of concrete and glass to create an uncompromisingly modern house. The placement well back on the lot provides privacy despite the expanses of glass and avoids shocking its traditional neighbors.

75 5757–5759 S. Blackstone Ave.
1899, Nimmons & Fellows

This double house presents a handsome Chicago interpretation of the Louis XIII style, with a flattened front and slightly bowed bays.

76 James Westfall Thompson House
5747 S. Blackstone Ave.
1899, Pond & Pond

The diaper pattern of bricks on the top floor was a popular

motif in the 1890s among architects inspired by the Arts & Crafts movement, because the design was derived from the materials themselves rather than from applied color or ornament. Pond & Pond, who designed many settlement houses, probably used the motif more than anyone else.

77 5701 & 5707 S. Blackstone Ave.
1905, Carl M. Almquist

This pair of typical six-flats has fluted columns supporting porches on all levels. Leaded-glass windows and brick quoins increase the grandeur.

78 St. Stephen's Church of God in Christ (Tenth Church of Christ, Scientist)
5640 S. Blackstone Ave.
1919, Coolidge & Hodgdon

University of Chicago architects Coolidge & Hodgdon gave this church a Classical facade, in a break from their campus Gothic. The shallow inward curve of the street wall draws people in and then cuts off views of the neighboring buildings, maximizing the potential of the midblock site.

79 5621 & 5611 S. Blackstone Ave.
1886, Flanders & Zimmerman

These sharply contrasting buildings were built for the same client, architect William Carbys Zimmerman himself. 5621 is a classic example of the Shingle Style, while 5611 is almost proto-Prairie, with its deep-set door and its porch hollowed out of the building's mass and inset with square columns.

80 **5603–5615 S. Kenwood Ave. and 1357–1361 E. 56th St.**
1903, Mann, MacNeille & Lindeberg
81 **5558 S. Kimbark Ave. and 1220–1222, 1226, 1228, 1234 E. 56th St.**
1904, Mann, MacNeille & Lindeberg

Several groups of cooperative row houses were designed for university faculty by this New York firm. Charles Riborg Mann was a professor of physics at the university and probably referred colleagues to his brother's firm. The group is noteworthy for its intact tile roof and for the variety of window and door treatments.

82 **William H. Ray Public School** (Hyde Park High School)
5631 S. Kimbark Ave.
1893, John J. Flanders
Assembly Hall *1915, Arthur F. Hussander*
Classroom addition (north side)
1955, John C. Christensen

This highly decorated Queen Anne school is distinguished by Flanders's signature bands of ornament and full-height octagonal bays rising to an unusually lively roofline.

83 **5748, 5752, 5756 S. Kimbark Ave.**
1985, David Swan

This group of detached houses is only a few years older than Swan's mammoth Egandale project, but the uniformly bland colors and smooth surfaces couldn't be more different from the riot of color and texture of the later work. These stucco and brick houses are starkly modern and geometric, recalling Art Deco forms in their sweeping curves and metal railings.

Hillel Foundation

84 **Hillel Foundation** (Arthur J. Mason House)
5715 S. Woodlawn Ave.
1904, Howard Van Doren Shaw
85 **Edgar Johnson Goodspeed House**
5706 S. Woodlawn Ave.
1906, Howard Van Doren Shaw

Shaw's Hyde Park and Kenwood houses demonstrate his admiration for the English Arts & Crafts movement, which flourished in Chicago beginning in the 1890s. Shaw had great respect for materials and craftsmanship and a deep appreciation of English vernacular residential architecture as well as classical and historical forms. At 5715 the treatment of the elaborate door surround and the inventive ornamentation on the pilaster capitals exemplify his freedom with the classical vocabulary.

86 **First Unitarian Church of Chicago**
5650 S. Woodlawn Ave.
1931, Denison B. Hull

This textbook example of English Perpendicular Gothic design fits in easily with the limestone facades and Gothic ornament of many Hyde Park residences and campus buildings. It was built around the Hull Memorial Chapel (1897, William A. Otis), which is now the south transept.

87 **Herbert Hugh Riddle House**
5626 S. Woodlawn Ave.
88 **Lewis W. Riddle House**
5622 S. Woodlawn Ave.
1912, Riddle & Riddle

Built for brothers who practiced architecture together, these houses share the same massing and push the entrance to one side, so that the street facade has only windows. Lewis's house is a sober Georgian composition, while Herbert's has a distinctly French flair. Don't miss the metal-and-glass entrance canopy, reminiscent of Hector Guimard's Art Nouveau design for a Paris Métro entrance.

89 Hyde Park Union Church
(Hyde Park Baptist Church)
5600 S. Woodlawn Ave.
1906, James Gamble Rogers

The congregation of this church was closely associated with founders of the University of Chicago, and its construction was financed largely by John D. Rockefeller. The massive orange sandstone facade on Woodlawn Ave. is anchored by square entry towers marked by round arches. The round-arch motif is repeated on the interior, which also has beautiful stained-glass windows by Louis C. Tiffany of New York and Charles J. Connick Studios of Boston.

90 Theodore F. Rice House
5554 S. Woodlawn Ave.
1892, Mifflin E. Bell

One of the neighborhood's best-preserved Queen Anne houses is distinguished by a wonderful color palette: the brownstone base harmonizes with the dark pink and gray tiles above.

91 United Campus Christian Ministry (University Church of the Disciples of Christ)
5655 S. University Ave.
1921, Howard Van Doren Shaw

This austere Gothic church is almost primitive. An unusual feature of its spare but lovely interior is the fireplace at the back of the west aisle.

92 5551 S. University Ave.
1937, George Fred Keck & William Keck

Here is timeless, first-generation modernism from the firm that had gained fame (but few commissions) for their futuristic House of Tomorrow at Chi-

5551 S. University Ave.

cago's 1933 Century of Progress Exposition. A three-flat, it is unrelated to any of its predecessors. The innovative louvers make curtains unnecessary and conserve energy. Even the garage doors are building blocks for the facade's simple geometry.

93 Lutheran School of Theology
1100 E. 55th St.
1966, Perkins & Will

A far cry from Collegiate Gothic, this triple-winged complex is a structural tour de force, with six concrete Vierendeel trusses (normally used for bridges) poured in pairs, 175 feet long and two feet thick. Three-piece steel rockers transfer the load to concrete pedestals carried on cruciform piers.

94 Chicago Child Care Society
5467 S. University Ave.
1963, Keck & Keck

The concrete floors extend beyond the glass walls and are perforated to provide a sunscreen.

95 St. Thomas the Apostle Roman Catholic Church
5472 S. Kimbark Ave.
1924, Barry Byrne
96 School
5467 S. Woodlawn Ave.
1929, Shattuck & Layer

This remarkable break from traditional Catholic church design was executed by Barry Byrne,

St. Thomas the Apostle School

who had previously worked for Frank Lloyd Wright. This affiliation with the Prairie School may account for the naturalistic hues of the bricks, the innovative massing, and the unique design of the sculpture and ornament, especially the terra-cotta surrounding the entry and windows. Alfonso Iannelli, an important sculptor who often collaborated with other Prairie School architects, worked closely with Byrne on the design of the facades and interior spaces.

Verticality has always been a meaningful metaphor in church design, and here the narrow lancet windows, doorway sculpture, and sculpted brick surfaces ascend dramatically to a richly ornamented roofline. The worship space is free of columns and has pews set close to and almost encircling the altar, which is pushed forward into the nave. The resulting proximity of celebrant and congregation anticipated Roman Catholic liturgical reforms of the early 1960s. Sculptor Alfeo Faggi designed the bronze stations of the cross with an expressive simplicity appropriate to the interior.

97 Augustana Evangelical Lutheran Church of Hyde Park
1151 E. 55th St.
1968, Loebl, Schlossman, Bennett & Dart

Edward D. Dart's solid design of interconnecting masses has a low and inviting entry to provide

shelter from the rush of traffic on 55th St. The sculpture of Christ (*Ecce Homo*, 1939) was Egon Weiner's first important work after emigrating from Europe in 1938. He also designed the St. Paul sculpture in the 1985 Memorial Garden.

98 Egandale Row Houses
E. 53rd to 54th Sts.; S. Ingleside Ave. to S. Drexel Ave.
1991, David Swan & Assocs.

A garish palette characterizes this block-square development of fifty town houses. It was named for the community that grew up around the estate of William Bradshaw Egan, a physician and state legislator who built a house on this block in 1847. The variety of colors and materials was allegedly inspired by turn-of-the-century developments such as 5200–5244 S. Greenwood Ave.; the developers claim that it reflects Hyde Park's cultural, intellectual, and racial diversity. If this ambitious multiculturalism resurfaces, perhaps it will be tempered by some aesthetic restraint.

99 5200–5244 S. Greenwood Ave.
1903, John C. Brompton

Charmingly deceptive, the entire block is lined with twenty row houses with set-back common walls mimicking detached houses. It was created by Charles Counselman, a local meat-packer, and Samuel E. Gross, an active real estate developer. Like Gross's contemporaneous Alta Vista Terrace on the North Side, the row features a variety of styles, materials, and colors—but with a remarkable effect of unity deriving from the common scale and setbacks.

100 Joseph A. Thomlinson House
5317 S. University Ave.
1904, Solon S. Beman

One of the neighborhood's most eccentric designs bears a great gambrel roof ornamented with stone brackets above a rock-faced stone facade.

101 53rd & University Town Houses
1119–1125 E. 53rd St.
1985, David Swan

The severe northern facade gives no clue to the personable southern side, where tiers of terraces overlook back gardens.

Heller House

102 Isidore Heller House
5132 S. Woodlawn Ave.
1897, Frank Lloyd Wright

This important early design by Wright has many of the radical features that characterize his slightly later Prairie School houses. The bands of windows tucked under the low horizontal eaves and the potential for cross-axial spatial relationships suggest what was to follow in the Robie House. The frieze by Richard W. Bock (an important collaborator of many Prairie architects) and the two-tone brick banding of the top story empha-size the horizontal divisions of the wall plane. Despite the narrow and deep I-shaped plan, the interior space is open and expansive because Wright pulled the dining room out to the south and created a long east–west hallway axis perpendicular to the entry. Unlike the frontal entries of most 1890s houses, the all-important entries to Wright's houses—here marked by relief sculpture—are frequently set into the side for privacy and to dramatize the entry process.

103 Henry C. Work Cottage
5317 S. Dorchester Ave.
1859, architect unknown

Look south from 53rd St. to see what is thought to be Hyde Park's oldest house, a tiny cottage that has long been part of the larger house facing Dorchester Ave. The original board-and-batten siding has been re-created; this and the steep pitch of the roof and of the lone dormer identify the style as Gothic Revival. Work was a renowned composer of Civil War and temperance songs.

104 Harper Court
S. Harper Ave. and E. 52nd St.
1965, Dubin, Dubin, Black & Moutoussamy

In the 1950s many Hyde Parkers feared that their community's reputation as a bohemian, artistic neighborhood was threatened by proposed urban renewal. This

Harper Court

small-scale shopping center was meant to provide affordable space for the many artists and craftspeople working in buildings on 55th St. slated for demolition. Although the rents proved too expensive for many of those displaced, this pleasant villagelike complex has thrived as a retail center and peaceful public space.

105 5312–5318 S. Hyde Park Blvd.
1908, Andrew Sandegren

The bulging glassy bays are an early form of the boxy sun-room additions that became so popular on flat buildings in the following two decades.

106 5451–5455 S. Hyde Park Blvd.
1907, Frommann & Jebsen

The carved Art Nouveau ornament is more reminiscent of Barcelona than Chicago on this fanciful example of a luxurious six-flat, built when the street was dominated by large single-family residences.

107 5487–5499 S. Hyde Park Blvd.
1908, Doerr & Doerr

This prototypical Hyde Park luxury six-flat has giant Classical columns supporting large open porches on the upper floors. This type of multibalconied six-flat is more common in Hyde Park than in any other area of the city.

108 5501–5503 S. Hyde Park Blvd.
1909, Henry W. Tomlinson

Tomlinson's residential and commercial buildings in Hyde Park frequently exhibit flared cornices and a robust modern interpretation of classical ornament. This particular building retains the most integrity, with its basement retail shops, iron railings, intact cornice, and other original features.

109 William B. Conkey House
5518 S. Hyde Park Blvd.
1888, attrib. to George W. Maher

This house presents several features typical of an idiosyncratic, highly decorative style. The window lintels are massive blocks of rough stone, so large that they seem structurally impossible. The second-floor window is pushed behind the wall plane, with a fat splayed column placed in front of it. The third-floor window is a variation on a Palladian theme, with the central section squeezed almost into oblivion. The rough stone and rock-faced brick are of a similar color and texture.

110 N. Anderson House
5522 S. Hyde Park Blvd.
1888, attrib. to George W. Maher

The facade has an unusual combination of pale yellow and green sandstone.

5451–5455 S. Hyde Park Blvd.

ⅧⅡ Windemere House
(Windemere East Hotel)
1642 E. 56th St.
1924, Rapp & Rapp

The 1920s were the golden age of residential hotels, and this lakefront area is particularly rich in fine examples. Designed to house both transient and permanent guests, the Windemere offered single rooms (many with kitchenettes), as well as suites that could be combined to create apartments of up to five rooms. Typically for this building type, all the architectural exuberance is concentrated on an elaborate entry pavilion.

ⅧⅡ 5517–5519 S. Cornell Ave.
1891, attrib. to George W. Maher

Built by real estate broker Alex F. Shuman, presumably to Maher's designs, these houses have wildly original ornament, with almost no repetition of forms or detail.

ⅧⅡ Sinai Temple
5350 S. South Shore Dr.
1940, Friedman, Alschuler & Sincere

The smooth surfaces of this severe International Style synagogue lack any decoration apart from incised lettering.

Accessible only to pedestrians, via the 57th St. footbridge over S. South Shore Dr., is a spot dear to Hyde Parkers.

ⅧⅡ Promontory Point Park
(55th St. Promontory)
55th St. at S. South Shore Dr.
1937, Alfred Caldwell

This point of land is the highlight of Burnham Park, which stretches north all the way to Grant Park, serving as a lakefront link between them. The area of this park had been filled in by 1926 but was not landscaped until after WPA funding became available in 1935. Alfred Caldwell, a follower of the Prairie School landscape tradition of Jens Jensen, envisioned a prairie and meadow landscape planted with native flowering trees. His de-

sign was restored following the point's fiftieth anniversary in 1987, including the previously unexecuted circular stone rings used for cookouts and benches that were modeled after Jensen's larger council rings.

ⅧⅡ David Wallach Fountain
1939, Elizabeth & Frank Hibbard

Wallach donated money to design a fountain for "man and beast." The husband-and-wife sculptors (who designed the marble base and the bronze doe, respectively) were both students of Lorado Taft at the School of the Art Institute. Elizabeth Hibbard was also an assistant at his Midway Studios.

ⅧⅡ Promontory Point Park Field House
*1937, Emanuel V. Buchsbaum
Renovated 1991, Chicago Park District*

This Lannon stone field house, with its circular lookout tower, was modeled after a lighthouse.

ⅧⅡ Promontory Apartments
5530 S. South Shore Dr.
1949, Ludwig Mies van der Rohe; Pace Assocs.; Holsman, Holsman, Klekamp & Taylor

This was Mies's first constructed high rise and his first collaboration with developer Herbert S. Greenwald, who became one of his most important clients. The original design had a curtain wall of steel and glass that was the forerunner of 860–880 N. Lake Shore Dr., but the postwar steel shortage dictated the use of concrete instead. The columns taper as they rise, giving visual expression to their decreasing structural load.

ⅧⅡ Montgomery Place
5550 S. South Shore Dr.
1991, Nagle, Hartray & Assocs.

Crisp red brick walls are punctuated by angled bay windows that maximize light and views, in a design influenced by Richard M. Bennett's 1350–1360 N. Lake Shore Dr. This luxurious high rise for seniors was built over an existing underground garage and

South Shore Cultural Center

was sited to minimize blockage of its neighbors' light and views.

119 South Shore Cultural Center (South Shore Country Club)
7059 S. South Shore Dr.
1916, Marshall & Fox
Renovated 1983, Norman De Haan Assocs.

Established in 1906, South Shore prospered along with the neighborhood to become one of the city's renowned country clubs, and Marshall & Fox's modest clubhouse (1906) was replaced with this palatial Mediterranean-style structure. Spacious and elaborately decorated corridors connect grand ballrooms to the north and south with a glazed solarium on the east, as well as dining and meeting rooms overlooking the lake. It is well worth a trip inside, especially to see the north ballroom, which is like an enormous glass box with a Wedgwood lid. The wall-to-wall windows could be raised to expand the space to the surrounding terrace. The splendid colonnaded driveway, on axis with the entrance gatehouse (unrestored), provides a grand approach. The sixty-five-acre property, purchased by the Chicago Park District in 1973, includes a beach, golf course, tennis courts, an outdoor stage, and a riding arena, as well as traces of the original bowling green and shooting area. The stables are now used by the Chicago Mounted Police. The abandoned shooting lodge to the

north was built at the same time as the main clubhouse.

120 Allan Miller House
7121 S. Paxton Ave.
1915, John S. Van Bergen

This extremely well preserved house is the only surviving building in Chicago by this Prairie School architect, most of whose work is found in the North Shore suburbs. Its open plan is derived from Wright's "Fireproof House for $5,000," but the generous seventy-five-foot lot width allowed Van Bergen to expand the cube with a large porch, giving the composition some of the expansiveness associated with suburban Prairie houses.

121 St. Philip Neri Roman Catholic Church
2126 E. 72nd St.
1928, Joseph W. McCarthy

The golden hues of Plymouth granite set off this Tudor Revival design. Bedford limestone is used for the carving around the entrance and the tracery in the large rose windows. The copper spire adds height to this large church, which is set on a landscaped base raised above the street.

122 Jeffery–Cyril Historic District
7100 block of S. Jeffery and S. Cyril Blvds.

The rejuvenation of this enclave provides an excellent example of the benefits available under mid-1980s tax incentives for historic preservation. The busy intersection of E. 71st St. and Jeffery Blvd. was developed in the late 1920s with six apartment buildings in widely varied styles. All but one had small to medium units (one to four rooms) marketed to middle-class tenants. Varying in height from five to thirteen stories, the buildings form a group that dominates the low-rise residential and commercial landscape. In 1987–1988 four of them were restored and modernized by a development subsidiary of South Shore Bank.

123 **E. 71st Place Building**
1966–1974 E. 71st Pl.
1928, Paul Frederick Olsen
Renovated 1987, Lisec &
Biederman

A Spanish Colonial Revival building of brick and terra-cotta, it has a two-story lobby on 71st Pl. and storefronts (altered) along Jeffery Blvd.

124 **Bedford Villa Apartments**
7130 S. Cyril Ave.
1929, Paul Frederick Olsen

This Gothic Revival apartment building has a distinctive entrance with gargoyles and fleurs-de-lis.

125 **Shore Manor/Eleanor Manor**
7150 S. Cyril Ave.
1928, Daniel J. Schaffner

This pair of Georgian Revival apartment buildings rises over an English basement that contains the lobbies.

126 **Highland Apartments**
7147 S. Jeffery Blvd.
1927, McNally & Quinn
Renovated 1987, Lisec &
Biederman

Gabled parapets and a traceried entrance give this brick-and-limestone structure a Tudor flavor.

127 **Jeffery–Cyril Apartments**
7144–7148 S. Jeffery Blvd.
1927, Julius J. Schwarz
Renovated 1988, Lisec &
Biederman

The two-story entryway of this Tudor building is decorated with crockets. Unlike its neighbors, it was originally a cooperative, with larger apartments of five to six rooms.

128 **Jeffery Terrace Apartments**
7130 S. Jeffery Blvd.
1929, Paul Frederick Olsen
Renovated 1987, Lisec &
Biederman

Although designed by the same architect as two other buildings in this group, this one represents a complete break with their

Jeffery Terrace Apartments

Kenna Apartments

historically inspired styles. It is a jazzy essay in Art Deco, with ornament created only by geometric shapes. Arcades along Jeffery Blvd. provide sheltered entries for the commercial spaces. Note the apartment entry surrounded by gold glazed tile.

129 Kenna Apartments
2214 E. 69th St.
1916, Barry Byrne & Ryan Co.

The unusually severe composition, perhaps influenced by Byrne's contact with California protomodernist Irving J. Gill in 1913, is enlivened by Alfonso Iannelli's wonderful ornament around the entrance and windows.

130 Jackson Park Highlands
Euclid, Bennett, & Constance Aves. between 67th & 71st Sts.

Named for its location atop a ridge, this middle-class residential neighborhood was established as an eighty-acre subdivision in 1905. It was developed by Frank I. Bennett, a Chicago alderman, lawyer, and realtor, and Charles J. Bour, an "advertising agent." Most of the houses were built between 1905 and 1940, and they present an impressive array of the styles—mostly revivalist—of the period. The design standards included minimum lot widths of fifty feet, a thirty-foot setback from the street, no alleys, and buried utilities. Facade materials were restricted to brick or stone, and roof materials to tile or slate. As a group, the houses retain an unusually high degree of architectural integrity, rewarding visitors with superbly handled materials, ornamental details, and early landscape and gardening features. This subdivision grew as automobile ownership was increasing; look down the original narrow, two-track cement driveways to see auto sheds that match the houses.

131 6700 S. Euclid Ave.
1952, Spitz & Spitz

One of the few postwar houses in this subdivision, this 1950s classic has a big front-entry fin.

132 6826 S. Euclid Ave.
1905, architect unknown

The two-story temple front proclaims its Greek Revival style, but in an unusual twist, the triangular pediment is half-timbered. There is a similar house at 6931.

133 6840 S. Euclid Ave.
1905, architect unknown

This is a good example of the simplification of Queen Anne forms after the turn of the century. The large bays are still present, but the massing is simpler and the facade is symmetrical.

134 6955 S. Euclid Ave.
1909, Frank D. Chase

This Tudor Revival house and matching auto shed show the influence of the English Arts & Crafts movement.

135 6956 S. Bennett Ave.
1936, Paul Schweikher

This International Style house in brick has metal-framed corner windows, a low roof with a central chimney, and glass blocks in windows on the north side. Schweikher practiced in Chicago from 1933, when his work was exhibited at the Museum of Modern Art, to 1953, when he left to teach at Yale University.

6956 S. Bennett Ave.

136 6926 S. Bennett Ave.
1908, William L. Pagels

Maher's influence is strong in this house, with its octagonal columns and hipped roof with a flanged segmental arch dormer.

137 6851 S. Bennett Ave.
1909, Chatten & Hammond

One of three houses in Jackson Park Highlands by this firm (the others are at 6757 and 6855 S. Euclid), this large Tudor house has a matching auto shed.

138 6841 S. Bennett Ave.
1915, Harlev & Aga

Among the unusual features of this eclectic house are brickwork that imitates half-timbering, and terra-cotta plaques (more commonly found on commercial buildings) stuck like postage stamps on the first-floor piers.

139 6737 S. Bennett Ave.
1927, Charles D. Faulkner

The first-floor windows of this neo-Classical house are each framed by an arch with a coat of arms and wreaths in relief on the tympanum.

140 6734 S. Bennett Ave.
1918, Zimmerman, Saxe & Zimmerman

This distinctive one-story house combines stylistic features of the Prairie School (a low profile and horizontal proportions), California Arts & Crafts (multiple roof planes), and Tudor (half-timbering). Like its neighbors, it is set back from the street and raised slightly above ground level on a terrace.

141 6829 S. Constance Ave.
1915, Edgar M. Newman

This Craftsman bungalow has very horizontal proportions and brackets supporting low eaves.

142 6840 S. Constance Ave.
1921, Luther W. McDonald

A more modest bungalow, this type proliferated in urban developments of the 1910s and 1920s.

143 6946 S. Constance Ave.
1924, Samuel S. Oman

This free adaptation of Classical and Gothic motifs has stylized columns, humorous animals, and a lion bearing a coat of arms.

144 New Regal Theatre
(Avalon Theatre)
1645 E. 79th St.
1927, John Eberson

This Austrian-born architect was known throughout the South and Midwest as "Opera House John" for his fantastic and exuberant theaters. He specialized in "atmospheric" theaters, with opulent, exotic, and evocative interiors well suited to the fantasy settings of 1920s movies. The Middle Eastern world created here was inspired by a Persian incense burner that Eberson found in a New Orleans antique shop. The exterior is equally lavish, covered with multicolored terra-cotta.

145 Oak Woods Cemetery

The Oak Woods Cemetery Association was formed in 1853. Like Chicago's other historic cemeteries, Graceland and Rosehill, it was located beyond the growing city but close to a railroad line. In 1866 the Illinois Central began operating a spur line to the cemetery. The association hired Adolph Strauch, superintendent of Spring Grove Cemetery in Cincinnati, to assist in the planning, thus ensuring that Oak Woods would reflect the most up-to-date thinking. Beyond establishing a parklike environment, Strauch promoted the idea known as the lawn plan, in which no walls, fences, curbing, or coping mark the edges of the plots. His plan for Oak Woods included three lakes surrounded by curving roadways and gently rising mounds.
—Joan Pomaranc

Oak Woods has one of Chicago's most significant concentrations of Civil War commemorations. The **A** Confederate Mound Monument, erected in 1893 and officially dedicated on Memorial Day, 1895, marks the North's largest burial site for Southern soldiers and sailors. The two-acre site, acquired by the federal government in 1867, marks the graves of 6,000 prisoners of war who died in Chicago's Camp Douglas of disease and deprivation. General John C. R. Underwood, a civil engineer and Confederate veteran, led the movement to build this memorial and designed it himself. The graves are arranged in concentric trenches around the sloping base of the forty-foot-tall monument. In 1911 bronze tablets bearing the names and ranks of the 4,275 men identified in official records were added to the mound. Atop a twelve-foot column, its capital carved to resemble a battlement, is a bronze sculpture of a Confederate infantryman, based on a figure in a painting entitled *Appomattox* by Confederate veteran John A. Elder.

The 1890s saw the erection of numerous monuments to the Civil War in both the North and the South. Sufficient time had passed for the national rift to have begun to heal, and those with firsthand memories of the war wanted to commemorate their expe-

Fuller Monument

rience before it was too late. In the northwest corner of the cemetery are plots held by the Soldiers' Home, Abraham Lincoln Post No. 91, Department of Illinois, the Grand Army of the Republic, and the Chicago Veterans Association. A statue of a Union soldier with a rifle (partially missing) and a cannon and shot marks the plot of the Soldiers' Home, which still stands on E. 35th St. A 1905 replica of Charles J. Mulligan's *Lincoln the Orator (The Gettysburg Lincoln)* of 1903 marks off the plot for members of a local post of the GAR, the major Union veterans' organization.

The tallest monument is the limestone obelisk marking the burial site of **B** William Hale ("Big Bill") Thompson, Chicago's mayor from 1915 to 1923 and from 1927 to 1931. A boorish lout with a theatrical manner, he opposed U.S. involvement in World War I and Prohibition at home, threatening to fire any policeman who interfered with a citizen's "personal liberty"—the selling or consumption of alcohol. Thompson's was one of the loudest roars in the Roaring Twenties. A gray granite mausoleum

is the final resting place of **C** Harold Washington, state legislator, Congressman, and the first African-American mayor of Chicago.

A simple granite column with four sloping sides marks the grave of architect **D** Solon Spencer Beman.

E George A. Fuller was trained as an architect but achieved fame as originator of the modern contracting system in building construction. His firm, based in Chicago with a branch in New York City, built the Monadnock Building and the Rookery in Chicago and the Flatiron (originally Fuller) Building in New York. Bruce Price designed the monument, the only work in Chicago by this New York architect. It is a limestone pergola of fluted columns on which rest three layers of supporting beams representing steel, stone, and wood construction. Curiously, on the underside of the topmost, or "wooden," beams, are carved stone rivets characteristics of modern steel-frame construction. The classical details convey an impression of a traditional, albeit somewhat peculiar, design.

Eastman Monument

The red granite monument to **F** **Jesse Owens** features the Olympic rings that recall his achievements at the 1936 Games in Berlin, at which he won the broad jump and the 100- and 200-meter dash.

Crossed baseball bats and a ball mark the grave of **G** **Adrian C. ("Cap") Anson,** a baseball player and manager of the Chicago White Stockings (forerunner of the Cubs) in the newly formed National League.

The monument to **H** **Gale Cramer,** a young train engineer who sacrificed himself to save his passengers, features a model of the train in which he died.

I The **Firmenich** family monument is a very tall statuary group that stands out dramatically at Symphony Lake. Atop a large, heavy base are three female figures representing Faith, Hope, and Charity.

J The **Eastman** monument features a life-size bronze figure of a woman in classical dress, bearing a wreath in her right hand while she leans mournfully against a pink granite slab.

K **Paul Cornell's** plot features a very large monument made of a material known as white bronze. In 1853 he founded the town of Hyde Park and cofounded Oak Woods Cemetery.

L The **Chapel and Crematory** (1903, William Carbys Zimmerman) is reminiscent of a rural English Gothic church but exhibits some Prairie School elements in its steeple and entrance porch. The **Tower of Memories** (1960) is a communal mausoleum and columbarium.

Cornell Monument

Oakwoods Cemetery Chapel

Prairie School architect **George C. Nimmons,** who specialized in industrial buildings, is buried here.

Along the south edge of Oak Woods are a group of Jewish cemeteries, each demarcated by a fence. These plots, held by congregations or fraternal organizations, resemble traditional European graveyards with close-set head- stones and no open space apart from walkways. In the cemetery proper, among another area of Jewish graves, is a monument known as the **Eternal Light.** In every synagogue burns an eternal light; this one is a memorial to victims of the Holocaust. Its base shaped like a Star of David, the red granite tower contains in its top a radioactive material that absorbs sunlight by day and glows at night.

BEVERLY/ MORGAN PARK

Morgan Park Area

103rd
28
Bethany Union Church
Bell Tower Lofts
104th
27
Chambers House
43
Parker House
26
104th
McKee House
42
25
CSU
Presidents House
Griffin Pl
10410 and 10541 S Hoyne
105th
41
Ridge Historical Society
Walden
Hale
29-39
Walter Burley Griffin Place
105th
Claremont
Oakley
Leavitt
Hamilton
Hoyne
Seeley
106th
23
22
Beacon School
Longwood
24
Tolles House
Wood
106th
107th
Drew
107th Pl
Bell
Blake House
Waterman House
Hale
Dickey House
Ingersoll-Blackwelder House
Kirsch House
108th Pl
19
18
1
2
German House
109th
Edgren House
Bell
Hoyne
Prospect
3
21
20
Walker Morgan Park Library Methodist
17
Esmond
4
Iglehart House
110th
Smith House
Longwood
6
Metra 111th St Station
5
Woods House
Ferguson House
Pryor
13
15
16
Bell
14
Morgan Park Church
12
2203 W 111th
Monterey
To I-57 to Loop
Homewood
11
Morgan Park Academy Gym
Lothair
8
11228 S Longwood
7
Clarke House
Hermosa
Montvale
Artesian
Western
112th Pl
113th
Hale
Homewood
Church
Edmaire
9
10
Thayer Houses

I f communities still adopted Latin mottos, Beverly–Morgan Park might bill itself as "Suburbia in Urbe." With its towering trees, broad lawns, and sprawling old houses, it looks more like an affluent North Shore suburb than a Chicago neighborhood. The hilly topography and winding streets also set it apart from the flat urban grid to the east. The small rail stations, which retain much of their charm despite heavy-handed remodelings, recall the area's origins as a commuter suburb.

Morgan Park is the older community. In 1844 an Englishman named Thomas Morgan bought a large tract of land along the Blue Island Ridge (the hill that rises west of Longwood Dr.) from 91st to 119th streets, which remain the north and south boundaries of the combined neighborhoods. It remained a sleepy farm community until 1869, when the Blue Island Land & Building Company bought the

Beverly Area

87th

88th

Western

Hetherington House
Reed House
Brewer House
59 Chap House
62
61 **60**
Hunt
Hopkins
58 Phillips Studio
Pleasant

89th
Beverly
Winchester
Paulina

90th
Frisby House
66
65
64 8958 S Hamilton
63 Brough House
57 Bennett House
Balzekas House
90th
Pike House **52**
Beverly Hills Metra Station

91st
91st
51

92nd
Belding House **56**
55 French House
92nd
Marshfield

92nd Pl

93rd
Winchester
Pleasant
Longwood
Vanderpoel
93rd

Western
Claremont
Oakley
Bell
Leavitt
Hamilton
Hoyne
Damen
Waid House **67**
Adams House **54**
53 Hilliard House
94th

95th
95th

96th
Winchester

97th
Tanner House **50**
97th
Vanderpoel
Prospect

98th
Hill House
49
Sawyer House **48**

99th
Walden

Hoyne
Seeley
Damen
Longwood
Evans House **47**
Beverly Glen Pkwy

100th
100th Pl
Olmsted House **40**

101st
101st
Wood
101st Pl

Blount House (2)
45
101st Pl
Horton House
46
102nd
102nd
Bethany Union Church
101st Pl

Western
Beverly Unitarian **44**
28

103rd
To I-57 and Loop ➡

land and hired another Englishman, Thomas F. Nichols, to lay out the subdivision of Morgan Park south of 107th St. The curving streets and generous greenswards of this area result from Nichols's picturesque planning principles.

Although not incorporated as a village until 1882, Morgan Park developed significantly in the 1870s. In the first year of the decade the Chicago, Rock Island & Pacific Railroad established a branch line that provided the area with convenient service to the Loop. Three institutions were established here in quick succession: the Morgan Park Military Academy, founded in 1873, which continues—minus the military aspect—to be a prominent preparatory school; the Chicago Female College, established in 1875; and the Baptist Union Theological Seminary, which moved here from Chicago's Douglas neighborhood in 1877. The presence of the seminary, led by Thomas W. Goodspeed and William Rainey Harper, raised hopes that the proposed University of Chicago might establish its new campus here. When the more centrally located Hyde Park was chosen instead, the seminary left with them to become the university's Divinity School. Morgan Park remained a quiet residential village whose community life centered on a handful of Protestant churches. Even a fiercely fought annexation to the city in 1914 did little to alter its subdued character.

The community of Beverly, also called Beverly Hills, developed slightly later but followed a similar pattern. It was part of the village of Washington Heights to the east, which was annexed to Chicago in 1890 but retained its own small-town identity. Like Morgan Park, it developed from east to west. In 1889 the Chicago, Rock Island & Pacific Railroad opened a station at 91st St. and named it Beverly Hills, which came to be the name for the whole community north of 107th St. along the Ridge. Residential development proceeded swiftly, with the biggest boom taking place in the 1920s.

North of 95th St., an important commercial artery, the enclave of North Beverly is the area's most exclusive community. The deep wooded lots on rolling hills shelter large Revival Style houses from the 1920s and 1930s. As geographically distant from the Loop as are the suburbs of Evanston and Riverside, North Beverly shares their sylvan sense of shelter.

—Laurie McGovern Petersen

1 Luther S. Dickey, Jr. House
10990 S. Prospect Ave.
1912, Chatten & Hammond

Set far back on a four-acre lot is a stellar example of the Arts & Crafts–influenced eclectic house often found in the North Shore suburbs. Picturesque elements— a half-timbered double gable, sloping brick buttresses and piers, and a flanged segmental entry arch—are freely combined into a masterfully integrated composition.

2 Ingersoll-Blackwelder House
10910 S. Prospect Ave.
1866; extensive additions 1877; architects unknown
3 German House
10924 S. Prospect Ave.
1884, E. J. German

The Ingersoll House is a catalog of the decorative possibilities of wood sheathing: clapboards laid horizontally, vertically, and even diagonally; applied fretwork; and shingles in three patterns. The

German House is comparatively restrained but adds a touch of half-timbering to the mix.

4 Ferguson House
10934 S. Prospect Ave.
1873, architect unknown
5 Woods House
10970 S. Prospect Ave.
1872, architect unknown

Deep fascia characterize these altered but charming Italianates.

6 111th St. Metra Station (Chicago, Rock Island & Pacific Railroad—Morgan Park Station)
111th St. and Hale Ave.
1891, John T. Long

Set on a large greensward, this station has a deliberately domestic scale and was meant to advertise the comfortable suburban character of early Morgan Park. The first floor was designed to be faced in brick but was constructed entirely of wood. Details such as a waiting-room fireplace survive, but overscaled asphalt siding obscures some of the charm.

Morgan Park Church of God in Christ

Like Prospect Ave., Longwood Dr. developed early as a fashionable street. Look to the top of the hill to see many of the oldest houses, which have long front yards stretching down to Longwood, frequently with newer houses on their lots at the base of the hill. Some now have addresses on Lothair Ave., one block to the west, and are best seen from this "back door" street.

7 Sarah D. Clarke House (W. S. Kiskaddon House)
11156 S. Longwood Dr.
1892, John Gavin

This prim Queen Anne dollhouse miniaturizes diverse stylistic elements with bracketed charm. The Italianate corner tower shrinks as it rises.

8 11228 S. Longwood Dr./11213 S. Lothair Ave.
Remodeled 1935, Charles D. Faulkner

Probably dating from the late nineteenth century, this house was completely transformed with a Jacobean brick-and-stone veneer and addition.

9 Thayer House (2)
11347 S. Lothair Ave.
1874, architect unknown
10 Thayer House (1)
11359 S. Lothair Ave./11410 S. Longwood Dr.
1873, architect unknown

Almost lost to view in leafy summer are these grand hilltop Italianates with their breathtaking eastward views.

11 Morgan Park Academy Gymnasium
2147–2155 W. 112th St.
1900, Dwight H. Perkins

The geometric end gables and some of the windows hint at Perkins's Prairie School affinities. This is the oldest extant building of Morgan Park Academy.

12 Morgan Park Church of God in Christ (Morgan Park Congregational Church)
11153 S. Hoyne Ave.
1916, Patton, Holmes & Flynn

Domestically scaled and comfortable, it is Chicago's best-preserved Craftsman church, here blended with Mission touches. The interior retains the original lanterns and woodwork.

13 Charles D. Iglehart House
11118 S. Artesian Ave.
1857; front addition 1870s; architects unknown

Tucked away on a mundane street of mid-twentieth-century brick houses is one of Chicago's earliest dwellings. The rear half of this Italianate house was a small cottage where Iglehart's daughter Mary was born in 1857—the first birth in Morgan Park. The house is in remarkably good condition for an 1870s frame building.

14 2203 W. 111th St.
1873, architect unknown

15 Justin A. Smith House
2204 W. 111th St.
1872, architect unknown

These early, altered houses share a cross-gabled massing, triangular second-floor window hoods, and the bracketed front gables so popular in early 1870s cottages. 2203 was formerly the Morgan Park Academy Headmaster's House. The Smith House was the birthplace of the University of Chicago, and the institution's founders held many meetings here.

16 Chicago Public Library—George C. Walker Branch
11071 S. Hoyne Ave.
1890, Charles S. Frost
Additions 1933, Doerr & Doerr

This is reminiscent of H. H. Richardson's suburban train stations, but the twin towers with inward-facing windows have a slightly pigeon-toed charm all their own. The end and rear rooms came later, and the interior has been completely remodeled.

17 Morgan Park United Methodist Church (Morgan Park Methodist Episcopal Church)
11000 S. Longwood Dr.
1913, Harry Hale Waterman
Addition 1926, Perkins, Fellows & Hamilton

Simple, powerful elements dominate this Craftsman church: the exaggeratedly broad gable, the anchoring tower, and the entry cut like a cave from the body of the church.

Along Longwood Dr. architects dealt with a problem rare in Chicago, the rolling lot. The houses nestle into, perch upon, strut across, or lord it over their hilltop sites with varying degrees of success.

18 Harry Hale Waterman House
10838 S. Longwood Dr.
1892, Harry Hale Waterman

With its terraced entry, it snuggles more cozily into the Ridge than any house on Longwood Dr. Punctuated by an exaggerated gable at the entry porch, the high hipped roof gives a whimsical sense of disproportion to this overgrown cottage, the architect's own home.

19 J. T. Blake House
2023 W. 108th Pl.
1894, Harry Hale Waterman

Typical of many of Waterman's charmingly irregular designs, the asymmetrical, steeply pitched gable roof and jutting stairway bay form an entrance facade combining stone, stucco, and wood.

Waterman House

20 Edgren House
11019 S. Bell Ave.
early 1880s, architect unknown

Two narrow wings meet stiffly at an angled wall that grows into a tower—a massing with French precedents that is little seen in Chicago.

21 Kirsch House
10920 S. Oakley Ave.
1888, architect unknown

Queen Anne meets the Kremlin in this exuberant house with a gilded turret.

22 Beacon Therapeutic School (E. J. Barker House)
10650 S. Longwood Dr.
1910, Harry Hale Waterman
Addition 1992, Phillip Peecher & Assocs.

The horizontal massing and simple lines show a Prairie School spirit worlds apart from the picturesque irregularity of Waterman's houses from the 1890s.

23 Ridge Historical Society (Herbert S. Graver House)
10616 S. Longwood Dr.
1922, John Todd Hetherington

The terraces take better advantage of the dramatic hilltop site than any house on the street.

24 Harry N. Tolles House
10561 S. Longwood Dr.
1911, Walter Burley Griffin

Though related to the houses on Griffin Pl., it has an altered porch, a relocated main entrance, glass block, and replaced window muntins that detract from its appearance.

25 Chicago State University—President's House (Frank Anderson House)
10400 S. Longwood Dr.
1924, architect unknown

This very formal, elegant rendition of 1920s Italian Renaissance Revival has simple Classical pediments above the first-floor openings.

26 Hiland A. Parker House
10340 S. Longwood Dr.
1894, Harry Hale Waterman

Site and style combine here for high drama. The base of huge rusticated brownstone blocks rises from the hill to form arches on the big semicircular porch. The tall roof, pierced with steeply pitched gabled dormers, exaggerates the height.

27 Bell Tower Lofts (Thirteenth Church of Christ, Scientist)
10317 S. Longwood Dr.
1916, Howard L. Cheney
Converted to apartments 1992, Stowell Cook Frolichstein

A ponderous Greek Revival box, this typical Christian Scientist church has taken on a new mission with its conversion to apartments.

28 Bethany Union Church
1750 W. 103rd St.
1927, Raymond M. Hood

The narrow facade of this severely simple church has been overwhelmed by the mundane support building to the west.

29 W. 104th Place/Walter Burley Griffin Place

In 1973 an article in the *Prairie School Review* revealed that detective work by architect Wilbert R. Hasbrouck and architectural historian Paul E. Sprague had uncovered a significant concentration of houses by Walter Burley Griffin in Beverly. The houses were all commissioned by Russell L. Blount, an aspiring developer whose early successes in selling houses designed by Griffin led to a string of projects. Griffin was at the height of his American career at the time; he had worked in Frank Lloyd Wright's studio from 1901 to 1905 and had a substantial solo practice, until he left for Australia in 1913 to design the capital city of Canberra.

Blount's association with Griffin began in 1909, when he commissioned a house for himself and his fiancée, to be built on her father's property on 104th Pl. Before the house was complete, he received an attractive offer for it from Edmund C. Garrity, leading him to commission a new one for himself next door (Blount House 1) and a speculative one down the block that was later sold to Harry G. Van Nostrand. In 1912–1913 Blount commissioned three more houses from Griffin: the Blount House (2), which became his by default when the intended purchaser reneged, and the Salmon and Jenkinson houses. For this last house Griffin was listed as providing "plans only," and it differs in several respects from the previous five, which are considered purer examples of his work.

Shortly after Griffin left for Australia, Blount built four other houses in the area, three based on the Van Nostrand House design (Williams, Hornbaker, Clarke) and one on the Salmon House (Fumeaux). Sales of the later houses never lived up to the expectations generated by the quick offers received for the first few, and by 1915 Blount was building undistinguished rows of cracker box houses.

This remarkable street, renamed Walter Burley Griffin Pl., reflects an innovative approach to the design of small, inexpensive houses. Griffin's houses are all one and a half or two stories, built of wood and stucco on a concrete basement, and have very compact square plans, similar to Wright's 1907 design of "A Fireproof House for $5,000." The living and dining rooms are defined, rather than separated, by a large fireplace; the kitchen is tucked into the remaining corner; and open porches extend the spaces outdoors. Griffin invariably covers the foundation with clapboards, often continuing them to the sill line of the first-floor windows. The porch's location is determined by the desire to give it at least one southern exposure. The windows are casements with robust wooden mullions in geometric patterns, sometimes quite elaborate. The roof is occasionally hipped but most often has a large open gable with extended ends that enhance its sheltering quality. Gables over the screened porches echo the main gable and add variety to the basic cube. This group is part of Griffin's rustic work, with rough brown siding, pale stucco, and naturally weathering shingles making the houses seem suited to their bucolic location.

30 Harry G. Van Nostrand House
1666 W. Griffin Pl.
1911, Walter Burley Griffin

The plan is a smaller version of the Garrity House and was reused in others. Except for an added front dormer, the house is in close to original condition. It is especially rewarding to see the porch still screened—as so many of them were—rather than enclosed.

31 Edmund C. Garrity House
1712 W. Griffin Pl.
1909, Walter Burley Griffin

The quick and profitable sale of this newlyweds' house launched

Garrity House

Blount House (1)

Blount on his career. The second-floor dormers were added later, although the mullion pattern was thoughtfully reproduced.

32 Russell L. Blount House (1)
1724 W. Griffin Pl.
1911, Walter Burley Griffin

When Blount's first house was sold to Garrity, he commissioned this replacement. The clapboard "hoop skirt" covering the foundation exaggerates the horizontal with inexpensive flair. Griffin grouped first-floor windows to break through the wall at all four corners.

33 Walter O. Salmon House
1736 W. Griffin Pl.
1912, Walter Burley Griffin

The virtually unaltered exterior features an unusual two-story screened porch.

34 Arthur G. Jenkinson House
1727 W. Griffin Pl.
1912, Walter Burley Griffin

The partial extension of the clapboard siding above the first-floor level may be Blount's alteration to Griffin's design. It is similar to the facade treatment of the Newland House, whose architect of record was Spencer & Powers.

35 William N. Clarke House
1731 W. Griffin Pl.
1913, Walter Burley Griffin

Blount shifted the Van Nostrand House plan ninety degrees here and moved the porch. The windows have lost their distinctive muntins.

36 Harry C. Furneaux House
1741 W. Griffin Pl.
1913, Walter Burley Griffin

This plan is a reversed version of the Salmon House but with a single-story porch and different details. The triangular roof brackets may have been inspired by those on the Newland House.

37 Harry F. Newland House
1737 W. Griffin Pl.
1912, Spencer & Powers

This house may have been begun by Griffin. The roof brackets and the extension of the clapboarding above the first floor are not found in his work.

38 William R. Hornbaker House
1710 W. 104th St.
1914, Walter Burley Griffin

This heavily altered variation of the Clarke House has had all the windows replaced and large dormers added.

39 Ida E. Williams House
1632 W. 104th St.
1913, Walter Burley Griffin

Despite the addition of a small dormer, this house retains much of its original appearance and still has a screened porch with the wood muntins. It is of the same plan and tiny dimensions as the Van Nostrand House.

40 Frank N. Olmsted House
1624 W. 100th Pl.
1910, Walter Burley Griffin

A reversal of the Blount House (1) plan, it has lost the "hoop skirt" clapboarding at the base.

10541 S. Hoyne Ave.

41 10410 and 10541 S. Hoyne Ave.
1917, Frank Lloyd Wright

These are products of American System Ready-Cut, a short-lived collaboration of Wright and Richards Bros. of Milwaukee that sold Wright designs prepackaged and ready to build. Novelist Sherwood Anderson was the company copywriter and touted the modestly priced houses as examples of an American architecture "as brave and direct as the country." These designs were derived from Wright's "Fireproof House for $5,000" but are far less successful schemes and were unsupervised by Wright. Other, more popular models included duplexes and bungalows.

McKee House

42 James R. McKee House
10415 S. Seeley Ave.
1908, John M. Schroeder

This house packs all its punch into one element, the projecting sunroom capped by a graceful broken arch. The simple entrance is hidden away on the side, behind the battered front wall.

43 George Chambers House
10330 S. Seeley Ave.
1874, architect unknown

This remarkably well preserved house is a classic suburban villa, complete with "French" tower. The garden veranda on the south side was meant to frame the view and provide a suitable vantage point for the beauties of nature.

Chambers House

44 Beverly Unitarian Church (Robert C. Givins House)
10244 S. Longwood Dr.
1886, architect unknown

Modeled after an Irish castle and built of Joliet limestone, this imposing edifice was the work of an early developer who wanted to give the area a fashionable image.

Beverly Unitarian Church

45 Russell L. Blount House (2)
1950 W. 102nd St.
1912, Walter Burley Griffin

The plan is the same as for the earlier Blount House (1), but the bedrooms have a cathedral ceiling that is echoed in the exterior trim. The family lived here from 1914 to 1916, when they sold it to Harry Furneaux and purchased *his* Griffin-designed house on Griffin Pl.

46 Horace Horton House
10200 S. Longwood Dr.
early 1890s, architect unknown

This house heralds the imposing Classical Revival that became popular with the 1893 World's Columbian Exposition.

47 Robert W. Evans House
9914 S. Longwood Dr.
1908, Frank Lloyd Wright

Here Wright builds onto the hill, not into it. The pinwheeling of forms around a central chimney is similar to that of his Ward W. Willitts House (1901) in Highland Park, Ill., but the stucco has been defaced with a layer of stone.

48 Frederick C. Sawyer House
9822 S. Longwood Dr.
1912, John Todd Hetherington
49 Bryson B. Hill House
9800 S. Longwood Dr.
1909, Albert G. Ferree

These Classically inspired mansions coexisted with the Prairie School and will never go entirely out of style.

50 Louis A. Tanner House
9640 S. Longwood Dr.
1909, Tallmadge & Watson

The simple but pleasing facade retains an element typical of this firm's smaller projects: the trellised porch with cutout balusters.

51 Beverly Hills Metra Station (Chicago, Rock Island & Pacific Railroad—Beverly Station)
91st St. & Prospect Sq.
early 1890s, Charnley & Evans

Only the picturesque towered and gabled massing hint at the Queen Anne character. Modernizations have removed the original small-paned windows and the elaborate cladding of shingles, textured stucco, and half-timbering.

Beverly Hills Metra Station

Pike House

52 E. S. Pike House
1826 W. 91st St.
1894, Harry Hale Waterman

Expect Hansel and Gretel to come tripping past this house set on the edge of the woods. Huge blocks of sandstone anchor the first floor and contrast with the light stucco above.

53 Edwin P. Hilliard House
9351 S. Pleasant Ave.
1894, Harry Hale Waterman

Like the Pike House, this small variation on Waterman's picturesque theme features a tower breaking through the curbed gambrel roof and half-timbered stucco over a heavy stone base. The half-timbering frames the edges of the windows, organizing the wall plane rather than fragmenting it.

54 William and Jesse M. Adams House
9326 S. Pleasant Ave.
1900, Frank Lloyd Wright

It is quiet by Wright standards but with a typically intriguing entry sequence.

55 William M. R. French House
9203 S. Pleasant Ave.
1894, William A. Otis

This Classical Revival house is sophisticated and straightforward among its picturesque Waterman-designed and oblique Wright-designed neighbors. The second-floor central doorway treatment is as elaborate as that on the first floor.

56 Hiram H. Belding House
9167 S. Pleasant Ave.
1894, Harry Hale Waterman

Described in *Inland Architect* as "Norman-French style," it has an

L-shaped plan with a prominent stair tower and corner entry, favorite Waterman elements.

57 Arthur J. T. Bennett, Jr. House
8944 S. Pleasant Ave.
1937, Murray D. Hetherington

Hallmarks of Hetherington's talents are the artfully integrated garage and the emphasis on site and landscape; the garden entrance is framed by a stone gate extending from the wall of the house. The conical corner-entrance tower and hipped roof pierced by arched dormers identify the style as French Provincial.

58 Madge Phillips Studio
8910 S. Pleasant Ave.
1954, William Carnegie

This is a latter-day version of the Walter Burley Griffin idiom as seen on 104th Pl. Although a sprawling single-story house rather than a compact cottage, it has the deep eaves and patterned wooden muntins of Griffin's distinctive style.

59 Ignatius Chap House
8831 S. Pleasant Ave.
1928, Homer G. Sailor

A dollhouse masquerading as a hacienda, it has a miniature entrance tower with blind arches. Note the painted tiles inset into the rough stucco.

60 Everett Robert Brewer House
2078 W. Hopkins Pl.
1924, Murray D. Hetherington

The irregular roofline, with its variegated slate hewn into random-sized slabs, evokes the craftsmanship of a preindustrial era. But the twentieth century asserts itself in the orderly arrangement of large windows in the projecting central section.

61 George W. Reed House
2122 W. Hopkins Pl.
1929, James Roy Allen

The irregular massing of this sprawling house, with four wings spinning off the central block, was probably intended to suggest an English country house

Hetherington House

If North Beverly is a symphony of architectural styles, here's the tuba. Everything is overblown: the five-foot eaves, the picture windows, and the first-floor coat of many colors that could have been the inspiration for Perma-stone. The finishing touch is the highly manicured yard, complete with marshmallow and corkscrew topiary.

enlarged over the centuries. The style is early Renaissance, with Classical details grafted onto medieval forms.

62 Murray D. Hetherington House
8918 S. Hamilton Ave.
1924, Murray D. Hetherington

Second-generation Beverly archi-tect Hetherington's home is en-dearingly and unself-consciously pretty. It's the perfect Cotswold cottage, from the irregular massing and roofline to the rough-hewn materials, to the flagstone-lined miniature streambed. Note the shield with the construction date in the stucco panel on the front.

63 James Alex Brough House
8929 S. Hamilton Ave.
1927, Murray D. Hetherington

This folksy stucco Spanish Revival home could be a stage set for *The Barber of Seville*, even down to the balcony.

64 8958 S. Hamilton Ave.
1951, Joseph Emil Hosek

65 S. P. Balzekas House
9000 S. Bell Ave.
1935, William Sevic

In this multilevel Prairie and Moderne mishmash, the flat roofs projecting at many levels shelter metal-framed corner casement windows.

66 Wilfome Frisby House
8959 S. Claremont Ave.
1937, Albert F. Heino

This Californian amalgam of Mis-sion, Moderne, and Craftsman elements would look more at home under palm trees and jaca-randas. The flat roof, reached by a flight of stairs above the entry, doubles as a porch. The corner casement windows are Art Mod-erne, but the heavily textured brick recalls the neighborhood's Revival houses.

67 Dan Everett Waid House
9332 S. Damen Ave.
1895, architect unknown

This lively Queen Anne house has an unusual triple-gable com-position that is symmetrical yet highly picturesque.

Balzekas House

PULLMAN/
ROSELAND

106th

Forrestville

North Pullman Row Houses

16

Langley

Champlain

Former North Pullman Fire Station

17

107th

Forest

Calumet

King Dr

Vernon

Eberhart

108th

Cottage Grove

109th

Pullman Administration Bldg

2

110th

Hotel Florence

Chicago Police Dept

← To Calumet Expwy (I-94) and Loop →

111th

I

King Dr

Vernon

3

Row Houses

Langley

Arcade Row

8

10

112th

Pullman Methodist (Greenstone Church)

Stables

5

9

4

6

Market Hall

13

Block House

Apt Bldg

11

"The Cottages"

Ellis

Holy Rosary

18

113th

Jimmy's Place II

21

15

7

Front

Row Houses

Pullman School

Champlain

12

Three-Flat Apartments

Forest

Two-Flats

23

Forrestville

St Lawrence

Honeymoon Row

14

Paradise Temple

Calumet

22

20

Front Street Saloon

24

19

Apartments

Schlitz Row

← 115th To Calumet Expwy (I-94) and Loop →

Kensington

25 Foster House
12147 S Harvard
13 blocks west;
6 blocks south

In 1878 the swampy land now locked between the Dan Ryan and Calumet expressways contained a few Dutch farms in the community of Roseland, high ground along what is now Michigan Ave., and fewer than twenty houses in the village of Kensington, centering on the railroad junction at 115th St. and Cottage Grove Ave. Five years later the population had soared to 7,000, most of whom were laborers drawn by new industry. The leading attraction was the company town of Pullman, begun by railroad car manufacturer George M. Pullman in April 1880 on 500 acres between the western edge of Lake Calumet and the Illinois Central Railroad right-of-way. Pullman's plans called for a model town set on the north and south sides of the Pullman Palace Car Co.'s works. Superior living quarters in a healthful setting far from urban problems, he believed, would attract good workers and enhance productivity. Pullman insisted that his venture was not philanthropy but good business, and he expected everything in the town—houses, stores, stable, and even the church—to bring in a return of 6 percent on investment.

Pullman's architect was Solon S. Beman, newly launched from the office of East Coast architect Richard M. Upjohn. His landscape designer was New Yorker Nathan F. Barrett, an avowed formalist whose work contrasted with the popular naturalism of Frederick Law Olmsted. Barrett's aesthetic gave the Pullman layouts their strongly French tone, with housing units arranged in carefully balanced sets, adorned with undulating walls like French pavilions, and oriented toward garden spaces. Beman's facades, of bricks made from Lake Calumet clay, reveal the French predilection for indicating the underlying construction, even if only with a course of black brick at a floor line. Slate-covered mansard stories equaling one-third the building's height are grace notes throughout the town.

Other developers capitalized on the popularity of this famous experiment, especially the West Pullman Land Association, formed in 1890 to exploit the area west of State St. and south of 119th St. One portion, Stewart Ridge, was reserved for large houses on spacious lots. But Pullman's paternalism as well as other ambitions for the area were thwarted by the depression of 1893 and by the notorious Pullman Strike of 1894. Workers' protests that rents remained high while wages were cut escalated into a national confrontation between railroad owners and the nascent railroad union led by Eugene V. Debs. The coup de grace came in 1898, when the Illinois Supreme Court found the company in violation of a state law forbidding businesses to own land in excess of their industrial needs. By 1907, the court-ordered sale of Pullman had been completed.

The communities of Pullman, Roseland, Kensington, and West Pullman grew during the industrial buildups of the world wars. Today they stagnate as their industries depart. The Pullman works closed in 1981, leaving behind an area that had seen rapid racial change in the 1960s. Residents strive to maintain their landmark town, wrested from developers by the Historic Pullman Foundation, which gained national landmark status for it and seeks its restoration. Meanwhile, the State of Illinois, which owns the Pullman Administration Building and the Florence Hotel, studies plans for a railroad museum.
—Mary Alice Molloy

■ Chicago Police
Department—Area 2
Detective Headquarters
727 E. 111th St.
*1981, City of Chicago, Dept. of
Public Works Bureau of Architecture,
Joseph W. Casserly, Chicago city
arch.; Murphy/Jahn, consulting arch.*

Panels as blue as a Chicago cop's uniform, layered in long stripes with clear and opaque glass block, form the durable, low-maintenance, energy-efficient walls of this justice factory. The police headquarters and a court complex have separate entries

Hotel Florence

around a shared court, enlivened by Loren Madsen's *Suspended Sentence* (1981). Composed of frosted-glass blocks, the sculpture is suspended from stainless-steel wire.

❷ Pullman Administration Building & Clock Tower
S. Cottage Grove Ave. north of E. 111th St.
1880, Solon S. Beman

Rooflines may be many and picturesque, but the massing remains rigidly, symmetrically French (the northern wing's southern mate is buried within later additions). The original focal point of the Pullman complex, it demonstrates the strong hold of French architectural principles on American architecture in the 1880s despite Queen Anne enthusiasms.

❸ Hotel Florence
11111 S. Forrestville Ave.
1881, Solon S. Beman

Named for Pullman's favorite daughter, this "large gingerbread country villa" with fifty guest rooms introduces the robust wooden embellishments on porches, gables, and stairs that characterize Beman's Queen Anne work. The trim is painted in "official" Pullman colors, two greens and a deep red, researched and reformulated by Pullman neighbor Sherwin-Williams. Go inside to see the restaurant and historically furnished rooms.

❹ Pullman United Methodist Church (Greenstone Church)
11211 S. St. Lawrence Ave.
1882, Solon S. Beman

The only significant importation of materials for Pullman was the serpentine rock quarried in New England for the town's only company-owned church. It was intended as a union church, with all denominations sharing the use and cost. This showpiece combines the peaked roofs of the Gothic with the round-arched openings and rock-faced masonry popularized by H. H. Richardson.

❺ Former Pullman Stables
11201 S. Cottage Grove Ave.
ca. 1881, Solon S. Beman

Time and unsympathetic readaptation have dimmed but not erased the charm of the wooden horses' heads, the wide entrance, and the shingle facing of this communal barn. It was erected to reduce town maintenance by keeping horses off most Pullman streets.

❻ Market Hall and Colonnade Apartments and Town Houses
E. 112th St. and S. Champlain Ave.
1892, Solon S. Beman

Four excruciatingly narrow curved units with bachelor apartments above arcades are book-ended with matching town houses in this touch of Italy.

They were inserted into the town fabric after a market hall on this site burned down. In the center is the remaining single story of the second Pullman Market Hall.

Colonnade Apartments

7 George M. Pullman Public School

11311 S. Forrestville Ave.
1910, Dwight H. Perkins

Beman's school was replaced by a distinctively Perkinsian stylized Gothic block, featuring thick terra-cotta copings and angle buttressing against rust brick walls.

8 Five-Room Row Houses

11145–11151 S. St. Lawrence Ave.
1880, Solon S. Beman

A significant contribution to 1880s residential design was Beman's plan for a five-room worker's cottage, introduced in this block of row houses, the first to be completed in Pullman. The house, which could range in width from fourteen to twenty-two feet, features a front parlor and rear kitchen/dining room on the main floor. Upstairs are a front bedroom and two small rear ones split by a skylit stair hall that leads to a water closet. Beman picturesquely grouped his row houses. Here a pair that shares a dormered, mansarded second story is linked with another pair in which an enhanced central element is topped with a purlin gable. No Pullman five-room house is unaltered; additions here include porches with details drawn from the Hotel Florence.

9 "Arcade Row" Houses

533–535 E. 112th St.
1881, Solon S. Beman

In Pullman the best buildings were placed in the most conspicuous locations. These two are the best-preserved examples in a row of gambrel-dormered, three-story row houses that faces the town's park. These units, large by Pullman standards, were not restricted to middle-class tenants. They were available to anyone who could afford the rents—whether the Pullman school principal, who lived at 533 in 1889, or the collection of carpenters and foremen for whom 535 was a boardinghouse.

10 Block House

704–706 E. 112th St.
ca. 1881, Solon S. Beman

Tenements anywhere else, they were called block houses in Pullman and offered individual rooms for rent. In a long row along the town's eastern edge, their low status and back-bench location called for simple common brick facades, and yet on each the third story featured an extended central section set off from the mansard roof. This building now houses two-bedroom apartments. Other surviving block houses are at 11127 S. Langley Ave. and at 614, 644–646 and 645–647 E. 113th St.

11 Corner Apartment Building

11261 S. Forrestville Ave.
ca. 1884–1886, Solon S. Beman

This nearly square corner building houses its third story under an unusually high, curbed mansard roof. Others are found along 113th St. at 11260 S. St. Lawrence Ave. and 11270 S. Champlain Ave.

12 Three-Flat Apartment Buildings

S. Langley Ave. between 113th and 114th Sts.
1880–1882, Solon S. Beman

An entire block of identical three-story, three-flat units stands with the backs of the units against the railroad tracks.

"The Cottages"

Although built of the most modest materials, they have some of Pullman's most formal layouts. In three places, units are pulled out to the sidewalk, creating two forecourts.

13 "The Cottages"
11218–11250 S. Langley Ave.
1880–1882, Solon S. Beman

Seventeen five-room row houses a mere fourteen feet wide demonstrate the great variety of facades that Beman and his associates such as Irving K. Pond designed in Pullman's early years for even the least expensive houses.

14 Flats on "Honeymoon Row"
11401–11403 S. Champlain Ave.
1888, Solon S. Beman

Ingenuity faltered as building continued in Pullman. These four-flat units employ common brick picked out with red brick in the manner of industrial housing worldwide in the late nineteenth century; the only relief is in the low conical roofs at the ends and midpoints. Each trapezoidal bay has three doors. The two on the sides opened into the main-floor flats, and the central one led to stairs to two upper units. There were originally four water closets at the rear of the main floor, one for each unit.

15 Five-Room Row Houses
11307–11309 S. Cottage Grove Ave.
1888, Solon S. Beman

Houses seen by the public from passing trains received special treatment, even when they were modest dwellings. These row houses have triangular bays, wide pedimented porches, and carefully balanced contrasts between light and dark brick that are unknown elsewhere in Pullman. The units to the south have the town's only roundheaded windows.

16 North Pullman Row Houses
10701–10739 S. Cottage Grove Ave.
ca. 1884–1885, Solon S. Beman

The first sight of Pullman from trains leaving Chicago was this picturesque row, which steps forward to follow the angle of the street. Anchored by a large corner rooming house and distinguished by particularly high false rooflines, the buildings share simple, flat, red-orange brick facades.

Fire Station

17 Former North Pullman Fire Station
623 E. 108th St.
1895, Solon S. Beman

With a limestone pedimented truck door, ranks of arched windows, and an attenuated hose-drying tower, this Renaissance fire station was the last gasp in Pullman construction. It reflects the prevailing mode of the 1890s as surely as the initial Pullman buildings document the previous decade.

18 Holy Rosary Roman Catholic Church
11300 S. Martin Luther King, Jr. Dr.
1890, Solon S. Beman

Built on Pullman-held land for company employees, this church replays in brick the Greenstone Church's round arched windows under peaked roofs and steep tower cap. But details such as the self-corbeling, the arched detailing on the tower, and the small rose window appear to reflect the communicants' Germanic background rather than the donor's preferences.

"Schlitz Row"—Front St. Saloon Building

"Schlitz Row" 19 Paradise Inn Store and Flats
400–410 E. 115th St.
1905, Frommann & Jebsen
20 Front Street Saloon Building
11444 S. Front St.
1907, Frommann & Jebsen
21 Jimmy's Place II
11402 S. Front St.
1906, Frommann & Jebsen
22 Apartments
11429–11431 S. Martin Luther King, Jr. Dr.
1906, Frommann & Jebsen
23 Two-Flats
11413, 11419, and 11425 S. Martin Luther King, Jr. Dr.
1906, Frommann & Jebsen

To keep its dry town safe from Demon Rum, the Pullman Company controlled a wide swath of surrounding land until forced by a court order to sell it in 1904.

The first on hand to buy was Edward G. Uihlein, Chicago agent for the Joseph Schlitz Brewing Co., which acquired two blocks immediately west of Pullman's residential portions. They were soon filled with saloons, a stable, and housing for workers seeking a way out from under the company thumb. Uihlein's buildings are common sights in old German neighborhoods and were designed to look familiar to their first patrons. They are ornamented with friezes of patterned brickwork in subtly varied colors, wide flat-arched window openings with contrasting brick voussoirs, copper flashing, and other architectural details drawn directly from industrial towns of 1870s Germany. The most representative example here is the large store-and-flats building at 400–410 E. 115th, with brick that is dark maroon at the base, greenish throughout the walls, and red around the windows. Before the train tracks were elevated, Schlitz's terra-cotta globe trademark, set high in a peaked dormer at the building's northeastern end, was as visible as a church steeple.

24 Paradise Temple Church of God in Christ (Shomre Hadath Synagogue)
11437–11445 S. Forest Ave.
1928, Harry L. Morse

This is a late example of the curved gable synagogue; the design was popularized by the Grande Synagogue of Paris, in the rue de la Victoire (1874, A. P. Aldrophe). But Morse used strictly twentieth-century Chicago materials: wire-cut brick, exposed concrete as trim, and an inset band of multicolored tiles.

25 Stephen A. Foster Residence and Stable
12147 S. Harvard Ave.
1900, Frank Lloyd Wright

The house with the hat marks Wright's brief flirtation with Japanese variations on the Shingle Style theme. The tall, brimmed roof is echoed in the dormers and all but swamps the shingle-clad base.

TOUR
INFORMATION

If you would like a knowledgeable human guide to help you explore Chicago's architecture, the following are some of the many opportunities to tour the city on foot or by bus, boat, bicycle, or elevated train. Note that all tours are subject to change, so always write or call first.

The most extensive architectural tour program in the metropolitan area is run by the **Chicago Architecture Foundation (CAF)**. Volunteer docents trained by CAF give daily tours of the Loop year-round; one tour covers early skyscrapers while a second highlights newer construction. From spring to fall, docents give tours in many Chicago neighborhoods and several suburbs. Most are walking tours, but bicycles, boats, and buses are also popular. "Elevated Chicago," a tour by elevated train, is offered in spring and fall. Throughout the warm months, tours of downtown, viewed from boats on the Chicago River, originate from the south bank of the river at S. Michigan Ave. and E. Wacker Dr. CAF also operates the Clarke House and Glessner House museums on Prairie Ave. as well as an exhibit gallery, book and gift store, and lecture hall at 224 S. Michigan Ave. For details, contact the Foundation at 224 S. Michigan Ave., Chicago 60604, or call 312/922-3432 (or 312/922-TOUR for recorded tour information).

Chicago

The **Landmarks Preservation Council of Illinois (LPCI)** has been presenting an annual "Tour of Chicago's Historic Churches and Synagogues" since 1981. Each year, the religious architecture of a particular community is chosen for touring on the first Sunday in May. The tours begin at one of the sites with a keynote speaker. For information, contact LPCI at 53 W. Jackson Blvd., Ste. 752, Chicago 60603, or call 312/922-1742.

The Michigan Ave. lobby of the **Auditorium Building** (now Roosevelt University) by Adler & Sullivan, 430 S. Michigan Ave., contains an exhibit on its history that may be visited whenever the building is open. Guided tours of the theater, which include a stop in the lobby, are offered Mondays, Tuesdays, and occasionally Wednesdays and Thursdays, depending on the theater schedule. For information and reservations, call 312/922-4046.

The **Charnley House**, by Frank Lloyd Wright, 1365 N. Astor St., is home to the Chicago Institute for Architecture and Urbanism and is operated by the Skidmore, Owings & Merrill Foundation. For information and tour reservations, call 312/951-8006.

The **Chicago Cultural Center**, 78 E. Washington St., is open to visitors every day of the week. Guided tours are offered on Tuesdays at 1:30 P.M. and Thursdays at 11 A.M. The City of Chicago Department of Cultural Affairs offers exhibits and programs; the private Museum of Broadcast Communications is here as well and open every day. Call 312/744-6630 for information.

The **Clarke House**, 1855 S. Indiana Ave., and H. H. Richardson's **Glessner House**, 1800 S. Prairie Ave., are open for tours given by the Chicago Architecture Foundation every Wednesday, Friday, Saturday, and Sunday. Call 312/922-3432 (or 312/922-TOUR for recorded tour information).

In Pullman, the **Historic Pullman Foundation** provides guides for touring the community on Sundays and runs an annual house tour on the second weekend in October. Tours begin at the Hotel Florence, 11111 S. Forrestville Ave., where the Foundation operates a restaurant. Contact the Foundation at 11111 S. Forrestville Ave., Chicago 60628, or call 312/785-8181.

Frank Lloyd Wright's **Robie House**, 5757 S. Woodlawn Ave., is the home of the office of the Alumni Association of the University of Chicago. Tours are given daily by student guides. Call 312/702-2175 for tour information.

Oak Park

The **Visitors Center** offers an orientation to Oak Park, maps, guidebooks, and tour tickets. It is open every day from 10 A.M. to 5 P.M. Write to the Visitors Center at 158 Forest Ave., Oak Park, Ill. 60302, or call 708/848-1500 for a brochure describing Oak Park tours.

The **Frank Lloyd Wright Home and Studio**, 951 Chicago Ave., Oak Park, Ill. 60302, has been fully restored and is open for tours every day. It may be visited by itself or as a package with the Forest Ave. walking tour of the exteriors of thirteen Wright-designed houses. Forest Ave. may also be toured with the help of a map or a self-guided cassette (available in English, Japanese, and German). For information, contact the Visitors Center. In the former garage of the Home and Studio is a book and gift store, the Gingko Tree Bookshop.

Pleasant Home, by George W. Maher, 217 S. Pleasant Ave., is open midday on Friday and on Saturday and Sunday afternoons for tours offered by the Pleasant Home Foundation. The Oak Park–River Forest Historical Society displays its collection on the second floor. Call 708/383-2654 for information on tours.

Unity Temple, by Frank Lloyd Wright, 875 Lake St., may be toured with the aid of a self-guided cassette on weekdays and with a guided tour on weekends. Call 708/848-6225 for information; tour availability may change to accommodate church events.

Wright Plus is an annual housewalk sponsored by the Frank Lloyd Wright Home and Studio Foundation and features guided tours of eight privately owned homes and two public buildings designed by Wright and his contemporaries. The tour, which quickly sells out, takes place on the third weekend in May. Tickets go on sale March 1. Contact the Visitors Center for more information.

PHOTO CREDITS

The position of photographs on a page has been abbrievated in the following manner: T, top; B, bottom; L, left; R, right.

THE SHAPING OF CHICAGO: P. 3 Lewis University Canal Collection; 4 Courtesy Chicago Historical Society; 5 Courtesy The Art Institute of Chicago; 6 Courtesy Chicago Historical Society; 8 Courtesy Chicago Historical Society; 10 Courtesy Chicago Historical Society; 11 Courtesy of the Commission on Chicago Landmarks; 14 Courtesy Chicago Historical Society; 15 Courtesy Chicago Historical Society; 17 Courtesy Chicago Historical Society; 19 Hedrich-Blessing photograph, courtesy Chicago Historical Society; 22 Courtesy Chicago Historical Society; 23T Courtesy Chicago Historical Society; 23B Photo by Ron Gordon; **THE LOOP:** P. 34 Hedrich-Blessing photograph, courtesy Chicago Historical Society; 36 Hedrich-Blessing photograph, courtesy Hedrich-Blessing; 37 Barbara Crane for the Commission on Chicago Landmarks; 38L Courtesy Chicago Historical Society; 38R Hedrich-Blessing photograph, courtesy Chicago Historical Society; 39 Courtesy Chicago Historical Society; 42 Bob Thall, courtesy The Art Institute of Chicago; 43 Courtesy of Chicago Park District Special Collections; 44 Hedrich-Blessing photograph, courtesy Chicago Historical Society; 45 Courtesy Chicago Historical Society; 46 Photo by Alice Sinkevitch; 47T Barbara Crane for the Commission on Chicago Landmarks; 47B Courtesy of the Commission on Chicago Landmarks; 49 Courtesy of the Commission on Chicago Landmarks; 50 Courtesy of the Commission on Chicago Landmarks; 52T Hedrich-Blessing photograph, courtesy Chicago Historical Society; 52B Hedrich-Blessing photograph, courtesy Chicago Historical Society; 53 Courtesy of the Commission on Chicago Landmarks; 54 Hedrich-Blessing photograph, courtesy Chicago Historical Society; 56 Courtesy of the Commission on Chicago Landmarks; 57 Courtesy of the Commission on Chicago Landmarks; 58 Hedrich-Blessing photograph, courtesy Chicago Historical Society; 59 Photo by Ron Gordon; 61 Courtesy of Chicago Historical Society; 62L Howard N. Kaplan, © HNK Architectural Photography, Inc.; 62TR Hedrich-Blessing photograph, courtesy Chicago Historical Society; 62BR Courtesy The Art Institute of Chicago; 63 Courtesy Chicago Historical Society; 65 Photo by David Clifton; 66 Howard N. Kaplan, courtesy of Holabird & Root; 67 Hedrich-Blessing photograph, courtesy Chicago Historical Society; 68 Bob Harr, Hedrich-Blessing; 69 Hedrich-Blessing photograph, courtesy Chicago Historical Society; 71 Hedrich-Blessing photograph, courtesy Chicago Historical Society; 72 Hedrich-Blessing photograph, courtesy Chicago Historical Society; 73 James R. Steinkamp, courtesy of Murphy/Jahn–Lester B. Knight & Associates, A Joint Venture; 75 Jim Hedrich, Hedrich-Blessing; 77L Hedrich-Blessing photograph, courtesy Chicago Historical Society; 77R James R. Steinkamp, Steinkamp/ Ballogg Photography, Chicago; 78 Courtesy Chicago Historical Society; 79T Nick Merrick, Hedrich-Blessing, courtesy of McClier; 79B Nick Merrick, Hedrich-Blessing, courtesy of McClier; 80 Photo by John Gronkowski; 82 James R. Steinkamp, courtesy of Murphy/Jahn; 83T Chicago Architectural Photographing Co. for the Commission on Chicago Landmarks; 83B Hedrich-Blessing photograph, courtesy Chicago Historical Society; 85 Photo by Harold A. Nelson; 86 Scott McDonald, Hedrich-Blessing; 87 Nick Merrick, Hedrich-Blessing; 88 Photo by Gregory Murphey; 89 Robert Shimer, Hedrich-Blessing, courtesy of Merchandise Mart Properties, Inc.; 91 Photo by Timothy Hursley; 92T © Judith Bromley; 92B Hedrich-Blessing photograph, courtesy Chicago Historical Society; 93 Hedrich-Blessing photograph, courtesy Chicago Historical Society; 94 Nick Merrick, Hedrich-Blessing; 95T Bob Thall for the Commission on Chicago Landmarks; 95B William Kildow Photography; **NORTH MICHIGAN AVENUE / STREETERVILLE:** P. 99 Steve Beal for the Commission on Chicago Landmarks; 100 Courtesy of the Commission on Chicago Landmarks; 101 Hedrich-Blessing photograph, courtesy Chicago Historical Society; 102L Courtesy of the Commission on Chicago Landmarks; 102R Courtesy Chicago Historical Society; 103T Courtesy of Harry Weese Associates; 103B Courtesy Chicago Historical Society; 104L Photo by Alice Sinkevitch; 104R Bob Thall for the Commission on Chicago Landmarks; 105T Steve Hall, Hedrich-Blessing; 105B George Lambros, courtesy of Loebl, Schlossman & Hackl; 106 Courtesy Chicago Historical Society; 107 Courtesy Chicago Historical Society; 109 Courtesy Chicago

Historical Society; 110 Courtesy of the Commission on Chicago Landmarks;
111L Hedrich-Blessing photograph, courtesy Chicago Historical Society; 111R
Bob Thall for the Commission on Chicago Landmarks; 112 Hedrich-Blessing
photograph, courtesy Chicago Historical Society; 114T Timothy Hursley, courtesy of Holabird & Root; 114B Gregory Murphey, courtesy of Perkins & Will;
115 David Urshel, courtesy of Bertrand Goldberg Associates; 116 Howard N.
Kaplan, © HNK Architectural Photography, Inc.; 117 Hedrich-Blessing photo-
graph, courtesy Chicago Historical Society; 118L Hedrich-Blessing photograph,
courtesy Chicago Historical Society; 118R © Wayne Cable, Cable Studios; 119
Nick Merrick, Hedrich-Blessing; **RIVER NORTH:** P. 123 Courtesy Chicago
Historical Society; 124 Courtesy Chicago Historical Society; 125T Russell
Phillips, courtesy of Holabird & Root; 125B Bob Thall for the Commission on
Chicago Landmarks; 126 William Kildow Photography; 127 Photo by William A.
Rooney; 128 Barbara Crane for the Commission on Chicago Landmarks; 129
Courtesy of the Commission on Chicago Landmarks; 130 Photo by Neal A.
Vogel; 131 Courtesy of the Commission on Chicago Landmarks; 132T Courtesy
Moody Bible Institute Archives; 132B Courtesy Chicago Historical Society; 133T
Photo by John Gronkowski; 133B Howard N. Kaplan, © HNK Architectural
Photography, Inc.; 134 Courtesy The Art Institute of Chicago; 135 Courtesy of
the Commission on Chicago Landmarks; 136L Photo by Neal A. Vogel; 136R
Courtesy Chicago Historical Society; 137 *The Far Side* © 1992 FAR WORKS, INC.
Reprinted with permission of UNIVERSAL PRESS SYNDICATE. All rights reserved.;
SOUTH LOOP: P. 141L Bob Harr, Hedrich-Blessing; 141R Leslie Schwartz
Photography; 142 Leslie Schwartz Photography; 143 Courtesy of the Com-
mission on Chicago Landmarks; 144 Photo by David Pilarczyk; 145 © Wayne
Cable, Cable Studios; 146 Photo by Ron Gordon; 147 Photo by John Gronkowski;
148T Ron Gordon for the Commission on Chicago Landmarks; 148B Photo by
Ron Gordon; 149 David Belle, courtesy of Bertrand Goldberg Associates; 150
Hedrich-Blessing photograph, courtesy Chicago Historical Society; 151 Marco
Lorenzetti, Hedrich-Blessing; **GOLD COAST/OLD TOWN:** P. 157 Courtesy of
the Commission on Chicago Landmarks; 159L Photo by David Clifton; 159R
Courtesy of Loebl, Schlossman & Hackl; 160 Barbara Crane for the Commission
on Chicago Landmarks; 161 Courtesy Chicago Historical Society; 162T Nick
Merrick, Hedrich-Blessing; 162B Hedrich-Blessing photograph, courtesy Chicago
Historical Society; 163T Barbara Crane for the Commission on Chicago
Landmarks; 163B Hedrich-Blessing photograph, courtesy Chicago Historical
Society; 164L Hedrich-Blessing photograph, courtesy Chicago Historical Society;
164R Courtesy Chicago Historical Society; 165T Courtesy of the Commission
on Chicago Landmarks; 165B Howard N. Kaplan, © HNK Architectural
Photography, Inc.; 167T Howard N. Kaplan, © HNK Architectural Photography,
Inc.; 167B Paul Zakoian, courtesy of Weese Langley Weese Architects Ltd.;
169T Photo by David Clifton; 169B Courtesy Chicago Historical Society; 170
Kate Roth Photography; 171 Mark Ballogg, Steinkamp/Ballogg Photography,
Chicago, courtesy of Holabird & Root; 172 Barbara Crane for the Commission
on Chicago Landmarks; 173 © Paul Warchol; 174 Barbara Crane for the
Commission on Chicago Landmarks; 175T Courtesy of Krueck & Sexton
Architects; 175B Photo by Bob Thall; 176 Mark Ballogg, Steinkamp/Ballogg
Photography, Chicago; 177 Courtesy Chicago Historical Society; 178L Photo by
Sandy Peterson; 178TR Hedrich-Blessing photograph, courtesy Chicago
Historical Society; 178BR Photo by Sandy Peterson; 179 Photo by David
Clifton; **LINCOLN PARK:** P. 184 Photo by Harold A. Nelson; 185 Leslie
Schwartz Photography; 186 © Boschke Photography; 187L Barbara Crane for
the Commission on Chicago Landmarks; 187R Leslie Schwartz Photography;
188 Leslie Schwartz Photography; 189T Courtesy The Art Institute of Chicago;
189B Kate Roth Photography; 190 Van Inwegen Photography; 191T Courtesy
Chicago Historical Society; 191B Photo by Harold A. Nelson; 192T Courtesy
Chicago Historical Society; 192B Photo © Don DuBroff/Chicago; 193L
Courtesy Chicago Historical Society; 193R © 1993 The Art Institute of Chicago.
All rights reserved.; 194L Hedrich-Blessing photograph, courtesy Chicago
Historical Society; 194R Kate Roth Photography; 195T Photo by David Clifton;
195B Courtesy of *The Elks Magazine*; 198 Courtesy The Art Institute of
Chicago; 199 Courtesy of Chicago Park District Special Collections; 200 Susan
Reich, courtesy of Lincoln Park Zoo; 201 Courtesy of Chicago Park District
Special Collections; **LAKEVIEW/UPTOWN/RAVENSWOOD:** P. 205T
Howard N. Kaplan, © HNK Architectural Photography, Inc.; 205B Hedrich-
Blessing photograph, courtesy Chicago Historical Society; 206L Bob Thall for the
Commission on Chicago Landmarks; 206R *Architectural Record*, v. 21, Feb. 1907;
207L Bob Thall for the Commission on Chicago Landmarks; 207R Bob Thall for
the Commission on Chicago Landmarks; 208L Kate Roth Photography; 208R
Kate Roth Photography; 210T Photostat line drawing by Schroeder Murchie
Laya Associates Ltd.; 210B Scott McDonald, Hedrich-Blessing; 211 Photo by

David Clifton; 212T Richard Nickel for the Commission on Chicago Landmarks; 212B Courtesy Chicago Public Schools; 214 Barbara Crane for the Commission on Chicago Landmarks; 215 Bob Thall for the Commission on Chicago Landmarks; 216 Photo by Barry Bebart; 217T Courtesy The Art Institute of Chicago; 217B Bob Thall for the Commission on Chicago Landmarks; 218 Barbara Crane for the Commission on Chicago Landmarks; 219T Howard N. Kaplan, © HNK Architectural Photography, Inc.; 219B Leslie Schwartz Photography; 221T William Kildow Photography; 221B Leslie Schwartz Photography; 222T © Fred Leavitt Photography; 222B Mark Ballogg, Steinkamp/Ballogg Photography, Chicago; 223L Leslie Schwartz Photography; 223R Photo by Ron Gordon; 224 Jim Hedrich, Hedrich-Blessing; 225T Courtesy Chicago Public Schools; 225B Photo by David Clifton; **EDGEWATER/ROGERS PARK:** P. 229T Photo by Ron Gordon; 229B © Fred Leavitt Photography; 230 Photo by David Vincent Forte, AIA; 231 Leslie Schwartz Photography; 232T William Kildow Photography; 232B Leslie Schwartz Photography; 233 Photo by Mati Maldre; 234 Courtesy Mundelein College Archives; 235 Photo © by Lawrence Okrent; 236 © George Lambros Photography; 237T Photo by Ron Gordon; 237B Photo by Mati Maldre; 238T Courtesy Chicago Public Schools; 238B Leslie Schwartz Photography; 239 © Fred Leavitt Photography; 240L © Fred Leavitt Photography; 240R © George Lambros Photography; 242L Photo by Barry Bebart; 242R Photo by Barry Bebart; 243T Bob Thall for the Commission on Chicago Landmarks; 243B Photo by Barry Bebart; **NORTHWEST SIDE:** P. 250L Barbara Crane for the Commission on Chicago Landmarks; 250R William Kildow Photography; 251 Photo by Dennis Pratt; 252L Photo by Felicity Rich; 252TR Andreas Simon, *Chicago, die Gartenstadt*, 1893; 252BR Photo by Felicity Rich; 253L Photo by Neal A. Vogel; 253R James R. Steinkamp, Steinkamp/Ballogg Photography, Chicago; 255T Courtesy of Chicago Park District Special Collections; 255B Courtesy of Chicago Park District Special Collections; 256 Barry Rustin Photography; 257L Photo by Sean J. Reidy; 257R Courtesy Chicago Historical Society; 258L Photo by Sean J. Reidy; 258R Photo by Felicity Rich; 258B Kate Roth Photography; 259 Barbara Crane for the Commission on Chicago Landmarks; 260 Steve Beal for the Commission on Chicago Landmarks; 261 © Fred Leavitt Photography; **CHICAGO–O'HARE INTERNATIONAL AIRPORT:** P. 264 James R. Steinkamp, courtesy of Murphy/Jahn; 265 Timothy Hursley, courtesy of Murphy/Jahn; 266 Hedrich-Blessing photograph, courtesy Chicago Historical Society; 267 James R. Steinkamp, Steinkamp/Ballogg Photography, Chicago; **NEAR WEST SIDE:** P. 272 Leslie Schwartz Photography; 273 Photo by Neal A. Vogel; 274 Elaine S. Baxton for the Commission on Chicago Landmarks; 275 Courtesy The Art Institute of Chicago; 276 Barbara Crane for the Commission on Chicago Landmarks; 278T Photo by Neal A. Vogel; 278B Photo by Felicity Rich; 280 University of Illinois at Chicago, The University Library, University Archives; 282T Photo by Neal A. Vogel; 282B Bob Thall for the Commission on Chicago Landmarks; 283 Howard N. Kaplan © HNK Architectural Photography, Inc.; 285 Leslie Schwartz Photography; 287 University of Illinois at Chicago, The University Library, University Archives; 288 © Judith Bromley; **GARFIELD PARK/AUSTIN:** P. 293 Photo by Ron Gordon; 295 Courtesy of Chicago Park District Special Collections; 296 Courtesy of Chicago Park District Special Collections; 298T Photo © Don DuBroff/Chicago; 298B Chicago Historic Resources Survey of the Commission on Chicago Landmarks; 299 Ben Altman/SPG; 300T Photo by Josh Goldman; 300B *Western Architect*, v. 21, Feb. 1915; 301 Photo by Alice Sinkevitch; 302 Photo by Josh Goldman; 303T Photo by Josh Goldman; 303B Photo by Neal A. Vogel; 304T Photo by David Clifton; 304B Copyright © Thom Clark; 305 Photo by Josh Goldman; 306 Photo by Neal A. Vogel; 307T Courtesy The Art Institute of Chicago; 307B Courtesy of Chicago Park District Special Collections; **OAK PARK:** P. 313L Photo by Suzette Bross; 313R Photo by Josh Goldman; 314 Photo by Josh Goldman; 315T Photo by Josh Goldman; 315B Leslie Schwartz Photography; 316 Courtesy of the Historical Society of Oak Park and River Forest; 317T Photo by Suzette Bross; 317B Photo © Don DuBroff/Chicago; 318 Marco Lorenzetti, Hedrich-Blessing; 319T Photo by Josh Goldman; 319B © 1991 Wayne Cable, Cable Studios, Inc.; 320 Suzette Bross; 321 © Wayne Cable, Cable Studios; 322 Photo by Josh Goldman; 323 Photo by Alice Sinkevitch; 324 Photo by Josh Goldman; 326T Courtesy of the Frank Lloyd Wright Foundation; 326B Photo by Thomas A. Heinz; 328T Photo by Alice Sinkevitch; 328B Donald G. Kalec, courtesy of The Frank Lloyd Wright Home and Studio Foundation; 329 Jon Miller, Hedrich-Blessing, courtesy of The Frank Lloyd Wright Home and Studio Foundation; 330 Photo by Thomas A. Heinz; 331T Photo by Josh Goldman; 331B © Wayne Cable, Cable Studios; 332 Photo by Alice Sinkevitch; 333 © Wayne Cable, Cable Studios; **LOWER WEST SIDE:** P. 340 Photo © by Lawrence Okrent; 341 Mark Ballogg, Steinkamp/Ballogg Photography, Chicago; 343 Courtesy Chicago Historical Society; 344 Photo by

GLOSSARY

Many architectural terms have several meanings. Only those primary to this book or relevant to Chicago's built environment are given here.

A

abacus the slab surmounting columns that supports roof beams; also the topmost element—square or round—of a column capital

acanthus a common Mediterranean plant whose spike-edged leaf is used for decorative purposes in Classical architecture, especially in Corinthian and Composite capitals

acroterion a decorative element placed at the corners and peak of a roof in Classical buildings

aedicula the framing of a door, window, niche, or shrine with a pair of flanking columns supporting a gable

Adam Style architecture and interior decoration derived from the work of the British architect Robert Adam (1728–1792); based on Classical motifs, it often included Etruscan, Egyptian, and Gothic elements expressed in a light, linear, precisely detailed, and elegant manner

American Foursquare a popular house type from around 1905 to 1930 that borrowed elements from the Prairie Style and is characterized by a two-story square mass, a full-width front porch, and deep eaves

anthemion a decorative motif based on the honeysuckle, common in Greek architecture

apse the extension of the nave, or central body, of a church that traditionally contains the altar

arcade a line of arches resting on columns or piers, forming an interior aisle or exterior covered walkway

arcuated supported by arches or arched vaults, as opposed to straight beams

Art Deco a decorative style whose name derives from the Exposition Internationale des Arts Décoratifs et Industriels Modernes held in Paris in 1925; it is characterized by verticality and by geometric, stylized floral, and Native American motifs, often given a sleek, metallic, machine-made appearance

art glass a general term for artistically designed panels of transparent or translucent pieces of leaded glass, either clear or colored

Art Moderne an alternate term for Art Deco that has come to describe its 1930s and 1940s form, which is characterized by horizontality, curves, and streamlined forms that give an impression of speed

Art Nouveau a decorative style of the 1890s and early 1900s, primarily in Continental Europe; it took its name from a Parisian gallery for modern decoration, L'Art Nouveau, opened in 1895 to promote design based on natural forms expressed through sinuous lines

Arts & Crafts a British (later American) movement of the late nineteenth century that sought to improve social conditions through the production of handmade, high-quality objects that respected indigenous traditions rather than increasingly mechanized production

ashlar squared blocks of stone laid in horizontal rows with vertical joints

atrium an interior space open to the sky or covered with a skylight

B

baldachin an altar canopy that may be suspended from the ceiling, supported by a wall, or freestanding; frequently a dome resting on four columns

balloon frame a wood framing system, invented in 1833, that used machine-cut two-by-fours fastened with machine-made nails, allowing for fast and easy assembly; the name was meant derisively, implying that such lightweight structures would blow away in the wind

baluster the vertical element in a balustrade

balustrade a decorative railing consisting of a horizontal rail atop vertical supports that are often resting on a bottom rail

bargeboard decorative wood trim cut into curvilinear shapes and attached to the projecting gable ends of a roof

Baroque European architecture of the seventeenth and early eighteenth centuries, characterized by effusive ornament, curved forms, and complex spatial effects; the English and French versions are more restrained and employ classical elements

basilica a rectangular hall, divided by two rows of columns into a central aisle, or nave, and flanking side aisles; entered through a small room, or narthex, at the short end of the building, it terminates in a rounded end, or apse; also a title bestowed by the Pope on certain Roman Catholic churches of historic, artistic, or spiritual merit whereby special privileges are granted

bascule (French for seesaw) Chicago's most common type of movable bridge, in which counterbalanced leaves pivot around a trunnion, or pin

battered a wall that recedes as it rises

Bauhaus a design school founded by Walter Gropius in Weimar, Germany, in 1919 in which artists and architects collaborated in developing an industrial aesthetic of worldwide influence

Beaux Arts a style of design and planning, based on classical prototypes and often expressed on a monumental scale, named for the École des Beaux-Arts in Paris, at which many American architects, including Louis H. Sullivan, were trained

Bedford limestone a sedimentary rock formed from shells and shell fragments cemented with calcite; quarried near Bedford, Indiana

Bedford sandstone a sedimentary rock composed of sandlike quartz grains cemented with silica or other oxides, resulting in a variety of colors; quarried near Bedford, Indiana

belt course a horizontal band across an exterior wall or around a building; also known as a string-course

berm an earthen mound, either freestanding or adjoining a wall

beveled cut with angled edges

blind arcade a decorative row of arches set against a solid wall

board-and-batten wood siding composed of flat boards laid flush, with the seam covered by a thin board, or batten

bollard a low, thick post, often used in a series, to prevent vehicles from entering an area; also used on docks and ships for securing ropes and lines

Bower-Barff process invented in England in the 1870s for creating a rust-resistant, gunmetal, blue-black finish on cast iron

broken pediment a triangular gable above a door or window in which the center segment is removed

bungalow a modest brick or stucco house, usually one-and-a-half stories high, derived from the Hindustani word *bangla*, meaning Bengalese; in Chicago it usually has a flat or segmental front and Prairie School details

Byzantine the domed, round-arched, and colorful architecture of Greece, Turkey, and other countries; after flourishing from the fifth to the fifteenth centuries, it was revived in the nineteenth and twentieth

C

caisson a foundation made by sinking a boxlike form under water or through waterlogged ground to bedrock and then filling it with concrete; also a recessed panel in a ceiling or cupola

campanile a bell tower, usually freestanding, alongside a church

cantilever a structural element, such as a beam, balcony, or roof, that projects beyond a supporting wall and is counterbalanced by a downward force behind the wall

capital the uppermost, usually decorated, part of a column

cartouche an ornamental enframement, often oval with an elaborately carved frame and central inscription

casement a window that opens outward on side hinges mounted on the frame

center-pivot swing bridge a bridge supported on a structural element, or pivot

chamfered cut at an angle

chancel that extension of the nave which lies beyond the crossing of the transepts and is the sanctuary of the church

châteauesque a late nineteenth-century style derived from sixteenth-century French country estates and characterized by hipped and dormered roofs and finely carved ornament with a mixture of Gothic and Renaissance details

Chicago Housing Authority a municipal not-for-profit corporation created in 1937 to manage federally subsidized or funded housing; commissioners are appointed by the mayor but it receives neither city funding nor tax levies

Chicago School a movement (1875–1910) in which architects and engineers developed the construction technology and design aesthetic of tall, steel-framed commercial buildings

Chicago window a three-part design, used in a steel-framed building and comprising a wide fixed pane flanked by narrow, movable sash windows

chords the straight elements in a truss or across a curve that provide rigidity

Churrigueresque a heavy, lavish style of late Baroque ornament popular in early eighteenth-century Spain, Mexico, and South America and named after the Churriguera family of Spanish architects

clapboard horizontal wood siding in which the grain runs lengthwise, planed with one edge thicker than the other, and overlapping with the thicker side at the bottom

clerestory the highest portion of the walls of a nave, pierced by windows

coffered ornamented with recessed panels that form a continuous pattern

Colonial Revival a historical style popular from the 1880s to the 1930s and based on the eighteenth-century American interpretation of contemporaneous, Classically derived British architecture

colonnette a small thin column, generally used to form a clustered or compound pier

columbarium a repository for cremated remains, containing vaults lined with recesses

common brick inexpensive, unglazed brick intended for side and rear walls and usually painted when used on facades

Composite column one of the five Classical orders, it combines the acanthus-leaf capital of the Corinthian order, the large scrolled volutes of the Ionic capital, and a fluted shaft

console a decorative scrolled bracket, usually supporting a horizontal element and generally taller than its depth

corbel table a series of projecting bricks or stones that extend progressively away from the building plane as they rise, and support a stringcourse or eaves

Corinthian column one of the five Classical orders; the capital consists of two rows of acanthus leaves topped by narrow arched volutes

cornice a decorative projection, generally along the edge of a roof

cornice return the extension of a cornice as it wraps around a gable or the sides of a building

courtyard building a U- or C-shaped building, generally three or four stories in height, constructed around a central landscaped courtyard facing the street

Craftsman initially, a monthly magazine (1901–1916) published by furniture manufacturer Gustav Stickley in Syracuse, New York, that interpreted the theories of the English Arts & Crafts movement and published writings by Prairie School architects; by extension, a style of design, also known as "Mission"

crenellation a defensive fortification along a roof consisting of alternating solid elements and voids; also known as a battlement

crockets in Gothic architecture, small upward-projecting decorative elements, often floral, placed along the edge of gables, spires, and steeples

cupola a small, often dome-shaped structure capping a roof

curtain wall the non-load-bearing skin that encloses a building's structural framework

D

Darlington sandstone a sedimentary rock quarried near Darlington, Indiana

dentils a type of molding consisting of small, rectangular, toothlike blocks

Doric column one of the five Classical orders, it consists of a plain, narrow, rounded capital and a fluted shaft that does not rest on a base

dormer a vertically set window or ventilation opening that projects from a sloping roof and possesses its own roof

drop pendant a knoblike ornamental element extending downward from the ceiling of a vault

Dryvit a modern stuccolike material used for coating buildings

E

eaves the lower edge of a roof that overhangs a wall

engaged pier a masonry supporting element built partially into a wall, rather than freestanding

English basement a very high basement, almost at street level

entablature the horizonal assemblage in Classical architecture that is carried by columns and comprises an architrave (lowest section), frieze (middle section), and cornice (upper section)

Euclid stone a blue-gray sandstone quarried near Euclid, Ohio, and used for foundations, bridgework, and flagstones

exedra a classical seating form, usually semicircular with a high back, either filling a niche or freestanding when outdoors

F

face brick very dense brick, frequently colored or glazed, that is used as facing

fascia a flat horizontal band or molding

Favrile a trademark registered by the Tiffany Glass & Decorating Co. in 1894 for its blown glass, "a composition of various colored glasses, worked together while hot"

Federal Revival a historical style popular between the 1880s and the 1930s and based on American architecture from around 1790 to 1830

finial an ornamental termination,

usually in a foliate form, atop a gable, spire, or other projection

flanged segmental arch a curve with ends that extend out from the arch in a straight line parallel to the ground

flatiron building a building reminiscent of an antique flatiron and shaped by its triangular site

Flemish bond a bricklaying pattern of alternating headers (short ends) and stretchers (long sides) centered on the brick above and below

fleur-de-lis a stylized lily originally used as an emblem of royalty and later, in churches, to represent the Holy Trinity

footprint a building's outline on the ground

four-plus-one a 1960s architectural phenomenon consisting of four stories of small, cheaply constructed apartments atop a floor of parking

frieze a decorative band of molding near the top of an interior wall or within an entablature; it may be flat or enriched with figures or patterned ornament

G

gable the triangular upper portion of a building's end; it may have curved, straight, or stepped sides

gambrel roof a ridged roof with a double pitch

gargoyle a projecting water spout carved in grotesque human or animal forms

Gibbsian surround a door or window opening, used by James Gibbs (1682– 1754), featuring a triple keystone and large and small quoins on either side

golden section a proportion thought to have aesthetic value and universal meaning; strictly defined as the ratio (about three to five) between two parts such that the smaller is to the larger as the larger is to the sum of the two

Gothic Revival a revival of medieval Gothic forms, such as the pointed arch and the spire, that began in the late eighteenth century and, although never dominant, persisted in changing contexts into the twentieth century

graystone a common Chicago residential-building type with a limestone front and Classical details

Greek Revival constituting, along with the Roman Revival, an influential American architectural style, beginning in the 1820s and persisting for almost a half century; characterized by the symmetrical arrangement of parts, columned entrance or portico, and pronounced cornice

greenstone also known as serpentine stone, essentially a hydrous silicate of magnesium that assumes various hues depending on the presence of other minerals

grisaille painting or stained glass executed in shades of gray

H

Hagia Sophia literally "holy wisdom," the epitome of Byzantine architecture, a church built in Istanbul in the fourth century, rebuilt in the sixth, and converted to a mosque in the fifteenth

half-timbering a wood framing technique of the Middle Ages, revived as a decorative motif in the nineteenth and twentieth centuries, in which the structural members appear on the exterior with an infill of masonry or plaster

header the short end of a brick

hip roof a roof with four sloping surfaces, supported by a rafter extending from each corner to a top ridge

hood molding a projecting molding above a door or window, originally intended to deflect water from the wall

I

impost block a masonry element placed above the capital of a column and supporting the end of an arch

Indiana limestone a calcite stone, virtually noncrystalline and of uniform character, quarried around Bedford and Bloomington, Indiana; its internal elasticity makes it ideal for carving; gray when freshly cut, it lightens as it dries and ages

inglenook a semienclosed seating area around a fireplace, usually with a built-in bench

International Style first used in a 1932 exhibit at the Museum of Modern Art in New York City, the term initially described a common design vocabulary free from regional or historical elements and characterized by cubic masses with white exterior coatings, asymmetrical compositions with cantilevered elements, and large windows, often in bands

Ionic column one of the five Classical orders, characterized by a fluted shaft and a capital of large scrolled volutes

Italianate typically an asymmetrical house with a tower; in Chicago usage, the typical tall and narrow house of the 1870s and 1880s usually with incised ornament in the lintels and bracketed cornices

J

Jacobethan (Jacobean + Elizab**ethan)** a revival style combining aspects of late sixteenth- and early seventeenth-century English design, characterized by varied rooflines, multiple chimneys, and clusters of tall rectangular windows with small panes

Joliet limestone the predominant rock found in northern Illinois, quarried in the vicinity of Joliet and Lemont, is a dolomite stone similar to limestone; buff when quarried, it becomes more yellow or golden with age; formerly termed limestone or marble because of its suitability for carving and polishing, it was also known as Athens marble and Lemont limestone

K

Kasota stone a very strong buff or rusty pink limestone quarried near Kasota and Mendota, Minnesota

keystone the wedge-shaped central stone, or voussoir, that locks an arch in place

L

Lake Superior sandstone quartz cemented with silica and iron oxides that may be reddish-brown, brown, or mottled with green or gray; quarried in northeastern Minnesota

lamella truss a truss patented in 1925 and used for large-span vaults in which the members are arranged in a diamond pattern

lancet window a narrow, sharply peaked window

Lannon stone limestone quarried near Lannon, Wisconsin, that has an off-white or yellowish hue with occasional darker segments; popular starting in the 1950s

lantern a superstructure, open to the air, atop a dome or roof and used for light or ventilation

lintel a horizontal member that traverses an opening in a wall

load-bearing an architectural element such as a wall or column that supports weight

loggia an arcade or gallery, roofed and open along one side, located on the front or side of a building

Longmeadow stone a fine-grained, brick-red sandstone quarried near East Longmeadow, Massachusetts

M

machicolation a projecting enclosure on a defensive wall or tower, supported on brackets or corbels and containing a hole for discharging missiles

mansard roof a roof with a double pitch on all four sides, generally with ornamental dormers in the lower section; named after the seventeenth-century Parisian architect François Mansart

mastaba the above-ground portion of an Egyptian tomb, consisting of a rectangular masonry structure with sloping walls and a flat top

meander a decorative pattern from Greek architecture consisting of a labyrinth of lines at right angles

Miesian pertaining to Ludwig Mies van der Rohe (1886–1969), the German architect who came to Chicago in 1938 and developed the steel and glass architecture with which his name is associated

Milwaukee brick a cream-colored face brick made in Milwaukee

Moorish arch also known as horseshoe arch, has a diameter greater than the opening that it spans

mosaic a surface decoration created by small pieces of cemented glass, stone, or tile laid in the form of patterns or representational pictures

motif-rhythm theory espoused by architect George W. Maher (1864–1926) in which a particular motif serves as the decorative organizing principle of a house

mullion a vertical member that separates (and often supports) the units of a window, door, or panel and is often used for decoration on a building's surface

N

nave the central section, or middle aisle, of a church

neo-Classical the readaptation and reuse of the principles of Greek and Roman architecture, including the concepts of logical construction and truth to materials

neo-Grec a mid to late nineteenth-century French architectural style that emulated Greek structural expressionism in masonry and cast iron

Norman the late nineteenth-century revival of the English Romanesque architecture of the late eleventh and twelfth centuries, characterized by massive stonework, round arches, and thick columns

O

oculus a round window or opening

ogee arch a pointed arch formed by the meeting of two elongated, flattened S-shaped curves

oriel a projecting bay window supported on brackets or corbels

P

Painted Ladies   wood-frame houses that display the multihued programs of authentic Victorian paint schemes or simply reflect a flair for the colorful

Palladian window   a three-part window named for the sixteenth-century Italian architect Andrea Palladio and comprising a central arched opening flanked by two shorter, narrower rectangular ones

papyriform capital   an Egyptian capital depicting or resembling papyrus flowers

parapet   the part of a wall projecting above a roof; also a low protective wall along any precipitous edge such as a balcony or bridge

parging   a plaster or mortar coating used to smooth or waterproof a brick or stone surface

pediment   the triangular end of a gable roof or a triangular or curved decorative panel over a door or window

pergola   a covered walkway consisting of columns or posts that support a lattice roof for climbing plants and vines

Perma Stone™   a molded, exterior-cladding product that resembles stone or masonry

Phoenix column   the trade name for a late nineteenth-century circular column composed of four or eight vertical segments of iron riveted together

piano nobile   the principal floor of a building, usually elevated above the ground floor and receiving the finest decoration

pier   a supporting element that carries a load

pilaster   a shallow, flattened pier that projects slightly from a wall and serves a decorative, rather than primarily structural, purpose

pilings   heavy beams used for foundations

pilotis   the French word for piling refers to a street-level column or pillar; a favorite form of the International Style

plat   a map of subdivided land, showing streets and lots

po-mo   shorthand for "postmodern," the 1970s and '80s architectural phenomenon in which historical references were applied to contemporary buildings

porte cochere (coach door)   a door permitting vehicles to enter a building; also the covered section of a driveway that allows people to pass from a vehicle to a doorway protected from weather

portico   a colonnade or roofed entrance porch

poured-in-place   concrete components formed where they are to be used, in contrast to precast or factory-made components

Prairie Style   the Chicago-based movement, primarily in domestic architecture, of the early twentieth century, centering around Frank Lloyd Wright; it rejected historical revival styles in favor of designs reflecting the midwestern environment and the needs of the modern age

Pratt through truss   an American truss with vertical members in compression flanked by diagonal members in tension

purlin   a horizontal timber, placed parallel to the walls and ridge beam atop a peaked roof and supporting the rafters

putti   chubby cherubs with wings

Q

quarter-sawn oak   boards cut from timbers that have been cut lengthwise into quarters and which show a variegated, attractive grain

quoins   decorative or reinforcing stones at the corner of a wall, frequently laid so that small and large sides, or faces, appear in alternation

R

rail grillage foundation   a foundation composed of beams arranged in alternating layers so as to form a grille

raked joint   joints between rows, or courses, of brick in which the mortar is cut back with a narrow tool

rectilinear Queen Anne   eclectic Queen Anne with a proto–Prairie School appearance

reentrant corners   corners that angle inward

refectory   a hall, originally in a religious institution or university, where meals are eaten

reinforced concrete   concrete poured into forms containing steel bars or netting that strengthen the material

relieving arch   an arch built into a wall over a lintel (or another arch) to distribute the weight of the wall above

reredos   a wall or screen of wood or stone, usually tall and highly decorative, that forms the back of an altar

reveal   the side of a window or door opening lying between the frame and the outer surface of the adjacent wall

Richardsonian Romanesque   the Romanesque Revival as influenced by Boston architect Henry Hobson Richardson (1838–1886) and his followers, characterized by heavy rusticated stone walls, round arches, and thick, often squat columns with foliate capitals

Roman brick high-quality, hard-burned face brick with thin, elongated proportions; popular with Prairie School architects

Romanesque the architecture of Western Europe from about the tenth to twelfth centuries, derived from Roman and Byzantine architecture and characterized by the round arch and massive walls

Rookwood the most famous American art pottery (1880–1967) of the Arts & Crafts movement, founded in Cincinnati by Maria Longworth Nichols

rose window a circular window with tracery radiating in spokes from a central roundel

rotated bay a corner bay placed at an angle to the adjacent walls

roundel a small circular panel, window, or plaque

rusticated masonry with strongly beveled and recessed borders, conspicuous joints, and often a textured finish

S

sash the framework in which movable window panes are set

scagliola a technique to imitate marble with pigmented plaster mixed with marble dust or chips and other materials

Scherzer rolling lift bridge a movable bridge invented by Chicago engineer William Scherzer, in which two leaves come together at the center of a river, opening and closing by rolling on rockers of cogs on runners or rails

Second Empire an eclectic style of the post–Civil War years, based on French architecture of the period of Emperor Napoleon III (1852–1870) and characterized by the mansard roof, dormers, central and end pavilions, and abundant ornamentation in the classical mode

setback the stepping-back of a skyscraper from property lines as it rises, the result of 1920s zoning codes that sought to maximize the light and air reaching street level

Sezession the Austrian and German version of the Art Nouveau movement, named for the secession of its followers in the 1890s from official academies, societies, and exhibitions

sidelight a fixed glass panel flanking a door or window

soffit the underside of such architectural elements as an arch, eave, or cornice

spandrel the roughly triangular area between two arches or above the curve of a single arch; in high-rise buildings, the area between a windowsill and the top of the window below

Spanish Baroque Revival a popular 1920s style that exploited the plastic qualities of glazed terra-cotta to imitate the exuberantly ornamented architecture of seventeenth- and eighteenth-century Spain

Spanish mission the architectural style of eighteenth-century Spanish religious settlements in the Southwest

Stick Style a predominantly residential style of the 1860s to 1890s characterized by exterior wood boards that delineate underlying structural members, asymmetrical massing, and broad porches or verandas

strapwork ornament composed of interlacing, folded, or ribbonlike bands

stretcher the long side of a brick

stucco an exterior coating material composed of portland cement, lime, and sand, generally applied wet and with a textured finish; also a fine grade of interior plaster used for decorative elements

T

teardown a building purchased in order to be demolished and replaced with a larger one

tempietto a small ornamental temple in the classical style

terrazzo a flooring made from chips of marble or other stones set into a mortar and polished to a smooth finish

terra-cotta (cooked earth) a fired clay material that can be molded or shaped, glazed with colors, or finished to resemble more expensive masonry materials

tourelle a small, generally narrow turret projecting from the corner of a wall, supported by corbels

transept in a cross-shaped church, the transverse arms that separate the nave from the chancel

travertine a cream-colored, porous marble used for flooring and wall facing that became particularly popular with International Style architects in the 1950s through the 1970s

trefoil arch a three-lobed arch

trompe l'oeil a realistically detailed painting technique that "fools the eye" and creates the illusion of reality

truss bridge a bridge composed of metal or wood elements arranged, in part, in triangles so as to support itself

two-flat or three-flat a widespread residential-building type having two or three stacked units and usually faced with brick

tympanum a triangular or semicircular space, often above a door or window, enclosed by the molding of a pediment or arch

U

urban renewal government-sponsored programs, authorized under the federal Housing Act of 1949 and persisting until the early 1970s, of acquiring land in severely deteriorated inner-city communities, relocating residents, demolishing existing structures, and selling the cleared land to private developers or institutions for new construction

V

vision glass transparent glass

volute a spiral scroll on a capital or console

voussoir one of the wedge-shaped or tapering elements making up an arch or vault

W

WPA murals the federal Works Progress Administration (1935–1943), as the major New Deal relief agency, employed artists to paint murals in public buildings

wainscot a wood or stone facing applied to the lower portion of an interior wall

Warren truss patented by the British engineer James Warren in 1848, this truss consists of diagonal members between the top and bottom chord, and was the preferred type for nineteenth-century railroad bridges

water table a sloping horizontal element between two vertical sections of a wall, designed to deflect water

weeping mortar excess mortar that by design has oozed out of joints between bricks

Z

ziggurat a pyramidal Mesopotamian temple with three to ten steppedback levels, each smaller than the one below

FOR FURTHER READING

This list is an introduction to the many publications on Chicago's (and Oak Park's) man-made environment. It includes many of the resources most frequently used by the writers of this book.

Adelman, William. *Touring Pullman.* 2d ed. Chicago: Illinois Labor History Society, 1977.

Bach, Ira J., and Mary Lackritz Gray. *A Guide to Chicago's Public Sculpture.* Chicago: University of Chicago Press, 1983.

Bach, Ira J., Susan Wolfson, and Charles E. Gregersen. *A Guide to Chicago's Train Stations, Present and Past.* Athens: Ohio University Press, 1986.

Berger, Miles L. *They Built Chicago: Entrepreneurs Who Shaped a Great City's Architecture.* Chicago: Bonus Books, 1992.

Blaser, Werner, ed. *Chicago Architecture: Holabird & Root, 1882–1992.* Basel: Birkhausen Verlag, 1992.

Block, Jean F. *Hyde Park Houses: An Informal History, 1856–1910.* Chicago: University of Chicago Press, 1978.

———. *The Uses of Gothic: Planning and Building the Campus of the University of Chicago, 1892–1932.* Chicago: University of Chicago Press, 1983.

Bluestone, Daniel. *Constructing Chicago.* New Haven: Yale University Press, 1991.

Bowly, Devereux, Jr. *The Poorhouse: Subsidized Housing in Chicago, 1895–1976.* Carbondale: Southern Illinois University Press, 1978.

A Breath of Fresh Air: Chicago's Neighborhood Parks of the Progressive Era, 1900–1925. Chicago: Chicago Public Library and Chicago Park District, 1989.

Brooks, H. Allen. *Frank Lloyd Wright and the Prairie School.* New York: George Braziller, 1984.

———. *The Prairie School: Frank Lloyd Wright and His Midwest Contemporaries.* Toronto: University of Toronto Press, 1972.

Bruegmann, Robert. *Holabird & Roche/Holabird & Root: An Illustrated Catalog of Works, 1880–1940.* 3 vols. New York: Garland, 1991.

Burnham Library of Architecture. *The Plan of Chicago, 1909–1979.* Chicago: Art Institute of Chicago, 1979.

Chappell, Sally A. Kitt. *Architecture and Planning of Graham, Anderson, Probst & White, 1912–1936: Transforming Tradition.* Chicago: University of Chicago Press, 1992.

Chicago: An Industrial Guide. Chicago: Public Works Historical Society, 1991.

Chicago and New York: Architectural Interactions. Chicago: Art Institute of Chicago, 1984.

Chicago Architects Design: A Century of Architectural Drawings from the Art Institute of Chicago. New York: Rizzoli, 1982.

Chicago Issue. *Abitare* (Milan) no. 256 (July–August 1987).

"Chicago, a Special Issue." *Architectural Review* (London) no. 968 (October 1977).

Chicago Department of Public Works. *Chicago Public Works: A History.* Chicago: City of Chicago, 1973.

Cohen, Stuart E. *Chicago Architects.* Chicago: Swallow Press, 1976.

Condit, Carl W. *Chicago, 1910–29: Building, Planning, and Urban Technology.* Chicago: University of Chicago Press, 1973.

———. *Chicago, 1930–70: Building, Planning, and Urban Technology.* Chicago: University of Chicago Press, 1974.

———. *The Chicago School of Architecture: A History of Commercial and Public Building in the Chicago Area, 1875–1925.* Chicago: University of Chicago Press, 1964.

Cudahy, Brian J. *Destination: Loop, the Story of Rapid Transit Railroading in and Around Chicago.* Brattleboro, Vt., and Lexington, Mass.: The Stephen Greene Press, 1982.

Darling, Sharon S. *Chicago Ceramics and Glass: An Illustrated History from 1871 to 1933.* Chicago: Chicago Historical Society, 1979.

———. *Chicago Furniture: Art, Craft and Industry, 1833–1983.* New York: W. W. Norton, 1984.

———. *Chicago Metalsmiths: An Illustrated History.* Chicago: Chicago Historical Society, 1977.

Duis, Perry R. *Chicago: Creating New Traditions.* Chicago: Chicago Historical

Society, 1976.

Frueh, Erne R., and Florence Frueh. *Chicago Stained Glass*. Chicago: Loyola University Press, 1983.

Gilbert, James. *Perfect Cities: Chicago's Utopias of 1893*. Chicago: University of Chicago Press, 1991.

Glibota, Ante, and Frederic Edelmann. *Chicago: 150 Years of Architecture, 1833–1983*. Paris: Paris Art Center, Musée-Galerie de la SEITA, 1983.

Grese, Robert E. *Jens Jensen: Maker of Natural Parks and Gardens*. Baltimore: Johns Hopkins University Press, 1992.

Grube, Oswald W., Peter C. Pran, and Franz Schulze. *100 Years of Architecture in Chicago: Continuity of Structure and Form*. Chicago: J. Philip O'Hara, 1976.

Hirsch, Susan E., and Robert I. Goler. *A City Comes of Age: Chicago in the 1890s*. Chicago: Chicago Historical Society, 1990.

Hoffmann, Donald. *The Architecture of John Wellborn Root*. Baltimore: Johns Hopkins University Press, 1973.

Holt, Glen E., and Dominic A. Pacyga. *Chicago: A Historical Guide to the Neighborhoods: The Loop and South Side*. Chicago: Chicago Historical Society, 1979.

Kunz, Richard. *Overhead and Underground: A Guide to Chicago's Rapid Transit*. Andover, N.J.: Andover Junction Publications, 1991.

Lanctot, Barbara. *A Walk Through Graceland Cemetery*. 3d ed. Chicago: Chicago Architecture Foundation, 1988.

Lane, George A. *Chicago Churches and Synagogues: An Architectural Pilgrimage*. Chicago: Loyola University Press, 1981.

Lowe, David. *Chicago Interiors: Views of a Splendid World*. Chicago: Contemporary Books, 1979.

———. *Lost Chicago*. Boston: Houghton Mifflin, 1975.

Lyden, Jacki, and Chet Jakus. *Landmarks and Legends of Uptown*. Chicago: n.p., 1980.

McBrien, Judith Paine. *Skyline: Chicago*. Wilmette: Perspectives Press, 1991–. A series of videotapes accompanied by guidebooks.

Manson, Grant C. *Frank Lloyd Wright to 1910: The First Golden Age*. New York: Reinhold, 1958.

Mayer, Harold M., and Richard C. Wade. *Chicago: Growth of a Metropolis*. Chicago: University of Chicago Press, 1969.

Miller, Ross. *American Apocalypse: The Great Fire and the Myth of Chicago*. Chicago: University of Chicago Press, 1990.

Moffat, Bruce. *Forty Feet Below: The Story of Chicago's Freight Tunnels*. Glendale, Calif.: Interurban Press, 1982.

Molloy, Mary Alice. *Chicago Since the Sears Tower: A Guide to New Downtown Buildings*. 3d rev. ed. Chicago: Inland Architect Press, 1992.

Morrison, Hugh. *Louis Sullivan, Prophet of Modern Architecture*. New York: Peter Smith, 1952.

Museum of Science and Industry. *A Guide to 150 Years of Chicago Architecture*. Chicago: Chicago Review Press, 1985.

Pacyga, Dominic A., and Ellen Skerrett. *Chicago, City of Neighborhoods: Histories and Tours*. Chicago: Loyola University Press, 1986.

Prairie in the City: Naturalism in Chicago's Parks, 1870–1940. Chicago: Chicago Historical Society, Chicago Park District, and Morton Arboretum, 1991.

Rader, Lauren Weingarden. *Faith and Form: Synagogue Architecture in Illinois*. Chicago: Spertus College of Judaica Press, 1976.

Riedy, James L. *Chicago Sculpture*. Chicago: University of Illinois Press, 1981.

Saliga, Pauline A., ed. *Fragments of Chicago's Past: The Collection of Architectural Fragments at the Art Institute of Chicago*. Chicago: Art Institute of Chicago, 1990.

———. *The Sky's the Limit: A Century of Chicago Skyscrapers*. New York: Rizzoli, 1990.

Schulze, Franz. *Mies van der Rohe: A Critical Biography*. Chicago: University of Chicago Press, 1985.

———, and Kevin Harrington. *Chicago's Famous Buildings*. 4th rev. ed. Chicago: University of Chicago Press, 1993.

Siry, Joseph. *Carson Pirie Scott: Louis Sullivan and the Chicago Department Store*. Chicago: University of Chicago Press, 1988.

Slaton, Deborah, ed. *Wild Onions: A Brief Guide to Landmarks and Lesser-Known Structures in Chicago's Loop*. Chicago: Association for Preservation Technology International, 1989.

Sprague, Paul E. *Guide to Frank Lloyd Wright and Prairie School Architecture in Oak Park*. 3d ed. Oak Park: Village of Oak Park, 1982.

Stamper, John W. *Chicago's North Michigan Avenue: Planning and Development, 1900–1930*. Chicago: University of Chicago Press, 1991.

Takayama, Masami. "The Structural Architecture of Chicago." *Process: Architecture* (Tokyo) no. 102 (April 1992).

University of Chicago. *A Walking Guide to the Campus.* Chicago: University Publications Office, 1991.

Viskochil, Larry A. *Chicago at the Turn of the Century in Photographs.* New York: Dover, 1984.

Wille, Lois. *Forever Open, Clear, and Free: The Struggle for Chicago's Lakefront.* 2d ed. Chicago: Henry Regnery, 1991.

Zukowsky, John, ed. *Chicago Architecture 1872–1922: Birth of a Metropolis.* Munich: Prestel Verlag, 1987.

———. *Chicago Architecture and Design 1923–1993: Reconfiguring an American Metropolis.* Munich: Prestel Verlag, 1993.

INDEX

Every building described in the Guide is listed as a primary entry in the index, both by the building's previous and current names. Street names beginning with "North," "South," "East," or "West" are alphabetized under those words; building and street names beginning with numbers are alphabetized as if spelled out. The names of persons, firms, organizations, and government offices involved in creating the works listed in the Guide appear in UPPER AND LOWER CASE SMALL CAPS. Unless otherwise indicated, they are architects or associated artists. Names of towns, historic districts, and communities within Greater Chicago appear in boldface. Major divisions and tours appear in BOLD UPPER CASE. A page reference in boldface indicates that an illustration of the building, area, or other work appears on that page.

The following abbreviations appear in the index:

add.	addition	H.S.	High School
alt.	altered	Hosp.	Hospital
Assn.	Association	M.S.	Middle School
Assocs.	Associates	Natl.	National
Apts.	Apartments	Pkwy.	Parkway
Ave.	Avenue	Pl.	Place
Bldg.	Building	P.S.	Public School
Blvd.	Boulevard	R.C.	Roman Catholic
Bros.	Brothers	Rd.	Road
Cem.	Cemetery	recon.	reconstructed
Co.	Company	rehab.	rehabilitated
Condos.	Condominiums	rem.	remodeled
conv.	converted	renov.	renovated
Corp.	Corporation	res.	restored
Ct.	Court	RR	Railroad/Railway
Dept.	Department	St.	Street
Dr.	Drive	Univ.	University
Expy.	Expressway		

All Souls Unitarian Church: 404
ALLEN, JAMES ROY
  George W. Reed House: 466–67
Allerton Hotel: **106**
Allerton House: **106**
ALMQUIST, CARL M.
  S. Blackstone Ave., Nos. 5701 & 5707:
    441
ALSCHULER, ALFRED S.
  Chemistry Bldg., Illinois Institute of
    Technology: 377
  Chicago Public Library—Henry E. Legler
    Regional Branch: **298**
  Chicago Public Library—Henry W.
    Austin Branch: 299
  Columbian Colortype Co.: 365
  Commissary Bldg.: 132
  Donohue Annex: 147
  E. 21st St., No. 320: 365
  E. Ohio St., No. 230: 117
  Finchley Bldg.: 48
  Harrison Hotel: 144
  Hudson Motor Co. of Illinois: **367**
  John R. Thompson Bldg.: 132
  John Sexton & Co.: **134**
  Kehilath Anshe Ma'ariv—Isaiah Israel
    Temple: 408, **409**
  London Guarantee & Accident Bldg.: 33
  Maurice L. Rothschild Bldg. (add.): 58
  Michigan-Ohio Bldg.: 104
  Mount Pisgah Missionary Baptist Church:
    402–3
  N. Michigan Ave., No. 360: 33
  O'Malley Bldg., DePaul Univ.: 48
  Pelouze Bldg.: 117
  Shops Bldg. (rem.): 50
  Sinai Temple: 402–3
  S. Michigan Ave., Nos. 2222–2228: **367**
  S. Michigan Ave., No. 2255 (add.):
    367–68
  Temple Isaiah Israel: 408
  Thomas Flyer Garage & Service Bldg.
    (add.): 367–68
  Wishnick Hall, Illinois Institute of
    Technology: 377
ALSCHULER, JOHN H.
  Kehilath Anshe Ma'ariv—Isaiah Israel
    Temple (add.): 408, **409**
  Temple Isaiah Israel (add.): 408, **409**
ALSCHULER & SINCERE
  Boiler Plant & Steam Generating Plant,
    Illinois Institute of Technology: 375
  S. Federal St., No. 3430: 375
Alta Vista Terrace: 212, 444
ALTMAN-SAICHEK ASSOCS.
  Chicago & North Western RR Office
    (renov.): 85–86
  City Colleges Bldg. (renov.): 85–86
  Theodore Ascher Bldg. (add.): 38
Alumni Memorial Hall, Illinois Institute of
  Technology: 377
American Airlines: 351
American Architect: 63, 131
American Book Co.: 365
American College of Surgeons—John B.
  Murphy Memorial Auditorium: 124
American Fat Stock show: 391
American Furniture Mart: **116**
American Institute of Architects: 193,
  422–23
American Institute of Architects, Chicago
  Chapter: 22
American Islamic College: **217**–18
American Luxfer Prism Co.: 391
American Medical Assn.: 123
American National Bank Bldg.: 81
American System Ready-Cut: 464
American Terra Cotta Co.: 223–24
American Youth and Independence Day
  Fountain: 348
  Amertorp torpedo plant: 19
Ames (Miner T.) House: 363
Ammann, Othmar H.: 351
AMMANN & WHITNEY (engineers)
  Trans World Airlines Hangar,

Chicago–Midway Airport: **351**
  W. 55th St., No. 5035: **351**
Ammon (Ernest) House: 190
Amoco Bldg.: 35, 108
Anderson, Peirce
  gravesite, Graceland Cem.: 216
Anderson, Sherwood: 464
Anderson (Frank) House: 461
Anderson (N.) House: 446
ANDRESEN, THEODORE
  Gustav Hottinger Flat: 208–9
Angel Guardian Croatian Catholic Church:
  240
Annex Bldg.: 38
Anshe Kenesseth Israel: **347**
Anshe Sholom Synagogue: 348
Anson, Adrian C. ("Cap")
  monument, Oak Woods Cem.: 454
Anti-Cruelty Society: **133**
Apfel (Arthur H.) House: **207**
Apparel Center: 89
Appomattox (Elder): 452
Aquarium & Fish Hatchery, Lincoln Park
  Zoo: 199
Aragon Ballroom: 221–22
ARAO, HIDEAKI
  Midwest Buddhist Temple: 175
Arby's: 106
"Arcade Row" Houses: 471
Archbishop Quigley Prep. Seminary: 126
Archer, William B. (Col.): 389
ARCHITECTS INTL.–CHICAGO
  Green Brier Apts. (renov.): 206
Architectural Forum: 237, 371
Architectural Record: 45, 229, 299, 348, 367,
  434, 437
Architecture & Art Laboratories, Univ. of
  Illinois at Chicago: **287**
Archway Amoco Gas Station: 171
Armour, Philip Danforth: 375
Armour Institute of Technology: 209, 214,
  374–**75**
Armour (Lester) House: 207
Armour (M. Cochran) House: **438**
Armour Mission: 375
Armour Square Park: 389
ARMSTRONG, W. SCOTT
  Plymouth Bldg. (rem.): 62
  S. Dearborn St., No. 417 (rem.): 62
ARNOLD, WESLEY A.
  Ernest Hall House: 325
  Fowler Methodist Episcopal Church: 344
  Greater Zion Hill Missionary Baptist
    Church: 344
  Wesley A. Arnold House: **314**
  William J. MacDonald House: 327
Arnold (Wesley A.) House: **314**
ARONER & SOMERS
  Anshe Kenesseth Israel: **347**
  Shepherd's Temple Missionary Baptist
    Church: **347**
Art Institute of Chicago: 14, 16, 36, 40, **42,**
  45, 59, 168, 277, 436
  Columbus Drive Addition: 42
  Daniel F. & Ada L. Rice Bldg.: 42
  Ferguson Bldg.: 42
  Goodman Theater: 42
  Morton Wing: 42
  Ryerson and Burnham Libraries: 42
  School: 42, 447
Arthur Dixon Transfer Co. Truck Garage:
  146
Arthur J. Schmitt Academic Center, DePaul
  Univ.: 184
Arthur S. Keating Sports Center, Illinois
  Institute of Technology: **377**
Asbury Plaza: 129
Association Bldg.: 81
Astor Court: **162**
Astor Tower: 163
Astor Tower Hotel: 163
ATKINSON & FITZGERALD
  N. Wabash Ave., No. 401: 52
  Sun-Times Bldg.: 52
Atrium Houses: 408–9

Holzaffel (Angelica) House: 230
HOLZER, J.
  Chicago Public Library Cultural Center: 37
  Marquette Bldg.: 9, 11, 65–**66**
*Homage to the Chicago School of
  Architecture* (Haas): 167
Home Builders Assn. of Greater Chicago:
  301
Home Insurance Bldg.: 12, 61
"Honeymoon Row," Flats on: 472
Honoré, Eliza
  gravesite, Graceland Cem.: 215
Honoré, Henry H.
  gravesite, Graceland Cem.: 215
HOOD & FOUILHOUX
  Tribune Tower (add.): 101–2
HOOD, RAYMOND: 102
  Bethany Union Church: 461
Horn, Gerald: 435
Horn, Milton: 124
Hornbaker (William R.) House: 462–63
HOROWITZ, WILLIAM M.
  Garrick Garage: 73
Horse Show Assn. Fountain: 318
Horton (Horace) House: 465
HORWITZ-MATTHEWS
  City Commons: 175–76
HOSEK, JOSEPH EMIL
  S. Hamilton Ave., No. 8958: 467
Hosp. Addition, Univ. of Illinois College
  of Medicine: 280
HOTCHKISS, ROY J.
  Medical Arts Bldg.: 318
  Scoville Block (1) (rem.): 317
Hotel Florence: 469–71, **470**
Hotel Inter-Continental Chicago: **103**
Hotel La Salle Public Garage: 84
Hotel Nikko Chicago: 73
Hotel St. Benedict Flats: **125**
Hottinger (Adolph) Flat: 208–9
Hottinger (Gustav) Flat: 208–9
Hottinger (Gustav) House: 208
Houghteling (James L.) Houses: **163**
House of Light: **173**
"House of Tomorrow," Century of
  Progress Exposition: 443
House with a Bay: **176**
Housing projects. See Chicago: housing
  projects
Howard (Joseph H.) House: 411
HOWELLS & HOOD
  N. Michigan Ave., No. 435: 101–2
Howells, John Mead: 102
HOWELLS, JOHN MEAD
  Tribune Tower (add.): 101–2
Hoyt (William H.) House: 440
HUBER, JOHN PAUL
  Holy Family Church (add.): 282
Huber, Julius H.: 230
HUBER, JULIUS H.
  Bryant Bldg. (add.): 70
  Cobbler Square: **179**
  Delaware Bldg. (add.): 70
  Edwin S. Hartwell Houses: 127
  Gustav Hottinger House: 208
  Herman C. Lammers House: 230
  Herman H. Hettler House (add. &
    rem.): 210
  Herman Kirchstein Houses: 190
  N. Lakewood Ave., No. 5222: 230
  Peter Peterson House: 190
  St. Procopius Church: 340
  Thomas Brown Houses: 380
  Western Wheel Works: **179**
Hudson Motor Co. of Illinois: 367
Hudson Studios: 187
HUEHL & SCHMID
  Medinah Temple: **123**, 128
  Peter M. Zuncker House: 256–57
  W. Stratford Pl., No. 606: 209
Hughitt, Marvin: 85
Hulbert, William A.
  gravesite, Graceland Cem.: 214
Hulburd (Charles Henry) & Charles C. Yoe
  Double House: 164

HULL, DENISON B.
  First Unitarian Church of Chicago: 442
Hull, George N.: 279
Hull (Charles J.) House: 287–**88**
Hull Court & Biological Laboratories, Univ.
  of Chicago: 429
Hull Gate, Univ. of Chicago: 429
Hull House: 18, 22, 270, 272, 286–**88**
Hull House Dining Hall: 287–**88**
Hull Memorial Chapel: 442
Humana–Michael Reese Hosp. & Medical
  Center: 357, 369–71
Humboldt Park: 248, 254–56, 290, 295,
  306, 346
Hundley, Elisha E.: 204
Hunt, Jarvis: 102
HUNT, JARVIS
  Lake Shore Athletic Club: 113
  McCormick Bird House, Lincoln Park
    Zoo: 200
  Northwestern Univ.—Lake Shore
    Center: 113
  Saddle and Cycle Club: 230–31
Hunt, Richard: 135, 403
Hunt, Richard Morris: 363, 423
Hunter (Edward S.) House: 372
HUSSANDER, ARTHUR F.
  Carl Schurz H.S. (add.): **260**–61
  Carter H. Harrison Technical H.S.: 346
  Edward Everett P.S.: 397
  Eugene Field P.S. (add.): **238**
  Hyde Park H.S. Assembly Hall: 442
  John Spry P.S. (add.): 346
  Lakeview H.S.: **212**
  Louis Nettelhorst P.S.: 209
  Maria Saucedo Magnet School: 346
  Nicholas Senn H.S.: 233
  Ravenswood P.S.: 223
  William H. Ray P.S. Assembly Hall: 442
HUSZAGH & HILL
  Aragon Ballroom: 221–22
  N. Lake Shore Dr., No. 1540: 160
  Uptown Bank Bldg. (add.): **221**
  Uptown Chicago Natl. Bank (add.): **221**
Hutchins (Eugene R.) House: 161
Hutchinson, Charles L.: 431
Hutchinson Court, Univ. of Chicago: 425,
  429–31
Hutchinson St. Landmark District: 218
Hyatt on Printers Row: 149
Hyatt Regency Chicago: 34
HYDE, ROBERT M.
  Charles A. Carlson House: 239, 302
  N. Ridge Ave., No. 7106: 239
Hyde Park: 13, 112, 187, 274, 312, 356,
  381, 400–401, 408, 410, 418–19,
  438–40, 442, 444–45, 447, 454, 457
Hyde Park Baptist Church: 443
Hyde Park Historical Society: 438
Hyde Park H.S.: 442
Hyde Park Redevelopment Project: 434,
  438–40
  Townhouses: **439**–40
HYDE PARK/SOUTH SHORE: *map*
  416–17, 416–55
Hyde Park Union Church: 443
HYLAND & CORSE
  Equitable Bldg.: 4, 84
  W. Washington St., No. 180: 84

I

"I Am" Temple: 84
I Will: 200
Iannelli, Alfonso: 35, 218, 444, 450
IBM Self Park: 123
Ida Noyes Hall, Univ. of Chicago: **432**
Iglehart, Mary: 459
Iglehart (Charles D.) House: 459
Iglesia Presbiteriana Emmanuel: 340
IIT Research Institute Tower, Illinois
  Institute of Technology: 375
Illinois & Michigan Canal: **3**–4, 39, 336, 387,
  389
Illinois Athletic Club [former] Bldg.: 38–39